the Unofficial Guide® to

the Best RV and Tent Campgrounds in Northwest & Central Plains

Alaska, Idaho, Iowa, Montana, Nebraska, North Dakota, Oregon, South Dakota, Washington, Wyoming, and British Columbia

Other Titles in the Unofficial Guide
Best RV and Tent Campgrounds Series

California & the West
Florida & the Southeast
Great Lakes States
Mid-Atlantic States
The Northeast
Southwest & South Central Plains
U.S.A.

Other Unofficial Guides

Beyond Disney: The Unofficial Guide to Universal, SeaWorld, and the Best of Central Florida

Inside Disney: The Incredible Story of Walt Disney World and the Man Behind the Mouse

Mini Las Vegas: The Pocket-Sized Unofficial Guide to Las Vegas

Mini-Mickey: The Pocket-Sized Unofficial Guide to Walt Disney World

The Unofficial Guides to Bed & Breakfasts and Country Inns:
California Great Lakes New England
Northwest Rockies Southeast Southwest

The Unofficial Guides to the Best RV and Tent Campgrounds:
California & the West Florida & the Southeast Great Lakes
Mid-Atlantic States Northeast Northwest Southwest U.S.A.

The Unofficial Guide to Branson, Missouri

The Unofficial Guide to Chicago

The Unofficial Guide to Cruises

The Unofficial Guide to Disneyland

The Unofficial Guide to Disneyland Paris

The Unofficial Guide to Florence, Rome, and the Heart of Italy

The Unofficial Guide to the Great Smoky and Blue Ridge Region

The Unofficial Guide to Golf Vacations in the Eastern U.S.

The Unofficial Guide to Hawaii

The Unofficial Guide to Las Vegas

The Unofficial Guide to London

The Unofficial Guide to New Orleans

The Unofficial Guide to New York City

The Unofficial Guide to Paris

The Unofficial Guide to San Francisco

The Unofficial Guide to South Florida, including Miami and the Keys

The Unofficial Guides to Traveling with Kids:
California Florida Mid-Atlantic New England and New York
Walt Disney World

The Unofficial Guide to Walt Disney World

The Unofficial Guide to Walt Disney World for Grown-Ups

The Unofficial Guide to Washington, D.C.

The Unofficial Guide to the World's Best Diving Vacations

the Unofficial Guide® to the Best RV and Tent Campgrounds in the Northwest & Central Plains

1st Edition

Alaska, Idaho, Iowa, Montana, Nebraska, North Dakota, Oregon, South Dakota, Washington, Wyoming, and British Columbia

Shane Kennedy & Christopher Parks

Hungry Minds™

Best-Selling Books • Digital Downloads • e-Books • Answer Networks • e-Newsletters
Branded Web Sites • e-Learning

New York, NY • Indianapolis, IN • Cleveland, OH

Please note that prices fluctuate in the course of time, and travel information changes under the impact of many factors that influence the travel industry. We therefore suggest that you write or call ahead for confirmation when making your travel plans. Every effort has been made to ensure the accuracy of information throughout this book and the contents of this publication are believed correct at the time of printing. Nevertheless, the publishers cannot accept responsibility for errors or omissions or for changes in details given in this guide or for the consequences of any reliance on the information provided by the same. Assessments of attractions and so forth are based upon the author's own experience and therefore, descriptions given in this guide necessarily contain an element of subjective opinion, which may not reflect the publisher's opinion or dictate a reader's own experience on another occasion. Readers are invited to write to the publisher with ideas, comments, and suggestions for future editions.

Your safety is important to us, so we encourage you to stay alert and be aware of your surroundings. Keep a close eye on cameras, purses, and wallets, all favorite targets of thieves and pickpockets.

Published by Hungry Minds, Inc.
909 Third Avenue
New York, NY 10022

Produced by Menasha Ridge Press
COVER DESIGN BY MICHAEL J. FREELAND
INTERIOR DESIGN BY MICHELE LASEAU

ISBN 0-7645-6252-5

ISSN 1536-9684

Manufactured in the United States of America

10 9 8 7 6 5 4 3 2

Contents

Part Three Supplemental Directory of Campgrounds 299

the Unofficial Guide® to

the Best RV and Tent Campgrounds in the Northwest & Central Plains

Introduction

Why Unofficial?

The material in this guide has not been edited or in any way reviewed by the campgrounds profiled. In this "unofficial" guide we represent and serve you, the consumer. By way of contrast with other campground directories, no ads were sold to campgrounds, and no campground paid to be included. Through our independence, we're able to offer you the sort of objective information necessary to select a campground efficiently and with confidence.

Why Another Guide to Campgrounds?

We developed *The Unofficial Guide to the Best RV and Tent Campgrounds in the Northwest and Central Plains* because we recognized that campers are as discriminating about their choice of campgrounds as most travelers are about their choice of hotels. As a camper, you don't want to stay in every campground along your route. Rather, you prefer to camp only in the best. A comprehensive directory with limited information on each campground listed does little to help you narrow your choices. What you need is a reference that tells you straight out which campgrounds are the best, and that supplies detailed information, collected by independent inspectors, that differentiates those campgrounds from all of the also-rans. This is exactly what *The Unofficial Guide to the Best RV and Tent Campgrounds* delivers.

The Choice Is All Yours

Life is short, and life is about choices. You can stay in a gravel lot, elbow to elbow with other campers, with tractor-trailers roaring by just beyond the fence, or with this guide, you can spend the night in a roomy, shaded site, overlooking a sparkling blue lake. The choice is yours.

The authors of this guide have combed the Northwestern and Great Plains states inspecting and comparing hundreds of campgrounds. Their objective was to create a hit parade of the very best, so that no matter where you travel, you'll never have to spend another night in a dumpy, gravel lot.

The best campgrounds in each state are described in detail in individual profiles so you'll know exactly what to expect. In addition to the fully profiled campgrounds, we provide a Supplemental Directory of Campgrounds that lists hundreds of additional properties that are quite adequate, but that didn't make the cut for the top 350 in the guide. Thus, no matter where you are, you'll have plenty of campgrounds to choose from. None of the campgrounds appearing in this guide, whether fully profiled or in the supplemental list, paid to be included. Rather, each earned its place by offering a superior product. Period.

Letters, Comments, and Questions from Readers

Many who use the Unofficial Guides write to us with questions, comments, and reports of their camping experiences. We appreciate all such input, both positive and critical. Readers' comments are frequently incorporated into revised editions of the Unofficial Guides and have contributed immeasurably to their improvement. Please write to:

The Unofficial Guide to the Best RV and Tent Campgrounds
P.O. Box 43673
Birmingham, AL 35243
UnofficialGuides@menasharidge.com

For letters sent through the mail, please put your return address on both your letter and envelope; the two sometimes become separated. Also include your phone number and email address if you are available for a possible interview.

How to Use This Guide

Using this guide is quick and easy. We begin with this introduction followed by "Campground Awards," a list of the best campgrounds for RVers, tenters, families, and more. Then we profile the best 350 campgrounds in the Northwest and Central Plains states. Next is a supplemental list of hundreds of additional campgrounds including details about prices, hookups, and more. Bringing up the rear is an alphabetical index of all campgrounds included in the guide.

Both the profiled section and the supplemental directory are ordered alphabetically, first by state and then by city. To see what campgrounds are available:

- Find the section covering the state in question.
- Within that section, look up the city alphabetically.
- Under the city, look up the campgrounds alphabetically.

You can choose and locate campgrounds in four different ways.

1. **Use the Map** If a city appears with a black, solid bullet on our map, at least one of our profiled or listed campgrounds will be located there. The converse is also the case: if the city has a hollow, outlined bullet, you can assume that we do not cover any campgrounds in that city.
2. **Check the Campground Profiles** In the section where we profile campgrounds, look up any city where you hope to find a campground. If the city isn't listed, it means we do not profile any campgrounds there.
3. **Check the Supplemental Directory of Campgrounds** Check for the same city in the supplemental listings.
4. **Use the Index** If you want to see if a specific campground is profiled or listed in the guide, look up the name of the campground in the alphabetical index at the back of the book.

When looking up campgrounds, remember that the best campgrounds are found in the profiled section; always check there first before turning to the Supplemental Directory of Campgrounds.

Understanding the Profiles

Each profile has seven important sections:

Campground Name, Address, and Contact Information In addition to the street address, we also provide phone and fax numbers as well as website and email addresses.

Ratings Using the familiar one- to five-star rating with five stars being best, we offer one overall rating for RV campers and a second overall rating for tent campers. The overall rating for each type of camper is based on a rough weighted average of the following eight individually rated categories:

Category	Weight
Beauty	15%
Site Privacy	10%
Site Spaciousness	10%
Quiet	15%
Security	13%
Cleanliness/upkeep	13%
Insect Control	10%
Facilities	14%

Beauty This rates the natural setting of the campground in terms of its visual appeal. The highest ratings are reserved for campgrounds where the beauty of the campground can be enjoyed and appreciated both at individual campsites and at the campground's public areas. Views, vistas, landscaping, and foliage are likewise taken into consideration.

Site Privacy This category rates the extent to which the campsites are set apart and/or in some way buffered (usually by trees and shrubs) from adjacent or nearby campsites. The farther campsites are from one another the better. This rating also reflects how busy the access road to the campsites is in terms of traffic. Campgrounds that arrange their sites on a number of cul-de-sacs, for example, will offer quieter sites than a campground where the sites are situated off of a busy loop or along a heavily traveled access road.

Site Spaciousness This rates the size of the campsite. Generally, the larger the better.

Quiet This rating indicates the relative quietness of the campground. There are three key considerations. The first is where the campground is located. Campgrounds situated along busy highways or in cities or towns are usually noisier, for example, than rural or wilderness campgrounds removed from major thoroughfares. The second consideration relates to how noise is managed at the campground. Does the campground forbid playing of radios or enforce a "quiet time" after a certain hour? Is there someone on site at night to respond to complaints about other campers being loud or unruly at a late hour? Finally, the rating considers the extent to which trees, shrubs, and the natural topography serve to muffle noise within the campground.

Security This rating reflects the extent (if any) to which management monitors the campground during the day and night. Physical security is also included in this rating: Is the campground fenced? Is the campground gated? If so, is the gate manned? Generally, a campground located in a city or along a busy road is more exposed to thieves or vandals than a more remote campground, and should more actively supervise access.

Cleanliness This rates the cleanliness, serviceability, and state of repair of the campground, including grounds, sites, and facilities.

Insect Control This rating addresses questions regarding insect and pest control. Does management spray or take other steps to control the presence of mosquitoes and other insect pests? Does the campground drain efficiently following a rain? Are garbage and sewage properly collected and disposed of?

Facilities This rates the overall variety and quality of facilities to include bath house/toilets, swimming pool, retail shops, docks, pavilions, playgrounds, etc. If the quality of respective facilities vary considerably within a given campground, inconsistencies are explained in the prose description of the campground.

Campground Description This is an informative, consumer-oriented description of the campground. It includes what makes the campground special or unique and what differentiates it from other area campgrounds. The description may additionally include the following:

- The general layout of the campground.
- Where the campground is located relative to an easily referenced city or highway.
- The general setting (wilderness, rural, or urban).
- Description of the campsites including most and least desirable sites.
- Prevailing weather considerations and best time to visit.
- Mention of any unusual, exceptional, or deficient facilities.
- Security considerations, if any (gates that are locked at night, accessibility of campground to non-campers, etc.).

Basics Key information about the campground including:

- *Operated By* Who owns and/or operates the campground.
- *Open* Dates or seasons the campground is open.
- *Site Assignment* How sites are most commonly obtained (first-come, first served; reservations accepted; reservations only; assigned on check-in, etc. Deposit and refund policy.
- *Registration* Where the camper registers on arrival. Information on how and where to register after normal business hours (late arrival).
- *Fee* Cost of a standard campsite for one night for RV sites and tent sites respectively. Forms of payment accepted. Uses the following abbreviations for credit cards: V = VISA, AE = American Express, MC = MasterCard, D = Discover, CB = Carte Blanche, and DC = Diner's Club International.
- *Parking* Usual entry will be "At site" or "On road," though some campgrounds have a central parking lot from which tent campers must carry their gear to their campsite.

Facilities This is a brief data presentation that provides information on the availability of specific facilities and services.

- *Number of RV Sites* Any site where RVs are permitted.
- *Number of Tent-Only Sites* Sites set aside specifically for tent camping, including pop-up tent trailers.
- *Hookups* Possible hookups include electric, water, sewer, cable TV, phone, and Internet connection. Electrical hookups vary from campground to campground. Where electrical hookups are available, the amperage available is stated parenthetically, for example: "Hookups: Electric (20 amps), water."
- *Each Site* List of equipment such as grill, picnic table, lantern pole, fire pit, water faucet, electrical outlet, etc., provided at each campsite.
- *Dump station, laundry, pay phone, restrooms and showers, fuel, propane, RV service, general store, vending, playground* Are these items or services available on site? Their respective fields indicate the answer.
- *Internal Roads* Indicates the road type (gravel, paved, dirt), and condition.
- *Market* Location and distance of closest supermarket or large grocery store.
- *Restaurant* Location and distance of closest restaurant.
- *Other* Boat ramp, dining pavilion, miniature golf, tennis court, lounge, etc.
- *Activities* Activities available at the campground or in the area.
- *Nearby Attractions* Can be natural or manmade.
- *Additional Information* The best sources to call for general information on area activities and attractions. Sources include local or area chambers of commerce, tourist bureaus, visitors and convention authorities, forest service, etc.

Restrictions Any restrictions that apply, including:

- *Pets* Conditions under which pets are allowed or not.
- *Fires* Campground rules for fires and fire safety.
- *Alcoholic Beverages* Campground rules regarding the consumption of alcoholic beverages.
- *Vehicle Maximum Length* Length in feet of the maximum size vehicle the campground can accommodate.
- *Other* Any other rules or restrictions, to include minimum and maximum stays; age or group size restrictions; areas off-limits to vehicular traffic; security constraints such as locking the main gate during the night; etc.

How to Get There Clear and specific directions, including mileage and landmarks, for finding the campground.

Supplemental Directory of Campgrounds

If you're looking for a campground within the territory covered in this guide and can't find a profiled campground that is close or convenient to your route, check the Supplemental Directory of Campgrounds. This directory of hundreds of additional campgrounds is organized alphabetically by state and city name. Each entry provides the campground's name, address, reservations phone, fax, website, number of sites, average fee per night, and hookups available.

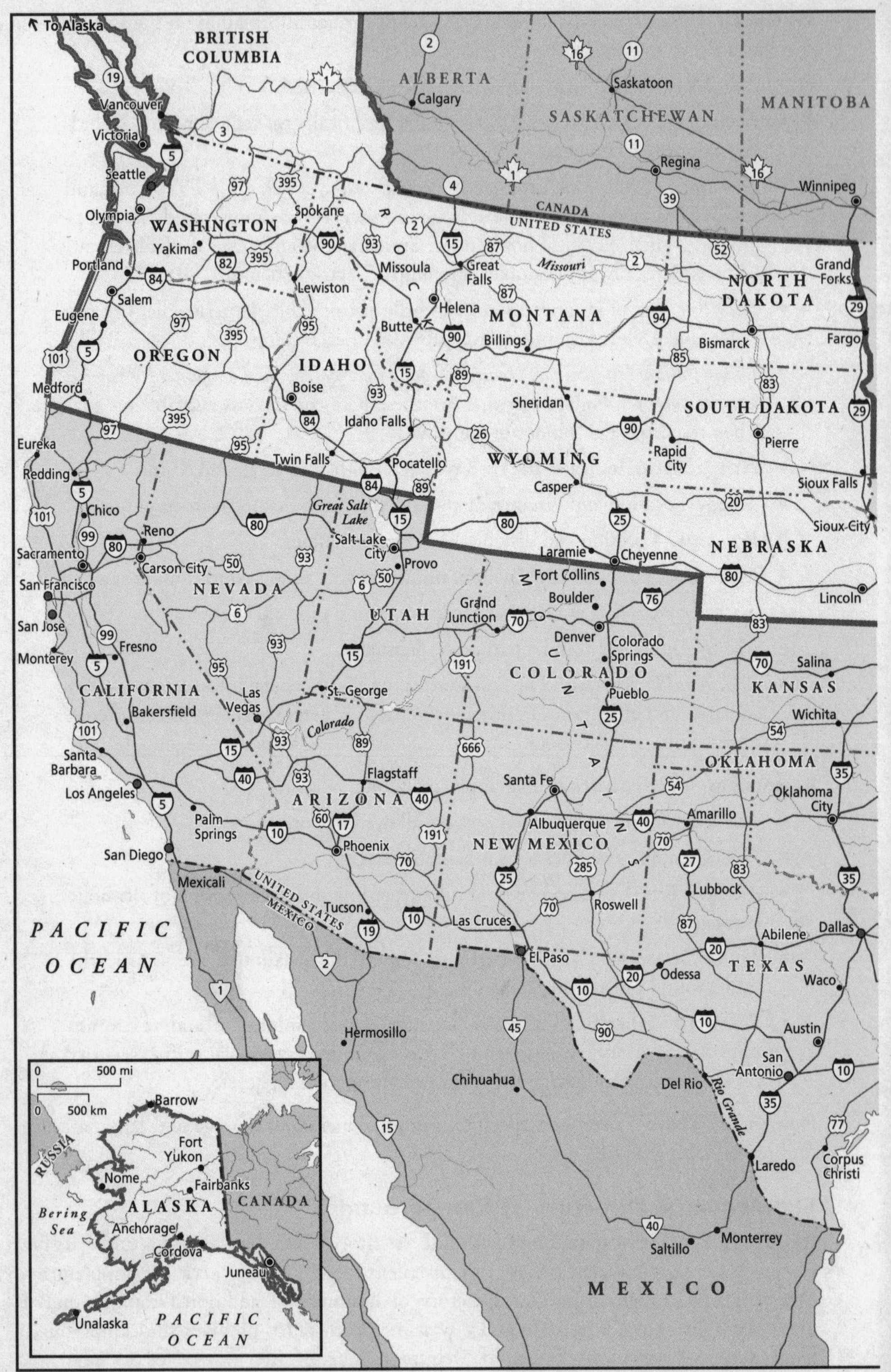
To Alaska
BRITISH COLUMBIA
ALBERTA
SASKATCHEWAN
MANITOBA
Calgary
Saskatoon
Regina
Winnipeg
Vancouver
Victoria
Seattle
Olympia
WASHINGTON
Yakima
Spokane
Portland
Salem
Eugene
OREGON
Medford
Lewiston
Missoula
Great Falls
Helena
Butte
MONTANA
Billings
IDAHO
Boise
Idaho Falls
Twin Falls
Pocatello
CANADA
UNITED STATES
Missouri
ROCKY MOUNTAINS
Grand Forks
NORTH DAKOTA
Bismarck
Fargo
SOUTH DAKOTA
Pierre
Rapid City
Sioux Falls
Sioux City
Sheridan
WYOMING
Casper
Laramie
Cheyenne
NEBRASKA
Lincoln
Eureka
Redding
Chico
Sacramento
San Francisco
San Jose
Monterey
Fresno
CALIFORNIA
Bakersfield
Santa Barbara
Los Angeles
Palm Springs
San Diego
Reno
Carson City
NEVADA
Las Vegas
Great Salt Lake
Salt Lake City
Provo
UTAH
St. George
Colorado
Grand Junction
Fort Collins
Boulder
Denver
Colorado Springs
COLORADO
Pueblo
Salina
KANSAS
Wichita
OKLAHOMA
Oklahoma City
ARIZONA
Flagstaff
Phoenix
Tucson
Santa Fe
Albuquerque
NEW MEXICO
Amarillo
Lubbock
Roswell
Las Cruces
El Paso
Abilene
Dallas
Odessa
TEXAS
Waco
Austin
San Antonio
Del Rio
Rio Grande
Laredo
Corpus Christi
Mexicali
UNITED STATES
MEXICO
PACIFIC OCEAN
Hermosillo
Chihuahua
Saltillo
Monterrey
MEXICO
0 500 mi
0 500 km
Barrow
RUSSIA
Fort Yukon
Nome
Fairbanks
ALASKA
CANADA
Bering Sea
Anchorage
Cordova
Juneau
Unalaska
PACIFIC OCEAN

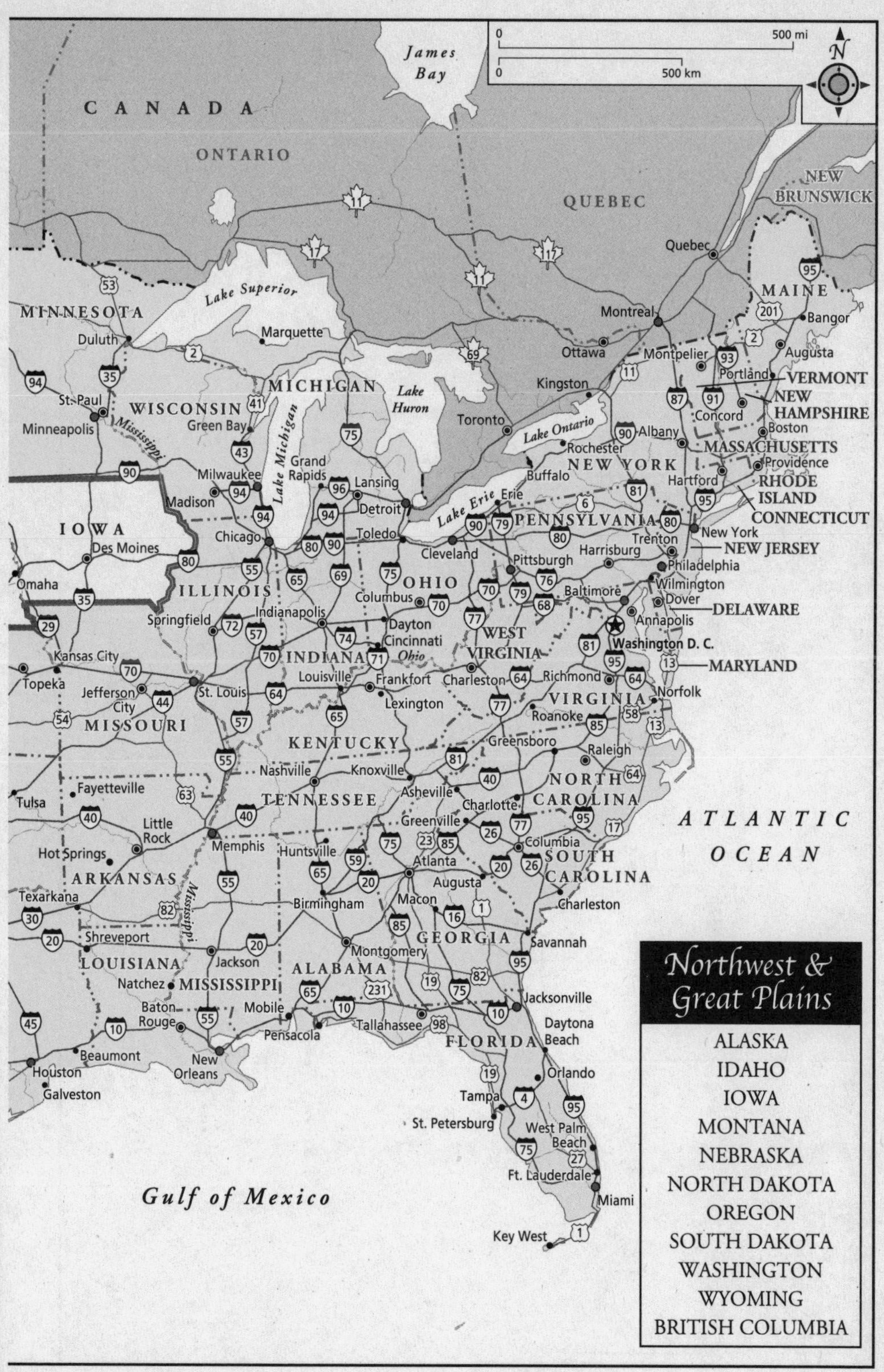
0
500 mi
0
500 km
N
James Bay
CANADA
ONTARIO
QUEBEC
NEW BRUNSWICK
Lake Superior
Lake Michigan
Lake Huron
Lake Ontario
Lake Erie
MINNESOTA
WISCONSIN
MICHIGAN
IOWA
ILLINOIS
INDIANA
OHIO
MISSOURI
KENTUCKY
TENNESSEE
ARKANSAS
LOUISIANA
MISSISSIPPI
ALABAMA
GEORGIA
FLORIDA
SOUTH CAROLINA
NORTH CAROLINA
VIRGINIA
WEST VIRGINIA
PENNSYLVANIA
NEW YORK
MAINE
VERMONT
NEW HAMPSHIRE
MASSACHUSETTS
RHODE ISLAND
CONNECTICUT
NEW JERSEY
DELAWARE
MARYLAND
Quebec
Montreal
Ottawa
Kingston
Toronto
Bangor
Augusta
Montpelier
Portland
Concord
Boston
Providence
Hartford
Albany
Rochester
Buffalo
Erie
New York
Trenton
Harrisburg
Philadelphia
Wilmington
Dover
Annapolis
Baltimore
Washington D. C.
Pittsburgh
Cleveland
Toledo
Detroit
Lansing
Grand Rapids
Marquette
Duluth
St. Paul
Minneapolis
Green Bay
Milwaukee
Madison
Chicago
Des Moines
Omaha
Springfield
Indianapolis
Columbus
Dayton
Cincinnati
Ohio
Mississippi
Kansas City
Topeka
Jefferson City
St. Louis
Louisville
Frankfort
Lexington
Charleston
Richmond
Norfolk
Roanoke
Greensboro
Raleigh
Nashville
Knoxville
Asheville
Charlotte
Greenville
Columbia
Tulsa
Fayetteville
Little Rock
Hot Springs
Memphis
Huntsville
Atlanta
Augusta
Birmingham
Macon
Charleston
Savannah
Texarkana
Shreveport
Jackson
Montgomery
Natchez
Mobile
Baton Rouge
New Orleans
Pensacola
Tallahassee
Jacksonville
Daytona Beach
Orlando
Tampa
St. Petersburg
West Palm Beach
Ft. Lauderdale
Miami
Key West
Beaumont
Houston
Galveston
ATLANTIC OCEAN
Gulf of Mexico
Northwest & Great Plains
ALASKA
IDAHO
IOWA
MONTANA
NEBRASKA
NORTH DAKOTA
OREGON
SOUTH DAKOTA
WASHINGTON
WYOMING
BRITISH COLUMBIA

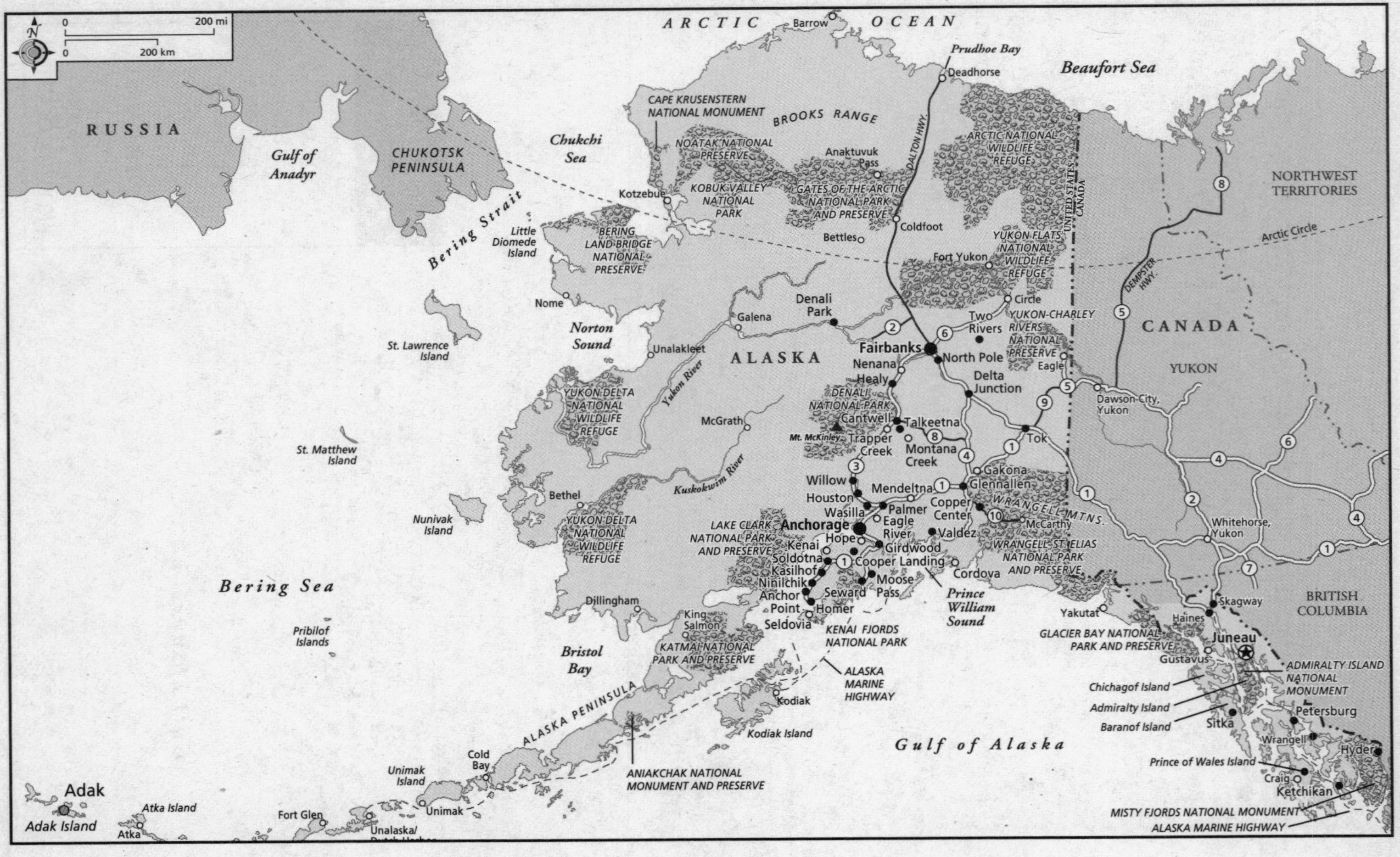
ARCTIC OCEAN
Beaufort Sea
Chukchi Sea
Bering Strait
Bering Sea
Norton Sound
Bristol Bay
Gulf of Alaska
Gulf of Anadyr
Prince William Sound
RUSSIA
CHUKOTSK PENINSULA
ALASKA
CANADA
YUKON
NORTHWEST TERRITORIES
BRITISH COLUMBIA
UNITED STATES
CANADA
Arctic Circle
BROOKS RANGE
WRANGELL MTNS.
ALASKA PENINSULA
0
200 mi
0
200 km
N
Barrow
Prudhoe Bay
Deadhorse
DALTON HWY.
DEMPSTER HWY.
CAPE KRUSENSTERN NATIONAL MONUMENT
NOATAK NATIONAL PRESERVE
KOBUK VALLEY NATIONAL PARK
GATES OF THE ARCTIC NATIONAL PARK AND PRESERVE
ARCTIC NATIONAL WILDLIFE REFUGE
YUKON FLATS NATIONAL WILDLIFE REFUGE
YUKON-CHARLEY RIVERS NATIONAL PRESERVE
BERING LAND BRIDGE NATIONAL PRESERVE
YUKON DELTA NATIONAL WILDLIFE REFUGE
DENALI NATIONAL PARK
LAKE CLARK NATIONAL PARK AND PRESERVE
WRANGELL-ST. ELIAS NATIONAL PARK AND PRESERVE
KENAI FJORDS NATIONAL PARK
KATMAI NATIONAL PARK AND PRESERVE
ANIAKCHAK NATIONAL MONUMENT AND PRESERVE
GLACIER BAY NATIONAL PARK AND PRESERVE
ADMIRALTY ISLAND NATIONAL MONUMENT
MISTY FJORDS NATIONAL MONUMENT
ALASKA MARINE HIGHWAY
Anaktuvuk Pass
Kotzebue
Coldfoot
Bettles
Fort Yukon
Circle
Little Diomede Island
Nome
Galena
Denali Park
Unalakleet
Yukon River
Kuskokwim River
McGrath
Bethel
Dillingham
King Salmon
St. Lawrence Island
St. Matthew Island
Nunivak Island
Pribilof Islands
Fairbanks
North Pole
Two Rivers
Nenana
Healy
Delta Junction
Eagle
Dawson City, Yukon
Cantwell
Talkeetna
Mt. McKinley
Trapper Creek
Montana Creek
Tok
Gakona
Glennallen
Willow
Houston
Mendeltna
Wasilla
Palmer
Eagle River
Copper Center
McCarthy
Anchorage
Hope
Girdwood
Valdez
Kenai
Soldotna
Kasilhof
Ninilchik
Anchor Point
Cooper Landing
Moose Pass
Seward
Homer
Seldovia
Cordova
Kodiak
Kodiak Island
Cold Bay
Unimak Island
Unimak
Fort Glen
Adak
Adak Island
Atka Island
Atka
Yakutat
Haines
Skagway
Whitehorse, Yukon
Juneau
Gustavus
Chichagof Island
Admiralty Island
Baranof Island
Sitka
Petersburg
Wrangell
Hyder
Prince of Wales Island
Craig
Ketchikan
1
2
3
4
5
6
7
8
9
10

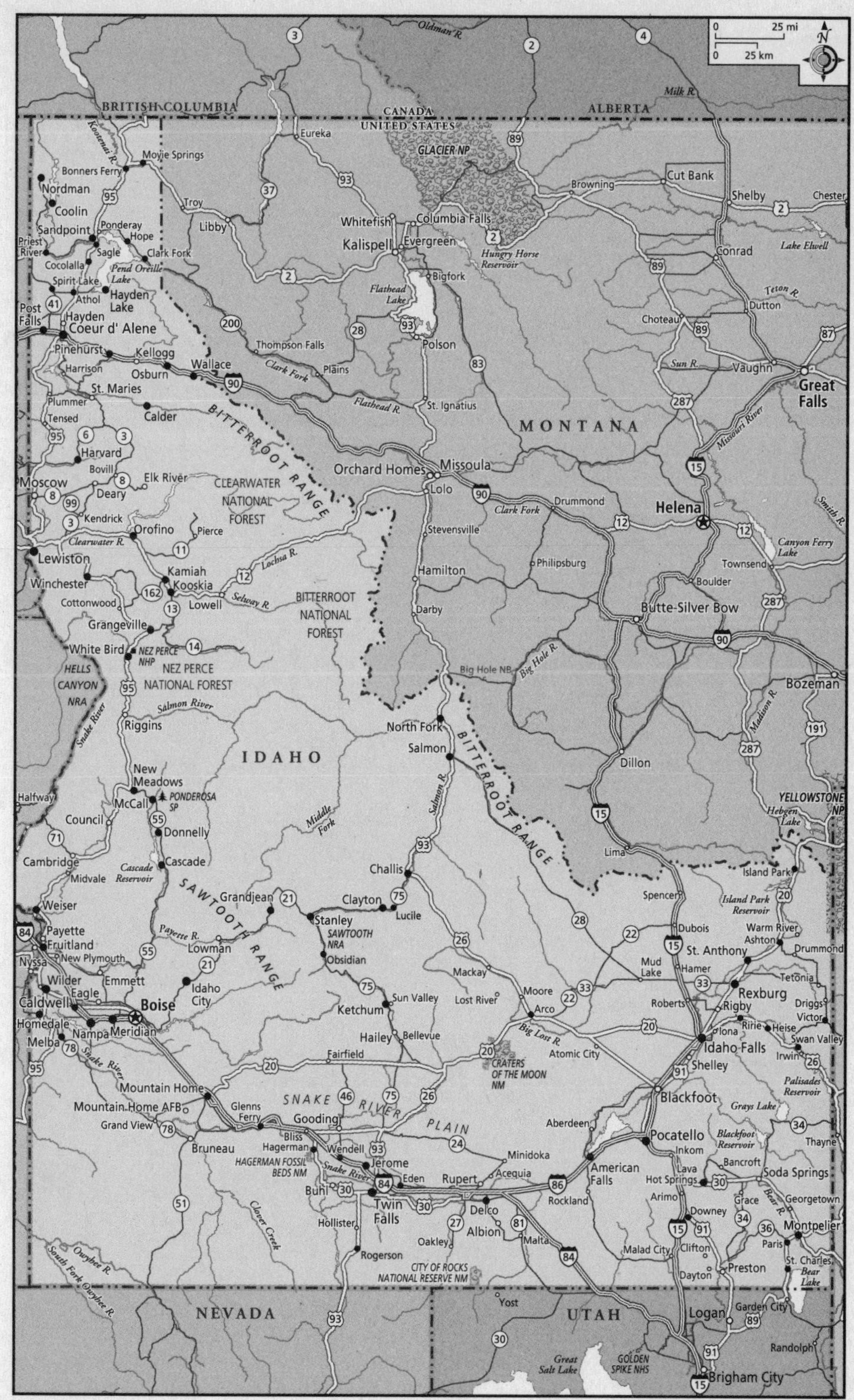

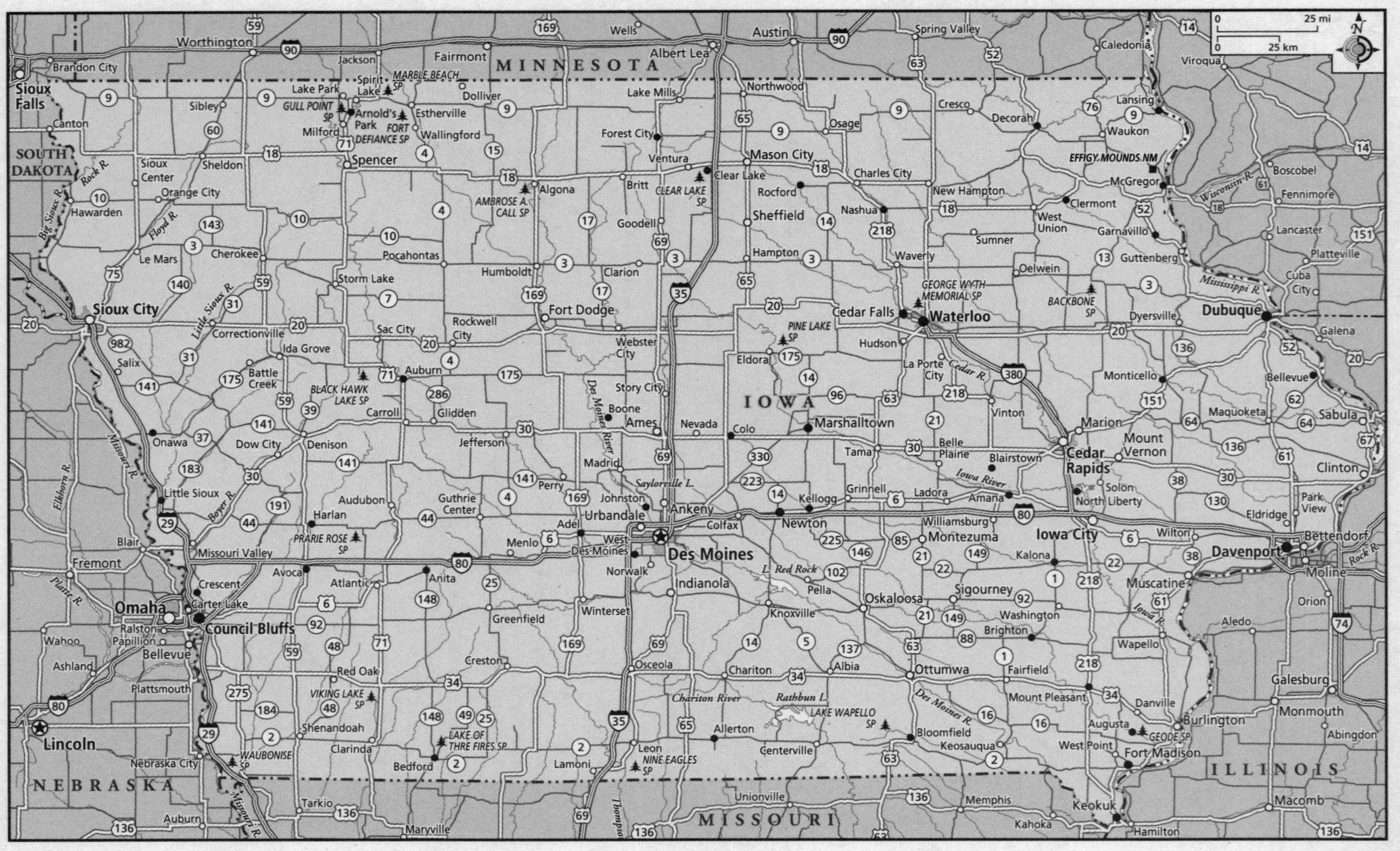

MINNESOTA
IOWA
ILLINOIS
MISSOURI
NEBRASKA
SOUTH DAKOTA
0 25 mi
0 25 km
N
Sioux Falls
Brandon City
Canton
Worthington
Albert Lea
Austin
Spring Valley
Fairmont
Wells
Jackson
Caledonia
Viroqua
Boscobel
Fennimore
Lancaster
Platteville
Galena
Cuba City
Sioux City
Dubuque
Waterloo
Cedar Falls
Cedar Rapids
Iowa City
Davenport
Bettendorf
Moline
Des Moines
West Des Moines
Council Bluffs
Omaha
Lincoln
Mason City
Clear Lake
Fort Dodge
Ames
Marshalltown
Newton
Ottumwa
Burlington
Fort Madison
Keokuk
Muscatine
Clinton
Decorah
McGregor
Spencer
Spirit Lake
Arnold's Park
Estherville
Storm Lake
Le Mars
Cherokee
Carroll
Denison
Harlan
Atlantic
Red Oak
Shenandoah
Clarinda
Creston
Osceola
Indianola
Knoxville
Pella
Oskaloosa
Grinnell
Kalona
Washington
Fairfield
Mount Pleasant
Galesburg
Monmouth
Macomb
EFFIGY MOUNDS NM
BACKBONE SP
PINE LAKE SP
CLEAR LAKE SP
GEORGE WYTH MEMORIAL SP
LAKE WAPELLO SP
LAKE OF THREE FIRES SP
NINE EAGLES SP
VIKING LAKE SP
WAUBONSIE SP
BLACK HAWK LAKE SP
PRARIE ROSE SP
GULL POINT SP
FORT DEFIANCE SP
MARBLE BEACH SP
AMBROSE A CALL SP
GEODE SP
Mississippi R.
Missouri R.
Des Moines River
Iowa River
Cedar R.
Big Sioux R.
Little Sioux R.
Rathbun L.
Saylorville L.
L. Red Rock
Chariton River
Platte R.

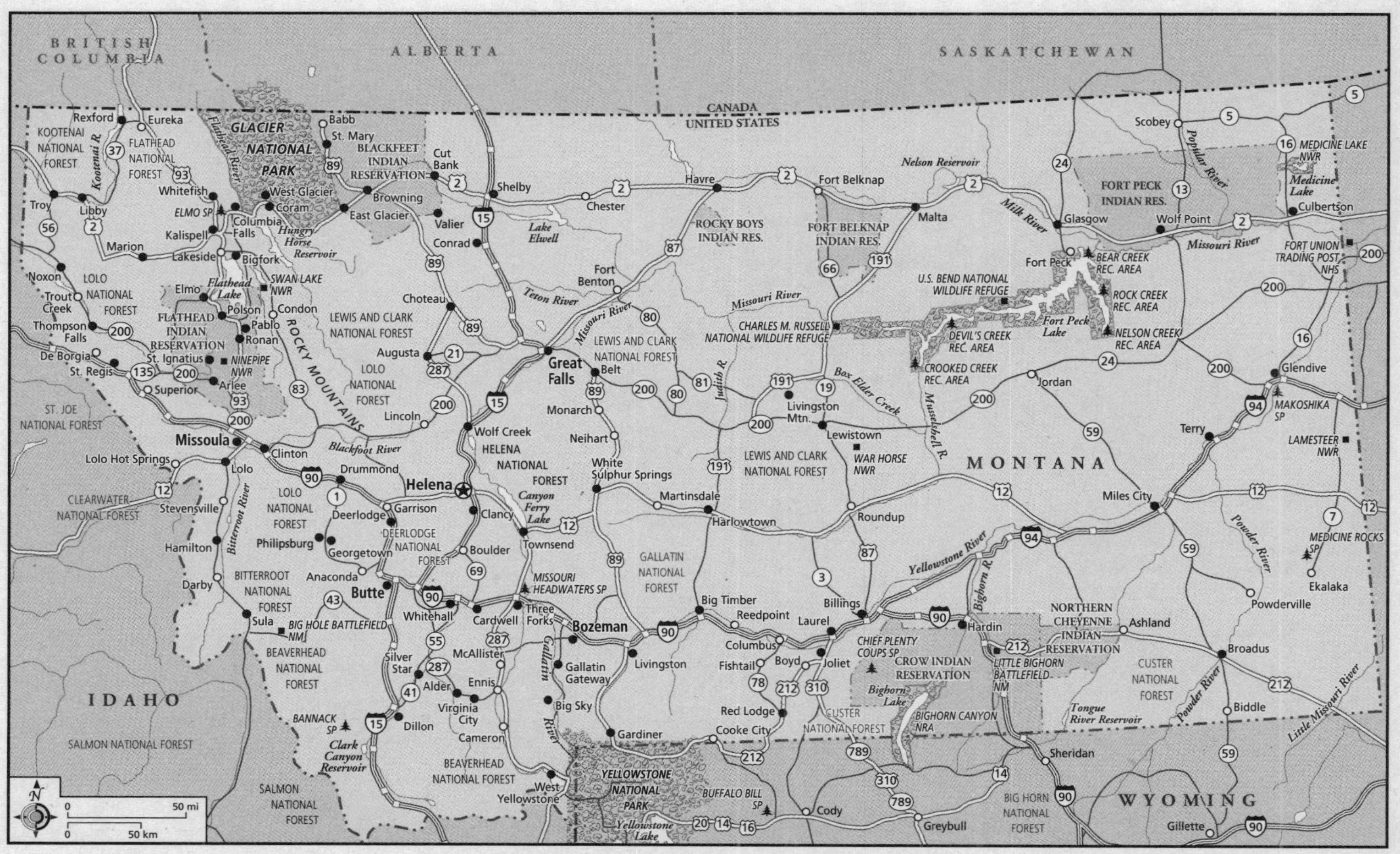
BRITISH COLUMBIA
ALBERTA
SASKATCHEWAN
CANADA
UNITED STATES
MONTANA
IDAHO
WYOMING
Rexford
Eureka
KOOTENAI NATIONAL FOREST
Kootenai R.
FLATHEAD NATIONAL FOREST
Flathead River
GLACIER NATIONAL PARK
Babb
St. Mary
BLACKFEET INDIAN RESERVATION
Cut Bank
Shelby
Chester
Havre
Fort Belknap
Nelson Reservoir
Malta
Milk River
Glasgow
Wolf Point
Scobey
Popular River
FORT PECK INDIAN RES.
MEDICINE LAKE NWR
Medicine Lake
Culbertson
Missouri River
FORT UNION TRADING POST NHS
Troy
Libby
Whitefish
ELMO SP
West Glacier
Coram
Columbia Falls
Hungry Horse Reservoir
Browning
East Glacier
Valier
Conrad
Lake Elwell
ROCKY BOYS INDIAN RES.
FORT BELKNAP INDIAN RES.
Fort Peck
BEAR CREEK REC. AREA
ROCK CREEK REC. AREA
NELSON CREEK REC. AREA
Fort Peck Lake
U.S. BEND NATIONAL WILDLIFE REFUGE
DEVIL'S CREEK REC. AREA
CROOKED CREEK REC. AREA
CHARLES M. RUSSELL NATIONAL WILDLIFE REFUGE
Kalispell
Marion
Lakeside
Bigfork
Noxon
LOLO NATIONAL FOREST
Trout Creek
Elmo
Flathead Lake
SWAN LAKE NWR
Polson
Condon
Thompson Falls
FLATHEAD INDIAN RESERVATION
Pablo
Ronan
De Borgia
St. Regis
St. Ignatius
NINEPIPE NWR
Arlee
Superior
ROCKY MOUNTAINS
LEWIS AND CLARK NATIONAL FOREST
Choteau
Augusta
LOLO NATIONAL FOREST
Teton River
Fort Benton
Missouri River
Great Falls
Belt
Monarch
Neihart
LEWIS AND CLARK NATIONAL FOREST
Judith R.
Livingston Mtn.
Lewistown
Box Elder Creek
Musselshell R.
WAR HORSE NWR
Jordan
Glendive
MAKOSHIKA SP
Terry
LAMESTEER NWR
ST. JOE NATIONAL FOREST
Missoula
Lolo Hot Springs
Clinton
Lolo
Blackfoot River
Lincoln
Wolf Creek
HELENA NATIONAL FOREST
Drummond
Helena
Garrison
Deerlodge
Clancy
Canyon Ferry Lake
White Sulphur Springs
Martinsdale
Harlowtown
LEWIS AND CLARK NATIONAL FOREST
Roundup
Miles City
Powder River
MEDICINE ROCKS SP
Ekalaka
CLEARWATER NATIONAL FOREST
Stevensville
Bitterroot River
Hamilton
Philipsburg
Georgetown
DEERLODGE NATIONAL FOREST
Boulder
Townsend
GALLATIN NATIONAL FOREST
Yellowstone River
Bighorn R.
Darby
BITTERROOT NATIONAL FOREST
Anaconda
Butte
MISSOURI HEADWATERS SP
Three Forks
Big Timber
Reedpoint
Billings
Laurel
Hardin
NORTHERN CHEYENNE INDIAN RESERVATION
Ashland
Powderville
Sula
BIG HOLE BATTLEFIELD NM
Whitehall
Cardwell
Bozeman
Columbus
CHIEF PLENTY COUPS SP
CROW INDIAN RESERVATION
LITTLE BIGHORN BATTLEFIELD NM
Broadus
BEAVERHEAD NATIONAL FOREST
Silver Star
McAllister
Gallatin River
Gallatin Gateway
Livingston
Fishtail
Boyd
Joliet
Bighorn Lake
CUSTER NATIONAL FOREST
Tongue River Reservoir
Biddle
Little Missouri River
Alder
Ennis
Big Sky
Red Lodge
BIGHORN CANYON NRA
BANNACK SP
Clark Canyon Reservoir
Dillon
Virginia City
Cameron
Gardiner
Cooke City
CUSTER NATIONAL FOREST
Sheridan
SALMON NATIONAL FOREST
BEAVERHEAD NATIONAL FOREST
West Yellowstone
YELLOWSTONE NATIONAL PARK
Yellowstone Lake
BUFFALO BILL SP
Cody
Greybull
BIG HORN NATIONAL FOREST
Gillette
N
0
50 mi
50 km

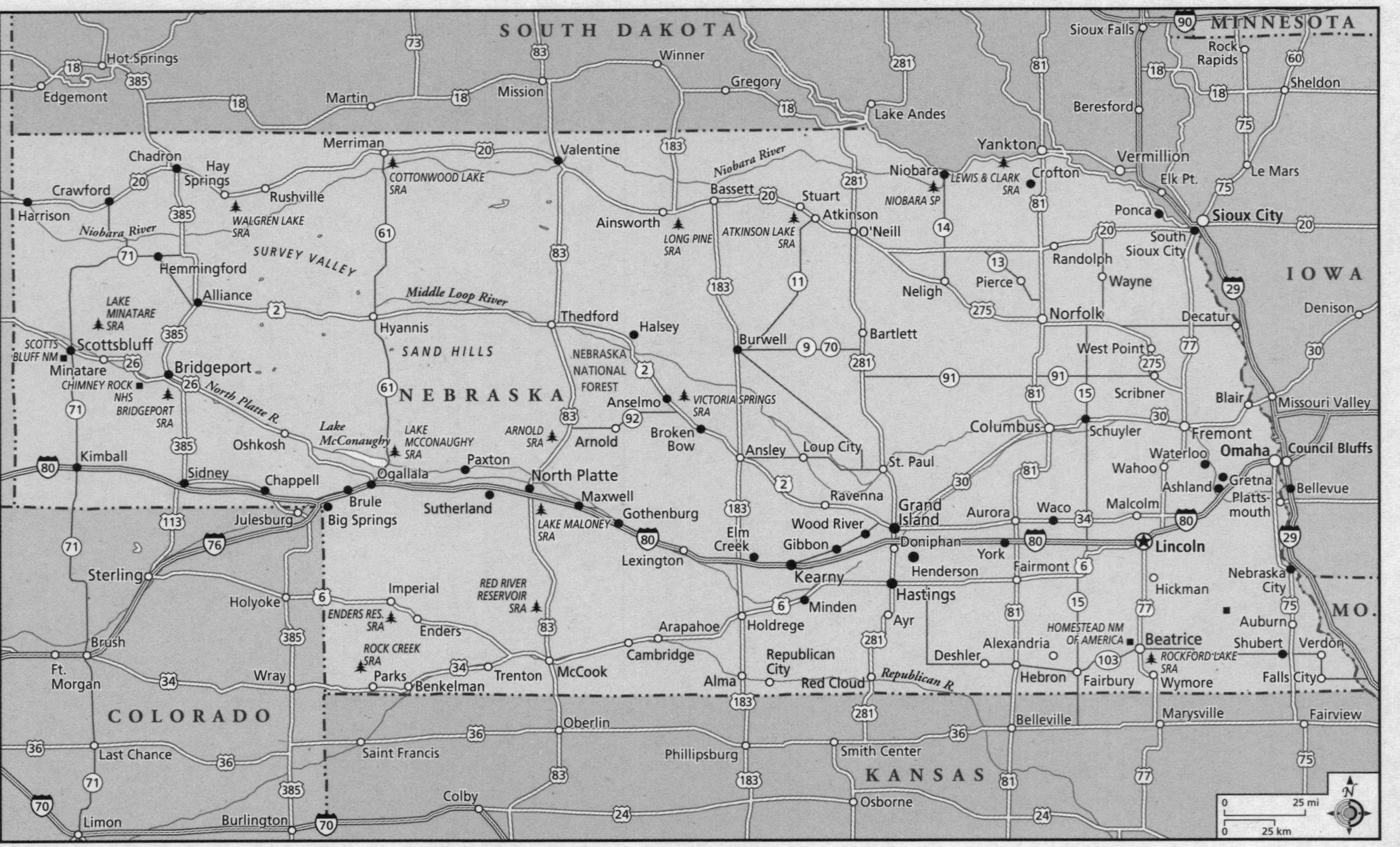
SOUTH DAKOTA
MINNESOTA
IOWA
MO.
NEBRASKA
KANSAS
COLORADO
Hot Springs
Edgemont
Martin
Mission
Winner
Gregory
Lake Andes
Sioux Falls
Rock Rapids
Sheldon
Beresford
Le Mars
Yankton
Vermillion
Elk Pt.
Sioux City
South Sioux City
Ponca
Niobara
LEWIS & CLARK SRA
NIOBARA SP
Crofton
Niobara River
Chadron
Hay Springs
Rushville
Crawford
Harrison
Niobara River
WALGREN LAKE SRA
Merriman
COTTONWOOD LAKE SRA
Valentine
Ainsworth
LONG PINE SRA
Bassett
Stuart
Atkinson
ATKINSON LAKE SRA
O'Neill
Neligh
Pierce
Randolph
Wayne
Norfolk
Decatur
Denison
SURVEY VALLEY
Hemmingford
Alliance
Middle Loop River
Thedford
Halsey
Burwell
Bartlett
West Point
Scribner
Blair
Missouri Valley
LAKE MINATARE SRA
SCOTTS BLUFF NM
Scottsbluff
Minatare
Bridgeport
CHIMNEY ROCK NHS
BRIDGEPORT SRA
Hyannis
SAND HILLS
NEBRASKA NATIONAL FOREST
NEBRASKA
Anselmo
VICTORIA SPRINGS SRA
North Platte R.
Lake McConaughy
LAKE MCCONAUGHY SRA
ARNOLD SRA
Arnold
Broken Bow
Oshkosh
Columbus
Schuyler
Fremont
Omaha
Council Bluffs
Waterloo
Wahoo
Ashland
Gretna
Bellevue
Plattsmouth
Kimball
Sidney
Chappell
Ogallala
Paxton
North Platte
Ansley
Loup City
St. Paul
Ravenna
Julesburg
Brule
Big Springs
Sutherland
Maxwell
LAKE MALONEY SRA
Gothenburg
Elm Creek
Wood River
Grand Island
Aurora
Waco
Malcolm
Lincoln
Lexington
Gibbon
Doniphan
York
Henderson
Kearny
Fairmont
Sterling
Imperial
RED RIVER RESERVOIR SRA
Hastings
Hickman
Nebraska City
Holyoke
ENDERS RES. SRA
Enders
Minden
Ayr
Arapahoe
Holdrege
Auburn
Brush
ROCK CREEK SRA
Cambridge
Alexandria
HOMESTEAD NM OF AMERICA
Beatrice
Shubert
Verdon
Ft. Morgan
Wray
Parks
Benkelman
Trenton
McCook
Republican City
Alma
Red Cloud
Republican R.
Deshler
Hebron
Fairbury
ROCKFORD LAKE SRA
Wymore
Falls City
Oberlin
Belleville
Marysville
Fairview
Last Chance
Saint Francis
Phillipsburg
Smith Center
Colby
Osborne
Limon
Burlington
0 25 mi
0 25 km
N

SASKATCHEWAN
MANITOBA
MINNESOTA
NORTH DAKOTA
SOUTH DAKOTA
CANADA
UNITED STATES
0 25 mi
0 25 km
N
Souris R.
Fortuna
Crosby
Noonan
Westby
Flaxton
Bowbells
Loraine
Mohall
Westhope
Bottineau
Dunseith
St. John
Rolla
Sarles
Rock L.
Perth
Rocklake
Wales
Langdon
Walhalla
Cavalier
Hamilton
Humboldt
Lancaster
Lake Bronson
Grenora
Alamo
Wildrose
Powers Lake
Kenmare
Maxbass
L. Darling
Overly
Loma
St. Thomas
Egeland
FORT UNION TRADING POST NHS
Upham
Barton
Wolford
Drayton
Stephen
Ray
White Earth
Donnybrook
Minot AFB
GEOGRAPHIC CENTER OF NORTH AMERICA
Rugby
Cando
Starkweather
Adams
Grafton
Argyle
Wheelock
Ross
Palermo
Des Lacs
Granville
Towner
Leeds
Churchs Ferry
Lawton
Minto
Williston
Minot
Surrey
Balta
Brinsmade
Dry L.
Devils Lake
Warren
Missouri River
New Town
Plaza
Velva
Bergen
Esmond
Lakota
Petersburg
Manvel
Arvilla
East Grand Forks
Alexander
Fairview
Parshall
Ryder
Kief
Anamoose
Oberon
Devils L.
SULLYS HILL NAT'L GAME PRES.
Warwick
Grand Forks
Watford City
Max
Harvey
Sheyenne
Pekin
Sheyenne R.
Reynolds
THEODORE ROOSEVELT NP
L. Sakakawea
FORT STEVENSON SP
Garrison
AUDUBON NWR
Fessenden
New Rockford
Binford
Sharon
Goose R.
Little Missouri R.
Pick City
Coleharbor
McClusky
Bowdon
Carrington
Mayville
Hillsboro
Killdeer
KNIFE RIVER INDIAN VILLAGES NHS
Halliday
Washburn
Kensal
Hannaford
Arrowwood L.
Clifford
Wild Rice R.
THEODORE ROOSEVELT NP (Elkhorn Ranch Site)
Beulah
Hazen
Pingree
Sibley
Pipestem Creek
Knife R.
Wilton
Wing
Tuttle
L. Ashtabula
Green River
Missouri River
Spiritwood Lake
THEODORE ROOSEVELT NP
Jamestown Res.
Eckelson
Belfield
Dickinson
Hebron
Bismarck
Medina
West Fargo
Beach
Medora
Jamestown
Valley City
Fargo
South Heart
Glen Ullin
Mandan
Menoken
Long L.
Steele
Golva
LITTLE MISSOURI NATIONAL GRASSLAND
Almont
Montpelier
Nome
Maple R.
Davenport
Streeter
Amidon
New England
L. Tschida
Heart R.
Napoleon
Jud
Dickey
FORT RANSOM SP
Sheyenne R.
Red River
Cannonball R.
Mott
Elgin
Flasher
Hazelton
Lisbon
Colfax
Solen
BEAVER LAKE SP
James R.
Marmarth
Leith
Fredonia
Edgeley
Verona
Linton
La Moure
Gwinner
Mooreton
Cedar Creek
Cannonball R.
Wishek
Bowman
Scranton
Strasburg
Merricourt
Oakes
Fort Yates
Ashley
L. Oahe
Hankinson
Hettinger
CEDAR RIVER NATIONAL GRASSLAND
Selfridge
Hague
Forbes
Ellendale
Ludden
Havana
Lemmon
McIntosh
McLaughlin
Long Lake
Herreid
Eureka
Frederick
Britton
Little Missouri R.
GRAND RIVER NATIONAL GRASSLAND
Grande R.
Leola
L. Traverse
Columbia Road Res.
Buffalo
Bison
Mobridge
Sisseton
Browns Valley
Camp Crook
Langford

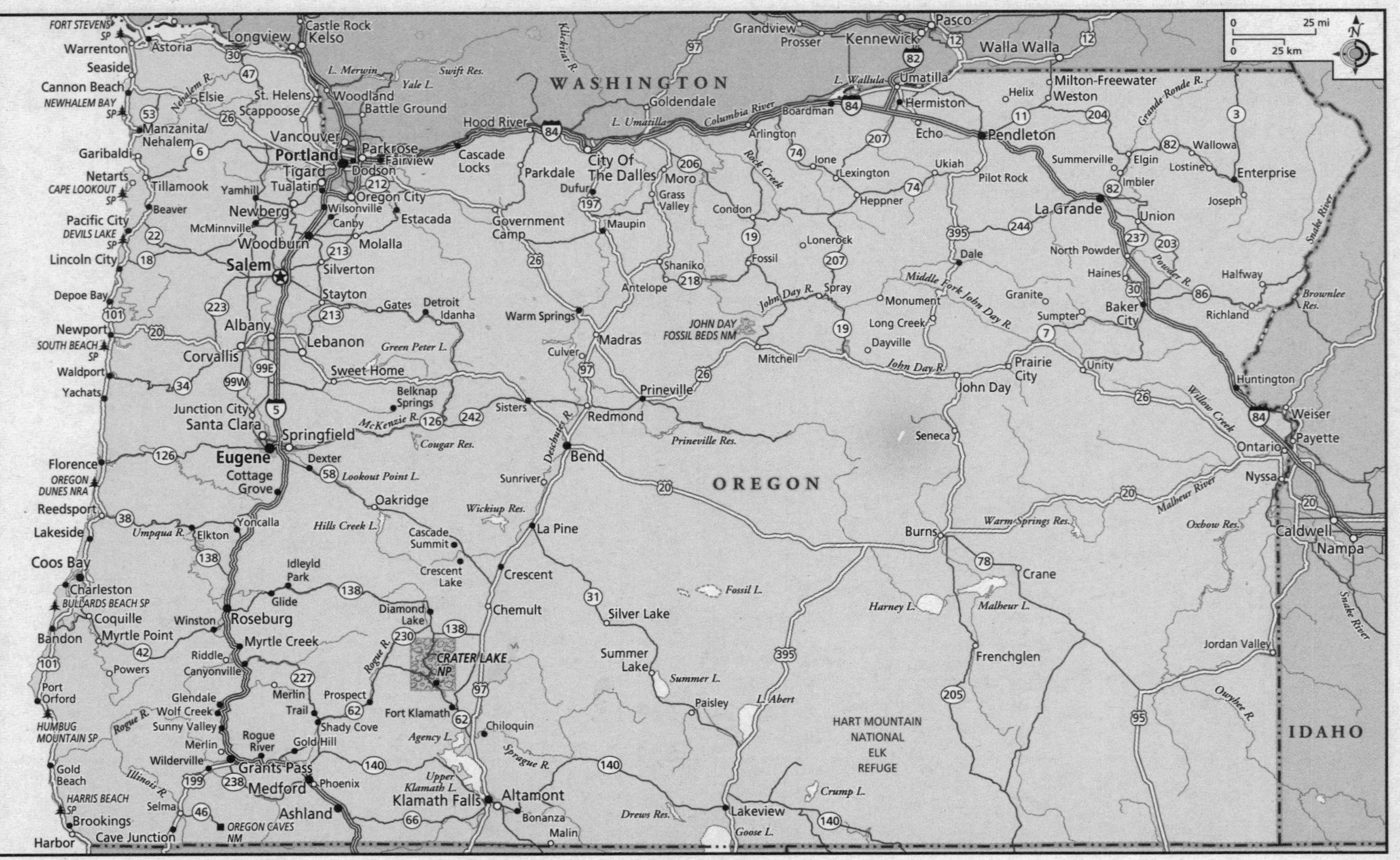

WASHINGTON
OREGON
IDAHO
0 25 mi
0 25 km
N
FORT STEVENS SP
Warrenton
Astoria
Longview
Castle Rock
Kelso
Seaside
Cannon Beach
NEWHALEM BAY SP
Nehalem R.
Elsie
St. Helens
Scappoose
Woodland
Battle Ground
L. Merwin
Yale L.
Swift Res.
Klickitat R.
Grandview
Prosser
Kennewick
Pasco
Walla Walla
Manzanita/ Nehalem
Garibaldi
Netarts
CAPE LOOKOUT SP
Tillamook
Vancouver
Portland
Parkrose
Fairview
Tigard
Dodson
Tualatin
Yamhill
Oregon City
Wilsonville
Canby
Estacada
Newberg
McMinnville
Woodburn
Molalla
Beaver
Pacific City
DEVILS LAKE SP
Lincoln City
Salem
Silverton
Stayton
Gates
Detroit
Idanha
Depoe Bay
Newport
SOUTH BEACH SP
Albany
Corvallis
Lebanon
Green Peter L.
Waldport
Yachats
Sweet Home
Belknap Springs
Junction City
Santa Clara
Springfield
McKenzie R.
Cougar Res.
Eugene
Florence
OREGON DUNES NRA
Dexter
Cottage Grove
Lookout Point L.
Oakridge
Reedsport
Lakeside
Umpqua R.
Elkton
Yoncalla
Hills Creek L.
Cascade Summit
Crescent Lake
Coos Bay
Charleston
BULLARDS BEACH SP
Coquille
Myrtle Point
Bandon
Idleyld Park
Glide
Winston
Roseburg
Myrtle Creek
Diamond Lake
Riddle
Canyonville
Powers
Port Orford
Rogue R.
CRATER LAKE NP
HUMBUG MOUNTAIN SP
Glendale
Wolf Creek
Sunny Valley
Merlin
Trail
Prospect
Fort Klamath
Shady Cove
Rogue River
Gold Hill
Wilderville
Grants Pass
Agency L.
Chiloquin
Gold Beach
HARRIS BEACH SP
Illinois R.
Selma
Medford
Phoenix
Upper Klamath L.
Klamath Falls
Altamont
Bonanza
Malin
Brookings
Harbor
Cave Junction
OREGON CAVES NM
Ashland
Hood River
Cascade Locks
Parkdale
City Of The Dalles
Dufur
Government Camp
Goldendale
L. Umatilla
Columbia River
Moro
Grass Valley
Maupin
Warm Springs
Shaniko
Antelope
Madras
Culver
JOHN DAY FOSSIL BEDS NM
Prineville
Sisters
Redmond
Deschutes R.
Bend
Prineville Res.
Sunriver
Wickiup Res.
La Pine
Crescent
Chemult
Silver Lake
Summer Lake
Summer L.
Paisley
L. Abert
Sprague R.
Drews Res.
Lakeview
Goose L.
Crump L.
HART MOUNTAIN NATIONAL ELK REFUGE
Fossil L.
Harney L.
Malheur L.
Crane
Frenchglen
Burns
Warm Springs Res.
Seneca
Arlington
Boardman
L. Wallula
Umatilla
Hermiston
Echo
Rock Creek
Condon
Ione
Lexington
Heppner
Lonerock
Fossil
Spray
John Day R.
Mitchell
Monument
Long Creek
Dayville
Ukiah
Pilot Rock
Dale
Middle Fork John Day R.
Granite
Sumpter
Prairie City
John Day
Unity
Helix
Milton-Freewater
Weston
Pendleton
Grande Ronde R.
Summerville
Elgin
Imbler
Wallowa
Lostine
Enterprise
Joseph
La Grande
Union
North Powder
Haines
Powder R.
Baker City
Halfway
Richland
Brownlee Res.
Snake River
Huntington
Willow Creek
Weiser
Payette
Ontario
Nyssa
Malheur River
Oxbow Res.
Caldwell
Nampa
Jordan Valley
Owyhee R.

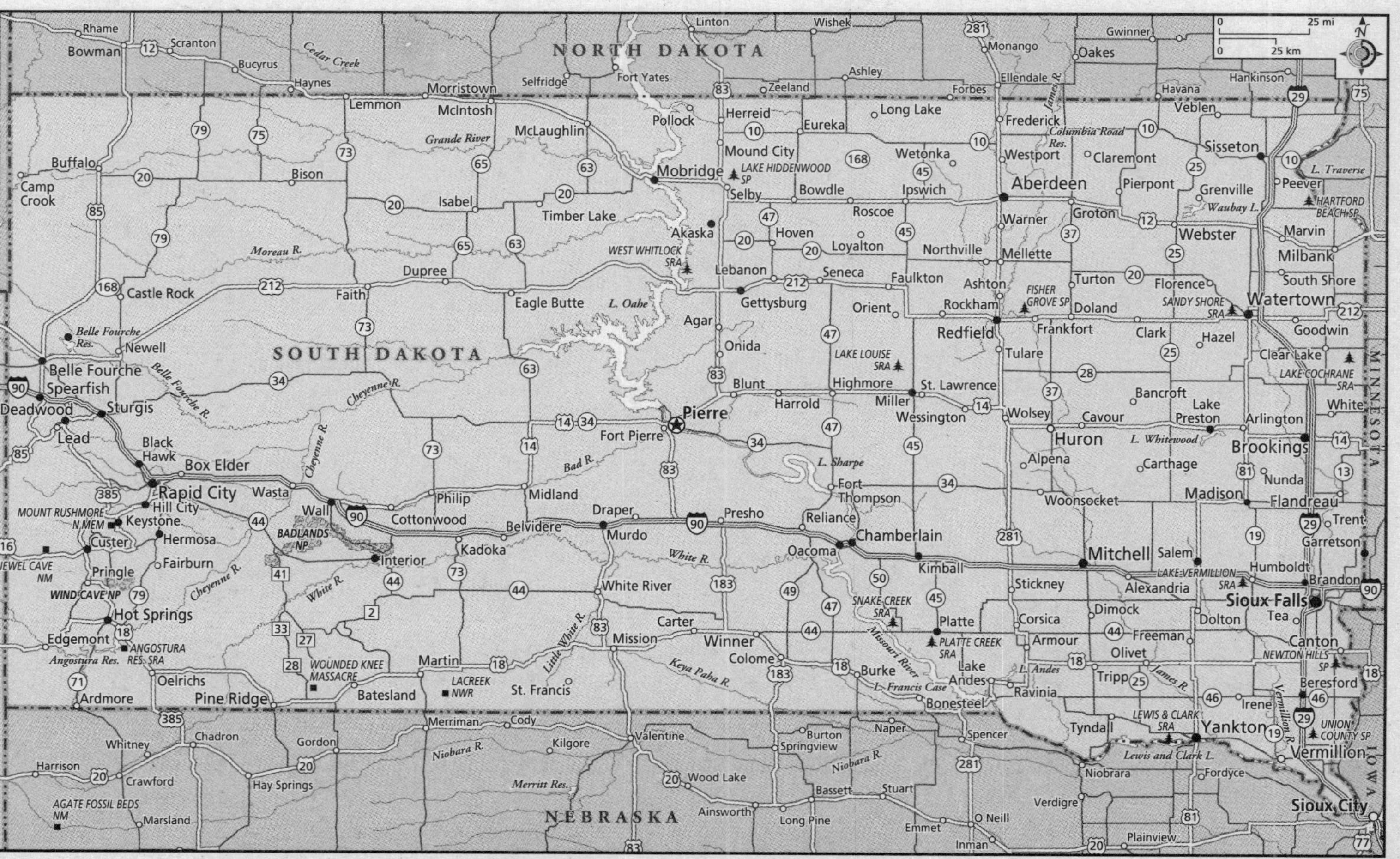
NORTH DAKOTA
SOUTH DAKOTA
NEBRASKA
MINNESOTA
IOWA
0 25 mi
0 25 km
Pierre
Rapid City
Sioux Falls
Aberdeen
Watertown
Brookings
Huron
Mitchell
Yankton
Vermillion
Sioux City
Mobridge
Chamberlain
Spearfish
Sturgis
Deadwood
Lead
Belle Fourche
Hot Springs
Custer
Keystone
Hill City
Wall
Philip
Murdo
Winner
Lemmon
Buffalo
Faith
Eagle Butte
Gettysburg
Redfield
Madison
Sisseton
Webster
Milbank
Flandreau
Pine Ridge
Martin
Fort Pierre
L. Oahe
Missouri River
BADLANDS NP
MOUNT RUSHMORE N.MEM
WIND CAVE NP
JEWEL CAVE NM
WOUNDED KNEE MASSACRE

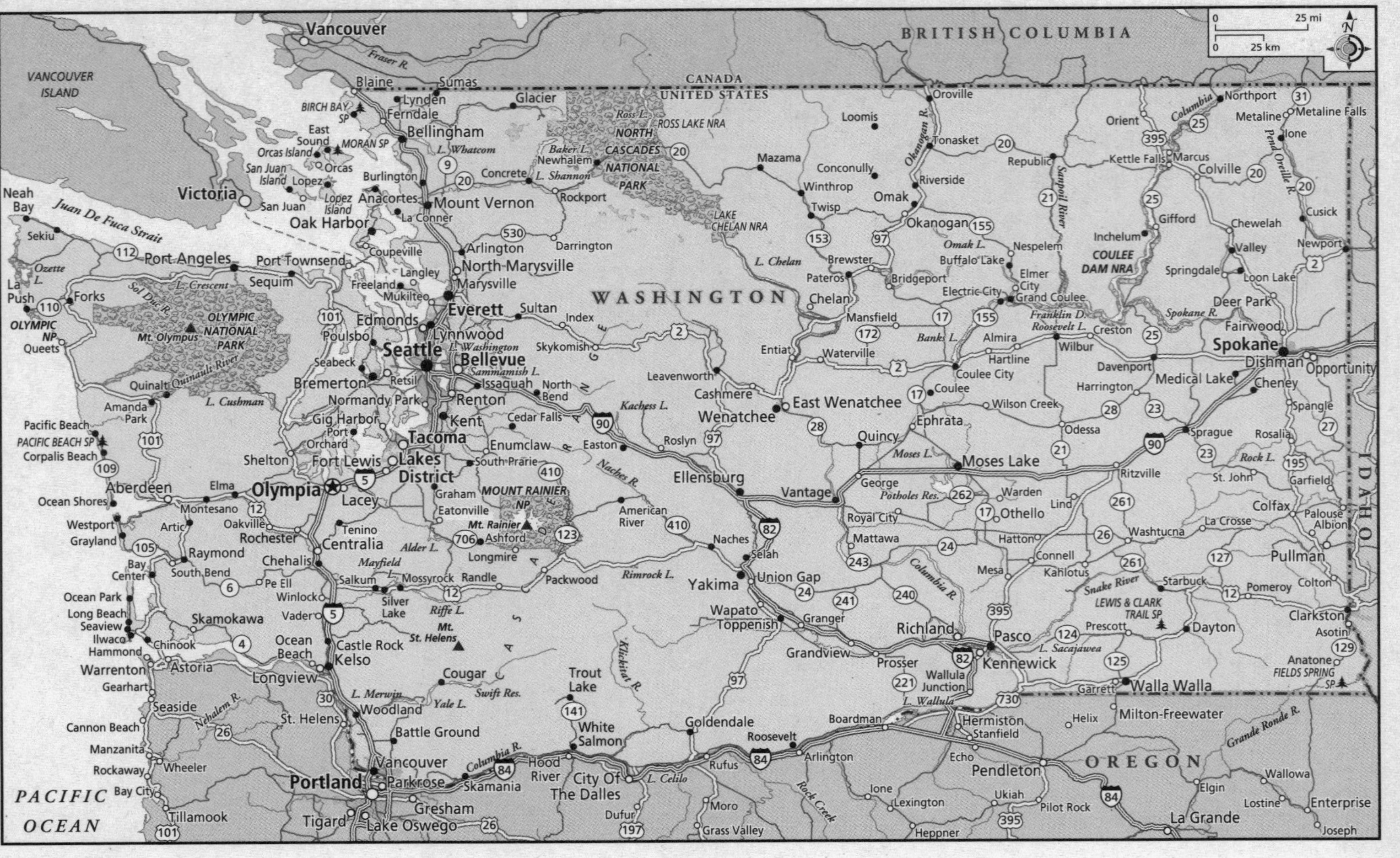

BRITISH COLUMBIA
CANADA
UNITED STATES
WASHINGTON
IDAHO
OREGON
PACIFIC OCEAN
VANCOUVER ISLAND
Juan De Fuca Strait
0 25 mi
0 25 km
N
Vancouver
Victoria
Blaine
Sumas
Lynden
Ferndale
Bellingham
Glacier
Oroville
Loomis
Tonasket
Republic
Orient
Northport
Metaline
Metaline Falls
Ione
Kettle Falls
Marcus
Colville
Cusick
Chewelah
Newport
Valley
Loon Lake
Springdale
Inchelum
Gifford
COULEE DAM NRA
Deer Park
Fairwood
Spokane
Dishman
Opportunity
Cheney
Medical Lake
Spangle
Rosalia
Garfield
St. John
Colfax
Palouse
Albion
Pullman
Colton
Pomeroy
Clarkston
Asotin
Anatone
FIELDS SPRING SP
Dayton
Starbuck
Prescott
Walla Walla
Garrett
LEWIS & CLARK TRAIL SP
Kennewick
Pasco
Richland
Wallula Junction
Milton-Freewater
Helix
Hermiston
Stanfield
Echo
Pendleton
Pilot Rock
Ukiah
La Grande
Elgin
Lostine
Wallowa
Enterprise
Joseph
Boardman
Arlington
Roosevelt
Rufus
Moro
Grass Valley
Ione
Lexington
Heppner
Goldendale
White Salmon
Trout Lake
Hood River
City Of The Dalles
Dufur
Skamania
Portland
Parkrose
Gresham
Tigard
Lake Oswego
Vancouver
Battle Ground
Woodland
St. Helens
Longview
Kelso
Castle Rock
Cougar
Mt. St. Helens
Astoria
Warrenton
Gearhart
Seaside
Cannon Beach
Manzanita
Rockaway
Wheeler
Bay City
Tillamook
Hammond
Ilwaco
Seaview
Chinook
Long Beach
Ocean Park
Skamokawa
Ocean Beach
Vader
Winlock
Silver Lake
Salkum
Mossyrock
Randle
Packwood
Chehalis
Centralia
Pe Ell
South Bend
Raymond
Bay Center
Grayland
Westport
Ocean Shores
Aberdeen
Montesano
Elma
Oakville
Rochester
Tenino
Olympia
Lacey
Fort Lewis
Lakes District
Shelton
Port Orchard
Gig Harbor
Tacoma
Normandy Park
Bremerton
Seabeck
Poulsbo
Retsil
Seattle
Bellevue
Renton
Kent
Issaquah
North Bend
Cedar Falls
Enumclaw
South Prarie
Graham
Eatonville
Ashford
Longmire
MOUNT RAINIER NP
Mt. Rainier
Edmonds
Lynnwood
Everett
Mukilteo
Marysville
North-Marysville
Arlington
Darrington
Sultan
Index
Skykomish
Leavenworth
Cashmere
Wenatchee
East Wenatchee
Entiat
Chelan
Pateros
Brewster
Bridgeport
Mansfield
Waterville
Ellensburg
Roslyn
Easton
Vantage
Yakima
Naches
Selah
Union Gap
Wapato
Toppenish
Granger
Grandview
Prosser
Quincy
George
Royal City
Mattawa
Moses Lake
Warden
Othello
Lind
Ritzville
Washtucna
La Crosse
Hatton
Connell
Kahlotus
Mesa
Odessa
Harrington
Davenport
Sprague
Wilbur
Creston
Almira
Hartline
Coulee City
Coulee
Ephrata
Wilson Creek
Grand Coulee
Electric City
Elmer City
Nespelem
Buffalo Lake
Okanogan
Omak
Riverside
Conconully
Mazama
Winthrop
Twisp
Mount Vernon
Burlington
Anacortes
La Conner
Concrete
Rockport
Newhalem
Oak Harbor
Coupeville
Langley
Freeland
Port Townsend
Sequim
Port Angeles
Sekiu
Neah Bay
La Push
Forks
Queets
Quinalt
Amanda Park
Pacific Beach
PACIFIC BEACH SP
Corpalis Beach
Artic
Orcas Island
East Sound
Orcas
Lopez
Lopez Island
San Juan Island
San Juan
BIRCH BAY SP
MORAN SP
OLYMPIC NATIONAL PARK
OLYMPIC NP
Mt. Olympus
NORTH CASCADES NATIONAL PARK
ROSS LAKE NRA
LAKE CHELAN NRA
Fraser R.
L. Whatcom
Baker L.
L. Shannon
Ross L.
L. Chelan
Okanogan R.
Omak L.
Sanpoil River
Columbia R.
Pend Oreille R.
Spokane R.
Franklin D. Roosevelt L.
Banks L.
Moses L.
Potholes Res.
Rock L.
Snake River
L. Sacajawea
L. Wallula
Grande Ronde R.
Rock Creek
L. Celilo
Klickitat R.
Rimrock L.
Naches R.
Kachess L.
L. Washington
Sammamish L.
L. Cushman
Quinault River
L. Crescent
Sol Duc R.
Ozette L.
Alder L.
Mayfield L.
Riffe L.
L. Merwin
Yale L.
Swift Res.
Nehalem R.

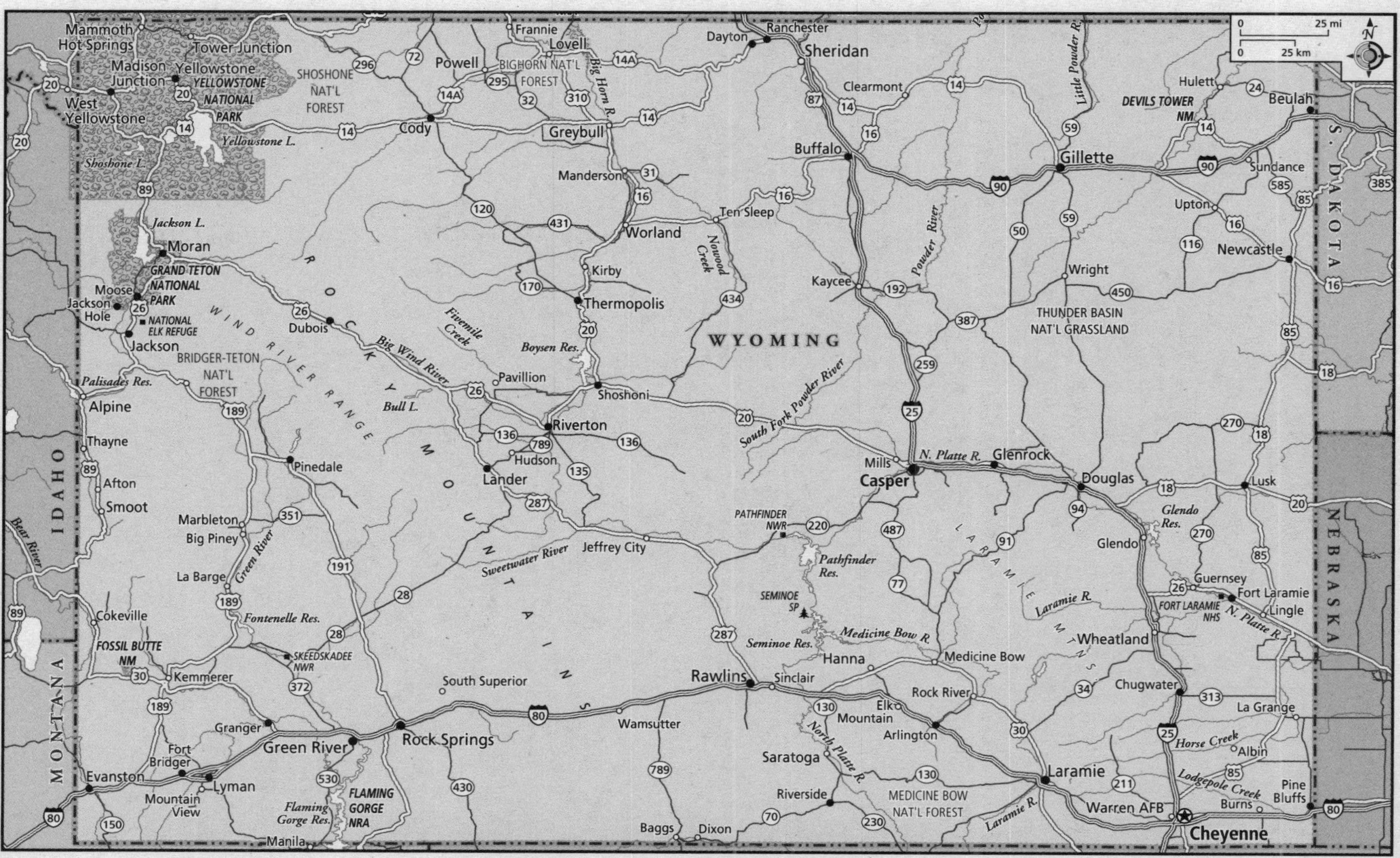
WYOMING
S. DAKOTA
NEBRASKA
IDAHO
MONTANA
ROCKY MOUNTAINS
LARAMIE MTNS
WIND RIVER RANGE
0 25 mi
0 25 km
N
Mammoth Hot Springs
Tower Junction
Madison Junction
Yellowstone
YELLOWSTONE NATIONAL PARK
West Yellowstone
Yellowstone L.
Shoshone L.
SHOSHONE NAT'L FOREST
Powell
Frannie
Lovell
BIGHORN NAT'L FOREST
Big Horn R.
Cody
Greybull
Dayton
Ranchester
Sheridan
Clearmont
Buffalo
Little Powder R.
DEVILS TOWER NM
Hulett
Beulah
Gillette
Sundance
Upton
Newcastle
Manderson
Worland
Ten Sleep
Nowood Creek
Powder River
Wright
Kaycee
THUNDER BASIN NAT'L GRASSLAND
Jackson L.
Moran
GRAND TETON NATIONAL PARK
Moose
Jackson Hole
NATIONAL ELK REFUGE
Jackson
Dubois
Big Wind River
Fivemile Creek
Kirby
Thermopolis
Boysen Res.
BRIDGER-TETON NAT'L FOREST
Palisades Res.
Alpine
Pavillion
Shoshoni
Bull L.
South Fork Powder River
Riverton
Hudson
Lander
Mills
Casper
N. Platte R.
Glenrock
Douglas
Lusk
Thayne
Afton
Smoot
Pinedale
Marbleton
Big Piney
Green River
La Barge
Bear River
Sweetwater River
Jeffrey City
PATHFINDER NWR
Pathfinder Res.
Glendo
Glendo Res.
Guernsey
Fort Laramie
FORT LARAMIE NHS
N. Platte R.
Lingle
Laramie R.
Cokeville
Fontenelle Res.
FOSSIL BUTTE NM
SKEEDSKADEE NWR
SEMINOE SP
Medicine Bow R.
Seminoe Res.
Wheatland
Kemmerer
Hanna
Medicine Bow
South Superior
Rawlins
Sinclair
Rock River
Chugwater
Elk Mountain
La Grange
Granger
Wamsutter
Arlington
Horse Creek
Albin
Fort Bridger
Green River
Rock Springs
Saratoga
North Platte R.
Laramie
Lodgepole Creek
Pine Bluffs
Evanston
Lyman
Burns
Mountain View
Flaming Gorge Res.
FLAMING GORGE NRA
Riverside
MEDICINE BOW NAT'L FOREST
Laramie R.
Warren AFB
Cheyenne
Manila
Baggs
Dixon

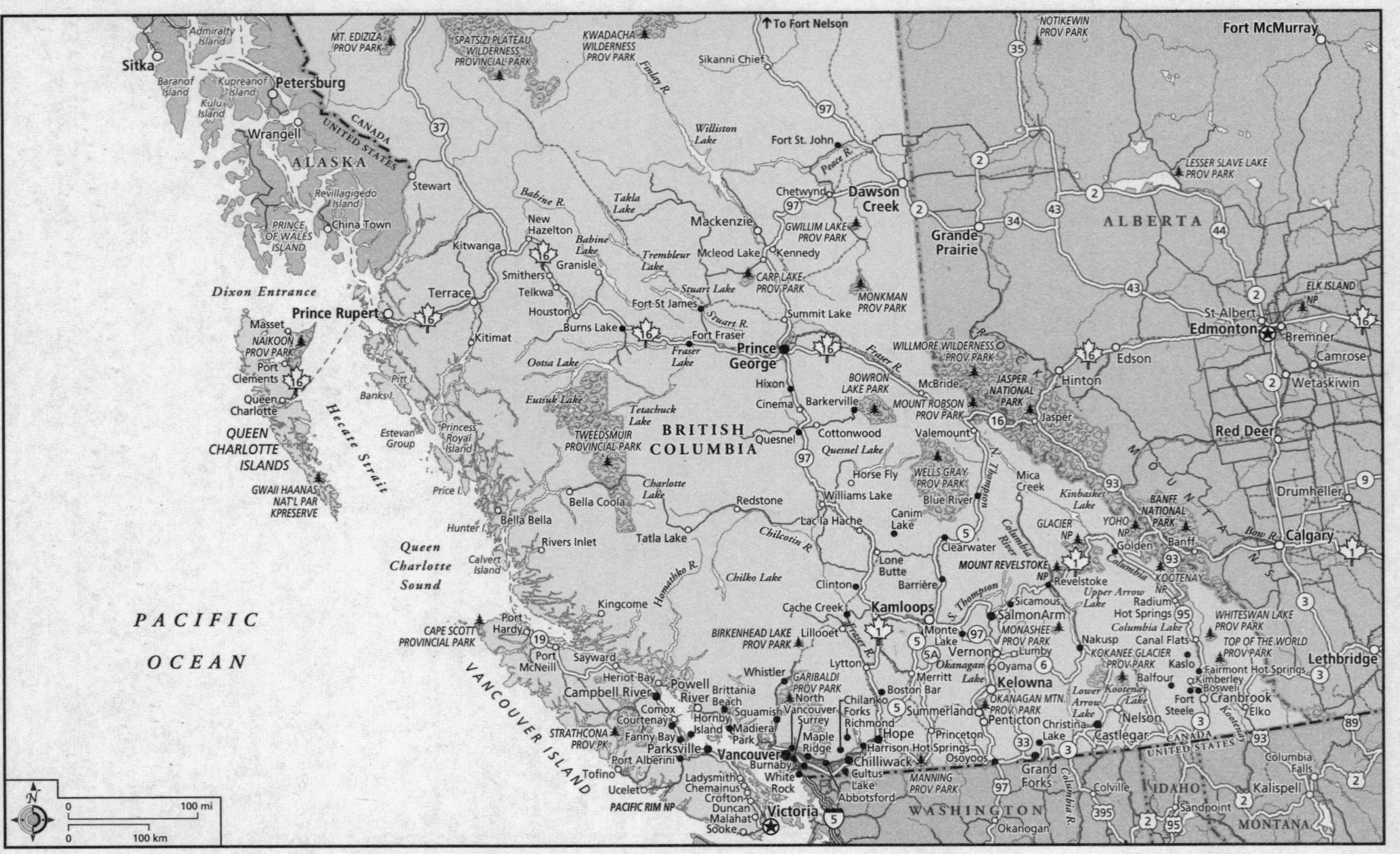
Sitka
Admiralty Island
Baranof Island
Kupreanof Island
Kulu Island
Petersburg
Wrangell
ALASKA
CANADA
UNITED STATES
Revillagigedo Island
China Town
PRINCE OF WALES ISLAND
MT. EDZIZA PROV PARK
SPATSIZI PLATEAU WILDERNESS PROVINCIAL PARK
KWADACHA WILDERNESS PROV PARK
Finlay R.
To Fort Nelson
Sikanni Chief
Williston Lake
Fort St. John
Peace R.
NOTIKEWIN PROV PARK
Fort McMurray
LESSER SLAVE LAKE PROV PARK
ALBERTA
Stewart
Babine R.
Takla Lake
Mackenzie
Chetwynd
Dawson Creek
GWILLIM LAKE PROV PARK
Grande Prairie
New Hazelton
Babine Lake
Trembleur Lake
Mcleod Lake
Kennedy
Kitwanga
Smithers
Granisle
CARP LAKE PROV PARK
MONKMAN PROV PARK
Dixon Entrance
Terrace
Telkwa
Stuart Lake
Houston
Fort St James
Stuart R.
Summit Lake
Prince Rupert
Masset
Kitimat
Burns Lake
Fort Fraser
Fraser Lake
Prince George
Fraser R.
WILLMORE WILDERNESS PROV PARK
St. Albert
Edmonton
ELK ISLAND NP
Bremner
Camrose
Wetaskiwin
NAIKOON PROV PARK
Port Clements
Ootsa Lake
Hixon
BOWRON LAKE PARK
McBride
Hinton
Edson
Queen Charlotte
Pitt I.
Banks I.
Eutsuk Lake
Tetachuck Lake
Cinema
Barkerville
MOUNT ROBSON PROV PARK
JASPER NATIONAL PARK
Jasper
Red Deer
QUEEN CHARLOTTE ISLANDS
Hecate Strait
Estevan Group
Princess Royal Island
TWEEDSMUIR PROVINCIAL PARK
BRITISH COLUMBIA
Quesnel
Cottonwood
Quesnel Lake
Valemount
Horse Fly
WELLS GRAY PROV PARK
Mica Creek
N. Thompson
Drumheller
GWAII HAANAS NAT'L PAR KPRESERVE
Price I.
Charlotte Lake
Bella Coola
Redstone
Williams Lake
Blue River
Kinbasket Lake
BANFF NATIONAL PARK
Hunter I.
Bella Bella
Lac la Hache
Canim Lake
YOHO NP
GLACIER NP
Bow R.
Calgary
Queen Charlotte Sound
Calvert Island
Rivers Inlet
Tatla Lake
Chilcotin R.
Clearwater
Golden
Banff
Columbia River
Lone Butte
MOUNT REVELSTOKE NP
Revelstoke
KOOTENAY NP
Homathko R.
Chilko Lake
Clinton
Barrière
Upper Arrow Lake
Radium Hot Springs
PACIFIC OCEAN
Kingcome
Cache Creek
Kamloops
S. Thompson
Sicamous
SalmonArm
WHITESWAN LAKE PROV PARK
Columbia Lake
CAPE SCOTT PROVINCIAL PARK
Port Hardy
BIRKENHEAD LAKE PROV PARK
Lillooet
Monte Lake
MONASHEE PROV PARK
Nakusp
Canal Flats
TOP OF THE WORLD PROV PARK
Port McNeill
Sayward
Lytton
Vernon
Lumby
KOKANEE GLACIER PROV PARK
Lethbridge
VANCOUVER ISLAND
Whistler
GARIBALDI PROV PARK
Merritt
Okanagan Lake
Oyama
Kaslo
Fairmont Hot Springs
Heriot Bay
Powell River
Brittania Beach
North Vancouver
Boston Bar
Kelowna
Balfour
Kimberley
Campbell River
Comox
Courtenay
Squamish
Chilanko Forks
OKANAGAN MTN. PROV. PARK
Lower Arrow Lake
Kootenay Lake
Boswell
Cranbrook
Hornby Island
Surrey
Richmond
Summerland
Penticton
Nelson
Fort Steele
Elko
Kootenay
STRATHCONA PROV PK
Fanny Bay
Madiera Park
Maple Ridge
Hope
Princeton
Christina Lake
Castlegar
Parksville
Harrison Hot Springs
Osoyoos
Vancouver
Chilliwack
Port Alberini
Burnaby
Cultus Lake
MANNING PROV PARK
Grand Forks
Columbia R.
Columbia Falls
Tofino
Ladysmith
White Rock
Chemainus
Abbotsford
Ucelet
Crofton
Duncan
Malahat
Sooke
Victoria
PACIFIC RIM NP
WASHINGTON
Okanogan
Colville
IDAHO
Sandpoint
Kalispell
MONTANA
N
0
100 mi
0
100 km

Campground Awards

ALASKA

Best RV Camping

Anchorage RV Park, Anchorage
Denali Grizzly Bear Cabins & Campground, Denali Park
Riverside Camper Park, Houston

Best Tent Camping

Granite Creek Campground, Anchorage
Williwaw Campground, Anchorage

Most Beautiful Campgrounds

Bayside RV Park, Valdez
Denali View North Campground, Wasilla
Granite Creek Campground, Anchorage
Mountain View RV Park, Palmer
Oceanview RV Park, Homer
Scenic View RV Park, Ninilchik
Seaview RV Park, Hope
Waterfront Park, Seward
Williwaw Campground, Anchorage

Most Private Campsites

Centennial Park Municipal Campground, Soldotna
Granite Creek Campground, Anchorage

Most Spacious Campsites

Granite Creek Campground, Anchorage
Williwaw Campground, Anchorage

Quietest Campgrounds

Granite Creek Campground, Anchorage

Cleanest Campgrounds

Anchorage RV Park, Anchorage
Denali Grizzly Bear Cabins & Campground, Denali Park
Montana Creek Campground, Anchorage
Oceanview RV Park, Homer
Williwaw Campground, Anchorage

Best Campground Facilities

Anchorage RV Park, Anchorage

Best Urban and Suburban Settings

Rainbow Denali RV Park, Denali Park
Ship Creek Landings RV Park, Anchorage

Best Mountain Settings

Bayside RV Park, Valdez
Bear Creek Campground, Seward
Denali Grizzly Bear Cabins and Campground, Denali Park
Denali View North Campground, Wasilla
Granite Creek Campground, Anchorage
Kenai Princess RV Park, Cooper Landing
Mountain View RV Park, Palmer
Oceanview RV Park, Homer
Rainbow Denali RV Park, Denali Park
Scenic View RV Park, Ninilchik
Seaview RV Park, Hope
Waterfront Park Campground, Seward
Williwaw Campground, Anchorage

Best Waterfront Settings

Bayside RV Park, Valdez
Oceanview RV Park, Homer
Scenic View RV Park, Ninilchick
Seaview RV Park, Hope
Waterfront Park Campground, Seward

ALASKA (continued)

Most Romantic Campgrounds

Denali View North Campground, Wasilla
Granite Creek Campground, Anchorage
Waterfront Park Campground, Seward
Williwaw Campground, Anchorage

Best Family-Oriented Campgrounds

Denali Grizzly Bear Cabins and Campground, Denali Park
Waterfront Park Campground, Seward

IDAHO

Best RV Camping

Prospector's Gold RV Park and Campground, Lucile
Riverfront Gardens RV Park, Lucile
Rivers Inn and RV, North Fork
Water's Edge RV Resort, Cascade

Best Tent Camping

Chalis Hot Springs, Chalis
Riverfront Gardens RV Park, Lucile

Most Beautiful Campgrounds

Boise National Forest, Southwestern Idaho Region 3
Bruneau Dunes State Park, Mountain Home
Dworshak State Park, Orofino
Idaho Panhandle Natioanl Forest, Idaho Panhandle
Lake Cascade State Park, Cascade
Payette National Forest, Central Idaho
Ponderosa State Park, McCall
Priest Lake State Park, Coolin
Red Rock R.V. and Camping Park, Island Park
Riverfront Gardens RV Park, Lucile
Rivers Inn and RV, North Fork
Sawtooth National Recreation Area, Ketchum
Swiftwater RV Park & Store, White Bird
Winchester Lake State Park, Winchester

Most Private Campsites

Boise National Forest, Southwestern Idaho Region 3
Chalis Hot Springs, Chalis
Heyburn State Park, Plummer
Huckleberry Campground, Calder
Idaho Panhandle Natioanl Forest, Idaho Panhandle
Payette National Forest, Central Idaho
Prospector's Gold RV Park and Campground, Lucile
Riverfront Gardens RV Park, Lucile
Rivers Inn and RV, North Fork
Sawtooth National Recreation Area, Ketchum
Swiftwater RV Park & Store, White Bird

Most Spacious Campsites

Boisé National Forest, Southwestern Idaho Region 3
Chalis Hot Springs, Chalis
Hells Gate State Park, Lewiston
Heyburn State Park, Plummer
High Adventure River Tours RV Park & Store , Hagerman
Idaho Panhandle Natioanl Forest, Idaho Panhandle
Payette National Forest, Central Idaho
Prospector's Gold RV Park and Campground, Lucile
Riverfront Gardens RV Park, Lucile
Rivers Inn and RV, North Fork
Sawtooth National Recreation Area, Ketchum

Quietest Campgrounds

Boise National Forest, Southwestern Idaho Region 3
Carmela Winery & Golf Course, Glenns Ferry
Heyburn State Park, Plummer
Huckleberry Campground, Calder
Idaho Panhandle Natioanl Forest, Idaho Panhandle
Payette National Forest, Central Idaho
Prospector's Gold RV Park and Campground, Lucile
Rivers Inn and RV, North Fork
Sawtooth National Recreation Area, Ketchum

Most Secure Campgrounds

Prospector's Gold RV Park and Campground, Lucile
Riverfront Gardens RV Park, Lucile
Rivers Inn and RV, North Fork
Water's Edge RV Resort, Cascade

IDAHO (continued)

Cleanest Campgrounds
Prospector's Gold RV Park and Campground, Lucile
Riverfront Gardens RV Park, Lucile
Rivers Inn and RV, North Fork
Swiftwater RV Park & Store, White Bird
Water's Edge RV Resort, Cascade

Best Campground Facilities
Prospector's Gold RV Park and Campground, Lucile
Riverfront Gardens RV Park, Lucile
Rivers Inn and RV, North Fork
Water's Edge RV Resort, Cascade

Best Rural, Farm, or Ranch Settings
Chalis Hot Springs, Chalis
Payette National Forest, Central Idaho

Best Urban and Suburban Settings
Anderson, Eden (Twin Falls)

Best Mountain Settings
Coeur d'Alene KOA RV, Tent & Kabin Resort, Couer d'Alene
Priest Lake State Park, Coolin
Red Rock R.V. and Camping Park, Island Park
Rivers Inn and RV, North Fork
Sawtooth Lodge, Grandjean
Sawtooth National Recreation Area, Ketchum

Best Waterfront Settings
Henry's Lake State Park, Island Park
Lake Cascade State Park, Cascade
Priest Lake State Park, Coolin
Water's Edge RV Resort, Cascade
Winchester Lake State Park, Winchester

Most Romantic Campgrounds
Boise National Forest, Southwestern Idaho Region 3
Idaho Panhandle Natioanl Forest, Idaho Panhandle
Payette National Forest, Central Idaho
Riverfront Gardens RV Park, Lucile
Rivers Inn and RV, North Fork
Sawtooth National Recreation Area, Ketchum

Best Family-Oriented Campgrounds
Idaho Falls KOA, Idaho Falls

Best Swimming Pools
Sawtooth Lodge, Grandjean
Three Island Crossing State Park, Glenn's Ferry

IOWA

Most Beautiful Campgrounds
Clearlake State Park, Clearlake
George Wyth State Park, Waterloo
Lewis and Clark State Park, Onawa
Saylorville Lake, Johnston
Springbrook State Park, Guthrie

Most Private Campsites
Onawa/Blue Lake KOA, Onawa
Saylorville Lake, Johnston
Springbrook State Park, Guthrie

Most Spacious Campsites
Onawa/Blue Lake KOA, Onawa
Saylorville Lake, Johnston
Springbrook State Park, Guthrie

Best Rural, Farm, or Ranch Settings
Onawa/Blue Lake KOA, Onawa

Best Urban and Suburban Settings
Cheyenne Koa, Cheyenne

Best Waterfront Settings
Clearlake State Park, Clearlake

Best Family-Oriented Campgrounds
Lewis and Clark State Park, Onawa
Skip-A-Way, Clermont
Timberland campground, West Des Moines

Best Swimming Pools
Clearlake State Park, Clearlake
George Wyth State Park, Waterloo
Springbrook State Park, Guthrie

MONTANA

Best RV Camping
Bismark KOA, Bismark
Madison River Cabins & RV, Cameron
Mountain Meadow Campground, Hungry Horse
Polson/Flathead Lake KOA, Polson
Timber Wolf Resort, Hungry Horse
Whitefish-Glacier KOA Kampground, Whitefish
Yellowstones Edge RV Park, Livingston

Best Tent Camping
Jefferson River Campground, Silver Star
Madison River Cabins & RV, Cameron
Mountain Meadow Campground, Hungry Horse
Polson/Flathead Lake KOA, Polson
Timber Wolf Resort, Hungry Horse
Whitefish-Glacier KOA Kampground, Whitefish
Yellowstones Edge RV Park, Livingston

Most Beautiful Campgrounds
Campground St. Regis, St. Regis
Flathead Lake State Park, Polson/Flathead Lake area
Glacier Campground, West Glacier
Glacier National Park, West Glacier
Lake Holter Recreation Area, Wolf Creek
Madison River and RV, Cameron
Mountain Meadow Campground, Hungry Horse
Paradise Valley KOA, Livingston
Pipestone Campground, Whitehall
Polson/Flathead Lake KOA, Polson
Timber Wolf Resort, Hungry Horse

Most Private Campsites
Campground St. Regis, St. Regis
Cardwell Store & RV Park, Cardwell
Glacier Campground, West Glacier
Mountain Meadow Campground, Hungry Horse
Yellowstone River RV Park & Campground, Billings
Yellowstones Edge RV Park, Livingston

Most Spacious Campsites
Campground St. Regis, St. Regis
Cardwell Store & RV Park, Cardwell
Glacier Campground, West Glacier
Helena Campground & RV Park, Helena
Mountain Meadow Campground, Hungry Horse
Yellowstone River RV Park & Campground, Billings
Yellowstones Edge RV Park, Livingston

Quietest Campgrounds
Mountain Meadow Campground, Hungry Horse
Shady Grove RV Park & Campground, Cut Bank
Timber Wolf Resort, Hungry Horse
Yellowstones Edge RV Park, Livingston

Most Secure Campgrounds
Illahe Campground, Gold Beach
Madison River Cabins & RV, Cameron

Most Secure Campgrounds
Mountain Meadow Campground, Hungry Horse
Polson/Flathead Lake KOA, Polson
Timber Wolf Resort, Hungry Horse
Whitefish-Glacier KOA Kampground, Whitefish
Yellowstones Edge RV Park, Livingston

Cleanest Campgrounds
Arrowhead Resort, Elmo
Campground St. Regis, St. Regis
Glacier Campground, West Glacier
Madison River and RV, Cameron
Madison River Cabins & RV, Cameron
Mountain Meadow Campground, Hungry Horse
Polson/Flathead Lake KOA, Polson
Yellowstones Edge RV Park, Livingston

Best Campground Facilities
Madison River Cabins & RV, Cameron
Mountain Meadow Campground, Hungry Horse
Polson/Flathead Lake KOA, Polson
Timber Wolf Resort, Hungry Horse
Whitefish-Glacier KOA Kampground, Whitefish
Yellowstones Edge RV Park, Livingston

Best Urban and Suburban Settings
Buffalo KOA Kampground, LLC, Buffalo

Best Mountain Settings
Glacier Campground, West Glacier
Glacier National Park, West Glacier
Mountain Meadow Campground, Hungry Horse
Whitefish-Glacier KOA Kampground, Whitefish

Best Waterfront Settings
Flathead Lake State Park, Polson/Flathead Lake area
Lake Holter Recreation Area, Wolf Creek

MONTANA (continued)

Most Romantic Campgrounds
Campground St. Regis, St. Regis
Glacier Campground, West Glacier
Mountain Meadow Campground, Hungry Horse

Best Family-Oriented Campgrounds
Whitefish-Glacier KOA Kampground, Whitefish

Best Swimming Pools
Arrowhead Resort, Elmo

NEBRASKA

Most Beautiful Campgrounds
Chadron State Park, Chadron
Fort Robinson State Park, Crawford
Lewis and Clark State Recreation Area, Crofton
Niobrara State Park, Niobrara

Best Rural, Farm, or Ranch Settings
Branched Oak State Recreation Area , Lincoln (Raymond)

Best Urban and Suburban Settings
Camp-A-Way, Lincoln

Best Family-Oriented Campgrounds
Double Nickel Campground, Waco
Eugene T Mahoney, Ashland

Best Swimming Pools
Lewis and Clark State Recreation Area, Crofton

NORTH DAKOTA

Best RV Camping
Crown Villa RV Park, Bend

Best Tent Camping
Bismark KOA, Bismark

Most Beautiful Campgrounds
Bismark KOA, Bismark
Fort Lincoln State Park, Mandan
Fort Stevenson State Park, Garrison
Graham's Island State Park, Cavalier
Icelandic State Park, Cavalier
Lake Metigoshe State Park, Bottineau
Lewis and Clark State Park, Epping
Turtle River State Park, Arvilla

Most Private Campsites
Bismark KOA, Bismark
Fort Stevenson State Park, Garrison
Graham's Island State Park, Cavalier
Jamestown KOA, Jamestown
Lake Metigoshe State Park, Bottineau
Larimore Dam Recreation Area and Campground, Larimore
Lewis and Clark State Park, Epping

Most Spacious Campsites
Bismark KOA, Bismark
Fort Stevenson State Park, Garrison
Graham's Island State Park, Cavalier
Jamestown KOA, Jamestown
Lake Metigoshe State Park, Bottineau
Larimore Dam Recreation Area and Campground, Larimore
Lewis and Clark State Park, Epping

Best Rural, Farm, or Ranch Settings
Icelandic State Park, Cavalier
Lewis and Clark State Park, Epping
Prairie Acres RV Park, Williston

Best Waterfront Settings
Lake Metigoshe State Park, Bottineau

Most Romantic Campgrounds
Bismark KOA, Bismark

Best Family-Oriented Campgrounds
Icelandic State Park, Cavalier
Turtle River State Park, Arvilla

OREGON

Best RV Camping
Kah Nee Ta Resort, Warm Springs
Mt. Hood Village, Portland
Pacific Shores Motorcoach Resort, Newport
RV Resort At Cannon Beach, Cannon Beach
Stokes-Thomas Lake City Park, Watertown

Best Tent Camping
Jessie M. Honeyman Memorial State Park Campground, Florence
Manzama Campground, Crater Lake National Park

Most Beautiful Campgrounds
Bear Creek Campground, Maupin
Cape Blanco State Park, Port Orford
Cape Lookout State Park, Netarts
Cape Perpetua Scenic Area, Yachats
Crater Lake Resort Fort Creek Campground, Fort Klamath
Diamond Lake Campground, Diamond Lake
Eel Creek Campground, Winchester Bay
Elk Lake Campground, Detroit
Emmigrant Springs State Park, Meacham
Farewell Bend State Recreation Area, Huntington
Historic Arizona Beach RV Park, Port Orford
Jessie M. Honeyman Memorial State Park Campground, Florence
Lake Owyhee State Park, Ontario
Manzama Campground, Crater Lake National Park
Natural Bridge Campground, Prospect
Oxbow Park, Gresham
Princess Creek Campground, Cascade Summit
Rocky Point Resort, Klamath Falls
Saddle Mountain State Park, Cannon Beach
Shelter Cove Resort and Marina, Cascade Summit
Thielsen View Campground, Diamond Lake
Nehalem Bay State Park, Manzanita/Nehalem

Most Private Campsites
Cape Lookout State Park, Netarts
Eagle Creek Campground, Bonneville
Eel Creek Campground, Winchester Bay
Elk Lake Campground, Detroit
Illahe Campground, Gold Beach
Natural Bridge Campground, Prospect
Oxbow Park, Gresham
Thielsen View Campground, Diamond Lake

Most Spacious Campsites
Bear Creek Campground, Maupin
Cape Blanco State Park, Port Orford
Crown Villa RV Park, Bend
Eel Creek Campground, Winchester Bay
Elk Lake Campground, Detroit
Head of the River Campground, Chiloquin
Illahe Campground, Gold Beach
Oxbow Park, Gresham
Riverside Campground, Sisters
Thielsen View Campground, Diamond Lake

Quietest Campgrounds
Cinder Hill Campground, Bend
Eel Creek Campground, Winchester Bay
Elk Lake Campground, Detroit
Lake of the Woods Resort, Klamath Falls
Lake Owyhee State Park, Ontario
Paulina Lake Campground, Bend
Thielsen View Campground, Diamond Lake

Most Secure Campgrounds
Corps of Engineers Downstream, Pierre
Kah Nee Ta Resort, Warm Springs
Mt. Hood Village, Portland
Oxbow Park, Gresham
Pacific Shores Motorcoach Resort, Newport

Cleanest Campgrounds
Cape Blanco State Park, Port Orford
Cape Lookout State Park, Netarts
Crown Villa RV Park, Bend
Illahe Campground, Gold Beach
Kah Nee Ta Resort, Warm Springs
Lincoln City KOA Campground, Lincoln City
Natural Bridge Campground, Prospect
Pacific Shores Motorcoach Resort, Newport
Phoenix RV Park, Salem
Thielsen View Campground, Diamond Lake

Best Campground Facilities
Crown Villa RV Park, Bend
Kah Nee Ta Resort, Warm Springs
Mt. Hood Village, Portland
Pacific Shores Motorcoach Resort, Newport

Best Rural, Farm, or Ranch Settings
Richardson Park, Eugene

OREGON (continued)

Best Mountain Settings

Mountain View RV Park, Pendelton

Saddle Mountain State Park, Cannon Beach

Best Waterfront Settings

Bastendorff Beach Campground, Coo's Bay

Diamond Lake Campground, Diamond Lake

Most Romantic Campgrounds

Cape Lookout State Park, Netarts

Eel Creek Campground, Winchester Bay

Elk Lake Campground, Detroit

Natural Bridge Campground, Prospect

Oxbow Park, Gresham

Thielsen View Campground, Diamond Lake

Best Family-Oriented Campgrounds

Astoria/Warrenton/Seaside KOA, Astoria

Bastendorff Beach Campground, Coo's Bay

SOUTH DAKOTA

Best RV Camping

Fort Worden State Park, Port Townsend

Best Tent Camping

Corps of Engineers Downstream, Pierre

Palisades State Park, Garretson

Stokes-Thomas Lake City Park, Watertown

Most Beautiful Campgrounds

Badlands National Park, Interior

Custer Mountain Cabins and Campground, Custer

Palisades State Park, Garretson

Rafter J. Bar Ranch Campground, Hill

Most Private Campsites

Corps of Engineers Downstream, Pierre

Oakwood Lakes State Park, Brookings

Palisades State Park, Garretson

Stokes-Thomas Lake City Park, Watertown

Most Spacious Campsites

Corps of Engineers Downstream, Pierre

Oakwood Lakes State Park, Brookings

Palisades State Park, Garretson

Stokes-Thomas Lake City Park, Watertown

Quietest Campgrounds

Custer Mountain Cabins and Campground, Custer

Most Secure Campgrounds

Beckler River Campground, Skyhomish

Best Rural, Farm, or Ranch Settings

Rafter J. Bar Ranch Campground, Hill

Best Urban and Suburban Settings

Rushmore Shadows Resort, Rapid City

Best Mountain Settings

Custer Mountain Cabins and Campground, Custer

Best Waterfront Settings

Oakwood Lakes State Park, Brookings

Most Romantic Campgrounds

Palisades State Park, Garretson

Best Family-Oriented Campgrounds

Horse Thief Campground and Resort, Hill City

Yogi Bear's Jellystone Park, Sioux Falls

Best Swimming Pools

Griffen Park, Pierre

WASHINGTON

Best RV Camping

Cheyenne KOA, Cheyenne

Hoh Rainforest Campground, Western Olympic National Park

Icicle River RV Resort, Leavenworth

Sunbanks Resort, Electric City

Trailer Inns RV Park, Seattle (Bellevue)

Trailer Inns RV Park, Yakima

Yakama Nation Resort RV Park, Yakima (Toppenish)

Yogi Bear's Camp Resort, Spokane

WASHINGTON (continued)

Best Tent Camping

Fort Flagler State Park, Port Townsend
Heart of the Hills Campground, Port Angeles (Olympic National Park)
Hoh Rainforest Campground, Western Olympic National Park

Most Beautiful Campgrounds

Altaire Campground, Port Angeles (Olympic National Park)
Beckler River Campground, Skyhomish
Birch Bay State Park, Birch Bay
Brooks Memorial State Park, Goldendale
Cougar Rock Campground, Longmire
Dash Point State Park, Federal Way (Tacoma)
Denny Creek Campground, North Bend
Dungeness Recreation Area, Sequim
Fields Spring State Park, Anatone
Fort Ebey State Park, Coupeville
Fort Flagler State Park, Port Townsend
Fort Worden State Park, Port Townsend
Hang Cove Campground, Kettle Falls
Harmony Lakeside RV Park, Silver Creek
Heart of the Hills Campground, Port Angeles (Olympic National Park)
Hoh Rainforest Campground, Western Olympic National Park
Icicle River RV Resort, Leavenworth
Illahee State Park, Bremerton
Lake Wenatchee State Park, Leavenworth
Larrabee State Park, Bellingham
Log Cabin Resort, Port Angeles
Lower Falls Recreation Area, Swift
Mora Campground, La Push
Ohanapecosh Campground (Mount Rainier National Park), Packwood
Panorama Point Campground, Baker Lake
Shadow Mountain Campground, Port Angeles
Sol Duc Resort, Port Angeles (Olympic National Park)
Spencer Spit State Park, Lopez
Steamboat Rock State Park Campground, Electric City
Sun Lakes State Park Campground, Coulee City
Takhlakh Campground, Randle

Most Private Campsites

American Heritage Campground, Olympia
Beacon Rock State Park, Skamania
Corral Pass Campground, Enumclaw
Dungeness Recreation Area, Sequim
Hang Cove Campground, Kettle Falls
Illahee State Park, Bremerton
Larrabee State Park, Bellingham
Lower Falls Recreation Area, Swift
Merrill Lake Campground, Cougar
Mora Campground, La Push
Panorama Point Campground, Baker Lake
Spencer Spit State Park, Lopez
The Cedars RV Resort, Ferndale

Most Spacious Campsites

Beacon Rock State Park, Skamania
Corral Pass Campground, Enumclaw
Dungeness Recreation Area, Sequim
Fields Spring State Park, Anatone
Fort Ebey State Park, Coupeville
Hang Cove Campground, Kettle Falls
Illahee State Park, Bremerton
Larrabee State Park, Bellingham
Lower Falls Recreation Area, Swift
Merrill Lake Campground, Cougar
Midway RV Park, Centralia
Mora Campground, La Push
Panorama Point Campground, Baker Lake
Spencer Spit State Park, Lopez

Quietest Campgrounds

Beacon Rock State Park, Skamania
Brooks Memorial State Park, Goldendale
Corral Pass Campground, Enumclaw
Hang Cove Campground, Kettle Falls
Hoh Rainforest Campground, Western Olympic National Park
Icicle River RV Resort, Leavenworth
Lower Falls Recreation Area, Swift
Merrill Lake Campground, Cougar
Mora Campground, La Push
Spencer Spit State Park, Lopez
Steamboat Rock State Park Campground, Electric City
Takhlakh Campground, Randle

Most Secure Campgrounds

Cheyenne KOA, Cheyenne
Evergreen Court Campground, Ocean Park
Fort Ebey State Park, Coupeville
Yogi Bear's Camp Resort, Spokane

Cleanest Campgrounds

Altaire Campground, Port Angeles (Olympic National Park)

WASHINGTON (continued)

Beacon Rock State Park, Skamania
Brooks Memorial State Park, Goldendale
Cougar Rock Campground, Longmire
Evergreen Court Campground, Ocean Park
Fields Spring State Park, Anatone
Illahee State Park, Bremerton
Larrabee State Park, Bellingham
Lower Falls Recreation Area, Swift
Panorama Point Campground, Baker Lake
Sandy Heights RV Park, Pasco
Trailer Inns RV Park, Seattle (Bellevue)
Trailer Inns RV Park, Yakima

Best Campground Facilities
Sunbanks Resort, Electric City
Trailer Inns RV Park, Seattle (Bellevue)
Trailer Inns RV Park, Yakima
Yakama Nation Resort RV Park, Yakima (Toppenish)
Yogi Bear's Camp Resort, Spokane

Best Rural, Farm, or Ranch Settings
Columbia Riverfront RV Resort, Vancouver
Snoqualmie River Campground and RV Park, Fall City

Best Mountain Settings
Shadow Mountain Campground, Port Angeles

Best Waterfront Settings
Birch Bay State Park, Birch Bay
Lake Pleasant RV Park, Seattle
Lake Wenatchee State Park, Leavenworth
Merrill Lake Campground, Cougar

Most Romantic Campgrounds
Dungeness Recreation Area, Sequim
Hang Cove Campground, Kettle Falls
Illahee State Park, Bremerton
Lower Falls Recreation Area, Swift
Mora Campground, La Push
Spencer Spit State Park, Lopez

Best Swimming Pools
Trailer Inns RV Park, Yakima

WYOMING

Best RV Camping
Country Campin' RV Park, Thermopolis

Most Beautiful Campgrounds
Grand Teton Park RV Resort, Moran
Grand Tetons, Moose
The Flagg Ranch Resort, Moran
Yellowstone National Park, Yellowstone National Park

Most Private Campsites
Buffalo KOA Kampground, LLC, Buffalo
Cheyenne KOA, Cheyenne
Country Campin' RV Park, Thermopolis
Lake DeSmet, Lake Stop Resort, Buffalo
Owl Creek, Riverton
Snake River Park KOA (Jackson/Hoback Junction KOA), Jackson Hole

Most Spacious Campsites
Buffalo KOA Kampground, LLC, Buffalo
Cheyenne KOA, Cheyenne
Country Campin' RV Park, Thermopolis
Lake DeSmet, Lake Stop Resort, Buffalo
Owl Creek, Riverton
Snake River Park KOA (Jackson/Hoback Junction KOA), Jackson Hole

Quietest Campgrounds
Country Campin' RV Park, Thermopolis

Most Secure Campgrounds
Country Campin' RV Park, Thermopolis

Cleanest Campgrounds
Cheyenne KOA, Cheyenne
Country Campin' RV Park, Thermopolis

Best Campground Facilities
Cheyenne KOA, Cheyenne

Best Rural, Farm, or Ranch Settings
Country Campin' RV Park, Thermopolis
Lyman KOA, Lyman
The Flagg Ranch Resort, Moran

Best Urban and Suburban Settings
Cheyenne KOA, Cheyenne

Best Mountain Settings
Grand Teton Park RV Resort, Moran
Grand Tetons, Moose

WYOMING (continued)

Best Family-Oriented Campgrounds
Cheyenne KOA, Cheyenne

Best Swimming Pools
Lyman KOA, Lyman
Rock Springs KOA, Rock Springs
Virginian Lodge and RV Resort , Jackson Hole

BRITISH COLUMBIA

Best RV Camping
Riverside RV Resort and Campground, Whistler

Best Tent Camping
Riverside RV Resort and Campground, Whistler

Most Beautiful Campgrounds
Alice Lake Provincial Park, Squamish
Brandywine Falls Provincial Park, Whistler/Squamish
Gold Creek Campground (Golden Ears Provincial Park), Maple Ridge
Nairn Falls Provincial Park, Pemberton
Porteau Cove Provincial Park, Britannia Beach
Sunnyside Family Campground, Cultus Lake

Most Private Campsites
Peace Arch RV Park, Vancouver (Surrey)

Cleanest Campgrounds
Riverside RV Resort and Campground, Whistler

Best Campground Facilities
Riverside RV Resort and Campground, Whistler

Best Rural, Farm, or Ranch Settings
Hazelmere RV Park and Campground, Vancouver (Surrey)

Best Waterfront Settings
Alice Lake Provincial Park, Squamish

Best Family-Oriented Campgrounds
Hope Valley Campground, Hope

Alaska

Alaska, seemingly the granddaddy of destinations for RVers and campers, lives up to its reputation as "the last frontier" in several ways. Glaciers, mountains, crystal-clear streams, and wildlife are certainly attractions that make you feel like you've entered another world. However, in Alaska you will also be entering another world of RV parks and campgrounds. After you cross the mountainous border, you notice the quality of both state and private campgrounds changes dramatically. Here, many private RV parks look like they were constructed hastily, without consideration for aesthetics and privacy. Bulldozed lots that sandwich vehicles together are more standard than not. State campgrounds and facilities aren't much better. Although generally more private, they tend to have bumpy roads, uneven campsites accommodating only the shortest of vehicles, few facilities, and no hookups.

Primitive though the campgrounds may be, they are nothing compared to the road system. If you look at a map of Alaska and see "highways," don't be fooled! Although most of the state's main roads are now paved (some just recently), what is a considered a highway in Alaska is a backcountry road to the rest of the nation. Except for **Anchorage** and **Fairbanks,** even modern thoroughfares are mostly narrow, single lanes without shoulders, curb banks, or passing areas. Factor in the many unexpected curves, a stargazing truck or trailer in front of you, slower speed limits, or the occasional moose blocking the way, and your travel time increases significantly. As a general rule, it would be very difficult to cover more than 300 miles in one day if you planned on making any pit stops. We recommend a three-week minimum stay to see Alaska, and many travel agencies and tour guides say that it takes at least two months to take in the primary attractions. Visitors are always surprised just how far it is from one civilized destination to another, and how slow the pace can be.

But we assure you that your trip will be worth every pothole, irregular campsite, and outhouse. The scenery in Alaska is unrivaled, and you will find yourself gasping and holding your breath countless times a day. In Alaska, just when you begin to think you've viewed **mountains** from every possible angle, suddenly you turn a corner to see a heart-stopping scene that makes you feel like you're glimpsing these giant rocky wonders for the first time. Add to this the massive hanging and piedmont **glaciers** that are visible right from the highway, the turquoise water of the lakes and streams, sprawling forests of spruce and birch, and seemingly endless fields of wildflowers, and you will feel certain that you have found heaven.

In addition, if viewing **wildlife** is your goal, there is nowhere like Alaska. Wake up early (we're talking between 4:30 and 7:00 am) to increase your chances of seeing moose by the roadside. Besides moose, there are caribou, Dall sheep, 300 varieties of migrating birds, whales, wolves, fox, coyotes, and bears are some of the animals you have a chance of glimpsing on your trip. But, of course, let's not forget the fish! Welcome, anglers, to the state where the fabled 98.5-pound King salmon and 395-pound halibut were caught. Fishing opportunities are as bountiful as mosquitoes in this state (and that means plenty bountiful).

The following facilities accept payment in checks or cash only:

Denali View North Campground, Wasilla
Granite Creek Campground, Anchorage
Montana Creek Campground, , Anchorage
Northern Nights RV Campground, Glennallen
Waterfront Park Campground, Seward

The following facility features 20 or fewer sites:

Granite Creek Campground, Anchorage

Campground Profiles

ANCHORAGE

Anchorage RV Park

1200 North Muldoon Rd., Anchorage 99506.
T: (907) 338-7275 or (800) 400-7275; F: (907) 337-9007; www.anchrvpark.com.

RV: ★★★★ | Tent: n/a

Beauty: ★★★	Site Privacy: ★★★
Spaciousness: ★★★	Quiet: ★★★★
Security: ★★★	Cleanliness: ★★★★★
Insect Control: ★★	Facilities: ★★★★★

Anchorage RV Park, located 15 minutes east of downtown, takes camping in Alaska to an entirely new level. This immaculate and well-maintained campground spoils RV travelers for all other parks. With 195 full-hookup sites, one might think that campers feel overcrowded here; however, plenty of birch and spruce trees, coupled with manicured flower gardens, make it easy to forget that you are at the largest campground in the state's largest city. And besides, one can always seek reprieve in the cedar-lined lounge area, where a fireplace, television, games, books, and coffee make guests feel like they are back home in their living rooms. For travelers who don't want to waste time shopping, Anchorage RV Park has a general store and gift shop right on the premises. And for those who can't quite get used to the cooler temperatures of the state, Anchorage RV Park offers bathrooms with heated floors to keep those toes toasty. Both back-in and pull-through sites are available, although the latter are a bit more expensive. We preferred the most wooded sites, numbers 101 through 115, but keep in mind these are quite far from the rest rooms and showers. Anchorage RV Park is located adjacent to Elmendorf Air Force Base, so if you hear a deep rumble, look up for F-16s flying daily maneuvers. Also keep your eyes peeled for the fox and moose that like this part of town.

Basics

Operated By: CIRI Alaska Tourism. **Open:** May 15–Sept. 15 or later depending on the weather. **Site Assignment:** Reservations are strongly suggested in June & July. A credit card number is required to hold a spot & a $10 fee is charged for cancellations with 30-day notice. Cancellations within 30 days are nonrefundable. **Registration:** Office hours are from 6 a.m.–10 p.m. If you arrive after hours, a map w/ your site assignment will be posted on the door & payment can be settled by 8 a.m. the next morning. If you don't have a reservation, maps w/ highlighted available spots will be posted. Choose a spot & pay in the morning. **Fee:** $30–$35 per night. **Parking:** At site.

Facilities

Number of RV-Only Sites: 195. **Number of Tent-Only Sites:** 0. **Hookups:** Electric (20, 30, 50 amps), water, sewer, cable, telephone. **Each Site:** Picnic table. **Dump Station:** Yes. **Laundry:** Yes, coin operated washers & dryers cost $1.50. Laundry soap & change dispensers are available. **Pay Phone:** Yes, several w/ a terrace & chairs. **Rest Rooms and Showers:** Yes. Facilities are clean, modern & heated. **Fuel:** Available 3 mi. down the road at Muldoon Texaco. **Propane:** Available at Muldoon Texaco. **Internal Roads:** Gravel, pristine condition. **RV Service:** There are several service centers in Anchorage including mechanics that will come to you. Inquire in the office. **Market:** A Fred Meyers is located a few mi. south on Muldoon. **Restaurant:** Several to choose from in Anchorage. Ask for suggestions at the front office. **General Store:** Yes. **Vending:** Soda, candy & newspaper dispensers located by the rest rooms. **Swimming Pool:** No. **Playground:** No. **Other:** There is a covered picnic & grill area on the west side of the campground. **Activities:** Inquire at campground. **Nearby Attractions:** The Native Heritage Center is just across the street & downtown Anchorage is a 15 minute drive. There is also a paved bike trail nearby. Information on activities & a variety of brochures can be found at the front office. **Additional Information:** www.anchrvpark.com.

Restrictions

Pets: Must be leashed. Waste bags are available throughout to clean up after pets. **Fires:** No fires allowed. **Alcoholic Beverages:** Prohibited in communal areas. **Vehicle Maximum Length:** None. **Other:** A list of rules is distributed upon check-in.

To Get There

Take the Glenn Hwy. to the Muldoon North Exit. Follow Muldoon north almost to the end of the road, where you will see the Elmendorf Air Force Base gates. Turn left just before these gates at the lighted Anchorage RV Park sign.

ANCHORAGE
Granite Creek Campground

Alaska Recreational Management, Inc., 800 East Diamond Blvd., Kenai Peninsula 99515. T: (907) 522-8368; F: (907) 522-8383; www.alaskacampground.com; arm@alaska.com.

RV: ★★★★ Tent: ★★★★★

Beauty: ★★★★★	Site Privacy: ★★★★★
Spaciousness: ★★★★★	Quiet: ★★★★★
Security: ★★★	Cleanliness: ★★★★
Insect Control: ★★	Facilities: ★★

If you are looking for a truly Alaskan camping experience, Granite Creek campground, tucked into a trio of Chugach mountain peaks, will not disappoint you. This campground is only a half-mile off the Seward Hwy.; but it can still be considered "off the beaten track," since Anchorage locals tend to occupy the campground on weekends, and out-of-state visitors rarely find their way here. You'll have to come prepared with plenty of food and fuel (as well as mosquito spray from mid-June to mid-July) because you will not find convenience stores or other amenities for at least 25 miles in any direction. However, the nature-lover will be entertained merely by listening to the rushing waters of Granite Creek, taking in the stunning views of the Chugach mountains, or identifying the lush variety of wildflowers that fill in the gaps between spruce trees. All sites are back-in, spacious, and private. However, the loop layout is a bit tight for extra-long vehicles, and it is not recommended for RVs 30 feet or longer. You'll find the most impressive views at sites 8, 11, 12, and 16, although a bad site does not exist at Granite Creek campground. Chances of spotting moose are high here, particularly if you are an early riser. Ask the campsite manager where to look.

Basics

Operated By: Owned by USFS & managed by Alaska Recreational Management, Inc. A campground manager is on-site during operating months. **Open:** The campground may be utilized all year-round, but is only managed & maintained from Memorial Day weekend–Sept. 15. Sometimes snowy conditions prohibit opening until mid-June. **Site Assignment:** This campground is first come first served only. **Registration:** Occupy a site & return-the entrance sign within 30 minutes, fill out a fee envelope & settle payment. Tear the stub off the envelope & make sure it is visible through your car or RV windshield. **Fee:** All sites are $10 per night. Holders of a Golden Age Passport pay half price. Campground has a 14-day limit per camper. **Parking:** At site.

Facilities

Number of RV-Only Sites: 19. **Number of Tent-Only Sites:** 0. **Hookups:** 2 hand operated water pumps for entire campground. **Each Site:** Picnic table, fire grate. **Dump Station:** No. **Laundry:** No. **Pay Phone:** No. **Rest Rooms and Showers:** Two pit toilets both cleaned & well maintained by a campground manager. **Fuel:** Girdwood, 27 mi. north, or Seward, 63 mi. south. **Propane:** No. **Internal Roads:** Gravel, sometimes impassible up until mid-June due to high sNowfall in the area. **RV Service:** Girdwood, 27 mi. north, or Seward, 63 mi. south. **Market:** None in area. Go to Girdwood, 27 mi. north or Moose Pass, 34 mi. south. **Restaurant:** None in area. Go to Girdwood, 27 mi. north, Portage Lake Lodge near Portage Glacier, or Summit Lake Lodge 18 mi. south. **General Store:** None in area. Go to Girdwood, 27 mi. north, or Moose Pass, 34 mi. south. **Vending:** No. **Swimming Pool:** No. **Playground:** No. **Other:** The Johnson Pass hiking trailhead can be found on the highway 0.5 mi. north, & is a great family hike. There is also an 8-mi. paved biking trail that begins there. **Activities:** Go fishing for Dolly Vardens in Granite Creek, or take a walk & look for the many moose that reside in the area. **Nearby Attractions:** Portage Glacier & the access road to Whittier are only 30 minutes away & the gold mining town of Hope, although a 40-minute drive, would be worth an afternoon trip. **Additional Information:** www.alaskacamp ground.com.

Restrictions

Pets: All pets should be leashed & under owner supervision. **Fires:** Fires in fire grates only. **Alcoholic Beverages:** No restrictions. **Vehicle Maximum Length:** None, but RVs over 30 ft. may have difficulties. **Other:** No more than 8 people per site. Firearms & fireworks are not allowed. Food that is not properly stored or left unattended is subject to citation. Bear-proof food lockers are available free of charge from the campground manager.

To Get There

Take the Seward Hwy. to mi. 63.5 and look for the large blue and white sign for Granite Creek Campground w/ an arrow directing you to Granite Creek Rd. Follow the road approximately 0.5 mi., and you will find a large entrance sign and fee box.

ANCHORAGE

Montana Creek Campground

816 Oceanview Dr., Montana Creek 99515. T: (907) 566-Camp or (907) 733-KAMP; montanacreekcampground@alaska.net

RV ★★★★ | Tent ★★★★

Beauty: ★★★★	Site Privacy: ★★★
Spaciousness: ★★★	Quiet: ★★★★
Security: ★★★	Cleanliness: ★★★★★
Insect Control: ★★	Facilities: ★★

If you've been traveling awhile and feel that all campgrounds look alike, Montana Creek will offer a refreshing change of pace. Attention to detail is what makes this campground stand out from the rest. Sheila Lankford, the owner and operator of the campground, tends her perennial gardens and campsite grounds personally, and vibrant displays of wildflowers and berries are sure to delight those with or without a green thumb. Sheila was born and raised on a homestead in this area, and she can offer guests great stories and solid traveling advice. Look for her with her dog Cody. Montana Creek Campground has 18 back-in/pull-through sites with electric hookups available in a grassy area adjacent the creek. All-sized rigs can be easily accommodated here. These sites all have new fire pits and grills, as well as lanterns for the evening hours. For smaller RVs, more scenic, dry camping is available in the meandering campground loops tucked into birch and spruce woods. Campers will enjoy the private, heavily treed sites that have been uniquely named after regular guests. Our favorite spot was "Hilton's Hotel" located right next to the serene Montana Creek bed.

Basics

Operated By: Owned & operated by Sheila Lankford. **Open:** May–Oct., exact days depend on snowmelt & weather conditions. **Site Assign-**

ment: This campground is first come first served only. Space is usually available, but it is recommended that you arrive by Friday afternoon if you are planning to stay the weekend. **Registration:** A self-registration board & pay box are situated at the entrance of the campground. Find a site & return-the front-pay. **Fee:** Electric hookup costs $18, dry camping is $12. There is a $6 charge to park for the day & fish. **Parking:** At site.

Facilities

Number of RV-Only Sites: 74. **Number of Tent-Only Sites:** 0. **Hookups:** Electric (30, 50 amps), potable water is available near the tackle shop. **Each Site:** Picnic table, grill, lantern pole, fire pit, & some w/ electrical outlets. **Dump Station:** Available 3 mi. north at Sunshine One Stop or 5 mi. south at Mat-Su RV Park. **Laundry:** No. **Pay Phone:** No. **Rest Rooms and Showers:** No showers or flushable toilets. Only portables are available, but they are extremely well maintained & clean. **Fuel:** Available at Sunshine One Stop 3 mi. north or Ship Creek Lodge 8 mi. south. **Propane:** Available at Sunshine One Stop 3 mi. north or Mat-Su RV Park 5 mi. south. **Internal Roads:** Gravel, well-maintained. **RV Service:** Talkeetna Auto Care is located 3 mi. north of the campground. **Market:** The Store is located one mi. north & has basic, albeit pricey, food & supplies. Sunshine One Stop is 3 mi. north & also stocks basic amenities. **Restaurant:** His & Hers Lounge & Restaurant located 3 mi. north. Also several restaurants to choose from in Talkeetna. The Store just north of the campground also has a small baker w/ soups & sandwiches. **General Store:** The Store one mi. north. **Vending:** No. **Swimming Pool:** No. **Playground:** No. **Other:** A paved walkway & pedestrian bridge allows guests views of Montana Creek & several access points to the creek offer excellent fishing opportunities for silvers, kings, pink (even numbered years), grayling, & trout. A tackle shop on site offers fishing gear for sale or for rent. **Activities:** Live music is available on the campground July 4th. Feature artists vary every year. The Talkeetna Bluegrass Festival takes place the first week of Aug. just five mi. north of the campground. **Nearby Attractions:** This campground is a hop, skip & a jump from the endearing town of Talkeetna (the town which the show *Northern Exposure* was designed after). In addition, information is available at the campground on dog sledding, flight seeing, fishing, & boating opportunities in the area.

Restrictions

Pets: Should be leashed at all times. **Fires:** Allowed in campground fire pits & grills. Sometimes high forest fire conditions trigger temporary fire restrictions. **Alcoholic Beverages:** No restrictions. **Vehicle Maximum Length:** None. **Other:** There are several resident bald eagles in this area. Ask about recent sightings.

To Get There

Take the Parks Hwy. to mi. 96.5 and look to the east. The large sign and a picnic table w/ a statue of two bear cubs sitting on it make this campground easy to find.

ANCHORAGE

Ship Creek Landings RV Park

150 North Ingra St., Anchorage 99520. T: (907) 277-0877 or reservations: (888) 778-7700; www.alaskarv.com; alaskarv@aol.com.

RV ★★	Tent ★★
Beauty: ★	Site Privacy: ★
Spaciousness: ★★	Quiet: ★★
Security: ★★★	Cleanliness: ★★★
Insect Control: ★★	Facilities: ★★★

Only blocks away from downtown, Ship Creek Landings offers guests a resting spot that is within minutes of the highlights of Alaska's largest city. However, this campground is not one to choose for its scenery or quality. Located in Anchorage's warehouse district, dilapidated buildings surround the area, and the Alaska railroad passes directly by. Looming power lines cut through the center of the campground, and even though the city's hub is so close, a steep hill and industrial traffic do not make walking ideal. All of this said, Ship Creek does offer full hookup camping, clean bathrooms and showers, and a convenient location. It is also within the vicinity of Anchorage's prime fishing creek—you guessed it, Ship Creek. This loop-shaped campground consists of mostly back-in sites, but four pull-throughs are also available for larger rigs. A separate area at the back of the campground offers respite for tenters only. Besides a steep birch-lined hill bordering one side of the campground, there is little plant life here. About five feet of grass separates individual spaces. We found no one site to be better than another. It is simply a choice between being next to a power line or a fence.

Basics

Operated By: Best of Alaska RV Parks, Alaska Travel Adventures. **Open:** May 1–Sept. 30. **Site Assignment:** Reservations are strongly suggested as the campground fills up quickly. The toll-free reservation number is for all of Alaska Travel Adventures' campgrounds, so have the name of the one you want in mind. **Registration:** Office hours are from 8 a.m.–8 p.m. If you arrive after hours, choose a spot that doesn't have a name card posted on the electrical outlet & pay by 9 a.m. the next morning. **Fee:** RVs $14–$32, tents $13. **Parking:** At site.

Facilities

Number of RV-Only Sites: 153. **Number of Tent-Only Sites:** 20. **Hookups:** Electric (30, 50 amps), water, sewer. **Each Site:** Picnic table. **Dump Station:** Yes. **Laundry:** Yes, coin operated washers for $1 & dryers for $1.25. Laundry soap can be purchased at the office. **Pay Phone:** Yes. **Rest Rooms and Showers:** Yes, flushable toilets & unlimited showers. **Fuel:** Available at Tesoro on 5th & Gambell. **Propane:** Available at Tesoro on 5th & Gambell. **Internal Roads:** Gravel, some potholes. **RV Service:** Several service stations available in Anchorage. **Market:** A Carrs/Safeway is located on 13th & Gambell. **Restaurant:** Several to choose from in Anchorage. Ask for suggestions & menus at the front office. We enjoyed the Glacier Brewhouse on 5th Ave. **General Store:** Basic items & snacks are for sale in the office. **Vending:** Soda & newspaper dispensers located by the office. **Swimming Pool:** No. **Playground:** No. **Other:** Inquire at campground. **Activities:** Inquire at campground. **Nearby Attractions:** Downtown Anchorage has many attractions. Visit the 4th Ave. Visitor Center for maps & brochures. Some tours can be booked at the campground. **Additional Information:** www.alaskarv.com.

Restrictions

Pets: Must be leashed & attended. **Fires:** No fires allowed. **Alcoholic Beverages:** No restrictions. **Vehicle Maximum Length:** None. **Other:** A list of rules is distributed upon check-in.

To Get There

Coming from the north, take the Glenn Hwy. to Anchorage and turn right on Ingra St. (Coming from the south, take the New Seward Hwy. to Anchorage. The highway will become a one-way street named Ingra.) Go the end of Ingra, down a steep hill, and turn left on 1st St. You will see the Ship Creek Landings sign on your left. If you cross the railroad tracks, you have gone too far.

ANCHORAGE
Williwaw Campground

USFS, 800 East Diamond Blvd., Portage 99515.
T: (877) 444-NRRS; www.reserveusa.com.

RV: ★★★★ | Tent: ★★★★★

Beauty: ★★★★★	Site Privacy: ★★★★★
Spaciousness: ★★★★★	Quiet: ★★★★
Security: ★★★	Cleanliness: ★★★★★
Insect Control: ★★	Facilities: ★★

Relatively new to the RV scene, this immaculate and newly paved campground is a stone's throw away from Portage and Whittier, as well as an ideal overnight stopover for travelers heading to Seward or Homer. Williwaw is a USFS campground, and therefore without hookups or other amenities—but waking up to the dynamic blue of the hanging Middle Glacier that is the campground backdrop is an experience sure to delight young and old alike. Campsites are spacious and private here and can easily accommodate the largest of RVs. With both pull-through and back-in spaces available, it is worth planning ahead and making reservations for a campsite with a view of the Glacier. We recommend sites 2–6 or 34–36.

Basics

Operated By: USFS. **Open:** Apr. 15–Sept. 30. **Site Assignment:** By reservation or on a space available basis. **Registration:** Occupy a site & return-the entrance sign within 30 minutes-fill out a fee envelope & settle payment. Tear the stub off the envelope & make sure it is visible through your RV windshield or on the front of your tent. **Fee:** $12 per single site & $18 for a double site. **Parking:** At site.

Facilities

Number of RV-Only Sites: 60. **Number of Tent-Only Sites:** Several. **Hookups:** None. **Each Site:** Picnic table, fire pit. **Dump Station:** No. **Laundry:** No. **Pay Phone:** No, go to Portage Glacier Lodge 1.5 mi. down the road. **Rest Rooms and Showers:** Several brand new pit toilets. No showers or wash facilities available. **Fuel:** None in area, fuel up in Anchorage or Girdwood before arriving. The next gas station will not be available until Seward. **Propane:** No. **Internal Roads:** Newly paved & in excellent condition. **RV Service:** No. **Market:** No. The closest market is 10 mi. north in Girdwood. **Restaurant:** Tidewater Cafe is at the Seward Hwy. & Portage Rd. junction. They are open from 8 a.m.–8 p.m. Portage Glacier Lodge is 1.5 mi. beyond the campground. This cafeteria-style restaurant has great soups & sells assorted varieties of homemade fudge. Hours are 9 a.m.–7 p.m. **General Store:** The closest general store is in Girdwood, 10 mi. north. **Vending:** No, but there is a soda & candy machine at Portage Glacier Lodge. **Swimming Pool:** No. **Playground:** No. **Other:** Check out the salmon spawning viewing area adjacent the campground, or take the pleasant Williwaw Nature trail to get a better look at the glacier. **Activities:** Inquire at campground. **Nearby Attractions:** Portage Lake & the Begich Boggs Visitor Center are just 1 1/2 mi. down the road. It is worth catching the movie Voices from the Ice at the visitor center (shown 20 minutes after every hour). Boat tours to the face of the Glacier are also available. Portage road then continues to Whittier but there is a fee to drive through the tunnel. Many people catch glacier boat tours out of Whittier. **Additional Information:** www.reserveusa.com.

Restrictions

Pets: All pets should be on leashed & under owner supervision. **Fires:** Fires in fire grates only. **Alcoholic Beverages:** Inquire at campground. **Vehicle Maximum Length:** None. **Other:** Inquire at campground.

To Get There

Take the Seward Hwy. to mi. 78. Although your map may say Portage, the town was destroyed in the 1964 earthquake and only a few dilapidated remnants remain. Turn north on Portage Rd. and go 5 mi. to the Williwaw Campground sign (not to be confused w/ the Williwaw Viewing Area sign that you'll see 0.25 mi. before the campground). Turn right at the sign, and you will find the entrance board and campsite manager just down the road.

COOPER LANDING

Kenai Princess RV Park

P.O.Box 676, Cooper Landing 99572. T: (907) 595-1425; www.princessalaskalodges.com.

RV ★★★ Tent n/a

Beauty: ★★★	Site Privacy: ★
Spaciousness: ★★	Quiet: ★★★
Security: ★★★	Cleanliness: ★★★★
Insect Control: ★★	Facilities: ★★★★

When you begin to feel the need to pamper yourself after long days on the highway, spend a night at the Kenai Princess RV Park for a bit of luxury. The park itself is nothing extraordinary; however, it's adjacent to the beautiful Kenai Princess Lodge, where RV guests are welcome to dine in the restaurant, enjoy an evening cocktail outside at the bar, use the facility exercise equipment, or dip into the indoor and outdoor Jacuzzis located on the grounds. During your time at this facility, you will feel like coach passenger who just got bumped to first class. A small campground tucked well away from the main roads, Kenai Princess RV Park is quiet and without traffic. The peak of Cecil Rhode Mountain makes for a stunning backdrop, and the glacial waters of the Kenai River are a just short walk away. The campground has a pleasant border of Sitka spruce, but the individual sites are without trees, and only about 10 feet separates campers. All sites are back-ins—the longest being 55 feet—so extra-large rigs might find the campground to be a tight squeeze. No sites stand out as superior or inferior, but we do recommend a spot that is away from the dump station since the tour busses going to and from the lodge utilize the area throughout the day and can be somewhat distracting.

Basics

Operated By: Princess Cruise Lines. **Open:** May 15–Sept. 15. **Site Assignment:** In June & July reservations are necessary. Spots are held w/ a credit card number & cancellations must be made at least 24 hours beforehand. Reservations are recommended for all months, but occasionally there are spaces available in the early & late days of the season. **Registration:** Office hours are from 8 a.m.–10 p.m. Call if you're going-be late & a map w/

your site assignment will be posted on the door. **Fee:** $22–$27 per night. Good Sam discounts available. **Parking:** At site.

Facilities

Number of RV-Only Sites: 28. **Number of Tent-Only Sites:** 0. **Hookups:** Electric (20, 30 amps), water, sewer. **Each Site:** Picnic table. **Dump Station:** Yes. **Laundry:** Yes, $2 per machine. **Pay Phone:** Yes. **Rest Rooms and Showers:** Yes, flushable toilets & coin-operated showers. $1.25 buys about 15 minutes. **Fuel:** Available in Cooper Landing 2.5 mi. away. **Propane:** Available in Cooper Landing. **Internal Roads:** Gravel, well-maintained. **RV Service:** No. **Market:** The Shrew's Nest in Cooper Landing has sundries, including unique Alaskan gifts. Larger supermarkets are available in Soldotna. **Restaurant:** The Kenai Princess lodge offers fine dining, or eat at the bar for a simpler venue. Gwin's Restaurant in Cooper Landing also comes recommended. **General Store:** Yes, at the campground. **Vending:** A soda machine is by the office. **Swimming Pool:** No. **Playground:** No. **Other:** A gift shop is located across from the lodge. **Activities:** Tours & charters can be booked from the lodge. Many include transportation. **Nearby Attractions:** Most visitors are in this region are passionate anglers as the Kenai River is one of the most famous salmon fishing rivers in the state. There are also several local hikes for all skill ranges, including a nature hike on the Kenai Princess Lodge grounds. There are lots of moose in this area—wake up early to find them along Bean Creek Rd. **Additional Information:** www.princessalaskalodges.com.

Restrictions

Pets: Must be leashed & supervised. **Fires:** No fires allowed. **Alcoholic Beverages:** No restrictions. **Vehicle Maximum Length:** Sites are 55 ft. in length & back-in. **Other:** All prices include use of lodge facilities.

To Get There

Take the Sterling Hwy. to mi. 47.7 just before the bridge crossing the Kenai River. You will see a sign for the Kenai Princess Wilderness Lodge and RV Park, followed by the Bean Creek Rd. turnoff to the right. Follow Bean Creek Rd. for 2 mi. and turn left at the lodge sign. Another sign directs you to the campground tucked just down the hill from the lodge.

DENALI PARK

Denali Grizzly Bear Cabins & Campground

P.O.Box 7, Denali Park 99755. T: (907) 683-2696; www.alaskaone.com/dengrzly.

RV: ★★★★ Tent: ★★★★

Beauty: ★★★★	Site Privacy: ★★★
Spaciousness: ★★★	Quiet: ★★★★
Security: ★★★	Cleanliness: ★★★★★
Insect Control: ★★	Facilities: ★★★★

If you're looking to capture some of the hearty Alaskan spirit from the days of yore, Denali Grizzly Bear Campground will make you feel like you're back in the pioneer times. One of the highlights of this campground is chatting with the workers here. Most of them are part of the Reisland clan, descendents of the family that homesteaded this land decades ago. Siblings and cousins now run the campground in the summer, and they have gone to great lengths to preserve some of the flavor of yesteryear. Take a few moments to admire the unique Alaska paraphernalia that decorates the general store and office. Almost everything you see has a story behind it. With several thickly wooded back-in sites (and two pull-through sites) available, all-sized rigs can be accommodated, but longer vehicles may have some difficulty maneuvering if they wander beyond their designated area. This campground has many loops and turns, making campers feel like they're much further away from the park highway than they really are. The rushing Nenana River that borders the campground, coupled with the snow-capped mountains in the background, complete the effect of being away from it all. Ask for a riverside site if possible.

Basics

Operated By: Owned & operated by the Reisland's. **Open:** May 15–Sept. 12, exact days depend on snowmelt & weather conditions. **Site Assignment:** Reservations are recommended, particularly in June & July. A one-night deposit is required to secure a campsite, & a 15% service fee is charged for cancellations. No refunds are given w/ 48 hours of the reserved date. Walk-ins are also welcome, just check into the office before settling into a site. **Registration:** Payments should be made at the front office prior-going-your site. Check-in is from 3-10 p.m. If you are not going-be able-make it during office hours (8 a.m.-10 p.m.) call ahead. A map will w/ your site assignment will be waiting for you on a pegboard outside the office. **Fee:** Each campsite (up to four people) is $17.50. Extra people are $3 each. An extra vehicle or tent is $1. Electric hookup is $5 per vehicle & water is $1 per vehicle. All major credit cards or cash accepted. **Parking:** At site for most spots. Some tent sites are walk-in only w/ designated parking in a separate area.

Facilities

Number of RV-Only Sites: 89. **Number of Tent-Only Sites:** Several. **Hookups:** Electric (30 amps), water, sewer. **Each Site:** Picnic table, electrical outlet, water faucet. **Dump Station:** Yes, two on campground property. **Laundry:** Yes, tokens available for purchase at campground office. Laundry soap is sold in the general store. **Pay Phone:** Yes, three. **Rest Rooms and Showers:** Three buildings w/ flushable toilets & pay showers are available to park guests. Shower is coin operated; five minutes cost 75 cents. Facilities are clean & accessible. **Fuel:** A Tesoro station is located in Denali Village 7 mi. north. **Propane:** Yes. **Internal Roads:** Dirt, curvy but well maintained. **RV Service:** A service garage is available just a mi. away. Ask the front desk to call & schedule a time for you. **Market:** Basic food items are available at the campground general store. The Park Mart in Denali Village is also fairly well stocked, but costly. **Restaurant:** Two restaurants available just across the highway at McKinley Village Resort. Several more restaurants to choose from in Denali Village. **General Store:** A well-stocked general store is located adjacent the office & includes coffee & rolls, ice cream, snacks & groceries, ice, liquor, & Alaskan gifts. Hours are 8 a.m–10 p.m. **Vending:** No. **Swimming Pool:** No. **Playground:** No. **Other:** There are 7 covered pavilions for picnics & barbeques. **Activities:** Inquire at campground. **Nearby Attractions:** The Denali National Park entrance is located 6 mi. north of the RV Park. In addition, a wide array of local tours can be booked in the front office. **Additional Information:** www.alaskaone.com/dengrzly.

Restrictions

Pets: Should not be left unattended. **Fires:** Restricted to pit areas only. **Alcoholic Beverages:** No restrictions. Liquor is sold in the campground general store. **Vehicle Maximum Length:** No restrictions, but only 2 pull-through sites available. **Other:** A list of sensible campground rules is distributed to all campers.

To Get There

Take the Parks Hwy. to mi. 231. When you near this mi., slow down—the large Denali Grizzly Bear Cabins & Campground sign on the west side of the road sneaks up on you suddenly.

DENALI PARK

Rainbow Denali RV Park

P.O.Box 777, Denali Park 99755. T: (907) 683-7777; F: (907) 683-7275; www.denalirainbowrvpark.com.

RV ★★ | Tent ★★

Beauty: ★★★	Site Privacy: ★
Spaciousness: ★★	Quiet: ★★
Security: ★★	Cleanliness: ★★★
Insect Control: ★★★	Facilities: ★★★

Located at the apex of Denali Village, the development of hotels, restaurants, and gift shops that has sprouted just outside the entrance of Denali National Park, Rainbow Denali RV Park puts you where the action is. Use this RV Park during your allotted time in Denali, and you will be able to grab a bagel and morning cup of coffee, catch a shuttle to the Park, book various tours around the area, go shopping, and find evening entertainment all within walking distance of your tent or RV. Rainbow Denali RV Park is simply a barren gravel lot set behind a boardwalk of tourist shops and attractions, but the facilities are clean, and there are plenty of back-in and pull-through sites that can accommodate all vehicles. There are no superior or inferior individual sites at this campground, as all share the same sweeping views of the Alaska Range and all are equidistant from the hubbub of Denali Village.

Basics

Operated By: Owned & operated by the amicable Ed Regan. **Open:** May 20–Sept. 20, exact days depend on snowmelt & weather conditions. **Site Assignment:** Either just show up or make reservations in advance. Sites can be held w/ a credit card, but must be canceled at least 24 hours beforehand if you can't make it. June & July are the busiest months. **Registration:** Check in at the front office before settling on a site. Office hours are 9 a.m.–9 p.m. If you arrive after hours, find a site & place your payment in the box located on the front of the office building. **Fee:** Full hookups cost $28, electric only is $25, & dry camping costs $18. Tents are $14. These prices include tax. After two nights, a 25% discount is given for subsequent nights. All major credit cards accepted. **Parking:** At site.

Facilities

Number of RV-Only Sites: 77. **Number of Tent-Only Sites:** 10. **Hookups:** Electric (20, 50 amps), water, sewer. **Each Site:** Picnic table, electrical outlet, water faucet. **Dump Station:** Yes. **Laundry:** Yes. **Pay Phone:** Yes. **Rest Rooms and Showers:** Flushable toilets & pay showers available to park guests. Shower is coin operated & costs $2. **Fuel:** The Park Mart Tesoro station is directly adjacent to the campground. **Propane:** Available at the Park Mart Tesoro station. **Internal Roads:** Gravel, flat & well maintained. **RV Service:** Available 11 mi. north in Healy. **Market:** The Tesoro station has convenience items available (at inconvenient prices!). **Restaurant:** Black Bear Cafe is next to the campground office. This Internet cafe is Notable for its soups & sandwiches. The carrot cake also comes recommended. **General Store:** Again, the Tesoro station is your best bet for basic items, but it is preferable to stock up on supplies before arriving in Denali. **Vending:** Soda machines are located on the boardwalk. **Swimming Pool:** No. **Playground:** No. **Other:** The boardwalk offers a jewelry shop, several gift stores, a one-hour photo gallery, & offices where rafting, horseback riding, flight seeing, & golfing tours can be booked. **Activities:** Inquire at campground. **Nearby Attractions:** The Denali National Park entrance is located just south of the RV Park. **Additional Information:** www.denalirainbowrvpark.com.

Restrictions

Pets: No restrictions. **Fires:** Restricted to pit areas only. **Alcoholic Beverages:** No restrictions. Ed only asks that you "behave.". **Vehicle Maximum Length:** None. **Other:** Inquire at campground.

To Get There

Take the Parks Hwy. to mi. 238. This mi., known unofficially as Denali Village, is a strip of hotels, restaurants, and gift shops for guests to the National Park. Rainbow Denali is smack in the center of this area. On the east side of the highway, look for a boardwalk of cabin-style shops and a large green sign that says Rainbow Denali (just to the left of the Tesoro Station).

FAIRBANKS
River's Edge RV Park & Campground

4140 Boat St., Fairbanks 99709. T: (907) 474-0286 or (800) 770-3343; F: (907) 474-3695; www.riversedge.net; reresort@alaska.net.

RV ★★★ Tent ★★★

Beauty: ★★★	Site Privacy: ★
Spaciousness: ★★	Quiet: ★★★
Security: ★★★	Cleanliness: ★★★★
Insect Control: ★★★	Facilities: ★★★★

River's Edge RV Park offers the style of camping guests are accustomed to finding in the lower 48 states. Clean, pristine, and modern, this campground allows guests easy access to downtown Fairbanks and nearby tourist attractions, while at the same time providing a tranquil setting on the Chena River. Rest rooms and showers are well maintained here, and the friendly atmosphere, coupled with the knowledge of campground staff regarding the general area, will impress guests. This vast horseshoe-shaped campground has several treed sites on the eastside with more open, grassy spots on the west. Back-ins and pull-through sites are available, with approximately 20 feet between sites. Larger vehicles are easily accommodated. Sites located near the office seemed heavily trafficked and a bit noisy. We preferred the riverside sites, especially sites B-9, D-17, and E-16.

Basics

Operated By: Owned & operated by husband & wife team Steve Frank & Linda Anderson. **Open:** Memorial Day weekend–Sept. 15. **Site Assignment:** General reservations can be made, but specific sites are not assigned until arrival. Reservations require advance payment in full. Drop-in guests are welcome & usually accommodated. **Registration:** Check-in is required at the office before obtaining a site. If you will be arriving after hours (7 a.m.–10 p.m.) call ahead. A map & instructions will be hung on a bulletin board for you-pick up when you arrive. **Fee:** Full hookups are $26.95 & partial hookups cost $23.95. Dry camping available for $15.95. Good Sam discounts available. **Parking:** At site.

Facilities

Number of RV-Only Sites: 179. **Number of Tent-Only Sites:** 10. **Hookups:** Electric (30 amps), water, sewer, modem access. **Each Site:** Picnic table. **Dump Station:** Yes. **Laundry:** Coin operated machines available. Purchase soap & get change in the front office. **Pay Phone:** Yes. **Rest Rooms and Showers:** Flushable toilets & clean showers available free of charge to all guests. **Fuel:** Available on Airport Way (0.25 mi. away) in several places. Fred Meyer is kNown to have the lowest prices. **Propane:** Available on Airport Way (0.25 mi. away) at several gas stations. **Internal Roads:** Gravel, well-maintained. **RV Service:** Several service stations available in Fairbanks. The front office will assist you in making calls. **Market:** Fred Meyer & Safeway are both located on Airport Way. Safeway is open 24 hours. **Restaurant:** The front office lists the daily specials for the nearby Chena's Restaurant & staff will happily make reservations for you. Sample menus for other Fairbanks restaurants are also available. **General Store:** A gift shop & some general items are located on site. Other shopping is abundant throughout Fairbanks. **Vending:** Soda machines & newspaper dispensers on site. **Swimming Pool:** No. **Playground:** No. **Other:** Walk to the banks of the Chena River & try your hand at catch-and-release if you're inclined. There is also a sunny deck area adjacent the office where you can relax & read the newspaper. **Activities:** Reservations for fishing & rafting tours, historical city tours, gold mine tours, & Riverboat Discovery tours can all be booked at the front office. Transportation is provided for most tours. **Nearby Attractions:** The Fairbanks CVB has a toll free number: (800) 327-5774 for information. They can also be visited at 550 First Ave. Lots of website information is also available at www.explorefairbanks.com. **Additional Information:** www.riversedge.net.

RESTRICTIONS

Pets: No restrictions. **Fires:** Because campground is in city limits, no fires are allowed. **Alcoholic Beverages:** No restrictions. **Vehicle Maximum Length:** None. **Other:** There is a one-week max. stay unless otherwise arranged by the campground manager.

TO GET THERE

From the Parks Hwy. take the East Fairbanks Exit. Take a left on Sportsmans Way and another left on Boat St. From the Richardson Hwy. take a left on Airport Way, cross University Ave., and turn right on Sportsmans Way. Take an immediate left onto Boat St. Blue camping signs will point you in the right direction.

GLENNALLEN

K.R.O.A. Kamping Resorts of Alaska

HC1 Box 2560, Glennallen 99588. T: (907) 822-3346; F: (907) 835-3346.

RV ★★★ Tent ★★★

Beauty: ★★★	Site Privacy: ★★★
Spaciousness: ★★★	Quiet: ★★★
Security: ★★★	Cleanliness: ★★★
Insect Control: ★★	Facilities: ★★★

This campground, the halfway point between Tok and Anchorage, is not a destination in itself, but rather a place to layover before journeying to your next checkpoint. However, the highway-weary traveler will find a surprisingly unique experience at K.R.O.A. Set in the gnarly black spruce forest with the sinuous Mendeltna Creek flowing by, the campground has a bit of a rustic, wild feel to it. Jerry and Carol, the hardy Alaskan owners who have been here for over 30 years, do not believe in the creature comforts of the rest of the world. Ask them about computers or highway improvements and they will grunt and remind you that, "This is Alaska!" However, Carol is happy to serve you a hot sourdough pancake breakfast in the charming log cabin lodge, and Jerry can be found working at the bar in the evening offering you a shot of whiskey. This campground has treed sites with plenty of back-ins and pull-throughs. The several loops and slightly bumpy road make some parts of the campground difficult for larger rigs, but ultimately all can be accommodated. The sites are not numbered and seem slightly scattered about. We preferred the creekside sites, but they are the furthest away from the showers and bathrooms. Overall, the campground is clean and on par with Alaska's other RV sites—it simply has a very "seasoned" feel to it.

BASICS

Operated By: Jerry Snow & Carol Adkins. **Open:** Year round. **Site Assignment:** Reservations are recommended for holiday weekends & July 4th. Deposits are required during busy times. Otherwise, there is usually room for RVers who just show up. The only exception might be if the campground is accommodating a caravan. **Registration:** Stop in the restaurant/office & pay before you park. If you arrive after hours, find a spot & settle payment in the morning. **Fee:** Full hookup is $17, dry camping is $10, & tents are $6. Cabins range from $35–$55 per night. Good Sam discounts available. Cash or CC accepted, no checks. **Parking:** At site.

FACILITIES

Number of RV-Only Sites: 60. **Number of Tent-Only Sites:** Several. **Hookups:** Electric (20 amps), water, sewer, phone access. **Each Site:** Picnic table. **Dump Station:** Yes. **Laundry:** Yes, coin operated. **Pay Phone:** No, but calling cards may be used in the office. Phone cards available for purchase in the restaurant. **Rest Rooms and Showers:** Family style bathrooms available in the restaurant & on the campground. Showers cost $1. **Fuel:** Yes, on site. **Propane:** No. **Internal Roads:** Gravel, a bit bumpy. **RV Service:** Closest is available in Glenallen. **Market:** Closest is in Glenallen. **Restaurant:** A restaurant & bar are on site & are open from 7 a.m. to 10 p.m. Carol makes the dough for the pizzas, & the cinnamon rolls come recommended. Sandwiches & simple meals are also available at relatively reasonable prices. **General Store:** Some basic items available for purchase in the restaurant. **Vending:** No. **Swimming Pool:** No. **Playground:** No. **Other:** Cozy cabins are available for rent if you want a night out of your camper/tent. **Activities:** Inquire at campground. **Nearby Attractions:** The Drunken Forest museum is on site. This is a fenced in collection of unusually shaped wood pieces & artifacts that have been found in the local area.

RESTRICTIONS

Pets: Jerry says make sure your pets don't eat his!. **Fires:** No restrictions. **Alcoholic Beverages:** No restrictions, alcohol available at the bar. **Vehicle Maximum Length:** None. **Other:** Inquire at campground.

TO GET THERE

Take the Glenn Hwy. to mi. 153. You'll see the log lodge and the wooden K.R.O.A. sign on the south side of the highway.

GLENNALLEN

Northern Nights RV Campground

P.O.Box 528, Glennallen 99588. T: (907) 822-3199; F: (907) 822-3199; www.alaska-rv-campground-glennallen-northernnights.net; nnites@yahoo.com.

 ★★★ 

Beauty: ★★★★	Site Privacy: ★★
Spaciousness: ★★	Quiet: ★★★
Security: ★★★	Cleanliness: ★★★★
Insect Control: ★★	Facilities: ★★★

Set just where the Glenn Hwy. T-bones the Richardson Hwy., Northern Nights is a convenient stopover for those en route to Tok, Fairbanks, Valdez, or Anchorage. This spruce-lined campground is tucked away from the roar of the trucks and cars on the highways and has a quaint, cozy atmosphere. It is a good place to refuel, get a hot meal in town, and make preparations for the following day's travel. As an added bonus, if you stay at Northern Nights on a Monday or Wednesday, you can join in on their free bonfire and dessert nights—an attraction worth timing your visit for. Northern Nights is a small campground with a parking lot layout. There are plenty of pull-through sites for larger vehicles, and tenters are able to enjoy a comfortable night's sleep at a padded tent spot. Sites are only about 10 feet apart, but a few young trees between each camping space provide a little more privacy. We recommend sites 13–18, simply because they are farthest away from the office and the incoming and outgoing RVs.

BASICS

Operated By: Richard & Tomi Hawes. **Open:** Apr. 10–Sept. 29. **Site Assignment:** Reservations are strongly recommended for June & July. No deposit is required but please call by 4 p.m. if you have to cancel. Visitors without reservations will be accommodated on a space available basis. **Registration:** Register at the front office before settling in. If you are going-arrive after hours, call ahead, & a map w/ your assignment will be left on the front door. For those without reservations, find a spot & settle payment before 9 a.m. the next morning. **Fee:** RVs are $19–$22, tents are $12. No credit cards accepted. **Parking:** At site.

FACILITIES

Number of RV-Only Sites: 18. **Number of Tent-Only Sites:** 5. **Hookups:** Electric (30 amps), water, phone access. **Each Site:** Picnic table, fire pit. **Dump Station:** Yes. **Laundry:** In the process of being constructed at the time of publication. **Pay Phone:** No, but calling cards can be used in the front office. **Rest Rooms and Showers:** In the process of being constructed at the time of publication. **Fuel:** A gas station is directly across the street. **Propane:** Available at the gas station. **Internal Roads:** Gravel, pot-holed in some areas. **RV Service:** The Glennallen Chevron has complete mechanical service. **Market:** Park's Place is 0.5 mi. down the road. **Restaurant:** Check out the Hitchin' Post one mi. west for $2.99 breakfasts & large burgers. The Great Alaskan Freeze & The Caribou Restaurant are other close dining options. **General Store:** Spark's general store is across the road, & the Hub of Alaska is just east of the campground. **Vending:** No. **Swimming Pool:** No. **Playground:** No. **Other:** Inquire at campground. **Activities:** Glennallen has a large 4th of July celebration complete w/ a parade, raft races, & a salmon bake. **Nearby Attractions:** The Glennallen Visitor Center, mi. 189 on the Glenn Hwy., can help you find hiking, hunting, & fishing opportunities. Hours are 8 a.m. to 7 p.m. in the summer, (907) 822-5555. **Additional Information:** www.alaska-rv-campground-glennallen-northernnights.net.

Restrictions

Pets: Must be leashed. Pet sitting is available for a small fee. **Fires:** Restricted to fire pits. Firewood is free!. **Alcoholic Beverages:** Glennallen is a dry city. One cannot purchase alcohol here, but if you have your own you may imbibe at your site. **Vehicle Maximum Length:** None. **Other:** Quiet hours are from 10 p.m.–6 a.m. No generators or radios during these times. Vehicle washing is also not allowed on site.

To Get There

Take the Glenn Hwy. to mi. 188.7. The campground is right at the Glenn/Richardson junction in the town of Glennallen on the north side.

HOMER

Oceanview RV Park

Geri Barling, Homer 99603. T: (907) 235-3951; F: (907) 235-1065; www.oceanview-rv.com; camp4fun@xyz.net.

RV ★★★	Tent ★★★
Beauty: ★★★★★	Site Privacy: ★★
Spaciousness: ★★	Quiet: ★★★
Security: ★★★	Cleanliness: ★★★★★
Insect Control: ★★★	Facilities: ★★★★

This full-hookup campground offers a magnificent panoramic view of Katchemak Bay and is conveniently located next to downtown Homer, the very last town on the Alaska highway system. Probably the cleanest and most modern facility on the Kenai Peninsula, Oceanview is an ideal place to get a hot shower, browse a well-stocked gift shop, and get a free cup of coffee in the morning. With both back-in and pull-through sites, Oceanview is a parking lot–style facility with few trees and little privacy between sites. However, the friendly atmosphere and numerous amenities make Oceanview an ideal resting spot. Reserve a waterside site if you can. Sites 26, 43, 64, 83, and 86 are recommended. For shade-lovers, ask for 17B.

Basics

Operated By: Geri Barling. **Open:** Apr. 1–Oct. 1. **Site Assignment:** By reservation or on a space available basis. Sometimes the entire park is booked by caravans, so a phone call is recommended. **Registration:** Do not occupy a site until you have registered at the front office. If you are going-be arriving after hours (8 a.m.–9 p.m. Monday through Saturday, 9 a.m.–8 p.m. Sunday) call ahead & the campground manager will make arrangements w/ you. **Fee:** Full **Hookups:** $26.95, electricity $19.95, & dry camping $14.95. Showers are included for all campers. There are no discounts or coupons, but seniors do receive a 10% discount at the gift shop. **Parking:** At site.

Facilities

Number of RV-Only Sites: 100. **Number of Tent-Only Sites:** 11. **Hookups:** Electric (30, 50 amps), water, cable, phone. **Each Site:** Trash can. **Dump Station:** Not on site. City dump is located just down the road. **Laundry:** Yes, coin-operated washers & dryers are available for $2. Change is available in the gift shop. **Pay Phone:** Yes. **Rest Rooms and Showers:** Flush toilets & hot showers available free of charge to all campers. Facilities are clean & well-maintained. **Fuel:** Available just a few blocks away at Tesoro. **Propane:** Available at Homer Tesoro. **Internal Roads:** Gravel roads in good condition. **RV Service:** Available in Homer. **Market:** Located eight blocks away & open 24/7. **Restaurant:** None on site, but several to choose from in downtown Homer. We recommend Sal's for sourdough french toast or Cups for lunch & dinner. **General Store:** No, but there is a gift shop w/ some basic food & camping items. **Vending:** Ice, soda, & newspaper machines are all available outside the front office. **Swimming Pool:** No. **Playground:** No. **Other:** There is a covered picnic area for large groups or grill parties. Guests can also take a walk down the hill to the beach for an up close look at the shimmering waters of Katchemak Bay. **Activities:** A fish-fry is hosted for campground guests every Fourth of July. **Nearby Attractions:** Find information at the Chamber of Commerce located on the Sterling Hwy. between Bartlett & Main St. Their number is (907) 235-7740. **Additional Information:** www.oceanview-rv.com.

Restrictions

Pets: All pets should be leashed & under owner supervision. More than two animals requires manager approval. **Fires:** No fires in the RV Park. **Alcoholic Beverages:** No restrictions. **Vehicle Maximum Length:** None. **Other:** RV Park guests can arrange for several boating & fishing charters at a 10% discount.

To Get There

Take the Sterling Hwy. to mi. 172.7. Just before you reach downtown Homer, you will see the RV park's large sign off to the right.

HOPE

Seaview RV Park

P.O.Box 110, Hope 99605. T: (907) 782-3300; F: (907) 782-3344; www.home.gci.net/~hopeak; hopeak@gci.net.

RV ★★ | Tent ★★

Beauty: ★★★	Site Privacy: ★
Spaciousness: ★★	Quiet: ★★
Security: ★★★	Cleanliness: ★★★
Insect Control: ★★★	Facilities: ★★★

The town of Hope is a tiny speck on the Alaska map that is often overlooked by tourists. However, the traveler who ventures off the Seward Hwy. and down the curvy 18-mile road to this vintage gold-mining community will not regret the detour. Seaview RV Park lies on the edge of Hope and is host to the downtown area's only bar and dinner restaurant. Sweeping views of the Turnagain Arm, coupled with a convenient placement, allow one to ignore the fact that the RV Park itself is a barren, crowded lot with back-in and pull-through sites to accommodate all vehicles. Since there is little to no privacy between sites (and because there is a bar next door) this is not a campground for a person who sleeps lightly. However, for the more sociable, Seaview RV Park is an ideal place to meet local Alaskans, fish for salmon in Resurrection Creek, and explore a few well-preserved remnants of the gold rush.

Basics

Operated By: Owned & operated by a friendly Australian, Greg Stanley-Harris. Sometimes you'll find him running the bar. **Open:** May 1–Sept. 20. **Site Assignment:** First come, first served or by reservation. There is usually plenty of space at the beginning & end of the season, but reservations are recommended from mid-July until the end of Aug. **Registration:** Occupy a site & find someone in the bar or restaurant for payment. If you arrive after hours simply pay the next day. This campground operates on the honor system. **Fee:** $10 per RV site, $15 w/ electric. Tents are $5. **Parking:** At site or on road.

Facilities

Number of RV-Only Sites: 28. **Number of Tent-Only Sites:** As many as can be squeezed in. **Hookups:** Electric (20, 30 amps), one water hose available on the side of the bar. **Each Site:** Electrical outlet, fire pit. **Dump Station:** No, but can go to Henry's One Stop 1 mi. down the road. **Laundry:** No, Henry's One Stop is available. **Pay Phone:** No, but calling cards can be used in the bar or restaurant. **Rest Rooms and Showers:** Several portables of dubious cleanliness are available. Showers can be taken at Henry's One Stop for a miniscule fee. **Fuel:** Hope has a gas station, but the availability of fuel is hit or miss & there are No set hours of operation. Fuel-up beforehand in Anchorage (when coming from the north) or Seward (when leaving the south). **Propane:** Available at Henry's One Stop. **Internal Roads:** Gravel, average condition. **RV Service:** None. **Market:** No. Hope has a small gift shop w/ the basics, but it is expensive here. **Restaurant:** The Seaview Restaurant is famed for its seafood chowder & homemade pasta sauces. Also featured at various times are exotic meats such as ostrich, caribou, musk ox, kangaroo, & rattlesnake. Discovery Cafe, the town's other restaurant, is just down the road &, unlike the Seaview Restaurant, is open for breakfast. **General Store:** Again, you'll find the basics at the local gift shop, but be prepared to pay a hefty price. **Vending:** No. **Swimming Pool:** No. **Playground:** No. **Other:** Inquire at campground. **Activities:** Ask in the restaurant or bar for Gold Rush Peck. This eccentric Alaskan will give you a two-hour gold panning lesson for $5. Fish for salmon in Resurrection Creek from mid-July through the end of the summer. From Aug. through mid Sep., pick raspberries along the Turnagain Arm or follow Hope Junction to the end of the road & hike the scenic Gull Rock Trail. **Nearby Attractions:** There are several nearby hiking trails that cater to all levels. Rafting trips & guided fishing tours are also available in the area. Inquire in the restaurant or bar. **Additional Information:** www.home.gci.net/~hopeak.

Restrictions

Pets: No restrictions. **Fires:** In fire pits only. Firewood is available for sale. **Alcoholic Beverages:** No restrictions. **Vehicle Maximum Length:** None. **Other:** Inquire at campground.

To Get There

Take the Seward Hwy. to mi. 56 just over the Canyon Creek Bridge and turn north at Hope junction. There is a large sign pointing the way. Follow the Hope Hwy. 16.9 mi. and turn right on Old Hope Rd. A short stretch on Old Hope brings you to Main St. Turn left and follow this road to its end.

HOUSTON

Riverside Camper Park

P.O.Box 87, Houston 99694. T: (907) 892-9020; F: (907) 892-9020; aksalmon@mtaonline.net.

RV ★★★★ Tent ★★★

Beauty: ★★★	Site Privacy: ★★★
Spaciousness: ★★★	Quiet: ★★★
Security: ★★★	Cleanliness: ★★★★
Insect Control: ★★	Facilities: ★★★★

Riverside Camper Park is a clean, tranquil park that offers the perfect break before going to the big city of Anchorage just an hour's drive away. This loop-shaped campground is just off the park highway and is conveniently located within walking distance of a restaurant, post office, grocery store, and service station. It can also be commended for its clean bathrooms and home-style showers. For fishing fans, bank fishing on the Little Susitna River is available all summer, and boat charters can be arranged at the campground. There are plenty of spacious back-in and pull-through sites available. Spruce and birch line Riverside Camper Park, but no trees or flowers separate the grassy campsites. Request the spots furthest from the highwa;. sites 27 and 28 are next to the water.

Basics

Operated By: Owned & operated by Kenny & Sheila Mortensen. **Open:** May–Sept., exact days depend on snowmelt & weather conditions. **Site Assignment:** Either just show up or make reservations in advance. Sites can be held w/ a credit card, but must be cancelled at least 24 hours beforehand if you can't make it. **Registration:** Check in at the front office before settling on a site. Office hours are 9 a.m.–9 p.m. If you arrive after hours, instructions are on the front gate for check-in. **Fee:** Full hookups cost $20. Good Sam & Military discounts given. All major credit cards accepted. **Parking:** At site.

Facilities

Number of RV-Only Sites: 56. **Number of Tent-Only Sites:** 2. **Hookups:** Electric (30 amps), water, sewer, modem access available in the front office. **Each Site:** Picnic table, electrical outlet, water faucet. **Dump Station:** Yes. **Laundry:** Yes, $1.50 to wash & $1.50 to dry. An iron & ironing board are available free of charge. **Pay Phone:** Yes, phone cards can also be purchase here. **Rest Rooms and Showers:** Clean & modern bathroom facilities are available free of charge to all guests. **Fuel:** There is a service station adjacent to the campground. **Propane:** Yes. **Internal Roads:** Gravel, well-maintained. **RV Service:** Available in Wasilla 15 mi. away. **Market:** Miller's Place is located next to the campground within easy walking distance. Items are cheaper in Anchorage, but immediate needs can be met here & fishing licenses are also available. Ice cream fans will find the largest soft-serve cones in Alaska at this market!. **Restaurant:** Hamburgers are available at Miller's Place. For more variety, The Houston Lounge is located just down the road. **General Store:** Miller's Place stocks a variety of basic supplies. **Vending:** Soda & candy machines, newspapers, & phone cards are all vendable items in the Riverside front office. One can also buy or trade from a large variety of used books here. **Swimming Pool:** No. **Playground:** No. **Other:** There is a boat ramp & bank access to the Little Susitna River, & horseshoe pits on site. **Activities:** The 3rd Saturday of Aug. is Houston's Annual Founder's Day. This is a community BBQ w/ games, activities, & the best fireworks display you've ever witnessed!. **Nearby Attractions:** This area of the state is famed for lake & river fishing. Houston is also renown for its fireworks stores.

Restrictions

Pets: No restrictions. **Fires:** Restricted to pit areas only. **Alcoholic Beverages:** No restrictions. **Vehicle Maximum Length:** None. **Other:** Barcley, the office pooch, is not much of a watch dog, but he is fun to pet & play with!.

To Get There

Take the Parks Hwy. to mi. 57.7. You cannot miss the tiny strip of convenience shops and the large, dark brown building w/ Riverside Camper Park displayed above the front door.

NINILCHIK

Scenic View RV Park

P.O.Box 39253, Ninilchik 99639. T: (907) 567-3909; www.scenicviewrv.com; scenicrv@yahoo.com.

RV: ★★★ Tent: ★★★

Beauty: ★★★★	Site Privacy: ★★
Spaciousness: ★★	Quiet: ★★★
Security: ★★★	Cleanliness: ★★★
Insect Control: ★★★	Facilities: ★★★

This campground is justly named. On a clear day, the view of the famous mountain trio I.R.S. (Iliamna, Redoubt, and Spur) will remind you why you came to Alaska. Although just off of the Sterling Hwy., Scenic View feels more remote than other RV Parks on the Kenai Peninsula, with very little development in the surrounding area. Scenic View would make a wonderful stopover on the way to Homer, as well as offer a great rest stop for adventurers who want to try their hand at digging up razor clams at the nearby Clam Gulch. Scenic View Campground is located on a gently sloping hill reaching downward toward the Cook Inlet. All sites here are back-in, but larger vehicles can be accommodated. There is about 5–10 feet between camping spots, and grass or shrub-covered strips separate sites. Request a site next to the ocean and away from the highway. Wherever you end up, you'll have an amazing view.

Basics

Operated By: Ann Musarra. **Open:** May 15–Sept. 1. **Site Assignment:** Reservations are strongly suggested. A credit card number is required to hold a spot & one night's charge will be applied to the card if cancellations are made within 24 hours. **Registration:** Office hours are from 7 a.m.–10 p.m. If you arrive after hours, occupy a spot & find Ann in the morning-settle payment. **Fee:** $12–$19 per night. **Parking:** At site.

Facilities

Number of RV-Only Sites: 27. **Number of Tent-Only Sites:** As many as can be squeezed in. **Hookups:** Electric (20, 30 amps), water, sewer, phone access. **Each Site:** None. **Dump Station:** Yes. **Laundry:** Yes, coin operated washers & dryers for $1.75. **Pay Phone:** No, calling cards may be used in the office. **Rest Rooms and Showers:** Yes. Showers are clean but cost $3. **Fuel:** Available 6 mi. west in Ninilchik. **Propane:** Available 6 mi. west in Ninilchik. **Internal Roads:** Gravel & in good condition. **RV Service:** Available in Ninilchik. **Market:** Available in Ninilchik. **Restaurant:** Available in Ninilchik, ask at the front desk for recommendations. **General Store:** No. **Vending:** No. **Swimming Pool:** No. **Playground:** No. **Other:** There is a shared picnic & BBQ area at the center of the campground. **Activities:** Fishing charters can be arranged at the front office. **Nearby Attractions:** Fishing, hunting, & clamming are the main activities that draw travelers to this area. The quaint Russian Orthodox town of Ninilchik is just a 15 minute drive away, & Homer, the famous "end-of-the-road" Alaskan town is another hour beyond that. **Additional Information:** www.scenicviewrv.com.

Restrictions

Pets: No restrictions. **Fires:** No restrictions. **Alcoholic Beverages:** No restrictions. **Vehicle Maximum Length:** None. **Other:** Inquire at campground.

To Get There

Simply take the Sterling Hwy. to mi. 127 and turn right at the large Scenic View sign.

PALMER

Mountain View RV Park

P.O.Box 2521, Palmer 99645. T: (907) 745-5747 or (800) 264-4582; F: (907) 745-1700; str@matnet.com.

RV ★★★ Tent ★★

Beauty: ★★★★	Site Privacy: ★
Spaciousness: ★★	Quiet: ★★★★
Security: ★★★	Cleanliness: ★★★
Insect Control: ★★★	Facilities: ★★★

We chose to feature this park because it is a bit off the beaten path, and during busy times when other RV parks are bursting at the seams, Mountain View RV Park will likely be able to accommodate you even at the last minute. This pleasant campground is located three miles off the Glenn Hwy. in Palmer and offers close and personal views of Marsh, Byers, and Lazy Mountains. With spacious, grassy sites and farms on either side, Mountain View RV Park feels more like a stay in the country than a wilderness getaway. Of course, one does have to overlook the many trucks, cars, and engine parts stored behind the campground office. Come here on the Fourth of July, when the owners throw their BBQ bash for the whole town, and you can join the festivities for free. Mountain View RV Park consists of mostly pull-through sites that easily accommodate all rigs. There are no trees on the campground, as the owners say this keeps away insects. Anywhere from 5 to 10 feet separates the sites. We found that sites 1–5 and 22–25 offered the best view of the mountains and were conveniently located.

Basics

Operated By: Red & Dee Starr. **Open:** May 1–Oct. 1. **Site Assignment:** When possible it is best to make reservations. No deposit is required, but please phone if you can't make it. Usually, there is also space for last minute arrivals who haven't called in advance. **Registration:** Office hours are from 8 a.m.-10 p.m. If you arrive after hours, a map w/ your site assignment will be posted on the door & payment can be settled the next morning. If you don't have a reservation, choose a spot & pay in the morning. **Fee:** Spaces are $20–$22 per night. This includes showers. Senior & Good Sam discounts available. **Parking:** At site.

Facilities

Number of RV-Only Sites: 119. **Number of Tent-Only Sites:** 0. **Hookups:** Electric (30 amps), water, sewer, phone access. **Each Site:** Picnic table. **Dump Station:** No. **Laundry:** Yes, coin operated washers are $2 & dryers cost $1.25. Laundry soap & change available in the front office. **Pay Phone:** Yes. **Rest Rooms and Showers:** Yes, 8 separate bathrooms & showers. **Fuel:** Available at Tesoro 3 mi. away. **Propane:** Available at Tesoro. **Internal Roads:** Gravel, good condition. **RV Service:** RV Service is available 10 mi. away in Wasilla. **Market:** A Carrs/Safeway is located 4 mi. away on the Glenn Hwy. The farm adjacent the campground (Arctic Organics) sells freshly picked produce every Friday from 5 p.m.–7 p.m. **Restaurant:** Several to choose from in Palmer. Ask for suggestions at the front office. **General Store:** No. **Vending:** Newspaper dispensers located by the office. **Swimming Pool:** No. **Playground:** No. **Other:** There is a covered picnic & grill area in the center of the campground. **Activities:** A 4th of July grill party is hosted on the grounds. It is free to guests. **Nearby Attractions:** The campground owner operates a boat tour to the Knik Glacier that is reputed to be the best new attraction in South Central Alaska. The Palmer reindeer farm is also very near. If you arrive on Labor Day weekend, the Alaska State Fairgrounds are only a few mi. away. Brochures of other local charters & tours can be found at the front office..

Restrictions

Pets: Must be supervised. **Fires:** No fires allowed except in the grill area. **Alcoholic Beverages:** No restrictions. **Vehicle Maximum Length:** None. **Other:** A list of rules is distributed upon check-in.

To Get There

Take the Glenn Hwy. to Palmer and turn east at the Old Glenn Hwy. stoplight (also called Arctic St.). There is a Tesoro station on the corner to use for a landmark. Go 2.8 mi. on the Old Glenn Hwy., over the Matanuska River, and look for the Mt. View RV Park Sign. Turn left at the sign (Smith St.) and follow this road around a sharp right turn. You will see the campground off to the left. For travelers coming from Anchorage, be sure not to take the first Old Glenn Hwy. Exit you see. Go all the way to Palmer, through the Parks Hwy. intersection, and the next light will be the Old Glenn Hwy. access point you're looking for.

SEWARD
Bear Creek Campground

P.O.Box 2209, Seward 99664. T: (907) 224-5725; F: (907) 224-2283; www.bearcreekrv.com; bearcreekrvpk@symbolseward.net.

RV ★★	Tent ★★
Beauty: ★★★	Site Privacy: ★
Spaciousness: ★★	Quiet: ★★★
Security: ★★★	Cleanliness: ★★★
Insect Control: ★★	Facilities: ★★

Just off the Seward Hwy., six-and-a-half miles before you arrive in the town of Seward, Bear Creek Campground offers the only full-hookup camping on the south side of the Kenai Peninsula. The campground itself is not much more than an expansive gravel lot carved out of spruce forest, but the Kenai Mountains are in view, and pristine Bear Lake is within walking distance. This campground is a less crowded alternative for travelers who want to avoid the throngs of RVs and tourists in Seward, particularly during the fishing months of June, July, and Aug. However, despite the campground's generally tranquil location, be forewarned of the early morning train that whistles when passing Bear Creek Rd.

Basics

Operated By: Owned & operated by Lynn Hettick. **Open:** All year. **Site Assignment:** Reservations accepted or just show up. No deposit is required to hold a spot, however, reservations cannot be made for July 4th. This day is first come first served only. **Registration:** Office is well marked & is open from 8 a.m.–9 p.m. If you arrive after hours, simply choose a site & settle payment the following day. **Fee:** Full hookups costs $28. Parking & facility use without hookup costs $20. Tent sites are $20. MC & D accepted. Good Sam, AAA, AARP, & military receive 10% discount. **Parking:** At site.

Facilities

Number of RV-Only Sites: 60. **Number of Tent-Only Sites:** Space available basis. **Hookups:** Electric (30 amps), water, sewer, cable, phone. **Each Site:** Picnic table, electrical outlet, water faucet, cable hookup (some have fire pits, but campground is currently in a "no fire" zone). **Dump Station:** Yes. **Laundry:** Yes. **Pay Phone:** Yes. **Rest Rooms and Showers:** Yes, campers are provided w/ a punch code to use facilities. **Fuel:** a gas station is located 0.5 mi. away from the campground. **Propane:** Yes. **Internal Roads:** gravel, sometimes in poor condition, particularly in the spring. **RV Service:** in Seward, 6.5 mi. **Market:** Eagle/Safeway in Seward; open 24 hours. **Restaurant:** several to choose from in Seward; ask for sample menus in the office. **General Store:** Convenience shop & liquor store on site. **Vending:** No. **Swimming Pool:** No, but if you're brave & like cold water you can jump into Bear Lake. **Playground:** No. **Other:** Inquire at campground. **Activities:** Jet-ski rentals available at the gas station. **Nearby Attractions:** Explore the nearby fishing weir & watch the spawning red salmon in Aug. **Additional Information:** www.bearcreekrv.com.

Restrictions

Pets: no restrictions. **Fires:** no fires currently allowed due to state regulations. **Alcoholic Beverages:** no restrictions. **Vehicle Maximum Length:** None. **Other:** Management is on site 24/7.

To Get There

Take the Seward Hwy. to mi. 6.5 (mileposts mark the entire highway) and begin looking for the large blue-and-white sign showing Bear Creek Campground w/ an arrow directing you to Bear Creek Rd. Follow Bear Creek Rd. 0.5 mi. over the railroad tracks, past Gary's Gas, and around the bend. The campground is clearly marked on the right side of the road.

SEWARD
Waterfront Park

Camp Management, P.O. Box 167, Seward 99664. T: (907) 224-4055; F: (907) 224-4088; www.sprd.org; campsprd@seward.net.

RV ★★★	Tent ★★★★
Beauty: ★★★★★	Site Privacy: ★
Spaciousness: ★★	Quiet: ★★
Security: ★★	Cleanliness: ★★
Insect Control: ★★★	Facilities: ★★★

This sprawling campground spans almost the entire Seward waterfront, and it's probably one of the most popular RV destinations on the Kenai Peninsula. Visitors will understand why when they arrive; the panoramic views of the Kenai Mountains and Resurrection Bay are breathtaking, and the variety of activities within walking distance from this campground will make you want to schedule more than one night here. Waterfront Park is always active with the hustle and bustle of tourists, and there is very little distance or privacy between RVs. However, you will be too busy sighting bald eagles, looking for whale spouts, and enjoying the ever-changing sunlight in the mountains to notice the crowds. Make reservations for a waterside campsite (sites 12–82 are best), and then bring your walking shoes and take the scenic paved trail either to the Small Boat Harbor, where you can watch the fisherman bring in their daily cache, or to downtown, where shopping and dining are bountiful.

Basics

Operated By: The City of Seward. **Open:** Apr. 15–Sept. 30. **Site Assignment:** Reservations can be made for caravans of 10 or more vehicles only. Everyone else is first come first served. Spaces fill up quickly on the 4th of July & for the Silver Salmon Derby the second week of Aug. **Registration:** Occupy a site & return-an entrance within 15 minutes-fill out a fee envelope & settle payment. Tear the stub off the envelope & make sure it is visible through your RV windshield or on the front of your tent. **Fee:** $15 for hookups, $10 for dry camping, $6 for tents. **Parking:** At site or extra parking on road.

Facilities

Number of RV-Only Sites: 400. **Number of Tent-Only Sites:** 50. **Hookups:** Electric (20, 30 amps), water (23 sites). **Each Site:** Picnic table, fire pit. **Dump Station:** Yes. **Laundry:** No, but there is a laundromat on C & Ballaine. **Pay Phone:** Yes, in the shower house, at the Harbor Master's Office or at City Hall. **Rest Rooms and Showers:** There are flush toilets in three locations & a shower house in the center of the campground (make sure & have $2 worth of quarters, as there are No change machines). Showers are also available at the Harbor Master's Office on the north end of the campground. **Fuel:** Tesoro is located on the Seward Hwy. when arriving in Seward. **Propane:** Available at Bay City Motors on 3rd Ave. or at the Seward Hwy. Tesoro station. **Internal Roads:** Gravel roads that become somewhat pitted during the rainy months of July & Aug. **RV Service:** Available at Bay City Motors on 3rd Ave. **Market:** Eagle Grocery is a 24-hour market just off the highway when you arrive in Seward. **Restaurant:** There are several to choose from. Try Ray's in the Small Boat Harbor for dinner or check out the baked goods at the Ranting Raving on 4th Ave. for breakfast. **General Store:** Fourth Ave. has all varieties of gift & supply shops. **Vending:** No. **Swimming Pool:** No. **Playground:** Yes. **Other:** There are two large picnic pavilions, a baseball diamond, a sand volleyball court, a scenic gazebo, & a paved walkway lined w/ placards showcasing Seward's history & geography. The public boat ramp is adjacent to the campground. **Activities:** Inquire at campground. **Nearby Attractions:** There is a lot to do in Seward including fishing, glacier boat cruises, hiking, shopping, sled dog rides, etc. Information booths are available downtown, at the Small Boat Harbor, or at the Chamber of Commerce Visitors Center just off the Seward Hwy. before you get to town. Call (907) 224-8051 for information. **Additional Information:** www.sprd.org.

Restrictions

Pets: All pets should be on leashes 6 ft. or less. **Fires:** Fires in fire pits only. **Alcoholic Beverages:** No alcoholic beverages allowed. **Vehicle Maximum Length:** No restrictions, back-in sites only. **Other:** Quiet hours between 11p.m. & 7 a.m.

To Get There

Take the Seward Hwy. to the town of Seward. When the speed limit drops to 20 mph, the Seward Hwy. becomes 3rd Ave. Take 3rd Ave. to D St. and turn left. D St. turns into Ballaine, and this street parallels the entire campground. There are several well-marked entrances on Ballaine St.

SOLDOTNA

Centennial Park Municipal Campground

City of Soldotna Parks & Recreation, 538 Arena Dr., Soldotna 99669. T: (907) 262-3151; F: (907) 262-3152; www.ci.soldotna.ak.us.

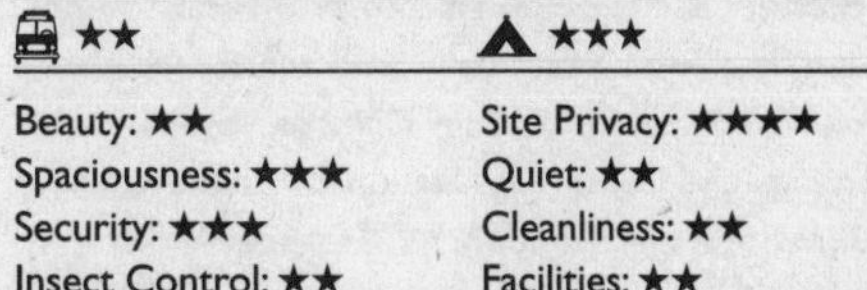

Beauty: ★★	Site Privacy: ★★★★
Spaciousness: ★★★	Quiet: ★★
Security: ★★★	Cleanliness: ★★
Insect Control: ★★	Facilities: ★★

If you are going to Alaska to fish, you might as well head straight for Centennial Park Municipal Campground in Soldotna. Located directly on the Kenai River, this campground includes a popular fishwalk where guests can cast for dolly vardens, red salmon, and king salmon within walking distance from their campsite. Be careful not to tell too many friends about this coveted fishing hole, since it is a favored area for locals and annually returning guests. Evenings at this campground are lively as fisherman fry up their daily catch and talk about "the one that got away". Centennial Park consists of a series of winding loops and is snugly tucked into a forest of spruce and birch. Vehicles of all sizes can be accommodated, but some of the curves will be a bit tight for larger RVs, and all sites are back-ins. Riverside sites are far superior to the inland ones. Campsites on the water include sites 6, 7, 9, 21, 23, 24, 25, 27–31, 84, 86, 88, 91, 93, 95, 97, 98, 100, and 102.

Basics

Operated By: City of Soldotna Parks & Recreation. **Open:** May 1–Oct. 1. If there is snow before Oct., the campground closes early. **Site Assignment:** Reservations are not accepted at this campground. Come early in the day to obtain a site. **Registration:** Choose a site from a map available at the registration area upon arrival, & pay before setting up camp. The registration booth is usually manned 24/7 during the high tourist season, but hours of operation are not set at the beginning & end of the camping season. **Fee:** RVs & tents are $9 a night. There is a $5 fee for day-use & a $7 charge for the boat launch. **Parking:** Cars can be kept at the site. Boat trailers are parked in a designated parking area.

Facilities

Number of RV-Only Sites: 180. **Number of Tent-Only Sites:** 14. **Hookups:** Potable water available at two campsground well houses. **Each Site:** Picnic table, fire grate. **Dump Station:** Two available on site, but the fee is $10. However, dumping is free of charge w/ a fuel purchase at the Soldotna Tesoro or Chevron. **Laundry:** No. **Pay Phone:** Yes. **Rest Rooms and Showers:** Several pit toilets. **Fuel:** Available in Soldotna. **Propane:** Available in Soldotna at any Chevron, Tesoro, or Thompson's Center Gas Station. **Internal Roads:** Gravel, average condition. **RV Service:** Available in Soldotna. **Market:** Fred Meyers & Safeway are two large & well-stocked grocery stores in Soldotna. Stock up on food items here as prices will be higher everywhere else on the Kenai Peninsula. **Restaurant:** All varieties to choose from in Soldotna. **General Store:** No. **Vending:** Soda machines available at the covered picnic area. Ice & newspapers can be purchased at the entrance. **Swimming Pool:** No. **Playground:** No. **Other:** A covered picnic area can accommodate large groups. **Activities:** There is a public boat launch & angler walk at the end of the campground. A small hut in the parking lot contains several brochures highlighting local charters & tours. Coffee can be purchased here for $1. **Nearby Attractions:** Fishing is definitely the highlight here, but non-anglers can inquire about other attractions at the Kenai Peninsula Visitor Center located on the Sterling Hwy. Their number is (907) 262-1337. **Additional Information:** www.ci.soldotna.ak.us.

Restrictions

Pets: Required to be on a leash at all times. **Fires:** In the designated fire grates only. Firewood is for sale at the entrance. **Alcoholic Beverages:** No restrictions. **Vehicle Maximum Length:** None. **Other:** Inquire at campground.

To Get There

Take the Sterling Hwy. through Soldotna to mi. 96. Here you will see the junction for Kalifornsky Beach Rd. Take this road west 0.1 mi. (just follow the vehicles pulling boats). You won't miss that campground sign on the right side of the road.

VALDEZ

Bayside RV Park

P.O.Box 466, Valdez 99686. T: (907) 835-4425 or (888) -835-4425; F: (907) 835-4425; www.alaska.net/~bayside1; bayside1@alaska.net.

RV ★★★ Tent ★★

Beauty: ★★★★★	Site Privacy: ★
Spaciousness: ★★	Quiet: ★★★
Security: ★★★	Cleanliness: ★★★★
Insect Control: ★★★	Facilities: ★★★★

Bayside RV Park is set amongst several other RV parks in Valdez, but this campground stands out for its cleanliness, friendly atmosphere, and waterfront campsites. Chuck Dennis, a retired Alaskan who does a lot of RVing himself, started this business as a way to meet people from around the world. If you're looking for information about the surrounding area, or are just in the mood to chat with someone, Chuck is the man to talk to. Bayside RV Park is basically an open gravel lot, but it's set on the edge of tranquil Prince William Sound with 360° views of the Chugach mountains. The campground is within walking distance from all the major attractions, and local tours can be booked directly through Chuck. There are no trees at this campground, so privacy is minimal, but this is the case at most RV parks in Valdez. At Bayside, the availability of full-hookup sites (plus cable) coupled with unlimited hot showers make this campground a welcome sight after driving the somewhat grueling Richardson Hwy. We preferred the waterside sites, odd numbers 1–41. Sites 45–66 are closer to the highway and tend to be a bit noisier. Both back-ins and pull-throughs campsites are available, and all size rigs can be accommodated.

Basics

Operated By: Charles C. Dennis. **Open:** May 1–Oct. 10, later if weather allows. **Site Assignment:** Reservations are recommended, particularly in June, July & Aug. However, visitors are also welcomed to just show up. If a campsite w/ hookups is not available, Chuck will still find space for you. **Registration:** Payments should be made at the front office prior-going-your site. If you are not going-be able-make it during office hours (8 a.m.–10 p.m.), find an open space & pay in the morning. **Fee:** RVs are $15–$24, Tents cost $12. Showers are included w/ all prices. **Parking:** At site.

Facilities

Number of RV-Only Sites: 89. **Number of Tent-Only Sites:** Several. **Hookups:** Electric (20, 30, 50 amps), water, sewer, cable, Internet access. **Each Site:** Picnic table. **Dump Station:** Yes. **Laundry:** Yes, $1.50 for washers & dryers. Change is available at campground office. **Pay Phone:** Yes, two. **Rest Rooms and Showers:** Home-style bathrooms have recently been installed & offer handicap accessible showers that are included w/ the camping price. Chuck suggests limiting showers to 20 minutes, but if it's been awhile since your last one, he doesn't mind if you take your time. **Fuel:** A Tesoro station is located just across the street. **Propane:** Yes. **Internal Roads:** Crushed rock. **RV Service:** A service garage is available in Valdez. Sometimes Chuck's brother is on-site & available to help w/ mechanical problems. **Market:** Eagle Grocery is a block away & is open from 5 a.m. to midnight. **Restaurant:** The Totem Restaurant is just across the street & is reputed to have the best breakfast in Valdez. **General Store:** No. **Vending:** Both soda & newspaper dispensers are located on the grounds. A microwave & coffee maker can be found in the office. **Swimming Pool:** No. **Playground:** No. **Other:** The public boat ramp is 0.25 mi. away. **Activities:** Not officially, but Chuck will gladly introduce you to his tamed squirrel, Squeaky. Put a peanut in your mouth, & Squeaky will climb on your shoulder to fetch it!. **Nearby Attractions:** Visit the Valdez Visitor Center for an impressive array of handouts & brochures regarding the surrounding area. They lay out a walking tour of Valdez as well as offer flyers that outline the general history of the area, the pipeline, & other interesting tidbits. **Additional Information:** www.alaska.net/~bayside1.

Restrictions

Pets: No restrictions. **Fires:** No restrictions. **Alcoholic Beverages:** No restrictions. **Vehicle Maximum Length:** None. **Other:** Inquire at campground.

To Get There

Take the Richardson Hwy. to Valdez. Just when you are in view of the town look to the left. You will see a light blue sign w/ Bayside RV Park in dark letters. It is the first RV Park you'll see.

WASILLA

Denali View North Campground

AK State Parks, Mat-su/CB Area, HC 32 Box 6706, Denali State Park 99654. T: (907) 745-3975; F: (907) 745-0938; www.dnr.state.ak.us/parks/units/denali1.htm.

RV ★★★ Tent n/a

Beauty: ★★★★★	Site Privacy: ★
Spaciousness: ★	Quiet: ★★★
Security: ★★	Cleanliness: ★★★★
Insect Control: ★★	Facilities: ★★

For many, one of the primary goals of visiting Alaska is to see the longest rock face in the world, Mt. McKinley (more commonly referred to as Denali by Alaskans). Unfortunately, 75% of the tourists who visit this area do not even get a glimpse of this elusive monolith, since it is usually cloaked in a thick layer of clouds. However, if you are willing to take a chance that during your visit the weather will break, then the Denali View North Campground is the place you'll want to be when the sun finally does shine.

Views of Mt. McKinley are the sole reason this campground was constructed, as there are no other attractions or guided activities for 30 miles in any direction. However, if the mountain does reveal itself, seeing it from this campground will be the highlight of your trip. A newly paved lot with extra-long pull-through sites makes this campground easily accessible to even the longest of vehicles. There are no hookups here, but a campground water pump is available, as well as regularly maintained outhouses. Some picnic tables and grill areas line the campground. There are also informational placards, a spotting scope, and benches to rest and enjoy the view. The campground is designed so that all RVs face the mountain. However, this really is a parking lot–style campground, and there is little to no space between sites.

Basics

Operated By: Denali State Park. **Open:** From snowmelt till the first snowfall (Approximately mid May–mid Sep.). **Site Assignment:** First come, first served. **Registration:** There is a self registration box located at the entrance. Park your vehicle & fill out a fee envelope shortly thereafter. Display the receipt in a visible area of your vehicle. **Fee:** $10 per night. **Parking:** At site.

Facilities

Number of RV-Only Sites: 23. **Number of Tent-Only Sites:** 0. **Hookups:** None. **Each Site:** None. **Dump Station:** No. **Laundry:** No. **Pay Phone:** No. **Rest Rooms and Showers:** Outhouses are available that are relatively clean. **Fuel:** The nearest fuel station is either north in Cantwell or south at Trapper Creek. **Propane:** No. **Internal Roads:** Newly paved & in excellent condition. **RV Service:** No. **Market:** No. **Restaurant:** Mary's McKinley View Lodge is located at mi. 134.5. **General Store:** No. **Vending:** No. **Swimming Pool:** No. **Playground:** No. **Other:** A short loop trail allows weary travels to walk & stretch their legs. **Activities:** Inquire at campground. **Nearby Attractions:** The entrance to the Denali State Park (not to be confused w/ Denali National Park) is located at mi. 132.2 & offers several hiking trails for all levels. Flightseeing, horsebackriding, & other area tours can be booked at Mt. McKinley Princess Lodge just up Mt. McKinley Princess Dr. at mi. 132.9. **Additional Information:** www.dnr.state.ak.us/parks/units/denali1.htm.

Restrictions

Pets: Must be leashed. **Fires:** Restricted to grill areas at the back of the campground. **Alcoholic Beverages:** No restrictions. **Vehicle Maximum Length:** None. **Other:** Campground rules & regulations are posted next to the fee box.

To Get There

Take the Parks Hwy. to mi. 162.7 and turn west at the Denali View sign. Since there are no landmarks before or after the campground, it can be difficult to find if you're not paying attention. A short paved road leads straight to the camp parking lot.

Idaho

A visit to Idaho is a journey in time, with much of the country looking exactly as it did for Lewis and Clark and early Native American tribes. Still, proud pines spiral into the cerulean blue, and bald eagles, prouder still, dare the limits of the mountain tops. As you wander into the backcountry wilderness, it's not hard to imagine that you're the first human to have ventured into these remote places. The number of Idaho parks, both state and private, and the diversity of Idaho's landscape offer a full spectrum of experience for all outdoor enthusiasts. From campsites accessible only by foot (where you're reminded that toilets are a modern amenity) to comfortable RV campgrounds, it's nearly impossible to escape the feeling of wilderness.

As you journey to your camping destinations, take the opportunity to enjoy the views provided by the Gem State. In the north, you might visit **Lake Coeur d'Alene** or **Lake Pend Oreille,** the largest lake in Idaho or you could motor along the **Lake Coeur d'Alene Scenic Byway**, making sure to stop at a scenic lookout to glimpse an eagle on the prowl. Take the **Northwest Passage Scenic Byway** and recapture moments of Lewis and Clark along 191 miles of their trail, and venture into **Hell's Canyon** where you can experience the sheer cliffs from water's edge. RV campers will enjoy a stop in **Kamiah** where the RV community is strong. In Central Idaho make a stop in the **Clear Lake Region** where you can stay at one of many Lewis and Clark Expedition campsites. Explore the area alone, take a guided tour, or horseback ride, or mountain bike through the remote territories. Drive the **Salmon River Scenic Byway,** with its awesome views of the **Sawtooth Mountains** and **Grand Tetons.**

Venturing east and southward, watch as the Idaho landscape transforms itself, as subtle desert colors begin to emerge and contrast with the deep evergreen. Ride the **Mesa Falls Scenic Byway** through the **Targhee National Forest** where glimpses of rushing waterfalls will beg for your attention. The **Bear Lake-Caribou Byway** takes you south past **Bear Lake**, **Minnetonka Caves,** and to the **Lava Hot Springs** established by the Bannock and Shoshone Tribes. Move farther south along the **Thousand Springs Scenic Byway** where you can visit the **City of Rocks.** Here, 60-foot granite pillars reach skyward like stalagmites from a cave floor. Nearby, the **Albion Mountain Range** provides a number of hiking, climbing, and wildlife-viewing experiences. Drive to the west along **Hells Canyon Scenic Byway** (it's short but steep) and visit southwest Idaho's **Bruneau Sand Dunes,** with sand peaks reaching 400 feet in height, the tallest dunes in North America. Choose a campsite in the **Payette National Forest** and enjoy the extensive hiking, biking, and fishing opportunities there. Wherever you travel, Idaho is sure to satisfy your spirit for adventure and quest for beauty if you seek more than the average camping experience.

The following facilities accept payment in checks or cash only:

- Bruneau Dunes State Park, Mountain Home
- Dent Acres Recreation Area, Orofino
- Elk Mountain RV Resort, Stanley
- Hells Gate State Park, Lewiston
- Lake Cascade State Park, Cascade

Campground Profiles

ATHOL

Farragut State Park

13400 East Ranger Rd., Athol 83801. T: (208) 638-2425; F: (208) 683-7416; www.idahoparks.org; FAR@idpr.state.id.us.

RV ★★★ Tent ★★★★

Beauty: ★★★★	Site Privacy: ★★★
Spaciousness: ★★★	Quiet: ★★★★
Security: ★★★★	Cleanliness: ★★★
Insect Control: ★★★★	Facilities: ★★★

Farragut State Park once served as a vital stop along the Pony Express route and was later purchased by the US Navy, which transformed it into the second-largest navel-training center in the world. Located only 14 miles north of Coeur d'Alene, this 4,000-acre state park is a perfect retreat, set in a forest of lodgepole pine, douglas fir, white pine, and western red cedar. Farragut State Park has five camping areas with 219 sites altogether. Its Snowberry Campground offers 44 hookup sites, with over 18 pull-throughs situated in a forest atmosphere. The eastern portion of the park is positioned on Idaho's largest lake, Lake Pend Oreille, with depths of 1,150 feet. The surrounding forest and mountain peaks are home to white-tail deer, black bear, coyote, and bald eagle. The elevation is 2,054 feet, offering crisp mornings and comfortable days. Each camping area has a camp host and day-use areas, and the marina gates are locked at 10 p.m.

BASICS

Operated By: Idaho Dept. of Parks & Recreation. **Open:** All year. **Site Assignment:** Reservations are recommended in the summer; $6 non-refundable reservation fee, which must be paid 5 days prior to arrival. **Registration:** In the visitors center. **Fee:** $12 no hookups, $16 w/ hookups. **Parking:** At site.

FACILITIES

Number of RV-Only Sites: 44. **Number of Tent-Only Sites:** 0. **Number of Multipurpose Sites:** 175. **Hookups:** Electric (30 amps), water. **Each Site:** Picnic table, fire pit. **Dump Station:** Yes. **Laundry:** No. **Pay Phone:** Yes. **Rest Rooms and Showers:** Yes. **Fuel:** No. **Propane:** No. **Internal Roads:** Mostly paved, some gravel. **RV Service:** 11 mi. south in Coeur d'Alene. **Market:** In Athol. **Restaurant:** In Athol. **General Store:** No. **Vending:** Yes. **Swimming Pool:** No, but there is lakefront swimming. **Playground:** Yes. **Other:** Visitor Center Park Museum, picnic areas, swimming area, model-airplane/glider flying field, boat launch & dock, amphitheater, Boy Scout monument, view points w/ coin-op. binoculars. **Activities:** Swimming, fishing (rainbow trout, bull trout, kokanee, machinaw, perch, blue gill, bass), boating, whitewater rafting, hiking, biking, hard path trails, volleyball, horseshoe pits, horseback riding, 18-hole golf course, shooting range, guided nature walks, interpretive programs, cross-country skiing. **Nearby Attractions:** Silverwood Theme Park, Lake Coeur d'Alene Cruises, Museum of North Idaho, Wild Water (water park). **Additional Infor-**

mation: Coeur d'Alene Chamber of Commerce, (208) 664-3194 or (877) 782-9232 or www.coeurdalene.org.

RESTRICTIONS

Pets: On 6-ft. leash only or confined, not tied to trees or vegetation, always attended. **Fires:** In fire pits only (fires may be prohibited due to weather, ask park official before starting any fire). **Alcoholic Beverages:** Yes. **Vehicle Maximum Length:** 60 ft. **Other:** Max. 8 people per site, 14-day limit, group camps available, check-out 1 p.m; tents must be pitched on tent pads; extra-vehicle fee of $5 per night.

TO GET THERE

15 mi. north of Coeur d'Alene or 17 mi. south of sandpoint off of Hwy. 95, turn west on Hwy. 54, park is directly off of Hwy. 54.

ATHOL

Silverwood RV Park

North 26225 Hwy. 95, Athol 83801. T: (208) 683-3400 ext. 139; F: (208) 683-2268; www.silverwood4fun.com; info@silverwood4fun.com.

RV ★★★ Tent ★★★

Beauty: ★★★	Site Privacy: ★★★
Spaciousness: ★★★	Quiet: ★★★
Security: ★★★	Cleanliness: ★★★
Insect Control: ★★★	Facilities: ★★★

If you are looking for a great time and enjoy the thrill of a roller coaster or a water flume, this is the park for you. Silverwood RV Park is operated in conjunction with Silverwood Theme Park, one of the Northwest's largest amusement parks, just north of Coeur d'Alene. The RV park is located adjacent to the theme parks main parking lot and offers discount admissions for its patrons. The campground consists of six wagon-wheel loops of 10–12 sites per loop, plus one larger main loop also with sites. The park offers both back-in and pull-through grass sites with paved trailer pads. The campground is clean and functional, with laundry and a convenience store. Silverwood campground's main function is to provide comfortable alternative lodging for the theme park customers. Security is handled through the main theme park, and the campground operates near full capacity all summer.

BASICS

Operated By: Silverwood Theme Park. **Open:** May–Oct. **Site Assignment:** By reservation. **Registration:** In RV office/general store. **Fee:** $21.42 first night, $19.35 the second, $18.28 per night for 3 or more nights. **Parking:** At site.

FACILITIES

Number of Multipurpose Sites: 126. **Hookups:** Electric (30 amps), water, sewer. **Each Site:** Picnic table. **Dump Station:** No. **Laundry:** Yes. **Pay Phone:** Yes. **Rest Rooms and Showers:** Yes. **Fuel:** No. **Propane:** No. **Internal Roads:** Gravel. **RV Service:** In Coeur D'Alene. **Market:** In Athol. **Restaurant:** In Athol. **General Store:** Yes. **Vending:** Yes. **Swimming Pool:** No. **Playground:** No. **Other:** Owned in junction to Silverwood Theme Park. **Activities:** Fishing, hiking, rafting, volleyball, horseshoe pits. **Nearby Attractions:** Silverwood Theme Park, Museum of North Idaho, Wild Waters, Farragut State Park. **Additional Information:** Silverwood Theme Park tickets sold at a discount, (208) 683-3400, www.silverwood4fun.com. Coeur d'Alene area Chamber of Commerce & Visitor's Center, (208) 664-3194, (877) 782-9232, www.coeurdalene.org.

RESTRICTIONS

Pets: On leash only, may not be left in RVs or tied (Kickaboo Dog & Cat Boarding available in town, (208) 683-3210). **Fires:** No open fires allowed. **Alcoholic Beverages:** In moderation. **Vehicle Maximum Length:** None. **Other:** Discounted admission tickets to Silverwood Theme Park.

TO GET THERE

15 mi. North of Coeur d'Alene, on Hwy. 95.

BOISE

Boise National Forest

1249 South Vinnell Way, Suite 200, Boise 83709. T: (208) 373-4100; F: (208) 373-4111; www.fs.fed.us/r4/boise; r4boiseinfo@fs.fed.us.

RV ★★★ Tent ★★★★

Beauty: ★★★★★	Site Privacy: ★★★★
Spaciousness: ★★★★	Quiet: ★★★★★
Security: ★★★	Cleanliness: ★★★
Insect Control: n/a	Facilities: ★★

If you enjoy outdoor activity, then Boise National Forest is the place to go. Surrounded by gorgeous scenery, there are breath-taking views in just about every direction. The sites are spacious, and quiet, as well as providing adequate privacy for the guests. All of the sites are equipped with on-site parking (most of them paved), fire pits, and picnic tables. There are any number of activities available, such as hiking, skiing, horseback riding, and backpacking, and even a ghost town nearby. The only thing to remember is that Boise National Forest is quite large and somewhat remote in spots, so be sure you keep an eye on your fuel levels.

BASICS

Operated By: US Forest Service. **Open:** Most are May–Sept. **Site Assignment:** Several are by reservation (877) 444-6777 or www.reserveusa.com, you may reserve 240 days in advance or self serve. **Registration:** Registration kiosk or camp hosts trailer. **Fee:** Sites vary in price from $5–$20 per night/ 6 max-a site. **Parking:** At site.

FACILITIES

Number of Multipurpose Sites: There are 70 campgrounds in the Boise National Forest, 6 to 200 sites each. (on average 12). **Hookups:** Potable water. **Each Site:** Level parking spurs (most are paved), picnic table, grated fire pit. **Dump Station:** Dumps are located in several locations through out the forest. **Laundry:** There are laundry facilities in the small communities scattered through out the forest, but Not at the individual campgrounds. **Pay Phone:** No. **Rest Rooms and Showers:** All the campgrounds have rest rooms, mostly w/ vaulted toilets. **Fuel:** The Boise National Forest is very large area & there are very few areas to fuel, & even less places w/ diesel. Please be careful. **Propane:** Can be found most anyplace that sales fuel. **Internal Roads:** Most are paved. **RV Service:** Boise. **Market:** There are groceries in most every small community within the forest. **Restaurant:** There are very few restaurants, please pack dinner, especially if you don't eat hamburgers & fries. **General Store:** No. **Vending:** No. **Swimming Pool:** No, but there are many areas on the rivers & lakes open to public for swimming. There are also many natural hot springs in the area. Please use caution, many of the hot springs are too hot for swimming & will cause second- & third-degree burns. **Playground:** No. **Other:** Horse camps (there is 1 commercial horse camp in Idaho City), Boise River, Payette River. **Activities:** Hiking, mountain biking, fishing, skiing, horseback riding, backpacking, mountaineering, visiting ghost towns, cross-country skiing. **Nearby Attractions:** Arrowrock Reservoir, Anderson Ranch Reservoir, Idaho Historical Museum, Boise Zoo. **Additional Information:** www.fs.fed.us/r4/boise.

RESTRICTIONS

Pets: On leash. **Fires:** In fire rings only (the forest may prohibit open fires due to weather conditions, always check w/ a ranger or camp host before starting any fires). **Alcoholic Beverages:** Allowed. **Vehicle Maximum Length:** Sites vary in size, the campgrounds on the national reservation service are better equipped to handle larger RVs. **Other:** Golden Access & Golden Age Passes are honored & can be purchased at any ranger station; 14-day limit.

TO GET THERE

Hwy. 21, mile post 38.5.

BOISE
United Campground

7373 Federal Way, Boise 83716. T: (208) 343-4379

RV: ★★ | Tent: n/a

Beauty: ★★	Site Privacy: ★★★
Spaciousness: ★★	Quiet: ★★
Security: ★★	Cleanliness: ★★
Insect Control: ★★★	Facilities: ★★

United Campground is located directly off I-84 in Boise. The campground is open to self-contained hard-shelled campers. There is no tent camping allowed. United Campground is a large facility with a full-service convenient store, fuel, and supplies. It is mostly gravel with sprouts of grass and a few trees. The sites are close together and moderate in size. This campground seems to cater to a lot of transient workers. Boise is a large metropolitan city as well as Idaho's state capital and offers a large variety of activities, festivals, and events. It is home to Boise State University, numerous museums, motor speedway, parks, and theater. There are tours available of the downtown area, as well as the state capital building and surrounding grounds. United Campground makes for a nice base camp while patrons enjoy all Boise has to offer.

BASICS

Operated By: Western Construction. **Open:** All year. **Site Assignment:** By reservation, no deposit required. **Registration:** In convenience store. **Fee:** $15. **Parking:** At site.

Facilities

Number of RV-Only Sites: 106. **Number of Tent-Only Sites:** 0. **Hookups:** Electric (20, 30, 50 amps), water, sewer. **Each Site:** Some sites have picnic tables. **Dump Station:** Yes. **Laundry:** Yes. **Pay Phone:** Yes. **Rest Rooms and Showers:** Yes. **Fuel:** Yes. **Propane:** Yes. **Internal Roads:** Gravel, in good condition. **RV Service:** In Boise. **Market:** In Boise. **Restaurant:** In Boise. **General Store:** Yes. **Vending:** Yes. **Swimming Pool:** No. **Playground:** Yes. **Other:** Convenient store & fuel on site. **Activities:** Horseshoes, playground. **Nearby Attractions:** Basque Museum & Cultural Center, Discovery Center of Idaho, Idaho Botanical Garden, Morrison-Knudsen Nature Center, Boise National Forest, zoo, shopping,dinning. **Additional Information:** Boise CVB, (800) 635-5240.

Restrictions

Pets: Not permitted. **Fires:** No open fires. **Alcoholic Beverages:** Allowed. **Vehicle Maximum Length:** 40 ft.

To Get There

From I-84 Exit 57, go east on Godwin Rd. and within 0.25 mi. turn right on Federal Way.

CALDER

Huckleberry Campground

1808 North Third St., Coeur d'Alene 83814. T: (208) 769-5030; F: (208) 769-5050; www.id.blm.gov/recreation/sites/huckle.htm.

RV ★★★ Tent ★★★★

Beauty: ★★★★	Site Privacy: ★★★★
Spaciousness: ★★★	Quiet: ★★★★★
Security: ★★	Cleanliness: ★★★
Insect Control: ★★★	Facilities: ★★

Located in the Idaho Panhandle National Forest along the St. Joe River, this BLM campground is a hidden treasure to campers looking for a beautiful spot to relax, fish, or bike. The scenery is spectacular and the area is full of history. Huckleberry Campground is just one of many BLM campgrounds in the area offers electrical and water hookups, paved trailer pads, and gravel tent pads. The campsites are private and very well maintained. The security of the campground is overseen by the local ranger, but a camp host is there during the summer season to assist with any needs that may arise. (Please note this is bear country). The air is crisp in the spring and fall, and days are warm in the summer. The St. Joe area is popular for its fly-fishing and elk hunting.

Basics

Operated By: Bureau of Land Management. **Open:** May–Oct. **Site Assignment:** Self serve. **Registration:** Self register at the cash box. **Fee:** $12 w/ hookups, $9 no hookups, $3 RV dump fee. **Parking:** At site.

Facilities

Number of Multipurpose Sites: 33. **Hookups:** Electric (30 amps), water. **Each Site:** Picnic table, fire pit. **Dump Station:** Yes. **Laundry:** No. **Pay Phone:** No. **Rest Rooms and Showers:** Vaulted toilets, no showers. **Fuel:** No. **Propane:** No. **Internal Roads:** Gravel. **RV Service:** Avery. **Market:** 35 mi. west in St. Maries. **Restaurant:** St. Joe in Marble Creek about 7 mi. east. **General Store:** No. **Vending:** No. **Swimming Pool:** No, but you may swim in the river. **Playground:** No. **Activities:** Fishing (horseshoe fly fishing), hiking, backpacking, non-motorized boating, hunting. **Nearby Attractions:** St. Joe Discovery Tour, Hobo Cedar Grove Botanical Area, Splash Dam, Marble Creek Interpretive Site, Big Creek National Recreation Trail. **Additional Information:** St. Maries Chamber of Commerce, (208) 245-3562.

Restrictions

Pets: On leash. **Fires:** In fire pits only (open fires may be restricted due to dry weather, check w/ the local forest ranger, (208) 245-2531). **Alcoholic Beverages:** Contained on site only. **Vehicle Maximum Length:** None. **Other:** 50% discount w/ Golden Age or Golden Access passport.

To Get There

Take Hwy. 3 north from St. Maries for not quite a mile, then right on St. Joe River Rd. (FH-50) to between mile markers 29 and 30.

CALDER (MARBLE SPRINGS)

St. Joes Lodge and Resort

RR 3 Box 350, Calder 83808. T: (208) 245-3462; F: (208) 245-3367.

RV ★★★ Tent ★★★

Beauty: ★★★★	Site Privacy: ★★
Spaciousness: ★★	Quiet: ★★★★
Security: ★★★	Cleanliness: ★★★
Insect Control: ★★★	Facilities: ★★★

Hidden away in the Idaho Panhandle National Forest along the St. Joe River is St. Joes Lodge and Resort. This small resort offers cabins, a six-room motel, 24 camping sites, and a warm, cozy rustic lodge with the best home-cooked food around. The campground sits on the riverbank surrounded by a diverse evergreen forest. The sites are hard-packed dirt and gravel with some grass, that indicative of a forest floor. Most RV sites are back-ins, with a few pull-throughs. Tent sites are fairly open along the river. The campground has a tubing outfitter and some fishing supplies. The area is home to many wildlife species, such as deer, elk, and bear and offers great hunting or photography. The area is also along the St. Joe Discovery Tour and the Marble Creek Interpretive Site. There are several national recreation-hiking trails and mountain-biking trails. Temperatures are cool during the evening, with comfortable summer days.

Basics

Operated By: Richard & Sharie Larson. **Open:** All year. **Site Assignment:** Reservations recommended. **Registration:** In the lodge. **Fee:** Tent $8, RV $18. **Parking:** At site.

Facilities

Number of RV-Only Sites: 24. **Number of Tent-Only Sites:** Open tent area. **Hookups:** Electric (30, 50 amps), water, sewer. **Each Site:** Picnic table, fire pit. **Dump Station:** No. **Laundry:** No. **Pay Phone:** Yes. **Rest Rooms and Showers:** Yes. **Fuel:** Yes. **Propane:** Yes. **Internal Roads:** Gravel. **RV Service:** 20 mi. east in Avery. **Market:** 20 mi. east in Avery. **Restaurant:** St. Joes Lodge. **General Store:** No. **Vending:** Yes. **Swimming Pool:** No, but you may swim in the river. **Playground:** No. **Other:** Riverfront beach area, tube rental, 6-room motel, & a cabin. **Activities:** Fly-fishing (cut throat & rainbow trout), tubing, hunting, mountain biking, whitewater rafting, horseback riding, hiking. **Nearby Attractions:** There are many outfitters in the area & a lot of scenic drives. **Additional Information:** North Idaho Visitors Information Center, (888) 333-3737; St. Maries Chamber of Commerce, (208) 245-3563, www.stmarieschamber.org.

Restrictions

Pets: On leash only. **Fires:** In fire pits only (fires may be prohibited due to weather, ask management before starting any fire). **Alcoholic Beverages:** Yes. **Vehicle Maximum Length:** 40 ft.

To Get There

33.5 mi. from St. Maries down FH-50 (St. Joe River Rd.).

CASCADE

Arrowhead Mountain Village

P.O. Box 387, Cascade 83611.T: (208) 382-4534

RV ★★★★ Tent ★★★

Beauty: ★★★★ Site Privacy: ★★★
Spaciousness: ★★ Quiet: ★★★★
Security: ★★★★ Cleanliness: ★★★★
Insect Control: ★★★★ Facilities: ★★★★

Located just within the Cascade city limits, this 115-site RV park is like a home to many returning seasonal visitors. Arrowhead Mountain Village is a pristine community catering to its guests. It offers full amenities, craft classes, totem-pole carving, and many other scheduled activities. Sites are comfortably spaced and most are shaded. The majority of the sites are pull-through, with a few back-ins along the Payette River. The river runs along the southern portion of the property, offering great fishing and non-motorized boating. The park provides a fish cleaning area and boat ramp. There is a central fire pit on the riverbank, available for campfires. The Cascade Reservoir is only a few miles north, attracting water-skiers, jet-skiers, and serious fishermen. Perch, coho salmon, and rainbow trout are only a few of the many fish found in the reservoir. A constant breeze comes from the adjacent mountains, making summer days very pleasant.

Basics

Operated By: Gerald & Bobbie Patterson. **Open:** May–Oct. 15. **Site Assignment:** Reservations recommended & held w/ credit card. **Registration:** In camp office. **Fee:** Tent $15, RV $20 per 2 people, extra people $2, children under age 6 free. **Parking:** At site.

Facilities

Number of RV-Only Sites: 110. **Number of Tent-Only Sites:** 5. **Hookups:** Electric (30, 50 amps), water, sewer, satellite TV. **Each Site:** Picnic tables. **Dump Station:** Yes. **Laundry:** Yes. **Pay Phone:** Yes. **Rest Rooms and Showers:** Yes. **Fuel:** Across the street. **Propane:** Yes. **Internal Roads:** Gravel. **RV Service:** 12 mi. North in Lake

Fork. **Market:** In Cascade. **Restaurant:** In Cascade. **General Store:** Yes. **Vending:** Yes. **Swimming Pool:** No. **Playground:** Yes. **Other:** 2 yurts (circular, Mongolian-style tent), pet area, boat launch & parking, cabins, flower garden, butterfly garden, rec hall, pavilion, fish-cleaning house, secure storage yard. **Activities:** Archery, horseshoes, craft classes, carving classes, ice-cream socials, many scheduled activities, fishing (perch, rainbow trout, coho salmon), hiking, boating, waterskiing, snowmobiling, golf, basketball, skeet shooting, horseback trips, fly-fishing trips, wagon rides. **Nearby Attractions:** Nature trails, Idaho Historical Railroads. **Additional Information:** Cascade Chamber of Commerce, (208) 382-3833, www.cascadeid.com.

RESTRICTIONS

Pets: On leash only. **Fires:** No open fires allowed, 1 central fire pit. **Alcoholic Beverages:** Allowed. **Vehicle Maximum Length:** None.

TO GET THERE

Located directly off of Hwy. 55, within the city limits of Cascade.

CASCADE
Lake Cascade State Park

P.O. Box 709, Cascade 83611.T: (208) 382-6544; F: (208) 382-4071; www.idahoparks.org; cas@idpr.state.id.us.

RV ★★★ | Tent ★★★

Beauty: ★★★★	Site Privacy: ★★
Spaciousness: ★★	Quiet: ★★★
Security: ★★★	Cleanliness: ★★★
Insect Control: ★★★★	Facilities: ★★

Lake Cascade State Park is composed of five camping areas surrounding the Cascade Reservoir. The Cascade Reservoir stretches over 20 miles bordered by grass plains and framed with timbered mountains. The reservoir is known for its constant mountain breeze and attracts waterskiers, jet-skiers, windsurfers, and sailors. It is stocked with trophy coho salmon, rainbow trout, and perch. Each campground is located along the banks of the reservoir. Campground areas range in size from 5 to15 acres, each offering a picnic table, fire pit, potable water, and toilet facilities. Lake Cascade State Park does not offer full hookups; however, it does offer 300 campsites accommodating trailers up to 55 feet. Each campsite has a registration box and charges a fee. Lake Cascade State Park has five boat launches, boat parking, and a marine dump. Stop at the Lake Cascade visitors center for a map of campsite locations. All day-use areas of the park are closed at 10 p.m.

BASICS

Operated By: Idaho Dept. of Parks & Recreation, Rick Brown Manager. **Open:** All year. **Site Assignment:** First come, first served; no reservations except groups. **Registration:** Self-serve at the entrance of each camping area (except for groups). **Fee:** $7–$9 (cash or check). **Parking:** At site.

FACILITIES

Number of Multipurpose Sites: 300 within 5 campground areas. **Hookups:** Water. **Each Site:** Picnic table, fire pit. **Dump Station:** 2 dump locations. **Laundry:** No. **Pay Phone:** On the west side of the lake. **Rest Rooms and Showers:** Vaulted toilets, no showers. **Fuel:** In Cascade. **Propane:** In Cascade. **Internal Roads:** Paved & packed dirt/gravel. **RV Service:** 12 mi. north in Lake Fork. **Market:** In Cascade. **Restaurant:** In Cascade. **General Store:** No. **Vending:** No. **Swimming Pool:** No pool, but there is swimming in the lake. **Playground:** Yes. **Other:** 3 yurts (circular, Mongolian-style domed tents for groups), lakefront beach, group picnic shelters, dump station, 5 boat launches. **Activities:** Fishing (rainbow trout, coho salmon), fly-fishing trips, windsurfing, sailing, boating, waterskiing, jet-skiing, swimming, whitewater rafting, horseback trips, horseshoes, skeet shooting, golf. **Nearby Attractions:** Boating, fishing, & hunting outfitters, snowmobile trails, cross-country nordic trails, flea market, biking trails. **Additional Information:** Cascade Chamber of Commerce, (208) 382-3833, www.cascadeid.com; Idaho Dept. of Parks & Recreation, (208) 334-4199.

RESTRICTIONS

Pets: On 6-ft. leash only. **Fires:** In fire pits only (fires may be prohibited due to weather, check w/ park officials before starting any fires). **Alcoholic Beverages:** Allowed. **Vehicle Maximum Length:** 55 ft. **Other:** Lake Cascade State Park circles all of Lake Cascade but not all the land is Cascade State Park—much of it is private, US Forestry, or US Bureau of Reclamation; read all posted signs for directions & instructions; max. 8 people per site, 14-day stay limit.

To Get There

The main entrance is located off Hwy. 55, approx. 4 mi. north of Cascade.

CASCADE
Pinewood Lodge Motel, RV Park and Storage

900 South Main, Cascade 83611.T: (208) 382-4948; F: (208) 382-5521; www.thepinewoodlodge.com; pinewood@micron.net.

RV: ★★★ Tent: ★★

Beauty: ★★★	Site Privacy: ★★
Spaciousness: ★★	Quiet: ★★★
Security: ★★★	Cleanliness: ★★★★
Insect Control: ★★★★	Facilities: ★★★★

Located within the city limits of Cascade, the Pinewood Lodge Motel, RV Park, and Storage offers a pleasant and comfortable atmosphere. The campground sits behind a charming motel and offers wooded sites, both pull-throughs and back-ins. Tent camping is available, but the sites are small and backed up to the fence line. The Pinewood Lodge is convenient to the Cascade Reservoir and Lake Cascade State Park. The Cascade area is renown for attracting water-skiers, boaters, and fishermen. The breeze on the reservoir is perfect for windsurfing and sailing. In the winter the area is popular for its nordic trails, cross-country snow skiing, and snowmobiling. The Pinewood Lodge offers a canoe shuttle, fish-cleaning facilities, and a large screened-in pavilion with a kitchen area and two gas grills. Staff is on duty around the clock, always willing to assist.

Basics

Operated By: Paul & Audrey Parton. **Open:** All year. **Site Assignment:** Reservations recommended & held w/ a credit card. **Registration:** Lodge office. **Fee:** Tent $15, RV $21 per 2 people, extra person $3, children under age 2 free; cash, credit cards, checks; 10% senior discount. **Parking:** At site.

Facilities

Number of RV-Only Sites: 36. **Number of Tent-Only Sites:** 9. **Hookups:** Electric (20, 30, 50 amps), water, sewer, cable. **Each Site:** Picnic table, some fire pit. **Dump Station:** Yes. **Laundry:** Yes. **Pay Phone:** Yes. **Rest Rooms and Showers:** Yes. **Fuel:** Across the street. **Propane:** Across the street. **Internal Roads:** Paved. **RV Service:** 12 mi. north in Lake Fork. **Market:** In Cascade. **Restaurant:** In Cascade, 2 within 300 yards. **General Store:** No. **Vending:** Yes. **Swimming Pool:** Yes. **Playground:** Yes. **Other:** Large screened pavilion w/ 2 gas grills, kitchen area, & fire place, fish-cleaning facilities, group fire ring, canoe shuttle. **Activities:** Basketball, horseshoes, boating, whitewater rafting, skeet trap shooting, hiking, fishing, fly-fishing trips, trail rides, wagon rides, sleigh rides. **Nearby Attractions:** Lake Cascade, Lake Cascade State Park, Gem State Rock Hunting, summer flee markets. **Additional Information:** Cascade Chamber of Commerce, (208) 382-3833, www.cascadeid.com; Big Creek Wilderness Outfitters, (208) 382-4872; Snowbank Outfitters, (208) 382-4872; snowmobile rentals, (208) 382-3465.

Restrictions

Pets: On leash only. **Fires:** In fire pits. **Alcoholic Beverages:** Allowed. **Vehicle Maximum Length:** Call ahead for details.

To Get There

Hwy. 55 on the south side of Cascade within the city limits.

CASCADE
Water's Edge RV Resort

P.O. Box 1018, Cascade 83611.T: (208)382-0120 or (800) 574-2038; F: (208) 382-3035; www.watersedgervpark.com; we2are1@cyberhighway.net.

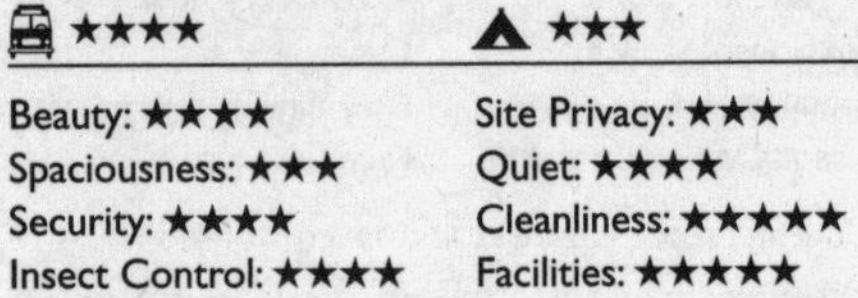

RV: ★★★★ Tent: ★★★

Beauty: ★★★★	Site Privacy: ★★★
Spaciousness: ★★★	Quiet: ★★★★
Security: ★★★★	Cleanliness: ★★★★★
Insect Control: ★★★★	Facilities: ★★★★★

Located on the beautiful Payette River and only a few short miles from the Cascade Reservoir, Water's Edge RV Resort is the ideal location for water-sport enthusiasts. Water's Edge offers free canoeing and kayaking from its own riverfront beach. There are 92 lakes and 169 streams in a 50-mile radius with trophy sockeye, chinook, and rainbow trout. The campground itself offers level gravel sites, with all the amenities, beautifully landscaped common areas, and a brand-new covered picnic pavilion. Water's Edge is famous for its evening campfires on the beach and the hot, fresh cinnamon rolls on summer weekend mornings. And Cascade is known for its cool mountain breeze, which makes summer days pleasant and evenings cool. In winter, the Cascade area offers miles of cross-country skiing and snowmobile trails.

Basics

Operated By: Ashley & Katrin Thompson. **Open:** May–Oct. **Site Assignment:** Reservations recommended & held w/ a credit card number. **Registration:** In camp office. **Fee:** Tent 19, RV $22–$29 per 2 people. Extra person $2. **Parking:** At site.

Facilities

Number of RV-Only Sites: 100. **Number of Tent-Only Sites:** 10. **Hookups:** Electric (30, 50 amps), water, sewer, cable, phone, Internet. **Each Site:** Picnic table. **Dump Station:** Yes. **Laundry:** Yes. **Pay Phone:** Yes. **Rest Rooms and Showers:** Yes. **Fuel:** No. **Propane:** Yes. **Internal Roads:** Gravel, in excellent condition. **RV Service:** 12 mi. north in Lake Fork. **Market:** In Cascade. **Restaurant:** In Cascade. **General Store:** Yes. **Vending:** Yes. **Swimming Pool:** No, but there is riverfront swimming. **Playground:** No. **Other:** 2 pavilions w/ grills, 2 riverfront fire pits, private riverfront beach (Payette River), cabins, covered picnic area, rec hall w/ kitchen area, free canoes & kayaks, fax & copier service, cinnamon rolls on Saturday morning in the summer. **Activities:** Canoeing, kayaking, beach volleyball, horseshoes, paddleboats, evening campfires, bird-watching, fishing (rainbow trout, perch, coho salmon), river nature walks, sailing, biking, hiking, windsurfing, whitewater rafting, skeet trap shoots, wilderness fly-fishing trips, horseback trips, wagon rides, golf. **Nearby Attractions:** Lake Cascade State Park. **Additional Information:** Cascade Chamber of Commerce, (208) 382-3833, www.cascadeid.com; Snowbank Outfitter, (208) 382-4872; Big Creek Wilderness Outfitter, (208) 382-4872.

Restrictions

Pets: On leash only. **Fires:** In central fire pits only. **Alcoholic Beverages:** Allowed. **Vehicle Maximum Length:** 40 plus.

To Get There

Directly off Hwy. 55 on the north side of Cascade.

CHALLIS

Challis Hot Springs

HC 63 Box 1779, Challis 83226. T: (208) 879-4442; www.scenicriver.com; fish@scenicriver.com.

RV ★★★★ Tent ★★★★★

Beauty: ★★★★ Site Privacy: ★★★★
Spaciousness: ★★★★ Quiet: ★★★★
Security: ★★★★ Cleanliness: ★★★★
Insect Control: ★★★★ Facilities: ★★★★

Nestled between the Lost River Range and Salmon River Mountains, this rustic campground is the perfect place to get away from the hubbub of city life. The 27 RV and 12 tent-only sites make a great base camp from which to explore a number of Idaho's spectacular resources, including the Frank Church River of No Return Wilderness, the Salmon River, and the Rocky Mountains. Wildlife frequently pass through the campgrounds, and the Salmon River, which is in easy walking distance, provides a great place to wet some lines. Though the campground is remote, campers can find most amenities in the town of Challis, including food, auto parts, and banking. Challis, the country seat of Custer County, is still the area's economic center of mines, ranches, and farms. This area is still known as one of the richest mineral belts in North America.

Basics

Operated By: Tom & Sandi Coates. **Open:** All year. **Site Assignment:** By reservation, 50% deposit required. **Registration:** In camp office. **Fee:** Tent $15.50, RV $21.50 per 2 people, extra person $6. **Parking:** At site.

Facilities

Number of RV-Only Sites: 27. **Number of Tent-Only Sites:** 12. **Number of Multipurpose Sites:** 4. **Hookups:** Electric (30 amps), water, sewer. **Each Site:** Picnic table, fire pit. **Dump Station:** Yes. **Laundry:** No. **Pay Phone:** Yes. **Rest Rooms and Showers:** Yes. **Fuel:** 3 mi. in Challis. **Propane:** 3 mi. in Challis. **Internal Roads:** Gravel, in good condition. **RV Service:** 3 mi. in Challis. **Market:** 3 mi. in Challis. **Restaurant:** Gourmet meals served once a week on site, & some Dutch-oven cooking, otherwise 3 mi. in Challis. **General Store:** Yes. **Vending:** No. **Swimming Pool:** Yes. **Playground:** Yes. **Other:** Natural hot water swimming pool open year-round, hot mineral pool, driving range, Dutch-oven cooking, beautiful bed-&-breakfast, nice pavilion, rafting outfitters, horseback outfitters, fly-fishing school. **Activities:** Swimming, fly fishing, rafting, golf, cross-country skiing, snowmobile trails. **Nearby Attractions:** Scenic drives, many recreational outfitters. **Additional Information:** Challis Chamber of Commerce, (208) 879-2771.

RESTRICTIONS

Pets: On leash only. **Fires:** In fire pits only (fires may be restricted due to dry weather, always ask management before starting any open fire). **Alcoholic Beverages:** Allowed. **Vehicle Maximum Length:** None.

TO GET THERE

Challis is at the junction of Hwy. 75 and Hwy. 93. From there go 3 mi. east on Hwy. 93 and turn left on Challis Hot Springs Rd.; this road will dead-end into the property. (There are excellent signs directing you into this property.)

COOLIN

Priest Lake State Park

314 Indian Creek Park Rd., Coolin 83821-9076. T: (208) 443-6710; www.idahoparks.org/parks/priest.html; PRI@idpr.state.id.us.

RV ★★★ Tent ★★★

Beauty: ★★★★	Site Privacy: ★★★
Spaciousness: ★★★	Quiet: ★★★
Security: ★★★★	Cleanliness: ★★★
Insect Control: ★★★★	Facilities: ★★★

If you are looking for abundance, spectacular scenery, and cool summer days, then Priest Lake State Park is the vacation spot for you. Priest Lake State Park offers two fully equipped campgrounds situated on a 19-mile lake of crystal-clear water. The campgrounds are under canopies of mature cedars and hemlocks that open to the panoramic view of Priest Lake and the Selkirk Mountain Range. Each site is comfortable in size and offers a sense of privacy. There are both pull-through and back-in sites available, as well as packed-sand trailer pads. Some sites are more level than others, and rain does seem to cause minor flooding. The area is home to diverse wildlife inhabitants (i.e. bears and moose), and it is wise to leave all food packed in a safe and secure place outside of your sleeping area. The campground is open year-round, with utilities functioning from spring until late fall. Activities differ with each season—from waterskiing in the summer to snowmobiling and cross-country skiing in winter. The park is fully staffed with park officials on duty around the clock.

BASICS

Operated By: Idaho State Parks. **Open:** All year. **Site Assignment:** First come, first served. **Registration:** Entrance gate. **Fee:** $12 no hookups, $16 w/ hookups. **Parking:** $ 4 extra-vehicle fee.

FACILITIES

Number of Multipurpose Sites: 151. **Hookups:** Electric (30 amps), water at both campgrounds. **Each Site:** Picnic table, fire pit. **Dump Station:** Yes. **Laundry:** Yes. **Pay Phone:** Yes. **Rest Rooms and Showers:** Yes. **Fuel:** Yes (also boat fuel). **Propane:** Yes. **Internal Roads:** Combination of sand & dirt (watch for water after hard rain). **RV Service:** No. **Market:** No. **Restaurant:** In Coolin. **General Store:** Yes. **Vending:** General store only. **Swimming Pool:** No, but you may swim in the lake. **Playground:** Yes. **Other:** Amphitheater, marina, picnic area, cabins, picnic shelters, day-use area. **Activities:** Fishing, swimming, boating, volleyball, horseshoes, guided walks, picking huckleberries, evening summer programs; skiing, ice-fishing, & snowmobiling in winter. **Nearby Attractions:** Lionhead. **Additional Information:** Idaho State Parks & Recreation, (208) 334-4199.

RESTRICTIONS

Pets: On 6-ft. leash only. **Fires:** In fire pits only (fires may be prohibited due to dry weather, check w/ park officials before starting any fire). **Alcoholic Beverages:** Allowed, if used w/ good judgement & in moderation. **Vehicle Maximum Length:** 50 ft. **Other:** 14-day limit.

TO GET THERE

From N US-95 to N US-2 to SH-57, then follow signs into the park.

COUER D'ALENE

Coeur d'Alene KOA RV, Tent, and Kabin Resort

East 10588 Wolf Lodge Bay Rd., Coeur d'Alene 83814. T: (208) 664-4471 or (800) 562-2609; F: (208) 765-4109; www.koa.com.

🚐 ★★★ ⛺ ★★★

Beauty: ★★★★ Site Privacy: ★★★
Spaciousness: ★★★ Quiet: ★★★★
Security: ★★★ Cleanliness: ★★★
Insect Control: ★★★★ Facilities: ★★★★

Positioned on the side of Coeur d'Alene Mountain and adjacent to Lake Coeur d'Alene, KOA RV, Tent, & Kabin Resort is ideal for recreation. The park is located directly off I-90, only nine miles east of Coeur d'Alene. The campground offers 89 RV sites and19 cabins terraced up the side of Coeur d'Alene Mountain, with 79 tent sites and 2 tepees in the valley. The grounds are nicely landscaped and the view is spectacular. Sites, however, are relatively close together, with pull-through sites offering little shade. All sites are gravel climbing the hill, and many are difficult to maneuver. A bird and wildlife sanctuary is found in the basin of the valley. The weather can change with a snap of a finger; evenings are cool. This KOA offers two adult-only hot tubs, and kayaking from a boat dock. The campground is patrolled on a regular basis.

Basics

Operated By: David & Karen Striker. **Open:** Apr. 1–Oct. 15. **Site Assignment:** Reservations recommended w/ 50% deposit. **Registration:** In camp store. **Fee:** Tent $19, RV $21–$29 per 2 people, $2.75 per extra person; cash, credit cards, checks. **Parking:** At site, very little extra.

Facilities

Number of RV-Only Sites: 86. **Number of Tent-Only Sites:** 79. **Hookups:** Electric (30 amps), water, sewer. **Each Site:** Picnic table, grill, fire pit. **Dump Station:** Yes. **Laundry:** Yes. **Pay Phone:** Yes. **Rest Rooms and Showers:** Yes. **Fuel:** No. **Propane:** Yes. **Internal Roads:** Gravel, in good condition. **RV Service:** 9 mi. west in Coeur d'Alene. **Market:** 9 mi. west in Coeur d'Alene. **Restaurant:** Steak house on the north frontage road about 0.5 mi., or in Coeur d'Alene. **General Store:** Yes, w/ snacks & homemade pizza. **Vending:** In general store only. **Swimming Pool:** Heated pool & 2 hot tubs. **Playground:** Yes. **Other:** Amphitheater, camp kitchen, tepees, cabins, non-motorized boat launch, kayak rentals. **Activities:** Outside movies, paddleboat, canoeing, kayaking, fishing, mini-golf, horseshoes, horseback riding, hiking, bike trails. **Nearby Attractions:** Silverwood Theme Park, Wild Water Slides, Silver Mountain Gondola ride, shopping, seaplane & helicopter rides, museums, parasailing, casinos. **Additional Information:** Coeur d'Alene Chamber of Commerce, (208) 664-3194, (877) 782-9232, www.coeurdalene.org.

Restrictions

Pets: On 6-ft. leash only, cleaned up after, always attended or a fee will be imposed; not allowed in any building or the pool area; pet walk provided. **Fires:** In fire pits only (fires may be prohibited during dry weather). **Alcoholic Beverages:** Allowed. **Vehicle Maximum Length:** None. **Other:** Free modem access.

To Get There

Exit 22 off I-90, go south on SR 97 for 0.5 mi. and turn left onto Wolf Lodge Bay Rd.

COEUR D'ALENE

Idaho Panhandle National Forest

3815 Schreiber Way, Coeur d'Alene 83815-8363.
T: (208) 765-7223; F: (208) 765-7307;
www.fs.fed.us/outernet/ipnf.

🚐 ★★★ ⛺ ★★★★

Beauty: ★★★★★ Site Privacy: ★★★★
Spaciousness: ★★★★ Quiet: ★★★★★
Security: ★★★ Cleanliness: ★★★
Insect Control: n/a Facilities: ★★

Camping in the Panhandle Idaho National Forest is for all outdoor enthusiasts, especially those who seek breathtaking views and pristine lakes and rivers. Most of the sites are accessible by cars and RVs (some even by boat), but this camping experience is relatively rustic for the most part. Whether you want to do some serious outdoor recreation or just to hang out under the pines (fir, spruce, cedar and hemlock, to name a few) and breathe the delicious northwest air, the beauty of this national forest will not disappoint. For the most part, you will find level parking spots at the campsites, but be prepared to do some research to choose the most practical site for your style of camping. These rural, quiet campgrounds will provide you with a private, gorgeous wonderland. Rock-climbing, hiking, hunting, fishing, and other such diversions will keep you busy.

Basics

Operated By: US Forest Service. **Open:** Most are May–Sept. **Site Assignment:** Several reservable,

(877) 444-6777 or www.reserveusa.com, 240 days in advance or self-serve. **Registration:** Registration kiosk or camp hosts trailer. **Fee:** $5–$20 per night; max. 6 per site. **Parking:** At site.

Facilities

Number of Multipurpose Sites: 60 campgrounds in the Idaho Panhandle National Forest, 6–35 sites each. **Hookups:** Potable water. **Each Site:** Level parking spurs (most are paved), picnic table, grated fire pit. **Dump Station:** In several locations throughout the forest. **Laundry:** In the small communities scattered throughout the forest, but not at the individual campgrounds. **Pay Phone:** No. **Rest Rooms and Showers:** Rest rooms, mostly w/ vaulced toilets; no showers. **Fuel:** Many places to fuel throughout the forest. **Propane:** Inquire at campground. **Internal Roads:** Most are paved. **RV Service:** Couer d'Alene. **Market:** Groceries in most every small community within the forest. **Restaurant:** Plenty of restaurants & a nice variety of dining. **General Store:** No. **Vending:** No. **Swimming Pool:** No, but many areas on the rivers & lakes open to public for swimming; many natural hot springs. (Use caution: many of the hot springs are too hot for swimming & will cause second- & third-degree burns.) **Playground:** No. **Other:** Many sites on lakes & rivers, excellent boating & blue-ribbon fishing. **Activities:** Hiking, mountain biking, fishing (Priest Lake, Lake Pend Oreille, St. Joe River), boating, waterskiing,swimming, lakefront beaches,backpacking, mountaineering, motorized bike trailheads, cross-country skiing, hunting. **Nearby Attractions:** Museum of North Idaho, Silverwood Theme Park, Stateline & Speedway, Fort Sherman Museum, Hells Canyon. **Additional Information:** North Idaho Visitors Center, (888) 333-3737.

Restrictions

Pets: On leash only. **Fires:** In fire rings only (the forest may prohibit open fires due to weather conditions, always check w/ a ranger or camp host before starting any fires). **Alcoholic Beverages:** Allowed. **Vehicle Maximum Length:** Sites vary in size, the campgrounds on the national reservation service are better equipped to handle larger RVs. **Other:** Golden Access & Golden Age Passes are honored & can be purchased at any ranger station; 14-day stay limit.

To Get There

I-90 passes right through the middle of the Idaho Panhandle National Forest. Coeur d'Alene is on I-90, acting as a hub for forest access.

DELCO
Village of the Trees

Exit 216, I-84, Delco 83323. T: (208) 654-2133; www.travelstop216.com; facility@travelstop216.com.

RV: ★★★ Tent: ★★★

Beauty: ★★ Site Privacy: ★★
Spaciousness: ★★★ Quiet: ★★★★
Security: ★★★ Cleanliness: ★★★★
Insect Control: ★★★ Facilities: ★★★★

Not quite an hour east of Twin Falls, off I-84 is Delco's, Village of the Trees. This is a moderately-sized, comfortable, and clean RV park. The sites are configured in rows with level, gravel parking spurs. The majority are pull-throughs, with a small lawn between sites. There are several, although not a lot, nice shade trees and a large, open tenting area separate from the RVs, with green grass and adequate shade. The tent area, however, is in plain view of the interstate and not the quietest spot. A large common area with playground is found by the pool; the camp store and restaurant are entrance to the park. There are not a lot of activities in Delco, but several state parks and the Sawtooth Nation Forest are only a short drive away.

Basics

Operated By: John & Gerry Temperley. **Open:** All year. **Site Assignment:** By reservations with credit card. **Registration:** In camp store. **Fee:** Tent $18, RV $25 per 4 people. **Parking:** At site.

Facilities

Number of RV-Only Sites: 120. **Number of Tent-Only Sites:** 30. **Hookups:** Electric (30, 50 amps), water, sewer. **Each Site:** Picnic table, grill. **Dump Station:** Yes. **Laundry:** Yes. **Pay Phone:** Yes. **Rest Rooms and Showers:** Yes. **Fuel:** Yes. **Propane:** Yes. **Internal Roads:** Gravel, in good condition. **RV Service:** 15 mi. in Burley. **Market:** In Burley. **Restaurant:** On site or in town. **General Store:** Yes. **Vending:** Yes. **Swimming Pool:** Yes, w/ hot tub. **Playground:** Yes. **Other:** Arcade, large recreation center, trout pond. **Activities:** Fishing, games, biking, nature walks. **Nearby Attractions:** City of Rocks, Lake Walcott State Park. **Additional**

Information: Mini-Cassia of Commerce, (208) 679-4793.

Restrictions

Pets: On leash only. **Fires:** In grills only, 1 central fire ring. **Alcoholic Beverages:** Allowed. **Vehicle Maximum Length:** None.

To Get There

I-84 Exit 216, directly off the ramp.

EDEN (TWIN FALLS)

Anderson Camp & RV Sales and Service

1188 East 99 US, Eden 83325. T: (208) 825-9800 or (888) 480-9400; F: (208) 825-9715; www.andersoncamp.cjb.net; andercmp@pmt.org.

RV ★★★★ Tent ★★★

Beauty: ★★★ Site Privacy: ★★★
Spaciousness: ★★★ Quiet: ★★★
Security: ★★★ Cleanliness: ★★★
Insect Control: ★★★★ Facilities: ★★★

This facility is more aptly described as a resort for campers rather than just a basic campground. Excellently maintained, the RV sites are spacious, with full hookups provided. For those who like to "rough it," a beautiful, open tent area is provided, with convenient access to laundry and shower facilities. Even though this campground is larger than most we've seen, it still manages to provide adequate privacy to the guests, as well as lots of peace and quiet. But the most attractive characteristic of this vacation spot is the huge list of activities. There is a water slide, mini-golf, and a game room, to name just a few. This park is a very popular spot, so be sure to make a reservation.

Basics

Operated By: Gerry & Carleen Miller. **Open:** All year. **Site Assignment:** By reservation. **Registration:** In camp office. **Fee:** Tent $17.50, RV $21.50 per 2 people, extra person $2. **Parking:** At site.

Facilities

Number of RV-Only Sites: 87. **Number of Tent-Only Sites:** Open tent area. **Hookups:** Electric (30, 50 amps), water, sewer. **Each Site:** Picnic table. **Dump Station:** Yes. **Laundry:** Yes. **Pay Phone:** Yes. **Rest Rooms and Showers:** Yes. **Fuel:** Yes. **Propane:** Yes. **Internal Roads:** Gravel, in good condition. **RV Service:** Next door. **Market:** In Twin Falls. **Restaurant:** On site, or in Twin Falls. **General Store:** Yes. **Vending:** Yes. **Swimming Pool:** Yes, w/ waterslide. **Playground:** Yes. **Other:** Natural hot water swimming pool, gas station, game room, large hall, fruit trees in season, homemade pizza. **Activities:** Waterslide, swimming, 18 bankshot basketball, mini-golf, square dancing, skiing, hiking, horseback riding. **Nearby Attractions:** Trout farms, Herrett Center, shopping. **Additional Information:** Twin Falls Chamber of Commerce, (208) 733-3974.

Restrictions

Pets: On leash only. **Fires:** No open fires, there is 1 central fire ring & a few grills. **Alcoholic Beverages:** Allowed. **Vehicle Maximum Length:** None.

To Get There

Located at mile post 204 on US Hwy. 95.

GLENNS FERRY

Carmela Winery & Golf Course

795 West Madison, P.O. Box 790, Glenns Ferry 83623. T: (208) 366-7531; F: (208) 366-2458; www.carmelawinery.com; info@carmelawinery.com.

RV ★★★ Tent ★★

Beauty: ★★★ Site Privacy: ★★★
Spaciousness: ★★★ Quiet: ★★★★★
Security: ★★★ Cleanliness: ★★★
Insect Control: ★★★ Facilities: ★★★

This tiny RV campground set between the Carmela Winery and Three Island Crossing State Park is little more than a cluster of hookup sites and a dump station. It's patronized almost exclusively by campers visiting the winery grounds, which, in addition to the fermented-grape-juice concern, also sports a golf course, gift shop, bar, and an excellent restaurant. There are no rest rooms at the campground itself, but you can use those at the winery's stone château across the street; showers are available at the nearby state park for $2. This is definitely just a stop-over while visiting the winery or passing through.

Basics

Operated By: Roger & Nancy Jones. **Open:** All year. **Site Assignment:** By reservation or walk-in. **Registration:** The Stone Château (the main building at the winery). **Fee:** $12. **Parking:** At site.

FACILITIES

Number of Multipurpose Sites: 15. **Hookups:** Electric (30 amps), water. **Each Site:** Some picnic tables. **Dump Station:** Yes. **Laundry:** No. **Pay Phone:** Yes. **Rest Rooms and Showers:** None in the campground area; rest rooms across the street at the Stone Château (winery), showers for $2 at the state park next door. **Fuel:** No. **Propane:** No. **Internal Roads:** Gravel, in good condition. **RV Service:** Limited local service. **Market:** In town. **Restaurant:** On-site; excellent restaurant at the Stone Château. **General Store:** Gift shop only. **Vending:** No. **Swimming Pool:** No. **Playground:** No, but large recreation area & playground at the state park next door. **Other:** Winery, restaurant, bar, banquet & conference rooms, gift shop, golf course. **Activities:** Wine-tasting, golf. **Nearby Attractions:** Three Island Crossing State Park, Oregon Trail History & Education Center. **Additional Information:** Glenns Ferry Chamber of Commerce, (208) 366-7345.

RESTRICTIONS

Pets: On leash only. **Fires:** No open fires. **Alcoholic Beverages:** Allowed. **Vehicle Maximum Length:** 45 ft.

TO GET THERE

I-84 to Glenns Ferry Exit; follow signs, winery is next door to Three Island State Park.

GLENNS FERRY

Three Island Crossing State Park

P.O.Box 609, Glenns Ferry 83623. T: (208) 366-2394; F: (208) 366-2060; www.idahoparks.org/parks/threeisland/html; thr@idpr.state.id.us.

RV ★★★★ | Tent ★★★

Beauty: ★★★★	Site Privacy: ★★★
Spaciousness: ★★★	Quiet: ★★★★
Security: ★★★★	Cleanliness: ★★★★
Insect Control: ★★★★	Facilities: ★★★

Three Island Crossing State Park is situated on the Oregon Trail where travelers moving west would cross the Snake River. You can see remnants of trail ruts and artifacts along the riverbank. Located only a few miles from I-84 in Glenns Ferry, this 513-acre park represents a piece of early American history. The park also is home to the Oregon Trail Three Island Crossing History and Education Center, where annually they reenact the crossing. The campground offers large shaded sites in two loops with large common areas of green grass. The park also offers a more primitive area with tepees. There is a day-use area with a riverfront swimming beach, picnic area, and grills. Sites are paved and level back-ins or pull-throughs. This park is located in high desert, so the days are warm and the nights are cool. Park officials and rangers are on duty 24 hours a day and are there to assist.

BASICS

Operated By: Idaho Dept. of Parks & Recreation. **Open:** All year. **Site Assignment:** First come, first served. **Registration:** At visitor center. **Fee:** $12 no hookups, $16 hookups, double camp sites $22, $5 extra-vehicle fee. **Parking:** At site.

FACILITIES

Number of Multipurpose Sites: 101. **Hookups:** Electric (20, 30 amps), water. **Each Site:** Picnic table, grated fire pit, grill. **Dump Station:** Yes. **Laundry:** No. **Pay Phone:** Yes. **Rest Rooms and Showers:** Yes. **Fuel:** No. **Propane:** No. **Internal Roads:** Paved. **RV Service:** No. **Market:** In Glenns Ferry. **Restaurant:** In Glenns Ferry or next door at the Carmela Vineyard. **General Store:** No. **Vending:** No. **Swimming Pool:** No. **Playground:** Yes. **Other:** 3 tepees, amphitheater, Oregon Trail Three Island Crossing History & Education Center, picnic shelters, grills, riverfront beach (Snake River), group picnic shelter. **Activities:** Fishing, hiking, weekend campfire program, swimming, guided nature walks. **Nearby Attractions:** Glenn's Ferry Historical Museum, Carmela Winery & Golf Club. **Additional Information:** Idaho Dept. of Parks & Recreation, (208) 334-4199; Glenns Ferry Chamber of Commerce, (208) 366-7345, www.cyberhighway.net/~gfcity; the second weekend in August Oregon Trail river-crossing reenactment takes place.

RESTRICTIONS

Pets: On leash only. **Fires:** In fire pits only. **Alcoholic Beverages:** Allowed. **Vehicle Maximum Length:** None. **Other:** Max. 8 people per site, 14-day stay limit.

TO GET THERE

I-84 to Exit 120, take a left, then take a left on First Ave., right on Commercial St., right on Madison Avenue, left into park.

GRANDJEAN
Sawtooth Lodge

130 North Haines, Boise 83712. T: (208) 259-3331 May–Oct. or (208) 344-2437 Oct. 15–May 15; www.sawtoothlodge.com.

★★★ ★★★★

Beauty: ★★★★ Site Privacy: ★★★
Spaciousness: ★★★ Quiet: ★★★★
Security: ★★★ Cleanliness: ★★★
Insect Control: ★★★ Facilities: ★★★

Situated in the Sawtooth National Forest, Sawtooth Lodge is a favorite destination amongst outdoor enthusiasts. Opened in 1927, Sawtooth Lodge offers a great place to relax and enjoy the serene beauty of the surrounding wilderness. Pines and spruce give background to a lovely meadow available for tent camping. The RV campground is a simple row of grass pull-through sites, shaded by towering mature pines. Well-maintained trails and majestic mountains envelope the property. The swimming-pool water is from a natural hot spring. The south fork of the Payette River and Trail Creek make for great fly fishing. Mornings are crisp with cool mountain air warming as the day progresses. Nights are chilly after sunset. Fresh home-style meals are served daily in the lodge, with ice-cream potatoes as a favorite desert. Cabins are available, and a there is a barn to board your horse.

BASICS

Operated By: Rodney & Linda Lockett. **Open:** Memorial Day weekend–Oct. 15. **Site Assignment:** Reservations highly recommended, 2-night min. on the weekend, 3-night min. over holidays. **Registration:** In camp lodge. **Fee:** Tent $6, RV $15 (pool is extra). **Parking:** At site.

FACILITIES

Number of RV-Only Sites: 22. **Number of Tent-Only Sites:** Open tent area. **Hookups:** Electric (20 amps, but for lights only), water, sewer. **Each Site:** Picnic tables. **Dump Station:** Yes. **Laundry:** No. **Pay Phone:** Yes. **Rest Rooms and Showers:** Yes. **Fuel:** 15 mi. south at the Sourdough Lodge. **Propane:** Yes. **Internal Roads:** Dirt & gravel. **RV Service:** Boise. **Market:** 40 mi. east in Stanley. **Restaurant:** In lodge, but with dinner reservations. **General Store:** Yes. **Vending:** General store only. **Swimming Pool:** Yes, natural hot spring water. **Playground:** No. **Other:** Lodge w/ cafe, barn, cabins, lovely open meadow. **Activities:** Fishing (trout & cutthroat), whitewater rafting, hiking, horseback riding, backpacking, mountain biking. **Nearby Attractions:** Natural hot springs, Sawtooth National Recreation Area. **Additional Information:** Stanley-Sawtooth Chamber of Commerce, (208) 744-3411 or (800) 878-7950, www.stanleycc.org.

RESTRICTIONS

Pets: On leash only (you may bring your horse, call about use of barn & fees). **Fires:** In grills only, there is a central fire pit (fire may be prohibited due to weather conditions, ask management before starting any fire). **Alcoholic Beverages:** Allowed. **Vehicle Maximum Length:** None.

TO GET THERE

Hwy. 21 between Lowman and Stanley in Grandjean. There is a sign right at the cross guards where they close parts of Hwy. 21 in the winter. Grandjean is 6 mi. back a narrow dirt road. Feel free to get a map of the Sawtooth Recreational area from either the Lowman or Stanley ranger station.

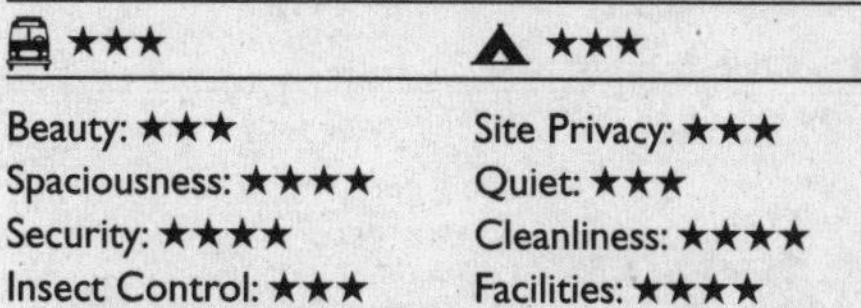

HAGERMAN
High Adventure River Tours RV Park & Store

1211 East 2350 South, Hagerman 83332. T: (800) 286-4123 or (208) 837-9005; www.inidaho.com.

★★★ ★★★

Beauty: ★★★ Site Privacy: ★★★
Spaciousness: ★★★★ Quiet: ★★★
Security: ★★★★ Cleanliness: ★★★★
Insect Control: ★★★ Facilities: ★★★★

High Adventure River Tours RV Park & Store is conveniently located off I-84 in Hagerman. It specializes in rafting trips and river tours of the Snake River and Snake River Canyon Area. The campground is located behind a small store/outfitter on level ground, with nice green grass. The campground is configured into rows, with the first row being an open lawn for tent camping. There are no trees on the tent lawn, and spaces are not divided out. The RV sites are all pull-throughs with level gravel parking spurs, divided by nice-size lawns and the occasional shade tree.

Hagerman is half way between Twin Falls and Boise. There are some wonderful geological finds in the area and excellent fishing. The staff at High Adventure River Tours RV Park & Store is friendly and inviting.

BASICS

Operated By: Private operator. **Open:** Mar.–Dec. **Site Assignment:** By reservations or first available. **Registration:** In camp store. **Fee:** Tent $4 per person, RV $20 per 2 people, extra person $1. **Parking:** At site.

FACILITIES

Number of RV-Only Sites: 26. **Number of Tent-Only Sites:** Open tent area. **Hookups:** Electric (20, 30, 50 amps), water, sewer. **Each Site:** Picnic table. **Dump Station:** Yes. **Laundry:** Yes. **Pay Phone:** Yes. **Rest Rooms and Showers:** Yes. **Fuel:** No. **Propane:** Yes. **Internal Roads:** Gravel, in good condition. **RV Service:** In Wendall. **Market:** In Wendall. **Restaurant:** Small, limited food service on site. **General Store:** Yes. **Vending:** Yes. **Swimming Pool:** No. **Playground:** Yes. **Other:** River tour outfitter. **Activities:** Rafting, river tours (Snake River), fishing, boating, hiking, horseshoes. **Nearby Attractions:** Hagerman Fossil Beds National Monument, Snake River Canyon, Blue Heart Springs, Box Canyon Springs, the Heron Rookery. **Additional Information:** Hagerman Valley Chamber of Commerce, (208) 837-9131.

RESTRICTIONS

Pets: On leash only. **Fires:** In grills only. **Alcoholic Beverages:** Yes. **Vehicle Maximum Length:** Call ahead for details.

TO GET THERE

I-84 Exit 141.

IDAHO CITY

Warm Springs Resort

P.O. Box 28, Idaho City 83631. T: (208) 392-4437

RV ★★★ Tent ★★

Beauty: ★★★ Site Privacy: ★★★
Spaciousness: ★★★ Quiet: ★★★★
Security: ★★★ Cleanliness: ★★★
Insect Control: ★★★★ Facilities: ★★★

Deep inside the Boise National Forest, about five miles south of Idaho City along the Payette River is Warm Spring Resort. This unique campground offers cabins, gravel RV sites, and an open tenting area. The highlight of the campground is a natural pebble-lined hot spring mineral pool. The pool stays a constant 98° and is open year-round.The RV sites are fairly close together and require leveling in most cases. The tenting area is a large, open grass field with a small stream. The area is rich in history and natural wonders, the forest is full of wildlife, flowers, and streams. This is a nice base camp for those wishing to fish, hunt, or bike. The days are very comfortable during the summer, but the evenings get very cool through the end of June. Security is overseen by the local forestry

BASICS

Operated By: Private Operator. **Open:** May 1–Labor Day Weekend, pool open year-round. **Site Assignment:** Reservations recommended. **Registration:** At pool desk. **Fee:** Tent $7.50 per 4 people, pool not included, RV $18 per 2 people & 2 swims per day, extra person $2; cash, credit, or in-state checks. **Parking:** At site.

FACILITIES

Number of RV-Only Sites: 22. **Number of Tent-Only Sites:** 38. **Hookups:** Electric (50 amps), water, sewer. **Each Site:** Some picnic table, some fire pit. **Dump Station:** Yes. **Laundry:** No. **Pay Phone:** Yes. **Rest Rooms and Showers:** Yes. **Fuel:** No. **Propane:** No. **Internal Roads:** Gravel, w/ some pot holes. **RV Service:** 23 mi. south in Boise. **Market:** In Idaho City. **Restaurant:** Small cafe w/ grill in the resort, or in Idaho City. **General Store:** No. **Vending:** No. **Swimming Pool:** Yes, natural hot-spring pool open year-round, stays a constant 98°. **Playground:** No. **Other:** Meeting rooms, cooking units, waterfront access, 2 cabins. **Activities:** Fishing, hiking, horseshoes, volleyball, cross-country skiing, rafting, boating, snowmobiling. **Nearby Attractions:** Boise Basin Historical Museum. **Additional Information:** Idaho City Chamber of Commerce, (208) 392-4148, www.idahocitychamber.com.

RESTRICTIONS

Pets: On leash only, not allowed in any buildings, cabins, or pool area. **Fires:** In fire pits or grills only. **Alcoholic Beverages:** Not permitted. **Vehicle Maximum Length:** None.

TO GET THERE

Located off Hwy. 21 about 4 mi. south of Idaho City (mile marker 37).

IDAHO FALLS

Idaho Falls KOA

1440 Lindsay Blvd., Idaho Falls 83402. T: (800) 562-7644 or (208) 523-3362; www.koa.com.

RV ★★★ Tent ★★★

Beauty: ★★★ Site Privacy: ★★★
Spaciousness: ★★★ Quiet: ★★★★
Security: ★★★★ Cleanliness: ★★★★
Insect Control: ★★★ Facilities: ★★★

This KOA campground, located in Idaho Falls, is one of the cleanest parks we've seen. The roads are gravel, but in excellent condition, and the facilities are well maintained. We preferred the RV sites over the tent sites in terms of beauty, but, both were spacious, private and quiet. The park offers all the amenities for our convenience, including a laundry on the premises. The range of activities is adequate to entertain the whole family, with the usual fishing, playground, and horseshoes, but the thing we liked best was the hot tub and sauna located in the park. For the sports fans, Idaho Falls is home to a minor league baseball team, and there are several area golf courses.

BASICS

Operated By: Private Operator. **Open:** All year. **Site Assignment:** By reservations or first available. **Registration:** In camp store. **Fee:** Tent $19–$22 per person, RV $24–$28 per 2 people, extra people $2. **Parking:** At site.

FACILITIES

Number of RV-Only Sites:. **Number of Tent-Only Sites:** 0. **Hookups:** Electric (20, 30, 50 amps), water, sewer. **Each Site:** Picnic table. **Dump Station:** Yes. **Laundry:** Yes. **Pay Phone:** Yes. **Rest Rooms and Showers:** Yes. **Fuel:** No. **Propane:** Yes. **Internal Roads:** Gravel, in good condition. **RV Service:** In town. **Market:** In town. **Restaurant:** There are many restaurants in town including several national chains. **General Store:** Yes. **Vending:** Store only. **Swimming Pool:** Yes, w/ hot tub & sauna. **Playground:** Yes. **Other:** Cabins, hot tub, sauna, snack bar. **Activities:** Game room, playground, fishing, mini-gold, horseshoes, volleyball, basketball. **Nearby Attractions:** Golf, professional baseball team. **Additional Information:** Idaho Falls Chamber of Commerce, (208) 523-1010.

RESTRICTIONS

Pets: On leash only. **Fires:** In grills only. **Alcoholic Beverages:** Allowed. **Vehicle Maximum Length:** Call ahead for details.

TO GET THERE

I-15 Exit 119 E 0.2 mi. to Lindsay.

ISLAND PARK

Henry's Lake State Park

HC 66 Box 20, Island Park 83429. T: (208) 558-7532

RV ★★★ Tent ★★★

Beauty: ★★★ Site Privacy: ★★★
Spaciousness: ★★★ Quiet: ★★★
Security: ★★★★ Cleanliness: ★★★
Insect Control: ★★★ Facilities: ★★

This beautiful park is surrounded on three sides by the Continental Divide in the rugged Targhee National Forest. The larger Island Park area offers most any kind of outdoor recreation imaginable, in any season, including hiking, snowmobiling, cross-country skiing, ATV-riding, snowshoeing, hunting, biking, and more. And if you want still more options, Yellowstone National Park is just 15 miles to the east. The Henry's Lake campground itself is nice but unremarkable, although that doesn't really matter—you'll spend most of your time marveling at the scenery. Trout-fishing is the main draw here; angling choices include Henry's Lake and the nearby Henry's Fork, Madison River, and Gallatin River. A boat ramp and docks are available for campers' use, but boaters should be careful of choppy water on the lake caused by occasionally unpredictable high winds. A three-mile hiking trail originates from the campground as well.

BASICS

Operated By: Private operator. **Open:** Call ahead for details. **Site Assignment:** First come, first served. **Registration:** In camp office. **Fee:** $22 w/ hookup, $18 no hookup. **Parking:** At site.

FACILITIES

Number of RV-Only Sites: 25. **Number of Tent-Only Sites:** 0. **Number of Multipurpose Sites:** 17. **Hookups:** Electric (20, 30 amps), water, sewer. **Each Site:** Picnic table, grated fire pit. **Dump Station:** Yes. **Laundry:** Yes. **Pay Phone:** Yes. **Rest Rooms and Showers:** Yes. **Fuel:** No.

Propane: No. **Internal Roads:** Paved. **RV Service:** Mobile RV service. **Market:** In town. **Restaurant:** In town. **General Store:** No. **Vending:** No. **Swimming Pool:** No. **Playground:** Yes. **Activities:** Fishing (rainbow trout, cutthroat, brook), hiking, golf. **Nearby Attractions:** Yellowstone National Park 16 miles east, Red Rock Lakes National Wildlife Refuge, Mesa Falls Scenic Byway. **Additional Information:** Idaho Dept. of Parks & Recreation (208) 334-4199.

Restrictions

Pets: On leash only. **Fires:** Inquire at campground. **Alcoholic Beverages:** Inquire at campground. **Vehicle Maximum Length:** Call ahead for details.

To Get There

From Hwy. 20 out of Idaho Falls go north approx. 80 mi. until you see park signs; go 2.5 mi. west to the entrance.

ISLAND PARK

Red Rock RV and Camping Park

HC 66 P.O. Box 7, Island Park 83429. T: (800) 473-3762 or (208) 558-7442; www.8004redrock.com.

RV ★★★★ Tent ★★★★

Beauty: ★★★★★	Site Privacy: ★★★
Spaciousness: ★★★	Quiet: ★★★★
Security: ★★★★	Cleanliness: ★★★★
Insect Control: ★★★	Facilities: ★★★

Only 20 miles from the western gateway to Yellowstone Park, Red Rock is situated in a pristine valley that offers panoramic views of the many 8,000–10,000-foot mountains in the area. Adjacent to Targhee National Forest and Henry's Lake State Park, Red Rock is a great base camp for every outdoor activity imaginable. For cycling enthusiasts, the Great Western Bike Trail borders the park. A working dude ranch with weekly rodeos is close by, and there's plenty of scenic driving for those who don't want to cozy to the many amenities available at Red Rock. Further afield, history buffs can visit Montana's Virginia City and Nevada City. Visitors wishing for a more "civilized" day-trip can travel south to Island Park.

Basics

Operated By: Gordon Glenn. **Open:** May 15–Sept. 20. **Site Assignment:** By reservation. **Registration:** In the general store. **Fee:** Tent $14, RV $16 per 2 people. **Parking:** At site.

Facilities

Number of RV-Only Sites: 44. **Number of Tent-Only Sites:** 6. **Hookups:** Electric (30 amps), water, sewer. **Each Site:** Picnic table, fire pit. **Dump Station:** Yes. **Laundry:** Yes. **Pay Phone:** Yes. **Rest Rooms and Showers:** Yes. **Fuel:** No. **Propane:** No. **Internal Roads:** Gravel, in good condition. **RV Service:** Mobile RV service. **Market:** 3 mi. in Island Park. **Restaurant:** The Model Ranch next door, or Island Park. **General Store:** Limited general store. **Vending:** No. **Swimming Pool:** No. **Playground:** Yes. **Other:** Fish photo gallery, Internet dataport in the office for checking e-mail only. **Activities:** Blue-ribbon trout fishing, boating, hiking, biking, bird- & wildlife-watching. **Nearby Attractions:** Meadow Vue Ranch, Lake Henry, Yellowstone National Park, Red Rock Lakes National Wildlife Refuge, The Great Western Bike Trail, Mesa Falls Scenic Byway. **Additional Information:** www.8004redrock.com.

Restrictions

Pets: On leash only. **Fires:** In grills or fire pits only. **Alcoholic Beverages:** Allowed. **Vehicle Maximum Length:** None. **Other:** Good Sam discount.

To Get There

From Hwy. 20 in Island Park turn west at mile post 398, follow signs on Red Rock Rd., approx. 5 mi.

JEROME

Twin Falls-Jerome KOA

5431 US 93, Jerome 83338. T: (800) 562-4169 or (208) 324-4169; F: (208) 324-7064; www.koa.com; twinkoa@filertel.com.

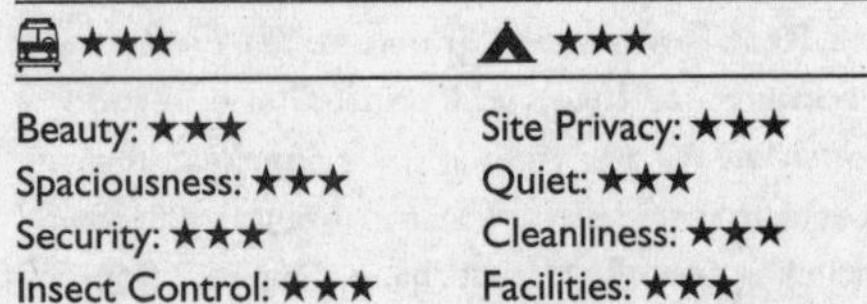

RV ★★★ Tent ★★★

Beauty: ★★★	Site Privacy: ★★★
Spaciousness: ★★★	Quiet: ★★★
Security: ★★★	Cleanliness: ★★★
Insect Control: ★★★	Facilities: ★★★

This KOA isn't as nice as some we have visited, but it is clean and well maintained. The RV and tent sites are medium sized, but still have some privacy and the park itself is quiet. Some of the RV sites offer full hookups, and all sites come equipped with a picnic table and grill. What this campground lacks in beauty, it makes up for in amenities. Over and above the normal activities usually found in parks, this KOA offers a hot tub, sauna, camp kitchen, and a snack bar. Nearby, guests can also try several more adventurous pastimes, like fishing on the Snake River, rafting, mountain biking, or waterskiing. If you'd like to visit, be sure to call ahead: this KOA is a "reservation-only" campground.

Basics

Operated By: Robert Tanner. **Open:** Mar. 20–Oct. 30. **Site Assignment:** By reservations with a credit card. **Registration:** In camp store. **Fee:** Tent $19, RV $25–$30 per 2 people, extra person $2.50. **Parking:** No extra parking.

Facilities

Number of RV-Only Sites: 69. **Number of Tent-Only Sites:** 21. **Hookups:** Electric (20, 30, 50 amps), water, sewer. **Each Site:** Picnic table, grill. **Dump Station:** Yes. **Laundry:** Yes. **Pay Phone:** Yes. **Rest Rooms and Showers:** Yes. **Fuel:** No, in town. **Propane:** Yes. **Internal Roads:** Gravel, in good condition. **RV Service:** 5 mi. west in Twin Falls. **Market:** In Twin Falls. **Restaurant:** On site or in town. **General Store:** Yes. **Vending:** No. **Swimming Pool:** Yes, w/ hot tub. **Playground:** Yes. **Other:** 6 cabins, sauna, hot tub, camp kitchen, snack bar. **Activities:** Mini-golf, horseshoes, games, fishing, rafting, hiking, mountain biking, waterskiing, boating. **Nearby Attractions:** Snake River, many outfitters, gold. **Additional Information:** Twin Falls Chamber of Commerce, (208) 733-3974.

Restrictions

Pets: On leash only. **Fires:** In grills only. **Alcoholic Beverages:** Allowed. **Vehicle Maximum Length:** 92 ft. w/ tow.

To Get There

From I-84 Exit 173, go 1 mi. north on US 93.

KETCHUM

Sawtooth National Recreation Area

HC 64 Box 8291, Ketchum 83340. T: (208) 727-5000 or (800) 260-5970; F: (208) 727-5029; www.fs.fed.us/r4/sawtooth/camplist.html or www.fs.fed.us/r4/sawtooth/; cgalvez@ff.fed.us.

RV ★★★	Tent ★★★★
Beauty: ★★★★★	Site Privacy: ★★★★
Spaciousness: ★★★★	Quiet: ★★★★★
Security: ★★★	Cleanliness: ★★★
Insect Control: n/a	Facilities: ★★

This campground is located in the heart of Sawtooth National Forest, which stretches for over two million acres, covering four mountain ranges that provide a scenic landscape in any direction, with more than 40 peaks over 10,000 feet in elevation. With over 300 mountain lakes and several major rivers, there are endless opportunities for fishing, bird-watching, and viewing wildlife. While the RV sites are quite peaceful and spacious, the campground's facilities are not very good. The campground's location is clearly its best-selling point. Prospective campers should note that this recreation area is very large, with very few gas stations. The campgrounds are open from May to September, and we recommend that you make reservations in advance.

Basics

Operated By: US Forest Service. **Open:** Mostly May–Sept. **Site Assignment:** Several are by reservation, (877) 444-6777, or self-serve. **Registration:** Registration kiosk or camp hosts trailer. **Fee:** Sites vary in price from $5–$20 per night/ max. 6 per site. **Parking:** At site.

Facilities

Number of Multipurpose Sites: 32 campgrounds suitable for RVs, 6–65 sites each. **Hookups:** Potable water. **Each Site:** Level parking spurs (most are paved), picnic table, grated fire pit. **Dump Station:** Dumps in several locations throughout the forest. **Laundry:** Laundry facilities in the towns of Hailey, Ketchum, Lowman, Sawtooth City, Stanley, Sunbeam, Redfish, Challis, Salmon, & Mackay. **Pay Phone:** No. **Rest Rooms and Showers:** Rest rooms, mostly w/ vaulted toilets. **Fuel:** The Sawtooth National Recreation Area is very large, with very few areas to fuel, even fewer places w/ diesel. **Propane:** Inquire at campground. **Internal Roads:** Most are paved. **RV Service:** Ketchum-Sun Valley. **Market:** Groceries in most every small community within the forest. **Restaurant:** Restaurants through the area, excellent dining in the Ketchum-Sun Valley. **General Store:** No. **Vending:** No. **Swimming Pool:** No, but many areas on the rivers & lakes open to public for swimming; natural hot springs. (Use caution: many hot springs are too hot for swimming & will cause second- & third-degree burns.) **Playground:** No. **Other:** Horse camps. **Activities:** Hiking, mountain biking, fishing, skiing, horseback riding, backpacking, mountaineering, visiting ghost towns, cross-country skiing. **Nearby Attractions:** Trail Creek Canyon,

Sun Valley, Sawtooth Fish. **Additional Information:** Central Idaho Rockies Assoc.

RESTRICTIONS

Pets: On leash only. **Fires:** In fire rings only (the forest may prohibit open fires due to weather conditions, always check w/ a ranger or camp host before starting any fires). **Alcoholic Beverages:** Allowed. **Vehicle Maximum Length:** Sites vary in size, the campgrounds on the national reservation service are better equipped to handle larger RVs. **Other:** Golden Access & Golden Age Passes are honored & can be purchased at any ranger station; 14-day stay limit.

TO GET THERE

The main roads in the recreation area are Hwy. 21 and Hwy. 75

LEWISTON

Aht Wy Plaza RV Park

17818 Nez Perce, Lewiston 83501. T: (208) 750-0231

RV: ★★★ Tent: ★★

Beauty: ★★★	Site Privacy: ★★★
Spaciousness: ★★	Quiet: ★★★
Security: ★★★	Cleanliness: ★★★
Insect Control: ★★★★	Facilities: ★★★

Aht Wy Plaza RV Park offers visitors to the Lewiston area a comfortable place to rest. This simple yet well-maintained RV park is conveniently located off Hwy. 95 on the Nez Perce Reservation, only five miles southeast of Lewiston. The campground offers level gravel and grass sites with varying degrees of shade. The tent area has just been expanded, so the foliage is young and there is little shade. The Clearwater River runs parallel to the property just across the highway. The Aht Wy Plaza offers Clearwater River Casino (next door) and free shuttle service to the Casino, as well as to Lapwai, Lewiston, and Clarkston. There are many nearby attractions, including the Nez Perce Historical Society Museum. Summers are warm during the day and cool in the evening; first snow is normally sometime in October. The park has a camp host in residence.

BASICS

Operated By: Nez Perce Tribal Enterprises. **Open:** All year. **Site Assignment:** Either by reservation or first available. **Registration:** In camp office. **Fee:** Tent $10, RV $15 per 4 people; cash, credit cards, checks. **Parking:** At site.

FACILITIES

Number of RV-Only Sites: 33. **Number of Tent-Only Sites:** 15. **Number of Multipurpose Sites:** 8. **Hookups:** Electric (20, 30, 50 amps), water, sewer, some phone. **Each Site:** Picnic table, grill. **Dump Station:** No. **Laundry:** Yes. **Pay Phone:** Yes. **Rest Rooms and Showers:** Yes. **Fuel:** No. **Propane:** No. **Internal Roads:** Gravel. **RV Service:** In Lewiston. **Market:** In Lewiston. **Restaurant:** In Lewiston. **General Store:** No. **Vending:** Yes. **Swimming Pool:** Yes. **Playground:** No. **Activities:** Fishing, hiking, swimming, whitewater rafting, hunting, skiing. **Nearby Attractions:** Hells Canyon, The Nez Perce National Historical Park & Museum, Clearwater River Casino. **Additional Information:** Lewiston Chamber of Commerce, (208) 734-3531 or (800) 473-3543, www.lewistonchamber.org.

RESTRICTIONS

Pets: Allowed. **Fires:** In fire pits only. **Alcoholic Beverages:** Allowed. **Vehicle Maximum Length:** None.

TO GET THERE

5 mi. south of Lewiston on Hwy. 95.

LEWISTON

Hells Gate State Park

3620A Snake River Ave., Lewiston 83501. T: (208) 799-5015 (office) or (208) 799-5016 (marina); F: (208) 799-5187; www.idahoparks.org; helgate@lewiston.com.

RV: ★★★★ Tent: ★★★

Beauty: ★★★	Site Privacy: ★★★
Spaciousness: ★★★★	Quiet: ★★★
Security: ★★★★	Cleanliness: ★★★★
Insect Control: ★★★★	Facilities: ★★★

Hells Gate State Park is a 960-acre facility located in the city limits of Lewiston. Hells Gate offers 96 campsites, in 3 circular loops. The sites are spacious and well shaded, both pull-throughs and back-ins available. The Snake River runs along the west side of the property, also serving as a boundary line between Idaho and Washington. Many of the campsites are in viewing distance of the river. The campground area is not as quiet as most due to Washington Hwy. 129 running directly across the river. Hells Gate offers a full-service marina with boat fuel and marine dump. Hells Gate is the opening to the Hells Canyon National Recreation Area. (At 9,393 feet, Hells Canyon is the deepest gorge in North America, surpassing the Grand Canyon.) Jet-boat tours of the canyon leave from the parks marina. Hells Gate is known for its moderate weather and has an elevation of only 733 feet. Camp rangers and camp host are available 24 hours a day, with day-use areas closing at 10 p.m. Quiet hours are strictly enforced.

Basics

Operated By: Idaho State Parks. **Open:** All year. **Site Assignment:** By reservation. **Registration:** Reservation can be made for a $6 non-refundable reservation fee. **Fee:** No hookups $12, w/ hookups $16, $5 extra-vehicle fee. Cash or check. **Parking:** At site.

Facilities

Number of RV-Only Sites: 64. **Number of Tent-Only Sites:** 0. **Number of Multipurpose Sites:** 28. **Hookups:** Electric (20, 30, 50 amps), water. **Each Site:** Picnic table, grated fire pit. **Dump Station:** Yes. **Laundry:** Yes. **Pay Phone:** Yes. **Rest Rooms and Showers:** Yes. **Fuel:** Boat Fuel Only. **Propane:** No. **Internal Roads:** Paved. **RV Service:** In Lewiston. **Market:** In Lewiston. **Restaurant:** In Lewiston. **General Store:** Yes. **Vending:** Yes. **Swimming Pool:** No. **Playground:** Yes. **Other:** 2 amphitheaters, counsel ring, covered pavilions, Riverside conference room, marina. **Activities:** Hells Canyon jet-boat tours, fishing, boating, picnicking, interpretive programs. **Nearby Attractions:** Nez Perce National Historical Park. **Additional Information:** www.idahoparks.org.

Restrictions

Pets: On leash only. **Fires:** In fire pits only (fires may be prohibited due to weather, ask park officials before starting any fire). **Alcoholic Beverages:** Allowed, but no kegs. **Vehicle Maximum Length:** None. **Other:** Max. 15 days in a 30-day period.

To Get There

From Hwy. 95 take Hwy. 12 towards Walla Walla, WA. Just before the bridge going into Washington make a left on Snake River Ave. (Hwy. 505); the park is 2.5 mi. on the right.

LUCILE

Prospector's Gold RV Park and Campground

P.O.Box 313, Lucile 83542. T: (208) 628-3773

RV ★★★★ Tent ★★★

Beauty: ★★★★	Site Privacy: ★★★★
Spaciousness: ★★★★	Quiet: ★★★★★
Security: ★★★★	Cleanliness: ★★★★★
Insect Control: ★★★★	Facilities: ★★★★★

Prospector's Gold is small in comparison to some other campgrounds we've visited, but none of the others can compete with the service here. The scenery is breath-taking and the facilities are exceptionally well kept. All of the sites are medium to large, quiet, and with ample privacy. The facilities available on-site are clean and more than adequate for anyone's needs. Activities center around outdoor activities, such as fishing, hunting (elk and deer), and panning for gold. There is a riverfront beach and a nearby outfitter for those who want to try whitewater rafting. Just remember that reservations are required.

Basics

Operated By: Tucker & Gay Lindsey. **Open:** All year. **Site Assignment:** By reservation. **Registration:** In camp office. **Fee:** $15–$16 per 2. **Parking:** At site.

Facilities

Number of RV-Only Sites: 24. **Number of Tent-Only Sites:** 10. **Hookups:** Electric (30, 50 amps), water, sewer. **Each Site:** Picnic table. **Dump Station:** Yes. **Laundry:** Yes. **Pay Phone:** Yes. **Rest Rooms and Showers:** Yes. **Fuel:** 9 mi. south in Riggins. **Propane:** In Riggins. **Internal Roads:** Gravel, in good condition. **RV Service:** Limited service in Riggins. **Market:** In Riggins. **Restaurant:** In the area & in Riggins. **General Store:** Yes. **Vending:** Yes. **Swimming Pool:** No, but there a riverfront beach. **Playground:** Yes. **Other:** Northwest Voyageurs rafting outfitters, contacts for jet-boat trip, video rental. **Activities:** Gold panning, fishing (salmon), hunting (deer & elk), horseshoes, volleyball, rafting, boating. **Nearby Attractions:** Scenic drives, Hells Canyon, Riggins, many outfitters. **Additional Information:** Riggins Chamber of Commerce, (208) 628-3778.

Restrictions

Pets: On leash only. **Fires:** No open fires. **Alcoholic Beverages:** Allowed. **Vehicle Maximum Length:** None. **Other:** Good Sam discount, group rates.

To Get There

Located at mile post 204 on US Hwy. 95.

LUCILE

Riverfront Gardens RV Park

HCO 1 Box 15, Lucile 83542. T: (208) 628-3777; F: (208) 628-3221; snmoore@cyberhighway.net.

RV ★★★★★ Tent ★★★★

Beauty: ★★★★★ Site Privacy: ★★★★
Spaciousness: ★★★★ Quiet: ★★★★
Security: ★★★★ Cleanliness: ★★★★★
Insect Control: ★★★★ Facilities: ★★★★★

Riverfront Gardens RV Park is an incredible work of art. Home of Stan and Norma Moore, this spectacular property could grace the cover of *Home and Garden Magazine.* The owners and horticulture students from the university in Boise have formally landscaped the entire campground. If fact, the grounds are so elegant you might want to bring along your best linen and china for dinner on the beach. All the sites are grass, with large shade trees strategically placed for optimal shade and growth. There is a riverfront beach area with a gazebo, fully equipped with a grill. The surrounding area is high desert, with very dry summers and cool winters. The Little Salmon River is famous for it chinook salmon. There are many fishing and rafting outfitters in the Riggins area, and great hunting in the fall.

Basics

Operated By: Stan & Norma Moore. **Open:** All year. **Site Assignment:** First come, first served. **Registration:** Self-serve envelopes at the entrance. **Fee:** Tents $15, RV $18 (cash). **Parking:** Very limited.

Facilities

Number of RV-Only Sites: 24. **Number of Tent-Only Sites:** Open tent area. **Hookups:** Electric (30 amps), water, sewer. **Each Site:** Some picnic tables. **Dump Station:** No. **Laundry:** No. **Pay Phone:** No. **Rest Rooms and Showers:** Yes. **Fuel:** No. **Propane:** No. **Internal Roads:** Gravel, in excellent condition. **RV Service:** 11 mi. south in Riggins. **Market:** 11 mi. south in Riggins. **Restaurant:** South to Riggins or North White Bird, there a snack shop/cafe in Lucile. **General Store:** No. **Vending:** No. **Swimming Pool:** No, but there is a riverfront beach w/ swimming. **Playground:** No. **Other:** Formal flower gardens, gazebo, riverfront beach, fax/copier service, handicapped equipped. **Activities:** Fishing (steelhead fishing Sept.–Mar., bass, sturgeon, & trout year-round), hunting (elk, deer, black bear, cougar, turkey, pheasant, chukar), whitewater rafting, jet-skiing. **Nearby Attractions:** Boat launch 0.25 mile, Hells Canyon National Recreation Area, Salmon River. **Additional Information:** Salmon River Chamber of Commerce, (208) 628-3778, www.rigginsidaho.com; cfriend@ctcweb.net.

Restrictions

Pets: On leash only. **Fires:** In fire pits only. **Alcoholic Beverages:** Allowed. **Vehicle Maximum Length:** None.

To Get There

Directly off Hwy. 95 at milepost 210.5, 11 mi. north of Riggins.

McCALL

Payette National Forest

800 West Lakeside Ave., McCall 83638. T: (208) 634-0700; F: (208) 634-0744; www.fs.fed.us/r4/payette; rbidiman@fs.fed.us.

RV ★★★ Tent ★★★★

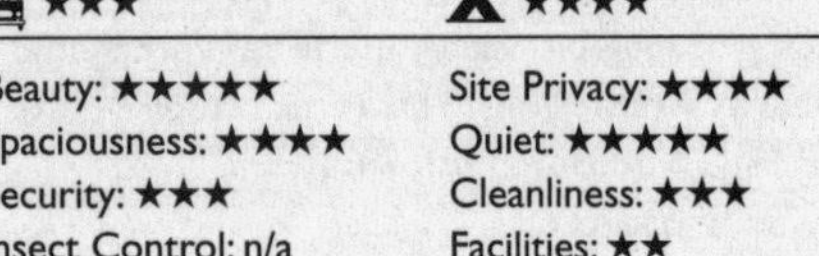

Beauty: ★★★★★ Site Privacy: ★★★★
Spaciousness: ★★★★ Quiet: ★★★★★
Security: ★★★ Cleanliness: ★★★
Insect Control: n/a Facilities: ★★

Rustic camping, clean air, stunning photo opportunities, and many ways to enjoy the dramatic terrain will serve to make campers at Payette brag to their friends. Many of the campsites accommodate RVs, all of them are tent-friendly. Most sites have a paved parking spot, but facilities are primitive to basic (and we mean basic). Surrounded by two deep river canyons, this remote area varies in altitude changes and climate, ranging from hot desert grasslands to conifer forests to snow-capped peaks. You can enjoy cross-country skiing, hiking, rock-climbing, hunting, fishing, and lots of outdoor recreation. Plan ahead, bring a good camera, and expect to find privacy, quiet, and legendary beauty.

Basics

Operated By: US Forest Service. **Open:** Most are May–Sept. **Site Assignment:** Several are by reservation, (877) 444-6777 or www.reserveusa.com, reservable 240 days in advance or self-serve. **Registration:** Registration kiosk or camp hosts trailer. **Fee:** $5–$20 per night; max. 6 per site. **Parking:** At site.

Facilities

Number of Multipurpose Sites: There are 22 campgrounds in the Payette National Forest, 6–35 sites each. **Hookups:** Potable water. **Each Site:** Level parking spurs (most are paved), picnic table, grated fire pit. **Dump Station:** Dumps are located in several locations throughout the forest. **Laundry:** In the small communities scattered throughout the forest, but not at the individual campgrounds. **Pay Phone:** No. **Rest Rooms and Showers:** Rest rooms mostly w/ vaulted toilets; no showers. **Fuel:** The Payette National Forest is a very large area with very few places to fuel, even fewer w/ diesel. **Propane:** Inquire at campground. **Internal Roads:** Most are paved. **RV Service:** McCall. **Market:** Groceries in most every small community within the forest. **Restaurant:** Very few, mostly café/grills & pizza. **General Store:** No. **Vending:** No. **Swimming Pool:** No, but many areas on the rivers & lakes open to public for swimming; natural hot springs. (Use caution: many hot springs are too hot for swimming & will cause second- & third-degree burns.) **Playground:** No. **Other:** Horse camps (1 commercial horse camp in Idaho City), Boise River, Payette River. **Activities:** Hiking, mountain biking w/ 6 trailheads, fishing, skiing, horseback riding w/ over 27 trailheads, backpacking, mountaineering, motorized bike trailheads, cross-country skiing. **Nearby Attractions:** Arrowrock Reservoir, Anderson Ranch Reservoir, Idaho Historical Museum, Boise Zoo, Ponderosa State Park. **Additional Information:** McCall Recreation Report, (208) 634-0409; Idaho Fish & Game, (208) 634-8137; McCall Area Chamber of Commerce, (208) 634-7631; Weiser Area Chamber of Commerce, (208) 549-0452.

Restrictions

Pets: On leash only. **Fires:** In fire rings only (the forest may prohibit open fires due to weather conditions, always check w/ a ranger or camp host before starting any fires). **Alcoholic Beverages:** Allowed. **Vehicle Maximum Length:** Sites vary in size, the campgrounds on the national reservation service are better equipped to handle larger RVs. **Other:** Golden Access & Golden Age Passes are honored & can be purchased at any ranger station; 14-day stay limit.

To Get There

From McCall, east and west off US 95, follow signs.

McCALL
Ponderosa State Park

P.O. Box 84, McCall 83638. T: (208) 634-2164; F: (208) 634-5370; www.idahoparks.org; PON@idpr.state.id.us.

RV ★★★ | Tent ★★★

Beauty: ★★★	Site Privacy: ★★★
Spaciousness: ★★	Quiet: ★★★
Security: ★★★★	Cleanliness: ★★★
Insect Control: ★★★	Facilities: ★★★

Ponderosa State Park, named for the 150-foot tall ponderosa pines that inhabit the diverse 1,400-acre area, is known as one of Idaho's favorite recreational spots. It is a sanctuary for the wildlife and a nesting ground for the osprey and the bald eagle. The park is on a large peninsula in the Payette Lake, with a public beach on its north end. The campground is the center of activity, with sites both primitive and developed. It is shaded by evergreens, and the ground is level. Sites are fairly close together, and the park reaches full capacity during the summer months. Most sites are located in one of three loops, are paved, and provide electricity. The park offers a large variety of activities for patrons of all ages, including paved walking paths, scheduled activities, and an education center. The weather is cool in the spring and fall, with dry, warm summers. The park is fully staffed around clock and camp host and rangers are always there to assist.

Basics

Operated By: Idaho Dept. of Parks & Recreation. **Open:** State park is open all year, the campgrounds are open Memorial Day weekend–the first snow (after Labor Day). **Site Assignment:** Reservations recommended, $6 non-refundable reservation fee to be paid 5 days prior to arrival. **Registration:** In visitors center. **Fee:** $12 water only, $16 electric & water, plus reservation fee. **Parking:** At site.

Facilities

Number of Multipurpose Sites: 137. **Hookups:** Electric (20, 30 amps), water. **Each Site:** Picnic table, grated fire pit. **Dump Station:** Yes. **Laundry:** No. **Pay Phone:** Yes. **Rest Rooms and Showers:** Yes. **Fuel:** No. **Propane:** No. **Internal Roads:** Paved. **RV Service:** In McCall. **Market:** In McCall. **Restaurant:** In McCall. **General Store:** No. **Vending:** Yes. **Swimming Pool:** No, but you may swim in the lake. **Playground:** Yes. **Other:** 2 yurts (a circular, Mongolian-style domed tent 20 ft. in diameter w/ a plywood floor, insulated & heated in the winter, sleeps 4–6 people), group picnic shelters, boat ramp, lakefront swimming. **Activities:** Fishing, hiking, biking, boating, horseshoes, volleyball, cross-country skiing, golf, interpretive programs, guided nature walks, hard path trail, youth programs for children 6–12. **Nearby Attractions:** Culture Center Museum, Meadow Creek natural hot springs, Brundage Mountain Ski Resort, scenic chair lifts, outdoor concerts, Cascade Reservoir, Payette lake. **Additional Information:** McCall Chamber & Visitor Bureau, (208) 634-7631 or (800) 260-5130, www.mccall-idchamber.org.

Restrictions

Pets: On 6-ft. leash only. **Fires:** In fire pits only (fires may be prohibited due to weather, ask park officials before starting any fire). **Alcoholic Beverages:** Allowed. **Vehicle Maximum Length:** Some spaces are up to 80 ft. **Other:** Max. 8 people per site, 14-day limit; group camps are available.

To Get There

Located 108 mi. north of Boise on Hwy. 55, you will need to follow signs once in McCall.

MOUNTAIN HOME

Bruneau Dunes State Park

HC 85 Box 41, Mountain Home 83647. T: (208) 366-7919; F: (208) 366-2844; www.idahoparks.org; BRU@idpr.state.id.us.

 ★★★★  ★★★

Beauty: ★★★	Site Privacy: ★★★
Spaciousness: ★★★	Quiet: ★★★★
Security: ★★★★	Cleanliness: ★★★★
Insect Control: ★★★★	Facilities: ★★★

Bruneau Dunes State Park is home to the largest single sand dune in North America, with a peak 470 feet above the lake surface. Situated in the high desert, Bruneau Dunes receives less than 10 inches of rain a year, with temperatures over a 100° in the summer to well below 0° in the winter. The park offers a unique feature, an observatory, as well as fascinating geological formations. There are two camping areas with electricity and water, both circular. The older campsite offers better shade and some covered picnic tables, while the new area offers larger pull-through sites and 50-amp hookups. However, the trees have not had time to mature. The park also has primitive camping near its horse coral for those campers wishing to take advantage of the equestrian trails. There are day-use areas in the park as well as great bluegill and large-mouth bass fishing in the lakes. The Natural Science Center and Observatory offers interpretive programs available with reservations.

Basics

Operated By: Idaho State Parks. **Open:** All year. **Site Assignment:** Yes. **Registration:** at visitor center. **Fee:** No hookups $12, hookups $16, equestrian camping $7; cash, checks. **Parking:** At site.

Facilities

Number of RV-Only Sites: 57. **Number of Tent-Only Sites:** 16. **Number of Multipurpose Sites:** 5. **Hookups:** Electric (30, 50 amps), water. **Each Site:** Picnic table, grill or grated fire pit. **Dump Station:** Yes. **Laundry:** No. **Pay Phone:** Yes. **Rest Rooms and Showers:** Yes. **Fuel:** No. **Propane:** No. **Internal Roads:** Paved. **RV Service:** In Mountain Home. **Market:** In Mountain Home. **Restaurant:** In Mountain Home. **General Store:** Yes. **Vending:** No. **Swimming Pool:** No. **Playground:** Yes. **Other:** Horse corral, picnic area, Bruneau Dunes State Park Astronomical Complex & Natural Science Center, Interpretive Services, non-motorized boat dock. **Activities:** Hiking, fishing, equestrian trails, picnicking. **Nearby Attractions:** 1 hour from Boise. **Additional Information:** Idaho State Parks & Recreation, Boise, (208) 334-4199.

RESTRICTIONS

Pets: On leash only. **Fires:** In fire pits only. **Alcoholic Beverages:** Yes. **Vehicle Maximum Length:** None. **Other:** 14-day limit.

TO GET THERE

From I-84 take Exit 90, bear right onto US 30 (Sunset Strip), south on SR 51, left (east) on SR 78, go about 3.4 mi. and turn right into park.

MOUNTAIN HOME

Golden Rule KOA

220 East 10th N, Mountain Home 83647. T: (800) 562-8695 or (208) 587-5111; www.koa.com.

RV ★★★	Tent ★★
Beauty: ★★	Site Privacy: ★★
Spaciousness: ★★	Quiet: ★★★
Security: ★★★	Cleanliness: ★★
Insect Control: ★★★	Facilities: ★★

The Golden Rule KOA is located in downtown Mountain Home. It is one of the smaller and older KOAs in the system and seems to cater more to longterm guest. It is centrally located within walking distance to the Mountain Home public park and pool as well as to restaurants. The campground has both pull-through and back-in sites, but due to the age of the park there is limited space for the new, larger RVs. The rest rooms are clean, kept locked at all times, and are available only to guests. There is a small store on premises, but not the normally large KOA-type gift shop. There is very limited space for children to play and there are several mobile homes within view. The staff is friendly and helpful; the weather is dry and windy; and Mountain Home is a delightful small community with an inviting atmosphere.

BASICS

Operated By: Private Operator. **Open:** Mar.–Nov. **Site Assignment:** By reservations or first available. **Registration:** In camp store. **Fee:** Tent $18–$19 per person, RV $26–$28 per 2 people, extra person $2.70. **Parking:** At site.

FACILITIES

Number of RV-Only Sites: 50. **Number of Tent-Only Sites:** 5. **Hookups:** Electric (20, 30, 50 amps), water, sewer, cable. **Each Site:** Picnic table, grill. **Dump Station:** Yes. **Laundry:** Yes. **Pay Phone:** Yes. **Rest Rooms and Showers:** Yes. **Fuel:** No. **Propane:** Yes. **Internal Roads:** Gravel, in good condition. **RV Service:** Terry RV on Hwy. 30. **Market:** Alberson, 1 block. **Restaurant:** Serval in walking distance. **General Store:** Yes. **Vending:** Store only. **Swimming Pool:** No, but the public city pool is 1 block away. **Playground:** Yes. **Other:** Game room. **Activities:** Fishing, golf. **Nearby Attractions:** City park within walking distance w/ pool, tennis, & recreation area. **Additional Information:** Mountain Home Valley Chamber of Commerce, (208) 837-9131.

RESTRICTIONS

Pets: On leash only. **Fires:** In grills only. **Alcoholic Beverages:** Allowed. **Vehicle Maximum Length:** Call ahead for details.

TO GET THERE

I-84 Exit 95 go towards Mountain Home on Hwy. 51 to third stop light, turn right on 2nd E St. to Chevron Station, right 2 blocks.

NORTH FORK

Rivers Inn and RV

P.O Box 68, North Fork 83466. T: (208) 865-2301; www.riversforkinn.com.

RV ★★★★★	Tent n/a
Beauty: ★★★★★	Site Privacy: ★★★★
Spaciousness: ★★★★	Quiet: ★★★★★
Security: ★★★★	Cleanliness: ★★★★★
Insect Control: ★★★	Facilities: ★★★★★

Twenty five miles south of the Montana, Idaho line off Hwy. 93, in the Salmon National Forest is the small Rivers Fork Inn and RV Park. This quaint eight-site campground is hands down the most naturally beautiful full hookup campground in the state. Its eight sites are all in a row, lined up only yards from the bank of the Salmon River. The veranda from the log lodge permit guests to view the merging of the North Fork River and Salmon River while gazing up into mountains of the Salmon National Forest. Both rivers are famous for their steelhead fishing, and the Joseph Pass Ski resort is only a few miles north. There are several fishing, hunting, and rafting outfitters in the area, and the snow skiing is wonderful in the winter. There is also a small hotel on the property of resort quality and the owners meticulously maintain the property. In addition, the owners are quite affable people and live full time on the property.

Basics

Operated By: Noel & Betty Stone. **Open:** All year. **Site Assignment:** By reservation or walk-in. **Registration:** In the lodge. **Fee:** $18. **Parking:** At site.

Facilities

Number of RV-Only Sites: 8. **Number of Tent-Only Sites:** 0. **Hookups:** Electric (30, 50 amps), water, sewer. **Each Site:** A few tables. **Dump Station:** No. **Laundry:** No. **Pay Phone:** Yes. **Rest Rooms and Showers:** No, campground was build for self contained RVs, there are rest rooms in the lodge. **Fuel:** No, in North Fork about 3 mi. **Propane:** No, in North Fork about 3 mi. **Internal Roads:** Gravel, in good condition. **RV Service:** Limited local service. **Market:** In town. **Restaurant:** In North Fork. **General Store:** No. **Vending:** Yes. **Swimming Pool:** No. **Playground:** No. **Other:** Large lodge, 8-room motel, all sites sit on the river. **Activities:** Mountain biking, hiking, fishing (property is on the Salmon River) & backs up to the Salmon National Forest. **Nearby Attractions:** Whitewater rafting, fishing tours, float trips, skiing both cross-country & downhill (10 miles for the ski resorts). There are several outfitters in the area. **Additional Information:** Salmon Valley Chamber of Commerce, (208) 756-2100.

Restrictions

Pets: On leash only. **Fires:** No open fires. **Alcoholic Beverages:** Allowed. **Vehicle Maximum Length:** 45 ft.

To Get There

From I-90 in Missoula, MT, the campground is 180 mi. south on Hwy. 93, 25 mi. south of the MT/ID border.

OROFINO

Dent Acres Recreation Area

P.O. Box 48, Ahsahka 83520. T: (208) 476-1261; F: (208) 476-1262; www.nww.usace.army.mil; eric.s.peterson@nww.usace.army.mil (project manager).

RV ★★★ | Tent ★★★★

Beauty: ★★★★	Site Privacy: ★★★
Spaciousness: ★★★	Quiet: ★★★★
Security: ★★★★	Cleanliness: ★★★
Insect Control: ★★★	Facilities: ★★★

Dent Acres Recreation Area sits on the east side of the Dworshak Reservoir, 19 miles northeast of Orofino. The Dworshak Dam is the largest straight-axis dam in North America and its reservoir has 54 miles of tree-lined shore. This 500 area recreation area offers 50 full-hookup campsites situated in an open meadow. The campgrounds consist of an "S," configuration offering both shaded and open sites. The elevation of the park is 1,600 feet, offering warm summer days and cool nights. Most sites are spacious and private, both pull-throughs and back-ins. Dent Acres Recreation Area offers trophy fishing (kokanee salmon, small mouth bass, and rainbow trout), 18 miles of hiking trials, and an additional 100 primitive campsites accessible only by boat. The park also has a full marina with boat dump. Park rangers and camp attendant are on duty 24 hours a day to provide you with any assistance.

Basics

Operated By: US Army Corp of Engineers (Walla Walla District). **Open:** Recreation area year-round, the campground Apr.–Nov. **Site Assignment:** Dent Acres Recreation Area uses the National Recreation Reservation Service (877) 444-6777, 60% of the campsites are reservable, www.reserveusa.com. **Registration:** See camp attendant. **Fee:** $16 (cash or check, unless using the reservation service). **Parking:** At site.

Facilities

Number of Multipurpose Sites: 50. **Hookups:** Electric (20, 30 amps), water, sewer. **Each Site:** Picnic table, fire pit. **Dump Station:** Yes. **Laundry:** No. **Pay Phone:** Yes. **Rest Rooms and Showers:** Yes. **Fuel:** 20 mi. in Orofino (except by boat & then Big Eddy Marina approx. 5 mi. down the res. **Propane:** 20 mi. in Orofino. **Internal Roads:** Paved. **RV Service:** 20 mi. south in Orofino. **Market:** 20 mi. south in Orofino. **Restaurant:** 20 mi. south in Orofino. **General Store:** No. **Vending:** Inquire at campground. **Swimming Pool:** No, you make swim in the reservoir. **Playground:** Yes. **Other:** Boat launch, floating marine dump, group shelters, weather station, camp attendant, boat parking. **Activities:** Fishing (kakanee salmon, small mouth bass, rainbow trout), hunting (elk, deer, black bear, cougar), boating, waterskiing, cross-country skiing, 18 miles of hiking trails, backpacking, mountain biking. **Nearby**

Attractions: Dworshak State Park, Dworshak National Steelhead Fish Hatchery, Clearwater County Museum, Lewis & Clark National Historic Trail. **Additional Information:** There are 100 primitive sites surrounding the Dworshak Reservoir, accessible only by boat, featuring picnic tables, fire pits, & vaulted toilets. Orofino Chamber of Commerce, (208) 476-4335, www.orofino.com.

Restrictions

Pets: On 6-ft. leash only. **Fires:** In fire pits only (fires may be prohibited due to weather, ask park official before starting any fire). **Alcoholic Beverages:** Yes. **Vehicle Maximum Length:** Some sites up to 50 ft. **Other:** Max. 8 people per site, 14-day limit.

To Get There

Hwy. 12 to Orofino, in Orofino there are signs to the Dworshak Reservoir Visitor Center. Please stop and obtain a map of the reservoir and recreation area. They will direct you into the area. The roads leading in to recreation area are narrow and curvy. It is 19 mi. from the visitors center into the recreation area. Please note the visitor center closes most days at 4 p.m.

OROFINO
Dworshak State Park

P.O. Box 2028, Orofino 83544. T: (208) 476-5994; www.idahoparks.org; DWO@idpr.state.id.us.

RV ★★★ Tent ★★★★

Beauty: ★★★★	Site Privacy: ★★★
Spaciousness: ★★★	Quiet: ★★★★
Security: ★★★	Cleanliness: ★★★
Insect Control: ★★★	Facilities: ★★

Located on the west side of the Dworshak Reservoir, Dworshak State Parks offers a spectacular secluded setting of pine forest and open meadows. This 105-campsite park is seated along side the Dworshak Reservoir with many walk-in tent sites right on the bank. The Dworshak Dam is the largest straight-axis dam in North America and its reservoir has 54 miles of tree-lined shore. The campground consists of three circular loops offering both shaded and open sites. The elevation of the park is 1,600 feet, translating into warm summer days and cool nights. Most sites are spacious and private, providing both pull-through and back-in sites. Dworshak State Park offers trophy fishing, miles of hiking trials, and a full service group camp. The park also offers weekend interpretive programs throughout the spring and summer in a large outdoor amphitheater. Park rangers and camp host are on duty 24 hours a day to provide you with any assistance.

Basics

Operated By: Idaho Dept. of Parks & Recreation. **Open:** All year (electric & water are only on Apr.–Oct.). **Site Assignment:** Some sites are reservable, there is a $6 non-refundable reservation fee. **Registration:** At entrance gate or see camp hosts. **Fee:** $12 no hookups, $16 w/ electric & water. **Parking:** At site.

Facilities

Number of RV-Only Sites: 45. **Number of Tent-Only Sites:** 20. **Number of Multipurpose Sites:** 40. **Hookups:** Electric (20, 30 amps), water. **Each Site:** Picnic table, fire pit. **Dump Station:** Yes. **Laundry:** No. **Pay Phone:** Yes. **Rest Rooms and Showers:** Yes. **Fuel:** No. **Propane:** No. **Internal Roads:** The main roads are paved, some of the campground loops are gravel. **RV Service:** 25 mi. south in Orofino. **Market:** 25 mi. south in Orofino. **Restaurant:** 25 mi. south in Orofino. **General Store:** No. **Vending:** No. **Swimming Pool:** No, but you may swim in the reservoir. **Playground:** Yes. **Other:** Marina, boat launch, boat parking, floating boat dump (shared w/ the corp of engineers), group picnic shelter, dry storage, Three Meadows Group Area w/ cabins, lodge, & kitchen facilities. **Activities:** Fishing (kakanee salmon, smallmouth bass, rainbow trout), weekend interpretive programs, hiking, swimming, boating, waterskiing, jet skiing. **Nearby Attractions:** Hunting (no hunting on state park property), Dent Acres Recreational Area, Dworshak National Steelhead Fish Hatchery, Clearwater County Museum, Lewis & Clark National Historic Trail. **Additional Information:** Idaho Dept. of Parks & Recreation, (208) 334-4199; Orofino Chamber of Commerce, (208) 476-4335, www.orofino.com.

Restrictions

Pets: On 6-ft. leash only. **Fires:** In fire pits only (fires may be prohibited due to weather, ask park official before starting any fire). **Alcoholic Beverages:** Allowed. **Vehicle Maximum Length:** 50 ft. **Other:** Max. 8 people per site; 14-day limit; group camps available; $4 extra-vehicle fee per night.

To Get There

Take Hwy. 12, 40 mi. east of Lewiston into Orofino. Stop at the visitor center or ranger station in Orofino, they will give you a map of the Dworshak reservoir and direct you to the park. The park is 26 mi. north of Orofino on the west side of the reservoir, the road is paved but narrow and curves.

OSBURN

Blue Anchor Trailer and RV Park

P.O.Box 645, Osburn 83849.T: (208) 752-3443 or (877) 590-7275; www.blueanchorrv.homestead.com; reservations@blueanchor-rv.com or manager@blueanchor-rv.com.

RV: ★★★ Tent: ★★★

Beauty: ★★★ Site Privacy: ★★★
Spaciousness: ★★★ Quiet: ★★★
Security: ★★★ Cleanliness: ★★★
Insect Control: ★★★ Facilities: ★★★

Tucked into the hills of Northern Idaho, Blue Anchor Trailer and RV Park is great for a cozy hideaway. The campground is abundant in evergreens providing shade and gorgeous scenery. The spring and summer months are the best time to visit because of the stunning foliage and warmer temperatures. The 24 pull-through RV sites are grassy and average in size compared to others in the area. Off Exit 57 on I-90 this campground is easily accessible. Surprisingly, in the nearby small town of Osburn there are attractions appealing to all age groups.

Basics

Operated By: Jim. **Open:** All year. **Site Assignment:** Reservations recommended. **Registration:** In general store. **Fee:** Tent $14, RV $17–$19. **Parking:** At site.

Facilities

Number of RV-Only Sites: 24. **Number of Tent-Only Sites:** Open tent area. **Hookups:** Electric (30, 50 amps), water, sewer. **Each Site:** Picnic tables, fire pit. **Dump Station:** Yes. **Laundry:** Yes. **Pay Phone:** Yes. **Rest Rooms and Showers:** Yes. **Fuel:** 1 mi. by I-90. **Propane:** 1 mi. by I-90. **Internal Roads:** Gravel. **RV Service:** Limited service in town. **Market:** In town. **Restaurant:** There are a few in town. **General Store:** Yes. **Vending:** No. **Swimming Pool:** No. **Playground:** Yes. **Other:** Dataport, river access. **Activities:** Volleyball, skiing, hiking nature trails, fishing, basketball, recreation area. **Nearby Attractions:** Wallace Melodrama, mining town tours & museums, Silver Mt. Ski Resort, many outfitters. **Additional Information:** Montana Visitors Information, (406) 649-2290.

Restrictions

Pets: On leash only. **Fires:** In fire pits only. **Alcoholic Beverages:** Allowed. **Vehicle Maximum Length:** None. **Other:** Good Sam Member.

To Get There

Exit 57 off I-90, follow signs.

PINEHURST

Kellogg/Silver Valley

801 North Division, Pinehurst 83850.T: (208) 682-3612; www.koa.com.

RV: ★★★★ Tent: ★★★

Beauty: ★★★ Site Privacy: ★★★
Spaciousness: ★★★ Quiet: ★★★★
Security: ★★★ Cleanliness: ★★★★
Insect Control: ★★★ Facilities: ★★★★

Only a few short mile away from the historic Silver Valley, directly off I-90 is the Kellogg/Silver Valley KOA. This well manicured campground offers a full array of services from cable TV and internet access to fishing and miniature-golf. There is a small stocked stream that runs through the campground adding ambiance. The campground is a completely gated community and patrons must have a code to enter the camping area. Campsites are moderate in size with gravel parking spurs. The further back you go into the campground, the smaller and closer together the sites get. There are both pull-through and back-in sites, with limited room for extra large big rigs. The area around the campground is full of silver mining history, several museums, and wonderful fishing and hiking. Summer days are warm and almost always windy.

Basics

Operated By: Mike & Kim Jones. **Open:** Apr. 15–Oct. 15. **Site Assignment:** By reservations held on a credit card number. **Registration:** In camp store. **Fee:** Tent $22–$24, RV $27–$34 per 2 people, extra people $2.50, children under 5 stay free. **Parking:** At site.

Facilities

Number of RV-Only Sites: 56. **Number of Tent-Only Sites:** 16. **Hookups:** Electric (30, 50 amps), water, sewer, cable, phone. **Each Site:** Picnic table, grated fire pit. **Dump Station:** Yes. **Laundry:** Yes. **Pay Phone:** Yes. **Rest Rooms and Showers:** Yes. **Fuel:** Next door. **Propane:** Next door. **Internal Roads:** Gravel, in good condition. **RV Service:** Inquire at campground. **Market:** In Pinehurst. **Restaurant:** In town. **General Store:** Yes. **Vending:** Yes. **Swimming Pool:** Yes, w/ hot tub. **Playground:** Yes. **Other:** 6 cabins, 1 pond front cottage, pedal boat dock, day-use area. **Activities:** Fishing, games, bikes, nature walks, fun cycles, pedal boats, croquet, golf. **Nearby Attractions:** Coeur d'Alene National Forest, Wallace, Idaho–Silver Capital of the World, Silverwood Theme Park, Idaho Panhandles, mtn. bike trails, Silver Mountain. **Additional Information:** Kellogg Chamber of Commerce, (208) 784-0821.

Restrictions

Pets: On leash only. **Fires:** In fire pits only. **Alcoholic Beverages:** Allowed. **Vehicle Maximum Length:** 75 ft. w/ tow. **Other:** Special holiday rates, KOA discount.

To Get There

I-90 Exit 45.

PLUMMER

Heyburn State Park

1291 Chatcolet, Plummer 83851. T: (208) 686-1308; F: (208) 686-3003; www.idahoparks.org/parks/heyburn.html; hey@idpr.state.id.us.

RV ★★★★ Tent ★★★

Beauty: ★★★★	Site Privacy: ★★★★
Spaciousness: ★★★★	Quiet: ★★★★★
Security: ★★★★	Cleanliness: ★★★★
Insect Control: n/a	Facilities: ★★★

Heyburn State Park was created from the Coeur d'Alene Indian Reservation by an act of Congress on April 28, 1908. It is the oldest State Park in the Pacific Northwest. The lakes provide an abundance of fish, the marsh areas are filled with waterfowl, and the heavily timbered slopes and open meadows are ideal for deer, bears and upland birds. Bird-watching is terrific at Heyburn, with osprey and blue heron as common as sparrows elsewhere. Trails for hikers or horseback riders are shaded by 400-year-old ponderosa pines. Heyburn has three campgrounds with sites that range from full hookup to primitive camping. The sites provide the ultimate get away, as they are quiet, spacious and clean. The campgrounds are open year-round and sites are available on a first come first serve basis.

Basics

Operated By: Idaho Dept. of Parks & Recreation. **Open:** All year. **Site Assignment:** First come, first served. **Registration:** Registration kiosk or entrance gate. **Fee:** $7–$22 depending on site & amenities. **Parking:** At site.

Facilities

Number of RV-Only Sites: 57. **Number of Tent-Only Sites:** 34. **Number of Multipurpose Sites:** 40. **Hookups:** Electric (30 amps), water, sewer. **Each Site:** Level parking spurs, picnic table, grated fire pit. **Dump Station:** Yes. **Laundry:** No. **Pay Phone:** Yes. **Rest Rooms and Showers:** Yes. **Fuel:** In the Rocky Point Day-Use Area. **Propane:** No, in town. **Internal Roads:** Most are paved. **RV Service:** St. Maries. **Market:** 5 mi. east in Plummer. **Restaurant:** Plummer or St. Maries. **General Store:** In the Rocky Point Day-Use Area. **Vending:** No. **Swimming Pool:** No, but there is a lakefront beach w/ swimming. **Playground:** Yes. **Other:** Boat launch, boat rentals, interpretive center, public docks, amphitheater, boat moorage, boat sewage station, cabins, group shelters. **Activities:** Hiking, boating, fishing, swimming, interpretive programming, audio scenic drives (pick tapes up at local ranger station). **Nearby Attractions:** Garnet digging, St. Joe's river, rafting & fishing outfitters. **Additional Information:** St. Maries Chamber of Commerce, (208) 245-3563.

Restrictions

Pets: On leash, not allowed on waterfront. **Fires:** In fire rings only (the forest service may prohibit open fires due to weather conditions, check w/ a ranger or camp host before starting any fires). **Alcoholic Beverages:** Allowed. **Vehicle Maximum Length:** 40 ft.

To Get There

Between Plummer & St. Maries, ID (SH 5, off US 95).

STANLEY

Elk Mountain RV Resort

Box 115, Stanley 83278. T: (208) 774-2202

RV: ★★★ Tent: ★★

Beauty: ★★★ Site Privacy: ★★
Spaciousness: ★★ Quiet: ★★★★
Security: ★★★ Cleanliness: ★★★
Insect Control: ★★★ Facilities: ★★★

Elk Mountain RV resort is a small private campground on the outskirts of the Sawtooth National Recreation Area. If offers a wooded ambiance amongst giant aged pine trees. The property is on a small slope; therefore sites are laid out in a non-uniformed manor. Tent sites are very close together and do not allow for very much privacy. Stanley and Redfish Lakes are in close proximity for trophy sockeye, chinook, and rainbow trout fishing. The Sawtooth recreation area offers miles of hiking trails, and mountain biking. There are several outfitters in the Stanley Area offering a vast assortment of activities from whitewater rafting trips, to guided fly-fishing expeditions. The campground offers a friendly and hospitable atmosphere, making this a great location to set up base camp or just relax and enjoy the summer. Days are warm with a nice mountain breeze, but bring a jacket for the evening.

BASICS

Operated By: Kenneth & Patti Butts. **Open:** Memorial Day–Labor Day. **Site Assignment:** Reservations recommended. **Registration:** In general store. **Fee:** Tents $15, RV $21.40 per 2 people, Cash & checks. **Parking:** At site.

FACILITIES

Number of RV-Only Sites: 20. **Number of Tent-Only Sites:** 5. **Hookups:** Electric (30 amps), water, sewer, phone. **Each Site:** Picnic table. **Dump Station:** No. **Laundry:** Yes. **Pay Phone:** No. **Rest Rooms and Showers:** Yes. **Fuel:** No. **Propane:** No. **Internal Roads:** Gravel. **RV Service:** None. **Market:** Stanley, ID. **Restaurant:** Stanley, ID. **General Store:** Yes. **Vending:** General store only. **Swimming Pool:** No. **Playground:** No. **Other:** Central fire pit. **Activities:** Hiking, rafting, fishing, hiking. **Additional Information:** Stanley-Sawtooth Chamber of Commerce, (208) 744-3411, (800) 878-7950, www.stanleycc.org.

RESTRICTIONS

Pets: Allowed. **Fires:** In fire pits only. **Alcoholic Beverages:** Not allowed. **Vehicle Maximum Length:** None.

TO GET THERE

Hwy. 21, about 5 mi. southwest of Stanley.

WHITE BIRD

Swiftwater RV Park & Store

HC 01 Box 24, White Bird 83554. T: (208) 839-2700 or (888) 291-5065; www.swiftwaterrvpark.com; jamie46@ctc.net.

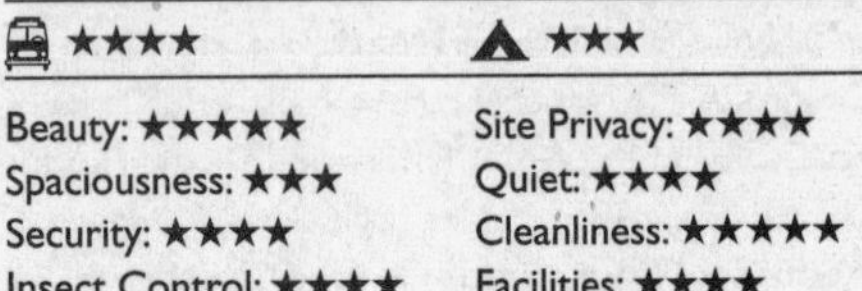

RV: ★★★★ Tent: ★★★

Beauty: ★★★★★ Site Privacy: ★★★★
Spaciousness: ★★★ Quiet: ★★★★
Security: ★★★★ Cleanliness: ★★★★★
Insect Control: ★★★★ Facilities: ★★★★

Swiftwater RV Park & Store is located in the Salmon River Valley, eight miles south of Grangeville. This quiet park has beautifully landscaped level sites, both pull-through and back-in. Situated in an open meadow on the banks of the Salmon River an attractive gazebo with fire pit and grill that overlooks the riverfront beach. White Bird is also located on the Lewis and Clark trail, with Meriweather Lewis being the first white man to visit the Salmon River Valley in 1805. Swiftwater is surrounded by recreational activities, and interesting historic areas. The area is home to many species of wildlife and offers trophy fishing and hunting. The weather is dry and the area is high desert, summer days can be very warm, with cool evenings. The owners live on the property and are there to assist in anyway.

BASICS

Operated By: Mark & Jamie Mortenson. **Open:** All year. **Site Assignment:** Reservations recommended. **Registration:** In the general store, located on the second floor. **Fee:** Tent $14, RV $18, per 2 people. Weekly & monthly rates available. $2.50 charge for extra people. **Parking:** At site.

FACILITIES

Number of RV-Only Sites: 27. **Number of Tent-Only Sites:** Open tent area. **Hookups:** Electric (30, 50 amps), water, sewer, satellite, phone. **Each Site:** Some picnic tables. **Dump Station:** Yes. **Laundry:** Yes. **Pay Phone:** Yes. **Rest Rooms**

and Showers: Yes. **Fuel:** No. **Propane:** Yes. **Internal Roads:** Gravel. **RV Service:** 8 mi. north in Grangeville. **Market:** No. **Restaurant:** 1 mi. North. **General Store:** Yes. **Vending:** No. **Swimming Pool:** No, but you may swim in the river. **Playground:** No. **Other:** TV room, gazebo w/ gas grill, central fire pit, river front beach. **Activities:** Fishing (chinook salmon, sockeye, rainbow trout,& perch), hiking, hunting, backpacking. **Nearby Attractions:** Rafting, skiing, snowmobiling, Hell's Canyon, Jet boating, kayaking, canoeing, guided hunting & fishing expeditions. **Additional Information:** www.swiftwaterrvpark.com.

RESTRICTIONS

Pets: Allowed. **Fires:** In central fire pit only. **Alcoholic Beverages:** Allowed. **Vehicle Maximum Length:** None.

TO GET THERE

From mile post 222 on Hwy. 95 at White Bird take a Hammer Creek turn off; campground is 0.5 mi. on the left.

WINCHESTER

Winchester Lake State Park

P.O.Box 186, Winchester 83555. T: (208) 924-7563; F: (208) 924-5941; www.idahoparks.org/parks/winchester.html; WIN@idpr.state.id.us.

RV: ★★★★	Tent: ★★★
Beauty: ★★★★	Site Privacy: ★★★
Spaciousness: ★★★	Quiet: ★★★
Security: ★★★★	Cleanliness: ★★★★
Insect Control: ★★★★	Facilities: ★★★★

Located in the Nez Perce Indian Reservation, Winchester Lake State Park is a beautiful 418-acre park on a 103-acre lake at the foot of the Craig Mountains. The park offers modern camping facilities and yurt rentals. The campground is configured in three loops on the west side of the lake. Campsites are both back-in and pull-through, with sites in loop A on the lake shaded by Douglas firs and ponderosa pines. The park offers boating, fishing (rainbow trout,) hiking trials, and biking trails in the summer; cross-country skiing, ice stating and ice fishing in the winter. In addition the park conducts educational programs and guided walks. Many different types of wildlife inhabit the park. The park staff is there to assist with any needs that may arise, along with volunteer host during the summer.

BASICS

Operated By: Idaho State Parks & Recreation. **Open:** All year. **Site Assignment:** First come, first served. **Registration:** Park office or self registration box at entrance gate. **Fee:** $12 no-hookups & $16 w/ hookups. **Parking:** Yes, but there is an extra vehicle fee of $3.

FACILITIES

Number of RV-Only Sites: 50. **Number of Tent-Only Sites:** 23. **Hookups:** Electric & water. **Each Site:** Picnic table, grated fire pit. **Dump Station:** 0.5 mi. in town. **Laundry:** No. **Pay Phone:** Yes. **Rest Rooms and Showers:** Yes. **Fuel:** No. **Propane:** No. **Internal Roads:** Paved. **RV Service:** No. **Market:** In Winchester. **Restaurant:** In Winchester. **General Store:** No. **Vending:** No. **Swimming Pool:** No. **Playground:** Yes. **Other:** Three yurts, lake side picnic area, non-motorized boat ramp, amphitheater. **Activities:** Fishing, picnicking, boating, hiking, wildlife viewing. **Nearby Attractions:** Inquire at campground. **Additional Information:** Idaho State Parks & Recreation, (208) 334-4199.

RESTRICTIONS

Pets: On leash only, dogs are not allowed on waterfront or day-use area of the park. **Fires:** In fire pits or grills only. **Alcoholic Beverages:** At sites only. **Vehicle Maximum Length:** 60 ft. **Other:** 15-day limit in a 30-day period.

TO GET THERE

From US 95 take right on US 95 business, then right on Camas St. and follow signs to park.

Iowa

If the state of Iowa registers at all to non-residents, it comes across as an endless field of corn where little, other than farming, ever happens. And yet, to view the Hawkeye state solely in this light is to ignore the many cultural and historical contributions Iowa has made to the nation. The 31st president of the United States (Herbert Hoover) was born here, as was famous TV personality Johnny Carson. Other notable Iowans include Grant Wood, Glenn Miller, and Ann Landers.

Before Europeans settled in Iowa, a number of Native American tribes livend in the area, including the Sauk, Mesquakie, Sioux, Potawatomi, Otoe, and Missouri, and before them, pre-historic ancestors roamed along the banks of the Mississippi. In 1673, the French explorers Louis Joliet and Father Jacques Marquette were the first Europeans to set foot in Iowa. As in other parts of the United States, pioneers soon came flooding into the state, displacing its native populations. Despite the lack of trees, pioneers remained to discover a land with exceedingly rich soil.

As settlement proceeded, Iowa became a melting pot of cultures. Between 1860 and 1870, the population of Iowa nearly doubled due to an influx of immigrants. Germans were the largest group of immigrants and could be found in every county in the state. Iowa also became home for many other nationalities, including Swedes, Norwegians, Danes, Dutch, Czechs, Italians, and Croatians. Most of these people came to farm, but, interestingly, a thriving coal industry also emerged, once making Iowa the major coal producer for the U.S.

The state has had its share of hard times. The coal industry collapsed in the early 1900s, leaving many towns deserted, and the stock market crash of 1929 led to many farmers losing their land. In spite of these setbacks, the citizens and the economy of Iowa ultimately prospered: the state is today the number one producer of corn and pork in the country.

Visitors to Iowa will find much to enjoy, including historic frontier forts, authentic American farms, and culturally rich cities.

In the southeast corner of the state, near **Cedar Rapids** (the second largest city), campers can visit the **Amana Colonies,** founded 150 years ago by Germans seeking religious freedom. Other sites include **Ushers Ferry Historic Village,** the **National Czech and Slovak Museum,** and the **Indian Creek Nature Center,** which has more than 11 miles of trails. About 50 miles away in **Davenport,** visitors can see the **Davenport Museum of Art's Grant Wood** collection as well as the **Adler Theater,** once part of the RKO theater chain. Outdoor enthusiasts will admire the many opportunities offered by the **Upper Mississippi River National Wildlife and Fish Refuge,** which runs along the state's eastern border.

The northeast section of Iowa stands in sharp contrast to the rest of the state. Instead of rolling hills and farmlands, this region, often referred to as **"Little Switzerland,"** has large forested swaths of land amidst its rugged geography. Outdoor enthusiasts will find much to do here, including paddling opportunities on the **Turkey, Upper Iowa,** and **Volga Rivers.** The access to the Mississippi also made this a valuable location for prehistoric Native Americans, as visitors will discover at the **Effigy Mounds National Monument.** For travellers seeking more cosmopolitan fare, **Cedar Falls/Waterloo** hosts many festivals, including the **Cedar Basin Jazz Festival** and **College Hill Arts Festival.**

Though lacking in major metropolitan areas, northwest Iowa has plenty to offer. There are numerous state parks and recreation areas within the Natural Lakes region, which was shaped by glacial activity thousands of years ago. **Gull Point State Park** and the **Lost Island Prairie Wetland Nature Center** are two recommended sites. Most winter outdoor activities center around cross-country skiing or snowmobile riding, but during the summer, visitors should seek out the **Inkpaduta Canoe Trail,** which follows the meandering **Little Sioux River.**

One of the richest regions in the state, the **Loess Hills,** is located in the southwest section of the state. Those wanting to see what the Iowa landscape looked like before European settlement should visit **Neal Smith National Wildlife Reserve,** where tall-grass prairie is being reintroduced along with natural herds of buffalo and other critters. The capital also offers numerous options for fun and recreation, including the **Des Moines Art Center** and the **Historic Jordan House.**

Campground Profiles

ADEL

Des Moines West KOA

3418 L Ave., Adel 50003. T: (515) 834-2729 or (800) KOA-2181; www.koa.com.

RV ★★★ Tent ★★★

Beauty: ★★★	Site Privacy: ★★★
Spaciousness: ★★★	Quiet: ★★★★
Security: ★★★★	Cleanliness: ★★★★
Insect Control: ★★★	Facilities: ★★★

Seventeen miles outside Des Moines and conveniently located directly off I-80 is the West Des Moines KOA. This KOA offers its patrons full amenities, a separate tent area, and all pull-through sites. Each site is has a level parking area and a small grass lawn. The campground is nicely landscaped and offers some shade. Hot coffee is served daily, just in time for an early morning dip in the pool. The area is rich in history, with numerous places to visit such as the Blank Park Zoo, the botanical center, and the now-famous bridges of Madison County. The staff is friendly and helpful, and the park offers excellent security. The park is open year round, but remember to pack according to the season; Iowa is bitterly cold and windy in the winter.

BASICS

Operated By: Howard & Katie Hudson. **Open:** Year round. **Site Assignment:** By reservation w/ credit card. **Registration:** In camp store. **Fee:** Tent $16, RV $18–$26; fee covers 2 people, $2. per additional guest, children under 5 free. **Parking:** At site.

FACILITIES

Number of RV-Only Sites: 110. **Number of Tent-Only Sites:** 70. **Hookups:** Electric (20, 30, 50 amps), water, sewer. **Each Site:** Picnic table. **Dump Station:** Yes. **Laundry:** Yes. **Pay Phone:** Yes. **Rest Rooms and Showers:** Yes. **Fuel:** No, in Adel or West Des Moines. **Propane:** No. **Internal Roads:** Paved, in good condition. **RV Service:** In West Des Moines. **Market:** 10 mi. in Castana, IA. **Restaurant:** In West Des Moines. **General Store:** Yes. **Vending:** No. **Swimming Pool:** Yes. **Playground:** Yes. **Other:** Cabins, fishing pond. **Activities:** Fishing, swimming, horseshoes. **Nearby**

Attractions: Living History Farms, State Capitol, John Wayne birthplace, Blank Park Zoo, botanical center, art & science center. Valley West Mall. **Additional Information:** West Des Moines Chamber of Commerce, (515) 225-6009.

RESTRICTIONS

Pets: On leash. **Fires:** No open fires. **Alcoholic Beverages:** Allowed. **Vehicle Maximum Length:** None. **Other:** $2 extra to run heat or a/c.

TO GET THERE

From I-80 Exit 106, go north 1 mi. on paved CR P-58.

CEDAR FALLS

Black Hawk Park

2410 West Lone Tree Rd., Cedar Falls 50613.
T: (319) 266-6813 or 266-0328; F: (319) 277-1536; www.co.black-hawk.ia.us/depts/conservation.html; conservation@co.black-hawk.ia.us.

RV ★★★★	Tent ★★★★
Beauty: ★★★★	Site Privacy: ★★★
Spaciousness: ★★★	Quiet: ★★★★
Security: ★★★★	Cleanliness: ★★★
Insect Control: ★★★	Facilities: ★★

Named after Chief Black Hawk of the Sauk Indian Tribe, Black Hawk Park is one of the largest county parks in the state. The park is part of a conservation area over 1,300 acres in size with a 142-site modern campground, complete with rest room facilities and showers. The sites are comfortable and well shaded by mature oak and other hardwoods. The park roads are paved and there are large sites, both pull-throughs and back-ins. Activities here include archery, a rifle range, and public hunting and fishing. There are even boat ramps. A full-time residential staff person and a host family are available to assist campers. The natural setting is a combination of woodland and prairie with a constant breeze.

BASICS

Operated By: Black Hawk County Conservation Board. **Open:** All year, weather permitting. **Site Assignment:** First come, first served & a small number of sites by reservation. **Registration:** Registration kiosk. **Fee:** $10–$13. **Parking:** At site.

FACILITIES

Number of Multipurpose Sites: 142. **Hookups:** Electric (20, 30, 50 amps), water. **Each Site:** Picnic table, fire pit. **Dump Station:** Yes. **Laundry:** No. **Pay Phone:** Yes. **Rest Rooms and Showers:** Yes. **Fuel:** No, in Cedar Falls. **Propane:** No, in Cedar Falls. **Internal Roads:** Paved, in good condition. **RV Service:** In Cedar Falls. **Market:** In Cedar Falls. **Restaurant:** In Cedar Falls. **General Store:** No. **Vending:** No. **Swimming Pool:** No. **Playground:** Yes. **Other:** 2 cabins, primitive camping, picnic shelters. **Activities:** Recreation trails, boating, rifle & pistol range, archery range, hunting, fishing, water activities, winter activities, ice fishing. **Nearby Attractions:** Sturgis Falls Celebrations, University of Northern Iowa Museum, the Grout Museums, Cedar Valley Nature Trail. **Additional Information:** Cedar Falls Chamber of Commerce, (319) 266-3593.

RESTRICTIONS

Pets: On leash. **Fires:** Fire pits only. **Alcoholic Beverages:** Allowed. **Vehicle Maximum Length:** 45 ft.

TO GET THERE

From Cedar Falls where US 218 and SR 58 meet, go north a little more than 1.7 mi., Turn left on East Lone Tree Rd and continue about 2.5 mi. to the campground.

CLEAR LAKE

Clear Lake State Park

2730 South Lakeview Dr., Clear Lake 50428. T: (515) 357-4212; F: (515) 357-4242; www.state.ia.us/parks; clear_lake@dnr.state.ia.us.

RV ★★★	Tent ★★★
Beauty: ★★★	Site Privacy: ★★
Spaciousness: ★★	Quiet: ★★★
Security: ★★★★	Cleanliness: ★★★
Insect Control: ★★★	Facilities: ★★

Located on the southeast shores of Clear Lake, this state park offers a verity of outdoor activities and is considered one of Northern Iowa's premiere recreation areas. The campground has over 215 sites in a series of loops surrounded by mature oaks and smaller vegetation. The park offers both pull-throughs and back-ins with level trailer pads, as well as modern rest rooms and showers. Clear Lake State Park offers a sandy beach perfect for swimming and tanning, along with many other water activities, all only a short walk for the main campground area. A large variety of fish can be caught in the lake, including walleye, catfish, and northern pike. Iowa's four distinct seasons include hot, dry summers, but it is never a bad idea to pack a rain jacket; sun screen and bug spray are imperitive. There is an entrance fee and camping permits are granted through self registration.

Basics

Operated By: Iowa Department of Natural Resources. **Open:** All year. **Site Assignment:** First come, first served. **Registration:** Self-registration at entrance gate. **Fee:** $16 w/ hookups, $11 no hookups. **Parking:** At site.

Facilities

Number of Multipurpose Sites: 215. **Hookups:** Electric (20, 30 amps). **Each Site:** Picnic table, grated fire pits. **Dump Station:** Yes. **Laundry:** No. **Pay Phone:** Yes. **Rest Rooms and Showers:** Yes. **Fuel:** At marina. **Propane:** At marina. **Internal Roads:** Paved, in good condition. **RV Service:** 10 mi. east in Mason City. **Market:** In Clear Lake or Mason City. **Restaurant:** In Clear Lake or Mason City. **General Store:** No, at nearby private marina. **Vending:** No, at nearby private marina. **Swimming Pool:** No. **Playground:** Yes. **Other:** Lodge w/ kitchen & rustic fireplace, enclosed picnic shelters, 900-ft. sandy beach. **Activities:** Fishing, boating, jetskiing, waterskiing, wind surfing, swimming, hiking, biking, cross-country skiing, snowmobiling, & ice sailing. **Nearby Attractions:** Iowa Trolley Park, shopping. **Additional Information:** Mason City Chamber of Commerce, (641) 423-5724.

Restrictions

Pets: Dogs on leash only, see web site for rules on horses & mules. **Fires:** In fire rings only. **Alcoholic Beverages:** At sites, beer & wine only. **Vehicle Maximum Length:** None. **Other:** No metal detectors in campground, max. 6 people per site.

To Get There

From I-35 Exit 193, take SR 106 (4th Ave. S.) west, turn left on S. Shore Dr., right onto 26th Ave. S., and left onto S. Lakeview Dr.

CLEAR LAKE

Oakwood RV Park

541 240th St., Clear Lake 50428. T: (641) 357- 4019

RV ★★★ | Tent n/a

Beauty: ★★★	Site Privacy: ★★
Spaciousness: ★★	Quiet: ★★★★
Security: ★★★★	Cleanliness: ★★★
Insect Control: ★★★	Facilities: ★★

Only a short drive from Clear Lake, Oakwood RV Park is ideal for visitors with large and long RVs. Campsites each have a gravel parking pad, a small lawn (some much larger than others), and many have a concrete patio with a picnic table. The campground offers full hookups with lockable rest room and shower facilities. As a result of an expansion, the two camping areas sit side by side, and the entire park backs up to a large corn field. There is a delightful small white church next door. However, this campground does have some strange regulations, and only accepts campers on reservations. There is no tent camping allowed, with or without an RV. The weather is warm in the summer and the grounds offer little shade. Campers are permitted one tow, and Clear Lake is a wonderful vacation spot to fish and boat.

Basics

Operated By: Bob & Lee Speakar. **Open:** All year. **Site Assignment:** By reservation, all charges are payable in advance. **Registration:** Camp office. **Fee:** $15 per two people, a $2 daily charge for extra people. **Parking:** At site.

Facilities

Number of RV-Only Sites: 68. **Number of Tent-Only Sites:** 0. **Hookups:** Electric (30, 50 amps), water, sewer, phone. **Each Site:** Picnic table, some fire pits. **Dump Station:** Yes. **Laundry:** Yes. **Pay Phone:** Yes. **Rest Rooms and Showers:** Yes. **Fuel:** No. **Propane:** Yes, but delivered on Friday's only. **Internal Roads:** Gravel, in fair condition. **RV Service:** 10.5 mi. in Mason City. **Market:** In Clear Lake. **Restaurant:** In Clear Lake. **General Store:** No. **Vending:** Yes. **Swimming Pool:** No. **Playground:** Yes. **Other:** Some concrete patios, rally room, game room, firewood sold. **Activities:** Games, hiking. **Nearby Attractions:** Fire museum, trolley tours, fishing, boating, golf. **Additional Information:** Clear Lake Chamber of Commerce, (641) 357-2159.

Restrictions

Pets: On leash at all times, no pets over 30 lbs. **Fires:** In fire pits only. **Alcoholic Beverages:** Allowed. **Vehicle Maximum Length:** Will accommodate very large RVs. **Other:** All RVs must be a 1987 model or newer & are subject to managers approval; firearms & firecrackers prohibited; no tent camping.

To Get There

From I-35 take Exit 193 south, merge onto SR 106 (4th Ave. S), go a little more than 1 mi. and turn left onto S. Shore Dr. Veer right, go another 0.5 mi. and turn left on 240th St. Look for campground.

CLERMONT

Skip-A-Way

3825 Harding Rd., Clermont 52135. T: (800) 728-1167; F: (563) 423-5239; www.gocamping.com/skipaway.

RV ★★★★ Tent ★★★

Beauty: ★★	Site Privacy: ★★
Spaciousness: ★★	Quiet: ★★★
Security: ★★★	Cleanliness: ★★★
Insect Control: ★★★	Facilities: ★★★★

With a little imagination and some foresight, Skip and Bev Baker have created a camper's playground at Skip-A-Way Resort. The hosts' aim, to make your stay comfortable and fun, is accomplished by providing a full range of amenities and a number of family and community activities. Enjoy a round of miniature golf, a game of Norwegian horseshoes, or a leisurely float down the Turkey River after an afternoon of fishing on Quarry Lake. Saturday evenings can be spent in the lodge watching a movie with other campers or bouncing through the campground on a wagon ride. Other scheduled events change each year and may include anything from square dancing to eating contests. For a truly unusual experience, spend a night in the rustic 1800s log cabin that is available for rent. With an eye for improvement, the owners continue to upgrade their campground with new landscaping, fresh paint, and added sites, making it increasingly popular. While walk-ins are welcome, it is best to reserve a site early, especially on holiday weekends. Certainly, the highlight of a stay here is the hosts eagerness to help guests have fun.

Basics

Operated By: Skip & Bev Baker. **Open:** May 1–Oct. 15. **Site Assignment:** Reservations taken. **Registration:** Call for reservations, otherwise at lodge. **Fee:** $14–$21. **Parking:** At site.

Facilities

Number of RV-Only Sites: 77. **Number of Tent-Only Sites:** 6. **Hookups:** Electric (20, 30, 50 amps), water, sewer. **Each Site:** None. **Dump Station:** Yes. **Laundry:** Yes. **Pay Phone:** Yes. **Rest Rooms and Showers:** Yes. **Fuel:** No. **Propane:** No. **Internal Roads:** Gravel. **RV Service:** Yes. **Market:** No. **Restaurant:** Yes. **General Store:** Yes. **Vending:** No. **Swimming Pool:** Yes. **Playground:** Yes. **Other:** Lake and river access. **Activities:** Mini golf, fishing (need license on river, but not for lake), swimming, boating, weekend movies. **Nearby Attractions:** 1800s log cabin for rent, Echo Valley Speedway. **Additional Information:** See website.

Restrictions

Pets: On leash. **Fires:** In fire rings only. **Alcoholic Beverages:** Allowed. **Vehicle Maximum Length:** Call for limits.

To Get There

From Hwy. 18, take Exit 3825.The campground is visible from the road.

DAVENPORT

Interstate RV Park

8448 North Fairmont, Davenport 52806. T: (563) 386-7292 or (888) 387-6573; F: (563) 386-7299; www.gocampingamerica.com/interstatervia/; interstatervia@gocampingamerica.com.

RV ★★★ Tent ★★

Beauty: ★★★	Site Privacy: ★★
Spaciousness: ★★	Quiet: ★★★★
Security: ★★★	Cleanliness: ★★★★
Insect Control: ★★★	Facilities: ★★★

Interstate RV Park is conveniently located for anyone wishing to visit the Davenport Metropolitan area. Wthin the city limits, this campground offers a full range of amenities. There are close to 100 sites, 15 of which are considered super sites, with extra parking space and 50-amp service (sites 80–97). The campground offers several activities, a large pool, and a gift shop. Interstate RV Park is next door to restaurants, fuel, and a large water park. Campsite's each have a gravel parking pad and light post, but some are tightly arranged, with little grass or shade. However, the grounds are well maintained. This campground is ideal for visitors wishing to see area attractions. The weather can be very warm in Davenport during the summer, and windy, so skin protection is a good idea. The office is staffed daily to assist campers.

Basics

Operated By: Private operator. **Open:** All year. **Site Assignment:** By reservation, credit card required for deposit. **Registration:** In office or drop box. **Fee:** $20–$25; fee covers 2 people, additional adults are $3 each, children $2. **Parking:** At site.

Facilities

Number of RV-Only Sites: 98. **Number of Tent-Only Sites:** 0. **Hookups:** Electric (20, 30, 50 amps), water, sewer. **Each Site:** Picnic table, light posts. **Dump Station:** Yes. **Laundry:** Yes. **Pay Phone:** Yes. **Rest Rooms and Showers:** Yes. **Fuel:** No, next door. **Propane:** Yes. **Internal Roads:** Gravel, in good condition. **RV Service:** In Davenport. **Market:** In Davenport. **Restaurant:** In walking distance or in Davenport. **General Store:** Yes. **Vending:** Yes. **Swimming Pool:** Yes, open June–Aug. **Playground:** Yes. **Other:** Enclosed group pavilion, dataport. **Activities:** Horseshoes, swimming. **Nearby Attractions:** Quad City Botanical Center, District Rock Island, several malls, President Casino, golf, Family Museum of Art. **Additional Information:** Davenport Chamber of Commerce, (563) 322-1706.

Restrictions

Pets: On leash. **Fires:** In fire pits only. **Alcoholic Beverages:** Allowed. **Vehicle Maximum Length:** None. **Other:** Good Sam honored.

To Get There

I-80 Exit 292, bear right on Northwest Blvd, then turn right onto the ramp and left onto N. Pine Street. Go 1.1 mi., turn right onto W. 49th St., then right on to N. Fairmount.

GUTHRIE

Springbrook State Park

2437 160th Rd., Guthrie Center 50115.T: (641) 747-3591; F: (641)747-3957; www.state.ia.us/parks/springbr.htm; springbrook@dnr.state.ia.us.

★★★★ ▲ ★★★★

Beauty: ★★★ Site Privacy: ★★★★
Spaciousness: ★★★★ Quiet: ★★★★
Security: ★★★★ Cleanliness: ★★★
Insect Control: ★★★ Facilities: ★★

If you're a serious outdoorsman, this park will suit your needs well. Operated by the Iowa Department of Natural Resources, it is open all year and is well maintained. The sites for both RVs and tents are very nice, being spacious, private, and quiet. Some of the RV sites have electric and water hookups, and all of the sites are equipped with a picnic table and grated fire pit. Activities within the park include fishing, boating, and hiking. There is also swimming, biking, water skiing and wind surfing in the summer. Nearby, visitors will find a golf course and river fishing. Reservations are not required.

Basics

Operated By: Iowa Department of Natural Resources. **Open:** All year. **Site Assignment:** First come, first served. **Registration:** Self-registration at entrance gate. **Fee:** $9-19 depending on site & hookups. **Parking:** At site.

Facilities

Number of RV-Only Sites: 81. **Number of Tent-Only Sites:** 0. **Number of Multipurpose Sites:** 40. **Hookups:** Electric (20, 30 amps), water. **Each Site:** Picnic table, grated fire pits. **Dump Station:** Yes. **Laundry:** No. **Pay Phone:** Yes. **Rest Rooms and Showers:** Yes. **Fuel:** In town. **Propane:** In town. **Internal Roads:** Paved, in good condition. **RV Service:** In Des Moines. **Market:** In Guthrie. **Restaurant:** There are several in the area. **General Store:** No. **Vending:** No. **Swimming Pool:** No, but there is a lake front beach. **Playground:** Yes. **Other:** 6 cabins, enclosed picnic shelters, boat ramps, boat rentals, beach, fishing dock, large group camp w/ kitchen, dinning hall, & meeting rooms. **Activities:** Fishing (walleye, muskie, yellow bass), boating, jet skiing, water skiing, wind surfing, swimming,miles of trails, in-line skating, hiking, biking in the summer. Part of The Central Iowa State Park Bike Route. **Nearby Attractions:** River fishing, golf. **Additional Information:** Panora Chamber of Commerce, (641) 755-3300.

Restrictions

Pets: Dogs on leash. **Fires:** In fire rings only. **Alcoholic Beverages:** Beer & wine only in sites. **Vehi-**

cle Maximum Length: None. **Other:** No metal detectors in campground; max of 6 people to a site.

To Get There

From I-80 Exit 86 go north on SR 25 for about 20 mi.(you will go through Guthrie Center) and east on SR 384 about 3 mi. into park.

IOWA CITY

Colony Country Campground

1275 Forever green Rd., Iowa City 52240.T: (319) 626-2221; www.gocampingamerica.com/colonycountry.

RV ★★★★ Tent ★★★

Beauty: ★★★★ Site Privacy: ★★★
Spaciousness: ★★★ Quiet: ★★★★
Security: ★★★ Cleanliness: ★★★★
Insect Control: ★★★ Facilities: ★★

This family owned campground is centrally located to many east Iowa points of interest such as the Hoover Historical Site and the Amana Colonies. The staff is friendly and more than willing to provide helpful tips on which attractions are worth visiting. The grounds are well kept, with meticulously groomed gravel roads and flowered grassy plots throughout. Most sites are tight and may be difficult to maneuver for oversized rigs. Many sites provide both privacy and shade. With plenty of activities on site such as basketball, volleyball, and horseshoes, leisure time at Colony Country is relaxing and plentiful.

Basics

Operated By: Private Operator. **Open:** Apr.–Nov 30. **Site Assignment:** By reservations or first available. **Registration:** In camp store. **Fee:** Tent $15, RV $22 per 4 people. **Parking:** At site.

Facilities

Number of RV-Only Sites: 29. **Number of Tent-Only Sites:** 20. **Hookups:** Electric (20, 30, 50 amps), water, sewer. **Each Site:** Picnic table. **Dump Station:** Yes. **Laundry:** Yes. **Pay Phone:** Yes. **Rest Rooms and Showers:** Yes. **Fuel:** No. **Propane:** No. **Internal Roads:** Gravel, in good condition. **RV Service:** In town. **Market:** In town. **Restaurant:** There are many restaurants in town. **General Store:** Yes. **Vending:** Store only. **Swimming Pool:** Yes, w/ hot tub & sauna. **Playground:** Yes. **Other:** Cabins, hot tub, sauna, snack bar, central Internet data port. **Activities:** Basketball, volleyball, playground. **Nearby Attractions:** Hoover Historic Site, Amana Colonies, Kalona & Iowa City/Coralville area. **Additional Information:** Iowa City Chamber of Commerce, (319) 337-9637.

Restrictions

Pets: On leash. **Fires:** Grills only. **Alcoholic Beverages:** Allowed. **Vehicle Maximum Length:** Big rigs welcome.

To Get There

I-15 Exit 119 E. Go 0.1 mi. to Lindsay.

JOHNSTON

Saylorville Lake

5600 NorthWest 78th Ave., Johnston 50131.T: (515) 276-4656 or (515) 964-0672 or Daily Lake Info (515) 276-0433; www.mvr.usace.army.mil/saylor/index.htm;jerry.l.demarce@usace.army.mil (project manager).

RV ★★★★ Tent ★★★★

Beauty: ★★★★ Site Privacy: ★★★★
Spaciousness: ★★★★ Quiet: ★★★★
Security: ★★★ Cleanliness: ★★★
Insect Control: ★★★ Facilities: ★★★

Approximately, ten miles north of Des Moines is the US Army Corp of Engineers Saylorville Lake Project. This 5950 acre area is a wonderful recreation haven for outdoor enthusiast. It features five campgrounds with over 500 camping sites. Camping sites have level paved parking pads and there is a variety of amenities including full hook ups on some sites. Modern rest rooms and showers can be found in all the camping areas. There are over 25 miles of biking trails, in addition to hiking and cross country ski trails. Boating and fishing are amongst the favorite activities with the project offering a full service marina, repair, and fuel. There is a year round visitor center and camping reservations are recommended. The area is a combination of woodland and prairie, and all the campsites are well groomed. There is a registration gate at the entrance to each camping area staffed by seasonal volunteers or corp employees.

Basics

Operated By: US Army Corps of Engineers. **Open:** The park is open year round, the campgrounds are open May–Sept. **Site Assignment:** The park is 60% reservable, the remainder are first come first served. Call the National Recreation reservation service toll free (877) 444-6777. **Registration:** At the entrance gate, or the registration kiosk. **Fee:** Camp fees range between $12 & $24 based on day of the week & amenities. **Parking:** At site.

Facilities

Number of Multipurpose Sites: over 100 in each campground, 558 total. **Hookups:** Electric (20, 30, 50 amps), water, sewer. **Each Site:** Picnic table, paved trailer pad, fire pit. **Dump Station:** Yes. **Laundry:** No. **Pay Phone:** Yes. **Rest Rooms and Showers:** Yes. **Fuel:** No. **Propane:** No. **Internal Roads:** Paved, in good condition. **RV Service:** In Des Moines. **Market:** In Des Moines. **Restaurant:** In Des Moines. **General Store:** Yes. **Vending:** Yes. **Swimming Pool:** No, but there are two beaches. **Playground:** Yes. **Other:** Two beaches, three boat ramps, picnic shelters, scheduled activities. **Activities:** Softball, bike trails, hiking trails, fishing, volleyball, horseshoes, swimming, boating, waterskiing, jet skiing, playground, horse trails, golf, winter recreation, scheduled activities, & nature program. **Nearby Attractions:** state capital, Historical Museum, botanical center, Des Moines zoo, Des Moines Science Center. **Additional Information:** West Des Moines Chamber of Commerce, (515) 225-6009.

Restrictions

Pets: On leash only (6 ft. maximum). **Fires:** In approved places only. **Alcoholic Beverages:** Yes, w/ discretion. **Vehicle Maximum Length:** 45 ft. **Other:** 50% discount w/ Golden Age or Golden Access passport.

To Get There

From I-35 Exit 96 go west on NE 126th Ave. for 7.2 mi., then turn left on NW Sheldahl Dr. go half mi. and continue south on N. 3rd St., 1 mi. later turn right on SR 415 go about 5 mi. and follow the signs to the area of the park you wish to visit or to the visitors center.

KELLOGG

Kellogg RV Park

1570 Hwy. 224 South, P.O. Box 380, Kellogg 50135. T: (641) 526-8535; F: (641)526-8060.

RV: ★★★ Tent: n/a

Beauty: ★★★	Site Privacy: ★★★
Spaciousness: ★★★	Quiet: ★★★
Security: ★★★	Cleanliness: ★★★
Insect Control: ★★★	Facilities: ★★★

Directly off I-80 halfway between Grinnell and Newtown, is the Kellogg Campground. Set in the backdrop of a small service station and adjacent to a large crop of corn, this small campground gives you the feeling of home. The campsites are arranged in a loop with a few in the center. All the campsites are large, level, and have gravel parking pads. Shaded by large, mature maple trees, most of the sites are pull-throughs and come with a barbeque grill. The lawn is plush and well kept, and the area is clean. The rest rooms and showers are located in the mini-mart (the Kellduff 5 and 10), and all campground patrons receive a $.10 per gallon discount on fuel. The campground is simple, warm, and a nice place to relax from a long day's drive. There is a small cafe in the mini-mart as well as basic supplies. The weather varies from season to season, but sun and bug protection are always a good idea.

Basics

Operated By: Richard Wenndt. **Open:** All year. **Site Assignment:** First come, first served. **Registration:** Inside the mini-mart. **Fee:** $11. **Parking:** At site.

Facilities

Number of RV-Only Sites: 23. **Number of Tent-Only Sites:** 0. **Hookups:** Electric (20, 30, 50 amps), water. **Each Site:** Picnic table, grill, light post. **Dump Station:** Yes. **Laundry:** No. **Pay Phone:** Yes. **Rest Rooms and Showers:** Yes. **Fuel:** Yes. **Propane:** Yes. **Internal Roads:** Gravel, in good condition. **RV Service:** 21 mi. in Marshalltown. **Market:** 8 mi. in either Grinnell or Newtown. **Restaurant:** On site or in Grinnell or Newton. **General Store:** Yes. **Vending:** At the mini-mart on property. **Swimming Pool:** No. **Playground:** Yes. **Activities:** Playground, walking, bicycling. **Nearby Attractions:** Inquire at campground. **Additional Information:** Grinnel Chamber of Commerce, (641) 236-6555, or Marshaltown Chamber of Commerce, (641) 792-5545.

Restrictions

Pets: On leash. **Fires:** Grills only. **Alcoholic Beverages:** Allowed. **Vehicle Maximum Length:** None.

To Get There

From I-80, take Exit 173 and go north on SR 224 about 0.2 mi. to the Kellduff 5 and 10.

ONAWA
Lewis and Clark State Park

21914 Park Loop, Onawa 51040. T: (712) 423-2829; F: 712-423-2829; www.state.ia.us/parks/lewisclk.htm; lewis_&_clark@dnr.state.ia.us.

RV ★★★ Tent ★★★

Beauty: ★★★ Site Privacy: ★★★
Spaciousness: ★★★ Quiet: ★★★
Security: ★★★ Cleanliness: ★★★
Insect Control: ★★★ Facilities: ★★★

Located in an "ox bow" on the Blue Lake, Lewis and Clark State Park is a delightful place to relax and enjoy a small piece of American history. In August of 1804, Lewis and Clark explored this area, making note of its natural beauty. The park features 81 camping sites, all with electrical hookups, along the lakeshore. Most sites have level parking pads and are back-ins, though there are some pull-throughs. The foliage is splendid in the spring, and the wind off the lake is crisp. The park, officially part of the Lewis and Clark National Trail, celebrates the Lewis and Clark festival around the second weekend in June, so call in advance for details and schedules. There are numerous activities available, including self-guided nature trails and a large lodge that's great for family gatherings. The park is well staffed and maintained. Winds in the area can be strong, so be prepared.

Basics

Operated By: Iowa Department of Natural Resources. **Open:** All year. **Site Assignment:** First come, first served. **Registration:** Self registration at kiosks. **Fee:** $16 hookups, $12 no hookups. **Parking:** At site.

Facilities

Number of Multipurpose Sites: 81. **Hookups:** Electric (20, 30 amps), water. **Each Site:** Picnic table, fire pit, trailer pad. **Dump Station:** Yes. **Laundry:** No. **Pay Phone:** Yes. **Rest Rooms and Showers:** Yes. **Fuel:** No. **Propane:** No. **Internal Roads:** Paved, in good condition. **RV Service:** 33 mi. northwest in South Sioux City. **Market:** In Onawa. **Restaurant:** In Onawa. **General Store:** No. **Vending:** Yes. **Swimming Pool:** No. **Playground:** Yes. **Other:** Beach, boat ramp, covered picnic tables, historic site. **Activities:** Fishing, hiking, biking, horseshoes, swimming, water activities, hunting. **Nearby Attractions:** The Kiwanis Railroad Depot Museum Complex, The Monona County Historical Museum, Lewis & Clark Festival. **Additional Information:** Onawa Chamber of Commerce, (712) 423-1801.

Restrictions

Pets: On leash. **Fires:** Yes in fire pits only. **Alcoholic Beverages:** Allowed. **Vehicle Maximum Length:** 45 ft.

To Get There

From I-29, take Exit 112 and go west on SR 175. Turn right on SR 324 and continue to the park.

ONAWA
Onawa/Blue Lake KOA

21788 Dogwood Ave., Onawa 51040. T: (712) 423-1633; F: 712-423-2494; www.koa.com; kampkoa@willinet.net.

RV ★★★★ Tent ★★★★

Beauty: ★★★★ Site Privacy: ★★★★
Spaciousness: ★★★★ Quiet: ★★★★
Security: ★★★★ Cleanliness: ★★★★
Insect Control: ★★★★ Facilities: ★★★★

Set in a rural area in the heart of the Loess Hills in western Iowa is the Onawa/Blue Lake KOA. This campground is situated on a 250-acre lake with excellent bass fishing and water-skiing. The campground offers large pull-through sites under a canopy of large oaks and other mature deciduous trees. It provides a full array of amenities and activities such as boating and swimming. The campground takes part in Lewis and Clark Festival activities in June, and there are fireworks over the lake on the 4th of July. The KOA is conveniently located near a public golf course, a Museum complex, and one of the most beautiful scenic byways in the country. The campground is well kept, and the service is friendly and helpful. It can be very windy, so don't forget your skin protection.

Basics

Operated By: Brian & Cherry Dye. **Open:** Apr.–Oct. 15. **Site Assignment:** By reservation, credit card required. **Registration:** In camp store. **Fee:** Tent $17, RV $21–$25; fees cover 2 people, $2 per additional guest, children under 5 free. **Parking:** At site.

Facilities

Number of RV-Only Sites: 54. **Number of Tent-Only Sites:** 11. **Hookups:** Electric (20, 30,

50 amps), water, sewer. **Each Site:** Picnic table, grated fire pits. **Dump Station:** Yes. **Laundry:** Yes. **Pay Phone:** Yes. **Rest Rooms and Showers:** Yes. **Fuel:** No. **Propane:** Yes. **Internal Roads:** Gravel. **RV Service:** 32 mi. in Sioux City. **Market:** In Onawa. **Restaurant:** In Onawa. **General Store:** Yes. **Vending:** No. **Swimming Pool:** Yes. **Playground:** Yes. **Other:** Cabins, fishing docks, boat rentals. **Activities:** Fishing, swimming, horseshoes, rowboating, paddleboating, basketball, volleyball. **Nearby Attractions:** Onawa Aquatic Center Monona County Historical Complex/Depot Museum, Monona County Arboretum, Loess Hills. **Additional Information:** Onawa Chamber of Commerce, (712) 423-1801.

Restrictions

Pets: On leash. **Fires:** In fire pits only. **Alcoholic Beverages:** Allowed. **Vehicle Maximum Length:** None. **Other:** 30-day limit.

To Get There

From I-29 Exit 112, merge west onto SR 175 and go about 1 mi. Turn left on to Dogwood Ave. and continue 1 mi.

ROCKFORD

George Wyatt Park

1st. Northwest, Rockford 50468. T: (641) 756-3618; www.netins.net/ricweb/community/rockford/rockford.htm.

RV ★★★ Tent ★★★

Beauty: ★★★	Site Privacy: ★★★
Spaciousness: ★★★	Quiet: ★★★★
Security: ★★★	Cleanliness: ★★★
Insect Control: ★★	Facilities: ★★★

George Wyatt Park, not to be confused with George Wyatt State Park, is a delightful small city park in the town of Rockford. This charming little park is located on the Shell Rock River at the edge of town. The campground is simple, with grass sites and mature trees, and overlooks the river. The park offers a small boat ramp for non-motorized boats and a lovely picnic area. There are also clean rest room facilities and warm showers. The price is great, and the town is full of charm and history. The area is known for its fossil beds, and there is a public pool and golf course in town. This is a wonderful hide away and a great value. The Rockford Fire Department is right next door, and although the city maintains the park, you could not ask for better security or nicer people.

Basics

Operated By: City of Rockford, Denny Ginther Manager. **Open:** Year round, weather permitting. **Site Assignment:** First come, first served. **Registration:** Self registration. **Fee:** $7. no hookups, $8 electric. **Parking:** At site.

Facilities

Number of RV-Only Sites: 8. **Number of Tent-Only Sites:** 0. **Number of Multipurpose Sites:** 16. **Hookups:** Electric (20, 30, 50 amps), water. **Each Site:** Some picnic tables. **Dump Station:** Yes. **Laundry:** No. **Pay Phone:** No. **Rest Rooms and Showers:** Yes. **Fuel:** No. **Propane:** No. **Internal Roads:** Paved & gravel. **RV Service:** 26 mi. away in Hanlontown. **Market:** In Rockford. **Restaurant:** In Rockford. **General Store:** No. **Vending:** No. **Swimming Pool:** No, but there is a public pool in town. **Playground:** Yes. **Other:** Small boat ramp, picnic area, river access. **Activities:** Fishing, hiking, biking. **Nearby Attractions:** The Rockford Fossil Beds, Rockfort Public Pool, golf, Iowa Trolley Park, Aladdin's Castle. **Additional Information:** Charles City Chamber of Commerce, (641) 228-4234.

Restrictions

Pets: On leash. **Fires:** In approved areas only. **Alcoholic Beverages:** Allowed. **Vehicle Maximum Length:** None.

To Get There

From Madison City on US 65, go east 9 mi. to US 18, then south on CR-S70 for another 5 mi. Follow the signs to the city park.

SPIRIT LAKE

Cenla RV Park

3400 US Hwy. 71, Spirit Lake 51360. T: (712) 336-2925; www.smithsrv.com.

RV ★★★ Tent ★★★

Beauty: ★★★	Site Privacy: ★★
Spaciousness: ★★	Quiet: ★★★
Security: ★★★	Cleanliness: ★★★
Insect Control: ★★★	Facilities: ★★★

Situated in the center of Iowa's lake region, Cenla RV Park is perfect for lake enthusiasts. The campground itself backs up to Center Lake, and there are five other lakes in very close proximity. Cenla RV Park has more than 100 RV sites with excellent amenities, activities, and a separate tenting cul-de-sac. The campground is laid out in a series of rows with both back-in and pull-through sites. Each site has a gravel parking pad, and several of the sites offer cable television from May through September. The campground features both shaded and open areas, as well as the lakeshore and two fishing docks. The Spirit Lake area is home to several lake beaches, fishing outfitters, boat rentals, and golf courses.

Basics

Operated By: Private operator. **Open:** Apr.–Oct. **Site Assignment:** By reservation, $25 deposits. **Registration:** In camp office. **Fee:** Tent $17.50, RV $21.50–$24.50. **Parking:** At site.

Facilities

Number of RV-Only Sites: 120. **Number of Tent-Only Sites:** 5. **Hookups:** Electric (30, 50 amps), water, sewer, cable. **Each Site:** Picnic tables, w/ some fire pits. **Dump Station:** Yes. **Laundry:** Yes. **Pay Phone:** Yes. **Rest Rooms and Showers:** Yes. **Fuel:** No. **Propane:** No. **Internal Roads:** Gravel & dirt. **RV Service:** 28 mi. in Worthington, MN. **Market:** In Spirit Lake. **Restaurant:** In Spirit Lake. **General Store:** Yes. **Vending:** Yes. **Swimming Pool:** Yes. **Playground:** Yes. **Other:** Game room, fish cleaning station. **Activities:** Volleyball, swimming, games. **Nearby Attractions:** Spirit Lake Fish Hatchery, The Ranch Amusement Park, Marble Beach State Park. **Additional Information:** Spirit Lake Chamber of Commerce, (712) 336-4978.

Restrictions

Pets: On leash. **Fires:** In fire pits only. **Alcoholic Beverages:** Allowed. **Vehicle Maximum Length:** None. **Other:** Good Sam honored.

To Get There

From I-90 Exit 73 in Jackson, Minnesota, go south on US Hwy. 71. The campground will be about 25 mi. directly off US Hwy. 71 in Spirit Lake, Iowa.

WATERLOO

George Wyth State Park

3659 Wyth Rd., Waterloo 50703. T: (319) 232-5505; F: (319) 232-1508; www.state.ia.us/parks; george_wyth@dnr.state.ia.us.

RV ★★★ Tent ★★★

Beauty: ★★★	Site Privacy: ★★
Spaciousness: ★★	Quiet: ★★★
Security: ★★★★	Cleanliness: ★★★
Insect Control: ★★★	Facilities: ★★

If you love water, biking, or fishing, then George Wyth State Park is a perfect spot to camp. The park is unique, because it offers patrons extraordinary water access. The campground is surrounded by the Cedar River to the south and George Wyth Lake to the northeast. There are wonderful sites right on the waters edge offering level trailer pads. Most sites are back-in sites, but there are a limited number of pull-through sites. There is a wonderful public beach area with concessions and boat rentals. The park offers a variety of multipurpose trails, which includes part of a lake-to-lake bike route that covers over 50 miles and links to Pine Lake. The campground offers self registration, and fees can be paid at the site. However, the park is staffed around the clock and someone is always there to assist. The park offers a broad spectrum of activities from swimming in the summer to cross-country skiing in the winter.

Basics

Operated By: Iowa Department of Natural Resources. **Open:** All year. **Site Assignment:** First come, first served. **Registration:** Self-registration at entrance gate. **Fee:** $16 hookups, $11 no hookups. **Parking:** At site.

Facilities

Number of Multipurpose Sites: 58. **Hookups:** Electric (20, 30 amps), water. **Each Site:** Picnic table, grated fire pits. **Dump Station:** Yes. **Laundry:** No. **Pay Phone:** Yes. **Rest Rooms and Showers:** Yes. **Fuel:** At Marina. **Propane:** At Marina. **Internal Roads:** Paved, in good condition. **RV Service:** In Waterloo. **Market:** In Waterloo. **Restaurant:** In Waterloo. **General Store:** No, but there is a concession stand at the beach. **Vending:** No. **Swimming Pool:** No. **Playground:** Yes. **Other:** Lodge w/ kitchen & rustic fireplace, enclosed picnic shelters, boat ramps, boat rentals, concession stand, beach, fish pier, 4 lakes & the Cedar River, 5.5 mi. of paved muti-purpose trails linked to a 45 mi. trail network. **Activities:** Fishing, boating, jet skiing, water skiing, wind surfing, swimming, in-line skating hiking, biking,cross-country skiing, snowmobiling, & ice sailing. **Nearby Attractions:** Lake-to-Lake State Park Bike Route (bike rentals), Grout Museum of History & Science, Ice House Museum, John Deere Tours. **Additional Information:** Waterloo Chamber of Commerce, (319) 233-8431.

Restrictions

Pets: Dogs on leash only, see web site for rules on horses & mules. **Fires:** In fire rings only. **Alcoholic Beverages:** At sites, beer & wine only. **Vehicle Maximum Length:** None. **Other:** No metal detectors in campground, max. 6 people to a site.

To Get There

From Waterloo, go west on US 218 (W. Washington St.), take the Broadway St. Exit, turn left onto Broadway St., and go 0.3 mi. to the park entrance.

WEST DES MOINES

Timberland Campground

3165 Ashworth Rd., Waukee 50263. T: (515) 987-1714; F: (515) 987-3455; www.timberlineiowa.com; timberr@aol.com.

RV ★★★ Tent ★★★

Beauty: ★★★	Site Privacy: ★★★
Spaciousness: ★★★	Quiet: ★★★
Security: ★★★	Cleanliness: ★★★
Insect Control: ★★★	Facilities: ★★★

Timberline Campground is a comfortable and relaxing get-away, conveniently located on the outskirts of Des Moines, less than two miles from I-80. It offers over 40 acres of scenic woodland, with mature shade trees and nature trails full of different wildlife. The campground provides a large selection of amenities, including a RV wash barn and an ice cream shop. There is a large pool, a full playground, and a rec room with games. The campsites are a nice size, most being fairly level pull-throughs. The campground has many nearby attractions, such as the botanical center, the Blank Park Zoo, and the bridges of Madison County. The weather can be windy, and you will most likely need sunscreen. The staff is kind, and there is a family-friendly atmosphere. All visitors must register in the office, and security is tight.

Basics

Operated By: Dick & Deborah Christensen. **Open:** Apr.–Nov. **Site Assignment:** By reservation, credit card & first night deposit required. **Registration:** In general store. **Fee:** Tent $16.80, RV $21–$24. **Parking:** At site.

Facilities

Number of RV-Only Sites: 100. **Number of Tent-Only Sites:** 16. **Hookups:** Electric (20, 30, 50 amps), water, sewer, phone. **Each Site:** Picnic table. **Dump Station:** Yes. **Laundry:** Yes. **Pay Phone:** No. **Rest Rooms and Showers:** Yes. **Fuel:** No. **Propane:** Yes. **Internal Roads:** Gravel, in good condition. **RV Service:** In Des Moines. **Market:** In Des Moines. **Restaurant:** In Des Moines. **General Store:** Yes. **Vending:** Yes. **Swimming Pool:** Yes. **Playground:** Yes. **Other:** Three camping cabins, pavilion, RV wash, game room. **Activities:** Swimming, playground, horseshoes, basketball. **Nearby Attractions:** State capital & historical museum, botanical center, art center, Des Moines zoo, Sugar Creek golf course. **Additional Information:** West Des Moines Chamber of Commerce, (515) 225-6009.

Restrictions

Pets: On leash (no large, aggressive breeds). **Fires:** Fire pits only. **Alcoholic Beverages:** Allowed. **Vehicle Maximum Length:** 45 ft. (the larger your RV the earlier you should make reservations).

To Get There

from I-80 Exit 117, go 1 mi. north and 0.5 mi. east; there are signs to follow.

Montana

As with much of the US, Montana was first inhabited by Native Americans, including the Arapaho, Assiniboine, and Cheyenne, among others. French trappers made inroads into the land as early as 1740, followed some years later by the Lewis and Clark Expedition in 1805.

Most of what is now Montana was turned over to the United States in the Louisiana Purchase of 1803. The Jesuits and various trading companies attempted to form permanent settlements here, but not until gold was discovered in the 1860s did great numbers of people begin to settle in the area. The wide open land in the eastern parts of the state drew another type of pioneer who helped settle the land—the cattle farmer.

The settling of Montana did not go easy. Native Americans did not give up their land willingly; pioneers appropriating Native American land were under constant threat of raids, which did not abate until the Wounded Knee Massacre in 1890. Settlers then caused their own strife, as rancher fought rancher during the infamous range wars in the late 1800s.

In the twentieth century, drilling for oil joined mining as a major source of revenue for the state, but enough people also recognized the need to preserve natural resources. In addition to Glacier National Park, many state parks and historic sites were created to preserve Montana's natural and cultural heritage.

Montana is comprised of six different regions, each with a distinct history and recreational offerings. The most western region, **Glacier Country,** is home to **Glacier National Park,** the **Flathead Indian Reservation,** and the town of Missoula, seen by many as the cultural, retail, and medical hub of western Montana. Home of the **University of Montana,** Missoula is the gateway to the Flathead and Bitterroot valleys. Numerous festivals are held in this region, including the famous **Testicle Festival,** an off-kilter culinary homage to mountain oysters (i.e. bulls bullocks).

The adjacent **Gold Country** is similar in geography to Glacier Country. The many mountains and valleys create a beautiful landscape, and numerous recreational possibilities abound, from hiking the **Continental Divide Trail** to skiing down spectacular slopes. The two largest towns in this region, Butte and Helena (Big Sky's capital), originated as mining towns. Many attractions in this area still reflect that heritage, including **Butte's World Museum of Mining** where visitors can see an authentic reproduction of an 1890s mining camp and can visit the numerous ghost towns around Helena.

To the west of Gold Country is Montana's most famous region, **Yellowstone Country**. While over 4 million people visit the nation's first national park each year, few venture north of the park, much to their loss. Those who do will find Bozeman. Located in the

Gallatin valley, this city is a significant agricultural center as well as home to the largest university in Montana's system. Several annual festivals enliven this college town, including the **Montana Winter Fair** and the **Sweet Pea Festival.** The region also hosts two key ski resorts—**Bridger Bowl** and **Big Sky.**

For those interested in raft trips, **Russell Country** is the place to visit. Rivers of all difficulty are paddled here, including the Madison, Gallatin, Yellowstone and the river that carried Lewis and Clark across the state, the Missouri. Lewis and Clark's progress west was stymied at the "great falls" along the Missouri, site now of Montana's third largest city. **Great Falls** is known as the Electric City for its many hydroelectric dams. While here, visitors can swing by the **Lewis and Clark National Historic Trail Interpretive Center** or by **Malmstrom Air Force Base,** location of the nation's first Minuteman Missile Complex.

Much of Lewis and Clark's journey through Montana passed through the Missouri River Country. This region is home to **Fort Belknap** and **Fort Peck Indian Reservations** as well as the 1.1 million-acre **Charles M. Russell National Wildlife Refuge.** Also known as the Montana Badlands, this area was once a lush wetland where dinosaurs roamed, but now provides a wealth of fossils from the dry landscape.

Located in the southeastern part of the state, **Custer Country** is probably most famous for one of the worst US military defeats. The Battle of Little Bighorn, sometimes referred to as Custer's Last Stand, took place not far from present day **Billings**. While other towns arose (and died) because of mining, Billings' existence is due to the railroad. Today it is a major shipping point for cattle and other agricultural products as well as home of **Montana State University-Billings.** Cultural offerings include the **Yellowstone Art Museum** and the **Western Heritage Museum.**

The following facilities accept payment in checks or cash only:

Canyon RV & Campground, Hungry Horse

Glacier National Park, West Glacier

Shady Grove RV Park & Campground, Cut Bank

Campground Profiles

ALDER

Alder/Virginia City KOA

P.O. Box 103, Alder 59710. T: (406) 842-5677 or (800) 562-1898; F: (406) 842-5564; www.koa.com; twernt@3rivers.net.

RV ★★★ Tent ★★★

Beauty: ★★★ Site Privacy: ★★★
Spaciousness: ★★★ Quiet: ★★★★
Security: ★★★★ Cleanliness: ★★★
Insect Control: ★★★ Facilities: ★★★

Over one hundred years ago, people visited this valley for one reason—gold. Not far from this KOA campground, Alder Gulch was one of the largest producers of gold in Montana. Modern-day visitors can still pan for gold or search for semi-precious stones while using this campground as a base. This campground is small, with 32 RV sites (hookups include electric, water, sewer, and some phones) and 18 tent-only sites. The sites are all grass. A daily pancake breakfast and ice cream social are available, and Sundays are steak nights. Several accessible rivers means outstanding fishing, and the campground is located in the heart of elk country—good news for hunters. Those leaning more toward history may want to visit nearby Virginia and Nevada City. Visitors can wander through an historic log-cabin village, or take an "historic" stage coach or steam engine ride through the landscape. Several festivals and gatherings occur locally, including Gold Rush Fever Days and the Cowboy & Indian Western Antique & Collectible Trade Show, so reservations are recommended far in advance.

BASICS

Operated By: Ed & Andy. **Open:** All year. **Site Assignment:** Reservations (800) 562-1898. **Registration:** In general store. **Fee:** Tent $20, RV $23–$28. **Parking:** At site.

FACILITIES

Number of RV-Only Sites: 32. **Number of Tent-Only Sites:** 18. **Hookups:** Electric (20, 30 amps), water, sewer, phone. **Each Site:** Picnic tables, grated fire pits. **Dump Station:** Yes. **Laundry:** Yes. **Pay Phone:** Yes. **Rest Rooms and Showers:** Yes. **Fuel:** Yes. **Propane:** Yes. **Internal Roads:** Gravel. **RV Service:** Sheridan. **Market:** Sheridan. **Restaurant:** Sheridan. **General Store:** Yes. **Vending:** In store only. **Swimming Pool:** No. **Playground:** Yes. **Other:** 1 cabin. **Activities:** Fishing (rainbow & brown trout), volleyball, horseshoes, hiking, rock hunting. **Nearby Attractions:** 9 mi. west of Virginia City, Nevada City, Museums, gold panning, tours. **Additional Information:** Virginia City Chamber of Commerce, (800) 829-2969.

RESTRICTIONS

Pets: On leash. **Fires:** Fire pits only. **Alcoholic Beverages:** Yes. **Vehicle Maximum Length:** None.

TO GET THERE

Located 0.25 mi. east of Alder on Hwy. 287.

BELT

Fort Ponderosa Family Campground and RV Park

568 Armington Rd., Belt 59412. T: (406) 277-3232; F: (406) 277-3309; shilo@3rivers.net.

RV ★★★★ Tent ★★★

Beauty: ★★★★	Site Privacy: ★★★
Spaciousness: ★★★	Quiet: ★★★★
Security: ★★★★	Cleanliness: ★★★★
Insect Control: ★★★★	Facilities: ★★★★

Fort Ponderosa Family Campground and RV Park is conveniently located directly off I-90 in Belt. The campground is situated on seven acres, with large shade trees and a blue ribbon trout stream. The campsites are level, gravel, and offered in both pull-through and back-in. The grass is green and well kept. In addition to the campsites, there are several mobile homes as well as the owner's home. Facilities include a large playground, pavilion, five-hole golf coarse, and room for children to play and ride bicycles. While it is well used, the campground is nice and peaceful. The community of Belt is a short drive from Great Falls, and there are a variety of outdoor activities in the area. Summer days are warm, the evenings cool, and the owner offers delightful conversation.

BASICS

Operated By: Jack Wiederrick. **Open:** May 1–Dec. 1. **Site Assignment:** By reservation. **Registration:** In camp office. **Fee:** Tent $16.75, RV $19–$25. **Parking:** At site.

FACILITIES

Number of RV-Only Sites: 45. **Number of Tent-Only Sites:** 20. **Hookups:** Electric (30 amps), water, sewer. **Each Site:** Picnic table. **Dump Station:** Yes. **Laundry:** Yes. **Pay Phone:** Yes. **Rest Rooms and Showers:** Yes. **Fuel:** No. **Propane:** Yes. **Internal Roads:** Gravel, in good condition. **RV Service:** 20 mi. west in Great Falls. **Market:** 2 mi. in town. **Restaurant:** 2 mi. in town. **General Store:** Yes w/ gift shop. **Vending:** Just the store. **Swimming Pool:** No. **Playground:** Yes. **Other:** 2 covered pavilions, 1 w/ BBQ, gift shop. **Activities:** Mini golf, swimming in Belt Creek, fishing (German, brown, & rainbow trout). **Nearby Attractions:** More fly fishing, fishing guide services, float trips, horseback riding, Smith River, Fort Benton, Great Falls, Sluice Box hiking Area, Clark National Forest, Memorial Falls. **Additional Information:** Great Falls Chamber of Commerce, (406) 761-4434.

RESTRICTIONS

Pets: On leash. **Fires:** In fire rings only. **Alcoholic Beverages:** Yes. **Vehicle Maximum Length:** None.

TO GET THERE

20 mi. southeast on Hwys. 87/89 (Armington Jct.) then 1 mi. north (follow signs).

BILLINGS

Yellowstone River RV Park & Campground

309 Garden Ave., Billings 59101. T: (406) 259-0878 or (800) 654-0878; F: (406) 248-1416; yellowstoneriver@hotmail.com.

RV ★★★★ Tent ★★★

Beauty: ★★★★ Site Privacy: ★★★★
Spaciousness: ★★★★ Quiet: ★★★★
Security: ★★★★ Cleanliness: ★★★★
Insect Control: ★★★ Facilities: ★★★

Often called the "Magic City," Billings is where the rustic adventure of the Wild West and the conveniences of a modern city converge. The town provides a number of activities for the passing traveler. The city is surrounded by six mountain ranges and offers a fine view of Montana scenery. Located on the Yellowstone River, this campground is beautifully landscaped, and all sites are arranged in rows and most are shaded. Sites are spacious, and the RV sites are separated from the tent sites but with little distinction. The nice lawn, clean surroundings, and quiet stillness contribute to a pleasing experience. River access and a nature trail compliment the campground, and amenities make this a more than comfortable stay. A large on-site antique display is a unique addition for avid collectors and curious visitors. Be sure to visit historical area attractions to give yourself a taste of the area's rich past.

BASICS

Operated By: Doug & Judy Barnes. **Open:** Apr.–Oct. **Site Assignment:** Reservations recommended. **Registration:** In general store. **Fee:** Tent $23.88, RV $29.08–$32.20 per 2 people, extra person $4. **Parking:** At site.

FACILITIES

Number of RV-Only Sites: 85. **Number of Tent-Only Sites:** 21. **Hookups:** Electric (20, 30, 50 amps), water, sewer. **Each Site:** Picnic table. **Dump Station:** Yes. **Laundry:** Yes. **Pay Phone:** Yes. **Rest Rooms and Showers:** Yes. **Fuel:** Less than 1 mi. **Propane:** Less than 1 mi. **Internal Roads:** Gravel. **RV Service:** Local service. **Market:** Locally. **Restaurant:** Several possibilities in Billings. **General Store:** Yes. **Vending:** General store only. **Swimming Pool:** No. **Playground:** Yes. **Other:** Arcade, gift shop, river access, Internet data port, recreation area. **Activities:** Nature walk, fishing, horseshoes. **Nearby Attractions:** Little Bighorn Battlefield National Monument, Pompeys Pillar National Historic Landmark, Beartooth Mountain Pass/Red Lodge, Bighorn Canyon National Recreation Area/Yellowtail Dam. **Additional Information:** Billings Chamber of Commerce, (406) 245-4111.

RESTRICTIONS

Pets: Leash only. **Fires:** No open fires. **Alcoholic Beverages:** Yes. **Vehicle Maximum Length:** None. **Other:** Good Sam, AAA, KOA, AARP, plus a other clubs discount.

TO GET THERE

From I-90 Exit 450, go west on SR-3 (S 27th St.) 0.2 mi., then left onto State Ave., left on to Sugur Ave., left onto Garden Ave. (total distance from I-90 is 3 mi.).

BOZEMAN

Bozeman KOA

81123 Gallatin Rd., Bozeman 59718. T: (406) 587-3030; F: (406) 582-9351; www.koa.com.

RV ★★★ Tent ★★

Beauty: ★★★ Site Privacy: ★★★
Spaciousness: ★★★ Quiet: ★★★
Security: ★★★★ Cleanliness: ★★★
Insect Control: ★★★ Facilities: ★★★

This campground is located within the Bozeman city limits, and it offers neither a purely wilderness experience nor a purely citified experience. A view of distant mountains, a trickling creek behind the on-site cabins, and a small collection of mature trees characterize the nature experience here, but it is quite accessible to the city. This campground works best as a base camp to explore Bozeman and the surrounding area. Nearby Gallatin Canyon provides some favored hiking, and proximity to Yellowstone Park, Lewis and Clark Caverns, and Red Rock Mine makes for some nice day trips. The 100 RV sites are more spacious than the 22 tent sites, and the tent sites sit cramped together, offering little privacy or shade. Sites L6–L11 and M1–M4 are arranged in rows, and all sites are grassy. Keep in mind that Bozeman is home to Montana State University, so avoid the area during graduation, unless of course, you are attending the graduation.

Basics

Operated By: Marvin Linde. **Open:** Apr.–Oct. 31. **Site Assignment:** By reservation. **Registration:** In camp store. **Fee:** Tent $26, RV $34–$36 per 2 people, extra person $3, children under 5 stay free. **Parking:** At site.

Facilities

Number of RV-Only Sites: 100. **Number of Tent-Only Sites:** 22. **Number of Multipurpose Sites:** 50. **Hookups:** Electric (30, 50 amps), water, sewer. **Each Site:** Picnic table. **Dump Station:** Yes. **Laundry:** Yes. **Pay Phone:** Yes. **Rest Rooms and Showers:** Yes. **Fuel:** No. **Propane:** Yes. **Internal Roads:** Gravel, in good condition. **RV Service:** In Bozeman. **Market:** In town. **Restaurant:** There are several in town. **General Store:** Yes. **Vending:** No, only in store. **Swimming Pool:** No, however they are next door to the indoor hot springs & pools. **Playground:** Yes. **Other:** Recreation Hall, cabins, camper kitchen, 15 cabins, & a creek. **Activities:** Swimming (next door), horseshoes, volleyball, basketball, fun cycles, mountain biking. **Nearby Attractions:** Museum of the Rockies, Yellowstone Park, Lewis & Clark Caverns. **Additional Information:** Bozeman Chamber of Commerce, (406) 586-5421.

Restrictions

Pets: On leash. **Fires:** In fire pits only. **Alcoholic Beverages:** Yes. **Vehicle Maximum Length:** None.

To Get There

I-90 (Exit 298) then 7 mi. south on Hwy. 85

CAMERON

Madison River Cabins & RV

1403 Hwy. 287 North, Cameron 59720. T: (406) 682-4890; F: (406) 682-4890; www.madisonriver.com; cabins@madison-river.com.

RV ★★★★ Tent ★★★★

Beauty: ★★★★★	Site Privacy: ★★★
Spaciousness: ★★★	Quiet: ★★★★
Security: ★★★★	Cleanliness: ★★★★★
Insect Control: ★★★★	Facilities: ★★★★★

A small but quaint family-run campground, Madison River Cabins & RV is nestled in the beautiful Madison Valley directly on the banks of the Madison River. This park makes for a very cozy, romantic get away or a great base for serious anglers. The campground is within easy reach of many famous trout streams—Madison, Gallatin, Beaverhead, and Henry's Fork Rivers. Each of the twelve unique cabins and RV sites has no shade, but they do offer great views of the adjacent Madison River and the distant mountains. The sites are level, have gravel parking spurs with some grassy areas, and have full-hookups. The Crazy Lady Outpost offers a variety of fishing supplies, licenses, and a large assortment of groceries. In addition, it houses the laundry facilities and rest rooms. The rest rooms and showers are the cleanest and best maintained of any campground in the state. Madison River Cabins and RV is less than an hour from the west entrance to Yellowstone National Park.

Basics

Operated By: Carol Salisbury. **Open:** Apr.–Oct. **Site Assignment:** By reservation. **Registration:** In fly shop. **Fee:** RV $19–$25. **Parking:** At site.

Facilities

Number of RV-Only Sites: 9. **Number of Tent-Only Sites:** Open tent area. **Hookups:** Electric (30 amps), water, sewer. **Each Site:** Picnic table. **Dump Station:** Yes. **Laundry:** Yes. **Pay Phone:** Yes. **Rest Rooms and Showers:** Yes. **Fuel:** No, 6 mi. south. **Propane:** No, 6 mi. south. **Internal Roads:** Gravel, in good condition. **RV Service:** Limited mobile service. **Market:** 35 mi. in either direction. **Restaurant:** Steak house next door. **General Store:** The Crazy Lady Outpost: rustic lodge fly shop w/ fishing tack, supplies, gift items & groceries. **Vending:** Just the store. **Swimming Pool:** No. **Playground:** Only a swing. **Other:** 12 fully furnished & unique cabins, all cabins & RV sites over look the Madison River, restaurant next door. **Activities:** Fly fishing & riverfront activities. **Nearby Attractions:** More fly fishing, fishing guide services, float trips, horseback riding, Yellowstone National Park, golf, hot springs, Historic Virginia City. **Additional Information:** Virginia City Chamber of Commerce, (800) 829-2969.

Restrictions

Pets: On leash. **Fires:** In fire rings only. **Alcoholic Beverages:** Yes. **Vehicle Maximum Length:** None.

To Get There

On Hwy. 287 north between Virginia City and West Yellowstone.

CARDWELL

Cardwell Store & RV Park

770 Hwy. 2 East, Cardwell 59721. T: (406) 287-5092; F: (406) 287-5092.

RV ★★★ Tent ★★★

Beauty: ★★★	Site Privacy: ★★★★
Spaciousness: ★★★★	Quiet: ★★★★
Security: ★★★	Cleanliness: ★★★
Insect Control: ★★★	Facilities: ★★★

Cardwell Store and RV Campground is located between Whitehall and Three Forks, directly off I-90. This simple campground is great for over night stays. It offers extra large, spacious sites, all of them pull-throughs arranged in a horseshoe configuration. They each have a level, gravel parking spur, full hook-ups, and a light post. To the east of the RV sites is a separate tent area with water and one cabin on the bank of a nice size stocked fishing pond. There is a large day use and picnic area, with lots of room for children to play. The grounds are well kept, and the rest rooms are clean. The campground has a large store, with fuel and movies to rent for the evening. The staff is friendly and inviting. There are many attractions in the area, including the Lewis and Clark Caverns.

BASICS

Operated By: Kipp & Dawn Huckaba. **Open:** All year, but the utilities are off Nov.–Feb. 28. **Site Assignment:** By reservation or walk-in. **Registration:** In camp store. **Fee:** Tent $10, RV $16–$18 per unit. **Parking:** At site.

FACILITIES

Number of RV-Only Sites: 36. **Number of Tent-Only Sites:** 10. **Hookups:** Electric (30, 50 amps), water, sewer. **Each Site:** Picnic table, light post. **Dump Station:** Yes. **Laundry:** Yes. **Pay Phone:** Yes. **Rest Rooms and Showers:** Yes. **Fuel:** Yes. **Propane:** Yes. **Internal Roads:** Gravel, in good condition. **RV Service:** 30 mi. west in Butte. **Market:** Whitehall. **Restaurant:** In Whitehall. **General Store:** Yes. **Vending:** Store only. **Swimming Pool:** No. **Playground:** No. **Other:** All pull-through sites, 1 cabin, stocked fishing pond, recreation area, picnic area, 1 tepee, movie rentals. **Activities:** Hiking, biking, fishing (trout), volleyball, horseshoes, small casino. **Nearby Attractions:** Lewis & Clark Caverns State Park, Madison Buffalo Jump State Park, Museum of the Rockies, Deer Lodge National Forest, hunting & fishing outfitters. **Additional Information:** Whitehall Chamber of Commerce, (406) 287-2260.

RESTRICTIONS

Pets: On leash. **Fires:** Tent area only. **Alcoholic Beverages:** Yes. **Vehicle Maximum Length:** 60 ft. **Other:** Group max 5 to a site.

TO GET THERE

I-90 Exit 256 on the east frontage road.

CHOTEAU

Choteau KOA

85 MT Hwy. 221, Choteau 59422. T: (406) 466-2615; F: (406) 466-5635; www.koa.com; rulonkoa@montana.com.

Tent ★★★

Beauty: ★★★	Site Privacy: ★★★
Spaciousness: ★★★	Quiet: ★★★★
Security: ★★★★	Cleanliness: ★★★
Insect Control: ★★★	Facilities: ★★★

Located 20 miles east of the Rocky Mountains on the Rocky Mountain Front, Choteau KOA is a great base camp for exploring the area. Campers are in easy reach of the one million acre Bob Marshall Wilderness and the Teton Spring Creek Bird Preserve. Those interested in dinosaurs should visit the Old Trail Museum in town, where visitors learn about the vast inland sea that covered this area 80 million years ago; if time permits, go on a dinosaur dig at Egg Mountain, available Jun.–Aug.

BASICS

Operated By: Shelly & Larry Rulon. **Open:** Apr. 1–Nov. 15. **Site Assignment:** By reservation. **Registration:** In camp store. **Fee:** Tent $17, RV $17-$23 per 2 people, extra person $2, children under 3 stay free. **Parking:** At site.

FACILITIES

Number of RV-Only Sites: 55. **Number of Tent-Only Sites:** 15. **Hookups:** Electric (20, 30, 50 amps), water, sewer. **Each Site:** Picnic tables, fire pits. **Dump Station:** Yes. **Laundry:** Yes. **Pay Phone:** Yes. **Rest Rooms and Showers:** Yes. **Fuel:** No, 1 mi. in town. **Propane:** No. **Internal Roads:** Gravel. **RV Service:** Limited service in town. **Market:** In town. **Restaurant:** In town. **General Store:** Yes. **Vending:** Yes. **Swimming**

Pool: No, but the public pool is less than 1 mi. **Playground:** 2 playgrounds. **Other:** 2 cabins, 3 tepees, a tent village, and data port. **Activities:** Mini-golf, horseshoes, large common area for games, game room, 9 hole golf course next door. **Nearby Attractions:** Fishing (Eureka Lake, Teton River), dinosaur digs, Bob Marshall Wilderness Complex, Old Trail Museum, Teton Spring Creek Bird Preserve. **Additional Information:** Choteau Chamber of Commerce, (800) 823-3866.

RESTRICTIONS

Pets: On leash. **Fires:** In fire rings only (fires may be prohibited due to dry weather; please always ask management before starting any open fires). **Alcoholic Beverages:** Yes. **Vehicle Maximum Length:** None.

TO GET THERE

From I-15 Exit 290, go west on US-89 for 40 mi., then bear right (west) on US-287 and follow in to Choteau. From Choteau, go east at the blinking light, 0.75 mi. on Hwy. 221.

COLUMBIA FALLS

La Salle RV Park

5618 Hwy. 2 West, Columbia Falls 59912. T: (406) 892-4668; F: (406) 892-4773.

RV: ★★★	Tent: ★★★
Beauty: ★★★	Site Privacy: ★★★
Spaciousness: ★★★	Quiet: ★★★★
Security: ★★★★	Cleanliness: ★★★★
Insect Control: ★★★★	Facilities: ★★★

Conveniently located off Hwy 2 about 5 miles southwest of Columbia Falls, the La Salle RV Park is a comfortable, clean, and well maintained campground with excellent service and friendly smiles. The seven acre property is divided into three areas: RV, tent, and cabins. The main entrance road is paved and loops around several rows of RV sites. Each RV site has a lush lawn and a level gravel parking pad. The tent area is in the back of the property with large sites divided by well-kept shrubs. In addition, there are 5 simple sleeping cabins. The campground is only 14 miles outside of Kalispell and 15 miles from the west entrance to Glacier National Park. The camping prices are one of the most reasonable in the area. The days are warm in the summer and evenings are cool. The owners live year-round on the property and are always there to assist.

BASICS

Operated By: Gordon, Carolynn & Andy Beloit. **Open:** All year. **Site Assignment:** Reservations recommended May–Oct., held w/ a credit card. **Registration:** In office/general store. **Fee:** Tent $15, RV $17–$20 per 4 people, extra person $2 (cash, credit, checks). **Parking:** At site.

FACILITIES

Number of RV-Only Sites: 52. **Number of Tent-Only Sites:** 8. **Hookups:** Electric (20, 30, 50 amps), water, sewer. **Each Site:** Picnic table, grated fire pits (tent sites, cabins). **Dump Station:** Yes. **Laundry:** Yes. **Pay Phone:** Yes. **Rest Rooms and Showers:** Yes. **Fuel:** 2 mi. northeast in Columbia Falls. **Propane:** 2 mi. northwest in Columbia Falls. **Internal Roads:** Paved & gravel. **RV Service:** 11 mi. south in Kalispell. **Market:** 2 mi. northeast in Columbia Falls. **Restaurant:** 2 mi. northeast in Columbia Falls. **General Store:** Yes. **Vending:** Yes. **Swimming Pool:** No. **Playground:** Yes. **Other:** 5 cabins, 1 tepee, lobby w/ color TV & Internet. **Activities:** Volleyball, basketball, horseshoes, group outings. **Nearby Attractions:** Glacier National Park 20 mi. northeast, water slides, go-kart tracks, fishing (rainbow trout, white fish), Hungry Horse Dam, Whitefish Lake, boating, whitewater rafting. **Additional Information:** Columbia Falls Area Chamber of Commerce, (406) 892-2072.

RESTRICTIONS

Pets: Leash only. **Fires:** Fire pit only in tent & cabin area (fires maybe prohibited due to weather; please ask management before starting any fire.). **Alcoholic Beverages:** Yes. **Vehicle Maximum Length:** 65 ft. total.

TO GET THERE

Eleven mi. northeast of Kalispell directly off Hwy. 2.

CONRAD

Pondera RV Park

510 South Maryland, Conrad 59425. T: (406) 278-5724; F: (406) 278-7644; www.conradrv.com; mail@conradrv.com.

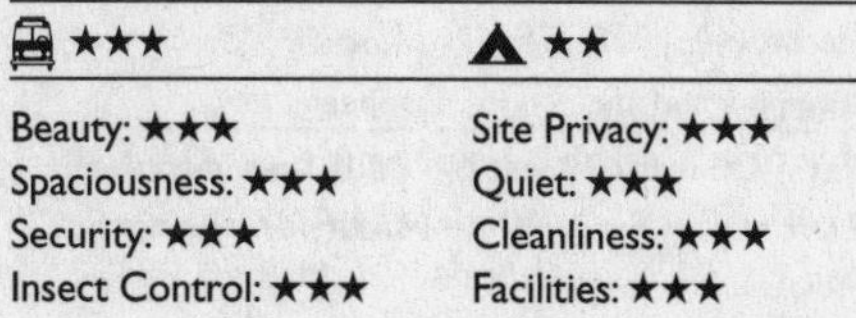

RV: ★★★	Tent: ★★
Beauty: ★★★	Site Privacy: ★★★
Spaciousness: ★★★	Quiet: ★★★
Security: ★★★	Cleanliness: ★★★
Insect Control: ★★★	Facilities: ★★★

Pondera RV Park is located in the center of Conrad, across from the city park. Pondera RV Park is a full-service facility with all the amenities looked for in an RV park. The sites are level and gravel. There is some grass and a few shade trees. Sites are close together and there are a few mobile homes. The area seems fairly quiet, and the park across the street has several activities: an Olympic-size public pool, large play ground, tennis courts and picnic areas. The campground is convenient to local restaurants, shopping, and repair. The Lewis and Clark Trail runs through Conrad, and the campground is not far from Glacier National Park, Great Falls, or Lake Holter Recreation Area. The area is very dry in the summer, and days can be very warm. This campground is not staffed during the day, and the owners show up around 4p.m.. There is a number on the bulletin board for emergencies.

Basics

Operated By: Ralph & Gladys Dunahoo. **Open:** All year. **Site Assignment:** By reservation or walk-in. **Registration:** The camp office. **Fee:** $18–$20 per unit. **Parking:** At site.

Facilities

Number of RV-Only Sites: 52. **Number of Tent-Only Sites:** 10. **Hookups:** Electric (30 amps), water, sewer, cable, phone. **Each Site:** Some picnic tables. **Dump Station:** Yes. **Laundry:** Yes. **Pay Phone:** Yes. **Rest Rooms and Showers:** Yes. **Fuel:** Less than 1 mi. **Propane:** Less than 1 mi. **Internal Roads:** Gravel, in good condition. **RV Service:** Limited local service. **Market:** In town. **Restaurant:** In town. **General Store:** No. **Vending:** Yes. **Swimming Pool:** Public pool located across the street. **Playground:** Located across the street in city park. **Other:** Internet data port, across from the Conrad Municipal Park: pavilions, grills, pool, tennis, & other activities. **Activities:** Park, pool, tennis, volleyball, horseshoes. **Nearby Attractions:** Golf, bowling, movies, dinosaur digs, hiking, fishing, an hour drive to Glacier National Park, community theater, horseback riding. **Additional Information:** Conrad Chamber of Commerce, (406) 278-7791.

Restrictions

Pets: On leash. **Fires:** No open fires. **Alcoholic Beverages:** Yes. **Vehicle Maximum Length:** 60 ft.

To Get There

Take Exit 339 off of I-15 and enter Conrad, Montana. Follow Main St. 11 Blocks. Turn Right on 7th. Go 1.5 blocks and look to your left.

CORAM

North American RV Park & Yurt Village

P.O. Box 130449, Coram 59913. T: (406) 387-5800 or (800) 704-4266; F: (406) 387-5888; narvpark@montana.com.

RV ★★★ Tent ★★

Beauty: ★★★ Site Privacy: ★★★
Spaciousness: ★★★ Quiet: ★★★★
Security: ★★★ Cleanliness: ★★★
Insect Control: ★★★★ Facilities: ★★★★

Located a few miles from the west entrance of Glacier National Park in the small community of Coram is the North American RV Park. This campground is ideal for those campers looking for a convenient base camp with up-to-date modern amenities. North America RV Park offers its patrons a clean, well-maintained facility with large, gravel, pull-through sites at the base of a huge mountain. There are few trees and little shade, but the satellite television reception is great. There is plenty of additional parking, and this campground caters to extra large motor coaches with tows. The tent sites lie along the back of the property in a sparsely grassy area by the mountain. The campground also has two rental yurts. Since this campground is in a valley with few trees, summer days can be very warm though the evenings tend to be very cool. The park office is open daily and there are also camp hosts to assist with any needs that may arise.

Basics

Operated By: Curt & Susan Sholar. **Open:** Apr.–Oct. **Site Assignment:** Reservations recommended. **Registration:** In camp office. **Fee:** Tent $17.50, RV $18.50–$24.50 per 4 people, extra person $3, Good Sam Club. (cash, credit, checks). **Parking:** At site.

Facilities

Number of RV-Only Sites: 101. **Number of Tent-Only Sites:** 12. **Hookups:** Electric (30, 50 amps), water, sewer, cable, phone. **Each Site:** Picnic table. **Dump Station:** Yes. **Laundry:** Yes. **Pay Phone:** Yes. **Rest Rooms and Showers:** Yes. **Fuel:** In Coram or West Glacier. **Propane:** In Coram or West Glacier. **Internal Roads:** Gravel. **RV Service:** 14 mi. southwest in Columbia Falls. **Market:** In Coram or West Glacier. **Restaurant:** In Coram or West Glacier. **General Store:** No. **Vending:** Yes. **Swimming Pool:** No. **Playground:** Yes. **Other:** 2 yurts (a circular, Mongolian-style domed tent w/ a plywood floor, sleeps 4–6 people). **Activities:** Picnic area, volleyball, horseshoes, North American Wildlife Museum. **Nearby Attractions:** Glacier National Park, House of Mystery, Hungry Horse Dam, golf, fishing tours, white water rafting, helicopter tours. **Additional Information:** Columbia Falls Area Chamber of Commerce, (406) 892-2072.

RESTRICTIONS

Pets: Leash only. **Fires:** Fire pits only (fires may be prohibited due to dry weather; please ask management before starting any fires.). **Alcoholic Beverages:** Yes. **Vehicle Maximum Length:** None.

TO GET THERE

Directly off US 2 about 5 mi. south of West Glacier.

CUT BANK

Shady Grove RV Park & Campground

P.O. Box 691, Cut Bank 59427. T: (406) 336-2475; F: (406) 336-2475; shdygrov@northerntel.net.

RV ★★★	Tent ★★★
Beauty: ★★★	Site Privacy: ★★★
Spaciousness: ★★★	Quiet: ★★★★★
Security: ★★★★	Cleanliness: ★★★★
Insect Control: ★★★★	Facilities: ★★★

Located on the east side of Glacier National Park in the flat farmland of Montana is Shady Grove RV Park and Campground. The air is sweet and the grass is green. There are beautiful mature trees that surround the property, and a feeling of home and family pervades the campground. The campsites form a circular perimeter around the property, with the Bomar's home in the center. There are clean and well-maintained facilities, and a small playground. All the sites are back-in but roomy in size and length. The tent sites are on lush grass and are well spaced for privacy. The park is a wonderful place to enjoy the stars on a cloudless night. The weather is typical of high desert, and is very dry in the summer. There are no open fires allowed in the campground. For extra security, the gates are closed in the evening. It is 30 miles to the east entrance of Glacier National Park.

BASICS

Operated By: Larry & Carole Bomar. **Open:** May 1–Oct. 1. **Site Assignment:** Reservations recommended, held w/ a credit card. **Registration:** Larry & Carole's home. **Fee:** Tent $12, RV $15 per 2 people, extra adult $2, Child 3–12 $1, under 3 stay free. (cash & check only). **Parking:** At site.

FACILITIES

Number of RV-Only Sites: 19. **Number of Tent-Only Sites:** 10. **Number of Multipurpose Sites:** 10. **Hookups:** Electric (20, 30 amps), water, sewer. **Each Site:** Picnic table. **Dump Station:** No. **Laundry:** No. **Pay Phone:** Yes. **Rest Rooms and Showers:** Yes. **Fuel:** 6 mi. east in Cut Bank. **Propane:** 6 mi. east in Cut Bank. **Internal Roads:** Gravel & grass. **RV Service:** 100 mi. in Great Falls. **Market:** 6 mi. east in Cut Bank. **Restaurant:** 6 mi. east in Cut Bank. **General Store:** No. **Vending:** Drinks & ice available at owners' home. **Swimming Pool:** No. **Playground:** Yes. **Activities:** Play Area, horseshoes, large open field great for playing ball. **Nearby Attractions:** Glacier National Park. **Additional Information:** www.visitmontana.com.

RESTRICTIONS

Pets: Leash only, some large breed restrictions. **Fires:** No open fires allowed. **Alcoholic Beverages:** In campers only. **Vehicle Maximum Length:** None.

TO GET THERE

Directly off Hwy. 2, 6 mi. west of Cut Bank.

DEER LODGE

Indian Creek RV Campground

745 Maverick Ln., Deer Lodge 59722. T: (406) 846-3848; www.indiancreekcampground.com; indiancreek@montana.com.

RV ★★★	Tent ★★★
Beauty: ★★★★	Site Privacy: ★★★
Spaciousness: ★★★	Quiet: ★★★
Security: ★★★★	Cleanliness: ★★★
Insect Control: ★★★	Facilities: ★★★

Indian Creek RV Campground is a great location for travelers with extra large motor-coaches or towed vehicles. Situated in the scenic Deer Lodge area, this park is less than an hour away from Yellowstone National Park. The campground offers level sites, 50 amp service, modem service and cable TV. There is a large recreation lodge with laundry, very well maintained rest rooms, and lounge. The campground sits on the banks of the Yellowstone River, and the view is spectacular. The staff is friendly and welcoming, and the climate is dry and breezy. In addition to Yellowstone, the Deer Lodge area has fine dinning, shopping, hot springs and much more. This is a wonderful place to mountain bike or hike. The Indian Creek RV Campground has a tendency to fill up early, so reservations are highly recommended.

BASICS

Operated By: Flicker Oil Company. **Open:** Apr. 15–Oct. 15. **Site Assignment:** By reservation. **Registration:** In camp office. **Fee:** Tent $13.52, RV $17–$19. **Parking:** At site.

FACILITIES

Number of RV-Only Sites: 50. **Number of Tent-Only Sites:** Open tent area. **Hookups:** Electric (30 amps), water, sewer, cable, phone. **Each Site:** Picnic table. **Dump Station:** Yes. **Laundry:** Yes. **Pay Phone:** Yes. **Rest Rooms and Showers:** Yes. **Fuel:** Next door. **Propane:** Yes. **Internal Roads:** Gravel, in good condition. **RV Service:** Mobile service from Butte. **Market:** In town. **Restaurant:** In town. **General Store:** Small w/ a few drinks. **Vending:** Just the store. **Swimming Pool:** No. **Playground:** Yes. **Activities:** Hiking, biking, enjoying views of Mt. Powell. **Nearby Attractions:** Grant-Kohrs Ranch National Historic Site, the Old Montana Prison Museum Complex. **Additional Information:** Deer Lodge Chamber of Commerce, (406) 846-2094.

RESTRICTIONS

Pets: On leash. **Fires:** No open fires. **Alcoholic Beverages:** Yes. **Vehicle Maximum Length:** 45 ft. w/tow. **Other:** Good Sam, KOA, discounts.

TO GET THERE

From I-90 Exit 184, go west on I-90 Bus 0.25 mi., make a left on Access Rd., follow signs 0.5 mi. down access road to 745 Maverick Ln.

ELMO

Arrowhead Resort

76076 Hwy. 93, Elmo 59915. T: (406) 849-5545; F: (406) 849-5545, ext. 51; www.webtize.com/arrowhead; arohed1_2@yahoo.com.

RV ★★★ Tent ★★★

Beauty: ★★★★ Site Privacy: ★★★
Spaciousness: ★★★ Quiet: ★★★★
Security: ★★★★ Cleanliness: ★★★★★
Insect Control: ★★★★ Facilities: ★★★★

Situated on Flathead Lake, the largest natural freshwater lake west of the Mississippi, Arrowhead Resort is a perfect retreat if you are looking for a quiet atmosphere in a pristine setting. Flathead Lake is fed by melting glaciers in the nearby Glacier National Park. Only 15 miles north of Polson, Arrowhead Resort overlooks Chief Cliff Mountain and Wild Horse Island. Arrowhead Resort is a delightfully manicured resort offering 40 pull-through grass sites, a swimming beach, and a marina. The breeze off the lake creates pleasant warm summer days and cool evenings. Charles and Ronnie Smith, the proprietors, live on the property throughout the season and are there to assist you in any way.

BASICS

Operated By: E. Charles & Ronnie Smith. **Open:** May 1–Sept. 30. **Site Assignment:** Reservations recommended, $16.50 Non-refundable deposit if less than 1 week, $25 deposit for more than 1 week. **Registration:** In camp office. **Fee:** Tent $12.50, RV $19.50–$20.50. **Parking:** At site.

FACILITIES

Number of RV-Only Sites: 40. **Number of Tent-Only Sites:** 2. **Hookups:** Electric (30, 50 amps), water, sewer. **Each Site:** Picnic table, some grills. **Dump Station:** Yes. **Laundry:** No. **Pay Phone:** You may use office phone. **Rest Rooms and Showers:** Yes. **Fuel:** 1 mi. in Elmo. **Propane:** 1 mi. in Elmo. **Internal Roads:** Gravel. **RV Service:** 25 mi. north in Kalispell. **Market:** 13 mi. south in Polson. **Restaurant:** 13 mi. south in Polson. **General Store:** No. **Vending:** In office, drinks & ice. **Swimming Pool:** No, you may swim in lake. **Playground:** No. **Other:** Marina, boat launch, boat rentals. **Activities:** Fishing, boating, waterskiing, jet skiing, parasailing. **Nearby Attractions:** Charter fishing trips, hunting, hiking, backpacking, Flathead Lake State Park. **Additional Information:** Polson Chamber of Commerce, (406) 883-5971.

RESTRICTIONS

Pets: Leashed only. **Fires:** In fire pits only. **Alcoholic Beverages:** Yes. **Vehicle Maximum Length:** None.

TO GET THERE

Located on Hwy. 93, 13 mi. north of Polson at the 76 mi. marker.

GARDINER

Yellowstone RV Park

P.O.Box 634, Gardiner 59030. T: (406) 848-7496; F: (406) 848-7496; www.visitmt.com.

RV ★★★	Tent ★★
Beauty: ★★★	Site Privacy: ★★
Spaciousness: ★★	Quiet: ★★★
Security: ★★★★	Cleanliness: ★★★
Insect Control: ★★★	Facilities: ★★★

Situated at the north entrance to Yellowstone National Park in breathtaking Paradise Valley, the Yellowstone RV Park is adjacent to the only park entrance open year-round. All sites look over the Yellowstone River, and because there are very few trees, each site has good views of the surrounding landscape. The park stays packed most of the year, so reserve way ahead of time. The mix of back-ins and pull-throughs is on level, gravel sites, organized in an oval shape. Locally, the town of Gardiner has many places to eat and shop. The park is 5 miles away from Mammoth Hot Springs and 55 miles away from Old Faithful

BASICS

Operated By: Venture West. **Open:** May 1–Nov. 1. **Site Assignment:** By reservation. **Registration:** In camp office. **Fee:** Tent $15–$21.50, RV $21.50–$30.50 per 6 people, extra person $4. **Parking:** At site.

FACILITIES

Number of RV-Only Sites: 46. **Number of Tent-Only Sites:** 10. **Hookups:** Electric (30 amps), water, sewer, cable. **Each Site:** Picnic table. **Dump Station:** Yes. **Laundry:** 2 laundry areas. **Pay Phone:** Yes. **Rest Rooms and Showers:** Yes. **Fuel:** In town. **Propane:** In town. **Internal Roads:** Gravel, in good condition. **RV Service:** Mobile RV Service (406) 646-9084. **Market:** In town. **Restaurant:** In town. **General Store:** No. **Vending:** Drinks. **Swimming Pool:** No. **Playground:** No. **Other:** Located on the Yellowstone River Basin. **Activities:** Hiking, biking, fishing. **Nearby Attractions:** Yellowstone National Park (this is as close as you can get to Yellowstone without going into the park), casino, trading post, shopping, fishing tours, park tours, Old Faithful, Roosevelt Arch. **Additional Information:** Gardiner Chamber of Commerce, (406) 848-7971, gardinerchamber@gomontana.com.

RESTRICTIONS

Pets: On leash. **Fires:** No open fires, grills in tent area. **Alcoholic Beverages:** Yes. **Vehicle Maximum Length:** 50 ft. **Other:** Good Sam, AAA, AARP, discounts.

TO GET THERE

On US 89S 1.3 mi. from the north gate to Yellowstone National Park.

GLENDIVE

Glendive RV Park and Campground

201 California St., Glendive 59330. T: (406) 377-6721; www.glendivervpark.com; larry@midrivers.com.

RV ★★★	Tent ★★★
Beauty: ★★★	Site Privacy: ★★★
Spaciousness: ★★★	Quiet: ★★★
Security: ★★★	Cleanliness: ★★★
Insect Control: ★★★	Facilities: ★★★

Located 33 miles west of the North Dakota border, Glendive offers the last bit of civilization before leaving the sprawling desert-like scenery of eastern Montana. Just a quick exit off of I-94, this campground might be a convenient stop as you journey to the next state. The chain-link fence, hodge-podge of buildings, and patchy grass found at the entrance are not aesthetically pleasing, but, luckily, the campsites are not located in close view. Sites 1–18 are arranged in three rows and are the farthest from the interstate and access road. However, they are not as spacious as sites 19–52, which are arranged in a horseshoe pattern. The inner horseshoe, sites 19–31, hug the playground, and sites 19 and 33 catch any incoming traffic. The separate tent area places tent campers closest to the interstate and hides them among occasional trees and sparse ground cover. Not far from the camp, Makoshika State Park (makoshika is the Sioux name for "bad lands") captures the subtle desert scenery of sandstone and sage, and is an interesting contrast to the Yellowstone experience. If you happen through during spring, be sure to catch the annual Buzzard Days festival celebrating the return of the turkey vultures.

Basics

Operated By: Larry Phillips. **Open:** Apr. 1–Dec. 1. **Site Assignment:** By reservation. **Registration:** In camp office. **Fee:** Tent $14, RV $21–$25 per 2 people, extra person charge $2, children under age 5 stay free. **Parking:** At site.

Facilities

Number of RV-Only Sites: 52. **Number of Tent-Only Sites:** 10. **Hookups:** Electric (20, 30, 50 amps), water, sewer, phone. **Each Site:** Picnic tables, fire pits. **Dump Station:** Yes. **Laundry:** Yes. **Pay Phone:** Yes. **Rest Rooms and Showers:** Yes. **Fuel:** Less than 1 mi. **Propane:** No. **Internal Roads:** Gravel, in good condition. **RV Service:** MIles City (70 mi.). **Market:** In town. **Restaurant:** On site. **General Store:** Yes. **Vending:** Yes. **Swimming Pool:** Yes. **Playground:** Yes. **Other:** On the Yellowstone River, 2 cabins w/ refrigerators, hot plates, running water, air-conditioning, cable TV, exercise bar, Internet data port. **Activities:** Horseshoes, basketball, volleyball, swimming, fishing, badminton. **Nearby Attractions:** Yellowstone River, boating, fishing, agate hunting, Makoshika State Park, self-guided walking tour of Glendive's downtown historic district. **Additional Information:** Glendive Chamber of Commerce, (406) 365-5601.

Restrictions

Pets: On leash. **Fires:** In fire pits only. **Alcoholic Beverages:** Yes. **Vehicle Maximum Length:** None. **Other:** Good Sam Park.

To Get There

North of I-94 Exit 215; you can see campground from the interstate.

HARDIN
Hardin KOA

RR 1, Hardin 59034. T: (406) 665-1635 or (800) 562-1635; www.koa.com; hardinkoa@aol.com.

 ★★★  ★★★

Beauty: ★★★ Site Privacy: ★★★
Spaciousness: ★★★ Quiet: ★★★★
Security: ★★★★ Cleanliness: ★★★★
Insect Control: n/a Facilities: ★★★

Hardin KOA is the perfect place for campers who have a taste for history. Within easy driving distance is Pompey's Pillar, a large, solitary plateau offering panoramic views of the surrounding countryside. The remnants of Native Americans pictographs can be found here, as well as the signature of Captain William Clark of Lewis and Clark fame. Also nearby is the Little Bighorn National Monument, site of the brutal battle between Custer's 7th Cavalry and the Sioux Indians. The 58 RV sites and 10 tent-only sites lie on mostly flat ground with minimal shade. Activities within camp include swimming, horseshoes, volleyball, and nightly movies during the summer. This camp fills up quickly during Little Big Horn Days each summer, so call ahead.

Basics

Operated By: Warren D. Hardy. **Open:** Apr. 1–Oct. 1. **Site Assignment:** By reservation. **Registration:** In camp store. **Fee:** Tent $15, RV $20.50–$21.50 per 2 people, extra person $1.50, children under 3 free. **Parking:** At site.

Facilities

Number of RV-Only Sites: 58. **Number of Tent-Only Sites:** 10. **Hookups:** Electric (30, 50 amps), water, sewer, cable. **Each Site:** Picnic table. **Dump Station:** Yes. **Laundry:** Yes. **Pay Phone:** Yes. **Rest Rooms and Showers:** Yes. **Fuel:** No. **Propane:** Yes. **Internal Roads:** Gravel, in good condition. **RV Service:** In Billings. **Market:** In town. **Restaurant:** There are several in town. **General Store:** Yes. **Vending:** No, only in store. **Swimming Pool:** Yes w/ hot tub. **Playground:** Yes. **Other:** 6 cabins, hot tub, snack bar, nightly summer BBQ's. **Activities:** Swimming, horseshoes, volleyball, basketball, nightly summer movies. **Nearby Attractions:** Fishing (Big Horn River), Big Horn National Monument, Little Big Horn Days June 20-25. **Additional Information:** Hardin Chamber of Commerce (406) 665-1672.

Restrictions

Pets: On leash. **Fires:** In fire pits only. **Alcoholic Beverages:** Yes. **Vehicle Maximum Length:** Limited sites for very large RVs.

To Get There

I-90 Exit 495, go north 1.5 mi. on Hwy. 47

HAVRE

Havre RV Park

1415 First St., Havre 59501. T: (406) 265-8861 or (800) 278-8861; www.havremt.com/duckinn/havre_rv_park.htm

RV ★★★ Tent ★★★

Beauty: ★★★	Site Privacy: ★★★
Spaciousness: ★★★	Quiet: ★★
Security: ★★★	Cleanliness: ★★★
Insect Control: ★★★	Facilities: ★★★

The Havre Campground, located in downtown Havre, is owned in conjunction with the Emporium Food and Fuel Store (Conoco), The Best Western Hotel, and The Duck Inn Restaurant and Casino. All of Havre Campground sites have concrete parking pads with full hookups and 50 amp service. They are configured in a large paved oval, surrounded by green grass and a wooden privacy fence. The only real drawback to this park is the railroad tracks that run behind the property. All campground guests are invited to use the pool, spa, sauna, and exercise room at the hotel, and rest rooms and shower are located inside the store. The campground office is located inside a refurbished train caboose and oversees the gate into the park. The restaurant serves three meals a day and is moderately priced. The Havre community offers tours of its downtown area and has an enriching history to share.

Basics

Operated By: Private Operator. **Open:** All year. **Site Assignment:** By reservation. **Registration:** In camp office. **Fee:** Tent $14, RV $27. **Parking:** At site.

Facilities

Number of RV-Only Sites: 50. **Number of Tent-Only Sites:** Open tent area. **Hookups:** Electric (20, 30, 50 amps), water, sewer. **Each Site:** Concrete parking pad, picnic tables. **Dump Station:** Yes. **Laundry:** Yes. **Pay Phone:** Yes. **Rest Rooms and Showers:** Yes. **Fuel:** Yes. **Propane:** Yes. **Internal Roads:** Paved. **RV Service:** Limited service in town. **Market:** In town. **Restaurant:** On site. **General Store:** Large Conoco. **Vending:** Yes. **Swimming Pool:** No, but free use of the pool & spa at the Best Western Great Northern Inn. **Playground:** Yes. **Other:** Emporium Food & Fuel Store (Conoco), saloon, The Best Western, The Duck Inn Restaurant, a small casino, & all sites have concrete parking pad w/ full hookups & 50 amp service. **Activities:** Casino, swim, spa, picnic, exercise room, sauna (located at the Best Western). **Nearby Attractions:** Bears Paw Mountains & battle field, Havre Beneath the Streets w/ daily tours of the town, Beaver Creek Park, several reservoirs w/ excellent fishing & boating. **Additional Information:** Havre Chamber of Commerce, (406) 265-4383.

Restrictions

Pets: On leash. **Fires:** No open fires. **Alcoholic Beverages:** Yes. **Vehicle Maximum Length:** None.

To Get There

From Hwy. 2, go east at 14th Ave

HELENA

Helena Campground & RV Park

5820 North Montana Ave., Helena 59602. T: (406) 458-4714; F: (406) 458-6001; www.helenacampgroundrvpark.com; info@helenacampgroundrvpark.com.

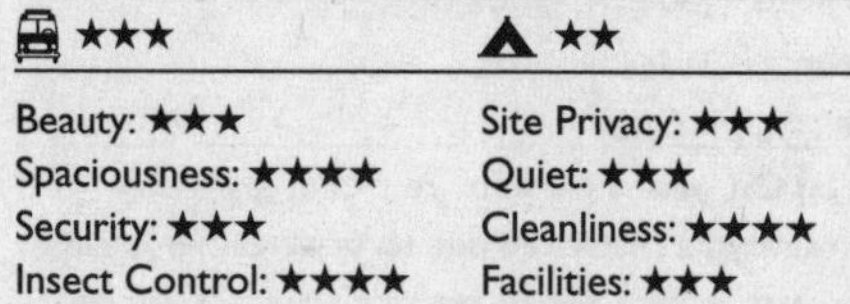

RV ★★★ Tent ★★

Beauty: ★★★	Site Privacy: ★★★
Spaciousness: ★★★★	Quiet: ★★★
Security: ★★★	Cleanliness: ★★★★
Insect Control: ★★★★	Facilities: ★★★

Welcome to the Capital city of Helena. The Helena Campground and RV Park is a mere three miles outside the city limits and is a comfortable vacation spot for those visitors wishing to visit the city and surrounding area. The campground is configured in rows containing both pull-through and back-in sites, which are well groomed with trailer pads. Tent sites have nice lawn areas, but are small with little privacy. There is also a tent corral with electricity and water, and a few cabins. During the peak season patrons may enjoy an all-you-can-eat breakfast, ice cream socials, and a dip in the pool. Canyon Ferry and Hauser Lakes are close by with tours and boating. The weather in Helena is dry and warm in the summer, with temperatures dropping in the evening. The campground has good security with someone always on the clock.

Basics

Operated By: Robert Dunlop. **Open:** Mar. 1–Oct. 31. **Site Assignment:** By reservation, w/ first night deposit. $5 cancellation fee. **Registration:** In camp office. **Fee:** Tent $22-23, RV $22–$29 per 2 people, extra person $6 children under 3 free, ac/heat $2 extra per night. **Parking:** Yes, extra vehicle $5.

Facilities

Number of RV-Only Sites: 100. **Number of Tent-Only Sites:** 29. **Hookups:** Electric (30, 50 amps), water, sewer. **Each Site:** Picnic tables, some grills, some fire pits. **Dump Station:** Yes. **Laundry:** Yes. **Pay Phone:** Yes. **Rest Rooms and Showers:** Yes. **Fuel:** In Helena. **Propane:** In Helena. **Internal Roads:** Paved & gravel. **RV Service:** In Helena. **Market:** In Helena. **Restaurant:** In Helena. **General Store:** Yes. **Vending:** In general store only. **Swimming Pool:** Yes (very large, open Memorial Day–Labor Day). **Playground:** Yes. **Other:** All tent sites have water, 3 cabins, tent village, recreation room, breakfast. **Activities:** Game room, swimming, fun cycles. **Nearby Attractions:** State Capitol Building, Holter Museum of Art, Boulder Hot Springs, St. Helena Cathedral, Elkhorn Ghost Town, Holter Lake & Recreation Area. **Additional Information:** Helena Chamber of Commerce, (406) 444-2654, (800)743-5362 or www.helenachamber.com.

Restrictions

Pets: On leash. **Fires:** In fire pits or grills only (fires may be restricted due to dry weather; please ask management before starting any fire.). **Alcoholic Beverages:** Yes. **Vehicle Maximum Length:** None. **Other:** Good Sam, AAA, & 30% discount to cyclist w/o vehicle.

To Get There

From I-15, take Lincoln Rd. Exit 200 (SR-279) west, take a left onto Montana Ave. Park is located 3 mi. down on your right.

HUNGRY HORSE

Canyon RV & Campground

9540 Hwy. 2 East, Hungry Horse 59919. T: (406) 387-9393; F: (406)387-9394; www.montanacampground.com; canyonrv@montanacampground.com.

 ★★★  ★★★

Beauty: ★★★★ Site Privacy: ★★★
Spaciousness: ★★ Quiet: ★★★★
Security: ★★★★ Cleanliness: ★★★★
Insect Control: ★★★ Facilities: ★★★

Only ten minutes away from the western entrance to Glacier National Park on the Flat Head River is Canyon RV & Campground. Canyon RV & Campground enjoys river frontage, great for trout fishing, and panoramic views of the snow-capped mountains. It is conveniently located near many of the attractions in the Hungry Horse–West Glacier area, including golf, the Hungry Horse Dam, and glacier helicopter tours. The campground is configured in a large loop with both back-in and pull-through sites. Sites, however, are relatively close together and tent sites lack privacy and shade. The air is crisp and dry, but be prepared for the cold any day of the year. The foliage is spectacular in the late spring, early summer, and the sunsets are magnificent. The owners stay on property during the operating season and are there to assist in any way.

Basics

Operated By: Steve & Dee Brown. **Open:** May 1–Sept. 30. **Site Assignment:** Reservations recommended held w/ a credit card number. **Registration:** In general store. **Fee:** Tent $16, RV $16–$22 per 2 people, extra person $3 (cash & checks). **Parking:** At site.

Facilities

Number of RV-Only Sites: 51. **Number of Tent-Only Sites:** 10. **Hookups:** Electric (20, 30, 50 amps), water, sewer. **Each Site:** Picnic table, some grills. **Dump Station:** Yes. **Laundry:** No. **Pay Phone:** Yes. **Rest Rooms and Showers:** Yes. **Fuel:** In Hungry Horse. **Propane:** In Hungry Horse. **Internal Roads:** Gravel. **RV Service:** In Hungry Horse, and there is a mobile service. **Market:** In Hungry Horse. **Restaurant:** In Hungry Horse. **General Store:** Yes. **Vending:** General store only. **Swimming Pool:** No. No swimming in the Flathead River. **Playground:** No. **Other:** 6 Cabins & 1 tepee, central fire ring. **Activities:** Fishing (bull trout, white fish, rainbow trout), horseshoes, hiking. **Nearby Attractions:** Glacier National Park 8 mi. northeast, House of Mystery, North American Wildlife Museum, go karts, helicopter tours, white water rafting, fishing tours. **Additional Information:** Columbia Falls Area Chamber of Commerce, (406) 892-2072.

Restrictions

Pets: Leash only. **Fires:** Fire ring only (fires maybe prohibited due to dry weather, please ask management before starting any fire.). **Alcoholic Beverages:** No alcoholic beverages allowed. **Vehicle Maximum Length:** 45 ft. plus.

To Get There

Directly off Hwy. 2 in Hungry Horse, 18 mi. northeast of Kalispell.

HUNGRY HORSE
Mountain Meadow Campground

P.O. Box 190442, Hungry Horse 59919. T: (406) 387-9125; F: (406) 387-9126; www.mmrvpark.com; camp@mmrvpark.com.

RV ★★★★★ Tent ★★★★

Beauty: ★★★★★	Site Privacy: ★★★★
Spaciousness: ★★★★	Quiet: ★★★★★
Security: ★★★★	Cleanliness: ★★★★★
Insect Control: ★★★★	Facilities: ★★★★★

Welcome to one of the most beautiful and pristine campgrounds in Montana. Located only a few short miles from the west entrance to Glacier National Park and the Hungry Horse Dam is Mountain Meadow Campground. High atop a mountain peak with a spectacular view of the Glacier Mountains, one finds cozy wooded camping sites, cabins with all the modern luxuries of a full service campground, and the rustic ambiance only nature can share. Large Douglas firs and cedars canopy each site and lend their sweet aroma to the air. The roads are wide, the sites are large, most are pull-through, and the trees are groomed. Tent sites are secluded and private. There is a large well-stocked fishing pond and large picnic area. The air is crisp and the breeze is inviting. Several nice restaurants are in walking distance as well as outfitters and helicopter tours. The office is staffed daily and the security is good.

Basics

Operated By: Dan & Sue Hussion. **Open:** May 1–Oct. 1. **Site Assignment:** Reservations recommended w/ credit card number. **Registration:** In general store. **Fee:** Tent $16.50, RV $21.50–$24.50 per 4 people, extra child $1.50, adult $3.(cash, credit, checks). **Parking:** At site.

Facilities

Number of RV-Only Sites: 51. **Number of Tent-Only Sites:** 11. **Hookups:** Electric (30, 50 amps), water, sewer. **Each Site:** Picnic table, grated fire pits. **Dump Station:** Yes. **Laundry:** Yes. **Pay Phone:** Yes. **Rest Rooms and Showers:** Yes. **Fuel:** In Coram. **Propane:** In Coram. **Internal Roads:** Graded dirt & sand, smooth & in excellent condition. **RV Service:** 10 mi. southwest in Columbia Falls. **Market:** In town. **Restaurant:** In town. **General Store:** Yes. **Vending:** Yes. **Swimming Pool:** No. **Playground:** Yes. **Other:** 2 cabins, stocked rainbow trout lake over looking the mountains, swings, modem hookup in the office. **Activities:** Fishing (rainbow trout), swing, hiking, biking. **Nearby Attractions:** 9 mi. from Glacier National Park, Hungry Horse Dam, Lion Lake, horseback riding, fly-fishing tours, white water rafting, helicopter tours. **Additional Information:** Columbia Falls Area Chamber of Commerce, (406) 892-2072.

Restrictions

Pets: Leash-only. **Fires:** Fire pits only (fires may be prohibited due to weather: please ask management before starting any fires.). **Alcoholic Beverages:** Yes. **Vehicle Maximum Length:** 45 ft plus. **Other:** Good Sam & AAA honored.

To Get There

Located directly off Hwy. 2 in Hungry Horse

HUNGRY HORSE
Timber Wolf Resort

9105 Hwy. 2 East, Hungry Horse 59919. T: (406) 847-9653 or (877) 846-9653; F: (406) 387-9654; www.timberwolfresort.com; elek@timberwolfresort.com.

RV ★★★★ Tent ★★★★

Beauty: ★★★★★	Site Privacy: ★★★
Spaciousness: ★★★	Quiet: ★★★★★
Security: ★★★★	Cleanliness: ★★★★
Insect Control: ★★★★	Facilities: ★★★★★

Nestled in a 20-acre forest only nine miles from the west entrance to Glacier National Park, Timber Wolf Resort is a true jewel. Timber Wolf offers a full service campground with excellent amenities, including a beautiful large gazebo with three barbeque grills, bike rentals, and a new playground. The campground has hiking trails and bike trails that connect to those in

Glacier National Park. Timber Wolf offers large gravel sites, both pull-through and back-in, with a natural forest floor and shade. In addition, they offer 15 beautiful camping cabins, a small bed and breakfast, and wonderfully secluded tent sites. The campground, while offering large sites, is not designed for huge (45 ft. plus) RVs. The resort is open year-round and the owners reside on the property. The winters are long, cold, and snowy, and the summers too short, but beautiful.

Basics

Operated By: Rob & Tracy Elek. **Open:** All year. **Site Assignment:** Reservations recommended. **Registration:** In general store or at the Elek's residence. **Fee:** Tent $16, RV $18–$23 (cash, credit, checks). **Parking:** At site.

Facilities

Number of RV-Only Sites: 24. **Number of Tent-Only Sites:** 10. **Hookups:** Electric (30, 50 amps), water, sewer. **Each Site:** Picnic table, grated fire pits. **Dump Station:** No. **Laundry:** No. **Pay Phone:** Yes. **Rest Rooms and Showers:** Yes. **Fuel:** In Hungry Horse. **Propane:** In Hungry Horse. **Internal Roads:** Gravel. **RV Service:** 10 mi. southwest in Columbia Falls. **Market:** In Hungry Horse. **Restaurant:** In Hungry Horse. **General Store:** Yes. **Vending:** Yes. **Swimming Pool:** No. **Playground:** Yes. **Other:** Large gazebo w/ 3 gas barbeques, Bed & Breakfast, 15 cabins. **Activities:** Hiking, horseshoes. **Nearby Attractions:** 9 mi. from Glacier National Park, Hungry Horse Dam, House of Mystery, helicopter tours, fly fishing (bull trout, rainbow trout), white water rafting,cross country skiing, Big Mountain Ski Resort. **Additional Information:** Columbia Falls Area Chamber of Commerce, (406) 892-2072.

Restrictions

Pets: Leash only (Please note that the owners have a beautiful, well-behaved & friendly retriever that has free reign of the property, but guestss pets must be on leash.). **Fires:** Fire pits only; fires may be prohibited due to weather: please ask management before starting any fires. **Alcoholic Beverages:** Yes. **Vehicle Maximum Length:** 45 ft.

To Get There

Located directly off Hwy. 2 in Hungry Horse, 20 mi. northeast of Kalispell.

LIVINGSTON

Paradise Valley KOA

163 Pine Creek Rd., Livingston 59047. T: (406) 222-0992 or (800) 562-2805; F: (402) 222-5911; www.koa.com; liv.koa@ycsi.net.

RV ★★★ Tent ★★★

Beauty: ★★★★★	Site Privacy: ★★★
Spaciousness: ★★★	Quiet: ★★★★
Security: ★★★★	Cleanliness: ★★★
Insect Control: ★★★	Facilities: ★★★★

The drive on I-90 to this KOA offers a pleasant combination of Montana's subtle sloping hills, expansive plains, distant cragged mountains, and towering pines, marking a transition in the journey toward Yellowstone National Park. On your way into Paradise Valley, you'll pass a sign that reads, "Don't get the gumps. It's only a few more bumps to KOA." Rest assured your camping experience here will keep you gump free. Located 8 miles south of Livingston, the campground is nestled at the foot of the Absaroka Mountains on the banks of the winding Yellowstone River. This KOA provides well-maintained, semi-private sites surrounded by huge cottonwood, Douglas fir, and quaking aspen. The campground offers the usual KOA comforts complete with morning coffee and inexpensive breakfasts. Yellowstone is a short 35 miles away, but you might find yourself tempted to enjoy the area attractions: challenge yourself to a white water rafting trip, enjoy a quiet fly fishing adventure, or hike one of the scenic trails.

Basics

Operated By: Terry & Diane Devine. **Open:** May 1–Oct. 15. **Site Assignment:** By reservation. **Registration:** In camp store. **Fee:** Tent $15–19, RV $23–$30 per 2 people, extra person $2.50, children under 7 free. **Parking:** At site.

Facilities

Number of RV-Only Sites: 47. **Number of Tent-Only Sites:** 22. **Hookups:** Electric (30, 50 amps), water, sewer. **Each Site:** Picnic table. **Dump Station:** Yes. **Laundry:** Yes. **Pay Phone:** Yes. **Rest Rooms and Showers:** Yes. **Fuel:** No. **Propane:** Yes. **Internal Roads:** Gravel, in good condition. **RV Service:** In Bozeman. **Market:** In town. **Restaurant:** There are several in town. **General Store:**

Yes. **Vending:** Only in store. **Swimming Pool:** Indoor w/ hot tub. **Playground:** Yes. **Other:** 23 cabins, 1 cottage, hot tub, snack bar, pavilion. **Activities:** Swimming, horseshoes, volleyball, basketball, fun cycles, mountain biking, rafting (outfitters next door). **Nearby Attractions:** 36 mi. from the North Gate to Yellowstone National Park, Scenic drives, horseback riding, hot springs, guided park tours, fly fishing trips, Yellowstone Gateway Museum. **Additional Information:** Livingston Chamber of Commerce, (406) 222-0850.

RESTRICTIONS

Pets: On leash. **Fires:** In fire pits only. **Alcoholic Beverages:** Yes. **Vehicle Maximum Length:** Limited sites for very large RVs.

TO GET THERE

I-90 Exit 333 towards Yellowstone, go south 10 mi. on Hwy. 89 to Yellowstone Rd.

LIVINGSTON

Yellowstone's Edge RV Park

3502 Hwy. 89, Livingston 59047. T: (406) 333-4036 or (800) 865-7322; F: (406) 333-4052; www.mtrv.com; edge@mtrv.com.

RV ★★★★★ | Tent ★★★★

Beauty: ★★★★	Site Privacy: ★★★★
Spaciousness: ★★★★	Quiet: ★★★★★
Security: ★★★★	Cleanliness: ★★★★★
Insect Control: ★★★★	Facilities: ★★★★★

As its name implies, Yellowstone's Edge RV Park is situated on the Yellowstone River, one of the longest free-flowing rivers in the United States and a great fly fishing destination to boot. The park's 81 RV and 13 tent-only sites don't have much in the way of shade, but they have great views of the river and surrounding landscape. Sites are close together, but with many return folks, this means the park is quite a friendly and neighborly place. The RV sites are divided evenly between pull-through and back-in, with electric, water, sewer, and phone hookups available. Tent sites have grass pads with picnic tables available at some. This is a great alternative to staying in Yellowstone, which is only a 35-mile drive south. Other activities within easy driving distance include Chico Hot Springs, Museum of the Rockies, Lewis and Clark Caverns, and Virginia City. Staying closer to camp, campers have the option to hike, fish, mountain bike, or play volleyball.

BASICS

Operated By: Chan & Pam Libbey. **Open:** May 1–Oct. 15. **Site Assignment:** By reservation. **Registration:** In camp store. **Fee:** Tent $16.50, RV $28.50 per 2 people. **Parking:** At site.

FACILITIES

Number of RV-Only Sites: 81. **Number of Tent-Only Sites:** 13. **Hookups:** Electric (30, 50 amps), water, sewer, phone. **Each Site:** Picnic table. **Dump Station:** No, all sites are on sewers. **Laundry:** Yes. **Pay Phone:** Yes. **Rest Rooms and Showers:** Yes. **Fuel:** 5 mi. south in Immigrant. **Propane:** Yes. **Internal Roads:** Gravel, in good condition. **RV Service:** In Bozeman. **Market:** In Livingston. **Restaurant:** There are several towards Bozeman. **General Store:** Yes. **Vending:** Yes. **Swimming Pool:** No. **Playground:** No. **Other:** Large lodge, recreation room, game room, 1 river suite, central fire ring, modem. **Activities:** Hiking, fishing (Yellowstone River), mountain biking, volleyball, game room, book exchange. **Nearby Attractions:** 36 mi. from the North Gate to Yellowstone National Park, scenic drives, horseback riding, hot springs, guided park tours, fly-fishing trips, Yellowstone Gateway Museum. **Additional Information:** Livingston Chamber of Commerce, (406) 222-0850.

RESTRICTIONS

Pets: On leash. **Fires:** No open fires. **Alcoholic Beverages:** Yes. **Vehicle Maximum Length:** Up to 90 ft. w/tow. **Other:** Good Sam discount, group rates.

TO GET THERE

Directly off Hwy. 89 in S. Livingston

POLSON

Polson/ Flathead Lake KOA

200 Irvine Flats Rd., Polson 59860. T: (406) 883-2151 or (800) 562-2130; F: (406) 883-0151; www.flatheadlakekoa.com; polsonkoa@bigsky.net.

RV ★★★★★ | Tent ★★★★

Beauty: ★★★★★	Site Privacy: ★★★
Spaciousness: ★★★	Quiet: ★★★★
Security: ★★★★	Cleanliness: ★★★★★
Insect Control: ★★★★	Facilities: ★★★★★

Built atop a hill, peering over the Flathead Lake is the Polson/Flathead Lake KOA. The view is magnificent and the air is crisp and cool. This KOA offers exceptional service and a lovely, clean, and well maintained property. Campsites offer level, gravel camping spurs, both back-in and pull-through, some lawn, and a terrific panoramic view of the Mission Mountains. There is a separate tent area, and if you prefer, there are sites in a tent village with water. The Polson KOA has a charming pool, spa, and snack bar. The Polson Koa is conveniently located to Glacier National Park and the National Bison Range. The Polson area has several places to rent boats or jet skis and offers outfitter services. The Flathead Lake is one of the largest naturally fed lakes in the country and offers recreation for every member of the family.

Basics

Operated By: Paul & Carlisa London. **Open:** Apr. 1–Oct. 15. **Site Assignment:** By reservation. **Registration:** In camp store. **Fee:** Tent $18.50–$20, RV $24–$32 per 2 people, extra person $5., children under 6 stay free. **Parking:** At site.

Facilities

Number of RV-Only Sites: 52. **Number of Tent-Only Sites:** 6. **Hookups:** Electric (30, 50 amps), water, sewer. **Each Site:** Picnic table. **Dump Station:** Yes. **Laundry:** Yes. **Pay Phone:** Yes. **Rest Rooms and Showers:** Yes. **Fuel:** No. **Propane:** Yes. **Internal Roads:** Gravel, in good condition. **RV Service:** Limited in town. **Market:** In town. **Restaurant:** There are several in town. **General Store:** Yes. **Vending:** No, only in store. **Swimming Pool:** Indoor w/ hot tub. **Playground:** Yes. **Other:** 6 cabins, 1 cottage, hot tub, snack bar, pavilion, camp kitchen, tent village, central fire ring, adult-only hot tub, pancake breakfast weekends & holidays. **Activities:** Swimming, horseshoes, volleyball, day tours. **Nearby Attractions:** Flathead Lake, great fishing & boating, boat rental, Wild Horse Island, several museums, short drive to Glacier National Park, The Polson Princess (50-ft. tour boat), whitewater float trips, guided fishing trips. **Additional Information:** Polson Chamber of Commerce, (406) 883-5969.

Restrictions

Pets: On leash. **Fires:** In fire pits only. **Alcoholic Beverages:** Yes. **Vehicle Maximum Length:** Limited sites for very large RVs.

To Get There

Half-mile north of Polson, just off Hwy. 93.

POLSON/FLATHEAD LAKE AREA

Flathead Lake State Park

490 North Meridian, Kalispell 59901.T: (406) 752-5501; www.fwp.state.mt.us/parks; dmonger@state.mtFla.

RV ★★★ Tent ★★★

Beauty: ★★★★	Site Privacy: ★★★
Spaciousness: ★★★	Quiet: ★★★
Security: ★★★★	Cleanliness: ★★★
Insect Control: ★★★	Facilities: ★★★

The Flathead Lake State Park consists of six areas and five campgrounds around the outer circumference of Flathead Lake. Flathead Lake is one of the largest natural lakes in the world with the Flathead River as its major tributary. Montana's Department of Fish, Wildlife and Parks operates these park units as well as several islands around this magnificent lake. The campgrounds are semi-developed with paved parking pads and great waterfront access. Finley Point is the only waterfront site with hookups. All of the sites are large back-in parking spaces. Yellow Bay is intended for tent camping only. It is the smallest and most private of the areas with only five camping sites. Each of the areas has entrance gates, water access, boat ramps, and someone on staff or a host at all times. The weather is cool in the evening and there is always a breeze.

Basics

Operated By: Montana Fish, Wildlife & Parks. **Open:** May–Sept. **Site Assignment:** Self serve & by reservation, (406) 751-7577. **Registration:** At park entrance. **Fee:** $8–$16 depending on residency & camp site. **Parking:** At site.

Facilities

Number of RV-Only Sites: 16. **Number of Tent-Only Sites:** 4 in Yellowbay. **Number of Multipurpose Sites:** 20 to 40 each in the other campgrounds. **Hookups:** Electric (30 amps), water (Finley Point Campground only). **Each Site:** Picnic table, fire pit or grill. **Dump Station:** In Wayfarers. **Laundry:** No. **Pay Phone:** In Wayfarers & Big Arm. **Rest Rooms and Showers:** Yes, but only in Wayfarers, Yellow Bay, & Big Arm (these are coin operated showers, 25 cents per 3 minutes.). **Fuel:** No. **Propane:** No. **Internal Roads:** Paved. **RV Service:** Kalispell. **Market:** Polson or Kalispell.

Restaurant: Polson or Kalispell. **General Store:** No. **Vending:** No. **Swimming Pool:** No, but you may swim in the lake. **Playground:** No. **Other:** Group camping, interpretive programs, boat launches, covered picnic areas, horse trails, Wild Horse Island accessible by boat. **Activities:** Swimming, fishing, hiking, waterskiing. **Nearby Attractions:** Ninepipes Museum, North America Wildlife Museum, Glacier National Park. **Additional Information:** Polson Chamber of Commerce, (406) 883-5970.

Restrictions

Pets: On leash. **Fires:** In approved pits & grills only. **Alcoholic Beverages:** Yes. **Vehicle Maximum Length:** 51 ft. **Other:** 7 day limit, you may purchase a MT state passport, which waves entrance fees.

To Get There

The Flathead State Park Units each have there own entrance. The entrances are all located around the perimeter of Flathead Lake. They are located either off US 93 or SR 35. For exact directions to the campground or area of your choice, please visit the web sight.

SILVER STAR

Jefferson River Guest Ranch and Campground

5162 State Hwy 41, Silver Star 59751. T: (406) 684-5225

RV ★★★	Tent ★★★★★
Beauty: ★★★★	Site Privacy: ★★★
Spaciousness: ★★★	Quiet: ★★★
Security: ★★★★	Cleanliness: ★★★★
Insect Control: ★★★★	Facilities: ★★★

Less than 30 miles from historic Virginia City, this campground is a beautiful 75-acre working ranch. Located on the Jefferson River, there are 15 RV sites. For tenters, the ranch offers open tenting most anywhere on the ranch. If you left your RV or tent at home, two fully-furnished cabins are available for rent (probably best to call ahead for reservations, especially in summer). The friendly folks who own the campground also own the Four Rivers Fishing Company. The campground, located on a half-mile stretch of the scenic and trout-rich Jefferson River, is a prime stop for trout fisherman.

Basics

Operated By: Greg & Janet Smith. **Open:** Apr. 1–Nov. 1. **Site Assignment:** By reservation, open tenting. **Registration:** In camp office or self registration. **Fee:** Tent $10, RV $15. **Parking:** At site.

Facilities

Number of RV-Only Sites: 15. **Number of Tent-Only Sites:** Open tent area. **Hookups:** Electric (30, 50 amps), water, sewer. **Each Site:** Picnic table, fire pits. **Dump Station:** No. **Laundry:** Yes, at the courtesy of the host. **Pay Phone:** Courtesy phone available. **Rest Rooms and Showers:** Yes. **Fuel:** About 2 mi. in Silver Star. **Propane:** No. **Internal Roads:** Combination of gravel & packed dirt. **RV Service:** In Butte. **Market:** In Twin Bridges. **Restaurant:** 10 mi. in either direction. **General Store:** No. **Vending:** Yes. **Swimming Pool:** No, but you may swim in river. **Playground:** No. **Other:** Located on Jefferson River. **Activities:** Blue-ribbon fly fishing, quilting, book exchange, mt. biking. **Nearby Attractions:** Horseback riding, Virginia City, hunting, gold panning, mt. biking. **Additional Information:** Whitehall Chamber of Commerce, (406) 287-2260.

Restrictions

Pets: Leash only. **Fires:** Fire pits only (fires may be prohibited due to dry weather: please ask management before starting any fire.). **Alcoholic Beverages:** Yes. **Vehicle Maximum Length:** 40 ft. **Other:** 14 day limit Memorial Day–Labor Day.

To Get There

Located between I-90 and I-15 on Hwy. 41.

ST. MARY

Johnson's Campground & RV Park

HC 72 10 St. Mary Rte., Browing 59417. T: (406) 732-4207; F: (406) 732-4453; www.glacierinfo.com & click on St.Mary.

RV ★★★	Tent ★★★
Beauty: ★★★	Site Privacy: ★★★
Spaciousness: ★★★	Quiet: ★★★★
Security: ★★★	Cleanliness: ★★★
Insect Control: ★★★	Facilities: ★★★

Upon a hilltop directly adjacent to the east entrance to Glacier National Park is Johnson Campground and RV Park. East of the Continental Divide, the St. Mary's area offers a diversified high desert terrain and hot summer days.

The campground sits atop a large hill overlooking the peaks of Logan Pass and circles back down the hill into a small grass and sand valley where there are several tent sites. The larger RV sites are located on top of the hill in an open clearing with a panoramic view of Glacier. The internal roads are gravel and dirt, which may hinder mobility into sites provided for smaller RVs and 5th wheelers. The campground has a very natural appearance and sites tend to be a bit rustic. In addition to the campground, there is a café, a covered picnic area with a grill, and a small motel. Someone is always on staff to assist with any need that may arise.

Basics

Operated By: The Johnson Family. **Open:** May–Oct. **Site Assignment:** Reservations recommended w/1 night deposit. **Registration:** In general store. **Fee:** Tent $14, RV $18–$25 per 2 people, extra person $3.50. Children under 12 stay free. (cash, credit, check) members of Good Sam. **Parking:** At site.

Facilities

Number of RV-Only Sites: 42. **Number of Tent-Only Sites:** 75. **Number of Multipurpose Sites:** 42. **Hookups:** Electric (20, 30 amps), water, sewer. **Each Site:** Picnic table, some fire pits. **Dump Station:** Yes. **Laundry:** Yes. **Pay Phone:** Yes. **Rest Rooms and Showers:** Yes. **Fuel:** Next door. **Propane:** Yes. **Internal Roads:** Gravel. **RV Service:** 50 mi. west in Kalispell. **Market:** 1 mi. southeast in St. Mary. **Restaurant:** In St. Mary, or on property. **General Store:** Yes. **Vending:** Yes. **Swimming Pool:** No. **Playground:** Yes. **Other:** 1 cabin, covered pavilion w/ kitchen facilities & 2 barbeque grills, small motel, cafe. **Activities:** Horseshoe pit, hiking, biking. **Nearby Attractions:** Glacier National Park (east entrance), hiking, backpacking, guided tours of the park, interpretive programs, helicopter tours, ballon tours. **Additional Information:** www.glacierinfo.com & click St.Mary.

Restrictions

Pets: Leash only. **Fires:** Fire pits only (fires may be prohibited due to weather; please ask management before starting any fire.). **Alcoholic Beverages:** At site only. **Vehicle Maximum Length:** Call ahead for details.

To Get There

Located in the heart of St. Mary on Hwy. 89, 0.25 mi. from the east entrance to Glacier National Park, (15 mi. northwest of Browing).

ST. MARY

St. Mary-Glacier Park KOA

106 West Shore, St. Mary 59417. T: (406)732-4122 or (800) 562-1504; F: (406) 732-4327; www.goglacier.com, www.koa.com; wsbrooke@goglacier.com.

RV ★★★ Tent ★★★

Beauty: ★★★	Site Privacy: ★★★
Spaciousness: ★★★	Quiet: ★★★★
Security: ★★★	Cleanliness: ★★★★
Insect Control: ★★★	Facilities: ★★★★

Directly at the east gate of Glacier and Waterton International Parks sits St. Mary KOA. The campground is an ideal base for families wishing to visit the national parks. Scenic Going-to-the-Sun Road is only a few miles away. St. Mary KOA is a full service modern campground with all the amenities including canoe, paddleboat, and kayak rentals. There are barbeque dinners in the evenings and pancakes for breakfast. The campground is large, but sites are small with little privacy between. Tent sites are in fields of aspen but a fair walk from the facilities. There is a nice hot tub with a spectacular mountain view. However, it is in close proximity to the dump. The weather is very warm and dry in the summer on the eastern side of the Continental Divide. The altitude is high, so the air may seem a bit thin. The view is spectacular and the staff is friendly.

Basics

Operated By: Will & Susan Brook. **Open:** May–Oct. **Site Assignment:** Reservations recommended, held w/a credit card number. **Registration:** In gift shop. **Fee:** Tent $21.95, RV $29.95–$36.95 plus 10% tax per 2 people.(cash, credit, checks) KOA value card 10% discount. **Parking:** At site.

Facilities

Number of RV-Only Sites: 60. **Number of Tent-Only Sites:** 64. **Number of Multipurpose Sites:** 10. **Hookups:** Electric (30, 50 amps), water, sewer. **Each Site:** Picnic table, some grated fire pits. **Dump Station:** Yes. **Laundry:** Yes. **Pay Phone:** Yes. **Rest Rooms and Showers:** Yes. **Fuel:** No.

Propane: Yes. **Internal Roads:** Gravel. **RV Service:** 126 mi. southeast in Great Falls. **Market:** In St. Mary. **Restaurant:** In St. Mary or on the property. **General Store:** Yes. **Vending:** General store only. **Swimming Pool:** No, but 2 hot tubs. **Playground:** Yes. **Other:** 25 camp cabins, 2 cottages, game room, gift shop, outdoor barbeque restaurant, 2 hot tubs, canoe rental, bike rental, car rental, group sites, Internet dataport in the gift shop. **Activities:** Fish (rainbow trout), canoe, bike, hike, game room, horseshoes, volleyball. **Nearby Attractions:** Glacier National Park (2 mi. from east entrance), hiking trails, mountain bike trails, horseback riding, nightly interpretive programs in Glacier. **Additional Information:** www.goglacier.com, www.koa.com.

Restrictions

Pets: Leash only. **Fires:** Fire pits only (fire may be prohibited due to weather; please ask camp staff before starting any fire). **Alcoholic Beverages:** Yes. **Vehicle Maximum Length:** None.

To Get There

From Hwy. 89 in St. Mary, look for huge KOA sign; turn down West Shore, and the KOA sits on the right hand side 1 mi. down.

ST. REGIS
Campground St. Regis

Drawer 8, St. Regis 59866. T: (406) 649-2470 or (888) 247-8734; www.campgroundstregis.com; moose@campgroundstregis.com.

 ★★★★  ★★★★

Beauty: ★★★★★	Site Privacy: ★★★★
Spaciousness: ★★★★	Quiet: ★★★★
Security: ★★★★	Cleanliness: ★★★★★
Insect Control: ★★★★	Facilities: ★★★★

Campground St. Regis is conveniently located off I-90 on the frontage road in St. Regis. This family oriented campground is nestled in a wooded setting, offering activities for all. Campground St. Regis is surrounded by mountains and is only a few miles from the St. Regis River. This campground offers large, spacious, shaded sites with some pull-throughs as long as 75 ft. They provide a large heated pool, game room, and video rentals. The weather offers summer days averaging in the 70s and evenings in the low 40s. There are two golf courses in the area, along with white water rafting, horseback riding, hunting, antique stores, and lots of fishing. St. Regis is the western gateway to the National Bison Range and the Flathead Lake Area.

Basics

Operated By: Gail Pierce & Tom Satterthwaite. **Open:** Apr. 16–Oct. 15. **Site Assignment:** Reservations recommended. **Registration:** In general store. **Fee:** Tent $17, RV $22. **Parking:** At site.

Facilities

Number of Multipurpose Sites: 75. **Hookups:** Electric (20, 30, 50 amps), water, sewer, phone, Internet. **Each Site:** Picnic table, some fire pits. **Dump Station:** Yes. **Laundry:** Yes. **Pay Phone:** Yes. **Rest Rooms and Showers:** Yes. **Fuel:** 1 mi. in St. Regis. **Propane:** Yes. **Internal Roads:** Gravel. **RV Service:** 24 mi. east in Superior. **Market:** In St. Regis. **Restaurant:** In St. Regis. **General Store:** Yes. **Vending:** General store only. **Swimming Pool:** Yes (Memorial Day–Labor Day). **Playground:** Yes. **Other:** Game room, video rental, fax service, horse boarding (must make reservations). **Activities:** Swimming, horseshoes, biking, hiking. **Nearby Attractions:** Fishing (St. Regis River or Flathead Lake), boating, hunting, golf, whitewater rafting, casinos. **Additional Information:** Montana Visitors Information, (406) 649-2290.

Restrictions

Pets: Leash only. **Fires:** Fire pits only. **Alcoholic Beverages:** Yes. **Vehicle Maximum Length:** None. **Other:** Good Sam & KOA discount.

To Get There

I-90 Exit 33, go north to 4-way and turn left onto Mullan Rd. Go 0.75 mi. and turn left on Little Joe Rd. Go 0.5 mi. and turn right on Frontage Rd.; campground is 0.5 mi. on right. There are excellent signs directing you from interstate Exit.

ST. REGIS
St. Regis KOA

105 Old Hwy. 10 East, St. Regis 59866. T: (406) 649-2122 or (800)562-4670; www.koa.com; koastregis@blackfoot.net.

★★★ ★★

Beauty: ★★★	Site Privacy: ★★★
Spaciousness: ★★★	Quiet: ★★★
Security: ★★★★	Cleanliness: ★★★
Insect Control: ★★★★	Facilities: ★★★★

Conveniently located on the frontage road

directly off I-90 in St. Regis, the St. Regis KOA is a unique experience. Of all the campgrounds in this book, the St. Regis KOA is the only campground with a "Caution Rabbit Crossing" sign at the entrance gate. The campground is full (I mean hundreds) of free-range domestic rabbits. There are paths and crossings and cute little shelters, all built for the rabbits. The facility itself is well maintained and clean. They offer all the modern amenities including a pool and driving range. There is a historic mining camp on the property to visit or use as a camping site. There is a camping kitchen, snack bar, and modem data port. The sites are a combination of grass and gravel, and there is a need for some leveling. The weather is comfortable in the summer and cold in the winter. There is someone on security duty around the clock.

Basics

Operated By: John & Louise Cochran. **Open:** All year. **Site Assignment:** Reservations recommended. **Registration:** In general store. **Fee:** Tent $16–$20, RV $27–$29 per 2 people, extra person $3. **Parking:** At site.

Facilities

Number of RV-Only Sites: 66. **Number of Tent-Only Sites:** 21. **Hookups:** Electric (30, 50 amps), water, sewer. **Each Site:** Picnic tables, some lantern poles. **Dump Station:** Yes. **Laundry:** Yes. **Pay Phone:** Yes. **Rest Rooms and Showers:** Yes. **Fuel:** 1 mi. in St. Regis. **Propane:** Yes. **Internal Roads:** Gravel. **RV Service:** 24 mi. east in Superior. **Market:** In St. Regis. **Restaurant:** In St. Regis. **General Store:** Yes. **Vending:** General store only. **Swimming Pool:** Yes (Memorial Day weekend–September 15). **Playground:** Yes. **Other:** Cabins, camp kitchen w/grill & microwave, historic mining camp (tent area), snack bar, dataport. **Activities:** Golf driving range, nature trails, fishing, hunting. **Nearby Attractions:** St. Regis River, golf, Flathead Lake, horseback riding. **Additional Information:** Montana Visitors Information, (406) 649-2290.

Restrictions

Pets: Leash only. **Fires:** Fire pits only. **Alcoholic Beverages:** Yes. **Vehicle Maximum Length:** None. **Other:** There are domestic rabbits all over this KOA, please watch for them on the road.

To Get There

I-90, Exit 33 in St. Regis, go north to 4 way, turn right on Frontage Rd., KOA sits 1 mi. down on your left.

THREE FORKS

Three Forks KOA

P.O. Box 15, Three Forks 59752. T: (406) 285-3611 or (800) 562-9752; www.koa.com.

RV ★★★★ Tent ★★★

Beauty: ★★★★ Site Privacy: ★★★
Spaciousness: ★★★ Quiet: ★★★
Security: ★★★★ Cleanliness: ★★★★
Insect Control: ★★★ Facilities: ★★★★

Nestled in a panoramic setting, this KOA is a very pleasant park indeed.The RV and tent sites are adequately sized, with lovely views of the countryside. Security is above average and the grounds are well maintained. Each site offers parking, picnic tables and fire pits, and some RV sites with full hookups. The campground also offers a good many family activities, including a petting zoo, ice cream parlor, and a pool table. For those guests on a working vacation, dataports are available. Nearby, there are golf courses, the Lewis and Clark Caverns, and the Headwater Heritage Museum, just to list a few. Reservations are recommended, however, because finding a place in the peak season is difficult.

Basics

Operated By: Tom Glorvigen. **Open:** Apr. 15–Oct. 15. **Site Assignment:** Reservations recommended. **Registration:** In general store. **Fee:** Tent $18, RV $22–$24 per 2 persons, extra person $3. **Parking:** At site.

Facilities

Number of RV-Only Sites: 56. **Number of Tent-Only Sites:** 21. **Hookups:** Electric (30, 50 amps), water, sewer. **Each Site:** Picnic tables, fire pits. **Dump Station:** Yes. **Laundry:** Yes. **Pay Phone:** Yes. **Rest Rooms and Showers:** Yes. **Fuel:** 1 mi. by I-90. **Propane:** 1 mi. by I-90. **Internal Roads:** Gravel. **RV Service:** 32 mi. in E. Bozeman. **Market:** 3 mi. in Three Fork. **Restaurant:** There are a few in town. **General Store:** Yes. **Vending:** General store only. **Swimming Pool:** Yes w/a slide. **Playground:** Yes. **Other:** Cabins, petting zoo (chickens & horses), ice cream, dataport. **Activities:** Volleyball,pool table, nature trails, fishing w/water access. **Nearby Attractions:** Headwater Heritage Museum, golf, Lewis & Clark Caverns, fishing, the Madison, Jefferson, & Missouri Rivers, fishing, hunting, & float trip outfitters. **Additional Information:** Montana Visitors Information, (406) 649-2290.

RESTRICTIONS

Pets: Leash only. **Fires:** Fire pits only. **Alcoholic Beverages:** Yes. **Vehicle Maximum Length:** None.

TO GET THERE

I-90 Exit 274 follow signs to KOA, less than 1 mi.

WEST GLACIER

Glacier Campground

P.O. Box 447, West Glacier 59936. T: (406) 387-5689 or (888) 387-5689; www.glaciercampground.com.

RV ★★★★	Tent ★★★★
Beauty: ★★★★★	Site Privacy: ★★★★
Spaciousness: ★★★★	Quiet: ★★★★
Security: ★★★★	Cleanliness: ★★★★★
Insect Control: ★★★★	Facilities: ★★★

Just outside the gates of Glacier National Park is Glacier Campground. This delightful campground is nestled in a mountain clearing surrounded by 40 acres of wooded area. The air is crisp and the view is spectacular. The campground consists of 175 wooded sites that are private, spacious and large enough for easy mobility. Sites are both back-in and pull-through, with gravel parking pads. The natural fir and pines stand tall, and overhanging branches do not seem to be a problem. Tent sites are private and offer a rustic ambiance. The campground is convenient to numerous lakes and rivers, restaurants, ski resorts, and other area activities. The weather is typical of high altitude areas, with dramatic temperature drops in the evening. The campground is staffed around the clock, with the office and lodge open daily.

BASICS

Operated By: George & Kathleen Flint. **Open:** May 15–Sept. 30. **Site Assignment:** Reservations recommended held w/a credit card number. **Registration:** In general store. **Fee:** Tent $17, RV $22 per 2 people, extra child ages 5–11, $1., extra adult $1.50(cash, credit, checks). **Parking:** At site.

FACILITIES

Number of RV-Only Sites: 50. **Number of Tent-Only Sites:** 50. **Number of Multipurpose Sites:** 75. **Hookups:** Electric (20, 30 amps), water, sewer. **Each Site:** Picnic tables, grated fire pits. **Dump Station:** Yes. **Laundry:** Yes. **Pay Phone:** Yes. **Rest Rooms and Showers:** Yes. **Fuel:** In West Glacier. **Propane:** Yes. **Internal Roads:** Mostly paved, some well-graded gravel. **RV Service:** Mobile Service ask in office. **Market:** In West Glacier. **Restaurant:** Next door & in West Glacier. **General Store:** Yes. **Vending:** General Store only. **Swimming Pool:** No. **Playground:** Yes. **Other:** Pavilion w/kitchen facilities, 5 cabins, level tent pads, beautiful rustic Lodge w/round central fire place & recreation room, large screen TV, area where large dogs may run. **Activities:** Horseshoes, volleyball, basketball, picnic area. **Nearby Attractions:** Glacier National Park, world class fly-fishing (Dolly Verden trout, eastern brook trout, western slope native cut throat, bull trout), white water rafting, helicopter tours, scenic drives, fishing tours, horseback riding, House of Mystery, North American Wildlife Museum. **Additional Information:** Columbia Falls Area Chamber of Commerce, (406) 892-2072, Glacier National Park (406) 888-7800, or www.areaparks.com.

RESTRICTIONS

Pets: Leash only. **Fires:** Fire pits only (fires may be restricted due to dry weather; please ask management before starting any fire.). **Alcoholic Beverages:** Yes. **Vehicle Maximum Length:** 45 ft.-plus.

TO GET THERE

Located directly off Hwy. 2 in West Glacier.

WEST GLACIER

Glacier National Park

Park Headquarters, West Glacier 59936. T: (406) 888-7800; F: (406) 888-7808; www.nps.gov/glac/home.htm; glac_info@nps.gov.

RV ★★★	Tent ★★★★
Beauty: ★★★★★	Site Privacy: ★★★
Spaciousness: ★★★	Quiet: ★★★
Security: ★★★★	Cleanliness: ★★★★
Insect Control: ★★★★	Facilities: ★★★★

Welcome to one of America's most pristine and bio-diverse parks. Glacier National Park stretches over a million acres, crosses the Continental

Divide, and is home too over 1,000 species of plants and some of the largest and smallest animals found below the Arctic Circle. Glacier National Park offers over 1,000 campsites in varying terrain. You may chose the mature Western Red Cedar and Hemlock Forests found in the west, to rolling grasslands and aspens found in the east. In order to preserve the natural setting and protect its wildlife inhabitants, Glacier National Park does not offer full hookup facilities. There are several dump stations located throughout the park. Most of Glacier's campgrounds are designed in loops, with an amphitheater somewhere in the middle offering evening interpretive programs. The weather in Glacier National Park varies from the east to the west, with more rain in the west, and warmer days in the east. Temperatures in the summer average high 70s for the day and drop into the low 40s during the evening. Remember, however, it can snow any day of the year. Camphosts attend to most campground areas, and rangers are on duty 24 hours a day.

Basics

Operated By: US National Park Service. **Open:** All year, most campsites are open May–the end of Sept.; there is primitive winter camping available. **Site Assignment:** 2 of the 13 campgrounds are reservable (Fish Creek on the west & St Mary on the east); the rest are on a first come basis; (800) 365-2267 or reservations.nps.gov. **Registration:** Register at information bulletin board for the selected campground, only pay 1 night at a time (see camp host for assistance). **Fee:** Fees range from $12–$17 per night (cash or check). **Parking:** At site.

Facilities

Number of Multipurpose Sites: 13 campgrounds vehicle-accessible w/ a total of 1,019 sites, 2 reservable campgrounds (Fish Creek & St. Mary) 328 sites. **Hookups:** Potable water. **Each Site:** Picnic table, grated fire pits. **Dump Station:** Yes. **Laundry:** Yes, located at the Swift Current Motor Inn in the Many Glacier area of the park also in West Glacier & St. Mary right outside the park gate. **Pay Phone:** Yes in designated service areas, but not individual campgrounds. **Rest Rooms and Showers:** There are rest rooms in all the campgrounds w/many campgrounds having flush toilets. Showers may be taken at the Swiftcurrent Motor Inn in the Many Glacier Area, or the Rising Sun Motor Inn in the Rising Sun Area (purchase shower tokens at any camp store or front desk). **Fuel:** There is no fuel in the park; you may purchase fuel in West Glacier (west entrance) or St. Mary (east entrance), also in Babb, MT; Waterton, Alberta; and Browning, MT. **Propane:** No. **Internal Roads:** Paved, gravel, & dirt. **RV Service:** In West Glacier. **Market:** Apgar, Lake McDonald, West Glacier, St. Mary, or Waterton. **Restaurant:** There are 8 restaurants located in the park, or West Glacier, & St. Mary. **General Store:** There are 10 gift shops/camp stores in the area. **Vending:** Yes in designated service areas, but not in individual campgrounds. **Swimming Pool:** No, but there are lakes & streams available for swimming. **Playground:** No. **Other:** Several boat launches, boat rentals (Lake McDonald, Apgar, Many Glaciers, Two Medicine), picnic areas, amphitheaters, 6 hotels, 10 gift shops, camera & film development shop, 3 visitor centers, many more primitive hike-in camp sites, ATM machines (Apgar, Lake McDonald Lodge, Many Glacier, St. Mary, West Glacier), back-country lodging (Granite Park Chalet, must have a reservation, (406) 387-5654 or www.ptinet/sperrychalet), worship services (check schedule for the ampitheather & denomination of your choice.). **Activities:** Scenic boat tours (Lake McDonald, Many Glacier, Rising Sun, Two Medicine), 700 mi. of maintained hiking trails & backpacking (permit required), bicycling (only permitted on roadways), horseback riding (Many Glacier & Lake McDonald), interpretive bus tours, scenic Going-to-the-Sun Road (vehicle or vehicle combinations may not be longer than 21 ft. × 8 ft. wide between Avalanche Campground & the Sun Point parking area, the park does offer shuttle service), stream fishing (western slope native cut throat, bull trout, lake trout), world class fly-fishing (Dolly Varden trout, eastern brook trout, arctic grayling), 1–7 day guided backpacking & hiking tours, interpretive programs nightly at the many amphitheaters in the park. **Nearby Attractions:** Whitewater rafting (West Glacier), balloon rides, helicopter tours. **Additional Information:** www.glacierparkinc.com, www.americanparks.net/glaciernationalpark.htm.

Restrictions

Pets: Leashed, or crated only. Pets are not permitted on trails, along lake shores, or in backcountry. **Fires:** In fire pits only; fires maybe restricted due to dry weather; please always ask park official before starting any fire. **Alcoholic Beverages:**

Yes w/discretion. **Vehicle Maximum Length:** Apgar 40 ft., Many Glacier, Fish Creek, St. Mary, Two Medicine 35 ft., Avalanche 26 ft., Sprague Creek 21ft. (no tow-in units). **Other:** 7-day limit per camp site; 8 people max. to a site; no more than 2 tents per site; group sites are available; special bike-camping sites are also available for $3 per night per person.

To Get There

West entrance is located off Hwy. 2 in West Glacier 23 mi. northeast of Kalispell; East entrance is located off Hwy. 89 in St. Mary, 17 mi. north of Browning. You may also enter the park in Waterson, Alberta, or off Hwy. 89 in Babb, MT.

WEST YELLOWSTONE
Lionshead RV Resort

1545 Targhee Pass Hwy., West Yellowstone 59758. T: (406) 646-7662

RV ★★★ Tent ★★★

Beauty: ★★★	Site Privacy: ★★★
Spaciousness: ★★★	Quiet: ★★★
Security: ★★★	Cleanliness: ★★
Insect Control: ★★★	Facilities: ★★

Lionshead has a little of everything, including a Super 8 Motel, casino, restaurants, and, of course, an RV park. Located on Denny Creek, the park offers excellent views of the surrounding mountains, and it's only eight miles west of Yellowstone Entrance. With a few exceptions, most of the 168 RV sites are pull-through, with electric, water, and sewer hookups available. Gravel roads wind between the grassy sites, but none of them are overly spacious or too cramped. Outdoor activities include anything imaginable, from whitewater rafting and mountain biking to horseback riding and fishing; winter visitors can cross-country ski or rent one of the resort's snowmobiles to explore the adjacent meadows. For enthusiastic hikers, the Continental Divide National Scenic Trail is close by.

Basics

Operated By: Private Operator. **Open:** Call ahead for details. **Site Assignment:** First come, first served. **Registration:** In camp office. **Fee:** $16–$27.50. **Parking:** At site.

Facilities

Number of RV-Only Sites: 168. **Number of Tent-Only Sites:** 26. **Hookups:** Electric (20, 30, 50 amps), water, sewer. **Each Site:** Picnic table, fire pits in tent sites. **Dump Station:** No. **Laundry:** Yes. **Pay Phone:** Yes. **Rest Rooms and Showers:** Yes. **Fuel:** Yes. **Propane:** Yes. **Internal Roads:** Gravel. **RV Service:** On site (the local RV mobile service is based from this campground). **Market:** In West Yellowstone. **Restaurant:** In West Yellowstone or on site. **General Store:** Yes. **Vending:** Yes. **Swimming Pool:** No. **Playground:** Yes. **Other:** Super 8 Hotel, dance hall, restaurant. **Activities:** Dances, fishing, hiking, book exchange, pool room. **Nearby Attractions:** Yellowstone National Park, IMAX, whitewater rafting, museums, shopping, Grizzly Discovery Center. **Additional Information:** West Yellowstone Chamber of Commerce, (406) 646-7701.

Restrictions

Pets: On leash only. **Fires:** Inquire at campground. **Alcoholic Beverages:** Inquire at campground. **Vehicle Maximum Length:** Call ahead for details.

To Get There

Located 7 mi. west of West Yellowstone on Hwy 20.

WEST YELLOWSTONE
Yellowstone Park/West Entrance KOA

P.O. Box 348, West Yellowstone 59758. T: (406) 646-7606 or (800) 562-7591; F: (406) 646-7606; www.koa.com/where/wy/26122.htm; ypkoa@aol.com.

RV ★★★★ Tent ★★★

Beauty: ★★★★	Site Privacy: ★★★
Spaciousness: ★★★	Quiet: ★★★
Security: ★★★★	Cleanliness: ★★★★
Insect Control: ★★★	Facilities: ★★★★

The perfect base camp for exploring Yellowstone's two million acres, Yellowstone Park KOA offers 166 RV sites and 73 tent-only sites within 6 miles of the west entrance. The newly paved road provides easy access throughout the grounds. Pancake breakfast and a chuckwagon dinner are available daily, in season (mid-June to Labor Day). There's not much campers can't do outside of camp, including hiking, white water rafting, and horseback riding. In-camp activities include mini-golf, basketball, and horseshoes. Bike rentals are available here as well. Nearby attractions include the Yellowstone IMAX Theater, Grizzly Discovery Center and Wolf Preserve, and Museum of the Yellowstone. A new indoor pool and spa provide comfort for those relaxing after a day of adventuring.

Basics

Operated By: Marvin & Carol Linde. **Open:** May 22–Oct. 1. **Site Assignment:** Reservations highly recommended. **Registration:** General Store. **Fee:** Tent $33, RV $27–$43. **Parking:** At site.

Facilities

Number of RV-Only Sites: 166. **Number of Tent-Only Sites:** 73. **Number of Multipurpose Sites:** 3. **Hookups:** Electric (30, 50 amps), water, sewer. **Each Site:** Picnic table, grated fire pits, some concrete patios. **Dump Station:** Yes. **Laundry:** Yes. **Pay Phone:** Yes. **Rest Rooms and Showers:** Yes. **Fuel:** No. **Propane:** Yes. **Internal Roads:** Paved. **RV Service:** Local service. **Market:** West Yellowstone. **Restaurant:** West Yellowstone (pancake breakfast & BBQ dinners served on site). **General Store:** Yes. **Vending:** Yes. **Swimming Pool:** Indoor pool & hot tub. **Playground:** Yes. **Other:** 58 cabins, camping kitchen, gifts, fresh fudge, Internet data port. **Activities:** Mini-golf, fun cycle & bike rentals, fishing, basketball, game room, Yellowstone tours. **Nearby Attractions:** Yellowstone National Park, IMAX, Museums, Grizzly Discovery Center, white water rafting, Teton Aviation Center, Yellowstone Historic Center. **Additional Information:** West Yellowstone Chamber of Commerce (406) 646-7701.

Restrictions

Pets: On leash. **Fires:** In fire pits only. **Alcoholic Beverages:** Yes. **Vehicle Maximum Length:** None.

To Get There

From West Yellowstone, go east 5 mi. on US 20 to the campground entrance.

WHITE SULPHUR SPRINGS

Conestoga Campground

P.O.Box 508, White Sulphur Springs 59645.
T: (406) 547-3890; F: (406) 547-3638;
www.ccmemberships.com;
info@ccmemberships.com.

RV ★★★ Tent ★★★

Beauty: ★★★	Site Privacy: ★★★
Spaciousness: ★★★	Quiet: ★★★★
Security: ★★★★	Cleanliness: ★★★
Insect Control: ★★★	Facilities: ★★★

This privately-owned campground is surrounded by the Big Belt, Little Belt, and Castle Mountains, and offers some of the most magnificent views in North America. While the site facilities are average, the campground's strongest selling point is its location. The campground is nestled between Yellowstone National Park and Glacier National Park, and provides easy access to these national treasures. The campground is also in close proximity to the world-famous Smith River along with numerous mountain lakes and streams filled with various species of fish. The locals boast that this unspoiled part of Montana has more elk and deer than people. There are more than 860 miles of hiking trails in seven mountain ranges. The campground is open from Apr. through Nov., and reservations can be made by phone.

Basics

Operated By: Roy & Linda Reich. **Open:** May 15–Oct. 15. **Site Assignment:** By reservation. **Registration:** In camp office. **Fee:** $21–$25 per 2 people, extra person $3 (special rate plans apply-members). **Parking:** At site.

Facilities

Number of RV-Only Sites: 41. **Number of Tent-Only Sites:** Open tent area. **Hookups:** Electric (20, 30, 50 amps), water, sewer. **Each Site:** Picnic tables. **Dump Station:** Yes. **Laundry:** Yes. **Pay Phone:** Yes. **Rest Rooms and Showers:** Yes. **Fuel:** No, 1 mi. in town. **Propane:** No. **Internal Roads:** Gravel. **RV Service:** Limited service in Townsend. **Market:** In town. **Restaurant:** In town. **General Store:** Yes. **Vending:** Yes. **Swimming Pool:** No. **Playground:** Yes. **Other:** Trout pond, all pull-through sites 25 x 80 ft., water in tent area, free shuttle service to many area activities. **Activi-**

ties: Games, picnicking, fishing. **Nearby Attractions:** Golf, teen center, hot mineral baths, many fishing & rafting outfitters, big game hunting, skiing, boating, several museums, Old Fort Logan. **Additional Information:** Meagher County Chamber of Commerce, (406) 547-2250.

Restrictions

Pets: On leash. **Fires:** No open fires. **Alcoholic Beverages:** Yes. **Vehicle Maximum Length:** None. **Other:** This is a special membership RV park, please refer to their web site or call for more information.

To Get There

66 mi. from I-90 Exit 340, head northeast on US 89 for 57 mi., then go north on US 12 for 9 mi., left onto SR 360 go 0.25 mi. and left or south on 8th Ave. Sw to entrance.

WHITEFISH

Whitefish-Glacier KOA Kampground

5121 Hwy. 93S, Whitefish 59937. T: (406) 862-4242 or (800) 562-8734; F: (406) 862-8967; www.koa.com; whitefishkoa@netscape.net.

RV: ★★★★ Tent: ★★★★

Beauty: ★★★★	Site Privacy: ★★★
Spaciousness: ★★★	Quiet: ★★★
Security: ★★★★	Cleanliness: ★★★★
Insect Control: ★★★★	Facilities: ★★★★★

Whitefish-Glacier KOA is a superb campground with amenities and activities for the entire family. Nestled in a scenic forest atmosphere two miles south of Whitefish, this campground is located in the Rocky Mountains, near Glacier National Park, the Flathead River, Whitefish Lake, and Big Mountain Ski Resort. The campground offers large comfortable sites, both pull-through and back-in. Tent sites are available in the woods or on a more open lawn area. The park features a large family entertainment center with an indoor/outdoor pool, game room, and pizzeria. The area is famous for its skiing and fishing, and has an abundance of hiking and biking trails (the campground rents bikes). In addition the campground has 10 cabins and a huge recreation hall that accommodates up to 500 people. The weather is cool through late June, so remember to pack warm. The campground offers 24-hour security and the staff is very friendly. Summers fill up quickly, so make reservations as far in advance as possible.

Basics

Operated By: Walt Staves. **Open:** All year. **Site Assignment:** Reservations recommended Apr.–Oct. held w/credit card number. **Registration:** In general store. **Fee:** Tent $20–$24 RV $25.50–$34.50 per 2 people, extra adult $4, children under 17 stay free. KOA Value card discount, & Good Sam honored (cash, credit, checks). **Parking:** At site.

Facilities

Number of RV-Only Sites: 15. **Number of Tent-Only Sites:** Open tent area. **Hookups:** Electric (30, 50 amps), water, sewer. **Each Site:** Picnic table, fire pits. **Dump Station:** No. **Laundry:** Yes, at the courtesy of the host. **Pay Phone:** Courtesy phone available. **Rest Rooms and Showers:** Yes. **Fuel:** About 2 mi. in Silver Star. **Propane:** No. **Internal Roads:** Combination of gravel & packed dirt. **RV Service:** In Butte. **Market:** In Whitefish. **Restaurant:** Buffalo Bob's Pizza Place on property; also in Kalispell or Whitefish. **General Store:** Yes. **Vending:** In restaurant or general store only. **Swimming Pool:** Yes, indoor w/child wading pool (open year-round). **Playground:** Yes. **Other:** Recreation center w/game room, 10 cabins, hot tub, restaurant. **Activities:** Paddle boats, volleyball, horseshoes, basketball, fun cycles, game room, hiking. **Nearby Attractions:** Big Mountain Ski Resort, Whitefish Lake, 18 mi. from Glacier National Park, boating, fishing (whitefish, cut throat), cross-country skiing, snow mobile trails, waterskiing, windsurfing. **Additional Information:** Whitefish Chamber of Commerce, (406) 862-3501.

Restrictions

Pets: Leash only. **Fires:** Fire pits only (fires may be prohibited due to dry weather: please ask management before starting any fire.). **Alcoholic Beverages:** Yes. **Vehicle Maximum Length:** 40 ft. **Other:** 14 day limit Memorial Day–Labor Day.

To Get There

Located directly off Hwy. 93, 4 mi. south of Whitefish.

WHITEHALL

Pipestone Campground

41 Bluebird Ln., Whitehall 59759. T: (406) 287-5224

RV ★★★ Tent ★★★

Beauty: ★★★	Site Privacy: ★★★
Spaciousness: ★★★	Quiet: ★★★★
Security: ★★★	Cleanliness: ★★★
Insect Control: ★★★	Facilities: ★★★

Located 16 miles east of Butte, just off of I-90, Pipestone Campground has 75 sites that offer a mix of pull-throughs and back-ins, some with complete hookups. The grounds are mostly open with a few scattered trees that provide little shade. Visitors will want to make sure to take advantage of the outdoor hot tub with a view of the snow-capped mountains. Activities such as horseshoes, swimming, tetherball and volleyball can help pass the time time. Those wanting to explore Butte will find several museums and interpretive centers dedicated to mining, including the World Museum of Mining, the Mineral Museum, and the Anselmo Mine Yard.

Basics

Operated By: Dan & Dianna Graves. **Open:** Apr. 1–Oct. 15. **Site Assignment:** Reservations accepted. **Registration:** In general store. **Fee:** $17.25–$21.75. **Parking:** At site.

Facilities

Number of RV-Only Sites: 75. **Number of Tent-Only Sites:** Open tent area. **Hookups:** Electric (20, 30, 50 amps), water, sewer, phone. **Each Site:** Picnic tables, some fire pits. **Dump Station:** Yes. **Laundry:** Yes. **Pay Phone:** Yes. **Rest Rooms and Showers:** Yes. **Fuel:** No. **Propane:** Yes. **Internal Roads:** Gravel, in good condition. **RV Service:** 18 mi. west in Butte. **Market:** 5 mi. east in Whitehall. **Restaurant:** 5 mi. east in Whitehall. **General Store:** Yes. **Vending:** Yes. **Swimming Pool:** Yes. **Playground:** Yes. **Other:** Cabins, RV wash, game room, mail service, large adult spa, Internet data port on pay phone. **Activities:** Swimming, campfires, volleyball, tetherball, horseshoes. **Nearby Attractions:** Fishing (rainbow trout), hunting, float trips, fishing tours. **Additional Information:** Whitehall Chamber of Commerce, (406) 287-2260.

Restrictions

Pets: On leash. **Fires:** In fire pits only (fires may be restricted due to weather; please ask management before starting any open fires.). **Alcoholic Beverages:** Yes. **Vehicle Maximum Length:** None.

To Get There

I-90 Exit 241, 16 mi. east of Butte, can be seen from interstate.

WOLF CREEK

Lake Holter Recreation Area

1383 Beartooth Rd., Wolf Creek 59648. T: (406) 494-5059; F: (406) 235-4314; www.mt.blm.gov.

RV ★★★ Tent ★★★

Beauty: ★★★	Site Privacy: ★★★
Spaciousness: ★★★	Quiet: ★★★
Security: ★★★	Cleanliness: ★★★
Insect Control: ★★★	Facilities: ★★★

Approximately 35 miles north of Helena, the highlight of this recreation area is its proximity to Holter Lake. With 56 grassy sites located on the lake, there is a good chance you might be able to enjoy some lakefront camping. The area provides plenty of opportunity for recreational activities, including hiking, horseback riding, and fishing. Gravel access and interior roads, scant landscaping, a propensity for high winds, and sparsely wooded surrounding hills make this campground wanting of scenery. However, this might well be a worthwhile stop for any avid fisher. Lake Holter, located on the Missouri River, is home to walleye, and the "Mighty Mo," known worldwide for its dry fly-fishing, runs wild with brown and rainbow trout. Definitely, this is a destination spot for a pleasing fishing experience.

Basics

Operated By: Bureau of Land Management. **Open:** All year. **Site Assignment:** First come, first served. **Registration:** Self serve. **Fee:** $8 per unit. **Parking:** At site.

Facilities

Number of Multipurpose Sites: 140. **Hookups:** Water. **Each Site:** Picnic tables; fire pits. **Dump Station:** Yes at Holter Lake Lodge for a fee. **Laundry:** No. **Pay Phone:** Yes. **Rest Rooms and Showers:** Rest rooms only. **Fuel:**

No. **Propane:** No. **Internal Roads:** Gravel. **RV Service:** Limited local service. **Market:** In town. **Restaurant:** Next door. **General Store:** No. **Vending:** No. **Swimming Pool:** No, but there is a beach on the lake. **Playground:** Yes. **Other:** Lake access, covered pavilion, lodge, 3 designated swimming areas, 2 multi-laned boat ramps, docks w/about 60 slips. **Activities:** Swimming, fishing, boating, jet skiing, waterskiing. **Nearby Attractions:** Several vacation ranches, blue ribbon fishing, the state capital, horseback riding, natural hot springs, ghost towns, Helena. **Additional Information:** Helena Chamber of Commerce, (406) 442-4120.

Restrictions

Pets: On leash. **Fires:** In fire pits only. **Alcoholic Beverages:** Yes. **Vehicle Maximum Length:** None. **Other:** 14 day stay limit.

To Get There

Take Exit 226 at Wolf Creek and follow Recreation Frontage Rd. northeast about 3 mi., then 2 mi. east on gravel road.

Nebraska

A motor coach, a bike, and a good horse are the best ways to experience Nebraska, America's gateway to the west. The most famous stories of adventure and transcontinental travel take you through the byways of Nebraska. Fur traders of the past navigated through this high plains state to avoid the mountain passes of Colorado as they ventured toward the Pacific. Famous trails such as the **Lewis and Clark, Oregon,** and **Mormon Trails** pass through this state. Nebraska was used for the first transcontinental railroad, as well as the Pony Express. Nebraska in many ways is a living museum. Every scenic byway tells a story and adds another piece to the puzzle of our American heritage. From the **Great Platte River Road Archway** to the famous **Oregon Trail Chimney Rock** landmark, the past comes alive.

Nebraska is also an outdoor enthusiast's paradise. The rivers and streams of Nebraska offer a variety of adventures. Whether you enjoy paddling, rafting, waterskiing, or sitting on the dock, there is a river for you, and if you are a serious angler, the waters of Nebraska are full of walleye, trout, and bass. If you enjoy biking and are looking for a wide-open scenic route, look no further. Nebraska has hundreds of miles of biking trails. You can pedal complete sections of the **Cowboy Trail** linking **Norfolk** and **Chadron,** or bike along the Platte River. And if you are an equestrian the trails are equally limitless. There are professional outfitters throughout the state, and the Nebraska state parks are wonderful base camps.

The state offers more than just the ruggedness of the west, however. There is a refined side of Nebraska as well—one devoted to the fine arts, offering world-class art museums of frontier paintings, sculptured gardens, symphonies, and theatre.

Recreational camping is the best way to see and experience the adventures Nebraska has to offer. The majority of full-service campgrounds are located of I-80, but you have to venture away from the interstate to fully appreciate the landscape and history. For impressive vistas of sweeping natural beauty, Nebraska state parks and recreation areas are some of the best in the country.

Campground Profiles

ASHLAND

Eugene T. Mahoney State Park

28500 West Park Hwy., Ashland 68003. T: (402) 944-2523; F: (402) 944-7604; www.ngpc.state.ne.us; etmsp@ngpc.state.ne.us.

RV ★★★ Tent ★★★

Beauty: ★★★	Site Privacy: ★★★
Spaciousness: ★★★	Quiet: ★★★★
Security: ★★★★	Cleanliness: ★★★
Insect Control: ★★★	Facilities: ★★

Offering large, shady sites near Owen Marina Lake, camping in Eugene T. Mahoney State Park can be enjoyed year-round. It is easily accessible due to its I-80 location midway between Lincoln and Omaha. For campers who don't want to travel far for activities, this is the place to be, with everything from a water slide to a new virtual reality game room located within the park. Winter recreation pursuits include ice skating from November through March in the Pavilion, fishing in the 10-acre, trout-stocked US West Lake, and downhill sledding. The centrally located theatre provides family fun with melodramas that run from Memorial Day weekend thru early November. Next door to the park is the new Strategic Air and Space Museum, the nation's foremost facility of its kind, with aircraft and missile exhibits.

BASICS

Operated By: Nebraska Game & Parks Commission. **Open:** Year-round. **Site Assignment:** First come, first served. **Registration:** Self-serve registration kiosks. **Fee:** $11–$12 depends on site & amenities, plus vehicle entrance fee. **Parking:** At site.

FACILITIES

Number of RV-Only Sites: 149. **Number of Tent-Only Sites:** 24. **Hookups:** Electric (20, 30 amps), water. **Each Site:** Picnic tables, fire pit. **Dump Station:** Yes, there is also a boat pump out on the marina. **Laundry:** Yes. **Pay Phone:** Yes. **Rest Rooms and Showers:** Yes. **Fuel:** Boat fuel only at the marina. **Propane:** No. **Internal Roads:** Paved. **RV Service:** 17 mi. in Elkhorn. **Market:** In Ashland. **Restaurant:** Peter Kiewit Lodge on site, the mariana, or in Ashland. **General Store:** The marina is open Memorial Day through Labor Day. **Vending:** Yes. **Swimming Pool:** Yes. **Playground:** Yes. **Other:** 51 cabin, 40 room lodge w/ full-service restaurant, water slide, hiking trails, 10 picnic shelters, one w/ electricity, fish-cleaning station, full service marina, Kountz Memorial Theater, observation tower, visitor center, indoor activity center, boat rental. **Activities:** Swimming, water slide, mini-golf, boating, fishing, hiking, arts & crafts, rock climbing simulator, indoor playground, hunting simulator, ball simulator, ice skating, picnics, driving range. **Nearby Attractions:** Gavins Point Dam, Lewis & Clark Visitor Center, The National Fish Hatchery, Lakeview Golf Course. **Additional Information:** Gretna Chamber of Commerce, (402) 332-3535.

RESTRICTIONS

Pets: On leash. **Fires:** In grills or fire pits only. **Alcoholic Beverages:** No alcoholic beverages allowed. **Vehicle Maximum Length:** 45 ft. **Other:** Nebraska State Park passes honored.

TO GET THERE

From I-80 Exit 426, go northwest on W. Park Hwy. then bear right on Park Dr.

CHADRON

Chadron State Park

15951 Hwy. 385, Chadron 69337-7353. T: (308) 432-6167; F: (308)432-6102; www.ngpc.state.ne.us; chadronsp@ngpc.state.ne.us.

RV ★★★ Tent ★★★

Beauty: ★★★	Site Privacy: ★★★
Spaciousness: ★★★	Quiet: ★★★★
Security: ★★★★	Cleanliness: ★★★
Insect Control: ★★★	Facilities: ★★

Situated near the Nebraska National Forest, Chadron State Park guarantees exceptional scenery. The fees are very reasonable, and there are no reservations required. The sites for both RVs and tents are average sized, with picnic tables and fire pits. The campground offers only adequate privacy, but there's lots of peace and quiet. As for activities available, Chadron has some very unusual and interesting pastimes for the family. There is an old-time fur trade demonstration, and arts and crafts, as well as archery, tennis, and a buffalo stew cookout by appointment. Nearby, guests will find the Dawes County Historical Museum, mountain biking, and golf.

Basics

Operated By: Nebraska Game & Parks Commission. **Open:** Year-round. **Site Assignment:** First come, first served. **Registration:** Self-serve registration kiosks. **Fee:** $3–$12 depends on site & amenities, plus vehicle entrance fee. **Parking:** At site.

Facilities

Number of RV-Only Sites: 70. **Number of Tent-Only Sites:** 18. **Hookups:** Electric (20, 30 amps), water. **Each Site:** Picnic tables, fire pit. **Dump Station:** Yes. **Laundry:** Yes. **Pay Phone:** Yes. **Rest Rooms and Showers:** Yes. **Fuel:** No. **Propane:** No. **Internal Roads:** Paved. **RV Service:** In town. **Market:** In town. **Restaurant:** There is a large variety of restaurant in town. **General Store:** Yes. **Vending:** Yes. **Swimming Pool:** Yes. **Playground:** Yes. **Other:** 22 cabins, hiking trails, biking trails, horseback riding, fishing pond, large picnic shelter w/ electricity, several hundred picnic tables & grills. **Activities:** Archery, horseback riding, old time fur trade demonstration, arts & crafts, Jeep rides, volleyball, tennis, fishing, Buffalo Stew Cookouts by appointment. **Nearby Attractions:** Museum of the fur trade, Nebraska National Forest, Dawes County Historical Museum, mountain biking, golf. **Additional Information:** Chadron Chamber of Commerce, (308) 432-4401.

Restrictions

Pets: On leash. **Fires:** In grills or fire pits only. **Alcoholic Beverages:** No alcoholic beverages allowed. **Vehicle Maximum Length:** 45 ft. **Other:** Nebraska State Park passes honored.

To Get There

From Chadron, take South Hwy. 385 for 8.4 mi., turn right on to park road.

CRAWFORD
Fort Robinson State Park

P.O.Box 392, Crawford 69339-0392. T: (308) 665-2900; F: (308)665-2906; www.ngpc.state.ne.us; ftrobsp@ngpc.state.ne.us.

RV ★★★ Tent ★★★

Beauty: ★★★ Site Privacy: ★★★
Spaciousness: ★★★ Quiet: ★★★★
Security: ★★★★ Cleanliness: ★★★
Insect Control: ★★★ Facilities: ★★

Fort Robinson State Park is a place in western tradition, made famous by men such Walter Reed and Red Cloud. The fort was established in 1874 as an active military post and remained so for the next 74 years. Today, Fort Robinson State Park is a living museum. Train, horseback, and jeep tours help tell of this western heritage. The park greets its visitors with resort-like accommodations with lodging and modern camping available. The internal roads are paved, and the campground offers large, paved camping spurs, well separated from neighbors. The park works hard at keeping the facilities clean and the lawn manicured. There are variety of activities taking place in the park and the surrounding area. Camping is on a first come, first served basis, so be sure to arrive early in order to get a site. There is full restaurant service in the Fort Robinson Inn during the summer. All visitor mush register at the entrance gate and pay an entrance fee.

Basics

Operated By: Nebraska Game & Parks Commission. **Open:** The park is open year-round, camping Apr.–Nov. **Site Assignment:** First come, first served. **Registration:** Self-serve registration kiosks. **Fee:** $8–$12 depends on site & amenities, plus vehicle entrance fee. **Parking:** At site.

Facilities

Number of RV-Only Sites: 100. **Number of Tent-Only Sites:** 25. **Hookups:** Electric (20, 30, 50 amps), water. **Each Site:** Picnic tables, fire pit. **Dump Station:** Yes. **Laundry:** Yes. **Pay Phone:** Yes. **Rest Rooms and Showers:** Yes. **Fuel:** No. **Propane:** No. **Internal Roads:** Paved. **RV Service:** 60 mi. in Scottsbluff. **Market:** In Crawford. **Restaurant:** At the lodge, or Sutler's Store on site (Memorial Day through Labor Day) or in town. **General Store:** Yes, Sutler's Store, Memorial Day–Labor Day. **Vending:** Yes. **Swimming Pool:** Yes. **Playground:** Yes. **Other:** 35 cabins, 22-room lodge w/ full-service restaurant, hiking trails, 4 picnic shelters, one w/ electricity, Fort Robinson Museum, trail side museum, meeting facilities, historic tours, bike rentals, over 100 picnic tables &

grills, modern horse stable (boarding available). **Activities:** Swimming, boating, fishing, hiking, horseback riding, (22,000 acres of horse trails), Jeep rides, Craft Center, horse drawn tour train, stagecoach rides, pony rides, rodeo. **Nearby Attractions:** Inquire at campground. **Additional Information:** Chadron Chamber of Commerce, (308) 432-4401.

Restrictions

Pets: On leash. **Fires:** In grills or fire pits only. **Alcoholic Beverages:** No alcoholic beverages allowed. **Vehicle Maximum Length:** 45 ft. **Other:** Nebraska State Park passes honored.

To Get There

The campground is off US 20 about 8 mi. west of Crawford.

CROFTON

Lewis and Clark State Recreation Area

5473 897 Rd., Crofton 68730-3290. T: (402) 388-4169; F: (402) 388-4696; www.ngpc.state.ne.us; lcsra@ngpc.state.ne.us.

RV ★★★ Tent ★★★

Beauty: ★★★	Site Privacy: ★★★
Spaciousness: ★★★	Quiet: ★★★★
Security: ★★★★	Cleanliness: ★★★
Insect Control: ★★★	Facilities: ★★

Straddling the northeast border with South Dakota, Lewis and Clark Lake offers a good place to fish and relax. On the Nebraska side of the lake, the recreation area is roughly divided into five parts. The Weigand-Burbach area is the most developed, featuring the bulk of the campsites (electric hookups, pull-throughs, some tent camping, etc.), a full-service marina, convenience store, swimming beach, and other amenities. This is going to be the first choice for most campers. Bloomfield is a smaller and more secluded area, with about 30 campsites with electric hookups, modern and primitive rest rooms, and a boat ramp; this place would be an acceptable second option if Weigand-Burbach is full or if you just want fewer neighbors. The Miller Creek and South Shore areas are primitive camping only, offering primitive rest rooms and boat ramps. The Deep Water area is nothing more than an access point with a parking lot.

Basics

Operated By: Nebraska Game & Parks Commission. **Open:** Year-round. **Site Assignment:** First come, first served. **Registration:** Self-serve registration kiosks, a few sites are reservable. **Fee:** \$3–\$12 depends on site & amenities, plus vehicle entrance fee. **Parking:** At site.

Facilities

Number of RV-Only Sites: 150. **Number of Tent-Only Sites:** 45. **Number of Multipurpose Sites:** 50. **Hookups:** Electric (20, 30 amps), water. **Each Site:** Picnic tables, fire pit. **Dump Station:** Yes, there is also a boat pump out on the marina. **Laundry:** Yes. **Pay Phone:** Yes. **Rest Rooms and Showers:** Yes. **Fuel:** Boat fuel only at the marina. **Propane:** No. **Internal Roads:** Paved. **RV Service:** 10 mi. in Yankton, SD. **Market:** In Yankton, SD. **Restaurant:** There is one restaurant in Crofton, but there are several in Yankton, SD. **General Store:** The marina is open Memorial Day through Labor Day. **Vending:** Yes. **Swimming Pool:** Yes. **Playground:** Yes. **Other:** 2 camping areas, swimming beach, 5 cabins, 4 boat ramps, 16 docks, 80 boat slips, boat fuel, marina, fish-cleaning station, picnic shelter w/electricity, over 200 picnic table & grills. **Activities:** Inquire at campground. **Nearby Attractions:** Gavins Point Dam, Lewis & Clark Visitor Center, the National Fish Hatchery, Lakeview Golf Course. **Additional Information:** Bloomfield City Clerk, (402) 373-4396.

Restrictions

Pets: On leash. **Fires:** In grills or fire pits only. **Alcoholic Beverages:** No alcoholic beverages allowed. **Vehicle Maximum Length:** 45 ft. **Other:** Nebraska State Park passes honored.

To Get There

From Crofton, drive north on Rte. 121 for 15 mi. Park entrance is on the left.

GOTHENBURG

Gothenburg KOA

P.O.Box 385, Gothenburg 69139. T: (308) 537-7387 or (800) 562-1873; www.koa.com.

RV ★★ Tent ★★

Beauty: ★★	Site Privacy: ★★
Spaciousness: ★★	Quiet: ★★★
Security: ★★★	Cleanliness: ★★★
Insect Control: ★★★	Facilities: ★★★

This KOA campground is located off I-80 Exit 211, a quarter of a mile south on Hwy. 47. This KOA is best used as an overnight stop. The RV and tent sites are not very spacious or private, and the facilities are merely adequate. However, the sites are nicely shaded with trees, and the Platte River provides excellent opportunities for fishing. The Campground is situated in close proximity to the Pony Express Station, Buffalo Bill's Guest Ranch. and the Sod House Museum. The campground is open from March to November, with sites assigned in advance through either phone or web reservations. KOA discount member rates apply.

BASICS

Operated By: Private Operator. **Open:** Mar. 15–Nov. 15. **Site Assignment:** By reservation. **Registration:** At Service Station/Convenience store. **Fee:** Tent $16–$20 RV $20–$28. per 2 people (cash or credit). **Parking:** At site.

FACILITIES

Number of RV-Only Sites: 33. **Number of Tent-Only Sites:** 15. **Number of Multipurpose Sites:** 14. **Hookups:** Electric (20, 30, 50 amps), water, sewer. **Each Site:** Picnic tables, few grills. **Dump Station:** Yes. **Laundry:** Yes. **Pay Phone:** Yes. **Rest Rooms and Showers:** Yes. **Fuel:** Yes. **Propane:** Yes. **Internal Roads:** Combination of gravel & pavement. **RV Service:** 33 mi. in North Platte. **Market:** Local. **Restaurant:** Local. **General Store:** Yes. **Vending:** General Store only. **Swimming Pool:** Yes. **Playground:** Yes. **Other:** Cabins, nature trail, Internet data port. **Activities:** horseshoes, nature walk, swimming. **Nearby Attractions:** Pony Express Station, Sod House Museum. **Additional Information:** Gothenburg Chamber of Commerce, (308) 537-3505.

RESTRICTIONS

Pets: On leash. **Fires:** No open fires, charcoal fires in grills only. **Alcoholic Beverages:** Yes. **Vehicle Maximum Length:** None.

TO GET THERE

Off I-80 Exit 211, 0.25 mi. south on Hwy. 47.

HASTINGS

Hastings Campground

302 East 26th St., Hastings 68901. T: (402) 462-5621; F: (402) 461-3892; billgilliland@inebraska.com.

 ★★★ ▲ ★★★

Beauty: ★★★ Site Privacy: ★★★
Spaciousness: ★★★ Quiet: ★★★
Security: ★★★★ Cleanliness: ★★★
Insect Control: ★★★ Facilities: ★★★

Located on the north edge of town, Hastings Campground has a semi-rural location situated among the cornfields. The 48 RV sites have hook-ups available, and the 15 tent-only sites round out the campground's offerings. There isn't any shade, but the owners have planted numerous trees to improve this new campground for future years. There are numerous outdoor recreation areas within easy driving distance (many located along the I-80 corridor), though most are fairly small. Hastings' main draws are its cultural and sports offerings. Numerous softball tournaments occur here, including the state championships, and the nearby Champions Sports and Recreation Center offers fun for the family as well as fitness buffs. Hastings also has the only symphony between Lincoln and Denver, and the Hastings Museum offers explorations into cultural and natural history, as well as an IMAX theater and planetarium. And those who remember drinking Kool-Aid as kids will by happy to know that the sweet, summer concoction got its start here.

BASICS

Operated By: Bill & Dorothy Gilliland. **Open:** Year-round. **Site Assignment:** By reservation, held on credit card number. **Registration:** Camp Office. **Fee:** Tent $16.75, RV $18.90–$22.16 per unit (cash, credit, check). **Parking:** At site.

FACILITIES

Number of RV-Only Sites: 48. **Number of Tent-Only Sites:** 15. **Hookups:** Electric (20, 30, 50 amps), water, sewer, cable tv. **Each Site:** Picnic tables. **Dump Station:** Yes. **Laundry:** Yes. **Pay Phone:** Yes. **Rest Rooms and Showers:** Yes. **Fuel:** No. **Propane:** No. **Internal Roads:** Gravel. **RV Service:** On site or 25 mi. in Grand Island. **Market:** In town. **Restaurant:** In town. **General Store:** Yes. **Vending:** No. **Swimming Pool:** Yes & two hot tubs. **Playground:** Yes. **Other:** TV room, RV wash, wild flower garden, arcade room, 3 cabins, horseshoes, storm shelter. **Activities:** Swimming, coin games, horseshoes. **Nearby Attractions:** Hastings Fun Park, Imax, Pioneer Village. **Additional**

Information: Hastings Chamber of Commerce, (402) 462-4159.

RESTRICTIONS

Pets: On leash. **Fires:** In grills or fire pits only. **Alcoholic Beverages:** Yes. **Vehicle Maximum Length:** None. **Other:** Good Sam, AAA, KOA.

TO GET THERE

From I-80 Exit 312, go south on US 34 for 14.6 mi., turn left into South Shore Dr., and continue east on CR 80 (East 26th St.) about 300 yards.

HENDERSON

Prairie Oasis

913 Rd. B, Henderson 68371. T: (402) 723-4310; prairie@telcoweb.net.

RV ★★★	Tent ★★★
Beauty: ★★★	Site Privacy: ★★
Spaciousness: ★★	Quiet: ★★★
Security: ★★★	Cleanliness: ★★★
Insect Control: ★★★	Facilities: ★★★

Located in Henderson, the Prairie Oasis is a pleasant and relaxing campground, especially at night. The campground offers 70 full-service pull-through sites, all of which are level and gravel. The campsites have nice lawns, and there are several large shade trees on the property. There is an open area used to accommodate larger RVs. A separate tent area is next to a swing set, with lush grass and good shade. There is a lake for fishing on the property, and four lakeside tent sites. The campground has one cabin, a small store, and a recreation room. The weather here is dry but comfortable most of the time. There are several historic attractions to see in the area. The campground staff is friendly and helpful, and fuel service is just around the corner.

BASICS

Operated By: Jacque & Valerie Stunich. **Open:** Apr.–Oct. **Site Assignment:** By reservation, held on credit card number. **Registration:** Camp Office. **Fee:** $18–$24 per two people. **Parking:** At site.

FACILITIES

Number of RV-Only Sites: 58. **Number of Tent-Only Sites:** 16. **Hookups:** Electric (20, 30, 50 amps), water, sewer. **Each Site:** Picnic tables, some grills. **Dump Station:** Yes. **Laundry:** Yes. **Pay Phone:** Yes. **Rest Rooms and Showers:** Yes. **Fuel:** No. **Propane:** No. **Internal Roads:** Gravel, in fair condition. **RV Service:** 30 mi. west in Grand Island. **Market:** 9 mi. east of York. **Restaurant:** 9 mi. east in York. **General Store:** Yes. **Vending:** No. **Swimming Pool:** No. **Playground:** Yes. **Other:** Fishing pond, camp store, free morning coffee. **Activities:** Fishing, volleyball, horseshoes, softball. **Nearby Attractions:** Lake View Park, golf. **Additional Information:** Henderson Chamber of Commerce, (402) 723-4228.

RESTRICTIONS

Pets: On leash. **Fires:** In grills or fire pits only. **Alcoholic Beverages:** Yes. **Vehicle Maximum Length:** None. **Other:** FMCA discount.

TO GET THERE

Off I-80 Exit 342, go 3 mi. south on Rte. 93A to Henderson. Rte. 93A becomes 17th St. through Henderson, then Rd. B as you leave downtown. Campground is on the right.

LINCOLN

Camp A Way

200 Ogden Rd., Lincoln 68521. T: (402) 476-2282 or 866 -719-CAMP; www.camp-a-way.com; jqueen@neb.rr.com.

RV ★★★	Tent ★★★
Beauty: ★★★	Site Privacy: ★★
Spaciousness: ★★	Quiet: ★★★
Security: ★★★	Cleanliness: ★★★★
Insect Control: ★★★	Facilities: ★★★

Located in the heart of Lincoln, Camp A Way is a pleasant metropolitan campground. Camp A Way is also a full-service RV park with an array of amenities. The campground offers 50-amp service, free cable, and phone hookups. There are plenty of large shade trees and nice-sized camping sites. Many of the sites are a combination of dirt and gravel, so some are more level than others. There are two sets of rest rooms in the campground; the set closest to the office is well kept and clean, whereas those in the rear needed some attention when we visited. Lincoln is the capital of Nebraska and a cultural center for the state. The community offers a variety of events, festivals, and celebrations, as well as fine restaurants, shopping, historical sites, and a zoo. There is also wonderful fishing and hiking in the area. The staff at Camp A Way is very respectable and welcoming.

BASICS

Operated By: Jacque & Valerie Stunich. **Open:** Year-round. **Site Assignment:** By reservation, held on credit card number. **Registration:** Camp Office. **Fee:** Tent $18, RV $18–$26.50 per 2 people, extra adult $2. (cash, credit, check). **Parking:** At site.

FACILITIES

Number of RV-Only Sites: 73. **Number of Tent-Only Sites:** 5. **Number of Multipurpose Sites:** 8. **Hookups:** Electric (20, 30, 50 amps), water, sewer, tv, phone. **Each Site:** Picnic tables, some grills & fire rings. **Dump Station:** Yes. **Laundry:** Yes. **Pay Phone:** Yes. **Rest Rooms and Showers:** Yes. **Fuel:** No. **Propane:** No. **Internal Roads:** Gravel, in good condition. **RV Service:** Local service. **Market:** Local. **Restaurant:** Local. **General Store:** Yes. **Vending:** Yes. **Swimming Pool:** Yes. **Playground:** Yes. **Activities:** Game room, swimming, basketball, horseshoes. **Nearby Attractions:** State Capitol Building, Devaney Center, zoo, National Museum of Roller Skating, Sheldon Art Gallery. **Additional Information:** Lincoln Chamber of Commerce, (402) 436-2350.

RESTRICTIONS

Pets: On leash. **Fires:** In grills or fire pits only. **Alcoholic Beverages:** Yes. **Vehicle Maximum Length:** None.

TO GET THERE

Off I-80 Exit 401, corner of 1st and Superior St.

LINCOLN

Branched Oak State Recreation Area

RR 2 Box 61, Raymond 68428. T: (402) 783-3400; F: (402) 783-0361; www.ngpc.state.ne.us; kinnamon@ngpc.state.ne.us.

RV ★★★ Tent ★★★

Beauty: ★★★	Site Privacy: ★★★
Spaciousness: ★★★	Quiet: ★★★★
Security: ★★★★	Cleanliness: ★★★
Insect Control: ★★★	Facilities: ★★

The largest of the Salt Valley areas, Branched Oak has nine camping areas spread out around a lake which stretches for almost four miles. Sites in the new campground are set in a straight line overlooking the lake. Trees are behind the sites, but they're too far away to provide much in the way of shade. Visitors with horses can use the three-mile multi-use trail on the south side of Branched Oak Lake and camp with their horses in Area 3. The 800-acre dog trail (about a mile from Area 9) has championship events, so call ahead for a schedule to avoid the crowds. Anglers will enjoy the variety of fish found in the lake, including bluegill, largemouth bass, and three species of catfish. The recreation area is also classified as a wildlife management area, so hunters arrive in the fall to hunt pheasants, quail, doves, and ducks.

BASICS

Operated By: Nebraska Game & Parks Commission. **Open:** Year-round. **Site Assignment:** First come, first served. **Registration:** Self-serve registration kiosks, or by reservation,$3 reservation fee. **Fee:** $3–$12 depends on site & amenities, plus vehicle entrance fee. **Parking:** At site.

FACILITIES

Number of RV-Only Sites: 206. **Number of Tent-Only Sites:** 287. **Number of Multipurpose Sites:** 71. **Hookups:** Electric (20, 30 amps), water. **Each Site:** Picnic tables, fire pit. **Dump Station:** Yes. **Laundry:** No. **Pay Phone:** Yes. **Rest Rooms and Showers:** Yes in areas one, four & at the pool. **Fuel:** Yes. **Propane:** Yes. **Internal Roads:** Paved. **RV Service:** in Lincoln. **Market:** in Lincoln. **Restaurant:** On site at the Marine or in Lincoln. **General Store:** Yes at the Marina. **Vending:** Yes. **Swimming Pool:** Yes. **Playground:** Yes. **Other:** 9 boat ramps, 49 fishing, 41 picnic shelters w/ over 600 picnic tables & grills. **Activities:** Fishing (walleye, blue gill, blue catfish, largemouth bass), boating, waterskiing, hiking, biking. **Nearby Attractions:** Lincoln Nebraska, shopping, golf, museums, movies. **Additional Information:** Lincoln Chamber of Commerce, (402) 436-2350.

RESTRICTIONS

Pets: On leash. **Fires:** In grills or fire pits only. **Alcoholic Beverages:** No alcoholic beverages allowed. **Vehicle Maximum Length:** 45 ft. **Other:** Nebraska State Park passes honored.

TO GET THERE

From I-80 Exit 388, go north on SR 103 for 5.5 mi., then east on US 34 for 1 mi. Take NW 140 St. for 6 mi. and then turn right (east) onto

West Branched Oak Rd. for 1.6 mi. and follow signs into park.

NIOBRARA

Niobrara State Park

P.O.Box 226, Niobrara 68760-0226. T: (402) 857-3373; F: (402) 857-3420; www.ngpc.state.ne.us; nsp@ngpc.state.ne.us.

RV ★★★ Tent ★★★★

Beauty: ★★★	Site Privacy: ★★★
Spaciousness: ★★★	Quiet: ★★★★
Security: ★★★★	Cleanliness: ★★★
Insect Control: ★★★	Facilities: ★★

Niobrara State Park is situated at the confluence of the Niobrara and Missouri Rivers on Nebraska's northeastern border. Visitors at this park have an opportunity to sample a wide range of outdoor recreation, including horseback trail rides, hiking, and fishing. The park offers numerous opportunities to observe wildlife such as white-tailed deer, wild turkeys, beavers, muskrats, and mink. The camping area extends along three miles of an extremely hilly, winding, one-way road, and it's interspersed with stands of elm, hackberry, and ash. Many sites are situated on elevated hills adjacent to the Niobrara River. The park is open year-round, although modern facilities, including cabins, are open from mid-April through mid-November. Reservations for all campsites may be made up to one year in advance.

Basics

Operated By: Nebraska Game & Parks Commission. **Open:** Year-round. **Site Assignment:** First come, first served. **Registration:** Self-serve registration kiosks. **Fee:** $8–$12 depends on site & amenities, plus vehicle entrance fee. **Parking:** At site.

Facilities

Number of RV-Only Sites: 69. **Number of Tent-Only Sites:** 50. **Hookups:** Electric (20, 30 amps), water. **Each Site:** Picnic tables, fire pit. **Dump Station:** Yes. **Laundry:** Yes. **Pay Phone:** Yes. **Rest Rooms and Showers:** Yes. **Fuel:** No. **Propane:** No. **Internal Roads:** Paved. **RV Service:** 30 mi. in Yanton, SD. **Market:** In town. **Restaurant:** In town. **General Store:** No. **Vending:** Yes. **Swimming Pool:** Yes. **Playground:** Yes. **Other:** 19 cabins, hiking trails, 9 picnic shelters, two w/ electricity, over 160 acres open for horseback riding, over 100 picnic tables & grills, 3 boat ramps, mountain bike trails, hiking trails. **Activities:** Swimming, boating, fishing, hiking, horseback riding, (160 acres of horse trails), guided float trips. **Nearby Attractions:** Smith Falls, golf, Ashfall State Historic site. **Additional Information:** Creighton Area Chamber of Commerce, (402) 358-3737.

Restrictions

Pets: On leash. **Fires:** In grills or fire pits only. **Alcoholic Beverages:** No alcoholic beverages allowed. **Vehicle Maximum Length:** 45 ft. **Other:** Nebraska State Park passes honored.

To Get There

The campground is about 3 mi. west of Niobrara on SR 12.

PONCA

Ponca State Park

88119 Spur 26-E, Ponca 68770. T: (402) 755-2284; F: (402) 755-2593; www.ngpc.state.ne.us; poncasp@ngpc.state.ne.us.

RV ★★★ Tent ★★★

Beauty: ★★★★	Site Privacy: ★★★
Spaciousness: ★★★	Quiet: ★★★★
Security: ★★★★	Cleanliness: ★★★
Insect Control: ★★★	Facilities: ★★

As you would expect from a state-operated park in this area, Ponca State Park is well run and situated in the midst of gorgeous scenery. The fees are very reasonable, and the available sites medium sized. Even though the camping area is fairly large, the sites still afford privacy and quiet for all guests. The biggest surprise regarding this park is the list of activities. Over and above the usual, Ponca offers golf, archery, waterskiing, hunting, and a special fishing clinic for the children on Sundays. The surrounding area isn't a disappointment either. Nearby, visitors to the park can hike the Lewis and Clark Trail; hunt deer, turkey, or duck; or stop by the Mid America Air Museum. Overall, this is a wonderful place to stay, and reservations are not required.

Basics

Operated By: Nebraska Game & Parks Commission. **Open:** Mid-Apr.–mid-Nov. **Site Assignment:** First come, first served. **Registration:** Camp

Office. **Fee:** $8 without hookups, $11–$12 w/ hookups, plus vehicle fee. **Parking:** At site.

FACILITIES

Number of RV-Only Sites: 75. **Number of Tent-Only Sites:** 72. **Number of Multipurpose Sites:** 10. **Hookups:** Electric (20, 30, 50 amps), water. **Each Site:** Picnic tables, fire pit. **Dump Station:** Yes. **Laundry:** No. **Pay Phone:** Yes. **Rest Rooms and Showers:** Yes. **Fuel:** No. **Propane:** No. **Internal Roads:** Paved in good condition. **RV Service:** 14 mi. in Sioux City. **Market:** Local or Sioux City. **Restaurant:** There are two restaurants in Ponca, or Sioux City. **General Store:** No. **Vending:** Yes. **Swimming Pool:** Yes (you may not swim in the river). **Playground:** Yes. **Other:** Lodge, 14 modern cabins, covered picnic shelters, boat ramps, scenic overlook, horse barn, horse trails, hiking trails, biking trails, golf course. **Activities:** Swimming, horseback riding, golf, fishing, hiking, organized activities Memorial weekend through Labor day, children fishing clinics on Sunday, boating, canoeing, rafting, waterskiing & tubing, archery range, outdoor education naturalist program. **Nearby Attractions:** Missouri River, Lewis & Clark Trail w/ 17 mi. of hiking trails, deer, pheasant, duck & turkey hunting, Mid America Air Museum, Sgt Floyd River Museum. **Additional Information:** Ponca Chamber of Commerce, (402) 755-2224.

RESTRICTIONS

Pets: Yes, w/ a 6 ft.- or under leash. **Fires:** In approved areas & fire pit. **Alcoholic Beverages:** No alcoholic beverages allowed in the State Park. **Vehicle Maximum Length:** 45 ft. **Other:** Annual vehicle passes accepted.

TO GET THERE

From I-29 Exit 144B, go west on US 75, which becomes US 20. Turn right on SR 12 go 12.5 mi. and follow signs into park (campground is 32.5 mi. from Sioux City and I-29).

SCOTTSBLUFF

Scottsbluff KOA

180037 KOA Dr., Scottsbluff 69361. T: (800) 562-0845 or (308)635-3760; www.koa.com.

RV ★★★ Tent ★★★

Beauty: ★★★	Site Privacy: ★★★
Spaciousness: ★★	Quiet: ★★★★
Security: ★★★★	Cleanliness: ★★★
Insect Control: ★★★	Facilities: ★★★

This KOA is rather small by comparison to others we've visited, but it still offers all the amenities of the larger campgrounds. The scenery is not spectacular by any means, but the property is pleasant and fairly clean. The RV and tent sites are small to average, but despite this fact, they still manage to provide a little privacy and a lot of quiet. Quite a few of the RV sites offer full hookups, and all sites come with picnic tables, grills, and fire pits. As a bonus to the guests, amenities on the premises include a dataport, game room, recreation room, and nature trails. Nearby, visitors can enjoy the Agate Fossil Beds, Fort Laramie, North Platte Valley Museum, or the local zoo.

BASICS

Operated By: Private Operator. **Open:** Apr. 15–Oct. **Site Assignment:** By reservation. **Registration:** Camp Office. **Fee:** Tent $16–$18 RV $20–$26 per 2 people (cash or credit). **Parking:** At site.

FACILITIES

Number of RV-Only Sites: 22. **Number of Tent-Only Sites:** 6. **Number of Multipurpose Sites:** 17. **Hookups:** Electric (20, 30, 50 amps), water, sewer. **Each Site:** Picnic tables, few grills & fire pits. **Dump Station:** Yes. **Laundry:** Yes. **Pay Phone:** Yes. **Rest Rooms and Showers:** Yes. **Fuel:** No. **Propane:** Yes. **Internal Roads:** Combination of gravel & pavement. **RV Service:** Local service. **Market:** Local. **Restaurant:** Local. **General Store:** Yes. **Vending:** General Store only. **Swimming Pool:** Yes. **Playground:** Yes. **Other:** Cabins, nature trail, Internet data port, recreation room. **Activities:** Game room, swimming, volleyball, basketball, horseshoes. **Nearby Attractions:** Scottsbluff National Monument, Agate Fossil Beds, North Platte Valley Museum, Fort Laramie, the zoo. **Additional Information:** Gothenburg Chamber of Commerce, (308) 537-3505.

RESTRICTIONS

Pets: On leash. **Fires:** In fire pits only. **Alcoholic Beverages:** Yes. **Vehicle Maximum Length:** None.

TO GET THERE

From I-80 Exit 59, take SR 17 north 0.2 mi. to SR 19. Follow SR 19 2 mi., then go north on US 30 for 0.3 mi. to US 385. Follow US 385 for 40 mi., then take US 26 west for another 42 mi. to KOA.

WACO

Double Nickel Campground

I-80 & Waco, Waco 68460. T: (402) 728-5558

RV ★★★ Tent ★★★

Beauty: ★★★ Site Privacy: ★★
Spaciousness: ★★ Quiet: ★★★
Security: ★★★ Cleanliness: ★★★
Insect Control: ★★★ Facilities: ★★★

The Double Nickel Campground is located one block south of I-80 in Waco. It is a moderately sized, privately owned facility with a lounge and meeting rooms attached. The campground has 103 sites that are basically gravel parking spurs with hookups. The area does have some grass and a fishing pond. There is a pool, a playground, and mini-golf. The internal roads were a bit rutty when we visited. However, the facilities in the campground were clean, though not manicured. The staff are friendly and helpful, and there are movies to rent. The park is quiet and seems genuinely family oriented. You can see the interstate from most campsites, and there is the possibility you may have to level out. The weather is dry here, and days in the summer are long and hot.

BASICS

Operated By: Craig & Shannon Runge. **Open:** Year-round. **Site Assignment:** By reservation, held on credit card number. **Registration:** Camp Office. **Fee:** Tent $16, RV $22–$24 per 2 people, extra person $1.50 (cash, credit, checks). **Parking:** At site.

FACILITIES

Number of Multipurpose Sites: 103. **Hookups:** Electric (20, 30, 50 amps), water, sewer. **Each Site:** Picnic tables. **Dump Station:** Yes. **Laundry:** Yes. **Pay Phone:** Yes. **Rest Rooms and Showers:** Yes. **Fuel:** No. **Propane:** No. **Internal Roads:** Gravel, in poor condition. **RV Service:** 35 mi. east Lincoln. **Market:** 8 mi. east in York. **Restaurant:** 8 mi. east in York. **General Store:** Yes. **Vending:** No. **Swimming Pool:** Yes. **Playground:** Yes. **Other:** Storm shelter, adult lounge (serve alcohol), mini-golf, fishing pond, videos, indoor meeting room. **Activities:** Swimming, fishing, videos, horseshoes. **Nearby Attractions:** Bruce L. Anderson Recreation Area, Kirkpatrick Wildlife Basin. **Additional Information:** York Chamber of Commerce, (402) 362-5531.

RESTRICTIONS

Pets: On leash. **Fires:** In grills or fire pits only. **Alcoholic Beverages:** Yes. **Vehicle Maximum Length:** None.

TO GET THERE

Off I-80 Exit 360, the campground is 1 block south of Waco.

WATERLOO

Two Rivers State Recreation Area

27702 F St., Waterloo 68069-7012. T: (402) 359-5165; F: (402) 359-9040; www.ngpc.state.ne.us.

RV ★★★ Tent ★★★

Beauty: ★★★ Site Privacy: ★★★
Spaciousness: ★★★ Quiet: ★★★★
Security: ★★★★ Cleanliness: ★★★
Insect Control: ★★★ Facilities: ★★

Adjacent to the Platte River just off NE 92 near Venice, Two Rivers State Recreation Area offers a wide range of campsites in five campgrounds, with primitive camping in two areas and sites for small groups in a third. Campgrounds are located near the river or one of the five ponds. This is a popular spot for canoe-campers travelling the 55-mile segment of the Platte River. Due to the location, most sites enjoy peace and quiet with deer, rabbits, and foxes often spotted. For campers who enjoy fishing, this is one of the few spots in the state that offers trout fishing. A wheelchair-accessible pier is provided. Railroad buffs will delight in ten cabooses donated by the Union Pacific Railroad, remodeled and restored, and now used as lodging in the park.

BASICS

Operated By: Nebraska Game & Parks Commission. **Open:** Apr.–Oct. **Site Assignment:** First come, first served. **Registration:** Self-serve registration kiosks. **Fee:** $8–$12 depends on site & amenities, plus vehicle entrance fee. **Parking:** At site.

FACILITIES

Number of RV-Only Sites: 93. **Number of Tent-Only Sites:** 39. **Number of Multipurpose Sites:** 63. **Hookups:** Electric (20, 30 amps), water. **Each Site:** Picnic tables, fire pit. **Dump Station:** Yes. **Laundry:** No. **Pay Phone:** Yes. **Rest Rooms and Showers:** Yes. **Fuel:** No. **Propane:** No. **Internal Roads:** Paved. **RV Service:** Local service. **Market:** In town. **Restaurant:** In town.

General Store: Yes. **Vending:** Yes. **Swimming Pool:** No, but there is a swimming beach w/ showers. **Playground:** Yes. **Other:** 10 Union Pacific train cabooses converted into cabins (no pets in cabooses), hiking trails, 2 picnic shelters, 2 w/ electricity, over 100 picnic tables & grills, boat ramps, 5 ponds, Platte River access, pull & take trout lake, mountain bike trails, hiking trails, fish cleaning station. **Activities:** Swimming, boating, fishing, hiking. **Nearby Attractions:** Strategic Air Command Museum. **Additional Information:** Elkhorn Chamber of Commerce, (402) 289-2678.

RESTRICTIONS

Pets: On leash. **Fires:** In grills or fire pits only. **Alcoholic Beverages:** No alcoholic beverages allowed. **Vehicle Maximum Length:** 45 ft. **Other:** Nebraska State Park passes honored.

TO GET THERE

From I-80 Exit 445 (in Omaha) go west on US 275 for 10.8 mi.; US 275 becomes SR 92, so continue for 2 mi., then turn left on CR 96 (S. 26th St), go 1 mi. and turn right onto CR 49 (F St.) into park.

WOODRIVER

Woodriver Motel and Campground

11774 South Hwy. 11, Woodriver 68883. T: (308) 583-2256

RV ★★★	Tent ★★
Beauty: ★★	Site Privacy: ★★
Spaciousness: ★★	Quiet: ★★★
Security: ★★★	Cleanliness: ★★★
Insect Control: ★★★	Facilities: ★★★

The Wood River Motel and Campground is conveniently located off I-80 in Woodriver. This campground is ideal for those people traveling through and looking for a comfortable, clean, simple place to spend the night. The Wood River Campground is located behind a truck stop and the Wood River Motel, and it offers well-spaced concrete parking spurs, separated by a lawn. There are a total of 30 sites, most of which are pull-throughs, each having its own lamp post. In addition, there are a few grills and an open tent area. The campground has a small playground, fishing pond, and clean facilities. There is a restaurant in the truck stop, and there's vending in the motel. The campground is open year-round, with the utilities turned off in the winter. The motel is privately run, and the owners live on the property. You must drive by the motel office in order to enter the RV park.

BASICS

Operated By: Deb Gerlach. **Open:** Year-round (water off in the winter). **Site Assignment:** By reservation. **Registration:** Motel front desk. **Fee:** Tent $9.50, RV $13.75 per unit (cash or credit). **Parking:** At site.

FACILITIES

Number of Multipurpose Sites: 30. **Hookups:** Electric (20, 30, 50 amps), water, sewer. **Each Site:** Picnic tables, few grills. **Dump Station:** Yes. **Laundry:** Yes. **Pay Phone:** Yes. **Rest Rooms and Showers:** Yes. **Fuel:** Next door. **Propane:** Next door. **Internal Roads:** Combination of gravel & pavement. **RV Service:** 18 mi. in Grand Island. **Market:** Local. **Restaurant:** Local. **General Store:** Truckstop next door. **Vending:** Yes. **Swimming Pool:** No. **Playground:** Yes. **Other:** 26 room motel. **Activities:** Fishing pond. **Nearby Attractions:** It is 17 mi. to Grand Island or Hastings. **Additional Information:** Grand Island Chamber of Commerce, (308) 382-9210.

RESTRICTIONS

Pets: On leash. **Fires:** No open fires, charcoal fires in grills only. **Alcoholic Beverages:** Yes. **Vehicle Maximum Length:** None.

TO GET THERE

Off I-80 Exit 300, merge left off Hwy. 11; the campground is behind the truck stop.

North Dakota

Although generally considered a Plains state, North Dakota offers a varied terrain loaded with unique opportunities for prospective campers to take advantage of the outdoors. After all, camping is said to be the most popular recreational activity within the state! In addition to its flat, rolling landscape, North Dakota has **four state forests** that are ideal habitats for moose and deer. The state is rich in wildlife and contains over **60 wildlife refuges,** more than any other state. Animals native to the state range from wild horses, sheep, bison, white-tailed deer, and eagles

North Dakota is divided into distinct geological areas: The Missouri Plateau, The Red River Valley, and the Drift Prairie. The Missouri Plateau is sculpted with colorful canyons, gorges, ravines, bluffs and buttes, while the Red River Valley and Drift Prairie serve as fertile farmlands. Added to the geological mix are North Dakota's numerous state parks and forests. Most of North Dakota's 18 state parks have camping and picnicking facilities. **Theodore Roosevelt National Park** is located in northwestern North Dakota and is one of six national parks found in the state

North Dakota is also filled with rivers and lakes, 171 to be exact. The major rivers are the Missouri, which flows south into the Mississippi, and the Red, which forms the border between North Dakota and Minnesota. Consequently, there are countless opportunities for fishing, boating, and waterfowl gazing. It is said that more ducks reproduce in North Dakota than anywhere in the nation.

The state's largest city is Fargo, which offers many of the modern conveniences while maintaining its rustic, western charm. Other prominent cities include **Bismark,** the capital, **Grand Forks,** home of the **University of North Dakota,** and **Pembina,** home of the newest state museum.

North Dakota is heaven on earth for lovers of the outdoors and is one of the most diverse wildlife areas in the country. In terms of camping, the state's only drawback is its winters, which are cold and long, to say the least! However, it is the ideal spot for winter activities such as snowmobiling, skiing, fishing, sledding, and skating.

The following facility features 20 or fewer sites:

Sportsmen's Centennial Park, Garrison

Campground Profiles

ARVILLA
Turtle River State Park

3084 Park Ave., Arvilla 58214. T: (701) 594-4445; F: (701) 594-2556; www.ndparks.com; trsp@stste.nd.us.

RV ★★★ Tent ★★★

Beauty: ★★★ Site Privacy: ★★★
Spaciousness: ★★★ Quiet: ★★★★
Security: ★★★★ Cleanliness: ★★★
Insect Control: ★★ Facilities: ★★

In the eastern part of the state, not far from Grand Forks, campers can find a nice mix of river recreation and mountain fun. Typical of nature-oriented camping in this climate, the time of year absolutely defines the vacation, with cross-country skiing in winter and water fun in the summer (mountain bikers ride whenever they will). This is a family place, and kids can even borrow fishing gear from the park office to try their luck in the rainbow trout–stocked Turtle River. The campground is fairly attractive, with average-sized back-in sites and varying privacy. The facilities are nothing special, but are totally adequate for both RV and tent campers (although facilities are limited during the off-season). We recommend this campground for families.

Basics

Operated By: The North Dakota Parks & Recreation Dept. **Open:** Year round, but the water is off Oct.–May in the campground. **Site Assignment:** By reservation in the summer, first come Oct.–Apr. **Registration:** At the entrance gate. **Fee:** $7 w/ no hookup, $12 w/ electric plus a $4 entrance fee per vehicle or annual park pass. **Parking:** At site.

Facilities

Number of Multipurpose Sites: 125. **Hookups:** Electric (30 amps), water. **Each Site:** Picnic table, grated fire pits. **Dump Station:** Yes. **Laundry:** No. **Pay Phone:** Yes. **Rest Rooms and Showers:** Yes. **Fuel:** No. **Propane:** No. **Internal Roads:** Paved. **RV Service:** 22 mi. in Grand Forks. **Market:** In Arvilla. **Restaurant:** In Arvilla or Grand Forks. **General Store:** Yes. **Vending:** Yes. **Swimming Pool:** No. **Playground:** Yes, several. **Other:** Camp Store, paved nature trails, 6 cabins, picnic shelters, 6 mi. of groomed cross-country ski trails. **Activities:** Hiking, fishing (rainbow trout), biking, sledding, cross-country skiing, wildlife viewing, special park programs. **Nearby Attractions:** Grand Forks 22 mi. east, golf. **Additional Information:** ND Parks & Recreation Dept., (701) 328-5357.

Restrictions

Pets: On leash. **Fires:** In fire pits or grills only; fires may be restricted due to weather conditions; please ask management before starting any open fires. **Alcoholic Beverages:** Yes. **Vehicle Maximum Length:** None.

To Get There

22 mi. west of Grand Forks directly off of Hwy. 2; there are excellent signs.

BISMARK
Bismark KOA

3720 Centennial Rd., Bismark 58501. T: (701) 222-2662; www.koa.com; bismkoa@aol.com.

RV ★★★★★ Tent ★★★★★

Beauty: ★★★★★ Site Privacy: ★★★★★
Spaciousness: ★★★★★ Quiet: ★★★★
Security: ★★★★ Cleanliness: ★★★★
Insect Control: ★★★ Facilities: ★★★★

Located just ten minutes from the state capitol, the Heritage Center, and the museums and art galleries of Bismarck, this KOA offers a comfortable camping experience. The 20-acre campground is spacious, and a nicely wooded area provides both site privacy and relaxing shade for activity wearied campers. Arranged in rows, most sites offer proximity to some campground amenity. Sites 1–10 border the playing fields but are close to nearby Centennial Road. Though they are closest to the frequented dog walk area, sites 71–78 are on the perimeter of the campground, farthest from the access road, and offer one of the only views of land without campers. Sites 100–115 offer a similar experience except that the tent campground occupies the adjacent "wilderness." With relatively mild summer temperatures, Bismarck is a nice family destination. The city itself provides a busy schedule of summertime activities, including a softball tournament, rodeo, United Tribes International Pow-Wow, and Folkfest. Depending on whether or not you plan to participate in the festivities or avoid the crowds, be sure to check dates for events before making plans to camp.

Basics

Operated By: Don & Pam Mueller. **Open:** May–Oct. **Site Assignment:** By reservation. **Registration:** In general store. **Fee:** Tent $15, RV $17–$20 per 2 people, $3. extra people, under 6 stay free. **Parking:** Limited.

Facilities

Number of RV-Only Sites: 80. **Number of Tent-Only Sites:** 34. **Number of Multipurpose Sites:** 0. **Hookups:** Electric (20, 30, 50 amps), water, sewer. **Each Site:** Picnic tables. **Dump Station:** Yes. **Laundry:** Yes. **Pay Phone:** Yes. **Rest Rooms and Showers:** Yes. **Fuel:** No, in town. **Propane:** No, in town. **Internal Roads:** Gravel. **RV Service:** In town. **Market:** In town. **Restaurant:** In town. **General Store:** Yes. **Vending:** Yes. **Swimming Pool:** Yes. **Playground:** Yes. **Other:** Picnic shelter, 4 cabins, jogging area, dataport by office. **Activities:** Swimming, basketball, volleyball, horseshoes, tennis, game room. **Nearby Attractions:** State Capital, Dakota Zoo, Heritage Center, Museums, golf, Fort Abraham Lincoln. **Additional Information:** www.koa.com.

Restrictions

Pets: On leash. **Fires:** 1 central fire ring. **Alcoholic Beverages:** Yes, in site only. **Vehicle Maximum Length:** None.

To Get There

From I-94, take Exit 276 (Eckelson) and go south less than 0.25 mi. on the left.

BOTTINEAU

Lake Metigoshe State Park

No. 2 Lake Metigoshe State Park Rd., Bottineau 58318. T: (701) 263-4651 office; www.ndparks.com; lmsp@state.nd.us.

RV ★★★★ Tent ★★★★

Beauty: ★★★★ Site Privacy: ★★★★
Spaciousness: ★★★★ Quiet: ★★★★
Security: ★★★★ Cleanliness: ★★★
Insect Control: ★★★ Facilities: ★★

Situated in the scenic Turtle Mountains on the shores of Lake Metigoshe, this campground was constructed by the Works Progress Administration (WPA) in the 1930s. The park's rolling hills, aspen forests, and small lakes make the site one of the most popular vacation spots in North Dakota. Lake Metigoshe is noted for its northern pike, walleye, and perch. The Old Oak Trail, a National Recreation Trail, is also found within the park's boundaries. The park has both modern and primitive camping, as well as picnic areas. The RV sites are spacious and private, providing a wonderful feeling of tranquility. Winter provides opportunities for snowmobiling, skating, sledding, and ice fishing. The park is open year-round, although water is turned off from October through May in the campground. The sites are assigned by reservation during the summer and first come first served from Oct. through Apr.

Basics

Operated By: The North Dakota Parks & Recreation Dept. **Open:** Year round, but the water is off Oct.–May in the campground. **Site Assignment:** By reservation in the summer, first come Oct.–Apr. **Registration:** At the entrance gate. **Fee:** $7 w/ no hookup, $12 w/ 30 amp, $14 w/ 50 amp. plus a $4 entrance fee per vehicle or annual park pass. **Parking:** At site.

Facilities

Number of Multipurpose Sites: 130. **Hookups:** Electric (30 amps), water. **Each Site:** Picnic table, grated fire pits. **Dump Station:** Yes. **Laundry:** No. **Pay Phone:** Yes. **Rest Rooms and Showers:** Yes. **Fuel:** No. **Propane:** No. **Internal Roads:** Paved. **RV Service:** 55 mi. South in Minot, ND. **Market:** There are 3 in town. **Restaurant:** There are several in town. **General Store:** No. **Vending:** Yes.

Swimming Pool: No, but there is a lake front beach. **Playground:** Yes, several. **Other:** 3 year-round cabins, group dorms (total cap. 120), kitchen, dining hall & auditorium, swim beach, boat ramp, fishing dock, picnic shelters, seasonal naturalist, canoe rentals, warming House, cross-country ski & snowshoe rentals. **Activities:** Hiking, fishing (walleye, chinook, trout, pike), boating, skiing, ice fishing in the winter, wildlife viewing, special park programs, cross-country skiing, sledding, mountain biking. **Nearby Attractions:** International Peace Garden, downhill & cross-country ski areas, Peace Garden State Snowmobile Trail, Golf courses, Turtle Mountains, J. Clark Salyer & Lords Lake National Wildlife Refuges, State Scenic Byway. **Additional Information:** ND Parks & Recreation Dept. (701) 328-5357.

Restrictions

Pets: On leash, but not on beach or public picnic areas. **Fires:** In fire pits or grills only; fires may be restricted due to weather conditions; please ask management before starting any open fires. **Alcoholic Beverages:** Yes. **Vehicle Maximum Length:** None.

To Get There

14 mi. northeast of Bottineau. From SR 5 go north on Lake Rd. 10.2 mi., make a right on SR 43 for 6.1 mi., then follow signs into park.

CAVALIER

Graham's Island State Park

152 South Duncan Dr., Devils Lake 58301.
T: (701) 766-4015; F: (701) 766-4311;
www.ndparks.com; dlsp@state.nd.us.

▲★★★★

Beauty: ★★★★ Site Privacy: ★★★★★
Spaciousness: ★★★★ Quiet: ★★★★
Security: ★★★★ Cleanliness: ★★★
Insect Control: ★★ Facilities: ★★

Of the three state parks on Devils Lake, this is the largest and most developed. Naturally, water sports are a big draw, and you can even do some serious ice fishing for yellow perch in the winter. Other catches in the warmer months may include walleye, northern pike and white bass. While you're tromping through the oak, ash, elm, and aspen in the surrounding hills, you may partake of some deer, wild turkey and other small game. The camping facilities are nothing spectacular, but they are certainly sufficient for RVs and tents, with plenty of recreation for all ages—heavy on the nature-appreciation, of course. The back-in sites vary in size, and the facilities are more limited in the winter, but with a little planning this would be a lovely destination anytime. The setting is rural, about nine miles from the town of Devils Lake, and near plenty of other diversions. Security is good, and privacy is superb at this campground. Take your parka or your swimsuit and enjoy.

Basics

Operated By: The North Dakota Parks & Recreation Dept. **Open:** Year round, but the water is off Oct.–May in the campground. **Site Assignment:** By reservation in the summer, (800) 807 4723 first come Oct.–Apr. **Registration:** At the entrance gate. **Fee:** $7 w/ no hookup, $12 w/ electric plus a $4 entrance fee per vehicle or annual park pass. **Parking:** At site.

Facilities

Number of Multipurpose Sites: 70. **Hookups:** Electric (30 amps), water. **Each Site:** Picnic table, grated fire pits. **Dump Station:** Yes. **Laundry:** No. **Pay Phone:** Yes. **Rest Rooms and Showers:** Yes. **Fuel:** No. **Propane:** No. **Internal Roads:** Paved. **RV Service:** Devils Lake. **Market:** Devils Lake. **Restaurant:** Devils Lake. **General Store:** Yes, Grahams Island. **Vending:** Yes. **Swimming Pool:** No. **Playground:** Yes, several. **Other:** Boat ramp (Grahams Island & Black Tiger Bay), picnic shelter, hiking trails (Grahams Island) & Sivert Thompson Activities Center (Grahams Island). **Activities:** Boating, fishing (walleye, northern pike, perch, & white bass), hiking, biking, self guided nature tours, interpretive programming, playgrounds, swimming, snowmobiling, cross-country skiing, & ice fishing. **Nearby Attractions:** Fort Totten State Historic Site, Sully's Hill National Game Preserve, Historic Downtown Devils Lake. **Additional Information:** ND Parks & Recreation Dept., (701) 328-5357.

Restrictions

Pets: On leash. **Fires:** In fire pits or grills only; fires may be restricted due to weather conditions; please ask management before starting any open fires. **Alcoholic Beverages:** Yes. **Vehicle Maximum Length:** None.

To Get There

To get to Grahams Island State Park, take Hwy. 2 north to Hwy. 19 south to Grahams Island

Rd. Continue south on Grahams Island Rd. to park entrance. Shelvers Grove State Recreation Area is 3 miles east of Devils Lake on Hwy. 2.

CAVALIER
Icelandic State Park

13571 Hwy. 5, Cavalier 58220. T: (701) 265-4561; F: (701) 265-4443; www.ndparks.com; isp@state.nd.us.

RV ★★★ | Tent ★★★

Beauty: ★★★ | Site Privacy: ★★★
Spaciousness: ★★★ | Quiet: ★★★★
Security: ★★★★ | Cleanliness: ★★★
Insect Control: ★★ | Facilities: ★★

It's not as cold as you think. But, then, neither is Iceland. Actually, this state park celebrates and preserves natural splendor and pioneer history, at the same time providing a good variety of recreation. In the northeastern corner of the sate, this rural spot on Lake Renwick offers plenty of water sports, and the northern pike are abundant. In the winter, plan to do your fishing through a hole in the ice (okay, it gets pretty cold). This is a well-rounded campground, with average facilities (that are more limited in the winter), comfortable for RVs and tents, relatively quiet, and secure. The medium-sized back-in sites offer a decent amount of privacy, and the old oak trees provide a good bit of shade, especially in the picnic area. Family-friendly recreation and wonderful wildlife viewing make this a delightful vacation spot. Depending on the crowd, this is a quiet, remote, secure campground where you can expect a peaceful and fun vacation.

Basics

Operated By: The North Dakota Parks & Recreation Dept. **Open:** Year round, but the water is off Oct.–May in the campground. **Site Assignment:** By reservation in the summer, (800) 807 4723 first come Oct.–Apr. **Registration:** At the entrance gate. **Fee:** $7 w/ no hookup, $12 w/ electric plus a $4 entrance fee per vehicle or annual park pass. **Parking:** At site.

Facilities

Number of Multipurpose Sites: 165. **Hookups:** Electric (30 amps), water. **Each Site:** Picnic table, grated fire pits. **Dump Station:** Yes. **Laundry:** No. **Pay Phone:** Yes. **Rest Rooms and Showers:** Yes. **Fuel:** No. **Propane:** No. **Internal Roads:** Paved. **RV Service:** In Cavalier. **Market:** In Cavalier. **Restaurant:** In Cavalier. **General Store:** No. **Vending:** Yes. **Swimming Pool:** No. **Playground:** Yes, several. **Other:** Boat ramp, picnic shelter, visitors center, historic buildings, historic artifacts, meeting room, & cabin. **Activities:** Boating, shore & ice fishing (northern pike), hiking, biking, self guided nature tours, interpretive programming, playgrounds, swimming, & artifacts exhibits on area's settlement. **Nearby Attractions:** Pembina County Historical Museum, Patton's Isle of Memories, Frostfire Mountain Ski Resort, golf, snowmobile trail, & scenic byway. **Additional Information:** ND Parks & Recreation Dept., (701) 328-5357.

Restrictions

Pets: On leash. **Fires:** In fire pits or grills only; fires may be restricted due to weather conditions; please ask management before starting any open fires. **Alcoholic Beverages:** Yes. **Vehicle Maximum Length:** None.

To Get There

Icelandic State Park is located 5 mi. west of Cavalier on Hwy. 5.

ECKELSON
Prairie Haven

10121 36th St. Southeast, Eckelson 58481. T: (701) 646-2267; www.prairie-haven.com; prairhvn@ictc.com.

RV ★★★ | Tent ★★★

Beauty: ★★★ | Site Privacy: ★★★
Spaciousness: ★★★ | Quiet: ★★★
Security: ★★★ | Cleanliness: ★★★
Insect Control: ★★★ | Facilities: ★★★

The onsite spring-fed lake, more aptly called a pond, compliments the quiet serenity of this park-like campground and offers a quaint experience slightly reminiscent of Thoreau's Walden. Sites here are spacious and most can accommodate double slide-outs. Though mature trees give ample shade and the uninterrupted grassy sites provide an expanse of pleasing green, the lack of bushes and trees between sites offers little privacy. Perhaps this is a ploy of hosts and owners Biff and Claudine Flowers to encourage guests to make new friends, but if you like eating dinner alone, you may have to venture elsewhere. The rustic architecture of the general store and one-room cabin add to the country ambiance of the campground. This campground offers a simple, pleasing experience to both RV and tent-campers alike and is a nice overnight stop.

Basics

Operated By: Biff & Claudine Flowers. **Open:** May–Oct. **Site Assignment:** By reservation. **Registration:** In general store. **Fee:** Tent $15, RV $17–$20 per 2 people, $3 extra person, under age 6 stay free. **Parking:** Limited.

Facilities

Number of Multipurpose Sites: 31. **Hookups:** Electric (20, 30, 50 amps), water, sewer. **Each Site:** Picnic tables. **Dump Station:** Yes. **Laundry:** Yes. **Pay Phone:** Yes. **Rest Rooms and Showers:** Yes. **Fuel:** Yes. **Propane:** No, 8 mi. in Sandborn. **Internal Roads:** Gravel. **RV Service:** 15 mi. in Jamestown. **Market:** 15 mi. in Jamestown. **Restaurant:** Snacks on property, or in Jamestown. **General Store:** Yes. **Vending:** Store Only. **Swimming Pool:** No. **Playground:** Yes. **Other:** Spring-fed lake, 2 cabins. **Activities:** Fishing, basketball, volleyball, horseshoes. **Nearby Attractions:** Inquire at campground. **Additional Information:** www.prairie-haven.com.

Restrictions

Pets: On leash. **Fires:** 1 central fire ring. **Alcoholic Beverages:** Yes, in site only. **Vehicle Maximum Length:** None.

To Get There

From I-94, take Exit 276 (Eckelson) and go south less than 0.25 mi. on the left.

EPPING

Lewis and Clark State Park

119th Rd. Northwest, Epping 58843. T: (701) 859-3071; F: (701) 859-3001; www.ndparks.com; lcsp@stste.nd.us.

RV: ★★★★ Tent: ★★★★

Beauty: ★★★★	Site Privacy: ★★★★
Spaciousness: ★★★★	Quiet: ★★★★
Security: ★★★★	Cleanliness: ★★★★
Insect Control: ★★★	Facilities: ★★★

A rural spot on an upper bay of the mighty Lake Sakakawea, this state park is of course named for the famous explorers, and you can find commemorations of the Lewis and Clark expedition here and there. In the northwest part of the state, this setting offers a striking view of the rugged buttes of the Badlands. Water sports and wildlife viewing are major draws, and the fishing is terrific as well. In addition to the healthy supply of walleye, sauger, and northern pike, you might occasionally discover a pallid sturgeon or a paddle-fish. This is a great place for tent and RV camping, with adequate facilities (although they are limited in the winter). As is the case with many state parks, this is a beautiful place to spend a vacation, with privacy, space and peace defining the campground, and a great variety of recreation for all ages in and around the park. History buffs and nature lovers alike will love it here.

Basics

Operated By: The North Dakota Parks & Recreation Dept. **Open:** Year round, but the water is off Oct.–May in the campground. **Site Assignment:** By reservation in the summer, first come Oct.–Apr. **Registration:** At the entrance gate. **Fee:** $7 w/ no hookup, $12 w/ electric plus a $4 entrance fee per vehicle, or annual park pass. **Parking:** At site.

Facilities

Number of Multipurpose Sites: 87. **Hookups:** Electric (30 amps), water. **Each Site:** Picnic table, grated fire pits. **Dump Station:** Yes, (there is also a marina dump for boats). **Laundry:** No. **Pay Phone:** Yes. **Rest Rooms and Showers:** Yes. **Fuel:** Yes, located at the marina. **Propane:** No. **Internal Roads:** Paved. **RV Service:** 19 mi. southeast of Williston. **Market:** 19 mi. southeast of Williston. **Restaurant:** In Garrison or snack bar at the marina. **General Store:** Yes, located at the marina. **Vending:** Yes at the marina. **Swimming Pool:** No. **Playground:** Yes, several. **Other:** Full service marina with ramps, fish cleaning station, picnic shelters, lake front beach, picnic area with grills, nature trails, slip rentals. **Activities:** Hiking, fishing (walleye, sauger, & northern pike), boating, skiing, ice fishing (perch & walleye), wildlife viewing, special park programs. **Nearby Attractions:** Buffalo Trail Museum, Fort. Buford, Fort Union. **Additional Information:** ND Parks & Recreation Dept., (701) 328-5357.

Restrictions

Pets: On leash. **Fires:** In fire pits or grills only; fires may be restricted due to weather conditions; please ask management before starting any open fires. **Alcoholic Beverages:** Yes. **Vehicle Maximum Length:** None.

To Get There

The park is 19 mi. southeast of Williston on Hwy. 1804; turn on CR 15 and it is mi. down on the left. There is excellent signage from Hwy. 1804.

GARRISON

Fort Stevenson State Park

1252-A 41st. Ave. Northwest, Garrison 58540. T: (701) 337-5576; F: (701) 337-5313; www.ndparks.com; fssp@stste.nd.us.

RV ★★★★ Tent ★★★★

Beauty: ★★★★ Site Privacy: ★★★★
Spaciousness: ★★★★ Quiet: ★★★★
Security: ★★★★ Cleanliness: ★★★
Insect Control: ★★★ Facilities: ★★

Located in the center of the state, on the eastern end of giant Lake Sakakawea, this park is a fisher person's paradise. Plenty of other water sports and nature appreciation is available to campers here, but the park hosts several annual fishing tournaments, and is known as the "walleye capital of North Dakota." Accordingly, the marina and fishing-related facilities outshine those in the campground, but both RVs and tents should be comfortable here. The facilities are more limited in the winter, but the park is fun year-round. Just a few miles from the small town of Garrison, the park is in a rural area, and its remoteness enhances the security as well as the general quiet and privacy. This is a typically lovely campground for a state park, and all ages should enjoy the experience, just so long as you're not trying to escape fishing folks.

Basics

Operated By: The North Dakota Parks & Recreation Dept. **Open:** Year-round, but the water is off Oct.–May in the campground. **Site Assignment:** By reservation in the summer, first come Oct.–Apr. **Registration:** At the entrance gate. **Fee:** $7 w/ no hookup, $12 w/ 30 amp, $14 w/ 50 amp. plus a $4 entrance fee per vehicle or annual park pass. **Parking:** At site.

Facilities

Number of RV-Only Sites: 107. **Number of Tent-Only Sites:** 35. **Number of Multipurpose Sites:** 0. **Hookups:** Electric (30, 50 amps), water. **Each Site:** Picnic table, grated fire pits. **Dump Station:** Yes, (there is also a marina dump for boats). **Laundry:** No. **Pay Phone:** Yes. **Rest Rooms and Showers:** Yes. **Fuel:** Yes, located at the marina. **Propane:** No. **Internal Roads:** Paved. **RV Service:** 4 mi. North in Garrison. **Market:** 4 mi. north in Garrison. **Restaurant:** In Garrison or snack bar at the marina. **General Store:** Yes, located at the marina. **Vending:** Yes at the marina. **Swimming Pool:** No, but there is a lakefront beach. **Playground:** Yes, several. **Other:** Full service marina with high & low water ramps, boat rentals, pavilions with grill, 3 cabins, lake front beach, picnic area with grills, meeting facilities, arboretum, prairie dog town. **Activities:** Hiking, fishing (walleye, chinook, trout, pike), boating, skiing, ice fishing in the winter, wildlife viewing, special park programs, cross-country skiing, in season bow hunting for white tail deer. **Nearby Attractions:** Broste Rock Museum, White Shield Powwow, golf, tennis. **Additional Information:** ND Parks & Recreation Dept., (701) 328-5357.

Restrictions

Pets: On leash, but not on beach or public picnic areas. **Fires:** In fire pits or grills only; fires may be restricted due to weather conditions; please ask management before starting any open fires. **Alcoholic Beverages:** Yes. **Vehicle Maximum Length:** None.

To Get There

Garrison is located on Hwy. 37, and the park is 4 mi. south on CR 15 on Lake Sakakawea's north shore.

GARRISON

Sportsmen's Centennial Park

P.O. Box 98, Garrison 58540. T: (701) 337-5377; www.visitmcleancounty.com.

RV ★★★ Tent ★★★

Beauty: ★★★★ Site Privacy: ★★★
Spaciousness: ★★★ Quiet: ★★★★
Security: ★★★★ Cleanliness: ★★★
Insect Control: ★★ Facilities: ★

Since it was only created in 1989, this park is still being developed and tweaked by its McLean County operators. However simple, its wide-open spaces make it a very attractive and peaceful property. Set near the shore of Lake Sakakawea, the campground's boat ramp and dock make it a good place for anglers, and there is a stocked trout pond ideal for younger fisherfolk. The park is adjacent to the DeTobriand Game Management Area, which makes the campground an ideal overnight stop for visiting hunters and wildlife enthusiasts. The hiking trail offers the typical North Dakota vistas of rolling plains and vaulted skies. Though facilities and amenities are sparse, the youth of the park means that they are relatively new and in good condition.

Basics

Operated By: McLean County Park Board, overseen by COE **Open:** Apr.–late Oct., depends on weather. **Site Assignment:** By reservation. **Registration:** In general store. **Fee:** $8 no hookups, $10 with hookups. **Parking:** At site.

Facilities

Number of RV-Only Sites: 20. **Number of Tent-Only Sites:** 0. **Number of Multipurpose Sites:** 90. **Hookups:** Electric (20, 30 amps), water. **Each Site:** Picnic table. **Dump Station:** No. **Laundry:** No. **Pay Phone:** Yes. **Rest Rooms and Showers:** Yes. **Fuel:** No. **Propane:** No. **Internal Roads:** Gravel. **RV Service:** Inquire at campground. **Market:** Garrison. **Restaurant:** Garrison. **General Store:** Yes. **Vending:** Yes. **Swimming Pool:** No (Lakefront beach with life guard). **Playground:** Yes. **Other:** Fish cleaning station, picnic shelters & 2 boat ramps. **Activities:** Softball, volleyball, boating, waterskiing, fishing, hiking, swimming, & biking. **Nearby Attractions:** Inquire at campground. **Additional Information:** McLean County Park Board.

Restrictions

Pets: On leash. **Fires:** In fire pits or grills only; fires may be restricted due to weather conditions, please ask management before starting any open fires. **Alcoholic Beverages:** Yes. **Vehicle Maximum Length:** None. **Other:** No garbage facilities, much carry out all garbage.

To Get There

One mi. west of the junction of Hwy. 37 and Hwy. 83, then 2 mi. south and 1 mi. west.

JAMESTOWN

Frontier Fort Campground

P.O. Box 143, Jamestown 58402-0143. T: (701) 252-7492

RV ★★★ Tent ★★★

Beauty: ★★★	Site Privacy: ★★★
Spaciousness: ★★★	Quiet: ★★★
Security: ★★★	Cleanliness: ★★★
Insect Control: ★★★	Facilities: ★★★

Frontier Fort is a solid middle-of-the-road campground attached to a small Western-themed tourist attraction called Frontier Village. Despite Frontier Village's general tackiness, it's hard not to marvel at the World's Largest Buffalo (a 26-foot-tall, 46-foot-long, 60-ton concrete behemoth). There's even a pair of normal-sized live buffalo you can hand-feed behind the gift shop. Depending as it does almost completely on traveling flocks of older RVers, facilities are limited at this campground during the off-season. Twenty-eight of the campsites are sizable pull-throughs. Besides Frontier Village attractions, there is little to see here.

Basics

Operated By: Tanata Enterprises Inc. (Charley, Liz, & Jim). **Open:** Year round. **Site Assignment:** By reservation. **Registration:** In general store. **Fee:** Tent $8.50, RV $16.50. **Parking:** At site.

Facilities

Number of RV-Only Sites: 46. **Number of Tent-Only Sites:** 0. **Number of Multipurpose Sites:** 20. **Hookups:** Electric (20, 30, 50 amps), water, sewer. **Each Site:** Picnic table. **Dump Station:** Yes. **Laundry:** Yes. **Pay Phone:** Yes. **Rest Rooms and Showers:** Yes. **Fuel:** No, but in town. **Propane:** No, but in town. **Internal Roads:** Combination pavement & gravel in good condition. **RV Service:** In town. **Market:** In Jamestown. **Restaurant:** On site, & in Jamestown. **General Store:** Yes. **Vending:** Yes. **Swimming Pool:** No. **Playground:** No. **Other:** Museum, bar, small zoo, buffalo, Village Trader Gift Shoppe. **Activities:** Museum, zoo, electronic gaming (adults only). **Nearby Attractions:** Frontier Village, old west stagecoach ride, dinner theater.

Restrictions

Pets: On leash. **Fires:** In fire pits or grills only; fires may be restricted due to weather conditions; please ask management before starting any open fires. **Alcoholic Beverages:** Yes. **Vehicle Maximum Length:** None. **Other:** RV clubs welcome.

To Get There

From I-94 take Exit 258, Go north on US 281 (about 0.5 mi.) to first stop light, then east on 17th St. entrance on right.

JAMESTOWN

Jamestown KOA

3605 80th Ave. South, Jamestown 58401-9511. T: (701) 252-6262; F: (701) 252-6249; www.rv.camping.com/nd/jamestownkoa or www.koa.com; ahc@pocketmail.com.

RV: ★★★★ Tent: ★★★★

Beauty: ★★★★ Site Privacy: ★★★★
Spaciousness: ★★★★ Quiet: ★★★★
Security: ★★★★ Cleanliness: ★★★
Insect Control: ★★ Facilities: ★★★

While this KOA offers the usual amenities and abundant opportunities for play, including bocci ball, tetherball, heated pool, and disc golf, it lacks anything particularly unique. Though the RV sites are spacious, the landscaping and design are modest. All RV sites are gravel, and sites1–6 are best if you are looking for a nicely shaded spot. Sites 1–18 are closest to the play equipment, and sites 19–36 are closer to the lodge and rest rooms. Smart planning places the play area and lodge between the sites and the frontage road to act as a buffer. Tent sites, designated separately from the RV sites, offer the most secluded and wooded experience. A nice feature is a half-mile walking trail on the perimeter of the campground. Jamestown, only two miles away, pays homage to the legendary buffalo and frontier spirit with its National Buffalo Museum and the World's Largest Buffalo and Frontier Village. This is a nice overnight stop to someplace else, but is probably not a destination for an extended stay.

Basics

Operated By: Ann Case. **Open:** May 1–Oct. 1. **Site Assignment:** By reservation (800) 562-6350, held on credit card number. **Registration:** In the general store. **Fee:** Tent $20., RV $25–$27 per 2 people, $3 per extra person. **Parking:** At site.

Facilities

Number of RV-Only Sites: 48. **Number of Tent-Only Sites:** 20. **Number of Multipurpose Sites:** 0. **Hookups:** Electric (20, 30, 50 amps), water, sewer, cable. **Each Site:** Picnic table. **Dump Station:** Yes. **Laundry:** Yes. **Pay Phone:** Courtesy phone. **Rest Rooms and Showers:** Yes. **Fuel:** No. **Propane:** No. **Internal Roads:** Gravel. **RV Service:** Jamestown. **Market:** Jamestown. **Restaurant:** Jamestown. **General Store:** Yes. **Vending:** Yes. **Swimming Pool:** Yes (Jun. 15–Aug. 15). **Playground:** Yes. **Other:** Cabins, gameroom. **Activities:** Tetherball, disc golf, bocci ball, basketball, horseshoes, & nature walk. **Nearby Attractions:** National Buffalo Museum & live herd, world's largest buffalo & frontier village. **Additional Information:** Jamestown Chamber of Commerce, (701) 252-4830.

Restrictions

Pets: On leash. **Fires:** In fire pits or grills only; fires may be restricted due to weather conditions; please ask management before starting any open fires. **Alcoholic Beverages:** Yes. **Vehicle Maximum Length:** None.

To Get There

I-94 to Exit 256, then west on South Frontage Rd. 1 mi.

LARIMORE

Larimore Dam Recreation Area and Campground

P.O. Box 268, Larimore 58251-0268. T: (701) 343-2078

RV: ★★★★ Tent: ★★★★

Beauty: ★★★★ Site Privacy: ★★★★
Spaciousness: ★★★★ Quiet: ★★★★
Security: ★★★★ Cleanliness: ★★★★
Insect Control: ★★ Facilities: ★★★

This pretty and well-run campground makes a good headquarters for exploring the nearby Grand Forks area. Anglers will relish the chance to fish for trout, bluegill, bullhead, walleye, and largemouth bass in the waters of the Turtle River. Other recreational options abound, of course. Campers can hike or bike the nature trails; there's even a paved bike path running from the town of Larimore to the dam itself, which makes for a good day trip in either direction. Seasonally, visitors can relax on the campground beach in warmer months, or enjoy snow sledding during the winter.

Basics

Operated By: Private operator. **Open:** Apr.–late Oct., depends on weather. **Site Assignment:** By reservation. **Registration:** In general store. **Fee:** $8 no hookups, $10 with hookups. **Parking:** At site.

Facilities

Number of Multipurpose Sites: 114. **Hookups:** Electric (20, 30 amps), water. **Each Site:** Picnic table, fire pits. **Dump Station:** Yes. **Laundry:** No. **Pay Phone:** Yes. **Rest Rooms and Showers:** Yes. **Fuel:** No. **Propane:** No. **Internal Roads:** Combination pavement & gravel in good condition. **RV Service:** Grand Forks. **Market:** In Larimore. **Restaurant:** In Larimore. **General Store:** Yes. **Vending:** Yes. **Swimming Pool:** No, but there is swimming beach. **Playground:** Yes. **Other:** Picnic shelters, Myra Arboretum, a gazebo, fishing dock, nature trail. **Activities:** Softball, volleyball, boating, waterskiing, fishing, hiking, swimming, & biking. **Nearby Attractions:** Inquire at campground.

Restrictions

Pets: On leash. **Fires:** In fire pits or grills only; fires may be restricted due to weather conditions; please ask management before starting any open fires. **Alcoholic Beverages:** Yes. **Vehicle Maximum Length:** None. **Other:** No garbage facilities, must carry out all garbage.

To Get There

Located 30 mi. west of Grand Forks on Hwy. 4.

MANDAN

Fort Lincoln State Park

4480 Fort Lincoln Rd., Mandan 58554. T: (701) 663-9571; F: (701) 633-9234; www.ndparks.com; falsp@stste.nd.us.

RV ★★★ | Tent ★★★

Beauty: ★★★	Site Privacy: ★★★
Spaciousness: ★★★	Quiet: ★★★★
Security: ★★★★	Cleanliness: ★★★
Insect Control: ★★	Facilities: ★★

This state park is interesting for both its military and Native American commemorative sites. What with Little Big Horn and Custer battle reminders, and the reconstructed On-A-Slant Indian Village, the cultural history here is intriguing. The view of the Missouri River from the trails is stunning, offering a full panorama in some places. The recreational opportunities include hiking, rainbow trout fishing, and wildlife viewing, with snowmobiling and cross-country skiing in the winter. Campers will find typical facilities for a state park, average-sized back-in sites and decent privacy, comfortable but not luxurious. It is a fairly quiet and secure campground, pleasant and generally peaceful. Keep in mind that facilities are limited in the winter, and bring along a history and/or anthropology friend to enhance your culturally enriching camping vacation.

Basics

Operated By: The North Dakota Parks & Recreation Dept. **Open:** Year round, but the water is off Oct.–May in the campground. **Site Assignment:** By reservation in the summer, (800) 807 4723 first come Oct.–Apr. **Registration:** At the entrance gate. **Fee:** $7 w/ no hookup, $12 w/ electric plus a $4 entrance fee per vehicle or annual park pass. **Parking:** At site.

Facilities

Number of Multipurpose Sites: 95. **Hookups:** Electric (30 amps), water. **Each Site:** Picnic table, grated fire pits. **Dump Station:** Yes. **Laundry:** No. **Pay Phone:** Yes. **Rest Rooms and Showers:** Yes. **Fuel:** No. **Propane:** No. **Internal Roads:** Paved. **RV Service:** 7 mi. north in Mandan. **Market:** 7 mi. north in Mandan. **Restaurant:** 7 mi. north in Mandan. **General Store:** Yes, in the commissary. **Vending:** Yes. **Swimming Pool:** No. **Playground:** Yes, several. **Other:** Camp Store, paved nature trails, 2 cabins, picnic shelters, trail riding concession, state snowmobile trailhead, On-a-Slant Mandan village Earthlodges & other historical buildings including the Custer House & commissary, museum, cross-country ski trails. **Activities:** Tours of Fort Lincoln, snowmobiling, Hiking, fishing (rainbow trout), biking, sledding, cross-country skiing, wildlife viewing, special park programs. **Nearby Attractions:** Grand Forks 22 mi. east, golf. **Additional Information:** ND Parks & Recreation Dept., (701)328-5357.

Restrictions

Pets: On leash. **Fires:** In fire pits or grills only; fires may be restricted due to weather conditions; please ask management before starting any open fires. **Alcoholic Beverages:** Yes. **Vehicle Maximum Length:** None.

To Get There

From I-94 Exit 152 go south on Sunset Dr. to Main St.; take a left on Main St. to 6th Ave.; then right on 6th Ave. 7 mi. to Fort Abraham Lincoln State Park.

MINOT

Minot KOA

5261 Hwy. 52 East, Minot 58701. T: (701) 839-7400; www.koa.com.

RV ★★★ Tent ★★★

Beauty: ★★★ Site Privacy: ★★★
Spaciousness: ★★★ Quiet: ★★★★
Security: ★★★★ Cleanliness: ★★★
Insect Control: ★★ Facilities: ★★★

This campground is really lovely, set in rolling hills and meadowland. The grounds are well manicured, clean and on-site security is great. Each site is medium to average size, which gives the guests privacy and quiet. It's somewhat smaller than other KOAs we've seen, with only 49 RV sites and 17 tent sites. However, we don't think this takes away from the campground at all. There are still all the amenities of the larger facilities, even a laundry, but without the crowd you'd find at a big park. There are plenty of things to do on site, as well as in town, but some of the more interesting attractions are Roosevelt Park and Zoo and Pioneer Village.

Basics

Operated By: Jerry & Sandy Boe. **Open:** Apr. 15–Oct. 15. **Site Assignment:** By reservation (800) 562-7421, held on credit card number. **Registration:** In the general store. **Fee:** Tent $15., RV $19–$21 per 2 people. **Parking:** At site.

Facilities

Number of RV-Only Sites: 49. **Number of Tent-Only Sites:** 17. **Number of Multipurpose Sites:** 0. **Hookups:** Electric (30 amps), water, sewer. **Each Site:** Picnic table. **Dump Station:** Yes. **Laundry:** Yes. **Pay Phone:** Yes. **Rest Rooms and Showers:** Yes. **Fuel:** No. **Propane:** No. **Internal Roads:** Gravel. **RV Service:** Minot. **Market:** Minot. **Restaurant:** There are several in town. **General Store:** Yes. **Vending:** Yes. **Swimming Pool:** No, but there is swimming at the Roosevelt Park & Zoo. **Playground:** Yes. **Other:** Cabins, gameroom. **Activities:** Mini-golf, go-carts, movies. **Nearby Attractions:** Roosevelt Park & Zoo, golf, Pioneer Village. **Additional Information:** Minot Chamber of Commerce, (701) 852-6000.

Restrictions

Pets: On leash. **Fires:** In fire pits or grills only; fires may be restricted due to weather conditions; please ask management before starting any open fires. **Alcoholic Beverages:** Yes. **Vehicle Maximum Length:** None.

To Get There

Go 2.25 mi. southeast on Hwy. 52 from Minot.

WILLISTON

Prairie Acres RV Park

2008 University Ave., Williston 58801. T: (701) 572-4860; jloomer@dia.net.

RV ★★★ Tent n/a

Beauty: ★★★ Site Privacy: ★★★
Spaciousness: ★★★ Quiet: ★★★★
Security: ★★★ Cleanliness: ★★★★
Insect Control: ★★★ Facilities: ★★★

Prairie Acres RV Park is located on the Montana, North Dakota line one mile west of Williston, ND. Prairie Acres offers a rural setting overlooking crop fields and summer wildflowers. All of Prairie Acres sites are grass, level, and pull-through, set on a large rectangular open lawn with few trees. The area is great for observing the stars and watching the summer evening lightning. Prairie Acres caters exclusively to people in RVs wishing to escape to a quiet and restful environment, no tenting allowed. Prairie Acres offers full service hookups with 50-amp receptacles, but there are no public rest rooms, showers, or laundry. This is a simple well-groomed campground for those visitors wishing for a comfortable nights sleep. There are no bells and whistles, just friendly people, and peace. The spring is cool, and the summer dry. The wind blows constantly.

Basics

Operated By: Orville C. Loomer. **Open:** May–Oct. **Site Assignment:** First come, first served. **Registration:** In camp office. **Fee:** $12. **Parking:** At site.

Facilities

Number of RV-Only Sites: 29. **Number of Tent-Only Sites:** 0. **Number of Multipurpose Sites:** 0. **Hookups:** Electric (30, 50 amps), water, sewer. **Each Site:** Picnic table. **Dump Station:** Yes. **Laundry:** No. **Pay Phone:** No. **Rest Rooms and Showers:** No. **Fuel:** No. **Propane:** No. **Internal Roads:** Paved. **RV Service:** 0.25 mi. in Williston. **Market:** In Williston. **Restaurant:** In

Williston. **General Store:** No. **Vending:** No. **Swimming Pool:** No. **Playground:** No. **Activities:** Inquire at campground. **Nearby Attractions:** Fort Union Trading Post National Historic Site, The James Memorial Center for the Visual Arts, Williston Community Center w/ indoor pool. **Additional Information:** Williston Area Chamber of Commerce, (701) 572-3767.

RESTRICTIONS

Pets: On leash. **Fires:** No open fires**Alcoholic Beverages:** Yes. **Vehicle Maximum Length:** None.

TO GET THERE

One mile west of Williston on Hwy. 2.

Oregon

Like its northern neighbor, Oregon exhibits amazing variety in terms of climates and ecosystems. Much of the I-5 corridor has plenty of rain, big forests and beautiful mountains. The **Cascade Range** divides the state into a temperate year-round wonderland on the west side and a forbidding desert on the east. Nearing the California border, the terrain morphs into arid, rolling hills.

West of the Cascade Mountains are the I-5 cities of **Portland, Salem,** and **Eugene,** and the Highway 101 coastline. State government and community involvement impact regional culture, making it surprisingly isolated. Portland resonates with cosmopolitan yet blue-collar vibes, combining fine arts venues, communities of foreign nationals, and funky things to do. Driving south down I-5, the next city is Salem, the surprisingly conservative capital of the state. The scenery along northern I-5—a mixture of forests, farms, and mountains—continues south past Eugene, home of the **University of Oregon** and one of the most liberal, earthy, scholarly concentrations of people of any city on the west coast.

The forestlands surrounding the I-5 corridor between Portland and **Roseburg** (the rafting capital of Oregon) are indescribable. **Mt. Hood** and the Umpqua River Valley (OR 38 to the coast from I-5) have must see status for all travelers.

Another area not to be missed is the coast. Hwy 101 runs the length of the coast to California with cut-throughs to I-5 every 60 to 100 miles. Starting in **Astoria,** the Oregon coast offers huge surf breaking against high rock cliffs and gnarled rock formations off shore. Rocky tidal pools at almost any beach hold all types of ecological wonders. During spring break and summer, traffic jams on two-lane 101 can get hairy. Oregon state parks litter the whole drive; make sure to see **Oswald West.** Another point of interest, **Newport** has an aquarium, an oceanography satellite of OSU, an enormous fishing fleet, a brewery, and a wax museum. South of **North Bend** and the **Oregon Dunes,** tourist traffic drops off, although the blue collar shipping, fishing, and logging villages have a certain charm to them and are worth seeing if time permits.

Driving east from Portland, I-84 follows the Columbia through the **Columbia River Gorge National Scenic Area.** Large rock formations, mountains, and, of course, the river make the drive appealing. Continuing on past the gorge, the scenery changes into flat, high-altitude plains and rolling hills along the Columbia and Snake Rivers. Eastern Oregon has very low population density and not many attractions, but there's plenty of beautiful scenery in both snowy winter and boiling summer weather.

The central part of the state has the second-largest tourism draw after the I-5 corridor (including the coast, the gorge and Mount Hood). In the **Bend-Sisters** area, recreation attractions include skiing, rafting, horseback riding, stream fishing, and drinking.

Driving south from Bend on Highway 97, day trips abound. Recreation comes in one flavor: outdoors. Lakes, national forests, and volcanoes sum up the attractions between Bend and **Klamath Falls.**

The following facilities accept payment in checks or cash only:

- Bastendorff Beach Campground, Coo's Bay
- Cinder Hill Campground, Bend
- Columbia River RV Park, Portland
- Diamond Lake Campground, Diamond Lake
- Paulina Lake Campground, Bend
- Portland-Dayton RV Park, Portland
- Princess Creek Campground, Cascade Summit
- Richardson Park, Eugene
- Harbor Vista Campground, Florence

The following facilities feature 20 or fewer sites:

- Eagle Creek Campground, Bonneville
- Elk Lake Campground, Detroit
- Illahe Campground, Gold Beach
- Riverside Campground, Sisters
- Saddle Mountain State Park, Cannon Beach

Campground Profiles

ASHLAND

Glenyan Campground of Ashland

5310 Hwy. 66, Ashland 97520. T: (541) 488-1785

RV ★★★ Tent ★★★

Beauty: ★★★	Site Privacy: ★
Spaciousness: ★★	Quiet: ★★★
Security: ★	Cleanliness: ★★★
Insect Control: ★★	Facilities: ★★★

Glenyan Campground, located in a scenic rural area six miles east of I-5, greets guests with a small pond shaded by medium-sized trees. The grounds, foliated with small cedars and shrubs, huge oaks and pines, birch, elm, willow, and thick blackberry brambles, sit nestled in the scruffy, rolling farmland foothills of the southern cascades. Sites within the campground contain a mixture of grass, moss, dirt, and very fine-grit gravel (about the size of kitty litter). All preferred sites back up to a gently flowing, clear stream and beyond that a lightly wooded hill. The stream helps to mask road noise in the sites arranged along it. Choice RV sites include 45–49 and 28–35. The best tent sites, 2–5, 39, D, E, and G, have some privacy; the RV sites do not. Avoid RV sites 58–63 and 26–15 as they catch the brunt of noise from a nearby road. The spring, summer, and fall necessitate reservations in this older park with well kept facilities; vacancies are more common in winter, despite relatively mild weather. The older game room has one large pool table and some classic arcade games.

BASICS

Operated By: Glenyan Campground. **Open:** All year. **Site Assignment:** First come, first served; reservation (required deposit is 1 night's stay; refund w/ 48-hours notice plus $2 cancellation fee). **Registration:** Office, after hours at drop box or in morning when office opens. **Fee:** Full $22, electric/cable $21, tent $17.50; fee covers 2 people, extra person $2; V, MC, cash. **Parking:** At site.

FACILITIES

Number of RV-Only Sites: 78. **Number of Tent-Only Sites:** 20. **Hookups:** Electric (20, 30 amps), water, sewer, cable. **Each Site:** Picnic table, fire ring. **Dump Station:** Yes. **Laundry:** Yes. **Pay Phone:** Yes. **Rest Rooms and Showers:** Yes. **Fuel:** No. **Propane:** Yes. **Internal Roads:** Paved. **RV Service:** No. **Market:** 4 mi. west in Ashland. **Restaurant:** 4 mi. west in Ashland. **General Store:** Yes. **Vending:** No. **Swimming Pool:** Yes. **Playground:** No. **Other:** Game room, meeting hall (capacity 40), horseshoes, badminton. **Activities:** Blackberry picking, bird-watching. **Nearby Attractions:** Emigrant Lake Recreation Area (across the street from campground; has a water slide), Oregon Shakespearean Festival (Feb.–Oct.), Britt Music Festival (summer), cabaret theater, Pacific Northwest Museum of Natural History. **Additional Information:** Ashland Chamber of Commerce, (541) 482-3486.

RESTRICTIONS

Pets: No more than 2, leash only. **Fires:** Fire pit/grill only. **Alcoholic Beverages:** Site only. **Vehicle Maximum Length:** 60 ft. **Other:** No clotheslines; only commercial RV awnings; quiet hours 10 p.m.–7 a.m.; no RV washer/dryer usage; no firearms.

TO GET THERE

From I-5 take Exit 14; drive 3.2 mi. southeast on Hwy. 66; Entrance is on right

ASTORIA

Astoria/Warrenton/Seaside KOA

1100 Northwest Ridge Rd., Hammond 97121. T: (503)861-2606 or (800)562-8506 for reservations; F: (503) 861-3209; www.koa.com; astoriakoa@aol.com.

RV ★★★ Tent ★★

Beauty: ★★	Site Privacy: ★★
Spaciousness: ★★	Quiet: ★★★
Security: ★★★	Cleanliness: ★★★
Insect Control: ★★	Facilities: ★★★★

Astoria/Warrenton/Seaside KOA, just across the street from gorgeous Fort Stevens State Park and south of Astoria a few miles off Hwy. 101, offers a bounty of family recreational activities within the property. These include a large, nice indoor pool, sandy playgrounds, an arcade with 14 machines and an Internet access terminal (20 cents a minute), nine holes of mini-golf in good condition, and a paved basketball court with opposing goals; all of these on top of regular and varying planned activities. The most visually appealing, flat, spacious sites on the property, the deluxe sites (sections B, C, D, E) have some foliage-generated privacy. The small number of grassy tent sites lack privacy, and this also applies to the rest of the RV sites: when full they create an almost treeless city of trailers. Sites J11–36 and sites K13–38 are quiet and isolated from the rest of the grounds along a lane ending in a cul-de-sac, but have the same privacy problems.

BASICS

Operated By: Recreational Adventures Campgrounds. **Open:** All year (some seasonal sites). **Site Assignment:** First come, first served; reservation (required deposit is 1 night's fee, 3 nights on holidays; refund w/ 24 hours notice, 1 week notice for holidays). **Registration:** At the office, after hours drop in front of office. **Fee:** Deluxe $37, water/electric/sewer $32, water/electric $30, tent village (w/ electricity) $25, tent w/ no hookups $23; fee covers 2 people, additional adults $3.95 per day, children ages 6–17 $2.95, children under age 5 free; off-season/weekday rates are $3 less;V, MC, D, cash. **Parking:** At site, limited off site.

FACILITIES

Number of RV-Only Sites: 230. **Number of Tent-Only Sites:** 26. **Hookups:** Electric (20, 30, 50 amps), water, sewer, cable, phone. **Each Site:** Picnic table, fire ring. **Dump Station:** No. **Laundry:** Yes. **Pay Phone:** Yes. **Rest Rooms and Showers:** Yes. **Fuel:** No. **Propane:** Yes. **Internal Roads:** Paved & grave. **RV Service:** No. **Market:** 5 mi. north in Astoria. **Restaurant:** 5 mi. North in Astoria. **General Store:** Yes. **Vending:** Yes. **Swimming Pool:** Yes. **Playground:** Yes. **Other:** Indoor Pool & hot tub, arcade, outdoor electric stoves w/full sized sinks, volleyball court, basketball court, horseshoes, stage, mini-golf; rec room, outdoor pavilion, fish cleaning station, bike rental, pancake house (open summers), board game & movie rentals. **Activities:** Multiple planned activities. **Nearby Attractions:** Columbia River Maritime Museum, Fort Clatsop National Memorial, Fort Stevens State Park, Flavel House Museum. **Additional Information:** Astoria-Warrenton Chamber of Commerce, (503) 325-6311 or www.old oregon.com

Restrictions

Pets: On leash only. **Fires:** In fire pits, grills only. **Alcoholic Beverages:** At site. **Vehicle Maximum Length:** 60 ft. **Other:** 3 night min. stay on blackout dates: Crab Festival Weekend (end of Apr.), Memorial Day, Fourth of July week, Labor Day, All weekends in July & Aug.

To Get There

After Astoria Suzuki Dealership on Hwy. 101, take next right on unmarked road with an ODOT KOA sign. Drive west 0.8 mi. and dead-end on S. Main St. Turn left and drive 0.2 mi., then take a right on Delaura Beach Rd. which turns into Ridge Rd. Follow for 3 mi.; entrance on the right across from state park.

BAKER CITY

Mountain View RV Park

2845 Hughs Ln., Baker City 97814. T: (541) 523-4824

RV ★★★ Tent ★★

Beauty: ★★★	Site Privacy: ★
Spaciousness: ★★	Quiet: ★★★
Security: ★★★	Cleanliness: ★★★★
Insect Control: ★★	Facilities: ★★★

Baker City has many RV parks, but none have faux-wild-west store-fronts like Mountain View RV Park's. The park is actually in better shape than appearances initially suggest; the facilities behind the facades are well maintained. Sites sit closer together than in some other parks. Mountain View has tall, older deciduous trees shading sites from the intense summer sun (trees are hard to find in eastern Oregon). The trees and grass below them create a kind of quaint park feel. Some sites have very limited views of the mountains on the horizon, limited by the perimeter fencing and older trees overhead. On one perimeter the park has a grassy tenting area; the sites have shade but like other sites on the grounds they lack privacy. RV sites on the perimeter provide good accomodations due to an absence of neighbors to the rear. The park stays open year-round, but winters bring extreme cold.

Basics

Operated By: Mt. View RV Park. **Open:** All year. **Site Assignment:** On arrival, reservation (required deposit is 1 night's fee; refund w/ 24 hours notice). **Registration:** At office, after hours night box at office. **Fee:** Full $22, tent $19; fee covers 2 people, extra person $2, extra child (ages 3–12) $1; Units using air-conditioning, 50 amp units, & units longer than 34 ft. add $1; V, MC, cash. **Parking:** At site, off site.

Facilities

Number of RV-Only Sites: 88. **Number of Tent-Only Sites:** 10. **Hookups:** Electric (20, 30, 50 amps), water, sewer, cable. **Each Site:** Picnic table. **Dump Station:** Yes. **Laundry:** Yes. **Pay Phone:** Yes. **Rest Rooms and Showers:** Yes. **Fuel:** No. **Propane:** Yes. **Internal Roads:** Paved. **RV Service:** No. **Market:** A few mi. away in Baker City. **Restaurant:** A few mi. away in Baker City. **General Store:** Yes, open seasonally. **Vending:** No. **Swimming Pool:** Yes. **Playground:** Yes. **Other:** Meeting room (reservable), indoor Jacuzzi. **Activities:** Inquire at campground. **Nearby Attractions:** Hell's Canyon, Hells Canyon National Scenic Byway, horseback riding, llama pack trips, Snake River Reservoirs (3), watersports, Alder House Museum. **Additional Information:** Baker County Visitor & Convention Bureau, (541) 523-3356.

Restrictions

Pets: On leash only. **Fires:** No fires. **Alcoholic Beverages:** At site. **Vehicle Maximum Length:** 73 ft.

To Get There

From I-84 Exit 302, turn south on North Cedar Dr. and follow for 0.7 mi. Turn right on Hughes Ln., drive 1 mi. and turn left into campground.

BEND

Bend Kampground

63615 North Hwy. 97, Bend 97701. T: (541) 382-7738 or for reservations (800) 323-8899

RV ★★★ Tent ★★

Beauty: ★★★	Site Privacy: ★
Spaciousness: ★★★	Quiet: ★★
Security: ★★	Cleanliness: ★★★★
Insect Control: ★★	Facilities: ★★★

Quick access to the greater Bend area and recreational facilities describe the advantages of staying at Bend Kampground, located just a few minutes northwest of Bend between Hwy. 97 and Hwy. 20. The irrigated campground consists of several rows of sites, all without privacy. The older, marginally maintained facilities within the grounds include a small arcade and a pool. The best gravel full hookup sites, pull-throughs 61–67, have grass perimeters and a little shade from the high desert sun. Back-in sites 18–24 have views of the distant mountains to the west. The worst RV sites, 40–47, consist of an area covered solely in gravel. The best grass tent sites within the grounds, letters H–K, have some shade but no privacy. Most tent sites have picnic tables with small, wall-less shelters, providing a canopy for diners from the blazing sun and infrequent rain. The usually cloudless summers here can be hot, winters bring good skiing conditions.

Basics

Operated By: Bend Kampground. **Open:** All year. **Site Assignment:** On arrival, reservation (deposit & refund policy varies depending on time of year & local events). **Registration:** At convenience store. **Fee:** Full $28, water/electric $24, tent $18; fee covers 2 people, extra adult $3, extra child (ages 3–18) $2; V, MC, cash. **Parking:** At site.

Facilities

Number of RV-Only Sites: 79. **Number of Tent-Only Sites:** 21. **Hookups:** Electric (30, 50 amps), water, sewer, cable. **Each Site:** Picnic table. **Dump Station:** Yes. **Laundry:** Yes. **Pay Phone:** Yes. **Rest Rooms and Showers:** Yes. **Fuel:** Yes. **Propane:** Yes. **Internal Roads:** Paved. **RV Service:** No. **Market:** 1 mile south. **Restaurant:** 1 mi. south. **General Store:** Yes. **Vending:** No. **Swimming Pool:** Yes. **Playground:** Yes. **Other:** Deli, horseshoes, volleyball, fishing pond (catch & release), tether ball, basketball, arcade. **Activities:** Swimming, fishing. **Nearby Attractions:** Pilot Butte, Deshutes Brewery, regional rodeos, national forests, all types of outdoor sports, horseback riding. **Additional Information:** Bend Chamber of Commerce, (541) 382-3221.

Restrictions

Pets: On leash only. **Fires:** Fire pits only. **Alcoholic Beverages:** At site. **Vehicle Maximum Length:** None.

To Get There

Located at north end of Bend on Hwy. 97, 0.25 mi. north of Mountain View Mall.

BEND
Cinder Hill Campground

P.O. Box 989, Bend 97709. T: (541) 383-4000; F: (541) 383-4700; www.fs.fed.us/r6/centraloregon/recinfo/camping/cinderhill.html.

RV: ★★★ Tent: ★★★★

Beauty: ★★★★	Site Privacy: ★★★
Spaciousness: ★★★	Quiet: ★★★★★
Security: ★★	Cleanliness: ★★★
Insect Control: ★★	Facilities: ★

Cinder Hill Campground, located at the end of the main access road passing through Newberry National Volcanic Monument, provides a wilderness camping environment easily accessible to larger rigs. Most sites sit situated along an avenue with loops branching from this straightaway. The start of the avenue has some of the best sites, numbered 1–16 and 34–40, and the area containing these has a low site density, some shade from evergreens, and some privacy from foliage. Site density increases as one travels deeper into the campground. Some sites have views of East Lake, and the best sites, numbers 27–33, have obscured views that avoid the late day glare plaguing many of the lakefront sites with unobstructed views. Sites numbered 65 and higher sit closer together than those in the front of the grounds. Facilities here are limited. Summers are hot but provide good fishing and swimming.

Basics

Operated By: High Lake Contractors. **Open:** May–Oct. **Site Assignment:** On arrival only. **Registration:** At self pay station. **Fee:** Regular site $10, premium site (usually paved, marked on site signpost) $12; cash. **Parking:** At site.

Facilities

Number of Multipurpose Sites: 110. **Hookups:** None. **Each Site:** Picnic table, fire ring. **Dump Station:** No. **Laundry:** No. **Pay Phone:** No. **Rest Rooms and Showers:** Rest rooms only. **Fuel:** No. **Propane:** No. **Internal Roads:** Paved. **RV Service:** No. **Market:** 30 mi. west. **Restaurant:** 30 mi. west. **General Store:** No. **Vending:** No.

Swimming Pool: No. **Playground:** No. **Other:** Boat ramp (2), hiking trails. **Activities:** Swimming, fishing, hiking, biking, boating, watching bubbles surface in the lake. **Nearby Attractions:** Bend, Deschutes National Forest, hiking, biking, boating, ecotourism. **Additional Information:** Bend Chamber of Commerce, (541) 382-3221.

Restrictions

Pets: On leash only (max. length 6 ft.). **Fires:** Fire pits only. **Alcoholic Beverages:** At site. **Vehicle Maximum Length:** 45 ft. **Other:** 14-day max. stay limit, Unlawful to clean fish in lakes or streams.

To Get There

From Bend, drive 23.5 mi. south on Hwy. 97, then 12.9 mi. east on Rd. 21 marked as leading to Newberry Caldera; Paulina, East Lakes.

BEND

Crown Villa RV Park

60801 Brosterhouse Rd., Bend 97702. T: (541) 388-1131

Beauty: ★★★★	Site Privacy: ★★
Spaciousness: ★★★★	Quiet: ★★★
Security: ★★	Cleanliness: ★★★★★
Insect Control: ★★	Facilities: ★★★★★

Crown Villa RV Park, off the Hwy. 97/20 Business Loop in Bend, provides a quiet, suburban setting for travelers. Not endowed with many in-house recreational activities, this park has more of an adult feel. The enormous, adjacent RV sites give the impression of camping on a golf course with ponderosa pines providing partial shade. The one common building, a club house and covered porch is equipped with an array of non-commercial propane grills. There's no privacy between sites, but site sizes make up for this. The best full hookup sites within the grounds, designated 447–458 and 461–471, back up to a fairway-like grassy area; many other sites have similar backyards but these have the largest. On the other hand, sites 601–610 provide a contrast to the rest of the park, as they make up an area of open gravel with electric hookups only. The park also has several tent sites in different areas, also open but with grass surfaces. Both fair weather and winter weather recreation abound in Bend.

Basics

Operated By: Crown Villa. **Open:** All year. **Site Assignment:** On arrival, reservation (required deposit is 1 night's fee; refund w/ 24-hours notice repayed w/ credits for future stay). **Registration:** At office. **Fee:** Full $38.50, electric/cable $33, dry $23, tent $19.25; V, MC, cash. **Parking:** At site.

Facilities

Number of RV-Only Sites: 131. **Number of Tent-Only Sites:** 16. **Hookups:** Electric (30, 50 amps), water, sewer, cable. **Each Site:** Picnic table. **Dump Station:** No. **Laundry:** Yes. **Pay Phone:** Yes. **Rest Rooms and Showers:** Yes. **Fuel:** No. **Propane:** Yes. **Internal Roads:** Paved. **RV Service:** No. **Market:** 2 mi. west on 97. **Restaurant:** 2 mi. west on 97. **General Store:** No. **Vending:** Yes. **Swimming Pool:** No. **Playground:** Yes. **Other:** Club house w/ TV, kitchen, covered BBQ area w/ propane grills (Non-commercial), horseshoes, volleyball, basketball, storage. **Activities:** Lounging. **Nearby Attractions:** City parks, Pilot Butte, Mt. Bachelor (Year-round skiing), Benham Falls, Newberry National Volcanic Monument, Oregon High Desert Museum, every type of outdoor recreation. **Additional Information:** Bend Chamber of Commerce, (541) 382-3221.

Restrictions

Pets: On leash only, no fighting breeds. **Fires:** No open fires. **Alcoholic Beverages:** At site. **Vehicle Maximum Length:** None. **Other:** Only newer (or well maintained) RVs allowed.

To Get There

Driving south on Hwy. 97, turn left on Brosterhouse Rd. (at traffic light near Hollywood Video), follow for 0.8 mi. Brosterhouse turns right (but is poorly marked) just after the Bend Trap Club on the left, continue to follow this road for 0.9 mi., park entrance is on the right.

BEND

Paulina Lake Campground

P.O. Box 989, Bend 97709. T: (541) 383-4001; F: (541) 383-4701; www.fs.fed.us/r6/centraloregon/recinfo/camping/paulinalake.html.

Beauty: ★★★★ Site Privacy: ★★
Spaciousness: ★★★ Quiet: ★★★★★
Security: ★★ Cleanliness: ★★★
Insect Control: ★★ Facilities: ★

Paulina Lake Campground, located within Newberry National Volcanic Monument, offers a rustic camping experience. No sites within this wilderness area campground have hookups of any sort. Some sites have paved while others have gravel surfaces, and all sites can accept a tent or RV; for tenting one can set up in the flat dirt area just off the parking area of each site. Sites are situated along several loops. Sites sit fairly close together with little privacy for RVs, but some privacy for tents generated by random trees and bushes. The longest sites, 38–53, sit in the back of the campground, near the lake with partial views of the lake and mountains on the opposite shore. Contrary to Forest Service estimates there are a few sites that can take rigs up to 45 feet long. The camground really doesn't have any objectively undesirable sites. Within Newberry National Volcanic Monument there exist four campgrounds, this one and Cinder Hill have the highest capacity for longer rigs. Of the other grounds, Little Crater consists of almost totally lakefront sites along a single straight-away in a secluded cove, East Lake has a mixture of sites positioned around a single loop.

Basics

Operated By: High Lake Contractors for National Forest Service. **Open:** May–Oct. **Site Assignment:** First come, first served. **Registration:** At self pay station. **Fee:** Regular site $10, premium site (usually paved, marked on site signpost) $12; cash. **Parking:** At site.

Facilities

Number of Multipurpose Sites: 68. **Hookups:** None. **Each Site:** Picnic table, fire ring. **Dump Station:** No. **Laundry:** No. **Pay Phone:** No. **Rest Rooms and Showers:** Rest room Only. **Fuel:** No. **Propane:** No. **Internal Roads:** Paved. **RV Service:** No. **Market:** 30 mi. west. **Restaurant:** 30 mi. west. **General Store:** No. **Vending:** No. **Swimming Pool:** No. **Playground:** No. **Other:** Boat ramp, hiking trails. **Activities:** Hiking, biking, swimming, fishing, basking in the sun. **Nearby Attractions:** hiking, biking, fishing, golf, ecotourism in the Bend area, rock climbing. **Additional Information:** Bend Chamber of Commerce, (541) 382-3221.

Restrictions

Pets: On leash only (max. length 6 ft.). **Fires:** Fire pits only. **Alcoholic Beverages:** At site. **Vehicle Maximum Length:** 45 ft. (listed smaller, but their are some sites w/ larger lengths). **Other:** 14 day max. stay limit, Unlawful to clean fish in lakes or streams.

To Get There

From Bend, drive 23.5 mi. south on Hwy. 97, then 12.9 mi. east on Rte. 21 marked as leading to Newberry Caldera; Paulina, East Lakes.

BONNEVILLE

Eagle Creek Campground

902 Roscoe Ave. Suite 200, Head River 97031.
T: (541) 308-1700

RV ★★★ Tent ★★★

Beauty: ★★★★ Site Privacy: ★★★★
Spaciousness: ★★★ Quiet: ★★★★
Security: ★★★ Cleanliness: ★★★★
Insect Control: ★★★ Facilities: ★★★

This campground sits just east of the Bonneville Dam. The campground can be easily missed by many Columbia Gorge travelers whose eyes are directed riverward to the massive plant that provides hydroelectric power to the metropolitan areas farther west. Despite its proximity to this hulking tribute to human engineering, Eagle Creek offers a woodsy setting amidst true fir, western red cedar, and hemlock, and provides access to some beautiful walks high above the river in the Columbia Wilderness. The nearby busy freeway quickly fades into oblivion as Eagle Creek Trail leaves the end of FSR 241 beside the campground and follows Eagle Creek for 13 miles to Wahtum Lake and the intersection with Pacific Crest National Scenic Trail. Along the way the trail passes high cliffs along Eagle Creek and waterfalls too numerous to mention. Several other trails and Forest Service roads lead off very near the campground to other points within the Columbia Wilderness.

Basics

Operated By: Mount Hood National Forest. **Open:** May–Oct. **Site Assignment:** First come, first served. **Registration:** self-registration on site. **Fee:** $10. **Parking:** At site.

Facilities

Number of RV-Only Sites: 17. **Number of Tent-Only Sites:** 0. **Hookups:** No. **Each Site:** Picnic table, fire ring & grill. **Dump Station:** No. **Laundry:** No. **Pay Phone:** No. **Rest Rooms and Showers:** Yes. **Fuel:** No. **Propane:** No. **Internal Roads:** Call ahead for details. **RV Service:** No. **Market:** No. **Restaurant:** No. **General Store:** No. **Vending:** No. **Swimming Pool:** No. **Playground:** No. **Activities:** Hiking. **Nearby Attractions:** Cascade Locks, Fort Dalles Museum, Crown Pointe Vista House & Observatory. **Additional Information:** Mt. Hood National Forest, (541) 308-1700.

Restrictions

Pets: On leash only. **Fires:** In fire rings only. **Alcoholic Beverages:** Allowed. **Vehicle Maximum Length:** 22 ft.

To Get There

From Portland, drive 33 mi. east on I-84 to the campground, it is 2 mi. past the town of Bonneville, just off of the interstate.

CANNON BEACH

RV Resort At Cannon Beach

P.O. Box 219, Cannon Beach 97110. T: (503) 436-2231 or (800) 847-2231; www.cbrvresort.com; info@cbrvresort.com.

RV ★★★★★ Tent n/a

Beauty: ★★★★	Site Privacy: ★★★
Spaciousness: ★★★	Quiet: ★★★
Security: ★★★	Cleanliness: ★★★★
Insect Control: ★★	Facilities: ★★★★

Just off of 101 on the west side of Cannon Beach sits the RV Resort at Cannon Beach. This well kept campground with plenty of trees provides a quiet escape from the bustle of the nearby resort town. The park has spacious, paved sites surrounded by grass and shaded by medium sized pines, maples and oaks. Quiet can be found in the back of the park in pull-through sites 84–89 and back-in sites 27–35 and 97–100. The campground has good views of the surrounding evergreen dotted hills, and on rainy days, beautiful patches of clouds and mist drift serenely around the tops of these hills. The indoor hot tub is big enough to accomodate a family reunion, and the rec room has two pool tables. This campground has a unique advantage of easy access; a city shuttle stops at the entrance to pick up tourists every half hour, with stops throughout the Cannon Beach area. Best times to visit are just before or after the on season in summer.

Basics

Operated By: RV Resort at Cannon Beach. **Open:** All year. **Site Assignment:** First come, first served; reservation (required deposit is 1st night's stay; refund w/ 72 hours notice). **Registration:** At mini-mart, after hours pay in morning. **Fee:** Summer $34, spring & fall $27, winter $23; fee covers 2 people & 2 vehicles, extra person (age 5 or older) $3, extra vehicle $3; V, MC, cash. **Parking:** At site.

Facilities

Number of RV-Only Sites: 100. **Number of Tent-Only Sites:** 0. **Hookups:** Electric (30, 50 amps), water, sewer, cable, central data port. **Each Site:** Picnic table, fire ring. **Dump Station:** No. **Laundry:** Yes. **Pay Phone:** Yes. **Rest Rooms and Showers:** Yes. **Fuel:** Yes. **Propane:** Yes. **Internal Roads:** Paved. **RV Service:** No. **Market:** Across 101 in Cannon Beach. **Restaurant:** Across 101 in Cannon Beach. **General Store:** Yes. **Vending:** No. **Swimming Pool:** Yes. **Playground:** Yes. **Other:** Reservable meeting room w/ TV, hot tub, basketball court, horseshoe pit, mini-storage, game room w/ 2 pool tables & 3 arcade games, free shuttle to Cannon Beach. **Activities:** Free hot dog roast Saturdays in summer, Thanksgiving potluck. **Nearby Attractions:** Beaches, Haystack Rock, Tillimook Rock Lighthouse, Sandcastle Day. **Additional Information:** Cannon Beach Visitor's Information Center, (503) 436-2623.

Restrictions

Pets: On leash only. **Fires:** Fire pits only. **Alcoholic Beverages:** At site. **Vehicle Maximum Length:** 60 ft. **Other:** Max. 8 people per site.

To Get There

From Hwy. 101, Campground is across from 2nd Cannon Beach Exit, turn (south bound-left) onto Sunset Blvd. After 200 feet turn left into entrance.

CANNON BEACH

Saddle Mountain State Park

P.O. Box 681, Cannon Beach 97110. T: (503) 368-5943

n/a ▲ ★★

Beauty: ★★ Site Privacy: ★★★
Spaciousness: ★★ Quiet: ★★
Security: ★★ Cleanliness: ★
Insect Control: ★★★ Facilities: ★★★

Want to enjoy the beach, see the mountains, and not get trampled by the crowds? Saddle Mountain is the answer. You have the best of both worlds at Saddle Mountain because you'll be less than 15 miles from the nearest coastal attractions of Cannon Beach and Seaside, well away from the crowded Coast Highway corridor, and only a 2.6-mile hike from superb views atop the highest peak in northwestern Oregon. Add to that a campground (albeit primitive) that is for tent campers only and nearly 3,000 acres of forests, with meadows, and creeks that you'll share with a number of woodland critters and several rare and endangered plant species. Saddle Mountain was a haven for certain species of plant life during the Ice Age, and much of the flora that has evolved today high on the flanks of this 3,283-foot peak is not found anywhere else. Alpine wildflowers put on one of the best shows of colors in the region in early to mid-June.

BASICS

Operated By: Oregon State Parks & Recreation. **Open:** Apr.–Oct. (depending on snow). **Site Assignment:** First come, first served, no reservations. **Registration:** self-registration on site. **Fee:** $10. **Parking:** At site.

FACILITIES

Number of RV-Only Sites: 0. **Number of Tent-Only Sites:** 10. **Hookups:** None. **Each Site:** Picnic table, fire pit, piped water. **Dump Station:** No. **Laundry:** No. **Pay Phone:** No. **Rest Rooms and Showers:** Vault toilets. **Fuel:** No. **Propane:** No. **Internal Roads:** Call ahead for details. **RV Service:** No. **Market:** No. **Restaurant:** No. **General Store:** No. **Vending:** No. **Swimming Pool:** No. **Playground:** No. **Activities:** Hiking. **Nearby Attractions:** Del Rey Beach, Hug Point, Arcadia Beach. **Additional Information:** Cannon Beach Visitor's Information Center, (503) 436-2623.

RESTRICTIONS

Pets: On leash only. **Fires:** In fire rings only. **Alcoholic Beverages:** Allowed. **Vehicle Maximum Length:** None. **Other:** No accommodations for RVs or trailers, but self-contained units are allowed in the parking lot.

TO GET THERE

Turn north on Saddle Mountain Rd. off of US 26 about 1.5 mi. east of Necanicum Junction. Drive 7 mi. to the campground.

CASCADE LOCKS

Ainsworth State Park Campground

P.O.Box 100, Corbett 97019. T: (503) 695-2301 or (503) 695-2261; www.oregonstateparks.org.

RV ★★★ ▲ ★★★

Beauty: ★★★★ Site Privacy: ★★
Spaciousness: ★★ Quiet: ★
Security: ★★ Cleanliness: ★★★
Insect Control: ★★ Facilities: ★★★

Ainsworth State Park, in the Columbia River Scenic Area east of Portland off I-84, provides a scenic location on the Oregon side of the gorge. This beautiful wooded campground has paved, terraced pull-throughs and a row of paved back-ins under the shade of cottonwoods and out-of-place coastal pines. The more spacious terraced sites, numbered A1–13, have tree-obscured views of surrounding cliffs. Facilities are limited in scope, and like all campgrounds in the gorge, train tracks run past the park to the north of the grounds. Still, Ainsworth is the quietest state park in the gorge. The few walk-in tent sites provide little privacy from other tenters, but are positioned away from the rest of the grounds. The loudest sites, the paved back-ins, sit closest to the railroad tracks, numbered B1-32.

BASICS

Operated By: Oregon State Parks & Recreation. **Open:** Mar. 16–the end of Oct. **Site Assignment:** First come, first served. **Registration:** At self pay station. **Fee:** Full $20, walk-in tent $13; V, MC, check, cash. **Parking:** At site.

Facilities

Number of RV-Only Sites: 42. **Number of Tent-Only Sites:** 5. **Hookups:** Electric (20, 30 amps), water, sewer, cable. **Each Site:** Picnic table, fire ring. **Dump Station:** Yes. **Laundry:** No. **Pay Phone:** No. **Rest Rooms and Showers:** Yes. **Fuel:** No. **Propane:** No. **Internal Roads:** Paved. **RV Service:** No. **Market:** 10 mile east in Cascade Locks. **Restaurant:** 10 mi. east in Cascade Locks. **General Store:** No. **Vending:** No. **Swimming Pool:** No. **Playground:** Yes. **Other:** Small Amphitheater, hiking trails. **Activities:** Seasonal interpretive programs, hiking, picnicking. **Nearby Attractions:** Bonneville Dam, Columbia Gorge Interpretive Center, Cascade Locks, hiking trails, Multnomah Falls. **Additional Information:** Portland Oregon Visitor's Assoc., 1-87-Portland.

Restrictions

Pets: On leash only (max. length 6 ft.). **Fires:** Fire pits only. **Alcoholic Beverages:** At site. **Vehicle Maximum Length:** 55 ft. **Other:** No firewood collecting.

To Get There

From I-84 Exit 35 turn right (south) off of ramp, access road dead-ends after 0.2 mi.; turn left and drive 0.2 mi.; entrance to campground is on the left marked with a sign.

CASCADE LOCKS
Cascade Locks KOA

841 Northwest Forest Ln., Cascade Locks 97014. T: (541) 374-8668

RV ★★★ Tent ★★★

Beauty: ★★★	Site Privacy: ★
Spaciousness: ★★★	Quiet: ★
Security: ★★	Cleanliness: ★★★
Insect Control: ★★	Facilities: ★★★

Cascade Locks KOA, located just a few miles off I-84 in the riverside hamlet of Cascade Locks, provides quick access to nearby manmade and natural wonders. Located in the heart of the Columbia River Gorge, this campground lacks views of the actual gorge, but has a view of its surrounding hills in Oregon. The wooded park, heavily shaded and colored by tall green Douglas firs, mossy oaks, and maples, sits next to a wood mill whose slight yet constant hum does not distract the peace-seeking camper as much as the nearby railroad track. The RV sites, both paved and gravel, afford little privacy, nor do the tent sites with the minimal exception of T21 and T16. Sites are arranged in a hodgepodge of rows, and the best RV sites with a view, 61–65 and 68–71, sit near the pool. The game room has several early-1990s video games. The playground has several pieces of equipment but also gets muddy.

Basics

Operated By: Cascade Locks KOA. **Open:** Feb.–Nov. **Site Assignment:** First come, first served; reservation (required deposit is 1 night's fee; refund w/ 72 hours notice). **Registration:** At office, after hours at drop box in front of office. **Fee:** Full: $28, water/electric: $27, tent $16; fee covers 2 people, extra person $3; V, MC, AE, D, check, cash. **Parking:** At site.

Facilities

Number of RV-Only Sites: 77. **Number of Tent-Only Sites:** 30. **Hookups:** Electric (20, 30, 50 amps), water, sewer, cable. **Each Site:** Picnic table, fire ring. **Dump Station:** Yes. **Laundry:** Yes. **Pay Phone:** Yes. **Rest Rooms and Showers:** Yes. **Fuel:** No. **Propane:** Yes. **Internal Roads:** Paved & gravel. **RV Service:** No. **Market:** 1 mile west. **Restaurant:** 1 mi. west. **General Store:** Yes. **Vending:** Yes. **Swimming Pool:** Yes. **Playground:** Yes. **Other:** Hot tub, rental cabins, arcade, meeting room. **Activities:** swimming, hot tubbing. **Nearby Attractions:** Cascade Locks, Bonneville Dam, Bridge of the Gods, The Sternwheeler, Columbia Gorge Scenic Highway. **Additional Information:** Portland Oregon Visitor's Assoc. 1-87-Portland.

Restrictions

Pets: On leash only, no more than 2 dogs. **Fires:** Fire pits only. **Alcoholic Beverages:** At site only. **Vehicle Maximum Length:** None. **Other:** No operating of mini bikes or dirt bikes; No fireworks or firearms.

To Get There

From I-84 Exit 44, the off-ramp becomes an unnamed road. Drive 0.75 mi. on this road and then turn left on Forest Ln. Follow Forest Ln. for 1 mi.; the entrance is on the left.

CASCADE SUMMIT
Princess Creek Campground

P.O. Box 208, Crecent 97733. T: (541) 433-3200; F: (541) 433-3224; www.fs.fed.us/r6/centraloregon/recinfo/camping/princesscreek.html.

RV ★★★ Tent ★★★★

Beauty: ★★★★★ Site Privacy: ★★★
Spaciousness: ★★★ Quiet: ★★★★
Security: ★ Cleanliness: ★★★
Insect Control: ★★ Facilities: ★

Princess Creek Campground, off Hwy. 58 and on the shores of Odell Lake, provides a no-frills alternative to camping in the area. The grounds don't have flush toilets, but there is potable water. Shaded by tall firs, the campground has a woodland feel and easy access to the lake. Organized into two loops, with sites on both sides of the road, the best dirt sites sit on the shoreline and just across the access road to the shore. These are numbered 12–32. Sites not on or near the lakefront sit near Hwy. 58, a road heavily traveled during the day but quiet at night. Summers provide the best time to visit, with fishing and good weather.

BASICS

Operated By: Recreation Resource Management. for National Forest Service. **Open:** May–Oct. (weather permitting). **Site Assignment:** On arrival. **Registration:** At self pay station. **Fee:** Regular site $10, Lakefront $12, second vehicle $12; in-state check, cash. **Parking:** At site.

FACILITIES

Number of Multipurpose Sites: 45. **Hookups:** None. **Each Site:** Picnic table, fire ring. **Dump Station:** No. **Laundry:** No. **Pay Phone:** No. **Rest Rooms and Showers:** Non flush, No showers. **Fuel:** No. **Propane:** No. **Internal Roads:** Paved. **RV Service:** No. **Market:** 7 mi. east on Hwy. 58. **Restaurant:** 7 mi. east on Hwy. 58. **General Store:** No. **Vending:** No. **Swimming Pool:** No. **Playground:** No. **Other:** Boat ramp. **Activities:** Fishing, boating, hiking. **Nearby Attractions:** Inquire at campground. **Additional Information:** www.fs.fed.us/r6/centraloregon/recinfo/camping/princesscreek.html.

RESTRICTIONS

Pets: On leash only (max. length 6 ft.). **Fires:** Fire pits only per fire conditions. **Alcoholic Beverages:** At site. **Vehicle Maximum Length:** 50 ft. **Other:** Harvest dead & down wood only, no chainsaw operation, no fish cleaning in lake, 14 day stay limit.

TO GET THERE

From Hwy. 58 westbound, entrance on left between mile 63 and mile 65.

CASCADE SUMMIT

Shelter Cove Resort and Marina

West Odell Lake Rd., Cascade Summit 97425. T: (541) 433-2548; www.sheltercoveresort.com; sheltercov@coinet.com.

RV ★★★ Tent ★★★

Beauty: ★★★★★ Site Privacy: ★★
Spaciousness: ★★★ Quiet: ★★★★
Security: ★★ Cleanliness: ★★★
Insect Control: ★★ Facilities: ★★★

Shelter Cove Resort and Marina, on the shore of Odell Lake in the Central Cascades and off Hwy. 58, provides excellent fishing opportunities in a quiet, shady, woodland setting. The grounds house many seasonal travelers that stay and fish the lake all summer. Semi private gravel and dirt sites within the grounds sit off three loops, but the best sites 29–33 and 38–47 lack good views of the lake, though they have more individual privacy than the rest of the sites. Sites 5–8A have good views of the lake and some privacy but sit near a high traffic area (for fishermen rush hour equals dawn). Avoid sites 9–12 and 23–28, they have a cramped feel without much privacy. Common areas have an open, spacious feel and the scenery is both lovely and rustic. In late July and early August, expect to see thru-hikers in the area coming off the Pacific Crest Trail. Summer necessitates reservations, walk up availability doesn't really exist here.

BASICS

Operated By: Shelter Cove Resort on Forest Service land. **Open:** Apr. 1–Oct. 30 or first snow fall. **Site Assignment:** On arrival, reservations highly recommended (required deposit is 1 night's stay or a third of stays longer than 4 days; refund less $10 w/ 10-days notice or 30-days notice for stays 2 weeks or longer). **Registration:** At office during business hours only unless w/ a reservation, w/ reservation info left outside. **Fee:** Non-electric RV or tent $12; extra sleeping units $10 (non-electric) or $19 (electric); moorage $10 per day; V, MC, AE, D, check, cash. **Parking:** At site, limited off site.

FACILITIES

Number of Multipurpose Sites: 20. **Number of RV-Only Sites:** 40. **Number of Tent-Only Sites:** 0. **Hookups:** Electric (30 amps). **Each Site:** Picnic table, fire ring. **Dump Station:** Yes. **Laun-**

dry: Yes. **Pay Phone:** Yes. **Rest Rooms and Showers:** Yes. **Fuel:** No. **Propane:** Yes. **Internal Roads:** Gravel. **RV Service:** No. **Market:** 9 mi. east. **Restaurant:** 9 mi. east. **General Store:** Yes. **Vending:** No. **Swimming Pool:** No. **Playground:** No. **Other:** Large fish freezer for storage of catch, fish cleaning station, power boat rentals, horseshoes, community fire pit, marine gasoline, boat launch, tons of moorage. **Activities:** Fishing, hiking, boating, cross country skiing in winter, occasional planned activities. **Nearby Attractions:** Fishing, hiking, boating, skiing, city of Eugene, lots of wilderness, Deshutes National Forest. **Additional Information:** Klamath County Dept. of Tourism, (800) 445-6732.

Restrictions

Pets: On leash only. **Fires:** Fire pits only. **Alcoholic Beverages:** Not allowed inside public buildings. **Vehicle Maximum Length:** None. **Other:** Quiet hours 10 p.m.–6 a.m.

To Get There

From Hwy. 58 west bound, turn left between mile 62 and 63 onto West Odell Lake Access Rd., drive 2 mi. and the entrance is on the left.

CHILOQUIN
Head of the River Campground

38500 Hwy. 97 North, Chiloquin 97624. T: (541) 783-4001

RV ★★★ Tent ★★

Beauty: ★★★★	Site Privacy: ★★
Spaciousness: ★★★★	Quiet: ★★★★
Security: ★★	Cleanliness: ★★★
Insect Control: ★★★	Facilities: ★★★

This campground is one of those little-known, out-of-the-way camping spots locals are afraid to trumpet because some sly, outdoor writer might include it in a guidebook. Located in the Winema National Forest, Visitors are more likely to encounter wildlife than fellow campers while staying at these rustic sites. Drinking water should be carried-in; otherwise, treat water available from the Williamson River. There is not much out here on this tableland of ponderosa pine, lodgepole pine, and assorted conifers except excellent trout fishing in the Williamson River and a crazy contingent of Forest Service roads that wander around the numerous buttes and flats. This area is relatively dry year-round. However, there is enough groundwater seeping to the surface from natural springs that wildflowers, such as fireweed, foxglove, lupine, and dandelion, line the banks of tiny creeks that quickly dry up after spring.

Basics

Operated By: Winema National Forest, Klamath Ranger District. **Open:** May–Oct. (depending on weather). **Site Assignment:** First come, first served, no reservations. **Registration:** not necessary. **Fee:** none. **Parking:** At site.

Facilities

Number of RV-Only Sites: 6. **Number of Tent-Only Sites:** 0. **Hookups:** No. **Each Site:** Picnic table, fire grill. **Dump Station:** No. **Laundry:** No. **Pay Phone:** No. **Rest Rooms and Showers:** Vault toilets. **Fuel:** No. **Propane:** No. **Internal Roads:** Call ahead for details. **RV Service:** No. **Market:** No. **Restaurant:** No. **General Store:** No. **Vending:** No. **Swimming Pool:** No. **Playground:** No. **Activities:** Fishing, hunting, hiking. **Nearby Attractions:** Inquire at campground. **Additional Information:** Klamath County Dept. of Tourism, (800) 445-6730.

Restrictions

Pets: On leash only. **Fires:** In fire rings only. **Alcoholic Beverages:** Allowed. **Vehicle Maximum Length:** 30 ft.

To Get There

Take Sprague River Hwy. northeast out of Chiloquin. Take a left onto Williamson River Hwy. at a about the 5-mi. point. Turn left onto FS 4648 the campground is 1 mi. on the left.

CHILOQUIN
The Waterwheel Campground

200 Williamson River Dr., Chiloquin 97624. T: (541) 783-2738

RV ★★★ Tent ★★

Beauty: ★★★	Site Privacy: ★
Spaciousness: ★★	Quiet: ★★
Security: ★★	Cleanliness: ★★★★
Insect Control: ★★	Facilities: ★★★

The Waterwheel Campground, on Hwy. 97 in the sparse outskirts of rural Chiloquin, offers an excellent location on the Williamson River for fishing and day trips to Crater Lake. The property is laid out in several parallel rows of sites. The best gravel full hookups sit in the middle of the park with some shade, pull-throughs numbered 1–6. There are some riverfront water/electric sites with nice views of the river and surrounding countryside, but not much shade. The grounds come complete with decorative, antiquated farm equipment. Located across a small bridge over the clear, brown-bottomed river stands a small island for tent camping, novel but not particularly flat in the shadiest areas of the island. Summers here can be intensely hot so plan for a high sun magnitude or visit at the beginning of the summer for the best experience.

BASICS

Operated By: The Waterwheel Campground. **Open:** All year. **Site Assignment:** On arrival, reservation (required deposit is 1 night's fee; refund w/ 48-hours notice). **Registration:** At office, after hours drop in front of office. **Fee:** Full $22, water/electric $19, tent $16; fee covers 2 people, extra person (age 5 or older) $1.50. **Parking:** At site.

FACILITIES

Number of RV-Only Sites: 28. **Number of Tent-Only Sites:** 6. **Hookups:** Electric (30, 50 amps), water, sewer. **Each Site:** Picnic table, fire ring. **Dump Station:** Yes. **Laundry:** Yes. **Pay Phone:** Yes. **Rest Rooms and Showers:** Yes. **Fuel:** No. **Propane:** Yes. **Internal Roads:** Gravel. **RV Service:** No. **Market:** 4 mi. north. **Restaurant:** Across street. **General Store:** Yes. **Vending:** Yes. **Swimming Pool:** No. **Playground:** Yes. **Other:** Horseshoes, boat ramp, fish cleaning station, rec room, boat dock. **Activities:** Fishing, boating. **Nearby Attractions:** Crater Lake National Park, city of Klamath Falls, fishing, boating. **Additional Information:** Klamath County Dept. of Tourism, (800) 445-6730.

RESTRICTIONS

Pets: On leash only. **Fires:** Fire pits only. **Alcoholic Beverages:** At site. **Vehicle Maximum Length:** 88 ft. **Other:** Quiet hours 10 p.m.–9 a.m., do not park on roadways.

TO GET THERE

From Hwy. 97 (north-bound turn left) between mile 251 and 253 onto Williamson River Dr., entrance to park immediately on left.

COO'S BAY

Bastendorff Beach Campground

181 South Broadway, Coos Bay 97420. T: (541) (888) 5353; www.co.coos.or.us/ccpark/main.html.

RV ★★★ Tent ★★★★

Beauty: ★★★	Site Privacy: ★★★
Spaciousness: ★★	Quiet: ★★★★
Security: ★	Cleanliness: ★★★
Insect Control: ★★	Facilities: ★★

Situated on the Pacific Ocean, this campground might be the perfect spot for recreation and relaxation. This 89-acre park provides easy access to the most desirable forms of natural entertainment. Navigate one of the scenic rivers or hike in the deep wilderness forest nearby. Catch a glimpse of a passing pod of whales as you enjoy the beaches and the ocean view. You will find great lake and river fishing and a convenient station to clean all of your day's catch. With picnic shelters, kitchens, and a large fire pit for grilling, you are sure to find plenty of the amenities you need to feel at home. Don't forget to let the kids visit the unique playground area. With a variety of activities along the spectrum of outdoor interests, this campground makes a great place for a family vacation, reunion, or group event.

BASICS

Operated By: Coos County Parks & Recreation. **Open:** All year. **Site Assignment:** First come, first served. **Registration:** At self pay station by vending machines. **Fee:** Water/electric $14, tent $10; extra vehicle $5; cash, check. **Parking:** At site.

FACILITIES

Number of RV-Only Sites: 56. **Number of Tent-Only Sites:** 25. **Hookups:** Electric (20, 30 amps), water, sewer, cable. **Each Site:** Picnic table, fire pit. **Dump Station:** Yes. **Laundry:** No. **Pay Phone:** Yes. **Rest Rooms and Showers:** Yes. **Fuel:** No. **Propane:** No. **Internal Roads:** Paved. **RV Service:** No. **Market:** 5 mi. north in Florence. **Restaurant:** 5 mi. North in Florence. **General Store:** No. **Vending:** Yes. **Swimming Pool:** No. **Playground:** No. **Other:** Basketball goal, horseshoe pit, pavilion w/ view of ocean, cabins, fish cleaning station. **Activities:** Hiking, picnicking, cleaning fish, horseshoes, basketball. **Nearby Attractions:** Charter fishing, Myrtlewood factories & shops, The Mill Resort & Casino, Oregon Dunes National Recreation Area, ATV rentals. **Additional Information:** Bay Area Chamber of Commerce, (800) 824-8486.

RESTRICTIONS

Pets: On leash only. **Fires:** Fire pits only. **Alcoholic Beverages:** At site. **Vehicle Maximum Length:** 45 ft. **Other:** Check out by 2 p.m.

TO GET THERE

From Hwy. 101 in downtown Coo's Bay, turn west (right from 101 southbound) onto Commercial Ave. Veer left when road forks at Dairy Queen, then immediatly right onto Central Ave. Drive 0.3 mi. and turn right at a yellow caution flasher; the road becomes Ocean Blvd. Drive 2.6 mi. to a red light, where the road dead ends; turn left onto Newmark Ave. Drive 0.5 mi.; at a yellow caution flasher turn left onto Empire Blvd. Continue 7 mi. on through Charleston. Turn right at a big sign for the park and the entrance is on the right atop the hill.

CRATER LAKE NATIONAL PARK

Manzama Campground

P.O.Box 158, Crater Lake 97604. T: (541)594-2511 ex. 3705; www.crater-lake.com.

RV ★★★ Tent ★★★★★

Beauty: ★★★★★	Site Privacy: ★★★
Spaciousness: ★★★	Quiet: ★★★★
Security: ★★	Cleanliness: ★★★★
Insect Control: ★★	Facilities: ★★★

Manzama Campground, concessionaire campground to Crater Lake National Park, has an excellent location for exploring all of the park's natural wonders. The campground is laid out in seven loops backing up to a canyon. There are a few sites with electric hookups, but most have no hookups. RV sites are pull-throughs (tent sites are back-ins) parallel, rather than perpendicular, to access roads. All sites have lots of room and some privacy. The campground has a very natural feel with lots of shade and foliage. Loops C and D have the best RV sites with lots of shade and some particularly large intrasite areas. The tenter-only G loop provides privacy for tenters with buffering shrubs and shady pines. RV-loop parking areas have gravel surfaces, while soft dirt is the rule for tents sites. Be aware that sites on the back perimeters of all loops sit on the edge of the canyon.

BASICS

Operated By: Estey Corp. for National Park Service. **Open:** Jun.–n–Sept. (snow melt–snow fall). **Site Assignment:** First come, first served. **Registration:** At kiosk, after hours pay in morning. **Fee:** RV $17, RV w/ electric $19, tent $15; fee covers 2 people, extra adult (18 or older) $3.50, max. site occupancy is 6 adults; V, MC, cash. **Parking:** At site.

FACILITIES

Number of RV-Only Sites: 84. **Number of Tent-Only Sites:** 143. **Hookups:** Electric (30 amps). **Each Site:** Picnic table, fire ring. **Dump Station:** Yes. **Laundry:** Yes. **Pay Phone:** Yes. **Rest Rooms and Showers:** Yes. **Fuel:** Yes. **Propane:** No. **Internal Roads:** Narrow paved. **RV Service:** No. **Market:** On site, limited groceries. **Restaurant:** 7 mi. North. **General Store:** Yes. **Vending:** No. **Swimming Pool:** No. **Playground:** No. **Other:** Amphitheater (interpretive programs). **Activities:** Hiking, interpretive programs, Jr. Ranger programs. **Nearby Attractions:** City of Klamath Falls, hiking, fishing, boating, National Park programs & facilities. **Additional Information:** Klamath County Dept. of Tourism, (800) 445-6728.

RESTRICTIONS

Pets: On leash only, not allowed on any trails. **Fires:** Fireplaces only. **Alcoholic Beverages:** At site. **Vehicle Maximum Length:** 42 ft. **Other:** Store food & food paraphernalia in vehicles Do not leave any food or cookware in open.

TO GET THERE

From the south entrance of the National Park (Hwy. 62), the campground is on the right just past the entrance gate

DETROIT

Elk Lake Campground

HC 73 Box 320, Mill City 97360. T: (503) 854-3366

Beauty: ★★★★★
Spaciousness: ★★★★★
Security: ★★★
Insect Control: ★★★
Site Privacy: ★★★★
Quiet: ★★★★★
Cleanliness: ★★★★
Facilities: ★★★

The word "foolhardy" may come to mind as you find yourself at the junction that leads to this gem of a spot in Willamette National Forest, about ten miles above the small, historic burg of Detroit. The road is decidedly rough but not impassable. As long as your exhaust system and oil pan sit high and secure, you should be okay. Elk Lake's campsites are strung along the shore of the lake. Tall stands of Douglas fir and western hemlock share the land with white fir, birches, Oregon grape, ferns, and trillium to offer a prime collection of natural cover. This campground may be tough to get to, but once you're there, peaceful Elk Lake makes for a terrific base camp while you enjoy the recreational options. For anyone who brings a boat into this remote area, Elk Lake is a nice spot to take in lazy kayaking or canoeing.

Basics

Operated By: Willamette National Forest. **Open:** Jul.–Sept. **Site Assignment:** First come, first served, no reservations. **Registration:** not necessary. **Fee:** none. **Parking:** At site, in parking lot, 4x4 recommended.

Facilities

Number of RV-Only Sites: 14. **Number of Tent-Only Sites:** 0. **Hookups:** No. **Each Site:** Picnic table, fire pit w/ grill. **Dump Station:** No. **Laundry:** No. **Pay Phone:** No. **Rest Rooms and Showers:** Vault toilets. **Fuel:** No. **Propane:** No. **Internal Roads:** Call ahead for details. **RV Service:** No. **Market:** No. **Restaurant:** No. **General Store:** No. **Vending:** No. **Swimming Pool:** No. **Playground:** No. **Activities:** Fishing, hiking, nonmotorized boating. **Nearby Attractions:** Battle Ax Mt., Mount Beachie. **Additional Information:** Information: (503) 854-3366.

Restrictions

Pets: On leash only. **Fires:** In fire rings only. **Alcoholic Beverages:** Allowed. **Vehicle Maximum Length:** None. **Other:** No low clearance RVs, no trash collection, fishing license required.

To Get There

From Detroit, drive north on FS 46 for 4.5 mi. to FS 4697. Follow this for 10 mi. to the campground. Stay to the left fork where FS 4697 and FS 4696 intersect at about 8 mi. The last 2 mi. are extremely rough.

DIAMOND LAKE

Diamond Lake Campground

2020 Toketee Ranger Station Rd., Idleyld Park 97447. T: (541) 498-2531; www.fs.fed.us/r6/umpqua/rec/cmp_gnd/cg3diaml.html.

RV ★★★ Tent ★★★★

Beauty: ★★★★★
Spaciousness: ★★★
Security: ★★
Insect Control: ★★
Site Privacy: ★★★
Quiet: ★★★★
Cleanliness: ★★★★
Facilities: ★

Diamond Lake Campground, located about ten minutes off Hwy. 230 on the shores of Diamond Lake, provides a particularly beautiful view of the summer sunset over the lake and mountains opposite the campground. This huge National Forest Campground covers over three miles of shoreline, but only has about six showers per gender, although more claim to be in the works and the existing ones are free (a rarity in campgrounds on publicly owned lands). The campground is organized into several loops diverging from a main access road which runs the span of the grounds. Sites have no hookups and can accept either a tent or RV. The best gravel-parking sites are on L loop with less site density, more shade, seclusion, and beautiful views. This is followed by K loop, which offers better than average space between sites. Loops M and G have the highest density with more open sites.

Basics

Operated By: National Forest Service. **Open:** May 15–Oct. 31 (weather permitting). **Site Assignment:** First come, first served; reservation (required deposit is 1 night's fee; refund w/ 72-hours notice less a $10 service charge. **Registration:** At office/entrance gate; After hours see notice posted at window, pay in morning. **Fee:** Regular site $10, shoreline $15, multiparty $20; cash upon arrival. **Parking:** At site, limited off site.

Facilities

Number of Multipurpose Sites: 238. **Hookups:** None. **Each Site:** Picnic table; Fire ring. **Dump**

Station: Yes. **Laundry:** No. **Pay Phone:** Yes. **Rest Rooms and Showers:** Yes. **Fuel:** No. **Propane:** No. **Internal Roads:** Paved. **RV Service:** No. **Market:** Small, nearby. **Restaurant:** Nearby, at a hotel. **General Store:** No. **Vending:** No. **Swimming Pool:** No. **Playground:** No. **Other:** Paved bike trails, Amphitheater, fish cleaning stations, boat ramp. **Activities:** Hiking, fishing, boating, biking, interpretive programs on weekends. **Nearby Attractions:** Crater Lake National Park, Douglas County Museum, Umpqua Valley Wineries, Roseburg, rafting, fishing, biking, covered bridges. **Additional Information:** Douglas County Information, (541) 672-3311.

Restrictions

Pets: On leash only (max. length 6 ft.). **Fires:** Fire pits only. **Alcoholic Beverages:** At site. **Vehicle Maximum Length:** 40 ft. **Other:** Quiet hours 10 p.m.–6 a.m.

To Get There

Located 80 mi. east of Roseburg on Hwy. 138, turn right onto Rd. 4795 (Diamond Lake Loop) at the north entrance to Diamond Lake Recreation Area. Proceed 2.5 mi. to the campground entrance. Diamond Lake may also be accessed via Hwy. 230 from Medford, or Hwy. 97 from Klamath Falls and Bend.

DIAMOND LAKE

Diamond Lake RV Resort

3500 Diamond Lake Loop, Diamond Lake 97731. T: (541) 793-3318; F: (541) 793-3088. www.diamondlakervpark.com.

RV ★★★ Tent n/a

Beauty: ★★★★	Site Privacy: ★
Spaciousness: ★★	Quiet: ★★★★
Security: ★★	Cleanliness: ★★★
Insect Control: ★★	Facilities: ★★

Diamond Lake RV Park, off of Hwy. 230 right at the 138/230 junction, offers full hookups in a beautiful natural recreation area. Sites sit in several lettered sections, some on islands and some on loops. The grounds are ungroomed, with some grass but more dirt. There exists a reasonable amount of shade provided by firs and pines, and the grounds retain the woodland feel characteristic of the area. All sites have gravel parking surfaces, but some have potholes and hills. The nicest back-in sites sit in section W, particularly sites 1–7 and 31–34. The whole section has the most space as well as good foliage for privacy and shade. The worst sections, H and F, have a cramped feel with not as much shade. There is a laundry facility, but it is quite basic.

Basics

Operated By: Diamond Lake RV Park on National Forest Service land. **Open:** May–Oct. 1. **Site Assignment:** On arrival, reservation (required deposit is 1 night's stay or $25 for an extended stay; refund less $3 w/ 48-hours notice). **Registration:** At office. **Fee:** Full $23.20; fee covers 2 people, extra adult $2, extra child (ages 2–15) $1, max. site occupancy is 1 family or 6 people; V, MC, cash. **Parking:** At site.

Facilities

Number of RV-Only Sites: 100. **Number of Tent-Only Sites:** 0. **Hookups:** Electric (30, 50 amps), water, sewer. **Each Site:** Picnic table, grated fire pits. **Dump Station:** Yes. **Laundry:** Yes. **Pay Phone:** Yes. **Rest Rooms and Showers:** Yes. **Fuel:** No. **Propane:** Yes. **Internal Roads:** Narrow paved. **RV Service:** No. **Market:** Across street. **Restaurant:** Across street. **General Store:** No. **Vending:** No. **Swimming Pool:** No. **Playground:** No. **Other:** Movie rentals, horseshoes, BBQ grills for loan (charcoal). **Activities:** Inquire at campground. **Nearby Attractions:** Diamond Lake, Crater Lake National Park, Umpqua National Forest, river rafting (Roseburg), fishing, city of Klamath Falls. **Additional Information:** Douglas County Information, (541) 672-3311.

Restrictions

Pets: On leash only, no loud or vicious dogs. **Fires:** Fire pits only. **Alcoholic Beverages:** At site. **Vehicle Maximum Length:** 45 ft. **Other:** No tents, check w/ office before cutting firewood.

To Get There

The campground is located 80 mi. east of Roseburg on Hwy. 138, or 85 mi. from Medford on Hwys. 62 and 230. The north entrance of Crater Lake National Park is 6 mi. south of Diamond Lake.

DIAMOND LAKE

Thielsen View Campground

2020 Toketez Ranger Station Rd., Idlewyld Park 97447. T: (541) 498-2531; www.fs.fed.us/r6/umpqua/rec/cmp_gnd/cg3diaml.html.

Beauty: ★★★★★ | Site Privacy: ★★★★
Spaciousness: ★★★★★ | Quiet: ★★★★★
Security: ★★★★ | Cleanliness: ★★★★★
Insect Control: ★★★ | Facilities: ★★★

With two other campgrounds across scenic Diamond Lake that can accommodate several hundred campers between them, chances are you won't find yourself alone out in this remote territory. However, this spacious campground offers a relatively private stay. Diamond Lake is an immensely popular area, particularly for trout fishermen, who troll the lake's crystalline waters. Great fishing notwithstanding, Diamond Lake's popularity can be attributed to a number of other factors. For starters, it is one of the largest natural lakes in Oregon. Add to this its proximity to some spectacular mountain scenery, and follow that up with blissfully warm, dry summer weather. Last but not least, factor in the proximity of Crater Lake National Park to the south. The area is a fantastic natural playgrounds that can turn the most resolute vacation planner into a miserable heap of indecision. The facilities here are limited, as is the norm in this national forest, but you won't need to spend a lot of time in the campground.

BASICS

Operated By: Umpqua National Forest. **Open:** May 15–Sept. 15. **Site Assignment:** First come, first served, no reservation. **Registration:** self-registration on site. **Fee:** $9. **Parking:** At site.

FACILITIES

Number of Multipurpose Sites: 60. **Hookups:** Water. **Each Site:** Picnic table, fire ring & grill. **Dump Station:** No. **Laundry:** No. **Pay Phone:** No. **Rest Rooms and Showers:** Vault toilets. **Fuel:** No. **Propane:** No. **Internal Roads:** Gravel **RV Service:** No. **Market:** No. **Restaurant:** No. **General Store:** No. **Vending:** No. **Swimming Pool:** No. **Playground:** No. **Activities:** Hiking, fishing, hunting, bird-watching, biking, canoeing, kayaking. **Nearby Attractions:** Crater Lake, North Umpqua River. **Additional Information:** Douglas County Information, (541) 672-3311.

RESTRICTIONS

Pets: On leash only. **Fires:** In fire rings only. **Alcoholic Beverages:** Allowed. **Vehicle Maximum Length:** 30 ft.

TO GET THERE

From Roseburg and I-5, take SR 138 east/southeast to Clearwater (about 50 mi.), at Clearwater the road leaves the North Umpqua and parallels Clearwater River. At the intersection with FS 4795, turn right and go around the north end of Diamond Lake to find the campground.

EUGENE

Eugene Kamping World RV Park

90932 South Stuart Way, Coburg 97408. T: (541) 343-4832 or (800)343-3008; F: (541) 343-5313.

★★  ★★

Beauty: ★★ | Site Privacy: ★
Spaciousness: ★★ | Quiet: ★★
Security: ★★ | Cleanliness: ★★
Insect Control: ★★ | Facilities: ★★★

Eugene Kamping World RV Park, located ten minutes north of downtown Eugene, provides vistas of the high, rolling hills on the eastern edge of the Willamette Valley. The grounds consist of a triangular arrangement with several rows of sites. The interior of the grounds lacks vegetation save the grass in between sites and a few flowering hardwoods, but the views from pull-through section D and pull-through sites C7–13 distract one's attention from the meager groundcover. The aforementioned paved sections have water and electric hookups. The best full hookup sites (paved) are E6–11. The lumpy grass and dirt tent sites T2–8 have some privacy created by wooden fences, the remainder of tent sites are in an open field. Essential facilities stay clean and well maintained.

BASICS

Operated By: Eugene Kamping World. **Open:** All year. **Site Assignment:** First come, first served; reservation (required deposit is 1 night's stay; refund w/ 24-hours notice). **Registration:** At office, after hours at night drop box in front of office. **Fee:** Full $22, water/electric $19.50, tents $15; fee covers 2 people & 2 vehicles, extra person (age 5 or older) $1.50, extra vehicle $1; V, MC, cash. **Parking:** At site.

FACILITIES

Number of RV-Only Sites: 110. **Number of Tent-Only Sites:** 40. **Hookups:** Electric (20, 30, 50 amps), water, sewer, cable. **Each Site:** Picnic table. **Dump Station:** Yes. **Laundry:** Yes. **Pay Phone:** Yes. **Rest Rooms and Showers:** Yes. **Fuel:** No. **Propane:** Yes. **Internal Roads:** Paved, gravel. **RV Service:** No. **Market:** 2 mi. north in Coburg. **Restaurant:** 2 mi. North in Coburg. **General Store:** Yes. **Vending:** Yes. **Swimming Pool:** No. **Playground:** Yes. **Other:** Volleyball court, basketball half court, central data port, mini golf, tetherball, horseshoes. **Activities:** Use of local recreational facilities. **Nearby Attractions:** Oregon Coast Lighthouses, The 20 Covered Bridges of Lane County, wineries, University of Oregon, Shelton-McMurphy-Johnson House. **Additional Information:** Convention & Visitors Assoc. of Lane County Oregon (800) 547-5445.

RESTRICTIONS

Pets: On leash only. **Fires:** Communal fire pits only. **Alcoholic Beverages:** At site only. **Vehicle Maximum Length:** None. **Other:** No tarps or other mats on the grass, no on-site vehicle repair.

TO GET THERE

From I-5 Exit 199 (southbound turn right) onto Van Duyn Rd. Drive 0.25 mi. west to South Stuart Way (marked with Eugene Camping World Sign), turn left and drive 1 block to entrance.

EUGENE
Richardson Park

90064 Coburg Rd., Eugene 97408. T: (541) 682-2000; www.co.lane.or.us/parks.

 ★★★★  ★★★

Beauty: ★★★	Site Privacy: ★★★
Spaciousness: ★★	Quiet: ★★★
Security: ★	Cleanliness: ★★★★
Insect Control: ★★	Facilities: ★★★

Richardson Park Campground, located in a quiet, rural county park 20 minutes west of Eugene and 8 miles off of Hwy. 99, offers very private sites and nearby access to a wide array of water sports. The enormous and marina-plentiful Fern Ridge Reservoir creates the eastern boundary of the county park. The campground is separated into two sections by a main access road and organized into several loops within each section. There is an eclectic mix of sites here, some private and some not. The best sites, 12, 13, 15, and 17–24, have privacy created by a dense mix of lime-green, moss encrusted pines, oaks, firs, and a thick bramble of secondary growth. Other sites stand totally open and adjacent. Those to avoid include 56–60 and 72–84. All paved sites have an area that will accommodate a tent, but there are no formal tent sites within the park. Winters mix mild and cold weather; summer brings better weather and is the best time to travel here.

BASICS

Operated By: Lane County Parks Division. **Open:** Apr. 15–Oct. 15. **Site Assignment:** First come, first served; reservation (541) 935-2005), (required deposit is 1 night's stay plus $10 non-refundable reservation fee; refund w/ 72-hours notice). **Registration:** At office, after hours see camp host. **Fee:** $16; xtra vehicle (more than 1 unit & 1 car) $5; cash, check. **Parking:** At site.

FACILITIES

Number of Multipurpose Sites: 88. **Number of RV-Only Sites:** 0. **Number of Tent-Only Sites:** 0. **Hookups:** Electric (30, 50 amps), water. **Each Site:** Picnic table, fire ring. **Dump Station:** Yes. **Laundry:** No. **Pay Phone:** Yes. **Rest Rooms and Showers:** Yes. **Fuel:** No. **Propane:** No. **Internal Roads:** Paved. **RV Service:** No. **Market:** 5 mi. west in Venita. **Restaurant:** 5 mi. west in Venita. **General Store:** No. **Vending:** No. **Swimming Pool:** No. **Playground:** Yes. **Other:** Small Amphitheater, boat & jet ski rentals, boat launch, short hiking trails, horseshoe pits, a lake. **Activities:** Swimming, fishing, boating, various planned activities during high volumes. **Nearby Attractions:** Fern Ridge Reservoir, The Bridges of Lane County, wineries, hiking trails, whitewater rafting, art & cultural events. **Additional Information:** Convention & Visitors Assoc. of Lane County Oregon, (800) 547-5445.

RESTRICTIONS

Pets: On leash only (max. length 6 ft.). **Fires:** At site. **Alcoholic Beverages:** At site only. **Vehicle Maximum Length:** None. **Other:** Vehicles must be parked on paved surfaces; site max. 8 people; 2-week stay limit.

To Get There

From I-5 Exit 194B, drive 3 mi. west on Hwy. 105/126 to West Eugene/Florence Exit for 99N/126W/6th Ave. Continue on 6th Ave for 5.2 mi., then turn left onto Clear Lake Rd. just after Beltline Hwy. underpass. Follow Clear Lake Rd. for 5 mi. to the entrance on the right.

FLORENCE
Harbor Vista Campground

3040 Delta Hwy. North, Eugene 97408. T: (541) 997-5987; www.co.lane.or.us/parks/harbor/harbor.htm.

RV ★★★ Tent n/a

Beauty: ★★★	Site Privacy: ★★★
Spaciousness: ★★	Quiet: ★★★★
Security: ★★	Cleanliness: ★★★
Insect Control: ★★	Facilities: ★★★

Harbor Vista Campground off of Hwy. 101 in residential Florence is distinguished by the seclusion of it's 38 water and electric sites from the outside world. Many of the deep, narrow, non-adjacent sites sit totally buffered on three sides by thick groves of woody deciduous shrubs including rhododendron. The paved sites sit on a loop and a roundabout. The roundabout has the most secluded sites, numbered 32, 34, and 35. The worst sites have little or no privacy, numbered 2–5 and 10–13. The grounds sit on a ridge overlooking the north jetty and a small, driftwood littered beach. None of this can be seen from any of the good sites due to thick vegetation, but there is a covered lookout on the ridge at the edge of the park. Spring and summer bring the best weather and flowers.

Basics

Operated By: Lane Co. Parks. **Open:** All year. **Site Assignment:** First come, first served; reservation (required deposit is 1 night's stay plus $10 non-refundable reservation fee; refund w/ 72-hours notice). **Registration:** At self pay station. **Fee:** $16, extra vehicle (more than 1 vehicle & 1 car) $5; cash, check. **Parking:** At site.

Facilities

Number of RV-Only Sites: 38. **Number of Tent-Only Sites:** 0. **Hookups:** Electric (20, 30, 50 amps), water. **Each Site:** Picnic table. **Dump Station:** Yes. **Laundry:** No. **Pay Phone:** Yes. **Rest Rooms and Showers:** Yes. **Fuel:** No. **Propane:** No. **Internal Roads:** Paved. **RV Service:** No. **Market:** 4 mi. east in Florence. **Restaurant:** 4 mi. east in Florence. **General Store:** No. **Vending:** No. **Swimming Pool:** No. **Playground:** Yes. **Other:** Coastal viewing area. **Activities:** hiking, picnicking. **Nearby Attractions:** Oregon Dunes National Recreation Area, Sea Lion Caves, Heceta Head Lighthouse, Oregon Coast Aquarium, beaches. **Additional Information:** Florence Chamber of Commerce, (541) 997-3128 or (800) 524-4864.

Restrictions

Pets: On leash only (max. length 6 ft.). **Fires:** Fire pits or grills only. **Alcoholic Beverages:** At site. **Vehicle Maximum Length:** 40 ft. **Other:** No firearms, fireworks; reservations must be made 14 days prior to arrival date.

To Get There

From Hwy. 101, southbound turn right onto Rhododendron (at light 1 block south of Safeway Grocery in Florence). Drive 3.8 mi. on Rhododendron, then turn left onto Jetty Rd. and drive for 1 block. Entrance is on right.

FLORENCE
Jessie M. Honeyman Memorial State Park Campground

84505 Hwy. 101 South, Florence 97439. T: (541) 997-3641 or (800) 551-6949; www.oregonstateparks.org.

RV ★★★★ Tent ★★★★★

Beauty: ★★★★★	Site Privacy: ★★★
Spaciousness: ★★★	Quiet: ★★★
Security: ★★	Cleanliness: ★★★★
Insect Control: ★★	Facilities: ★★★

Jessie M. Honeyman Memorial State Park Campground, located on Hwy. 101 a few minutes south of Florence, has a camping area as big as the name is long. The heavily forested park has many semi-private sites. Unfortunately most full hookup sites lack privacy. These make up the section open to ATVs in the winter (H loop). Further, avoid C loop with it's close proximity to the highway, and sites 283–299. The rest of the campground receives shade from tall cedars and firs, and gains privacy from the dense groves of huckleberry, salal, and rhododendron. As it is with most Oregon publicly owned camping property, the grounds have a very natural, woodland appearance. Tent sites and RV sites differ very little; both have paved parking and a flat side area of dirt and moss. The best time to visit is late spring when the rhododendron are in bloom all over the Florence area.

BASICS

Operated By: Oregon State Parks & Recreation. **Open:** All year (some seasonal areas). **Site Assignment:** First come, first served; reservation (required deposit is 1 night plus non refundable reservation fee; refund w/ 48-hours notice). **Registration:** At entrance gate or self pay station. **Fee:** Full $20, water/electric $19, tent $16; V, MC, check, cash. **Parking:** At site.

FACILITIES

Number of RV-Only Sites: 166. **Number of Tent-Only Sites:** 191. **Hookups:** Electric (20, 30 amps), water, sewer, cable. **Each Site:** Picnic table, fire ring. **Dump Station:** Yes. **Laundry:** No. **Pay Phone:** Yes. **Rest Rooms and Showers:** Yes. **Fuel:** No. **Propane:** No. **Internal Roads:** Paved. **RV Service:** No. **Market:** 5 mi. north in Florence. **Restaurant:** 5 mi. North in Florence. **General Store:** Yes. **Vending:** No. **Swimming Pool:** No. **Playground:** No. **Other:** Kayak & paddle boat rentals, reservable meeting hall, reservable outdoor pavilion, boat ramp (day use), pedestrian dune access. **Activities:** Fishing, hiking, lake swimming, interpretive programs, boating, sand boarding, winter dune buggy & ATV access. **Nearby Attractions:** Sea Lion Caves, Oregon Dunes National Recreation Area, the covered bridges of Lane County, Haceta Head Lighthouse. **Additional Information:** Florence Chamber of Commerce, (541) 997-3128 or (800) 524-4864.

RESTRICTIONS

Pets: On leash only (max. length 6 ft.). **Fires:** Fire pits only. **Alcoholic Beverages:** At site only. **Vehicle Maximum Length:** 50 ft. **Other:** Max. stay 14 days in winter, 10 days in summer.

TO GET THERE

Located 3 mi. south of Florence on Hwy. 101. Driving southbound, entrance is on right. Upon entering park, road forks; take left fork and pay attention to one-way signs; follow this road into the campground.

FORT KLAMATH

Crater Lake Resort Fort Creek Campground

P.O.Box 457, Fort Klamath 97626. T: (541) 381-2349; F: (541) 381-2343; www.craterlakeresort.com; CrtrLkRst@aol.com.

RV ★★★★ Tent ★★★

Beauty: ★★★★	Site Privacy: ★
Spaciousness: ★★	Quiet: ★★★★
Security: ★	Cleanliness: ★★★★
Insect Control: ★★	Facilities: ★★

Crater Lake Resort, the closest private land campground to the south entrance of the National Park, has a quaint, country feel. The park has few recreational opportunities on site due to it's location, though it does have several canoes free to use for patrons wanting to explore the nearby creek. The best RV sites in the park sit on Fort Creek, numbered 12–23. The tenting area has no delineated sites, but can fit quite a few tents and has lots of grass and shade. The whole park has an open feel, with little sense of privacy. The worst sites sit on the edge of Hwy. 62 and are subject to infrequent but irritating road noise. In the summer, mosquitos breed in nearby creeks and the weather is hot, so consider visiting during the late spring or early fall.

BASICS

Operated By: Crater Lake Resort. **Open:** Apr 1–Nov 1. **Site Assignment:** On arrival, reservation (required deposit is 1 night's fee; refund w/ 2-weeks notice). **Registration:** At office, after hours ring bell outside office. **Fee:** Full $20, water/electric $18, tent $5 per person; RV fee covers 2 people, extra person $2; V, MC, cash, personal check. **Parking:** At site, limited off site.

FACILITIES

Number of RV-Only Sites: 23. **Number of Tent-Only Sites:** 40. **Hookups:** Electric (30, 50 amps), water, sewer. **Each Site:** Picnic table. **Dump Station:** No. **Laundry:** Yes. **Pay Phone:** Yes. **Rest Rooms and Showers:** Yes. **Fuel:** No. **Propane:** No. **Internal Roads:** Gravel. **RV Service:** No. **Market:** 2 mi. northwest in Fort Klamath. **Restaurant:** 2 mi. Northwest in Fort Klamath. **General Store:** Yes. **Vending:** Yes. **Swimming Pool:** No. **Playground:** Yes. **Other:** Volleyball, horseshoes, canoes (free to guests), basketball, air hockey, ping pong, fooseball, meeting hall. **Activities:** Fishing, canoeing, swimming (in creek, cold). **Nearby Attractions:** Crater Lake National Park, Williamson River, Collier Logging Museum, fish hatchery, Agency lake. **Additional Information:** Klamath County Dept. of Tourism, (800) 445-6731.

RESTRICTIONS

Pets: On leash only. **Fires:** Fire pits only. **Alcoholic Beverages:** At site. **Vehicle Maximum Length:** None.

TO GET THERE

Located a few miles southeast of town on Hwy. 62, located at mile marker 92.

GOLD BEACH

Illahe Campground

29279 Ellensburg Ave., Gold Beach 97444. T: (541) 247-3600; www.fs.fed.us/r6/siskiyou

RV ★★★★ Tent ★★★★

Beauty: ★★★★	Site Privacy: ★★★★
Spaciousness: ★★★★	Quiet: ★★★
Security: ★★★★★	Cleanliness: ★★★★★
Insect Control: ★★★★	Facilities: ★★★

Just past the wilderness section of the Rogue River lies Illahe Campground. Nearby competitor campgrounds provide water access, and thus draw the greater crowds. But at Illahe, where a short, rough trail leads to a rugged shoreline, the relative inaccessibility of the river keeps the crowds away-that is, as long as you don't come from mid-June, when the jet boat racers take over the area, through the end of July. Campsites at Illahe have a thick buffer of vegetation that gives the sites a feeling of solitude. The area near the campground entrance is grassy and open, dotted with a few apple and plum trees. Campground hosts encourage guests to take the fruit when it ripens, because if the campers don't get it, the bears likely will. (Sensible campers will store food out of sight and out of reach of the critters.)

BASICS

Operated By: Gold Beach Ranger District, Siskiyou National Forest. **Open:** All year. **Site Assignment:** First come, first served, no reservations. **Registration:** self-registration on site. **Fee:** $5. **Parking:** At site.

FACILITIES

Number of RV-Only Sites: 14. **Number of Tent-Only Sites:** 0. **Hookups:** None. **Each Site:** Picnic table, fire ring. **Dump Station:** No. **Laundry:** No. **Pay Phone:** No. **Rest Rooms and Showers:** Yes. **Fuel:** No. **Propane:** No. **Internal Roads:** Call ahead for conditions. **RV Service:** No. **Market:** No. **Restaurant:** No. **General Store:** No. **Vending:** No. **Swimming Pool:** Yes. **Playground:** No. **Activities:** Hiking, boating, swimming. **Nearby Attractions:** Whitewater rafting on the Rogue River. **Additional Information:** Siskiyou National Forest, (541) 858-2200.

RESTRICTIONS

Pets: On leash only. **Fires:** In fire rings only. **Alcoholic Beverages:** Allowed. **Vehicle Maximum Length:** 22 ft.

TO GET THERE

From Gold Beach, turn east on Jerry's Flat Rd. north of town and on the south side of the Rogue River. Follow it as it turns into FSR 33 for 35 mi. At the junction after crossing the river, where Agness is left and Powers is straight, veer right on CR 375. Illahe Campground is 2 mi. on the right.

GRANT'S PASS

Riverpark RV Resort

2956 Rogue River Hwy., Grants Pass 97527. T: (541) 479-0046 or (800) 677-8857; F: (541) 471-1448; www.mullendesign.com; info@mullendesign.com.

RV ★★★★ Tent n/a

Beauty: ★★★★	Site Privacy: ★
Spaciousness: ★★★	Quiet: ★★★
Security: ★★	Cleanliness: ★★★★
Insect Control: ★★	Facilities: ★★★

On the banks of the Rogue River just a couple of miles south of Downtown Grants Pass travelers find an outdoor art museum, or is it an RV park? It's actually both; the owner/operator/avid sculptor of Riverpark RV Resort uses metal and wood to fill his campground with sculptures demonstrating both down home crafty and contemporary artsy styles. The flat concrete sites shaded by tall mossy hardwoods have grass perimeters, and the grounds have some garden-like qualities including a large number of rose bushes in the public areas. Riverpark RVs 20 sites, numbered 5–24, are on the bank of a calm stretch of the Rogue, and of these numbers 5–12 sit furthest from a nearby road. On the negative side, all sites lack privacy. Avoid sites 25–29 and J–Q; these are located too close to the office, dump station, and entrance. Winters here stay mild; summer usually brings crowds and some hot days.

Basics

Operated By: Riverpark RV Resort. **Open:** All year. **Site Assignment:** First come, first served; reservation (required deposit is 1 night's stay; refund w/ 24-hours notice). **Registration:** At office, after hours follow instructions on office door. **Fee:** $22; fee covers 2 people, extra person $3. **Parking:** At site.

Facilities

Number of RV-Only Sites: 47. **Number of Tent-Only Sites:** 0. **Hookups:** Electric (20, 30 amps), water. **Each Site:** Picnic table, trash can. **Dump Station:** Yes. **Laundry:** Yes. **Pay Phone:** Yes. **Rest Rooms and Showers:** Yes. **Fuel:** No. **Propane:** No. **Internal Roads:** Paved. **RV Service:** No. **Market:** 3 mi. north in Grant's Pass. **Restaurant:** 3 mi. North in Grant's Pass. **General Store:** No. **Vending:** No. **Swimming Pool:** No. **Playground:** No. **Other:** Horseshoe pit, tennis court, sculptures. **Activities:** Swimming, fishing, tennis, horseshoes. **Nearby Attractions:** The Applegate Trail Interpretive Center, Hellgate Jetboat Excursions, rafting, fishing, golf, museums. **Additional Information:** Grants Pass Visitor Information, (800) 547-5927.

Restrictions

Pets: On leash only, limit 2 dogs. **Fires:** No open fires. **Alcoholic Beverages:** At site. **Vehicle Maximum Length:** None. **Other:** No vehicle washing.

To Get There

From I-5 Exit 55, drive 1.8 mi. west on Hwy. 199, turn left and drive 0.2 mi. south on Parkdale Dr. Then turn left onto Rogue River Hwy. and follow it for 2 mi. to the entrance on the left.

GRESHAM

Oxbow Park

3010 Southeast Oxbow Pkwy., Gresham 97080. T: (503) 663-4708

RV ★★★★ Tent ★★★★

Beauty: ★★★★★ Site Privacy: ★★★★
Spaciousness: ★★★★ Quiet: ★★★★
Security: ★★★★★ Cleanliness: ★★★★
Insect Control: ★★★★ Facilities: ★★★

Oxbow Park sets a prime example of what a metropolitan park can and should be. The grounds are a sprawling 1,000 acres of dense forests, grassy clearings, sandy riverbanks, and sheer canyon walls. Old-growth forest alone covers 180 acres. Native salmon spawn within a quarter-mile of camping areas on Sandy River, known as the top-rated winter steelhead stream in Oregon. Wildlife abounds in the park, and a full-time naturalist employed year-round, is busiest in summer with a heavy schedule of public and private programs. The first order of business once you get settled into your site is to explore the trails on foot. There are roughly 15 miles of trails that follow Sandy River and wind throughout the park. Even at the height of the summer season, you'll be amazed at how quickly you can find seclusion.

Basics

Operated By: Multnomah County Parks. **Open:** All year. **Site Assignment:** First come, first served, no reservations. **Registration:** daily fee collected each night, 1-time fee-enter park. **Fee:** $10. **Parking:** At site.

Facilities

Number of RV-Only Sites: 0. **Number of Tent-Only Sites:** 45. **Hookups:** None. **Each Site:** Picnic table, freestanding barbecue pit. **Dump Station:** No. **Laundry:** No. **Pay Phone:** Yes. **Rest Rooms and Showers:** Vault toilets. **Fuel:** No. **Propane:** No. **Internal Roads:** Call ahead for details. **RV Service:** No. **Market:** No. **Restaurant:** No. **General Store:** No. **Vending:** No. **Swimming Pool:** Yes. **Playground:** Yes. **Other:** equestrian area, group camps, interpretive programs. **Activities:** Hiking, horseback riding trails, fishing boating (non-motorized watercraft only).

Nearby Attractions: Crown Point Vista House. **Additional Information:** County info line, 503.823.4000 or www.co.multnomah.or.us

RESTRICTIONS

Pets: No. **Fires:** In fire rings only. **Alcoholic Beverages:** not permitted. **Vehicle Maximum Length:** 35 ft. **Other:** No ATVs, guns or fireworks.

TO GET THERE

Take the Wood Village Exit 16 off I-84 in Gresham. Go south to Division St., turn left and continue to Oxbow Parkway. From here follow the signs down to the park.

HUNTINGTON

Farewell Bend State Recreation Area

23751 Old Hwy. 30, Huntington 97907. T: (541) 869-2365 or (800) 551-6949 or reservations (800) 452-5687; www.oregonstateparks.org/park7.php.

RV ★★★★ Tent ★★

Beauty: ★★★★	Site Privacy: ★★★
Spaciousness: ★★	Quiet: ★★★
Security: ★	Cleanliness: ★★★
Insect Control: ★	Facilities: ★★★

Farewell Bend State Park is set on an irrigated, flat arm of the Snake River, and it makes a great stopover for whitewater rafters on their way to Idaho or Utah. The campground has two sections, A and B; both campgrounds have sites on the river. Sites A42–A52 (even numbers only) have shade and some privacy; section B has three premium sites on the river with gas grills and patios but without cover from the intense sun. The tenting area has 45 drive in "primitive" sites with lots of shade, but no privacy or protection from occasional road noise. Remember that sites near the water receive, at times, copious amounts of wind, and that the high altitude summer sun here will burn skin very quickly. Winters in this part of Oregon are long and cold. Call before arrival to make sure the area has not flooded, as this is a recurring problem.

BASICS

Operated By: Oregon State Parks & Recreation. **Open:** All year. **Site Assignment:** On arrival, reservation (required deposit is 1 night plus non refundable reservation fee; refund w/ 48-hours notice). **Registration:** At self pay station. **Fee:** Electric $15, preferred electric $17, tepee $27, covered wagon $27; extra vehicle $7; V, MC, cash. **Parking:** At site.

FACILITIES

Number of RV-Only Sites: 91. **Number of Tent-Only Sites:** 45. **Hookups:** Electric (20, 30 amps), water, sewer. **Each Site:** Picnic table, fire ring. **Dump Station:** Yes. **Laundry:** No. **Pay Phone:** Yes. **Rest Rooms and Showers:** Yes. **Fuel:** No. **Propane:** No. **Internal Roads:** Paved. **RV Service:** No. **Market:** East in Pendleton. **Restaurant:** East in Pendleton. **General Store:** No. **Vending:** No. **Swimming Pool:** No. **Playground:** No. **Activities:** Boating, fishing, relaxing, bird-watching, interpretive programs. **Nearby Attractions:** Snake River Reservoirs, watersports, Ontario. **Additional Information:** Ontario Chamber of Commerce, (541) 889-8012.

RESTRICTIONS

Pets: On leash only (max. length 6 ft.). **Fires:** Fire pits only. **Alcoholic Beverages:** At site. **Vehicle Maximum Length:** 40 ft.

TO GET THERE

From I-84 Exit 353, eastbound turn right onto Hwy. 30, to park entrance, 1 mi.

KLAMATH FALLS

Klamath Falls KOA

3435 Shasta Way, Klamath Falls 97603. T: (541) 884-4644 or (800) 562-9036; www.koa.com.

RV ★★★ Tent ★★★

Beauty: ★★	Site Privacy: ★
Spaciousness: ★★	Quiet: ★
Security: ★★★	Cleanliness: ★★★
Insect Control: ★★	Facilities: ★★★

Klamath Falls KOA, located in southeast Klamath Falls a few minutes off the 97 business loop, affords quick access to municipal attractions. The grounds have several rows of sites, and back up to the levee of an irrigation canal. All of the flat, privacy lacking sites have partial views of nearby arid, rolling hills. The best RV sites, full hookup pull-throughs 30–47, have grass islands and a little shade provided by birch and other hardwoods. Tent sites 72–84 have grass surfaces, lots of shade, and also back up to the levee. There are also some grass water/electric and no hookup multi-use sites with a good amount of shade. The worst sites within the park, numbers 5–9, have no shade or grass. The pool within the campground is small but adequate, while the laundry is enormous. Visit during the mild fall or spring months, summers bring hot, arid weather and intense sunlight.

Basics

Operated By: Klamath Falls KOA. **Open:** All year. **Site Assignment:** On arrival, reservation (required deposit is 1 night's stay; refund w/ 72-hours notice). **Registration:** At office, after hours at drop box in front of office. **Fee:** Full $25 (50 amp add $2), water/electric $23, RV w/ no hookups $21, tent $20; fee covers 2 people, extra adult (age 10 or older) $3, extra child (age 6–9) $2, max. site occupancy is 6 people; V, MC, cash. **Parking:** At site.

Facilities

Number of RV-Only Sites: 63. **Number of Tent-Only Sites:** 19. **Hookups:** Electric (30, 50 amps), water, sewer, cable. **Each Site:** Picnic table. **Dump Station:** Yes. **Laundry:** Yes. **Pay Phone:** Yes. **Rest Rooms and Showers:** Yes. **Fuel:** Yes. **Propane:** Yes. **Internal Roads:** Gravel, some deteriorating pavement. **RV Service:** No. **Market:** 1 block away. **Restaurant:** 1 Block away. **General Store:** Yes. **Vending:** Yes. **Swimming Pool:** Yes. **Playground:** Yes. **Other:** Game room (a few mid-1980s era games, ping pong), meeting room, horseshoes, volleyball, jogging trail on top of levee. **Activities:** swimming. **Nearby Attractions:** Crater Lake National Park, Klamath County Museum, Favell Museum, Upper Klamath Lake, Lava Beds National Monument, hunting. **Additional Information:** Klamath County Dept. of Tourism, (800) 445-6733.

Restrictions

Pets: On leash only, no fighting breeds. **Fires:** No open fires. **Alcoholic Beverages:** Sites only. **Vehicle Maximum Length:** None.

To Get There

From Hwy. 97 Jct. with Hwy. 97 Business/Hwy. 39 in north Klamath Falls, drive 2.7 mi. south on Hwy. 97 Business. Turn right on Washburn Way. Drive 0.8 mi. and turn left at intersection with Schlotzki's Deli onto Shasta Way. Continue 0.5 mi. and KOA entrance is on the left.

KLAMATH FALLS

Lake of the Woods Resort

950 Harriman Rte., Klamath Falls 97601. T: (541) 949-8300; F: (541) 949-8229; www.lakeofthewoods.com; lowresort@earthlink.net.

RV ★★★★ Tent ★★★

Beauty: ★★★★	Site Privacy: ★
Spaciousness: ★★	Quiet: ★★★★★
Security: ★	Cleanliness: ★★★★
Insect Control: ★★	Facilities: ★★★★

Lake of the Woods Resort, a few minutes off of Hwy. 140 and 40 miles north of Klamath Falls, provides a variety of outdoor recreational activities for all seasons. The campground area has open, flat sites on several islands, and a few sites on the perimeter. The best dirt tent sites, A–E, sit on the perimeter near the back of the campground while the best wood chip surfaced RV full hookups, 3–9, sit on one of the islands. Tent sites F–M and RV sites 10–20 have a more disorganized and crowded feel. The whole resort stays very shady with a large number of old firs and pines towering overhead. The campground and the common areas of the resort have a very spacious, open, woodland feel. The marina rents a variety of boats including pontoon boats and even a sail boat. While the camp area has no scenic views, the common areas, beaches and restaurant have beautiful, peaceful vistas of the Lake of the Woods and its far, wooded shores. Any time of the year makes a good time to visit, as the grounds provide year-round recreation opportunities.

Basics

Operated By: Lake of the Woods Resort for the National Forest Service **Open:** All year. **Site Assignment:** On arrival, reservation (required deposit is 50% of stay upon making reservation, 100% due 30 days before arrival; refund w/ 10-days notice less $15 cancellation fee). **Registration:** At office. **Fee:** RV $14, tent $12, extra vehicle $4, pets $5; V, MC, cash. **Parking:** At site.

Facilities

Number of RV-Only Sites: 23. **Number of Tent-Only Sites:** 23. **Hookups:** Electric (30 amps), water, sewer. **Each Site:** Picnic table, fire pit. **Dump Station:** Yes. **Laundry:** Yes. **Pay Phone:** Yes. **Rest Rooms and Showers:** Yes. **Fuel:** Yes.

Propane: Yes. **Internal Roads:** Dirt w/ wood chips. **RV Service:** No. **Market:** In Klamath Falls. **Restaurant:** On site. **General Store:** Yes. **Vending:** No. **Swimming Pool:** No. **Playground:** No. **Other:** Marina w/ supplies, horseshoes, amphitheater, restaurant & bar, beach, boat rentals (an assortment of powered & Non), mountain bike rentals, moorage, movie rentals, VCR rentals, BBQ rentals, hiking & biking trails, lake swimming area, ice skate rentals, snowshoe rentals. **Activities:** Swimming, hiking, biking, fishing, boating, dining, occasional planned activities, cross country skiing, snowshoeing, ice skating, snow mobiling. **Nearby Attractions:** City of Klamath Falls, Upper Klamath Lake, Crater Lake National Park, boating, winter sports, fishing, hiking. **Additional Information:** Klamath County Dept. of Tourism, (800) 445-6734.

RESTRICTIONS

Pets: On leash only. **Fires:** Fire pits only. **Alcoholic Beverages:** Not in public buildings. **Vehicle Maximum Length:** None. **Other:** No cutting of firewood.

TO GET THERE

Between mile 37 and mile 39 on Hwy. 140, turn (westbound-left) onto Dead Indian Memorial Dr. Follow 1 mi. and then turn right onto an unnamed road marked with "Resort" ODOT sign. This road dead ends into the resort.

KLAMATH FALLS

Rocky Point Resort

28121 Rocky Point Rd., Klamath Falls 97601. T: (541) 356-2287; F: (541) 356-2222; www.rockypointoregon.com; rvoregon@aol.com.

RV ★★★ Tent ★★

Beauty: ★★★★★	Site Privacy: ★★
Spaciousness: ★★	Quiet: ★★★★
Security: ★	Cleanliness: ★★★
Insect Control: ★★	Facilities: ★★★

Rocky Point Resort, off of Hwy. 140 a half hour northwest of Klamath Falls, offers a quiet lakeside retreat. Located on Upper Klamath Lake, the resort rents both powered and non-powered boats for fishing or sightseeing. The small campground has a cramped feeling, but houses some nice shaded pull-throughs, numbered 1–4, with partial views of the beautiful lake, it's offshore marshes, and the arid, partially forested hills on the far shore. Shaded back-in sites 12–15 have the best lake views, sitting on an access road just off the main area of the grounds. The restaurant has beautiful views from both the dining room and outside porch. RV sites have gravel, and tent sites have dirt surfaces. Although the main tent sites, 30–33, sit on the lake's edge they have no privacy or shade. Additionally, avoid unattractive and shadeless sites 25–28, which also lack hookups.

BASICS

Operated By: Rocky Point Resort on NFS leased land. **Open:** Apr. 1–Nov. 1. **Site Assignment:** On arrival, reservation (required deposit is 50% of reservation; refund w/ 2 weeks notice). **Registration:** At office, after hours pay in morning. **Fee:** Full $20, water/electric $18, tent $14; fee covers 2 people, extra person $2, max. site occupancy is 4 adults or 1 family of 5; pets $1; V, MC, cash, check. **Parking:** At site.

FACILITIES

Number of RV-Only Sites: 29. **Number of Tent-Only Sites:** 5. **Hookups:** Electric (30 amps), water, sewer. **Each Site:** Picnic table, fire ring. **Dump Station:** Yes. **Laundry:** Yes. **Pay Phone:** Yes. **Rest Rooms and Showers:** Yes. **Fuel:** No. **Propane:** No. **Internal Roads:** Gravel. **RV Service:** No. **Market:** 40 mi. south in Klamath Falls. **Restaurant:** On site. **General Store:** Yes. **Vending:** No. **Swimming Pool:** No. **Playground:** No. **Other:** Ping pong, horseshoes, boat rentals (powered & non), boat launch, basketball, restaurant, moorage. **Activities:** Fishing, boating, swimming. **Nearby Attractions:** Crater Lake National Park, Favell Museum of Western Art & Native American Artifacts, rodeos, theatre, golf, Collier State Park & Logging Museum. **Additional Information:** Klamath County Dept. of Tourism, (800) 445-6729.

RESTRICTIONS

Pets: On leash only. **Fires:** Fire pits only. **Alcoholic Beverages:** At site. **Vehicle Maximum Length:** 40 ft. **Other:** Clean all game & fish in the fish-cleaning station.

TO GET THERE

From Hwy. 140, turn right on Rocky Point Rd. between mile 43 and mile 45; follow road for 2.8 mi. When road forks take right fork; entrance to resort is on the left just past fork.

LA GRANDE

Hot Lake RV Resort

65182 Hot Lake Ln., La Grande 97850. T: (541) 922-2699

RV ★★★★ Tent ★★

Beauty: ★★★★ Site Privacy: ★
Spaciousness: ★★★ Quiet: ★★★★
Security: ★ Cleanliness: ★★
Insect Control: ★★ Facilities: ★★

Hot Lake RV Resort, located in a peacefully scenic area, has some of the best views in Eastern Oregon. The park sits in a very flat area in a valley. From the campground, guests have views of the surrounding grassy, golden brown, rolling hills, complete with a train visible miles away. Save the occasional, distant train noises, the campground is quiet; there being nothing around to generate noise. Gravel sites on the perimeters have the best views, these include sites 82–100 and 40–49. The totally unobscured views from these sites provide enchanting, big sky sunsets and, at night, a stunning view of the heavens. With an organizational scheme of parallel rows, the RV section has some large pull-throughs, but the section lacks shade or privacy. The grassy tent area sits across a nearby stream, shaded by small, deciduous trees, but also lacks intersite privacy. The pool area needs more upkeep than it receives. Visit right before or after summer for the best weather conditions, summers here can be scorching.

BASICS

Operated By: Hot Lake Campground. **Open:** All year. **Site Assignment:** On arrival, reservation. **Registration:** At office, after hours see drop by office. **Fee:** Full $24, tent $12; fee covers 2 people, extra adult $2, children free; V, MC, Cash. **Parking:** At site.

FACILITIES

Number of RV-Only Sites: 100. **Number of Tent-Only Sites:** Open tent area. **Hookups:** Electric (20, 30 amps), water, sewer. **Each Site:** None. **Dump Station:** No. **Laundry:** Yes. **Pay Phone:** Yes. **Rest Rooms and Showers:** Yes. **Fuel:** No. **Propane:** No. **Internal Roads:** Gravel. **RV Service:** No. **Market:** 5 mi. away in La Grande. **Restaurant:** 5 mi. away in La Grande. **General Store:** Yes (seasonal hours). **Vending:** No. **Swimming Pool:** Yes. **Playground:** No. **Other:** Spa. **Activities:** Inquire at campground. **Nearby Attractions:** Golf, Anthony Lakes Mt. Resort & Recreation Area, Winom-Frazier Off Highway Vehicle Trail Complex, Spout Springs Ski Area. **Additional Information:** Union County Chamber of Commerce, (541) 963-8588.

RESTRICTIONS

Pets: On leash only. **Fires:** No fires. **Alcoholic Beverages:** At site. **Vehicle Maximum Length:** None. **Other:** No washing vehicles in park.

TO GET THERE

From I-84 Exit 265, drive 4.8 mi. east on Hwy. 203 South. The campground is listed by a small ODOT sign. Pass the sign, turn right onto Hot Lake Ln. (gravel); drive 0.5 mi. to the campground.

LINCOLN CITY

Lincoln City KOA Campground

5298 Northeast Park Ln., Otis 97368. T: (541) 994-2961; F: (541) 994-9454.

RV ★★★★ Tent ★★★

Beauty: ★★★ Site Privacy: ★★
Spaciousness: ★★★ Quiet: ★★★★
Security: ★★ Cleanliness: ★★★★★
Insect Control: ★★ Facilities: ★★★

Lincoln City KOA Kampground, a few miles off of 101 just north of Lincoln city, offers a quiet and serene retreat from surrounding beach culture. The grounds, shaded by pine and fir trees, and bordered on one side by a stream and all other sides by dense blackberry brambles, possess both terraced and field-set gravel pull-through and back-in sites. The terraced sites provide more of a feeling of spaciousness than the field sites. The best back-ins, 23–36 (some full hookup, some water/electric), and the best pull-throughs, 8–16, rise up the terraced hill to the entrance. None of the sites afford much privacy. Preferable tent sites, numbers 51–63, lie along the clear, gently flowing stream at the edge of the field. Many water/electric sites double as tent sites (be wary of sites where leaky motor homes have previously parked). Avoid the trailer city–like sites numbered 64–87. The playground here is large and well equipped and the grounds are very quiet.

Basics

Operated By: Lincoln City KOA. **Open:** All year. **Site Assignment:** First come, first served; reservation (required deposit is 1 night's stay; refund w/ 24 hrs notice). **Registration:** At office, after hours in drop box in front of office. **Fee:** Full $25, water/electric $23, tent $20; fee covers 2 people, extra person $3, max. site occupancy is 6; V, MC, AE, D, cash. **Parking:** At site.

Facilities

Number of RV-Only Sites: 56. **Number of Tent-Only Sites:** 15. **Hookups:** Electric (20, 30 amps), water, sewer, cable. **Each Site:** Picnic table. **Dump Station:** Yes. **Laundry:** Yes. **Pay Phone:** Yes. **Rest Rooms and Showers:** Yes. **Fuel:** No. **Propane:** Yes. **Internal Roads:** Gravel. **RV Service:** No. **Market:** 5 mi. west in Lincoln City. **Restaurant:** 5 mi. west in Lincoln City. **General Store:** Yes. **Vending:** Yes. **Swimming Pool:** No. **Playground:** Yes. **Other:** Horseshoes, game room, volleyball, basketball, tetherball. **Activities:** Berry picking, ice cream socials & other planned activities, wildlife viewing (elk). **Nearby Attractions:** Devil's Lake, beaches, Cascade Head Scenic Research Area, charter fishing, whale-watching. **Additional Information:** Lincoln City Chamber of Commerce, (541) 994-3070.

Restrictions

Pets: On leash only. **Fires:** Fire pits only. **Alcoholic Beverages:** At site only. **Vehicle Maximum Length:** 60 ft. **Other:** No multi-room tents; no hanging tarps from trees; Don't drive through unoccupied sites; Quiet hours 10 p.m. to 6 a.m.

To Get There

Headed south on Hwy. 101: Just past Faith Baptist church, 1 mi. south of the junction of Hwy. 18 and US 101, turn left onto East Devil's Lake Rd. and follow for 1 mi.; turn left on Park Ln. The entrance is on the right.

MANZANITA/NEHALEM

Nehalem Bay State Park

9500 Sandpiper Ln., Nehalem 97131. T: (503) 368-5154 or (800) 551-6949; www.oregonstateparks.org.

RV ★★★★ Tent ★★★

Beauty: ★★★★	Site Privacy: ★★★
Spaciousness: ★★	Quiet: ★★★★
Security: ★★	Cleanliness: ★★★
Insect Control: ★★	Facilities: ★★★

Nehalem Bay State Park, positioned in between the tiny villages of Nehalem and Manzanita, makes up for its lack of commerce with access to natural beauty. Campers need hike only a few hundred feet over the dunes to find themselves on beautiful, narrow, driftwood covered beaches of the great blue Pacific. The campground, divided into six loops, sits in a grove of short coastal pines that provide privacy for the sites. There are no official tent sites, save those reserved for coastal thru-hikers and bikers, but all of the campground sites have flat grassy areas to accommodate a tent. Sites vary significantly in width, and all have flat, paved areas for RVs. Avoid sites F41, F43, E34, E36, E40, E42, D36, D38, C38, C40, C47, B24, B34, B36, A25, and A27 as they are next to beach access trails (high traffic). Sacrificing some privacy, C43–46, B24–33, and A17–24 have the best views of the lovely, undeveloped surrounding coastal hills.

Basics

Operated By: Oregon State Parks & Recreation. **Open:** All year. **Site Assignment:** First come, first served; reservation (required deposit is 1 night plus nonrefundable reservation fee; refund w/ 48-hours notice). **Registration:** At entrance gate or self pay station. **Fee:** $21, extra vehicle (more than 1 unit & 1 vehicle) $7; V, MC, cash. **Parking:** At site.

Facilities

Number of Multipurpose Sites: 277. **Hookups:** Electric (20, 30 amps), water. **Each Site:** Picnic table, fire ring. **Dump Station:** Yes. **Laundry:** No. **Pay Phone:** Yes. **Rest Rooms and Showers:** Yes. **Fuel:** No. **Propane:** No. **Internal Roads:** Paved. **RV Service:** No. **Market:** 5 mi. north in Manzanita. **Restaurant:** 5 mi. North in Manzanita. **General Store:** No. **Vending:** No. **Swimming**

Pool: No. **Playground:** Yes. **Other:** Amphitheater, horse camp, boat launch, beach, airstrip, non-motorized traveler camp. **Activities:** Nightly interpretive programs, day time Jr. Ranger programs, other various planned activities (all above listed are seasonal). **Nearby Attractions:** Oswald West State Park, Nehalem Bay Winery, bike rentals. **Additional Information:** Nehalem Bay Area Chamber of Commerce, (503) 355-2335.

Restrictions

Pets: On leash only (max. length 6 ft.). **Fires:** Fire pits only. **Alcoholic Beverages:** At site only. **Vehicle Maximum Length:** 50 ft. **Other:** Quiet hours 10 p.m.–6 a.m.; stay away from driftwood on the beach, it can cause drowning.

To Get There

From Hwy. 101, turn right at the Texaco near Nehalem, drive 0.3 mi. to first stop, then turn right. Drive another 1.4 mi. to next stop and turn right into the park entrance. Drive 1 mi. and turn right at the wooden sign.

MAUPIN

Bear Creek Campground

16400 Champion Way, Sandy 97055. T: (503) 622-7674; www.reserveusa.com/nrrs/or/brsg.

RV: ★★★ Tent: ★★★★

Beauty: ★★★★★	Site Privacy: ★★
Spaciousness: ★★★★	Quiet: ★★★★
Security: ★	Cleanliness: ★★★
Insect Control: ★★	Facilities: ★

Bear Creek Campground, a National Forest Service Campground off Hwy. 26 in the southeast corner of the Mt. Hood National Forest, offers a quiet wooded respite to the weary traveler. This campground has facilities just above the primitive line, which is code for non-flush toilets. Still, the little campground has some charm, being a good distance away from anything but the trees. Gravel back-in sites with no hookups make up the whole of the campground with the exception of one pull-through. The campground is shaded, but not canopied, by tall spruce and pine, and sometimes receives visits from bears and stray livestock. Sites 12-20 sit the furthest from any roads, the grounds do get the occasional noise from passing vehicles on nearby, but lightly-traveled, Hwy. 216. The best time to visit has to be the summer months when the nearby rafting season is in full swing. The campground can get full on the weekends from people trying to escape the tourist bustle of Maupin.

Basics

Operated By: 1000 Trails for the National Forest Service. **Open:** Maintained mid-May–mid-Sept. **Site Assignment:** Walkup, reservation. **Registration:** W/ host; at self pay station if host not available. **Fee:** $10, extra vehicle $5. **Parking:** At site.

Facilities

Number of Multipurpose Sites: 21. **Hookups:** None. **Each Site:** Picnic table, fire ring. **Dump Station:** No. **Laundry:** No. **Pay Phone:** No. **Rest Rooms and Showers:** Non-flush only. **Fuel:** No. **Propane:** No. **Internal Roads:** Paved. **RV Service:** No. **Market:** 7 mi. east on 216. **Restaurant:** 24 mi. east in Maupin. **General Store:** No. **Vending:** No. **Swimming Pool:** No. **Playground:** No. **Activities:** Hiking. **Nearby Attractions:** Rafting on the Deschutes from Maupin, Mt. Hood National Forest, Mt. Hood, Portland. **Additional Information:** Mt. Hood Area Chamber of Commerce, (888) 622-4822.

Restrictions

Pets: On leash only. **Fires:** Fire pits only. **Alcoholic Beverages:** At site. **Vehicle Maximum Length:** 32 ft. **Other:** Collecting of dead & down wood allowed, no chainsaw operation within campground, No off road vehicles allowed in campground.

To Get There

From junction of Hwy. 26 and Hwy. 216 (72 mi. east of Sandy), take Hwy. 216 east and follow for 4 mi. Turn right at sign for Bear Creek Campground just before a ranger station; drive 0.1 mi. on a gravel road. Entrance is on right.

MCKENZIE BRIDGE

Trail Bridge Campground

57600 McKenzie Hwy., McKenzie Bridge 97413. T: (541) 822-3381; www.fs.fed.us/r6/willamette.

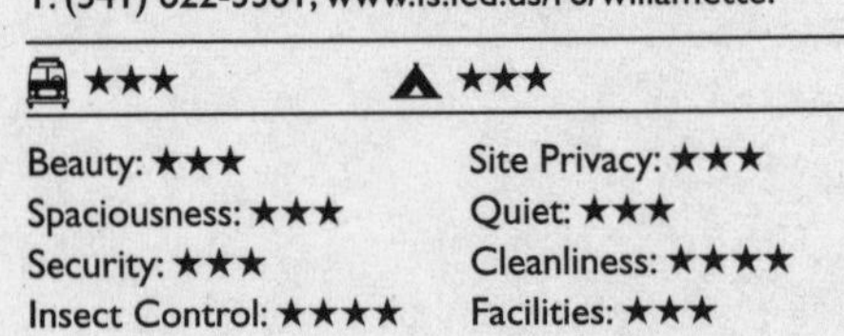

RV: ★★★ Tent: ★★★

Beauty: ★★★	Site Privacy: ★★★
Spaciousness: ★★★	Quiet: ★★★
Security: ★★★	Cleanliness: ★★★★
Insect Control: ★★★★	Facilities: ★★★

Think of Trail Bridge as the ultimate scenic drive, complete with campground. You can make it as short as 130 miles if your starting point is Redmond, or quite a bit longer if you are coming from points west and want to make more than a frenetic weekend of it. The drive takes you along one of Oregon's most prized trout streams, over two historic and scenic mountain passes, through a diverse assortment of picturesque landscapes ranging from alpine meadows to high desert grasslands, past many unusual geologic formations, across two of the state's largest national forests, and between two designated wildernesses. Trail Bridge Campground is located on Trail Bridge Reservoir, a small depository of McKenzie River headwaters and a good stopping point in the journey. Flowing pure and cold out of Clear Lake (a natural lava-dam lake just west of lava beds contained within Mount Jefferson Wilderness), the McKenzie River attracts both the drift boat community and vast numbers of rafters, kayakers, and canoeists who appreciate the McKenzie's gentle grade. The campground is split almost evenly between RV- and tent-only sites. Each site has a picnic table, a fire grill, and electricity, but there are no other hookups or special amenities. Rest rooms and showers are adequate, without frills.

Basics

Operated By: Willamette National Forest. **Open:** May–Oct. **Site Assignment:** First come, first served. **Registration:** self-registration. **Fee:** $6. **Parking:** At site.

Facilities

Number of RV-Only Sites: 21. **Number of Tent-Only Sites:** 26. **Hookups:** None. **Each Site:** Picnic table, fire grill, electricity. **Dump Station:** No. **Laundry:** No. **Pay Phone:** No. **Rest Rooms and Showers:** Yes. **Fuel:** No. **Propane:** No. **Internal Roads:** Call ahead for details. **RV Service:** No. **Market:** No. **Restaurant:** No. **General Store:** No. **Vending:** No. **Swimming Pool:** Yes. **Playground:** No. **Activities:** Fishing, boating, hiking, picnicking. **Nearby Attractions:** Trout fishing. **Additional Information:** Willamette National Forest, (541) 822-3381.

Restrictions

Pets: On leash only. **Fires:** In fire rings only. **Alcoholic Beverages:** Allowed. **Vehicle Maximum Length:** None. **Other:** Must follow local fishing regulations.

To Get There

Take SR 126 from Eugene or Redmond to McKenzie Bridge. Follow this road north until it becomes SR 26 in McKenzie Bridge. Continue driving to Trail Bridge Reservoir and the campground.

MEACHAM

Emmigrant Springs State Park

P.O.Box 85, Meacham 97859. T: (541)983-2277 or (800) 551-6949 or for horse camp or cabin reservations (800) 452-5687; www.oregonstateparks.org/park23.php.

RV ★★★ Tent ★★★

Beauty: ★★★★★	Site Privacy: ★★
Spaciousness: ★★	Quiet: ★★★★
Security: ★	Cleanliness: ★★★
Insect Control: ★★	Facilities: ★★★

Emmigrant Springs State Park in eastern Oregon, makes a beautiful base for exploring the area or just taking a night off of the interstate. Unlike many campgrounds in the region, this semi-arid, high altitude location has shade; sites sit underneath towering ponderosa pines and other evergreens. Although quiet, the area still has a close proximity to the interstate, making some sites louder than others. Sites B14–B5 and A18–A26 have the most protection from this noise. Sites have a mixture of gravel and paved surfaces, and all lack privacy. The park has an amphitheater and horse camp, but surrounding recreation outside the park is limited. Because of the higher altitude, the park has a milder climate than the surrounding desert, so a coat might be necessary when staying the night. And remember, eastern Oregon has cold weather nine months of the year.

Basics

Operated By: Oregon State Parks & Recreation. **Open:** Mar.–Nov. **Site Assignment:** On arrival, reservation (required deposit is1 night plus non refundable reservation fee; refund w/ 48-hours notice). **Registration:** At self pay station. **Fee:** Full $15, tent $13, extra vehicle $7; V, MC, cash, check. **Parking:** At site.

FACILITIES

Number of RV-Only Sites: 18. **Number of Tent-Only Sites:** 33. **Hookups:** Electric (20, 30 amps), water, sewer. **Each Site:** Picnic table, fire ring. **Dump Station:** Yes. **Laundry:** No. **Pay Phone:** Yes. **Rest Rooms and Showers:** Yes. **Fuel:** No. **Propane:** No. **Internal Roads:** Paved. **RV Service:** No. **Market:** Pendleton, 26 mi. west. **Restaurant:** Pendleton, 26 mi. west. **General Store:** No. **Vending:** No. **Swimming Pool:** No. **Playground:** No. **Other:** Amphitheater, horse camp. **Activities:** Interpretive programs during summer. **Nearby Attractions:** Trees. **Additional Information:** Pendleton Chamber of Commerce, (541) 276-7411.

RESTRICTIONS

Pets: On leash only (max. length 6 ft.). **Fires:** Fire pits only. **Alcoholic Beverages:** At site. **Vehicle Maximum Length:** 40 ft. **Other:** Bikes not permitted on hiking trails.

TO GET THERE

From I-84 Exit 234 (eastbound), drive straight towards Meacham, 0.8 mi, and turn left into the park.

NETARTS

Cape Lookout State Park

13000 Whiskey Creek Rd. West, Tillamook 97141.
T: (503) 842-4981

RV ★★★ Tent ★★★★

Beauty: ★★★★★	Site Privacy: ★★★★
Spaciousness: ★★★	Quiet: ★★★★
Security: ★★★★	Cleanliness: ★★★★★
Insect Control: ★★★	Facilities: ★★★

Situated on one of the most scenic capes in the Northwest, Cape Lookout State Park is located just south of Netarts on the Three Capes Scenic Dr. that encompasses two other magnificent headlands (Cape Meares on the north and Cape Kiwanda on the south). These are also state parks but are limited to day-use activities. Collectively these three areas cover more than 2,500 acres of coastal rain forest, sheer cliffs, wide sandy beaches and dunes, narrow spits, rocky points and outcroppings, protected bays, and estuaries. To accommodate the sizable numbers of seashore enthusiasts, the well-maintained and efficiently designed Cape Lookout State Park offers a whopping 185 tent sites and 54 RV sites, many of which are accessible all year. In addition, it offers hikers and bikers a separate area not far from the central camping grounds. Group camps are also available, as well as a meeting hall.

BASICS

Operated By: Oregon State Parks & Recreation. **Open:** All year. **Site Assignment:** First come, first served; reservation. **Registration:** self registration on site. **Fee:** $13–$20. **Parking:** At site.

FACILITIES

Number of RV-Only Sites: 54. **Number of Tent-Only Sites:** 185. **Hookups:** Water, electric, sewer. **Each Site:** Picnic table, fire pit & grill, piped water, shade trees. **Dump Station:** Yes. **Laundry:** No. **Pay Phone:** Yes. **Rest Rooms and Showers:** Yes. **Fuel:** 10 mi. (in Tillamook). **Propane:** 10 mi. (in Tillamook). **Internal Roads:** Call ahead for details. **RV Service:** No. **Market:** 10 mi. (in Tillamook). **Restaurant:** 10 mi. (in Tillamook). **General Store:** 10 mi. (in Tillamook). **Vending:** No. **Swimming Pool:** No. **Playground:** No. **Other:** 10 rental units, firewood. **Activities:** Beachcombing, hiking, walking, fishing, evening & historic programs. **Nearby Attractions:** Tillamook Cheese Factory. **Additional Information:** Information: (503) 842-4981 or (503) 842-3182.

RESTRICTIONS

Pets: On leash only. **Fires:** In fire rings only. **Alcoholic Beverages:** Allowed. **Vehicle Maximum Length:** None.

TO GET THERE

From Tillamook, drive southwest on Netarts Hwy. and follow signs the entire way for Cape Lookout State Park, total distance from Tillamook is 10 mi.

NEWPORT

Pacific Shores Motorcoach Resort

6225 North Coast Hwy. 101, Newport 97365.
T: (541)265-3750 or (800)333-1583; www.outdoor-resorts.com; stay@pacificshoresrv.com.

RV ★★★★ Tent n/a

Beauty: ★★★	Site Privacy: ★
Spaciousness: ★★★	Quiet: ★★
Security: ★★★★★	Cleanliness: ★★★★★
Insect Control: ★★	Facilities: ★★★★★

Pacific Shores Motor coach Resort, on the northern edge of Newport and the coastal side of Hwy. 101, is a newly renovated family oriented beach resort. Many of the individual sites are privately owned but rented out when not occupied. The well equipped facilities include a large indoor pool, several saunas, a hilly chip-and-putt six-hole golf area (with maintained grass) and a three story high viewing tower to watch whales playing off the coast. The park sits on cliffs above the beach and has beach access. The best (and also most expensive) sites, numbered 141, 161–168, 185, and 186, have a view of the Pacific and an outcropping to the south, finishing with a lighthouse. Additionally, sites 26–34 have a view slightly obscured by tall pines. Particular sites to avoid, located next to Hwy. 101, include 1–16, 237–252, and 76–93. The spacious, paved, grass bordered, shadeless sites have wide access roads. Summer months make up the busiest and best time to visit.

Basics

Operated By: Outdoor Resorts of America, Inc. **Open:** All year. **Site Assignment:** On arrival, reservation (required deposit is 1 night's stay; refund w/ cancel before 1 p.m. on arrival date). **Registration:** At office, after hours at guardhouse. **Fee:** Main $35, clubhouse $45, view $55; fee covers 4 people, extra person $5; cash, check; V, MC. **Parking:** At site.

Facilities

Number of RV-Only Sites: 203. **Number of Tent-Only Sites:** 0. **Hookups:** Electric (20, 30, 50 amps), water, sewer, cable. **Each Site:** Picnic table. **Dump Station:** No. **Laundry:** Yes. **Pay Phone:** Yes. **Rest Rooms and Showers:** Yes. **Fuel:** No. **Propane:** No. **Internal Roads:** Paved (wide). **RV Service:** No. **Market:** 2 mi. south in Newport. **Restaurant:** 2 mi. south in Newport. **General Store:** Yes. **Vending:** Yes. **Swimming Pool:** Yes. **Playground:** Yes. **Other:** 2 hot tubs, 3 saunas, 6 hole chip & putt golf, arcade (w/ 2 pool tables), reservable large meeting room, enclosed viewing tower. **Activities:** Bingo, weekly dinners, occasional live entertainment, wine & cheese socials, salt water swimming & fishing. **Nearby Attractions:** Yaquina Head Lighthouse, beaches, Oregon Coast Aquarium, Historic Bayfront, Ripley's Believe it or Not, Undersea Gardens, The Wax Works. **Additional Information:** Newport Chamber of Commerce, (800) 262-7844.

Restrictions

Pets: On leash only, no more than 2 per site. **Fires:** Communal fire pit only. **Alcoholic Beverages:** At site. **Vehicle Maximum Length:** None. **Other:** Min. Vehicle Length 25 ft., no 5th wheels, motorcoaches only, towed secondary vehicles ok.

To Get There

From southbound on Hwy. 101, park is located on right-hand side just north of Newport City limits and 3 mi. north of Hwy. 101 junction with Hwy. 20.

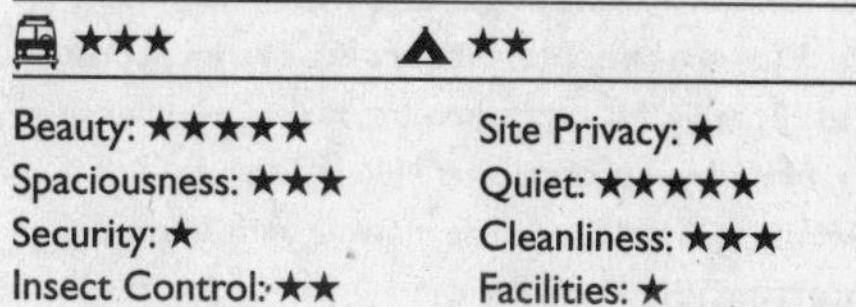

ONTARIO

Lake Owyhee State Park

P.O. Box 247, Adrian 97901. T: (541) 339-2331; www.oregonstateparks.org/park14.php.

RV ★★★ Tent ★★

Beauty: ★★★★★	Site Privacy: ★
Spaciousness: ★★★	Quiet: ★★★★★
Security: ★	Cleanliness: ★★★
Insect Control: ★★	Facilities: ★

Lake Owyhee State Park, located in the absolute middle of nowhere in the desert, eastern-central part of the state, provides a scenic and quiet place to spend a few days. The park can only be accessed by *small* rigs and cars, the road is too narrow and treacherous for anything longer than 25 feet. Created by a dam, the artificial lake plays host to fishing, summer water sports, and provides irrigation to nearby farmers. The campground's location, far from agrarian, sits in what was once a lush canyon. Downstream from the dam (on the way to the campground) the canyon still has such a look and feel. The area before the dam provides some of the most interesting and beautiful scenery in the surrounding area. The state park has two campgrounds, one with water/electric hookups and one with no hookups. All sites have good views of the surrounding, arid, sage-covered, red hills. The campground has little shade, and no privacy; the summer sun here packs a punch. Also, the remote location means no services and lots of bugs. Visit during late spring or late summer for the best conditions; reiterating: *do not attempt this trip in a large rig or during freezing weather; the road has steep, treacherous curves without guardrails.*

Basics

Operated By: Oregon State Parks & Recreation. **Open:** Mid Apr.–Oct. (weather permitting). **Site Assignment:** On arrival. **Registration:** At self pay station. **Fee:** Water/electric $15, tent $13, overflow or primitive $10, extra vehicle $7; V, MC (cash preferred as credit machine is unreliable). **Parking:** At site.

Facilities

Number of RV-Only Sites: 80. **Number of Tent-Only Sites:** 10. **Hookups:** Electric (20, 30 amps), water. **Each Site:** Picnic table, fire ring. **Dump Station:** Yes. **Laundry:** No. **Pay Phone:** No. **Rest Rooms and Showers:** Yes. **Fuel:** Marine only (Seasonal). **Propane:** No. **Internal Roads:** Paved, gravel. **RV Service:** No. **Market:** 30 mi. north. **Restaurant:** 30 mi. North. **General Store:** Yes (seasonal). **Vending:** No. **Swimming Pool:** No. **Playground:** No. **Other:** Boat ramp. **Activities:** Boating, fishing, swimming, hiking, wildlife viewing. **Nearby Attractions:** Hiking, fishing, swimming, boating, wildlife viewing. **Additional Information:** State Park, (541) 339-2331.

Restrictions

Pets: On leash only (max. length 6 ft.). **Fires:** Fire pits only; small fires only, pay attention to wildfire conditions. **Alcoholic Beverages:** At site. **Vehicle Maximum Length:** 25 ft. **Other:** Small fires only, pay attention to wildfire conditions.

To Get There

From Hwy. 201, turn west at Owyhee Junction onto Owyhee Ave. for 5 mi., then turn south (left) onto Owyhee Dam Cutoff Rd. for 22 mi. to the park. *Warning:* Parts of this road are steep and narrow with sharp corners, and with limited visibility. Please use caution.

PACIFIC CITY

Cape Kiwanda RV Park

P.O.Box 129, Pacific City 97135. T: (503) 965-6230; F: (503) 965-6235; www.pacificcity.net/capekiwandarvpark; capekiwanda@oregoncoast.com.

RV: ★★ Tent: ★★

Beauty: ★★	Site Privacy: ★
Spaciousness: ★★	Quiet: ★★★
Security: ★	Cleanliness: ★★
Insect Control: ★★	Facilities: ★★

Cape Kiwanda RV Park across from Haystack Rock and a few miles off of 101 in Pacific City provides a modest resting place amidst great natural beauty. Across the street the public beach has tidal pools, colorful sedimentary rock cliffs, a giant sand dune to climb, and the majestic, monolithic Haystack Rock offshore. The campground has flat, adjacent gravel sites surrounded by more gravel and sand, lots of yard junk (all that's missing is a ceramic gnome) and backs up to evergreen-forested hills. The property has few trees and therefore little shade. The best RV sites are A12–14 because they have a view of the rock, and 112, 113 for their size. Courtyard sites 5, 6, and 7 also have good distant views but are visually appalling at short range. The tent sites are flat and grassy and back up to the forest at the rear of the park, but the only ones with any privacy at all are T12–15.

Basics

Operated By: Cape Kiwanda RV Park. **Open:** All year, some seasonal areas. **Site Assignment:** First come, first served; reservation (required deposit is 1 night's stay; refund w/ 48-hours notice). **Registration:** At office, after hours at drop outside office. **Fee:** Full $25, water/electric $23, tent $16; V, MC, cash. **Parking:** At site.

Facilities

Number of RV-Only Sites: 168. **Number of Tent-Only Sites:** 22. **Hookups:** Electric (30, 50 amps), water, sewer, cable. **Each Site:** Picnic table. **Dump Station:** Yes. **Laundry:** Yes. **Pay Phone:** Yes. **Rest Rooms and Showers:** Yes. **Fuel:** No. **Propane:** Yes. **Internal Roads:** Gravel. **RV Service:** No. **Market:** South in Pacific City. **Restaurant:** South in Pacific City. **General Store:** Yes. **Vending:** Yes. **Swimming Pool:** No. **Playground:** Yes. **Other:** Reservable rec room w/ kitchen, shuffleboard. **Activities:** Bingo, crafts (seasonal & on demand). **Nearby Attractions:** Haystack Rock, beaches, fishing, hang gliding. **Additional Information:** Pacific City Chamber of Commerce, (503) 965-6161.

Restrictions

Pets: On leash only. **Fires:** Fire rings only. **Alcoholic Beverages:** At site only. **Vehicle Maximum Length:** None.

To Get There

From Hwy. 101, turn west off 101 onto Three Capes Scenic Dr. (Brooten Rd.) just south of Cloverdale and follow for 2 mi. to a blinking red light. Turn left onto Pacific Ave, drive 2 blocks and then turn right onto Cape Kiwanda Dr. Follow for 0.4 mi.; entrance is on the right.

PENDLETON
Mountain View RV Park

1375 Southeast 3rd, Pendleton 97801. T: (541) 276-1041 or (866) 302-3311; F: (541) 966-8820; rvpdt@oregontrail.net.

RV: ★★★★ Tent: ★

Beauty: ★★★★ Site Privacy: ★
Spaciousness: ★★★ Quiet: ★★
Security: ★★★★ Cleanliness: ★★★★
Insect Control: ★★ Facilities: ★★★

Mountain View RV Park in Pendleton has nice vistas and easy interstate access. Arranged in several parallel rows, the newer part has flat, paved, grass bordered sites, both with and without views. Unfortunately none of the sites have any shade or privacy. The best RV sites sit on a perimeter, numbers 52–70, that have an open view of the golden, rolling hills and dry flatlands to the south. The huge sky in this part of the countryside makes the scenery particularly impressive. The tenting section consists of a small grassy area with little shade and no intersite privacy. The park has very limited in-house recreation, but makes a good base for exploring the area or for stopping overnight on the long trek through eastern Oregon. Winters here bring extremely cold temperatures and summers just the opposite; late Spring and early fall provide the most comfortable climate.

Basics

Operated By: Mt. View RV Park. **Open:** All year. **Site Assignment:** On arrival, reservation (required deposit is1 night stay; refund w/ 24-hours notice). **Registration:** At office, after hours at drop or pay in morning. **Fee:** Premium $25, full $22, tent $15; fee covers 2 peopl, extra person (age 6 or older) $2; V, MC, check, cash. **Parking:** At site, limited off site.

Facilities

Number of RV-Only Sites: 100. **Number of Tent-Only Sites:** 6. **Hookups:** Electric (30, 50 amps), water, sewer, cable. **Each Site:** Picnic table. **Dump Station:** Yes. **Laundry:** Yes. **Pay Phone:** Yes. **Rest Rooms and Showers:** Yes. **Fuel:** No. **Propane:** Yes. **Internal Roads:** Paved. **RV Service:** No. **Market:** North in Pendleton. **Restaurant:** North in Pendelton. **General Store:** No. **Vending:** No. **Swimming Pool:** No. **Playground:** Yes. **Other:** Meeting room (reservable), storage. **Activities:** Watching the sky. **Nearby Attractions:** All types of outdoor sports, casino gambling, Tamastslikt Cultural Institute (confederated tribes). **Additional Information:** Pendleton Chamber of Commerce, (541) 276-7411.

Restrictions

Pets: On leash only (max. quantity 2; max. weight 40 lbs.each). **Fires:** No open fires. **Alcoholic Beverages:** At site. **Vehicle Maximum Length:** None. **Other:** Max. 6 people per site.

To Get There

From I-84 Exit 210, (eastbound turn right), turn south from the exit ramp and drive 1 block. Turn right on SE Nye and drive a short distance, turning right on SE 3rd St. This road dead-ends into the RV park after 0.2 mi.

PENDLETON
Wildhorse RV Park

72781 Hwy. 331, Pendleton 97801. T: (541) 966-1891

RV: ★★★ Tent: ★★

Beauty: ★★★ Site Privacy: ★
Spaciousness: ★★★ Quiet: ★★★
Security: ★ Cleanliness: ★★★★
Insect Control: ★★ Facilities: ★★★

Wild Horse Resort, in Pendleton, makes a great place to camp for the gambling enthusiast. Located on reservation lands, the campground operates in conjunction with the casino down the road. The flat setting has an enormous canvas of a sky, but not much in the way of shade, or for that matter high growing foliage. Most RV sites have paved surfaces but all lack privacy; the resort has a basic layout of parallel rows over a grassy field. Wild Horse has a tenting section consisting of a grassy area but sites lack borders, shade, or privacy. The facilities within walking distance of campsites have a good maintenance schedule, but are few in number. And of course a shuttle runs between the campground and the closest recreation, as mentioned above, the casino. The campground provides services all year but winters here bring bitter cold.

Basics

Operated By: Wild Horse Resort. **Open:** All year. **Site Assignment:** On arrival, reservation (required deposit is during events $50; refund w/ 10-days notice). **Registration:** At office, after hours drop in office door. **Fee:** 30 amp or tent $19, 50 amp $21; V, MC, cash. **Parking:** At site, limited off site.

Facilities

Number of RV-Only Sites: 100. **Number of Tent-Only Sites:** Open tent area. **Hookups:** Electric (30, 50 amps), water, sewer. **Each Site:** Picnic table. **Dump Station:** Yes. **Laundry:** Yes. **Pay Phone:** Yes. **Rest Rooms and Showers:** Yes. **Fuel:** No. **Propane:** No. **Internal Roads:** Paved. **RV Service:** No. **Market:** In Pendleton. **Restaurant:** Next door at Casino. **General Store:** No. **Vending:** Yes. **Swimming Pool:** Yes. **Playground:** No. **Other:** Free continental breakfast, casino. **Activities:** Gambling. **Nearby Attractions:** Pendleton Underground Tours, Pendleton Woolen Mills, Tamastslikt Cultural Institute, Pendleton Round-Up, Happy Canyon Hall of Fame, Umatilla County Historical Society Museum. **Additional Information:** Pendleton Chamber of Commerce, (541) 276-7411.

Restrictions

Pets: On leash only. **Fires:** No fires. **Alcoholic Beverages:** Not allowed. **Vehicle Maximum Length:** None. **Other:** No tents in RV sites.

To Get There

From I-84 Exit 216, turn north and drive 0.7 mi.; the casino is on the right. Turn right at the casino and drive past the casino; campground entrance is on the right.

PORT ORFORD
Bandon-Port Orford KOA

46612 Hwy. 101, Langlois 97450. T: (541) 348-2358; www.koacampgrounds.com/where/or/37116.htm.

RV ★★★ Tent ★★★★

Beauty: ★★★★	Site Privacy: ★★★
Spaciousness: ★★★	Quiet: ★★★
Security: ★	Cleanliness: ★★
Insect Control: ★★	Facilities: ★★★

Bandon-Port Orford KOA, ten miles north of Port Orford on Hwy. 101, offers both quiet, wooded sites for smaller vehicles and family-oriented recreation. The older grounds, canopied by fir, pine, and the occasional cedar, have good intersite privacy due to dense, low lying groves of green vegetation including huckleberries. Not suited for huge rigs, the gravel and grass sites are not uniformaly flat and the facilities are older but in good condition. The sites sit in rows lettered A–F, the quietest of which have numbers greater than four. The best tent sites sit near the back, numbered A10–12, and the best RV sites sit in the middle, water/electric pull-throughs B5–7 and full hookup pull-throughs E7 and E11. The best time to visit the shady campground is during the warm summers. Near the coast, beach access requires a 15-minute drive at the shortest distance.

Basics

Operated By: Bandon -Port Orford KOA. **Open:** All year. **Site Assignment:** First come, first served; reservation (24 hour cancellation policy, 1-week on holidays). **Registration:** At office, after hours at drop box. **Fee:** Full $28, water/electric $26, tent $22; fee covers 2 people & 2 vehicles, extra person $3, max. site occupancy is 8 people per site, extra vehicle $5; V, MC, D, cash, check. **Parking:** At site.

Facilities

Number of RV-Only Sites: 36. **Number of Tent-Only Sites:** 30. **Hookups:** Electric (20, 30 amps), water, sewer, cable. **Each Site:** Picnic table, fire ring. **Dump Station:** Yes. **Laundry:** Yes. **Pay Phone:** Yes. **Rest Rooms and Showers:** Yes. **Fuel:** No. **Propane:** Yes. **Internal Roads:** Gravel. **RV Service:** No. **Market:** 10 mi. south in Port Orford. **Restaurant:** 10 mi. south in Port Orford. **General Store:** Yes. **Vending:** Yes. **Swimming Pool:** Yes. **Playground:** Yes. **Other:** Basketball goal, volleyball net, horseshoe pit, arcade, rec room. **Activities:** (On seasonal demand) pancake breakfast every morning, ice cream social & train ride every night, line dancing, berry picking. **Nearby Attractions:** Cape Blanco Lighthouse, whale-watching, charter fishing, cranberry bogs. **Additional Information:** Greater Port Orford North Curry Chamber of Commerce, (541) 332-8055.

Restrictions

Pets: On leash only. **Fires:** In fire pits only. **Alcoholic Beverages:** At site only. **Vehicle Maximum Length:** 36 ft. **Other:** No pets in rest rooms.

To Get There

The grounds are located 10 mi. north of Port Orford between Bandon and Port Orford on the western side of the highway (south bound turn right), marked by large sign.

PORT ORFORD

Cape Blanco State Park

P.O. Box 1345, Port Orford 97465. T: (541) 332-6774; www.prd.state.or.us.

RV ★★★ Tent ★★★★

Beauty: ★★★★★ Site Privacy: ★★★
Spaciousness: ★★★★ Quiet: ★★★
Security: ★★★★ Cleanliness: ★★★★★
Insect Control: ★★★ Facilities: ★★★

This state park covers 1,895 acres of forested headlands and wildflower fields that flood the area with color in late spring and early summer. The lush vegetation of Cape Blanco is kept green by the year-round temperate marine climate that brings in half of the total annual precipitation between December and February. This makes it an ideal place to enjoy during the off-season and to avoid at peak times. The summer tourist season along the Oregon Coast-all 360 miles of it-is lovely weatherwise, and the scenery is consistently spectacular, but it is one of those experiences you could learn to hate. There is little relief from the crowds, campgrounds fill up quickly (including Cape Blanco), and the main north/south route (US 101) is one long, nearly unbroken procession of RVs and trailers.

Basics

Operated By: Oregon State Parks & Recreation. **Open:** All year. **Site Assignment:** First come, first served, no reservations. **Registration:** In camp office. **Fee:** $18. **Parking:** At site.

Facilities

Number of RV-Only Sites: 54. **Number of Tent-Only Sites:** 54. **Hookups:** Electric. **Each Site:** Picnic table, fire grill, electricity. **Dump Station:** Yes. **Laundry:** Yes. **Pay Phone:** Yes. **Rest Rooms and Showers:** Yes. **Fuel:** No. **Propane:** Yes. **Internal Roads:** Call ahead for details. **RV Service:** Yes. **Market:** No. **Restaurant:** No. **General Store:** Yes. **Vending:** No. **Swimming Pool:** Yes. **Playground:** No. **Other:** 4 reservable log cabins, horse camping. **Activities:** Fishing, hiking, horseback riding. **Nearby Attractions:** Oregon Islands National Refuge, Dunes of Bandon, New river, Blacklock point, Tower Rock, Oregon Coast Trail, lighthouses. **Additional Information:** Port Orford Chamber of Commerce, (541) 332-8055 or www.portorfordregion.com.

Restrictions

Pets: On leash only. **Fires:** In fire rings only. **Alcoholic Beverages:** not permitted. **Vehicle Maximum Length:** None.

To Get There

From Port Orford, drive north on US 101 to Cape Blanco Hwy., and then go 5 mi. west to the state park campground.

PORT ORFORD

Historic Arizona Beach RV Park

36939 Hwy. 101, Port Orford 97465. T: (541) 332-6491

RV ★★★★ Tent ★★★

Beauty: ★★★★★ Site Privacy: ★
Spaciousness: ★★★ Quiet: ★★★
Security: ★★★ Cleanliness: ★★★
Insect Control: ★★ Facilities: ★★

There are campgrounds in the Port Orford and Gold Beach Area with nicer facilities and shadier sites than those found at Historic Arizona Beach RV Park, located on Hwy. 101 between the two cities. However, Arizona Beach is the only park in the area, and possibly on the Oregon Coast, with beach back-ins. The grounds consist of two sections on either side of 101 with an underpass connecting them, and the east side backs up to steep wooded coastal hills. But on the west side sit 38 water/electric sites at sea level, five or so feet off a narrow, gray sand beach. The grass and dirt sites, numbered 112–165, have breathtaking views of the big, crashing Pacific surf and surrounding hills, and very easy beach access. The RV sites on either side lack privacy; some beach side tent sites have privacy, numbered 6–10. The park, located right across the street from Prehistoric Gardens (plaster dinosaurs), recently changed hands and the new management has plans for facility improvement. Late spring is less crowded than summer, summer has better weather.

Basics

Operated By: Arizona Beach RV Park. **Open:** All Year (but up–owner). **Site Assignment:** Reservable (required deposit is 1 night's stay; refund w/ 7-days notice), first come first served. **Registration:** At office, after hours see office window for varying directions. **Fee:** Waterfront $26, other RV $23, tent $16; V, MC, check, cash. **Parking:** At site, off site parking ample.

Facilities

Number of RV-Only Sites: 125. **Number of Tent-Only Sites:** 30. **Hookups:** Electric (20, 30 amps), water, sewer. **Each Site:** Picnic table, fire ring. **Dump Station:** Yes. **Laundry:** Yes. **Pay Phone:** Yes. **Rest Rooms and Showers:** Yes. **Fuel:** No. **Propane:** Yes. **Internal Roads:** Dirt & gravel. **RV Service:** No. **Market:** North or south 15 mi. in Bandon or Port Orford. **Restaurant:** North or south 15 mi. in Bandon or Port Orford. **General Store:** Yes. **Vending:** Yes. **Swimming Pool:** No. **Playground:** Yes. **Other:** Large reservable rec room, basketball goal, chipping range, horseshoes, tide pools(on beach), beach, discount tickets to Prehistoric Gardens, crab nets, fishing equipment rentals. **Activities:** Fishing, crabbing, golfing, body boarding, surfing, planned activities, gold panning, berry picking, whale-watching (seasonal & inconsistent). **Nearby Attractions:** Prehistoric Gardens, Bandon Cheese Factory, golf, charter fishing, cranberry bogs. **Additional Information:** Bandon Chamber of Commerce, (541) 347-9616.

Restrictions

Pets: On leash only. **Fires:** Fire pits only, no beach fires. **Alcoholic Beverages:** At site. **Vehicle Maximum Length:** None. **Other:** No gathering, cutting of firewood; no mechanized vehicles on beach.

To Get There

Entrance marked by large sign on east side of Hwy. 101, 14 mi. north of Gold Beach, opposite from Prehistoric Gardens. If you can see a big green Tyrannosaurus Rex in your side view mirrors, you missed it.

PORTLAND

Columbia River RV Park

10649 Northeast 13th Ave., Portland 97211. T: (503) 285-4397 or (888) 366-7725; F: (503) 285-4397.

RV: ★ Tent: n/a

Beauty: ★	Site Privacy: ★
Spaciousness: ★★	Quiet: ★
Security: ★★★	Cleanliness: ★★★★
Insect Control: ★★	Facilities: ★★

Columbia River RV Park, situated just off of I-5 and a short walk from its wide namesake river, is not a family-oriented park. If more than four people travel with you (no breaks for kids) you *have* to a second site. This new, defoliated park has flat paved sites and close proximity to downtown Portland, but no privacy. Sites arrangement consists of a perimeter surrounding parallel rows divided by access roads. Small sections of grass separate the sites. Sites 129–145 and 98–114 get the least public road noise; sites 24–68 get the most. Worse than traffic or frequent commercial jets from nearby Portland International Airport are the Air National Guard fighter jets breaking the sound barrier right over the property, no site has immunity from frequent aerial auditory assault. The park sits in a hole and does not have a good view of anything. On the bright side, the campground has good hookups and is located within easy striking distance of Portland.

Basics

Operated By: Columbia River RV Park. **Open:** All year. **Site Assignment:** First come, first served; reservation. **Registration:** At office, after hours at drop box by office. **Fee:** $22; fee covers 2 people, xtra person $2, max. site occupancy is 4 people; cash, check, no credit. **Parking:** At site.

Facilities

Number of RV-Only Sites: 152. **Number of Tent-Only Sites:** 0. **Hookups:** Electric (20, 30, 50 amps), water, sewer, cable. **Each Site:** Concrete pad. **Dump Station:** Yes. **Laundry:** Yes. **Pay Phone:** Yes. **Rest Rooms and Showers:** Yes. **Fuel:** No. **Propane:** No. **Internal Roads:** Paved. **RV Service:** No. **Market:** 2 mi. west in Jantzen Beach. **Restaurant:** 2 mi. west in Jantzen Beach.

General Store: No. **Vending:** Yes. **Swimming Pool:** No. **Playground:** No. **Other:** Reservable Rec room w/ a kitchen. **Activities:** Inquire at campground. **Nearby Attractions:** Saturday Market, Children's Museum, The Grotto, Sternwheeler Columbia Gorge, Portland Art Museum. **Additional Information:** Portland Oregon Visitor's Assoc. 1-87-PORTLAND.

RESTRICTIONS

Pets: On leash only, under 20 lbs. **Fires:** No open fires. **Alcoholic Beverages:** At site. **Vehicle Maximum Length:** None. **Other:** Only RV models ten years or younger; no boats or tow dolly's.

TO GET THERE

From I-5 Exit 307 to Marine Dr. East. Follow Marine Dr. east for 1.4 mi. to 13th Ave.; entrance is on the right across from the yacht club.

PORTLAND
Janzen Beach RV Park

1503 North Hayden Island Dr, Portland 97217.
T: (503) 289-7626 or (800) 443-7248

RV ★★ Tent n/a

Beauty: ★★	Site Privacy: ★
Spaciousness: ★★	Quiet: ★
Security: ★★★	Cleanliness: ★★★
Insect Control: ★★	Facilities: ★★★

Jantzen Beach RV Park, in Northwest Portland just off I-5, is located on Hayden Island, a short walk away from public transit, and adjacent to a well kept trailer park. The flat, paved sites are delineated manicured grass, shrubs and trees. Many of the trees flower in the spring, but theylack sufficient height to provide much of shade. The RV section has two distinctly different areas. The first area, sites 801–844 and A–D, makes up two cramped and unattractive rows back to back. The second consists of comparatively more spacious sites. The best sites, 903–922 and 859–871, have the most isolation from the surrounding noise of the city. These sites may or may not be available depending on demand for monthly accommodations. Although security is marginal, the convenient urban location's only real downfall, found directly overhead, is one of Portland International's Exit corridors. You can expect a low altitude jumbo jet screaming over about once every ten minutes during busier times of day.

BASICS

Operated By: Jantzen Beach RV Park. **Open:** All year. **Site Assignment:** First come, first served; reservation (required deposit is 1 night's stay; refund w/ 24-hours notice). **Registration:** At office, after hours pay in morning. **Fee:** back-in $24, pull-through $26, fee covers 2 people; extra person $1; V, MC, cash, check. **Parking:** At site.

FACILITIES

Number of RV-Only Sites: 169. **Number of Tent-Only Sites:** 0. **Hookups:** Electric (20, 30, 50 amps), water, sewer, cable, central data port. **Each Site:** Picnic table. **Dump Station:** Yes. **Laundry:** Yes. **Pay Phone:** Yes. **Rest Rooms and Showers:** Yes. **Fuel:** No. **Propane:** No. **Internal Roads:** Paved. **RV Service:** No. **Market:** 1 mile east by interstate. **Restaurant:** Across Hayden Island Dr. **General Store:** Yes. **Vending:** Yes. **Swimming Pool:** Yes. **Playground:** Yes. **Other:** basketball court, rec room, pool table. **Activities:** swimming, frolicking. **Nearby Attractions:** Burnside Park, Powell's Bookstore, Oregon Zoo, brewpubs, Vancouver, Columbia River gorge. **Additional Information:** None.

RESTRICTIONS

Pets: On leash only. **Fires:** No open fires. **Alcoholic Beverages:** At site only. **Vehicle Maximum Length:** None.

TO GET THERE

From I-5 Exit 308, drive 0.5 mi. west on Hayden Island Dr.; entrance is on the right across from a large strip mall.

PORTLAND
Mt. Hood Village

65000 East Hwy. 26, Welches 97067. T: (503) 622-4011; www.mthoodvillage.com; mhoodv@mthood village.com.

RV ★★★★ Tent ★★

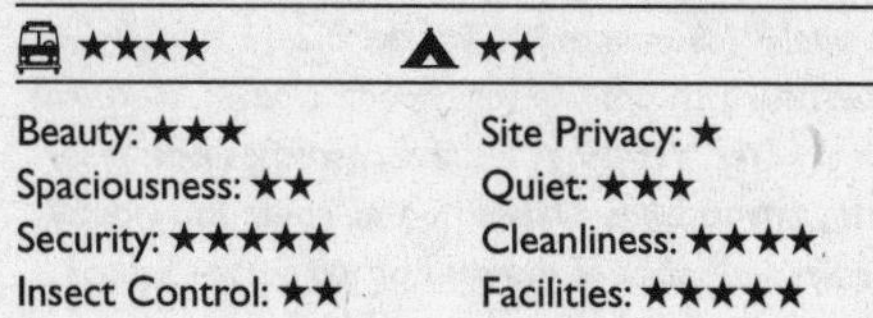

Beauty: ★★★	Site Privacy: ★
Spaciousness: ★★	Quiet: ★★★
Security: ★★★★★	Cleanliness: ★★★★
Insect Control: ★★	Facilities: ★★★★★

Mt. Hood Village, located on Hwy. 26 southeast of Portland, offers an amazing number of resort amenities within close proximity to the scenic National Forest Area. These facilities include, among others, a large indoor pool, tons of exercise equipment, resident massage therapists, and a very large lodge and outdoor pavilion for meetings of all sizes. The campground has several different sections offering different hookups, and these sections all have outdoorsy names. The best gravel, back-in, full-hookup sites can be found in Vine Maple Hollow, numbered 82–100; these adjacent sites, shaded by birch and pine, offer the most seclusion from the rest of the busy grounds. Conversely, the worst sites also sit in this section near a high traffic area of the park, numbered 8–50. There exist some quality water/electric sites, numbers 38–70, in the section deemed Hemlock Meadows; these sites are perhaps the shadiest on the property. All sections within the park make an attempt at maintaining the wooded feel of the surrounding country-side. The grounds only have slim opportunities for tent camping, with the tent sites consisting of gravel and crushed shale.

Basics

Operated By: Grayco Resources, Inc. **Open:** All year. **Site Assignment:** On arrival, reservation (required deposit is 1 night's fee; refund w/ 48-hours notice of reservation). **Registration:** At entrance gate, after hours use phone at gate-call attendant. **Fee:** Full $32, water/electric $29, group tent $40, tent $20; fee covers 6 people w/ 1 unit & 1 vehicle, extra vehicle $2 per stay; V, MC, D, AE, personal checks, cash. **Parking:** At site, some off site.

Facilities

Number of RV-Only Sites: 361. **Number of Tent-Only Sites:** 18. **Hookups:** Electric (20, 30, 50 amps), water, sewer, cable. **Each Site:** Picnic table, fire ring. **Dump Station:** Yes. **Laundry:** Yes. **Pay Phone:** Yes. **Rest Rooms and Showers:** Yes. **Fuel:** Yes. **Propane:** Yes. **Internal Roads:** Paved & gravel. **RV Service:** No. **Market:** 2 mi. east on 26. **Restaurant:** On site for breakfast, lunch. **General Store:** Yes. **Vending:** Yes. **Swimming Pool:** Yes. **Playground:** Yes. **Other:** Game room (no video games, indoor pool, indoor hot tub (large), saunas (1 per gender, small), cardio room, freeweight room, fireside room (small meeting room), lodge (enormous meeting room), huge outdoor pavilion w/ tables & tents, basketball, volleyball (sand), cabins, cottages, pedal carts (2 & 4 person), massage therapy. **Activities:** Weekend planned activities, swimming, ping-pong, pool, foos ball, fishing, use of facilities. **Nearby Attractions:** Mt. Hood National Forest, Portland, winter sports. **Additional Information:** Mt. Hood Area Chamber of Commerce, (888) 622-4822.

Restrictions

Pets: On leash only. **Fires:** Fire pits only. **Alcoholic Beverages:** At site, not allowed inside common areas. **Vehicle Maximum Length:** None. **Other:** Washing vehicles allowed in site w/ biodegradable soap.

To Get There

Take I-84 East to Exit 16 (Wood Village, Gresham, Mt. Hood). Drive south about 6 mi., then turn left (east) onto Burnside St. Burnside turns into Hwy. 26 East in about 1 mi. Take Hwy. 26 through the town of Sandy. About 15 mi. East of Sandy, the entrance will be on the right.

PORTLAND
Pheasant Ridge RV Park

8275 Southwest Elligsen Rd., Wilsonville 97070. T: (503) 682-7829 or (800) 532-7829; F: (503) 682-9043; www.pheasantridge.com; terri@pheasant ridge.com.

RV ★★★ Tent ★★

Beauty: ★★★	Site Privacy: ★★
Spaciousness: ★★★	Quiet: ★★
Security: ★★	Cleanliness: ★★★★
Insect Control: ★★	Facilities: ★★★★

Pheasant Ridge RV Park, one-half hour south of Portland on I-5, provides a good place for people wanting to daytrip to surrounding areas. The terraced sites climb a hill to views of the surrounding developed hill country, providing a feeling of inter-site spaciousness. Young pines also scale the hill alongside the paved, grass-enclosed sites. The pines afford a sense of privacy but not much shade. Sites with the best view sit at the top of the grounds, numbered 86–90 and 104–109. The campground was approved for its compliance with the Americans with Disabilities Act (although dumpsters are a long hike from most sites) and the indoor hot tub has a Hoyer lift for disabled access; the indoor pool does not. Several groups meet at the grounds in the rec room and open their doors to visitors, and these include (although schedules vary) a barbershop quartet on Tuesday nights, a men's Sunday morning prayer group, and a women's Wednesday morning craft and sewing circle.

Basics

Operated By: Pheasant Ridge RV Park. **Open:** All year. **Site Assignment:** First come, first served; reservation (deposit 1 night's stay; refund w/ 24-hours notice). **Registration:** At office, after hours ring bell. **Fee:** $27 plus $1 per person; V, MC, checks. **Parking:** At site 1.

Facilities

Number of RV-Only Sites: 130. **Number of Tent-Only Sites:** 0. **Hookups:** Electric (20, 30, 50 amps), water, sewer. **Each Site:** Picnic table. **Dump Station:** No. **Laundry:** Yes. **Pay Phone:** Yes. **Rest Rooms and Showers:** Yes. **Fuel:** No. **Propane:** Yes. **Internal Roads:** Paved. **RV Service:** No. **Market:** North up I-5 3 mi. **Restaurant:** North up I-5 3 mi. **General Store:** Yes. **Vending:** Yes. **Swimming Pool:** Yes. **Playground:** No. **Other:** Hoyer lift for hot tub, exercise room, horseshoe pit, hot tub. **Activities:** BBQs & various planned activities. **Nearby Attractions:** End of the Oregon Trail Interpretive Center, wineries, Powell's Bookstore, Wilsonville Family Fun Center. **Additional Information:** Portland Oregon Visitor's Assoc. 1-87-PORTLAND.

Restrictions

Pets: On leash only, no larger than 40 lbs, no more than 2. **Fires:** No open flames. **Alcoholic Beverages:** At site. **Vehicle Maximum Length:** 45 ft. **Other:** No skateboards.

To Get There

From I-5 Exit 286, drive 0.25 mi. east on Elligsen Rd.; entrance is on the left.

PORTLAND

Portland Fairview RV Park

21401 Northeast Sandy Blvd., Fairview 97024.
T: (503) 661-1047 or (877) 777-1047; F: (503) 665-4643; portlandrv@aol.com.

 ★★★ ▲ n/a

Beauty: ★★★ Site Privacy: ★
Spaciousness: ★★★ Quiet: ★
Security: ★★ Cleanliness: ★★★★
Insect Control: ★★ Facilities: ★★★★

The common areas of Portland Fairview RV Park, located about 15 minutes east of Portland off I-84 in the suburb of Fairview, are graces with flowers in the spring and early summer. Within this well manicured but shadeless park one finds flowering white pear trees, purple heather, camellias, a couple of low lying rose hedges, and several varieties of carefully shaped conifers. The grounds have five terraced levels providing views of the surrounding developed hill country. A clear stream cascading gently over rocks into a pond shaded by weeping willows is a visual focal point. Up a hill from the pond sit the prettiest (although not the quietest) sites, numbered 215-220. These shady sites can accommodate small RVs (around 25 ft). The campground's only shortcoming is the active railroad track 20 feet off the back perimeter. Sites 385–396 and 399–407 have the quietest views of the hills. None of the paved, grass bordered sites have visual privacy.

Basics

Operated By: Commonwealth Investors, Inc. **Open:** All year. **Site Assignment:** First come, first served; reservation (deposit to guarantee: 1 night's stay; refund w/ 24-hours notice). **Registration:** At office, after hours at drop in office door. **Fee:** $25.44; fee covers 2 people, extra person $1.06; 7th night stay free w/ 6 nights paid in advance; V, MC, check, cash. **Parking:** At site.

Facilities

Number of RV-Only Sites: 407. **Number of Tent-Only Sites:** 0. **Hookups:** Electric (20, 30, 50 amps), water, sewer, cable. **Each Site:** Picnic table. **Dump Station:** No. **Laundry:** Yes. **Pay Phone:** Yes. **Rest Rooms and Showers:** Yes. **Fuel:** No. **Propane:** No. **Internal Roads:** Paved. **RV Service:** No. **Market:** 5 mi. east in Troutdale. **Restaurant:** 5 mi. east in Troutdale. **General Store:** No. **Vending:** Yes. **Swimming Pool:** Yes. **Playground:** Yes. **Other:** Reservable rec room & log cabin meeting room rentals, basketball court, horseshoes, pool table, hot tub, exercise room. **Activities:** Inquire at campground. **Nearby Attractions:** The Columbia River Gorge National Scenic Area, Classical Chinese Garden, Oregon Museum of Science & Industry, Mt. Hood. **Additional Information:** Portland Oregon Visitor's Assoc. 1-87-Portland.

Restrictions

Pets: On leash only, limit 2 dogs. **Fires:** No open fires. **Alcoholic Beverages:** Not allowed. **Vehicle Maximum Length:** 45 ft. **Other:** No tents; bicycles allowed only on paved streets; only camping units appearing 20 years or younger are allowed, no tents.

To Get There

From I-84 Exit 14, drive 0.25 mi. north on 207th St.; this dead-ends into Sandy Blvd. Turn right on Sandy and drive another 0.25 mi.; entrance is on the left.

PORTLAND
Portland-Dayton RV Park

16205 Southeast Kreder Rd., Dayton 97114. T: (503) 864-2233; www.sites.onlinemac.com/pdrp/rv-park; pdrp@macnet.com.

RV: ★★★ Tent: n/a

Beauty: ★★ Site Privacy: ★
Spaciousness: ★★★ Quiet: ★★
Security: ★★ Cleanliness: ★★★★
Insect Control: ★★ Facilities: ★★★

Portland-Dayton RV Park, just off of Hwy. 99 West on the Hwy. 18 bypass, has a location close to the local wineries halfway between Portland and Salem. The landscaped grounds have a long way to grow; the young trees do not provide much shade or privacy, but location plus free corn more than makes up for this. The owner of the grounds plants corn in an adjacent field in several cycles every summer, and guests can pick it free of charge. The best back-in sites, numbered 10–25, sit adjacent to this field and wrap around the back perimeter of the park. Most of the park consists of row after row of pull-throughs surrounded by a four-sided block of back-ins. All sites are paved and surrounded by well-kept grass. Within walking distance of the grounds flows the Yamhill River. The trip to downtown Dayton is further but still possible on foot.

Basics

Operated By: Portland-Dayton RV Park. **Open:** All year. **Site Assignment:** First come, first served; reservation (no deposit required). **Registration:** At office, after hours drop in office door. **Fee:** $25.44; fee covers 2 people, extra person $2; 7th night stay free w/ 6 nights paid in advance; check, cash. **Parking:** At site.

Facilities

Number of RV-Only Sites: 190. **Number of Tent-Only Sites:** 0. **Hookups:** Electric (30, 50 amps), water, sewer, cable. **Each Site:** Picnic table. **Dump Station:** No. **Laundry:** Yes. **Pay Phone:** Yes. **Rest Rooms and Showers:** Yes. **Fuel:** No. **Propane:** No. **Internal Roads:** Paved. **RV Service:** No. **Market:** 4 mi. south in Dayton. **Restaurant:** 4 mi. south in Dayton. **General Store:** Yes. **Vending:** No. **Swimming Pool:** Yes. **Playground:** No. **Other:** Exercise-rec-meeting room, horseshoe pit, corn field. **Activities:** Potlucks, corn picking, gold panning. **Nearby Attractions:** Wineries, Portland. **Additional Information:** Portland Oregon Visitor's Assoc. 1-87-PORTLAND.

Restrictions

Pets: On leash only; small or medium dogs limit 2. **Fires:** No open fires. **Alcoholic Beverages:** At site. **Vehicle Maximum Length:** 40 ft. **Other:** Exercise equipment for adults only, no firearms, fireworks.

To Get There

Southbound on 99W, take first Hwy. 18 Exit for Dayton, drive 0.75 mi. Entrance on left.

PORTLAND
Roamers Rest RV Park

17585 Southwest Pacific Hwy., Tualatin 97062. T: (503) 692-6350 or (877) 4RV-PARK; F: (503) 691-6998.

RV: ★★★★ Tent: n/a

Beauty: ★★★ Site Privacy: ★
Spaciousness: ★★ Quiet: ★★★
Security: ★★ Cleanliness: ★★★★
Insect Control: ★★ Facilities: ★★★★

Southwest of Portland, in between the city and wine country on the Tualatin River, is Roamers Rest RV Park. The lower level of the park, a rectangular perimeter of sites with a central road, lays on a bank of the slow moving murky green river. Lush green ferns, cedars, oak, and cottonwood climb a steep hill from the river sites to a small alternate section of the grounds. The latter section has thick growth on three sides; the former has 25 waterfront sites. Also on the grounds are some protected wetlands that consist of ponds surrounded by cattails. These house many different species of birds, making the park popular for avid bird-watchers. The best sites for bird-watching, numbered 34–29, sit across from one marshy pond. Portland public transit stops nearby, providing access to many parts of the city.

Basics

Operated By: Roamer's Rest RV Park, LLC. **Open:** All year. **Site Assignment:** First come, first served; reservation (required deposit is 1 night's stay; refund w/ 24-hours notice. **Registration:** At office, after hours pay in morning. **Fee:** Full $24; fee covers 2 people, xtra person (age 5 or older) $2; V, MC, cash. **Parking:** At site, no parking on internal roads.

Facilities

Number of RV-Only Sites: 93. **Number of Tent-Only Sites:** 0. **Hookups:** Electric (20, 30, 50 amps), water, sewer, cable, phone. **Each Site:** Pavement. **Dump Station:** No. **Laundry:** Yes. **Pay Phone:** Yes. **Rest Rooms and Showers:** Yes. **Fuel:** No. **Propane:** No. **Internal Roads:** Paved. **RV Service:** No. **Market:** North on Hwy. 99. **Restaurant:** North on Hwy. 99. **General Store:** No. **Vending:** Yes. **Swimming Pool:** No. **Playground:** No. **Other:** Loaner books, protected wetlands. **Activities:** Bird-watching, fishing. **Nearby Attractions:** Portland Rose Gardens, Japanese Gardens, World Forestry Center Museum, Oregon Zoo, wineries. **Additional Information:** Portland Oregon Visitor's Assoc. 1-87-PORTLAND.

Restrictions

Pets: On leash only, no more than 2 dogs per site. **Fires:** No open fires. **Alcoholic Beverages:** At site. **Vehicle Maximum Length:** 40 ft. **Other:** No skates, skateboards, generators, or vehicle maintenance.

To Get There

From I-5 Exit 292 (junction with Hwy. 217), drive 2 mi. north on Hwy. 217 then 5 mi. south on Hwy. 99W; entrance is on the right just past the Tualatin River.

PROSPECT

Natural Bridge Campground

47201 Hwy. 62, Prospect 97536. T: (541) 560-3623

RV ★★★★ Tent ★★★★

Beauty: ★★★★★ Site Privacy: ★★★★★
Spaciousness: ★★★ Quiet: ★★★★
Security: ★★★★ Cleanliness: ★★★★★
Insect Control: ★★★★ Facilities: ★★★

Natural Bridge is so named for the unique feature adjacent to it. It is at this point that the upper Rogue disappears from sight and runs underground for 200 feet. The campground sits virtually on top of water flowing beneath it. Natural Bridge is one of several campgrounds in the vicinity that is located on the banks of the Rogue or on small creeks that feed it. Given its proximity to Crater Lake, this area can be quite busy in the summertime, with the larger, more developed campsites filling up first. The surrounding Rogue River National Forest is characterized by dense forests of Douglas fir and sugar pine that soften the contours of the high plateau upon which the forests grow. This rugged land is full of thick vegetation, laced with over 450 miles of trails within the national forest. Getting lost can happen easily. Make sure you have a good topographic or Forest Service map with you when you head out for lonely and distant spots.

Basics

Operated By: Rogue River National Forest. **Open:** May–Oct. **Site Assignment:** First come, first served, no reservations. **Registration:** not necessary. **Fee:** None. **Parking:** At site.

Facilities

Number of RV-Only Sites: 16. **Number of Tent-Only Sites:** 0. **Hookups:** No. **Each Site:** Picnic table, fire pit w/ grill. **Dump Station:** No. **Laundry:** No. **Pay Phone:** No. **Rest Rooms and Showers:** Vault toilets. **Fuel:** No. **Propane:** No. **Internal Roads:** Call ahead for details. **RV Service:** No. **Market:** No. **Restaurant:** No. **General Store:** No. **Vending:** No. **Swimming Pool:** No. **Playground:** No. **Activities:** Hiking, backpacking. **Nearby Attractions:** Rogue River. **Additional Information:** Information: (541) 560-3623 May–early Nov.

Restrictions

Pets: On leash only. **Fires:** In fire rings only. **Alcoholic Beverages:** Allowed. **Vehicle Maximum Length:** 22 ft.

To Get There

Travel northeast on SR 62 (about 32 mi. from Medford), from the Prospect turnoff. Continue north on SR 62 another 12 mi. or so to FS 300; turn left and the campground is 1 mi. in.

SALEM
Phoenix RV Park

4130 Silverton Rd. Northeast, Salem 97305. T: (503) 581-2497 or (800) 237-2497; F: (503) 391-2705; phoenixRVPK@aol.com.

RV ★★★★ Tent n/a

Beauty: ★	Site Privacy: ★
Spaciousness: ★★★	Quiet: ★★
Security: ★★★	Cleanliness: ★★★★★
Insect Control: ★★	Facilities: ★★★

Phoenix RV Park, located just off I-5 on the northeast side of Salem has the feel of a newly developed suburban community. The young campground occupies an L-shaped field of large paved sites surrounded by juvenile shrubs, small trees, and very well maintained grass. The sites come minus shade or privacy, but the convenient location more than makes up for this. The newly furbished, spacious, indoor facilities include two large laundry rooms and a kitchen. One would be hard pressed to find a campground with better access to Metropolitan Salem. The grocery store and RV service on either side of the grounds, as well as nearby bus routes only add to the park's convenient location. The campground is surrounded by privacy fencing and has night security. Sites 25-41 and 47-71 stay surprisingly quiet considering the urban location. The rec room has a Stairmaster, treadmill, two pinball games, and an assortment of jigsaw puzzles.

Basics

Operated By: Phoenix RV Park. **Open:** All year. **Site Assignment:** First come, first served; reservation (required deposit is1 night's stay; refund w/ 24-hours notice). **Registration:** At office, after hours at drop box outside office. **Fee:** $25; fee covers 2 people, extra person (age 3 or older) $2. **Parking:** At site.

Facilities

Number of RV-Only Sites: 107. **Number of Tent-Only Sites:** 0. **Hookups:** Electric (20, 30, 50 amps), water, sewer, cable. **Each Site:** Picnic table. **Dump Station:** No. **Laundry:** Yes. **Pay Phone:** Yes. **Rest Rooms and Showers:** Yes. **Fuel:** No. **Propane:** Yes. **Internal Roads:** Paved (wide). **RV Service:** No (next door). **Market:** Next door. **Restaurant:** 0.25 mi. east. **General Store:** Yes. **Vending:** Yes. **Swimming Pool:** No. **Playground:** Yes. **Other:** Multipurpose room. **Activities:** Watching traffic from park entrance. **Nearby Attractions:** State Capital, Silvercreek Falls, antique shops, Hallie Ford Museum of Art/Willamette University, Marion County Historical Society Museum. **Additional Information:** Salem Convention & Visitor's Assoc., (503) 581-4325 or (800) 874-7012.

Restrictions

Pets: On leash only (max. length 6 ft.), no fighting breeds; dogs over 25 lbs must be approved by mgmt. **Fires:** No open fires or charcoal. **Alcoholic Beverages:** At site. **Vehicle Maximum Length:** None. **Other:** No motor or generator usage, no fireworks or lethal weapons, no parking anywhere other than registered sites, no clotheslines, no business operations legal or otherwise without approval of mgmt.

To Get There

From I-5 Exit 256, drive 0.25 mi. east on Market St., then turn left on Lancaster Dr. Follow for 1.25 mi. then turn right onto Silverton Rd. Entrance is on the right after 1 block.

SALEM
Salem Campground and RV

3700 Hagers Grove Rd. Southeast, Salem 97301. T: (800) 826-9605 or (800) 825-9605; F: (503) 581-9945.

RV ★★★ Tent ★

Beauty: ★★	Site Privacy: ★
Spaciousness: ★★	Quiet: ★
Security: ★★	Cleanliness: ★★★
Insect Control: ★★	Facilities: ★★★

In the southeast corner of Salem, just off I-5 in what used to be a walnut grove, stands Salem Campground and RV. The convenient location consists of a grassy field with paved sites, and has some shade but no intersite privacy. The shade-providing trees consist primarily of poplar and walnut trees. Unfortunately walnut gathering can prove difficult as the local squirrels provide worthy competition with the winning advantages of reach and speed. The campground, which offers easy access to Cascade Gateway Park, features a swimming hole and a couple of fishing ponds. Tent sites sit on a beautifully flat, shady, grassy knoll. right next to the interstate. A grove of trees and the tent sites buffer much of the RV section from the interstate. The best RV sites are in areas A, B, C, D, E, and F; the sections D, E, and F have more shade but are closer to the interstate. Quieter sections A, B, and C have a good view of Home Depot. Sections G-K have smaller sites and lack visual appeal. Avoid them. Summers bring warmer weather, more metropolitan events, and crowds; visit during the late spring.

Basics

Operated By: Salem Campground and RVs. **Open:** All year. **Site Assignment:** first come first served; reservation (required deposit is 1 night's stay to guarantee space; refund w/ 48-hours notice). **Registration:** At office, after hours at drop box outside office. **Fee:** Full $21, water/electric $20, RV w/ no hookups $14, tent-only sites $15, fee covers 2 people, extra person (age 3 or older) $2;V, MC, D, cash. **Parking:** At site.

Facilities

Number of RV-Only Sites: 185. **Number of Tent-Only Sites:** 32. **Hookups:** Electric (20, 30, 50 amps), water, sewer, central data port. **Each Site:** Picnic table. **Dump Station:** Yes. **Laundry:** Yes. **Pay Phone:** Yes. **Rest Rooms and Showers:** Yes. **Fuel:** No. **Propane:** Yes. **Internal Roads:** Paved. **RV Service:** No. **Market:** 0.25 mile northwest. **Restaurant:** 0.25 mi. Northwest. **General Store:** Yes. **Vending:** Yes. **Swimming Pool:** No. **Playground:** Yes. **Other:** Basketball court, game room, trail under interstate to Cascade Park (has fishing, swimming). **Activities:** swimming, fishing in Cascade Park. **Nearby Attractions:** Adelman Peony Gardens, Oregon Garden, Bush House Museum, Jensen Arctic Museum, wineries. **Additional Information:** Salem Convention & Visitor's Assoc., (503) 581-4325 or (800) 874-7012.

Restrictions

Pets: On leash only, no fighting breeds. **Fires:** No open fires, charcoal in tent area only. **Alcoholic Beverages:** At site. **Vehicle Maximum Length:** None. **Other:** No repairing or washing of vehicles, no parking in grass, no tents in hookup sites, no laundry hanging, no tarps or canopies draped over RVs or cars.

To Get There

From I-5 Exit 253, drive 0.25 mi. west on Hwy. 22, then turn left on Lancaster Dr. Follow for 0.25 mi. and turn right on Hager's Grove Rd., which dead-ends into the park.

SISTERS

Black Butte Resort

25635 Southwest FSR 1419, Camp Sherman 97730. T: (541)595-6514 or (877)595-6514; F: (541) 595-5971; www.blackbutte-resort.com; almills@myexcel.com.

RV ★★★★ Tent ★★

Beauty: ★★★★	Site Privacy: ★
Spaciousness: ★★	Quiet: ★★★★
Security: ★	Cleanliness: ★★★★
Insect Control: ★★	Facilities: ★★★

Black Butte Resort, located west of Sisters off Hwy. 20, offers a serene setting within a resort community centered on fly-fishing and outdoor activities. The small campground consists of a grass field shaded by aspens, birch, and pine with a beautiful, unobstructed view of the butte providing the campground's name. Facilities are basic, but the campgrounds proximity to outdoor recreation and the cities of Sister and Bend, increase its appeal. Sites are distributed along both sides of a loop road. The best of the gravel and dirt sites sit on the back perimeter, numbered 3–8, with lots of shade but no view of the butte. Nearby are a reservation-only five star restaurant and a general store with a small selection of quality wines. No-hookup sites 23 and 24 A and B are less spacious back-ins, but have the best views of the nearby butte.

Basics

Operated By: Black Butte Resort. **Open:** All year. **Site Assignment:** On arrival, reservation (required deposit is 1 night's stay; refund w/ 14-days notice). **Registration:** At office, after hours pay in morning. **Fee:** Full $24, water/electric $19, dump station use $5; fee covers 2 people, extra person (age 6 or older) $3. **Parking:** At site.

FACILITIES

Number of RV-Only Sites: 31. **Number of Tent-Only Sites:** 0. **Hookups:** Electric (30, 50 amps), water, sewer. **Each Site:** Picnic table. **Dump Station:** Yes. **Laundry:** Yes. **Pay Phone:** No. **Rest Rooms and Showers:** Yes. **Fuel:** No. **Propane:** No. **Internal Roads:** Gravel. **RV Service:** No. **Market:** 0.1 mile east (Well stocked convenience store). **Restaurant:** 0.1 mi. east (5 star, reservations only). **General Store:** No. **Vending:** No. **Swimming Pool:** No. **Playground:** No. **Other:** Horseshoe pit, meeting room (w/ kitchen, electric organ), book & game loans. **Activities:** Hiking, biking (trails across road from park). **Nearby Attractions:** Deshutes National Forest, hiking, fishing, boating, city of Sisters, city of Bend, horseback riding, Sisters Rodeo. **Additional Information:** Sisters Area Chamber of Commerce, (541) 549-0251.

RESTRICTIONS

Pets: On leash only. **Fires:** Fire pits only. **Alcoholic Beverages:** At site. **Vehicle Maximum Length:** 40 ft. (call if over 40 for availability). **Other:** Laundry closed Sundays from noon to 4 p.m.

TO GET THERE

From Hwy. 20 westbound, turn right on Forest service road marked Camp Sherman-Metolius River. This turn is located between mile 91 and 92 about 15 minutes west of Sisters. Follow this road for 2.5 miles, when road forks take the left fork and drive 2.6 miles on FR 1419. This road continues through a stop, goes right at the stop sign. The park entrance is on the right.

SISTERS

Mountain Shadow RV Park

540 Hwy. 20 West, Sisters 97759. T: (541)549-7275

RV: ★★★ Tent: n/a

Beauty: ★★	Site Privacy: ★
Spaciousness: ★★	Quiet: ★★
Security: ★★★	Cleanliness: ★★★★
Insect Control: ★★	Facilities: ★★

Mountain Shadow RV Park on Hwy. 20 sits just east of the quaint town of Sisters adjacent to a Comfort Inn. The park is laid out in several sets of parallel rows, plus sites around the perimeter of, a very flat field. The newer park lacks shade, privacy, or views, but has well maintained facilities, easily navigable access roads, an indoor pool, and possibly the largest rest rooms of any RV park in Oregon. Tenting is not allowed within the park. All sites have full hookups with nightly phone service available for an extra fee. The best of the paved, grass-bordered sites, back-ins numbered 1–16 and 76–84, are on the boundary of the park. Mountain Shadow also has some exceptionally long pull-throughs, numbered 60-75. Avoid the trailer-city like setting of back-in sites 17–42. Since the park is open year-round, those willing to camp in the winter can sample a variety of snow sports nearby.

BASICS

Operated By: Choice Hotels, inc. **Open:** All year. **Site Assignment:** On arrival, reservation (required deposit is 1 night's stay; refund w/ 24-hours notice). **Registration:** At office, after hours pay in morning. **Fee:** $27.95, phone add $3; fee covers 3 adults, extra adult $3; D, AM, V, MC, cash. **Parking:** At site.

FACILITIES

Number of RV-Only Sites: 105. **Number of Tent-Only Sites:** 0. **Hookups:** Electric (20, 30, 50 amps), water, sewer, cable, phone. **Each Site:** Picnic table, grill riser. **Dump Station:** No. **Laundry:** Yes. **Pay Phone:** Yes. **Rest Rooms and Showers:** Yes. **Fuel:** No. **Propane:** No. **Internal Roads:** Paved. **RV Service:** No. **Market:** 2 mi. east. **Restaurant:** Next door. **General Store:** No. **Vending:** Yes. **Swimming Pool:** Yes. **Playground:** No. **Other:** Hot tub, wading pool, meeting/TV room w/ kitchen, horseshoes, 2 covered picnic pavilions. **Activities:** Swimming. **Nearby Attractions:** Paintball, Rock Climbing, rafting, boating, pretty much anything related to outdoor sports Bend or Sisters has it, Deshutes Brewing Company (Bend), horseback riding, Sisters Rodeo (first weekend in Jun.). **Additional Information:** Sisters Area Chamber of Commerce, (541) 549-0251.

RESTRICTIONS

Pets: On leash only. **Fires:** Off ground in portable fire place, grills only. **Alcoholic Beverages:** At site.

Vehicle Maximum Length: None. **Other:** Rest rooms closed between 10 p.m.–7 a.m.

To Get There

Located on Hwy. 20, 1 mi. northeast of Sisters; entrance is on left if driving northbound.

SISTERS

Riverside Campground

P.O. Box 249, Sisters 97759. T: (541) 549-7700

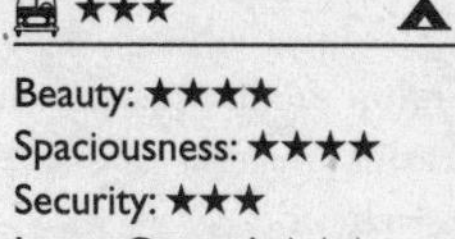

★★★ ★★★

Beauty: ★★★★	Site Privacy: ★★★
Spaciousness: ★★★★	Quiet: ★★★★
Security: ★★★	Cleanliness: ★★★
Insect Control: ★★★	Facilities: ★★★

Ah, the magical and mysterious Metolius. Welling up clear and bright from a tiny underground spring at the base of Black Butte, the river provides one of the finest trout habitats around before emptying into Lake Billy Chinook. The number of campgrounds on or near the Metolius is staggering, and are there primarily to serve the abundance of anglers. In addition to Riverside, there are Camp Sherman, Allingham, Smiling River, Pine Rest, Gorge, Allen Springs, Pioneer Ford, and Lower Bridge. Dominating the landscape in various stages of geologic splendor are the snowcapped peaks to the west. In order from north to south, they are Mount Jefferson, Mount Washington, North Sister, Middle Sister, South Sister, and last but not least even with its forlorn name, Broken Top. Highlights of a stay at Riverside Campground include short walks to Metolius Spring and Jack Creek Spring, the Metolius River Canyon near Camp Sherman, and the Wizard Falls Fish Hatchery.

Basics

Operated By: Concessionaire. **Open:** Apr.–Oct. **Site Assignment:** First come, first served, no reservations. **Registration:** self-registration on site. **Fee:** $8. **Parking:** At access road, about 200–400 yards from the campground.

Facilities

Number of RV-Only Sites: 16. **Number of Tent-Only Sites:** 0. **Hookups:** No. **Each Site:** Picnic table, fire grill. **Dump Station:** No. **Laundry:** No. **Pay Phone:** No. **Rest Rooms and Showers:** Vault toilets. **Fuel:** No. **Propane:** No. **Internal Roads:** Call ahead for details. **RV Service:** No. **Market:** No. **Restaurant:** No. **General Store:** No. **Vending:** No. **Swimming Pool:** No. **Playground:** No. **Activities:** Fishing, biking, hiking. **Nearby Attractions:** Mountains, lakes. **Additional Information:** Information: (541) 549-2111.

Restrictions

Pets: On leash only. **Fires:** In fire rings only. **Alcoholic Beverages:** Allowed. **Vehicle Maximum Length:** 21 ft. **Other:** 14 day limit on stay.

To Get There

Take SR 126/US 20 (Santiam Hwy.) north of Sisters to its intersection with FS 14 (Camp Sherman Rd.). Turn right, and follow FS 14 around the base of Black Butte to FS 900. The camp is less than 1 mi. north on this road.

SISTERS

Sisters/Bend KOA

67667 Hwy. 20 West, Bend 97701. T: (541) 549-3021 or reservations (800)562-0363; F: (541) 549-8144.

★★★★ ★★★

Beauty: ★★★★	Site Privacy: ★★
Spaciousness: ★★	Quiet: ★★★
Security: ★★	Cleanliness: ★★★★
Insect Control: ★★	Facilities: ★★★★

From the frontal appearance, Sisters/Bend KOA located on Hwy. 20 doesn't look very attractive. But upon closer examination, one finds quality facilities. Within the grounds there is an eclectically themed nine-hole mini-golf course, a pool with a beautiful surrounding deck, and a movie room complete with the biggest of big screen TVs and surround sound. The office/store also rents DVDs and videocassettes. In the camping area one finds many low juniper trees, adding a musty, pine fragrance to the air. Some areas have grass, but for the most part there is little cover. Sites are arranged in parallel rows. The full hookup area consists of gravel surfaces; tent sites 17–19 and 5–8 have grass while 92–100 have dirt surfaces. Avoid tent sites 92–94 as they sit near a road; the general overflow area also sits near Hwy. 20. Sites afford little privacy or shade.

Basics

Operated By: Sisters/Bend KOA. **Open:** Closed Jan.–Feb. **Site Assignment:** On arrival, reservation (required deposit is 1 night's stay; refund less $10 service charge: 24-hours notice. **Registration:** At office, after hours drop located out front of office. **Fee:** Full $29,water/electric $28, dry $25; fee covers 2 people, extra adult $9, children 4–17 $2, students 18–20 $3; extra vehicle $1;V, MC, cash. **Parking:** At site.

Facilities

Number of RV-Only Sites: 100. **Number of Tent-Only Sites:** 20. **Hookups:** Electric (20, 30, 50 amps), water, sewer. **Each Site:** Picnic table, fire ring (overflow section lacks these). **Dump Station:** Yes. **Laundry:** Yes. **Pay Phone:** Yes. **Rest Rooms and Showers:** Yes. **Fuel:** No. **Propane:** Yes. **Internal Roads:** Gravel. **RV Service:** No. **Market:** 4 mi. west in Sisters. **Restaurant:** 4 mi. west in Sisters. **General Store:** Yes. **Vending:** Yes. **Swimming Pool:** Yes. **Playground:** Yes. **Other:** 9-hole mini golf, ping pong, volleyball, basketball, spa, movie room, fishing pond, movie/DVD rental, deli. **Activities:** Swimming, fishing, nightly movies. **Nearby Attractions:** Sisters Rodeo (first weekend Jun.), Camp Sherman, fly-fishing, rafting, horseback riding, hiking, Deshutes National Forest, Bend. **Additional Information:** Sisters Area Chamber of Commerce, (541) 549-0251.

Restrictions

Pets: On leash only, not allowed on grass & some sections of park. **Fires:** Fire pits only. **Alcoholic Beverages:** At site. **Vehicle Maximum Length:** None. **Other:** Tie dogs to own RV only, must be attended.

To Get There

Located 3 mi. southeast of Sisters on Hwy. 20; westbound, entrance on left.

STANFIELD

Pilot RV Park

2125 Hwy. 395 South, Stanfield 97875. T: (541) 779-2136

RV: ★★ Tent: n/a

Beauty: ★ Site Privacy: ★
Spaciousness: ★★★ Quiet: ★★
Security: ★★★ Cleanliness: ★★★★
Insect Control: ★★ Facilities: ★

Pilot RV in Stanfield has convenient access from the interstate and all the truckin'-culture a camper could ever want, but little else. As a place to pull in late and leave early, Pilot RV works perfectly. The campground has perimeter fencing and sits adjacent to a truck stop providing limited, but always open, services. Because of it's location, ambient noise does exist but nothing of the magnitude of, say, an RV park in north-central Portland. The sites themselves have flat, paved surfaces and wide, grass borders but no shade or privacy. Though the park is open year-round, be mindful that in this region winters often bring freezing weather and the peak of summer can be sweltering.

Basics

Operated By: Pilot RV. **Open:** All year. **Site Assignment:** On arrival, reservation. **Registration:** At office or self pay station. **Fee:** Full $18; fee covers 2 people, extra person $5;V, MC, cash. **Parking:** At site.

Facilities

Number of RV-Only Sites: 40. **Number of Tent-Only Sites:** 0. **Hookups:** Electric (20, 30, 50 amps), water, sewer, cable. **Each Site:** Picnic table. **Dump Station:** Yes. **Laundry:** Yes. **Pay Phone:** Yes. **Rest Rooms and Showers:** Yes. **Fuel:** Yes. **Propane:** No. **Internal Roads:** Paved. **RV Service:** No. **Market:** North on Hwy. 395. **Restaurant:** North on Hwy. 395. **General Store:** Yes. **Vending:** Yes. **Swimming Pool:** No. **Playground:** No. **Other:** Truck stop. **Activities:** Inquire at campground. **Nearby Attractions:** Pendleton. **Additional Information:** Pendleton Chamber of Commerce, (541) 276-7411.

Restrictions

Pets: On leash only. **Fires:** No fires. **Alcoholic Beverages:** At site. **Vehicle Maximum Length:** 40 ft.

To Get There

From I-90 Exit 188, drive north to Pilot Station

WARM SPRINGS

Kah Nee Ta Resort

P.O.Box K, Warm Springs 97761. T: (541) 553-1112 or (800) 554-4SUN; F: (541) 553-1071; www.Kah-Nee-TaResort.com; margos@bendnet.com.

RV ★★★★★ Tent n/a

Beauty: ★★★★ Site Privacy: ★
Spaciousness: ★★ Quiet: ★★★★
Security: ★★★★★ Cleanliness: ★★★★★
Insect Control: ★★ Facilities: ★★★★★

Ka-Nee-Ta resort, twenty minutes east of Warm Springs, is among the best destination parks in the Northwest. An astounding array of recreational activities operated under the resort's dominion, and shuttles every half hour to move visitors to and fro, provide plenty of incentive for an extended stay. Facilities include a top-notch health spa, an enormous pool, a water slide, horse stables with trail rides, and a casino; the facilities are well maintained and frequently crowded. No tents are allowed on the property, but the RV section has 51 flat, paved, full hookup spaces. The only slightly unattractive sites are number 18-26 (even numbers only) for their lack of surrounding grass. The rest have nice grassy areas, well manicured and creating an oasis-like feel in the middle of the high desert. Unfortunately there is little shade. Without an RV, lodging options include a hotel and concrete-floored tepees (your own bedding is required for the latter). Early summer provides the most opportune time to visit, August especially can reach temperatures up to and over 100 degrees Fahrenheit.

Basics

Operated By: Confederated Tribes of Warm Springs. **Open:** All year. **Site Assignment:** On arrival, reservation (required deposit is 1 night's stay; refund w/ 72-hours). **Registration:** At office (village gate); after hours at lodge front desk. **Fee:** Full $38, tepee $70 ($50 refundable deposit on tepees); fee covers 2 people plus 1 unit & 1 car, extra person (age 7 or older) $6, extra vehicle $5; 2 night min. on weekends, 3 on holidays; V, MC, AE, D, check, cash. **Parking:** At site, limited off site.

Facilities

Number of RV-Only Sites: 51. **Number of Tent-Only Sites:** 0. **Hookups:** Electric (30, 50 amps), water, sewer, cable. **Each Site:** None. **Dump Station:** Yes. **Laundry:** Yes. **Pay Phone:** Yes. **Rest Rooms and Showers:** Yes. **Fuel:** No. **Propane:** Yes. **Internal Roads:** Paved. **RV Service:** No. **Market:** 11 mi. west in Warm Springs. **Restaurant:** 1 mi. east at resort lodge. **General Store:** Yes. **Vending:** Yes. **Swimming Pool:** Yes. **Playground:** Yes. **Other:** Arcade, mini-golf ($6 adults, $3 kids & seniors), basketball, picnic pavilion (small), huge pool, water slide, 2 small spas, kiddie pool, golf course, horseback riding ($20/person), kayaking trips ($20/person), tennis, bike rentals, shuttles around resort every half hour, arts & crafts, planned activities, volleyball, full service health spa, Indian Head Casino, gear rentals for most activities. **Activities:** Hiking, biking, horseback riding, swimming, relaxing, kayaking, gambling. **Nearby Attractions:** Outside of the resort, not much save National Forests, Native Cultural Events & Museum at Warm Springs. **Additional Information:** Ka Nee Ta Resort, (541) 553-1112.

Restrictions

Pets: On leash only (campground only). **Fires:** Pits only. **Alcoholic Beverages:** In areas where children are not present. **Vehicle Maximum Length:** 73 ft. **Other:** Be culturally sensitive; Fires here can get out of hand very quickly, keep even cigarette butts under control.

To Get There

From Hwy. 26 West in Warm Springs, turn right on Rte. 3 (marked with a big Kah-Nee-Tah sign, just after Texaco, westbound). Drive 10 mi. on Rte. 3; at bottom of a hill with lots of switchbacks, turn right onto Rte. 8 (marked with a large Kah-Nee-Tah sign). Drive 1.5 mi. and the entrance is on the right. There is an alternate route about 15 minutes northwest of Warm Springs that ends up in the same place and is marked in a similar way.

WINCHESTER BAY

Eel Creek Campground

855 Hwy. 101, Reedsport 97467. T: (541) 271-3611; www.reserveusa.com.

RV ★★★★ Tent ★★★★

Beauty: ★★★★★ Site Privacy: ★★★★★
Spaciousness: ★★★★ Quiet: ★★★★★
Security: ★★★★ Cleanliness: ★★★★
Insect Control: ★★★ Facilities: ★★★

Eel Creek is just one of many campgrounds that are clustered in the Florence/Reedsport/Coos

Bay stretch of US 101. Heavy vegetation helps absorb traffic sounds and provides lovely secluded, sandy-bottomed sites. Though no sires are designated "tent-only," tenters are free to choose from among the campgrounds all-purpose sites. Ocean breezes help keep insects to a minimum. Aside from its vegetation-lush private sites, Eel Creek's strongest selling point is the absence of off-road vehicle access to the dunes. If you want peace and quiet as part of your dunes experience, make sure you're not hiking in an area where they rent dune buggies. Eel Creek backs up against some of the largest dunes in the 46-mile-long protected beach. Always shifting, always changing, there are dunes that reach as high as 600 feet. Slog your way to the top of one of these monsters and look out over a most spectacular sight. Headquarters for Oregon Dunes National Recreation Area is right on US 101 at the junction of State Rte. 38 in Reedsport. This is a well-stocked information bureau. The exhibits are worth a look, too.

Basics

Operated By: Siuslaw National Forest, Oregon Dunes National Recreation Area. **Open:** May 14–Sept. 15. **Site Assignment:** First come, first served; reservation during the summer. **Registration:** self-registration or camp host collects. **Fee:** $13. **Parking:** At site.

Facilities

Number of Multipurpose Sites: 52. **Number of RV-Only Sites:** 0. **Number of Tent-Only Sites:** 0. **Hookups:** No. **Each Site:** Picnic table, fire grill. **Dump Station:** No. **Laundry:** No. **Pay Phone:** No. **Rest Rooms and Showers:** Yes. **Fuel:** No. **Propane:** No. **Internal Roads:** Call ahead for details. **RV Service:** No. **Market:** No. **Restaurant:** No. **General Store:** No. **Vending:** No. **Swimming Pool:** No. **Playground:** No. **Activities:** Hiking, beach. **Nearby Attractions:** Dean Creek Elk Viewing Area. **Additional Information:** Information: (541) 271-3611.

Restrictions

Pets: On leash only. **Fires:** In fire rings only. **Alcoholic Beverages:** Allowed. **Vehicle Maximum Length:** 35 ft.

To Get There

From Reedsport, drive south on US 101 for 12 mi. The campground entrance is on the ocean side.

YACHATS

Cape Perpetua Scenic Area

P.O. Box 274, Yachats 97498. T: (541) (563) 3211

 ★★★ ▲ ★★★

Beauty: ★★★★★	Site Privacy: ★★
Spaciousness: ★★★	Quiet: ★★★★
Security: ★★★★	Cleanliness: ★★★★
Insect Control: ★★★★	Facilities: ★★★

Both Cape Perpetua and the nearby town of Yachats (pronounced yah hots) have long been the vacation destination favored by Oregonians who choose the small town's relative seclusion amidst some of the coast's most awe-inspiring scenery. The Cape Perpetua Campground is actually two campgrounds managed by the Forest Service (as is the rest of the Scenic Area). Both are quite close to the Visitor Center, and the only difference between them is that one is an individual-site complex and the other accommodates groups of up to 50 people. Privacy is not great—mostly provided by spruce with little ground cover. On the other hand, the ocean breezes blow right through and keep insects to a minimum. Cape Perpetua is an enormously popular whale-watching spot in the wintertime. Although the campgrounds are not open, the visitor center has interpretive programs for the whale-watching crowd. The Cape Perpetua Viewpoint 800 feet above the sea provides a bird's-eye look in all directions over this breathtaking panorama.

Basics

Operated By: Concessionaire, under contract w/ Siuslaw National Forest. **Open:** May–Oct. **Site Assignment:** First come, first served, no reservations. **Registration:** self registration on site. **Fee:** $12–$14. **Parking:** At site.

Facilities

Number of RV-Only Sites: 38. **Number of Tent-Only Sites:** 0. **Hookups:** No. **Each Site:**

Picnic table, fire grill, electricity. **Dump Station:** No. **Laundry:** No. **Pay Phone:** Yes. **Rest Rooms and Showers:** Yes. **Fuel:** No. **Propane:** No. **Internal Roads:** Call ahead for details. **RV Service:** No. **Market:** No. **Restaurant:** No. **General Store:** No. **Vending:** No. **Swimming Pool:** No. **Playground:** No. **Other:** Group camping. **Activities:** Hiking, biking, tide pool walks. **Nearby Attractions:** Visitor's center, whale-watching, Devil's Churn, Captain Cook's Chasm. **Additional Information:** Information: (541) 563-3211.

RESTRICTIONS

Pets: On leash only. **Fires:** In fire rings only. **Alcoholic Beverages:** Allowed. **Vehicle Maximum Length:** 22 ft.

TO GET THERE

From Yachats, drive 3 mi. south on US 101. The entrance is on the non- ocean side.

South Dakota

Located in the north-central part of the United States, South Dakota is generally considered part of the Midwest. The east part of the state, with its flat or rolling soils, resembles the landscape of other states in the Midwest, while the western section lies on the Great Plains. South Dakota is filled campgrounds that take advantage of its magnificent scenery, rich natural resources, and varied wildlife.

The state's largest cities are **Sioux Falls; Rapid City,** which serves as the center of the state's resort area; and **Pierre,** where city and country collide. The Missouri River divides the state into its two major regions. The other major river is Big Sioux River. South Dakota is covered with countless other rivers and lakes providing limitless opportunities to enjoy fishing and boating.

While the bulk of South Dakota's population lies in the east, the crown jewels of the state are clearly in the southwestern part, though beautiful spots exist throughout the state. The **Badlands** and **Black Hills** typically draw the most tourists. The Black Hills are a region of deeply eroded gullies of colorful, fantastic shapes. Within are five national parks, waterfalls, abundant wildlife, acclaimed recreational trails, and trout fishing. Bison and wild horses still roam free here. The **Black Hills Caverns** and **Black Hill Maze** offer great fun for families. **Badlands National Park** is a 244,000-acre park of spires, pinnacles, buttes, and gorges. This gorgeous area was created by millions of years of erosion.

Other intriguing places include **Mt. Rushmore National Memorial,** which has the stone-carved faces of four U.S. presidents; **Jewel Cave National Monument; Wind Cave National Park,** one of the oldest caves in the world; and **Dell Rapids,** known for its beautiful scenery. One can also spend time at **Buffalo Gap** or **Grand River National Grasslands,** regions set aside to protect the state's complex ecosystem. **The Corn Palace** in **Mitchell** is a unique building that celebrates the state's rich agriculture. Finally, the state boasts of being the home of "Sue," the world famous T-rex fossil.

The state's national forests, national parks, and state parks all have facilities for camping, fishing, picnicking, and hunting. The weather is definitely a matter of extremes—cold, long winters and hot summers.

The following facilities accept payment in checks or cash only:

Mystery Mt. Resort, Rapid City

Campground Profiles

BROOKINGS

Oakwood Lakes State Park

46109 202nd St., Bruce 57220. T: (605) 627-5441; F: (605) 627-5258; www.state.sd.us/gfp/sdparks; oakwoodstp@gfp.state.sd.us.

RV ★★★★ Tent ★★★★

Beauty: ★★★★	Site Privacy: ★★★★
Spaciousness: ★★★★	Quiet: ★★★★
Security: ★★★★	Cleanliness: ★★★★
Insect Control: ★★★	Facilities: ★★

Located where Native Americans once gathered for summer camp, Oakwood Lakes State Park presents a small piece of early American history in a beautiful scenic setting. Level, asphalted camping pads under a canopy of trees make for a relaxing getaway. Within a stone's throw away are eight glacial lakes that are excellent for all water sports. In addition, there are miles of hiking trails, three Native American burial grounds, and the restored cabin of the first settler in the area, Samuel Mortimer. The campground is set in a figure-eight configuration, with most sites being back-ins. There are a limited number of pull-through sites. There is also a horse camp for those wishing to travel with their horses. Summer days average in the 80s, with nights cooling to the 50s. June is an excellent time to visit, before the bugs hatch. There is an employee in residence in addition to a camp host, offering the best of security.

BASICS

Operated By: South Dakota Game, Fish, & Parks Dept. **Open:** All year; water turned off in winter. **Site Assignment:** By reservation (800) 710-CAMP. **Registration:** At entrance booth. **Fee:** $10–$13 per camping unit (no more than 2 units per site) plus entrance fee. **Parking:** At site.

FACILITIES

Number of RV-Only Sites: 0. **Number of Tent-Only Sites:** 0. **Number of Multipurpose Sites:** 69. **Hookups:** Electric (20, 30 amps), potable water. **Each Site:** Picnic table, grated fire pits. **Dump Station:** Yes. **Laundry:** No. **Pay Phone:** Yes. **Rest Rooms and Showers:** Yes. **Fuel:** No. **Propane:** No. **Internal Roads:** Paved. **RV Service:** 17 mi. southeast in Brookings. **Market:** In Brookings. **Restaurant:** In Brookings. **General Store:** No. **Vending:** No. **Swimming Pool:** No, however there is a riverfront beach for swimming. **Playground:** Yes. **Other:** Boat ramp, picnic shelters w/ grills, amphitheater, cabins, 2 group camp areas, hiking trail, interpretive shelter, visitor center, canoe rentals. **Activities:** Water & snow skiing, boating, swimming, interpretive programs, hiking, fishing (walleye, northerns, bass), volleyball, weekly park programs, hay rides, junior naturalist program, Sunday worship services. **Nearby Attractions:** State Agricultural Heritage Museum, McCrory Gardens. **Additional Information:** South Dakota State Parks, (605) 773-3391 or Brookings Chamber of Commerce, (605) 692-6125.

RESTRICTIONS

Pets: On leash. **Fires:** In fire pits only; fires may be restricted due to weather conditions; please ask management before starting any open fires. **Alcoholic Beverages:** Yes. **Vehicle Maximum Length:** None. **Other:** 14-day stay limit.

TO GET THERE

From I-29 7 mi. north of Brookings, take Exit 140. Go west on Hwy. 30 (this will turn into CR 6) about 10 mi.; you will see a large sign for Oakwood Lake State Park. Turn north and follow signs to the campground.

CUSTER

Custer Mountain Cabins and Campground

P.O. Box 472, Custer 57730. T: (800) 239-5505 or (605) 673-5440; www.rapidnet.com/~phn.

RV ★★★ Tent ★★★★

Beauty: ★★★★★	Site Privacy: ★★★
Spaciousness: ★★★	Quiet: ★★★★★
Security: ★★★★	Cleanliness: ★★★★
Insect Control: ★★★	Facilities: ★★

Custer Mountain Cabins and Campground is an exquisite private facility. It offers deluxe modern cabins and a charming campground nestled deep in the Black Hills, two miles east of Custer. The Black Hills offer breathtaking scenic drives, wonderful wildlife, Custer State Park, and Mt. Rushmore. The campground is situated on 50 acres of pristine land encircled by stands of black hill spruces. The RV area is located in a loop near the front of the grounds, and it has both pull-through and back-in sites. Each site has a gravel camping pad, but expect to have to level it out. Large tent sites can be found among the trees, giving tent campers more seclusion and privacy. The air is crisp in the morning, and summer days are pleasant. Visitors can experience a vast array of recreational and historic activities. Inviting hosts are available to assist you with all your vacation needs.

Basics

Operated By: Paul Nordstrom. **Open:** All year; water is turned off in winter. **Site Assignment:** By reservations; deposit required for cabins only. **Registration:** In general store. **Fee:** Tents $17, RV $23 per unit. **Parking:** At site.

Facilities

Number of RV-Only Sites: 21. **Number of Tent-Only Sites:** 40. **Hookups:** Electric (30, 50 amps), water, sewer, cable. **Each Site:** Picnic table, some fire pits. **Dump Station:** Yes. **Laundry:** Yes. **Pay Phone:** Yes. **Rest Rooms and Showers:** Yes. **Fuel:** 2 mi. in Custer. **Propane:** 2 mi. in Custer. **Internal Roads:** Gravel, w/ some bumps. **RV Service:** There is a mobile service based out of Rapid City. **Market:** 2 mi. in Custer. **Restaurant:** 2 mi. in Custer or in Custer State Park. **General Store:** Yes. **Vending:** General store only. **Swimming Pool:** No. **Playground:** Yes. **Other:** Very nice cabins & summer vacation homes. **Activities:** Large open recreation field, hiking, biking. **Nearby Attractions:** Custer State Park, Flinstone Village, Mt. Rushmore. **Additional Information:** Custer Chamber of Commerce, (605) 673-2244.

Restrictions

Pets: In campsites only, not in cabins. **Fires:** In designated fire pits or grills only; fires may be restricted due to weather conditions; please ask management before starting any open fires. **Alcoholic Beverages:** Yes. **Vehicle Maximum Length:** None.

To Get There

The campground is 2 mi. east of Custer on Hwy. 16A.

CUSTER

Custer State Park

HC 83, Box 70, Custer 57730. T: (605) 255-4515; F: (605) 255-4460; www.state.sd.us/sdparks or www.custerresorts.com; craig.pugsley@state.sd.us or e-mail@custerresorts.com.

RV ★★★ Tent ★★★★

Beauty: ★★★★	Site Privacy: ★★★
Spaciousness: ★★★	Quiet: ★★★★
Security: ★★★★	Cleanliness: ★★★
Insect Control: ★★★	Facilities: ★★

Custer State Park is a 73,000-acre resort in the heart of the Black Hills. Created in 1913 as a game reserve, this magnificent park has become world-renowned as a showcase of the area's natural resources and wildlife. The park was named after George A. Custer, who was enthralled by the region's uncommon natural beauty. The park has eight campgrounds, including a horse camp where your equine friend is more than welcome. The majority of the campgrounds have level asphalt camping pads, potable water, laundry, evening programs, fishing, and nearby swimming. Most of the campgrounds are arranged in loops, many with sites overlooking streams, mountains, or forests. The state park works in conjunction with Custer State Park Resort Co. to offer restaurant service, group events, jeep tours, and other additional activities. There are hiking and biking trails throughout the park, as well as excellent trout fishing. The weather is typical of the area, experiencing warm summer days and cooling in the evening. The park has very tight security, and all vehicles are required to have a park license obtainable at any entrance gate.

Basics

Operated By: South Dakota Dept. of Game, Fish & Parks. **Open:** All year. **Site Assignment:** By reservation (800) 710-2267. **Registration:** At the information station, located at the entrance to each campground. **Fee:** $12–$14 depending on which of Custers' campground you choose, plus a gate fee. **Parking:** At site.

Facilities

Number of Multipurpose Sites: There are 26–71 sites per campground, 354 total sites. **Hookups:** Potable water. **Each Site:** Picnic table, grated fire pits. **Dump Station:** Yes, it is located just east of the Game Lodge Resort in the maintenance complex. **Laundry:** Yes, located in Blue Bell, Game Lodge, Grace Coolidge, & Sylvan Lake. **Pay Phone:** Yes, in service area & most camping areas. **Rest Rooms and Showers:** Yes. **Fuel:** Yes, located near Blue Bell, Grace Lodge, Grace Coolidge. **Propane:** No, but in Custer. **Internal Roads:** Most roads are paved. **RV Service:** In Custer. **Market:** Sylvan Lake General Store, within the park. **Restaurant:** There are serval places to eat within the park. **General Store:** There are 3 general stores, Coolidge, Sylvan Lake, Blue Bell. **Vending:** Soft drinks. **Swimming Pool:** No, however there are 4 park beaches: Center Lake, Legion Lake, Sylvan Lake, & the Game Lodge Pond; life jackets are advised, & jumping from cliffs & rocks is strictly prohibited. **Playground:** No. **Other:** Cabins, Peter Norbeck Visitor Center, Wildlife Station Visitor Center, Black Hills Play House, 3 chapels, several restaurants, Sylvan Auditorium, mountain bike rentals, boat rentals, art gallery. **Activities:** Horseback riding, fishing (perch, crappie, bullhead, walleye, bass), boating, 4 swimming beaches, family evening programs, guided nature walks, gold panning, junior naturalist programs, interpretive trails, special events, scenic drives, Buffalo Safari Jeep Rides, Black Hills Playhouse, mountain biking. **Nearby Attractions:** Mt. Rushmore, scenic drives, Crazy Horse Memorial, natural hot springs, rodeos, shopping, museums. **Additional Information:** Custer Chamber of Commerce; (605) 673-2244; for tickets to the Black Hills Playhouse, (605) 255-4141 or www.blackhillsplayhouse.com.

Restrictions

Pets: On Leash. **Fires:** In fire pits only; fires may be restricted due to weather conditions; please ask management before starting any open fires. **Alcoholic Beverages:** Yes. **Vehicle Maximum Length:** None. **Other:** 14-day stay limit.

To Get There

There are 7 entrances into this park. It is 22.3 mi. from Rapid City following Hwy. 16A south, 10.2 mi. from Hermosa following Hwy. 36 west, or you may take the scenic Needles Hwy. Most all of the campgrounds are located directly off Hwy. 16A inside the park boundaries.

GARRETSON

Palisades State Park

25495 485th Ave., Garretson 57030. T: (605) 594-3824; F: (605) 594-2369; www.state.sd.us/gfp/sdparks; palisades@gfp.state.sd.us.

RV: ★★★★ Tent: ★★★★★

Beauty: ★★★★★	Site Privacy: ★★★★
Spaciousness: ★★★★	Quiet: ★★★★
Security: ★★★★	Cleanliness: ★★★★
Insect Control: ★★	Facilities: ★★★

Palisades State Park is nestled in a unique landscape of quartzite spires cut by Split Rock Creek. It has become famous for its geological wonders and legends of the infamous Jessie James eluding a posse through Devils Gulch. Palisade State Park is located near Garretson, which has a history as unique as the land. The campground is a large loop, with both back-in and pull-through sites. The sites are spaced for optimal privacy, each with a paved parking pad and a spectacular view. The campground is well shaded with a variety of foliage. Many of the sites overlook Split Rock Creek and the magnificent quartzite spires. Palisade State Park is known for its rock climbing, and many climbers practice their scaling and rappelling. Like most of South Dakota summers, temperatures here average in the 80s, and it tends to be dry. Palisade State Park has around-the-clock security with a manager in residence.

Basics

Operated By: South Dakota Fish, Game, & Parks Dept. **Open:** All year; water may be turned off in winter. **Site Assignment:** By reservation (800) 710-CAMP. **Registration:** At the entrance gate-of the park. **Fee:** $10 no hookup, $13 w/ electric. **Parking:** At site.

Facilities

Number of Multipurpose Sites: 36. **Hookups:** Electric (20, 30 amps), potable water. **Each Site:** Picnic table, grated fire pits. **Dump Station:** Yes. **Laundry:** No. **Pay Phone:** Yes. **Rest Rooms and Showers:** Yes. **Fuel:** No. **Propane:** No. **Internal Roads:** Paved. **RV Service:** 15 mi. southwest in Sioux Falls. **Market:** Garretson or Sioux Falls. **Restaurant:** Garrettson or Sioux Falls. **General Store:** No. **Vending:** Yes. **Swimming Pool:** No. **Playground:** Yes. **Other:** Picnic area, cabins, amphitheater, 3 trails, pavilions, 1.2 billion-year-old Sioux quartzite spires, 1908 historic bridge. **Activities:** Guided hikes, summer weekend recreation programs, junior naturalist program & ECHOES program, repelling & rock climbing, fishing, s& volleyball, horseshoes. **Nearby Attractions:** Golf, Sioux Falls, Devil's Gulch, Great Plains Zoo, Jesse James River Runs (pontoon rides). **Additional Information:** Garretson Chamber of Commerce, (605) 594-6721.

Restrictions

Pets: On leash only. **Fires:** In fire pits only; fires may be restricted due to weather conditions; please ask management before starting any open fires. **Alcoholic Beverages:** Yes. **Vehicle Maximum Length:** None. **Other:** 14-day stay limit; limit of 6 people per camping site.

To Get There

From I-90 take Exit 406, go north on Hwy. 11 for 8.5 mi. then turn right and follow the signs into the park.

GETTYSBURG

West Whitlock Recreation Area

HC 3, Box 73A, Gettysburg 57442. T: (605)765-9410; F: (605) 765-2747; www.state.sd.us/gfp/sdparks/whitlock/whitlock.htm; whitlockrec@state.sd.us.

 ★★★ ▲ ★★★

Beauty: ★★★ Site Privacy: ★★★
Spaciousness: ★★★ Quiet: ★★★★
Security: ★★★★ Cleanliness: ★★★
Insect Control: ★★★ Facilities: ★★

Twenty-two miles west of Gettysburg in South Dakota's Great Lake Region, West Whitlock Recreation Area is situated on the Lake Oahe Reservoir. First explored by Lewis and Clark, this area is a small, hidden treasure and a sportsman's sanctuary. The park offers a variety of coordinated interpretive and educational programs. Lake Oahe Reservoir has over 2,000 acres of shoreline, making it ideal for boating, jet skiing, fishing, or diving. Anglers can find walleye, northern pike, chinook salmon, and bass. There is also a large variety of hunting game including pheasant, grouse, deer, and antelope. The campground is one large loop with back-in, level parking pads. Mature trees are found throughout the campground area, providing shade and adding ambiance. The weather is warm during the summer and cold in the winter. The late spring is a great time to visit before the insects come to life.

Basics

Operated By: South Dakota Game, Fish, & Parks Dept. **Open:** All year; water turned off in winter. **Site Assignment:** First come, first served. **Registration:** At entrance booth. **Fee:** $8–$11 per camping unit (no more than 2 units per site), plus entrance fee. **Parking:** At site.

Facilities

Number of Multipurpose Sites: 103. **Hookups:** Electric (20, 30 amps), potable water. **Each Site:** Picnic table, grated fire pits. **Dump Station:** Yes. **Laundry:** Next door. **Pay Phone:** Yes. **Rest Rooms and Showers:** Yes. **Fuel:** Next door. **Propane:** Next door. **Internal Roads:** Paved. **RV Service:** 22 mi. in Gettysburg. **Market:** In Gettysburg. **Restaurant:** Next door or in Gettysburg. **General Store:** No. **Vending:** Yes. **Swimming Pool:** No, but there is a swimming beach on Lake Oahe. **Playground:** Yes. **Other:** Cabins, fish-cleaning station, cross-country ski trail, boat ramp, beach, picnic area, pavilion, interpretive center, Arikara Lodge replica. **Activities:** Water & snow skiing, boating, swimming, interpretive programs, hiking, fishing (walleye, northerns, bass), biking. **Nearby Attractions:** Whitlock salmon spawning & imprinting station; annual Civil War festival. **Additional Information:** Gettysburg Chamber of Commerce, (605) 765-9309.

Restrictions

Pets: On leash. **Fires:** In fire pits only; fires may be restricted due to weather conditions; please ask management before starting any open fires. **Alcoholic Beverages:** Yes. **Vehicle Maximum Length:** None. **Other:** 14-day stay limit.

To Get There

From Gettysburg on US 212, go 18 mi. (stay on 212, do not get on 83), then take 1804N (right). Travel for 4 mi. until the pavement ends. Turn left and follow road into the park. Watch for signs.

HILL

Rafter J. Bar Ranch Campground

Box 128, Hill City 57745. T: (605)574-2527 or (888) 723-8375; F: (605) 574-3950; www.rafterj.com; info@rafter.com.

RV ★★★★ Tent ★★★★

Beauty: ★★★★★	Site Privacy: ★★★
Spaciousness: ★★★	Quiet: ★★★★
Security: ★★★★	Cleanliness: ★★★
Insect Control: ★★★	Facilities: ★★★

Located in the Black Hills, Rafter J. Bar Ranch is a huge full-service camping facility. It is divided into five camping areas, each under a canopy of large ponderosa pines. The camping areas each share beautiful commons, bike trails, hiking trails, and open meadows. The camping areas are large loops; three have their own rest rooms, showers, and laundry. Campsites, however, are not well spaced, nor are they any larger than most campground sites despite the enormous acreage of the property. The ranch offers lots of amenities, including fuel, fishing licenses, horseback riding, bike rentals, and an information center. In addition to being inclusive, it is in very close proximity to Mt. Rushmore, the Crazy Horse monument, and Custer State Park. Summer temperatures average in the mid 80s, with evenings dropping into the 60s. The ranch has staff on duty around the clock and several host families to assist with any need that may arise.

BASICS

Operated By: Tom George. **Open:** May 1–Oct. 1. **Site Assignment:** By reservations held on a credit card. **Registration:** In camp office. **Fee:** Tent $23, RV $30–$32 for 2 people; extra people $3, children under age 8 free; no personal checks. **Parking:** At site.

FACILITIES

Number of RV-Only Sites: 160. **Number of Tent-Only Sites:** 17. **Hookups:** Electric (30, 50 amps), water, sewer, satellite TV w/ HBO, ESPN (limited number). **Each Site:** Picnic table, grated fire pits. **Dump Station:** Yes. **Laundry:** Yes. **Pay Phone:** Yes. **Rest Rooms and Showers:** Yes. **Fuel:** Yes. **Propane:** Yes. **Internal Roads:** Combination of paved & gravel. **RV Service:** Mobile repair service. **Market:** In Hill City. **Restaurant:** Snack bar on property or there are restaurants all over the Black Hills. **General Store:** Yes. **Vending:** Yes. **Swimming Pool:** Yes, & hot tub. **Playground:** Yes. **Other:** Internet data port in information room. **Activities:** Trail rides, swimming, hot tub, fishing, hiking, bike rental. **Nearby Attractions:** Mt. Rushmore, Custer State Park, Needles Dr., Iron Mountain Rd., Borglum Story Museum, Hungry Horse. **Additional Information:** Hill City Chamber of Commerce, (605) 574-2368.

RESTRICTIONS

Pets: On leash. **Fires:** Fire pits or grills only; fires may be restricted due to weather conditions; please ask management before starting any open fires. **Alcoholic Beverages:** Yes. **Vehicle Maximum Length:** None. **Other:** 14-day stay limit; 1 family unit per site; Good Sam Club.

TO GET THERE

The campground is located on Sylvan Lake–Needles Rd. (SD Hwy. 87) between the towns of Custer and Hill City.

HILL CITY

Horse Thief Campground and Resort

Needles Hwy. 87, Hill City 57745. T: (605) 574-2668 or (800) 657-5802; F: (605) 547-4376; www.horsethief.com; camp@horsethief.com.

RV ★★★★ Tent ★★★★

Beauty: ★★★★	Site Privacy: ★★★
Spaciousness: ★★★	Quiet: ★★★
Security: ★★★★	Cleanliness: ★★★
Insect Control: ★★★	Facilities: ★★★

Deep in the groves of the Black Hills is a beautiful, 50-acre camping heaven, nestled in mountains, pines, streams, and ponds. Horse Thief Campground and Resort is a secluded family getaway conveniently located near Custer State Park, Mt. Rushmore, and the Scenic Needles Hwy. The campground is a full-service facility, with both pull-through and back-in sites, a lodge, and a pool with a breathtaking view. The campground consists of an RV area where you may choose open or wooded campsites. The tent-camper's section is spectacular, with wooded campsites and a huge common area. In addition to superb camping, Horse Thief is also a horse camp—meaning there are accommodations available for equine family members. However, advance reservations must be made if traveling with your horse. The temperatures in the area average in the mid 80s for the summer and 30s in the winter. There is an entrance gate and excellent security.

BASICS

Operated By: Bob & Vicki Irvine. **Open:** May 15–Sept. 15. **Site Assignment:** By reservation held on a credit card. **Registration:** In general store. **Fee:** Tent $17, RV $20–$29 for 2 people, extra person $2.50, children under age 5 stay free. **Parking:** At site.

FACILITIES

Number of RV-Only Sites: 54. **Number of Tent-Only Sites:** 43. **Hookups:** Electric (30 amps), water, sewer, phone, TV sites. **Each Site:** Picnic table, some fire pits. **Dump Station:** Yes. **Laundry:** Yes. **Pay Phone:** Yes. **Rest Rooms and Showers:** Yes. **Fuel:** No. **Propane:** No. **Internal Roads:** Gravel w/ some bumps & parts that are not level. **RV Service:** Mobile service. **Market:** Hill City. **Restaurant:** In Hill City. **General Store:** Yes. **Vending:** No. **Swimming Pool:** Yes. **Playground:** Yes. **Other:** Huge central fire ring, fax & copy service. **Activities:** Hiking, fishing, biking. **Nearby Attractions:** Mt. Rushmore, Custer State Park, Crazy Horse, museums, hot springs, Harney Peak. **Additional Information:** South Dakota Tourism, (800) 843-1930.

RESTRICTIONS

Pets: Dogs on a short leash only; horses allowed; must show a valid health certificate for all animals; horses must have proof of current negative Coggins test. **Fires:** In approved fire pits only; fires may be restricted due to weather conditions; please ask management before starting any open fires. **Alcoholic Beverages:** Yes. **Vehicle Maximum Length:** None. **Other:** Good Sam, AAA.

TO GET THERE

From the south side of Hill City, go 3 mi. south on US 16/385; the campground entrance is on the right.

INTERIOR

Badlands National Park

P.O. Box 6, Interior 57750-0006. T: (605) 433-5361; F: (605) 433-5404; www.nps.gov/badl; badl_information@nps.gov.

 ★★★ 

Beauty: ★★★
Site Privacy: ★★★
Spaciousness: ★★★
Quiet: ★★★
Security: ★★★
Cleanliness: ★★★
Insect Control: ★★
Facilities: ★

Set in the midst of what might be described as "peaks and valleys of delicately banded colors" (Thaddeus Culbertson) is the Badlands National Park campground. The wind is strong, and the terrain is a mixture of dirt and sand, yet there is an unbelievable biodiversity of both plant life and wildlife. This includes the largest remaining mixed-grass prairie in our country. The campground itself consists of two general camping loops, one group camp loop, and an amphitheater. The summers are dry and hot and the ground is brown, but in spring all is green and alive. There are no hookups in Badlands National Park; sites do have level, paved camping pads, tables on concrete pads, and wind guards. The campground is located inside the park gates, and there is a camp host during the summer months. The park offers a verity of educational and interpretive programs, including a night sky interpretive area.

BASICS

Operated By: US National Park Service. **Open:** All year. **Site Assignment:** First come, first served. **Registration:** Register at the information bulletin board; see camp host for assistance. **Fee:** $10 per site for up to 6 people; not to exceed 2 tents, or 2 vehicles per site). **Parking:** At site.

FACILITIES

Number of Multipurpose Sites: 96. **Hookups:** Potable water. **Each Site:** Picnic table, wind shelters, & patios. **Dump Station:** Yes. **Laundry:** No. **Pay Phone:** Yes. **Rest Rooms and Showers:** Yes. **Fuel:** No, 4 mi. in Interior. **Propane:** No, 30 mi. northwest in Wall. **Internal Roads:** Paved. **RV Service:** 30 mi. Northwest in Wall. **Market:** 30 mi. northwest in Wall. **Restaurant:** Cedar Pass Lodge (open mid-Apr. through mid-Oct.), or in Interior. **General Store:** Visitors center w/ ice & vending. **Vending:** No. **Swimming Pool:** No. **Playground:** No. **Other:** Amphitheater, Cedar Pass Lodge, Ben Reifel Visitor Cener. **Activities:** Ben Reifel Visitor Center w/ movies, & exhibits, horseback riding, hiking, day & evening interpretive programs, Jr. Ranger programs, guided walks. **Nearby Attractions:** Pine Ridge Indian Reservation, 80 mi. from the Black Hills & Mt. Rushmore. **Additional Information:** www.nps.gov/badl.

RESTRICTIONS

Pets: On leash; pets are not allowed in visitor centers, prairie dog towns, or Badl&s Wilderness Area. **Fires:** No open fires; fires may be restricted due to weather conditions; please ask management before starting any open fires. **Alcoholic Beverages:** Yes. **Vehicle Maximum Length:** None. **Other:** Golden Age & Golden Access Discounts; 14-day stay limit.

TO GET THERE

From I-90 Exit 131, take Hwy. 240 south about 8 mi.

INTERIOR

Badlands/White River KOA

HRC 54 Box 1, Interior 57750. T: (605) 433-5337 or (800) 562-3897; F: (605) 433-5337; www.koa.com; koa@gwtc.

RV ★★★★ Tent ★★★

Beauty: ★★★	Site Privacy: ★★★
Spaciousness: ★★★	Quiet: ★★★★
Security: ★★★★	Cleanliness: ★★★★
Insect Control: ★★★	Facilities: ★★★

Only a few miles from the Badlands National Park in the small community of Interior is the manicured landscape of the Badlands KOA. As with most KOAs, this is a full-service campground, with some of the only shade trees in the area. Due to the hard work of the owners and ongoing irrigation, the Badland KOA offers green grass and shade. There is a nice pool, mini-golf, and a courtesy phone. The campground is laid out in a series of rows and loops, with the majority of the sites being pull-through. The owners' private residence is in the middle of the property. In addition, several tent sites have electric and water hookups in what KOA refers to as a tent village. Please make note that is this campground is in a very small community, and the nearest services are 32 miles away in Wall.

BASICS

Operated By: Steve & Janet Snyder. **Open:** Apr. 22–Oct. 16. **Site Assignment:** By reservation held on a credit card. **Registration:** In general store. **Fee:** Tent $18, RV $23–$25 for 2 people, extra people $2.50, age 5 & under free. **Parking:** At site.

FACILITIES

Number of RV-Only Sites: 84. **Number of Tent-Only Sites:** 60. **Hookups:** Electric (20, 30, 50 amps), water, sewer. **Each Site:** Picnic table, some fire pits. **Dump Station:** Yes. **Laundry:** Yes. **Pay Phone:** Yes. **Rest Rooms and Showers:** Yes. **Fuel:** No. **Propane:** No. **Internal Roads:** Gravel. **RV Service:** 32 mi. Northwest in Wall, SD. **Market:** 32 mi. northwest in Wall, SD. **Restaurant:** In Interior; pancake breakfast served during summer season at the campground. **General Store:** Yes. **Vending:** Soft drinks. **Swimming Pool:** Yes. **Playground:** Yes. **Other:** Internet data port in laundry, 8 cabins, game room. **Activities:** Fishing, hiking, horseshoes, basketball. **Nearby Attractions:** Badl&s National Park, Pine Ridge Indian Reservation, fossil digging. **Additional Information:** South Dakota Tourism, (800) 843-1930.

RESTRICTIONS

Pets: On leash. **Fires:** In fire pits or grills only; fires may be restricted due to weather conditions; please ask management before starting any open fires. **Alcoholic Beverages:** Yes. **Vehicle Maximum Length:** None.

TO GET THERE

From I-90 take Exit 131, take SD 240/Badland Loop into the Badlands National Park, then take SD 377, which will become SD 44. The campground is approximately 6 mi. south of the Badlands National Park's south gate on Hwy. 44. It is approximately 10 mi. from I-90.

PIERRE

Corps of Engineers Downstream

P.O. Box 997, Pierre 57501. T: (605) 224-5862; F: (605) 224-5945; www.reserveusa.com (reservations).

RV ★★★★ Tent ★★★★★

Beauty: ★★★★	Site Privacy: ★★★★
Spaciousness: ★★★★	Quiet: ★★★★
Security: ★★★★★	Cleanliness: ★★★★
Insect Control: n/a	Facilities: ★★

Corps of Engineers Downstream is a huge park located about ten miles outside of Pierre on the Oahe Dam, encompassing both the Missouri River and Lake Oahe. The Corps of Engineers Downstream Recreation Area is broken into three campgrounds with over 300 sites between them. Each site has a paved camping pad and is under a forest of mature cottonwoods and willows. There are large common areas in each campground, complete with playgrounds and comfort stations with hot showers. The campgrounds are in loops and have both pull-through and back-in sites. There is a full-service marina on the property, as well as a restaurant, convenience store, and bait shop. Each campground has a camp host, and there is a staffed entrance booth for your protection. There are four distinct seasons in Pierre, with temperatures on summer days averaging in the mid 80s. Bring insect repellent if visiting in the late summer; otherwise, the deer flies will eat you for lunch.

Basics

Operated By: US Corp of Engineers. **Open:** May–Oct. 31. **Site Assignment:** By reservations, all fees payable at that time; call National Recreation Reservation Service, (877) 444-6777 or refer to website; fees for cancellations & no-shows will apply. **Registration:** Self-registration or at the guard shack. **Fee:** $14 per site, no more than 8 people per site. **Parking:** At site.

Facilities

Number of Multipurpose Sites: 206. **Hookups:** Electric (30, 50 amps); potable water (but not on every site). **Each Site:** Picnic table, grated fire pits. **Dump Station:** Yes. **Laundry:** No. **Pay Phone:** Yes. **Rest Rooms and Showers:** Yes. **Fuel:** At the marina. **Propane:** At the marina. **Internal Roads:** Paved. **RV Service:** In Pierre. **Market:** In Pierre. **Restaurant:** At the marina, or in Pierre. **General Store:** At the marina. **Vending:** Yes. **Swimming Pool:** No, but there is a huge swimming beach on the Missouri River. **Playground:** Several. **Other:** Picnic area, Oahe Marina, archery range, rifle range, Oahe Chapel, visitors center. **Activities:** Swimming, archery, nature trails, boating, jet skiing, waterskiing, biking. **Nearby Attractions:** Fort Pierre, South Dakota Discovery Center & Aquarium, state capitol, Capitol Grounds Arboretum Trail, South Dakota Cultural Heritage Center. **Additional Information:** Pierre Chamber of Commerce, (605) 224-7361.

Restrictions

Pets: Yes. **Fires:** Fire pits only; fires may be restricted due to weather conditions; please ask management before starting any open fires. **Alcoholic Beverages:** Yes. **Vehicle Maximum Length:** None. **Other:** 50% discount w/ Golden Age or Golden Access passport.

To Get There

From Fort Pierre take Hwy. 83N to just before the river; take a left on Hwy. 14. Go about 1 mi. and take a right on 1806. The campground is about 5 mi. on the right. There are signs all the way from Fort Pierre.

PIERRE

Griffen Park

715 East Dakota Ave., Pierre 57501. T: (605) 773-7445

RV ★★★ Tent ★★★★

Beauty: ★★★	Site Privacy: ★★
Spaciousness: ★★	Quiet: ★★
Security: ★★★	Cleanliness: ★★★
Insect Control: n/a	Facilities: ★★

Welcome to the state capital of Pierre, and a unique city park that offers three free nights of camping with electricity. Griffen Park is located in downtown Pierre, just a few blocks from the Capitol Building. This beautiful city park offers both a public pool and a swimming beach on the Missouri River. There are six tennis courts, 12 horseshoe pits, several picnic shelters, a softball field, a full basketball court, and a marina next door. The RV camp area is not much more than a dirt parking lot, and at the time of our visit, the showers needed some cleaning, but the park overall is very well kept and clean. The tent area is striking, as it overlooks the river. For the amenities and activities offered for free, this is a wonderful park. The weather is breezy around the riverfront, so pack a jacket.

Basics

Operated By: City of Pierre. **Open:** All year. **Site Assignment:** First come, first served. **Registration:** Read information board. **Fee:** Free (3-night limit). **Parking:** At site.

Facilities

Number of RV-Only Sites: 6. **Number of Tent-Only Sites:** 10. **Hookups:** Electric (20, 30 amps). **Each Site:** Picnic table. **Dump Station:** Yes. **Laundry:** No. **Pay Phone:** Yes. **Rest Rooms and Showers:** Yes; keep in mind that this is a public city park; there is a shower in the rest rooms located by the River Front beach & at the pool, but you will probably find that they don't meet your standards for cleanliness. **Fuel:** No. **Propane:** No. **Internal Roads:** Paved. **RV Service:** Local service. **Market:** In town. **Restaurant:** Within walking distance. **General Store:** No. **Vending:** Yes, located by the pool or across the street at the hospital. **Swim-**

ming Pool: Yes, large city pool w/ lifeguard. **Playground:** Yes. **Other:** Large riverfront beach w/ lifeguard, on the Missouri River, covered picnic tables overlooking the river, scheduled & planned recreation, marina next door. **Activities:** Volleyball, 6 tennis courts, swimming (river or pool), horseshoes, basketball, boating, waterskiing, softball field. **Nearby Attractions:** Shopping, State Capitol, arboretum, South Dakota Cultural Center, South Dakota Discovery Center & Aquarium. **Additional Information:** Pierre Chamber of Commerce, (605) 224-7361 or www.pierrechamber.com.

Restrictions

Pets: On leash; this is a city park. **Fires:** No open fires; fires may be restricted due to weather conditions; please ask management before starting any open fires. **Alcoholic Beverages:** Yes. **Vehicle Maximum Length:** None. **Other:** 3-day stay limit.

To Get There

From the junction of US 83 & Sioux St, go east 5 blocks on Sioux St. to Washington, then go south 2 blocks.

RAPID CITY
Black Hills Jellystone RV Park

7001 South Hwy. 16, Rapid City 57702-8903.
T: (605) 341-8554 or (800) 558-2954;
www.jellystone.com.

★★★ ★★★

Beauty: ★★★	Site Privacy: ★★★
Spaciousness: ★★★	Quiet: ★★★
Security: ★★★	Cleanliness: ★★★★
Insect Control: ★★★	Facilities: ★★★

Yogi Bear and the Schneidermans welcome you their Black Hills Jellystone RV Park in Rapid City. This campground is convenient to area attractions, a nearby water park, many restaurants, Custer State Park, and Mt. Rushmore. The campground consists of level, open campsites in a rectangular configuration of several long rows, with grass and small trees separating individual sites. Sites are relatively close together, and tent sites are located very close to high-traffic areas in the campground. The majority of the sites are pull-throughs, with 12 cabins located at the front of the property. The campground offers many amenities, including children's activities, movies, a pavilion, gazebo, and a wagon train. This campground is an ideal base for travelers wishing to explore the Black Hill region. Summers days in the area have average temperatures in the mid 80s, dropping to the 60s at night. The first full week of Aug. is the Sturgis Rally, and reservations must be made about a year in advance for that time.

Basics

Operated By: Keith & S&i Schneiderman. **Open:** May 15–Oct. 1. **Site Assignment:** By reservations held w/ credit card. **Registration:** In general store. **Fee:** Tent $18, $25–$31 for 2 people. extra people $3. **Parking:** At site.

Facilities

Number of RV-Only Sites: 46. **Number of Tent-Only Sites:** 31. **Number of Multipurpose Sites:** 17. **Hookups:** Electric (30, 50 amps). **Each Site:** Picnic table, fire pits. **Dump Station:** Yes. **Laundry:** Yes. **Pay Phone:** Yes. **Rest Rooms and Showers:** Yes. **Fuel:** No. **Propane:** No. **Internal Roads:** Gravel. **RV Service:** In Rapid City. **Market:** In Rapid City. **Restaurant:** In Rapid City. **General Store:** Yes. **Vending:** Soft drinks. **Swimming Pool:** Yes. **Playground:** Yes. **Other:** 12 cabins, pavilion. **Activities:** Hot tub, swimming, pool table, game room, book exchange, children's activities. **Nearby Attractions:** Mt. Rushmore, Black Hills Maze & Amusements, Reptile Gardens. **Additional Information:** Rapid City Chamber of Commerce, (605) 343-1744.

Restrictions

Pets: On leash. **Fires:** In fire pits or grills only; fires may be restricted due to weather conditions; please ask management before starting any open fires. **Alcoholic Beverages:** Yes. **Vehicle Maximum Length:** None. **Other:** No generators.

To Get There

The campground is located 4 mi. south of Rapid City on Hwy. 16.

RAPID CITY
Mystery Mt. Resort

13752 South Hwy. 16 West, Rapid City 57702.
T: (605) 342-5368 or (800)658-2267; F: (605) 348-2561; www.blackhillsresorts.com; mmresort@rapidnet.com.

Beauty: ★★★★
Site Privacy: ★★
Spaciousness: ★★
Quiet: ★★★★
Security: ★★★
Cleanliness: ★★★
Insect Control: ★★★
Facilities: ★★

Mystery Mountain Resort is situated on the outskirts of Rapid City, on Hwy. 16 near the Black Hills and Mt. Rushmore. Mystery Mountain is a combination of campground, cabins, bunkhouses, and furnished reunion cottages capable of sleeping ten. The campground is integrated with other buildings, and it's configured mostly in rows. There are both pull-through and back-in sites. Many sites have concrete patios and parking pads, while other sites could use some updating and are not very level. The majority of the campground is under a canopy of pine and offers excellent shade. The campground is conveniently located near many area attractions, restaurants, state parks, and Mt. Rushmore. The weather is typical of most places in the region, with temperatures in summer averaging in the mid 80s during the day. Please also note the first full week of August is the Sturgis Rally Week; special rates will be in effect, and reservations need to be made as much as a year in advance for this time—preferably at the end of the preceding year's rally.

Basics

Operated By: Blackhills Resorts. **Open:** All year. **Site Assignment:** By reservation. **Registration:** In resort office. **Fee:** Tents $17–$22, RV $25–$32, for 2 people. **Parking:** At site.

Facilities

Number of RV-Only Sites: 75. **Number of Tent-Only Sites:** 42. **Hookups:** Electric (30, 50 amps), water, sewer. **Each Site:** Picnic table, fire pit. **Dump Station:** 2 dump stations. **Laundry:** Yes. **Pay Phone:** Yes. **Rest Rooms and Showers:** Yes. **Fuel:** No. **Propane:** No. **Internal Roads:** Gravel. **RV Service:** In Rapid City. **Market:** In Rapid City. **Restaurant:** In Rapid City. **General Store:** Yes. **Vending:** Soft drinks. **Swimming Pool:** Yes, w/ hot tub. **Playground:** Yes. **Other:** Cabins, bunkhouse, guest houses, reunion cottages, maid service. **Activities:** Basketball, horseshoes, swimming, hiking. **Nearby Attractions:** Mt. Rushmore, Childrens Science Center, Crystal Cave Park, Flintstone's Bedrock City, Cosmos of the Black Hills, Bear Country USA, Black Hills Caverns. **Additional Information:** Rapid City CVB, (800) 487-3223 or tourist@rapidcitycvb.com).

Restrictions

Pets: On leash. **Fires:** In provided fire pits or grills only; fires may be restricted due to weather conditions; please ask management before starting any open fires. **Alcoholic Beverages:** Yes. **Vehicle Maximum Length:** None.

To Get There

The campground is located 11 mi. south of Rapid City, directly off US 16W.

RAPID CITY

Rushmore Shadows Resort

P.O. Box 1696, Rapid City 57709. T: (605) 343-4544; F: (605) 348-9323; rshadows@enetis.net.

RV ★★★ Tent ★★★

Beauty: ★★★
Site Privacy: ★★
Spaciousness: ★★
Quiet: ★★★
Security: ★★★★
Cleanliness: ★★★
Insect Control: ★★★
Facilities: ★★★

Rushmore Shadow Resort is located on Hwy. 16W near Rapid City, just 16 miles from Mt. Rushmore. The resort campground is a large facility with open common areas and activities. There is a clubhouse, large heated pool, park models, and a convenience store. The campground consists of over 200 sites, laid out much like a residential subdivision with several major streets. The streets are private, and only registered guests are permitted past the registration office. Most sites are gravel with some grass between, but they are relatively close together. The common areas are generally well groomed, with a lot of room for recreation. Next door is the Old McDonald Farm, with red barns and goats that walk an overhanging bridge. The weather is not quite as extreme as the in the heart of the Black Hills, with daytime temperatures average in the mid 80s in the summer, dropping into the 60s at night.

Basics

Operated By: Private operator. **Open:** May 15–Sept. 14. **Site Assignment:** By reservation; office open 9 a.m.–5 p.m. **Registration:** At registration office. **Parking:** At site.

Facilities

Number of RV-Only Sites: 235. **Number of Tent-Only Sites:** 0. **Hookups:** Electric (20, 30 amps), water, sewer. **Each Site:** Picnic table, some grills, some fire pits. **Dump Station:** Yes. **Laundry:** Yes. **Pay Phone:** Yes. **Rest Rooms and Showers:** Yes. **Fuel:** No. **Propane:** Yes. **Internal Roads:** Combination of paved & gravel. **RV Service:** Mobile. **Market:** In Rapid City. **Restaurant:** On site or in Rapid City. **General Store:** Yes. **Vending:** Yes. **Swimming Pool:** Yes. **Playground:** Yes. **Other:** Clubhouse, Internet data port, grill, bonfire pit, barn, picnic shelter. **Activities:** Volleyball, swimming, basketball, horseshoes. **Nearby Attractions:** Badl&s National Park, Chapel in the Hills, Dinosaur Park, Museum of Geology. **Additional Information:** Rapid City CVB, (605) 343-1744, www.rapidcitycvb.com.

Restrictions

Pets: No pets allowed. **Fires:** In designated fire pits or grills only; fires may be restricted due to weather conditions; please ask management before starting any open fires. **Alcoholic Beverages:** Yes. **Vehicle Maximum Length:** None.

To Get There

The campground is located directly off Hwy. 16W in Rapid City as you are heading out of town.

SIOUX FALLS

Yogi Bear's Jellystone Park

26014 478th Ave., Brandon 57005. T: (605) 332-2233; F: (605) 332-2233; www.gocampingamerica.com/yogisiouxfalls; jellystonesiouxfalls@gocampingamerica.com.

RV ★★★	Tent ★★★
Beauty: ★★★	Site Privacy: ★★★
Spaciousness: ★★★	Quiet: ★★★
Security: ★★★★	Cleanliness: ★★★★
Insect Control: ★★★	Facilities: ★★★

Directly off I-90 only five miles east of Sioux City, Yogi Bear's Jellystone Campground is a full-service, modern facility offering a multitude of amenities and activities for the entire family. The campground is conveniently located for travelers wishing to enjoy the Sioux Falls area and neighboring state parks. The campground offers all modern hookups, including cable and phone. There are two main sections to the campground, and roads are laid out in rows. There is a tree between most sites, but at the time of our visit, they were very young and afforded little to no shade. That will obviously change with time. Most sites are pull-throughs, and there is little interference for those who wish to receive satellite TV. The campground is open year-round; however, there are limited hookups in the winter. The weather in this part of the state goes from one extreme to the other—very warm and dry in summer, and ice-cold in winter. The owners are on site during busy season, and security is good.

Basics

Operated By: Bruce Aliets. **Open:** All year; water turned off in winter. **Site Assignment:** By reservation, (800) 638-9043. **Registration:** In general store. **Fee:** Tent $16, RV $26–$28 for 2 people, extra people $2, kids age 4 & under stay free. **Parking:** At site.

Facilities

Number of RV-Only Sites: 112. **Number of Tent-Only Sites:** 33. **Hookups:** Electric (20, 30, 50 amps), water, sewer, cable, phone. **Each Site:** Picnic table, grated fire pits. **Dump Station:** Yes. **Laundry:** Yes. **Pay Phone:** Yes. **Rest Rooms and Showers:** Yes. **Fuel:** No, just down the street. **Propane:** Yes. **Internal Roads:** Gravel. **RV Service:** In Sioux Falls. **Market:** In Sioux Falls. **Restaurant:** Snack bar on site or restaurants in town. **General Store:** Yes. **Vending:** Yes. **Swimming Pool:** Yes, & hot tub. **Playground:** Yes. **Other:** 5 cabins, hot tub, indoor theatre, pavilion, arcade game room, nightly visits by Yogi, picnic area. **Activities:** Swimming, 19-hole mini-golf, volleyball, peddle bikes, planned activities in the summer, summer Sunday morning pancake breakfast. **Nearby Attractions:** Thunder Road Family Fun Park, Great Plains Zoo & Delbridge Museum, *USS South Dakota* Battleship Memorial, Falls Park. **Additional Information:** Sioux City CVB, (800) 333-2072.

Restrictions

Pets: On leash. **Fires:** In fire pits only; fires may be restricted due to weather conditions; please ask management before starting any open fires. **Alcoholic Beverages:** Yes. **Vehicle Maximum Length:** None.

To Get There

From I-90 at Exit 402, go 0.25 mi. north on City Rd. 121; the park is located on the right.

WATERTOWN

Stokes-Thomas Lake City Park

90 South Lake Dr., Watertown 57201. T: (605)882-6264

RV ★★★★★ Tent ★★★★★

Beauty: ★★★★ Site Privacy: ★★★★
Spaciousness: ★★★★ Quiet: ★★★★
Security: ★★★★ Cleanliness: ★★★★
Insect Control: n/a Facilities: ★★★

Stokes-Thomas Lake City Park is one of South Dakota's wonderful city parks. It reflects the pride South Dakota places on its towns and offers the local population, as well as travelers, a beautiful place for recreation. Stokes-Thomas is located on Lake Kampeska, about five miles out of Watertown. Watertown is a known for its rich grain fields and grasslands. The park is kept in pristine condition, with lush green grass and 42 paved camping pads, all under an awning of large, mature oak trees. New in the summer of 2002 is the introduction of full-hookup sites with all the amenities. Stokes-Thomas Lake City Park has a large boat ramp, a swimming beach, and three picnic shelters. This park is a fantastic weekend getaway. The weather is pleasant for water sports in the summer, and there is a manager in residence.

Basics

Operated By: Watertown Parks, Recreation & Forestry Dept., Kelly Stugis, Manager. **Open:** All year. **Site Assignment:** First come, first served. **Registration:** In park office. **Fee:** $13–$15 per site (limit 6 people per site). **Parking:** At site.

Facilities

Number of Multipurpose Sites: 43. **Hookups:** Electric (20, 30 amps), water, sewer. **Each Site:** Picnic table, fire pits. **Dump Station:** Yes. **Laundry:** No. **Pay Phone:** Yes. **Rest Rooms and Showers:** Yes. **Fuel:** No. **Propane:** No. **Internal Roads:** Paved. **RV Service:** In Watertown. **Market:** In Watertown. **Restaurant:** In Watertown. **General Store:** No. **Vending:** Yes. **Swimming Pool:** No, but there is a roped-off swimming beach on Lake Kampeska. **Playground:** Yes. **Other:** Boat launch, 3 picnic shelters, park manager's home/office. **Activities:** Boating, swimming, fishing, softball field, s& volleyball, horseshoes, basketball. **Nearby Attractions:** Golf, Thunder Road Family Fun Park, Bramble Park Zoo & Discovery Center. **Additional Information:** Watertown Area Chamber of Commerce, (800) 658-4505, or www.watertownsd.com.

Restrictions

Pets: On leash. **Fires:** In fire pits only; fires may be restricted due to weather conditions; please ask management before starting any open fires. **Alcoholic Beverages:** Yes. **Vehicle Maximum Length:** None. **Other:** 9-day stay limit; 5-day stay limit on holiday weekends.

To Get There

From the junction of US 81 and Hwy. 20 in Watertown, go 3 mi. northwest on Hwy. 20 to South Lake Dr.

YANKTON

Lewis & Clark Recreation Area, Resort, and Marina

43349 SD Hwy. 52, Yankton 57078. T: (605) 668-2985; F: (605) 668-3069; www.state.sd.us/gfp/sdparks; yanktonstp@gfp.state.sd.us.

RV ★★★ Tent ★★★

Beauty: ★★★ Site Privacy: ★★★
Spaciousness: ★★★ Quiet: ★★★★
Security: ★★★★ Cleanliness: ★★★
Insect Control: ★★★ Facilities: ★★

Located in one of South Dakota's most popular recreation areas, the campground at Lewis & Clark Recreation Area is a full-service modern resort facility. It's located on the Missouri River, five miles from Yankton, just north of the South Dakota/Nebraska border. Lewis & Clark Resort is broken into three areas. There's a campground consisting of 386 level, asphalted camping sites in several loop configurations, with grass common areas and plenty of trees for shade. You'll also find a concession area equipped with a marina, lodging, dining, and theater. Lastly, Gravins Point is the horse camp and day-use section of the park. The park offers many organized activities for all ages, and it rents anything from RVs to bikes. So, pack your insect repellent and sun screen, and whether you enjoy horseback riding or jet skiing down the Missouri River, Lewis & Clark Recreation Area can provide it all. During the warmer summer months, insects can be a problem. Security is excellent.

Basics

Operated By: South Dakota Game, Fish, & Parks Dept. **Open:** All year; water turned off in winter. **Site Assignment:** By reservation, (800) 710-CAMP. **Registration:** At entrance booth. **Fee:** $10–$15 per camping unit (no more than 2 units per site) plus entrance fee. **Parking:** At site.

Facilities

Number of Multipurpose Sites: 380. **Hookups:** Electric (20, 30 amps), potable water. **Each Site:** Picnic table, grated fire pits. **Dump Station:** Yes. **Laundry:** No. **Pay Phone:** Yes. **Rest Rooms and Showers:** Yes. **Fuel:** Yes, at the Marina. **Propane:** Yes, at the Marina. **Internal Roads:** Paved. **RV Service:** In Yankton. **Market:** In Yankton. **Restaurant:** Harbor Lights Restaurant on site or in Yankton. **General Store:** Yes, at the Marina. **Vending:** Yes. **Swimming Pool:** There is a pool at the Lewis & Clark Resort Hotel for guests, & there are 3 riverfront beaches available for swimming. **Playground:** Yes. **Other:** Lewis & Clark Resort Hotel, Harbor Lights Restaurant, Lewis & Clark Playhouse, marina, cabins, Horse Trail Camp, several boat ramps, convenience store, bicycle rental, boat rental, showers at the beach, picnic shelters w/ grills, amphitheater. **Activities:** Waterskiing, boating, swimming, interpretive programming, hiking, fishing (walleye, northerns, bass), 6 mi. of bike trails, 4 mi. of equestrian trails, fishing guide service, volleyball, archery, weekly park programs. **Additional Information:** South Dakota State Parks, 523 E. Capitol, Pierre, SD 57501, (605) 773-3391, or Yankton Chamber of Commerce, (605) 665-3636.

Restrictions

Pets: On leash. **Fires:** In fire pits only; fires may be restricted due to weather conditions; please ask management before starting any open fires. **Alcoholic Beverages:** Yes. **Vehicle Maximum Length:** None. **Other:** 14-day stay limit.

To Get There

The park is located 6 mi. west of Yankton, directly off SD Hwy. 52.

Washington

Washington State, a beautiful place to tour year-round, boasts a variety of different natural and urban environments to explore. While the most popular region for tourism is the I-5 corridor, astounding natural beauty, cultural events, and man-made curiosities await across the state.

The I-5 corridor, the most widely traveled (and also promoted) section of the state, contains **Seattle, Tacoma, Olympia, Bellingham,** the Canadian border, the volcanoes, access to the **North Cascades** and **Olympic Peninsula,** and **Vancouver** (Washington). This region has mild, temperate weather all year and lots of rain.

Cities and natural attractions along the I-5 corridor abound. The northwestern region is especially beautiful, with the **San Juan Islands, Victoria** (Canada), and Bellingham. The region's geography blends mountains to the east, myriad inlets and bays to the west, and mountains rising from the islands beyond. Bellingham houses **Western Washington University** and is an interesting, small, college town. The absolute best views in the region can be had from overlooks on **Chuckanut Drive.** If you're in a small enough vehicle, continue on south through the beautiful Skagit county farmland as the road makes its way back to the interstate.

A major geographic region of the state, the Olympic Peninsula has tremendous natural beauty, vibrancy, and diversity. **Port Angeles** has the most services of any city on the northern peninsula, provides the best access to the Olympic Mountains, and, along with the surrounding area, handles the bulk of the tourist traffic. If you can only visit one area in the state, go see the peninsula; you won't be sorry.

Traveling east across Washington, the climate and environment change dramatically. The Northern Cascades have snow on the ground year-round in some places. The mountainous belt drops a couple of thousand feet into high-altitude deserts. The red earth of north-central Washington is home to a mix of desert, valleys, canyons, farms, rivers, lakes, and the occasional ponderosa pine forest. The coulee region has scenery different from any other area, with many pullouts and vistas along **Banks Lake Road.** South-central Washington has a flat, desolate, arid terrain with lots of farms and wineries. The Yakima region of the state produces copious amounts of wine and makes a popular tourist destination. In both central and eastern Washington, lake fishing draws a lot of travelers.

Moving east from south-central Washington, the landscape changes to rolling hills around the Idaho border and the Snake River area. Moving north to **Spokane,** the landscape changes yet again to smoothly rolling farms and dry ponderosa pine forests. Although a popular escape for locals, the eastern side of the state receives very little state-sponsored tourism PR (a fact not lost on residents). Coincidentally, goods and services on the eastern side of the state don't cost quite as much as in the Puget Sound region (particularly hotels and restaurants), but the tourism infrastructure is not as developed as it is around Seattle.

The following facilities accept payment in checks or cash only:

Denny Creek Campground, North Bend
Vancouver RV Park, Vancouver
Van Mall RV Park, Vancouver

The following facilities feature 20 or fewer sites:

Mounthaven Resort, Ashford
Merrill Lake Campground, Cougar
Corral Pass Campground, Enumclaw
Evergreen Court Campground, Ocean Park
Sol Duc Resort, Port Angeles (Olympic National Park)

Campground Profiles

ANATONE
Fields Spring State Park

P.O. Box 37, Anatone 99401. T: (509) 256-3332; www.parks.wa.gov.

RV ★★★ Tent ★★★★

Beauty: ★★★★★ Site Privacy: ★★★
Spaciousness: ★★★★★ Quiet: ★★★★
Security: ★★★★ Cleanliness: ★★★★★
Insect Control: ★★ Facilities: ★★★

Anatone is quite small. It is the last stop for any kind of services before continuing on to Field's Spring State Park. Beyond Field's Spring to the south lies wilderness, national forest, and wild river canyons. Sitting on a basalt foundation at 4,000 feet on the eastern edge of Washington's Blue Mountains, Field's Spring State Park is a place of unusual beauty in an otherwise harsh and rugged terrain. Escaping the heat of the summer is one of the biggest draws to Field's Spring. Although the park sits on what is essentially an arid, desert-like plateau, with prickly pear cactus growing down along the Grande Ronde's banks, the difference in elevation makes all the difference in temperature. While Clarkston and Lewiston swelter in 100-degree agony in midsummer, Field's Spring rarely gets above a tolerable 85. Field's Spring is a true oasis in a region otherwise parched for camping options.

BASICS

Operated By: Washington State Parks & Recreation Commission. **Open:** All year, weather permitting. **Site Assignment:** First come, first served. **Registration:** Self-registration. **Fee:** $5–$11. **Parking:** At site.

FACILITIES

Number of Multipurpose Sites: 20. **Hookups:** None. **Dump Station:** Yes. **Laundry:** No. **Pay Phone:** Yes. **Rest Rooms and Showers:** Yes. **Fuel:** 31 mi. in Clarkston. **Propane:** 31 mi. in Clarkston. **Internal Roads:** Paved. **RV Service:** No. **Market:** 31 mi. in Clarkston. **Restaurant:** Yes. **General Store:** 31 mi. in Clarkston. **Vending:** No. **Swimming Pool:** No. **Playground:** Yes. **Other:** 2 lodges, 2 kitchen shelters w/ electricity, 2 sheltered fire circles, teepee camp (6 can be reserved for $20 per night). **Activities:** Environmental Learning Center, hiking, biking, horseshoe pits, softball field, volleyball fields, hang gliding, paragliding. **Nearby Attractions:** Puffer Butle, Snake River. **Additional Information:** www.parks.wa.gov.

RESTRICTIONS

Pets: On leash. **Fires:** In fire pit. **Alcoholic Beverages:** Allowed. **Vehicle Maximum Length:** Call ahead for details.

TO GET THERE

From Clarkston (roughly 110 mi. south of Spokane), follow SR 129 south through Asotin and Anatone for about 25 mi. to the park entrance.

ASHFORD

Mounthaven Resort

38210 SR 706 East, Ashford 98304. T: (360) 569-2594 or (800) 456-9380; www.mounthaven.com; info@mounthaven.com.

★★★★  ★

Beauty: ★★★★ Site Privacy: ★
Spaciousness: ★★★ Quiet: ★★★
Security: ★ Cleanliness: ★★★★
Insect Control: ★★ Facilities: ★★

Mounthaven Resort, half a mile west of the entrance to Mount Ranier National Park, offers a beautiful woodland setting. The quaint park lacks on-site indoor recreation, but people don't often come to the area to "stay at home". Seventeen shady RV sites are arranged in two rows. The intimate campground sits among cedars and firs, and is visited by friendly deer. Adjacent sites have dirt surfaces and come in a variety of sizes. Sites 6–13 make up the nicest sites in the park, due to size and quiet; sites 1–5 sit near the sometimes busy Hwy. 706. The campground also has an array of cabins for travelers looking for indoor accomodations. Visit during the early or late summer shoulder seasons for optimal conditions.

BASICS

Operated By: Mt. Haven Resort. **Open:** All year. **Site Assignment:** On arrival or by reservation (deposit required for holidays, 15-days cancellation notice for refund). **Registration:** At office, late arrivals pay in morning. **Fee:** Full $20, extra campers (more than 4) & dogs $2; V, MC, cash. **Parking:** At site.

FACILITIES

Number of RV-Only Sites: 17. **Number of Tent-Only Sites:** 1. **Hookups:** Electric (20, 30 amps), water, sewer. **Each Site:** Picnic table, fire ring. **Dump Station:** Yes. **Laundry:** Yes. **Pay Phone:** Yes. **Rest Rooms and Showers:** Yes. **Fuel:** No. **Propane:** No. **Internal Roads:** Gravel, dirt. **RV Service:** No. **Market:** Convenience stores, 1–5 mi.; larger store 30 mi. west. **Restaurant:** 1–5 mi. **General Store:** No. **Vending:** Yes. **Swimming Pool:** No. **Playground:** Yes. **Other:** Cabins, firewood, horseshoes, volleyball, basketball, badminton, board games, hot tub (by reservation only, $10 per hour for 2 people). **Activities:** Mt. Rainier. **Nearby Attractions:** Mt. Rainier. **Additional Information:** Mount Ranier NPS Office, (360) 569-2212.

RESTRICTIONS

Pets: On leash only, 2 per site max. **Fires:** In fire pits only. **Alcoholic Beverages:** At site only. **Vehicle Maximum Length:** None.

TO GET THERE

Located on SR 706, 0.5 mi. west of the southwestern park gate (Nisqually entrance).

BAKER LAKE

Panorama Point Campground

2105 WA Rte. 20, Sedro Woolley 98284. T: (360) 856-5700; www.fs.fed.us/r6/mbs or www.reserveusa.com.

★★★ 

Beauty: ★★★★★ Site Privacy: ★★★★
Spaciousness: ★★★★ Quiet: ★★★
Security: ★★★★ Cleanliness: ★★★★★
Insect Control: ★★★ Facilities: ★★★

Many purist northwest wilderness goers purposefully overlook camping options at places like Baker Lake simply because they don't feel that they're truly getting a pristine experience if they're within earshot of mechanized sounds. In the case of Panorama Point Campground, midway up the western shore, that sound will most likely be the gentle buzz of small outboard motors as fishermen putt-putt around in search of the best spots to hook their daily catch. They have their choice of such delights as rainbow, cutthroat, or Dolly Varden trout; kokanee salmon; and whitefish. This is, indeed, a fisherman's lake. But one can hardly complain that there's no getting away from civilization here thanks to miles and miles of Forest Service roads and trails that can lead you to soothing hot springs and deep into two designated wildernesses, a national recreation area, and a national park. Just make sure you have a good map and trail guides of the area before you find yourself at the mercy of the purists.

Basics

Operated By: Mount Baker-Snoqualmie National Forest; Conservation Resources, Inc. **Open:** May–mid-Sept. **Site Assignment:** Reservations required, call (877) 444-6777. **Registration:** Self-registration on-site. **Fee:** $7–$12. **Parking:** At site.

Facilities

Number of Multipurpose Sites: 16. **Hookups:** Water. **Dump Station:** No. **Laundry:** No. **Pay Phone:** No. **Rest Rooms and Showers:** Vault toilets. **Fuel:** 6 mi. in Concrete. **Propane:** 6 mi. in Concrete. **Internal Roads:** Paved. **RV Service:** No. **Market:** 6 mi. in Concrete. **Restaurant:** 6 mi. in Concrete. **General Store:** 6 mi. in Concrete. **Vending:** No. **Swimming Pool:** No. **Playground:** No. **Activities:** Fishing, hiking, backpacking, skiing, climbing. **Nearby Attractions:** Hot Springs, Mt. Baker, designated wildernesses, Mt. Shuksan. **Additional Information:** www.fs.fed.us/r6/mbs or www.reserveusa.com.

Restrictions

Pets: On leash only. **Fires:** In fire pits only. **Alcoholic Beverages:** Allowed. **Vehicle Maximum Length:** 21 ft. **Other:** Permit required for overnight backpacking or to park at trailhead; 2-day minimum weekend stay, 3-days on holidays.

To Get There

Drive north on Baker Lake Rd. from its junction with SR 20, about 6 mi. west of Concrete (named for the primary industry that converts local limestone into cement).

BELLINGHAM

Larrabee State Park

245 Chuckanut Dr., Bellingham 98226. T: (360) 676-2093; www.parks.wa.gov.

RV ★★★ Tent ★★★★

Beauty: ★★★★★	Site Privacy: ★★★★
Spaciousness: ★★★★	Quiet: ★★★
Security: ★★★	Cleanliness: ★★★★★
Insect Control: ★★★	Facilities: ★★★

Located on 1,885 acres along the saltwater shores of Samish Bay south of Bellingham, Larrabee is the oldest state park in Washington. Its designation in 1915 has kept protected throughout the years such a lush growth of northwest foliage that it is difficult not to feel you have ventured miles into a remote and primeval place. There are plenty of hiking trails, pebbled beaches, and rocky tide pools to explore, and sea kayaking is also an option, with numerous coves, bays, points, rocks, and islets within easy paddling range. For freshwater anglers, both Fragrance Lake and Lost Lake are stocked, but you have to take a two-mile trail to reach them. If you simply want fresh air and a look at the lay of the land, take a drive up Cleator Rd. to 1,900-foot Cyrus Gates Overlook for the best possible view of the San Juans. For views of Mount Baker and the North Cascades, take the short trail to the East Overlook.

Basics

Operated By: Washington State Parks & Recreation Commission. **Open:** All year. **Site Assignment:** First come, first served; reservations accepted mid-May–mid-Sept. **Registration:** Self-registration. **Fee:** $12–$17. **Parking:** At site.

Facilities

Number of RV-Only Sites: 26. **Number of Tent-Only Sites:** 59. **Hookups:** Electric, water, sewer. **Each Site:** Picnic table, fire pit w/ grill, shade trees. **Dump Station:** Yes. **Laundry:** No. **Pay Phone:** Yes. **Rest Rooms and Showers:** Yes. **Fuel:** 1 mi. **Propane:** 1 mi. **Internal Roads:** Paved. **RV Service:** No. **Market:** 1 mi. **Restaurant:** 1 mi. **General Store:** 1 mi. **Vending:** No. **Swimming Pool:** Yes. **Playground:** Yes. **Other:** Boat launch, security, amphitheater, working train track that runs through the park. **Activities:** Boating, hiking, fishing, diving, clamming & crabbing. **Nearby Attractions:** Frangrance Lake, Lost Lake. **Additional Information:** www.parks.wa.gov.

Restrictions

Pets: On leash only. **Fires:** In fire pits only. **Alcoholic Beverages:** In designated areas. **Vehicle Maximum Length:** None.

To Get There

Drive north on I-5 to the turnoff for Chuckanut Dr. and Fairhaven. Follow the signs to SR 11, and head south. The entrance to the park is about 7 mi. on the right.

BIRCH BAY

Birch Bay State Park

4105 Helwig, Birch Bay 98230. T: (360) 371-2800 or (888) 226-7688 for reservations; www.parks.wa.gov.

Beauty: ★★★★★ Site Privacy: ★★
Spaciousness: ★★ Quiet: ★★★
Security: ★★★ Cleanliness: ★★
Insect Control: ★★ Facilities: ★★

Birch Bay State Park, incorporates an old growth forest and bay beach, both of the astounding Northwest Washington mainland variety, to provide a scenic place to stay on the U.S. side of the border. Just minutes from Blaine, the park makes a good central base for touring the surrounding area. The campground has two sections, one with a water view and the other surrounded by dense forest. The northern side of the campground (particularly sites 21, 22, 25, 63, 64, and 67) has the best view of the bay, but it also has some traffic noise during the day. The southern side has less noise and no view. Quite a few impressively large trees shade both sections, but sites lack privacy. All sites have mixed surfaces (gravel and dirt). The weather here is simple: cold and rainy. Feel special if the forecast comes out otherwise.

Basics

Operated By: Washington State Parks & Recreation. **Open:** All year (some sites seasonal). **Site Assignment:** On arrival, reservations May 15–Sept. 15 (1 night's stay deposit, 48-hours cancellation notice less $11 fee). **Registration:** At self pay station. **Fee:** Utility $19, standard $13, extra person (more than 4) $2, extra car; $6; V, MC, cash. **Parking:** At site.

Facilities

Number of RV-Only Sites: 18. **Number of Tent-Only Sites:** 0. **Number of Multipurpose Sites:** 148. **Hookups:** Electric (20, 30 amps), water. **Each Site:** Grill, picnic table. **Dump Station:** Yes. **Laundry:** No. **Pay Phone:** Yes. **Rest Rooms and Showers:** Yes. **Fuel:** No. **Propane:** No. **Internal Roads:** Paved, gravel. **RV Service:** No. **Market:** 6 mi. north in Birch Bay. **Restaurant:** 6 mi. North in Birch Bay. **General Store:** No. **Vending:** Yes. **Swimming Pool:** No. **Playground:** No. **Other:** Boat ramp, beach, basketball court. **Activities:** Shellfishing (Red Tide Hotline, (800)-562-5632). **Nearby Attractions:** Birch Bay Golf Club, water slides, scenic tours, whale-watching tours, kayaking, fishing charters, Canada, Bellingham, Mt. Baker. **Additional Information:** Bellingham/Whatcom County Visitor's Bureau, (360) 671-3990 or www.bellingham.org.

Restrictions

Pets: On leash only. **Fires:** In fire pits only. **Alcoholic Beverages:** At sites & picnic areas only. **Vehicle Maximum Length:** 55 ft. **Other:** No firewood gathering, no metal or glass on beaches; 10-day max. stay limit May–Sept., 20-day max. stay limit Oct.–Apr.

To Get There

From I-5 Exit 270, turn west onto Birch Bay Dr. and drive west 3 mi. At a stop sign, turn left on Blaine and drive south 2 mi. At a stop sign turn right on Bay Rd. and travel west 1 mi. At another stop sign, turn left on Jackson and drive 0.2 mi. south to Helwig Dr. Continue 1 mi. on Helwig to the park entrance and 0.3 mi. further to the campground.

BREMERTON

Illahee State Park

3540 Bahia Vista, Bremerton 98310. T: (360) 902-8500 or (360) 478-6460; www.parks.wa.gov.

RV ★★ Tent ★★★★

Beauty: ★★★★★ Site Privacy: ★★★★
Spaciousness: ★★★★ Quiet: ★★★★
Security: ★★★★ Cleanliness: ★★★★★
Insect Control: ★★★ Facilities: ★★

Situated on a high bluff that guards the southern entrance to Port Orchard Bay, Illahee State Park is a gem of a destination roughly an hour by ferry west of Seattle and about a half hour drive north from Tacoma. Illahee is a perfect retreat amidst towering and densely clustered maples, cedars, Douglas fir, madrona, dogwood, and rhododendron. Ferns, huckleberry, blackberry, and salmonberry provide heavy doses of understory for each of the picturesque and very private campsites. After setting up camp, with the sound of seagulls screeching overhead, take one of the park trails that leads down to the waterfront. At low tide, the clamming can be quite good. Crabbing and oystering are options, but check with park officials before eating any shellfish.

Basics

Operated By: Washington State Parks & Recreation Commission. **Open:** All year. **Site Assign-**

ment: First come, first served. **Registration:** Self-registration. **Fee:** $5–$15. **Parking:** At site or in main lot.

Facilities

Number of RV-Only Sites: 1. **Number of Tent-Only Sites:** 24. **Hookups:** None. **Each Site:** Fire grill, picnic table, water, shade trees. **Dump Station:** Yes. **Laundry:** No. **Pay Phone:** Yes. **Rest Rooms and Showers:** Yes. **Fuel:** 1 mi. **Propane:** 1 mi. **Internal Roads:** Paved. **RV Service:** No. **Market:** 1 mi. **Restaurant:** 1 mi. **General Store:** 1 mi. **Vending:** No. **Swimming Pool:** Yes. **Playground:** Yes. **Other:** Boat launch, mooring buoys, dock, covered kitchen. **Activities:** Horseshoe, ball field, boating, swimming, saltwater fishing, bird-watching. **Nearby Attractions:** Scandinavian Poulsbo, Trident Submarine Warfare Base in Bangor, golf courses, Thomas Kemper Brewing Company, antique malls in Port Orchard. **Additional Information:** www.parks.wa.gov.

Restrictions

Pets: On leash only. **Fires:** In fire pits only. **Alcoholic Beverages:** In designated areas. **Vehicle Maximum Length:** 30 ft.

To Get There

From the ferry terminal, follow SR 303 north (Warren Ave.) to SR 306 (Sylvan Way). Turn right, and follow the signs to Illahee. Total distance from the ferry terminal is about 3 mi. From Tacoma, cross the Tacoma Narrows Bridge on SR 16 and follow it for about 25 mi. to Bremerton. Take the City Center Exit (SR 304), which zigzags confusingly through town. Just keep making the obvious zigzags until you reach SR 303 (Warren Ave.). Turn left, and follow the directions above.

CASTLE ROCK

Seaquest State Park

Spirit Lake Hwy., Castle Rock 98611.T: (206) 274-8633 or (800) 452-5687 for reservations; www.parks.wa.gov

RV ★★ Tent ★★★★

Beauty: ★★★★	Site Privacy: ★★★
Spaciousness: ★★	Quiet: ★★★
Security: ★★	Cleanliness: ★★
Insect Control: ★★	Facilities: ★★

Seaquest's only drawback is it's accessibility to the interstate. Situated just off I-5, the park is 60 miles north of Portland and 100 miles south of Seattle. Still, the park is a great base camp for exploring Mount St. Helens, the famous volcano that erupted in 1980. The Mount St. Helen's Visitor Center, located across from the park entrance, offer exhibits on the cultural and historical significance of the area as well as the eruption and ensuing recovery of the area. The 475-acre park borders a one-mile section of Silver Lake. Additionally, visitors can enjoy year-round the playground and ball fields as well as the eight miles of woodland trails suitable for hiking and bicycling.

Basics

Operated By: Washington State Parks & Recreation Commission. **Open:** All year. **Site Assignment:** First come, first served; reservations (May 15–Sept. 15 (1 night's fee deposit, 48-hours cancellation policy, less $11 cancellation fee). **Registration:** At entrance or self pay station. **Fee:** Utility site $20, standard site $14, extra person (more than 4) $2, extra car $6; V, MC, check, cash. **Parking:** At site.

Facilities

Number of RV-Only Sites: 34. **Number of Tent-Only Sites:** 53. **Hookups:** Electric (20, 30 amps), water, sewer. **Each Site:** Picnic table, fire ring. **Dump Station:** Yes. **Laundry:** No. **Pay Phone:** Yes. **Rest Rooms and Showers:** Yes. **Fuel:** No. **Propane:** No. **Internal Roads:** Paved & gravel. **RV Service:** No. **Market:** 5 mi. east by I-5. **Restaurant:** 5 mi. east by I-5. **General Store:** No. **Vending:** No. **Swimming Pool:** No. **Playground:** Yes. **Other:** Horseshoe pit. **Activities:** Hiking. **Nearby Attractions:** Fishing, Mt. St. Helen's Visitor Center, Castle Rock Exhibit Hall, Mt. St. Helens Cinedome Theater, Mt. St. Helens. **Additional Information:** Castle Rock Chamber of Commerce, (360) 274-6603.

Restrictions

Pets: On 6-ft. leash only. **Fires:** Fire rings only. **Alcoholic Beverages:** At site only. **Vehicle Maximum Length:** 40 ft. **Other:** One camping unit (max. 8 people) per site, quiet hours 10p.m.–6:30 a.m.

To Get There

From I-5 Exit 49 Drive East on Hwy. 504 towards for 5.3 mi., the entrance is on left.

CENTRALIA

Midway RV Park

3200 Galvin Rd., Centralia 98531. T: (360) 736-3200; F: (360) 736-6695; www.midwayrv.com; midwayrv @cen.quik.com.

★★★★ n/a

Beauty: ★★★	Site Privacy: ★
Spaciousness: ★★★★	Quiet: ★★
Security: ★★★	Cleanliness: ★★★★
Insect Control: ★★	Facilities: ★★

Midway RV in Centralia has the nicest accomodations among RV parks located roughly halfway between Portland and Puget Sound. The grounds have friendly, yet not overdone, landscaping with small, manicured conifers, red Japanese Maples, and maintained grass. Sites don't have substantial privacy and lack shade, also the city location has some noise. Still, the pleasant grounds and the limited facilities have a well-maintained, newer look, and sites have lots of space. Back-ins on the back perimeter row, numbers 12-24, have the longest diagonal measurements. The rows of sites also have wide access roads. The best time to tour in the region is late summer when weather is the most amicable.

Basics

Operated By: Midway RV. **Open:** All year. **Site Assignment:** On arrival, reservations (deposit: 1 night stay; refund: 72 hours notice of cancellation). **Registration:** At office, late arrivals see sign outside office. **Fee:** $23, extra campers (more than 2) $2, Family rate $25 (2 adults & up to 3 children); V, MC, cash, personal check. **Parking:** At site.

Facilities

Number of RV-Only Sites: 60. **Number of Tent-Only Sites:** 0. **Hookups:** Electric (30, 50 amps), water, sewer, cable. **Dump Station:** No. **Laundry:** Yes. **Pay Phone:** Yes. **Rest Rooms and Showers:** Yes. **Fuel:** No. **Propane:** Yes. **Internal Roads:** Paved. **RV Service:** No. **Market:** Down the street. **Restaurant:** Down the street. **General Store:** Yes. **Vending:** Yes. **Swimming Pool:** No. **Playground:** No. **Other:** Horseshoes, movies for loan, restaurant, rec room, meeting room (reserveable). **Activities:** Monthly potluck. **Nearby Attractions:** The Vintage Antique Motorcycle Museum, skiing, wineries, casino gambling, golf, Puget Sound & big cities, Washington's Pacific coast. **Additional Information:** Centralia, Chehali,s & Greater Lewis County Chamber of Commerce, (360) 748-8885.

Restrictions

Pets: On leash only. **Fires:** No open fires. **Alcoholic Beverages:** At site only. **Vehicle Maximum Length:** None. **Other:** Do not park in grassy areas or vacant spaces.

To Get There

From I-5 Exit 82, drive west on Harrison Ave. to Galvin Rd. Turn left and continue driving for about 0.3 mi. Midway RV Park is on the left side of the road.

CLARKSTON

Granite Lake RV Resort

306 Granite Lake Dr., Clarkston 99403. T: (509) 751-1635 or reservation (800) 989-4578; F: (509) 751-1652; www.granitelakervresort.com; rvresort@clarkston.com.

★★★ n/a

Beauty: ★★★★	Site Privacy: ★
Spaciousness: ★★★	Quiet: ★★
Security: ★★	Cleanliness: ★★★★
Insect Control: ★★	Facilities: ★★

Granite Lake RV Resort in Clarkston (and on the Snake River) has beautiful views but very strong sunlight, no trees, and occasional air pollution from nearby industries. The park sits in downtown Clarkston and very near the Idaho-Washington border. Across the river from the campground, green, steep, rolling hills of grass drop from high altitude to the river's edge, dominating the surrounding landscape; so, the best sites, 23–38, sit on the riverbank. Consisting of a one-way loop, the whole grounds ofer little privacy, in-house recreation, shade, or much landscaping other than grass. The park has large, flat, paved sites surrounded by grass and the occasional shrub. Between the river and the park runs a bike trail, and the newer, well-maintained park has easy access to services and nearby recreation like Hell's Canyon. Summers here bring scorching, dry heat, and winters bring snow. Nights in the summer can be cool, so always have a jacket handy.

Basics

Operated By: Granite Lake Resort. **Open:** All year. **Site Assignment:** On arrival, reservation (deposit: 1 night stay; refund 72 hours notice). **Registration:** At office, after hours pay in morning. **Fee:** For 2 adults, 2 children under 14 years old, Waterfront full $27, Interior full $24, extra adult $3, 3 adults max per site, 1 pet free, second pet $1/day; V, MC, cash. **Parking:** At site.

Facilities

Number of RV-Only Sites: 75. **Number of Tent-Only Sites:** n/a. **Hookups:** Electric (20, 30, 50 amps), water, sewer, cable. **Dump Station:** No. **Laundry:** Yes. **Pay Phone:** Yes. **Rest Rooms and Showers:** Yes. **Fuel:** No. **Propane:** No. **Internal Roads:** Paved. **RV Service:** No. **Market:** A few blocks west. **Restaurant:** A few blocks west. **General Store:** No. **Vending:** Yes. **Swimming Pool:** No. **Playground:** No. **Activities:** Inquire at campground. **Nearby Attractions:** Hells Canyon, Dinner cruises, golf, casinos. **Additional Information:** Clarkston Chamber of Commerce, (800) 993-2128.

Restrictions

Pets: On leash only, no fighting breeds. **Fires:** No open fires. **Alcoholic Beverages:** At site only. **Vehicle Maximum Length:** 42 ft. **Other:** No skateboards, scooters.

To Get There

From Snake River Bridge (WA-ID border) drive 0.3 mi. on Hwy. 12 west, turn right onto 5th St. which dead-ends behind Costco; entrance on right.

CONCONULLY

Liar's Cove Resort

P.O. Box 72, Coconully 98819. T: (509) 826-1288 or (800) 830-1288; www.omakchronicle.com/liarscove; liarscr@televar.com.

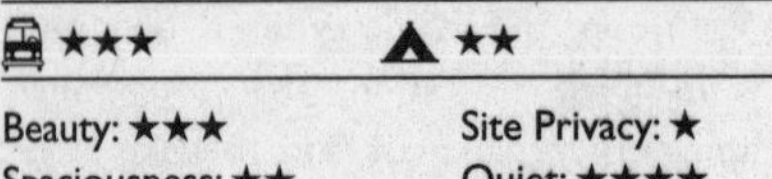

Beauty: ★★★ Site Privacy: ★
Spaciousness: ★★ Quiet: ★★★★
Security: ★★ Cleanliness: ★★★
Insect Control: ★★★ Facilities: ★★★

Liar's Cove RV Park, 15 minutes north of Omak, offers beautiful vistas, quiet, and fishing. The campground sits on the edge of emerald-green Conconully Reservoir, surrounded by ponderosa pines, and beautiful Northern Cascade foothills covered intermittently with evergreens and grass rise sharply from the far shore. Arranged in several terraces, the park extends all the way to the lake's edge, where the best views and most spacious gravel sites (L1–L8) can be found. The whole park lacks shade or privacy between sites and the tent area consists of a small square of mostly gravel and a little grass. The least-spacious RV sites sit on the uppermost terrace (sites 1–10). The area has full-fledged winters; the best weather moves in during the summer.

Basics

Operated By: Liar's Cove Resort. **Open:** Apr. 1–Nov. 1. **Site Assignment:** First come, first served; reservations (deposit: 1 night stay; refund: 72 hours cancellation, 2 weeks for holidays). **Registration:** At office; after hours pay in the morning. **Fee:** Rates for 2 people, Lakefront Full: $21, Middle & upper terrace full & tent: $20, extra person: $2, 7th Day free; V, MC, cash. **Parking:** At site.

Facilities

Number of RV-Only Sites: 30. **Number of Tent-Only Sites:** 10. **Hookups:** Electric (20, 30 amps), water, sewer. **Each Site:** Picnic table, fire ring. **Dump Station:** No. **Laundry:** No. **Pay Phone:** Yes. **Rest Rooms and Showers:** Yes. **Fuel:** No. **Propane:** No. **Internal Roads:** Gravel. **RV Service:** No. **Market:** 20 mi. south in OkaNogan. **Restaurant:** 0.5 mi. North in Conconully. **General Store:** Yes. **Vending:** Yes. **Swimming Pool:** No. **Playground:** No. **Other:** Boat launch, pontoon, paddle, row, & motor boat rentals, fish cleaning station. **Activities:** swimming, fishing, boating. **Nearby Attractions:** Snowmobiling, fishing, mining exhibitions, Colville Indian Reservation, historical points of interest. **Additional Information:** Conconully Chamber of Commerce (877)-826-9050.

Restrictions

Pets: On leash only. **Fires:** In fire pits only. **Alcoholic Beverages:** At site only. **Vehicle Maximum Length:** None. **Other:** Holidays minimum three night stay, Quiet Hours 10 p.m.–7a.m.

To Get There

Off Hwy. 20/2nd Ave S. in Okanogan.

COUGAR

Merrill Lake Campground

601 Bond Rd., Castle Rock 98611. T: (360) 577-2025

Beauty: ★★★★ Site Privacy: ★★★★
Spaciousness: ★★★★★ Quiet: ★★★★★
Security: ★★ Cleanliness: ★★★★
Insect Control: ★★★ Facilities: ★★

Campers who were enjoying the serene quiet of Merrill Lake on the fateful May morning when Mount St. Helens erupted must have been doing so with one eye nervously fixed in the direction of the mountain (which is roughly six air miles to the northeast). When the mountain blew, those lucky enough to have chosen a weekend outing on the south side probably thought that the plume of ash rising to an eventual height of 63,000 feet was the extent of the show. It wouldn't be until they returned home later that evening that television news reports showed them the full extent of the horror. Today, more than a decade later, Merrill Lake Campground sits in wooded isolation just outside the boundaries of Gifford Pinchot National Forest and Mount St. Helens National Volcanic Monument. In summer, most of the tourist throngs inundate Mount St. Helens from the north, leaving you free to explore lands around the geologic wonder in relative solitude.

BASICS

Operated By: Dept. of Natural Resources. **Open:** Memorial Day–Nov. 30. **Site Assignment:** First come, first served. **Registration:** Not necessary. **Fee:** None. **Parking:** At site.

FACILITIES

Number of RV-Only Sites: 0. **Number of Tent-Only Sites:** 7. **Hookups:** None. **Each Site:** Picnic table, fire grill, tent pad. **Dump Station:** No. **Laundry:** No. **Pay Phone:** No. **Rest Rooms and Showers:** Pit toilets. **Fuel:** No. **Propane:** No. **Internal Roads:** No. **RV Service:** No. **Market:** No. **Restaurant:** No. **General Store:** No. **Vending:** No. **Swimming Pool:** No. **Playground:** No. **Other:** Boat launch, disabled access. **Activities:** Boating, fishing, hiking, biking, caving, bird-watching. **Nearby Attractions:** Mount St. Helens, Ape Cave, Cedar Flats Northern Research Natural Area.

RESTRICTIONS

Pets: On leash. **Fires:** In fire pit. **Alcoholic Beverages:** Allowed. **Vehicle Maximum Length:** Call ahead for details. **Other:** RVs prohibited.

TO GET THERE

Take Lewis River Rd. east from Woodland off I-5 to the small settlement of Cougar. Turn north, away from Yale Lake, onto FR 81, and travel 4.5 mi. to the access road that leads to the campground.

COULEE CITY

Sun Lakes Park Resort

34228 Park Ln. Rd. Northeast, Coulee City 99115. T: (509) 632-5291; www.sunlakesparkresort.com.

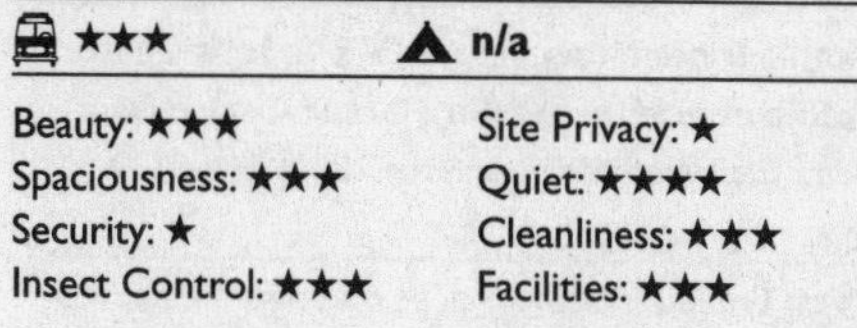

★★★ n/a

Beauty: ★★★ Site Privacy: ★
Spaciousness: ★★★ Quiet: ★★★★
Security: ★ Cleanliness: ★★★
Insect Control: ★★★ Facilities: ★★★

Sun Lakes Park Resort, a concessionaire (leased) campground located in the Sun Lakes State Park complex south of Coulee City, provides a less-rustic alternative to the state park campground next door. When compared to the park, the irrigated campground has more organization, a little more shade, longer and more spacious sites, and a cheaper base rate for full hookups. The full-hookup gravel sites lack privacy, but they have obscured views of surrounding coulee walls through the many old paper birch that shade the park. Cramped back-in sites 81–108 adjoin in the rear; the best back-ins, sites 1–16, sit on the perimeter of a grassy area. The most spacious pull-through sites, 41–80, can accommodate most large rigs. Easy access to fishing and exploration of surrounding natural wonders make this spot popular; visit just before or after summer school break to avoid both crowds and high-altitude winter weather.

BASICS

Operated By: Sunlakes Park Resort, INC. **Open:** Apr.–Sept. **Site Assignment:** Walkups, reservations starting Jan 1 for upcoming season (deposit 1 night's rate/ refund: 7 day confirmation or cancellation. **Registration:** At office, after hours pay in morning. **Fee:** For 4 people, sites 1–16 $24, sites 17–108 $22; V, AE, D, MC, cash. **Parking:** At site.

FACILITIES

Number of RV-Only Sites: 108. **Number of Tent-Only Sites:** n/a. **Hookups:** Electric (20, 30, 50 amps), water, sewer. **Each Site:** Picnic table. **Dump Station:** Yes. **Laundry:** Yes. **Pay Phone:** Yes. **Rest Rooms and Showers:** Yes. **Fuel:** No. **Propane:** Yes. **Internal Roads:** Paved, gravel. **RV**

Service: No. **Market:** 5 mi. north in Coulee City. **Restaurant:** 5 mi. North in Coulee City. **General Store:** Yes. **Vending:** No. **Swimming Pool:** Yes. **Playground:** Yes. **Other:** Mini golf, boat launch & dock, 9 hole golf course, paddle & row boat rentals, fish cleaning station. **Activities:** Hiking, fishing, boating, swimming, bird-watching, picnicking, golfing. **Nearby Attractions:** Grand Coulee Dam, tons of lakes for fishing, two golf courses, hiking trails, rock climbing, various local events, Coulee Dam Casino, Coville Tribes Museum, Dry Falls Visitor's Center. **Additional Information:** Grand Coulee Dam Area Chamber of Commerce, (800) 268-5332.

RESTRICTIONS

Pets: On leash only, no dogs on grass. **Fires:** No open fires. **Alcoholic Beverages:** At site only. **Vehicle Maximum Length:** None. **Other:** Cannot guarantee specific space numbers; check in 3p.m., check out 2:45 p.m.

TO GET THERE

From the junction of Hwy. 17 and Hwy. 2 south of Coulee City, drive 3.8 mi. SW on Hwy. 17; 1.8 mi. south of Dry Falls Visitor Center, turn left onto Park Lake Rd., follow 1.1 mi., entrance on the right.

COULEE CITY

Sun Lakes State Park Campground

34875 Park Lake Rd. Northeast, Coulee City 99115. T: (509)-632-5583; www.parks.wa.gov; infocent@parks.wa.gov.

RV ★★ Tent ★★

Beauty: ★★★	Site Privacy: ★
Spaciousness: ★★	Quiet: ★★★★
Security: ★★	Cleanliness: ★★★
Insect Control: ★★★	Facilities: ★★

Sun Lakes State Park south of Coulee City off of Hwy. 17 offers convenient access to many outdoor recreational activities. Many of these activities exist within the state park complex or a short walk from the campground. Most of the gravel sites have no hookups, but there are 18 gravel, full-hookup sites, and sites 49–51 have the most space and shade. Every site lacks privacy, but sites 26–33 sit in a slightly secluded area away from the rest of the grounds. An arid mix of sage-crusted hills and forbidding coulee walls make up nearby scenery, and the sun can be intense here. Sites 62–66, 163–170, and 177–180 have little to no shade. Black locust, birch, and maple create partial shade for most other sites. The flowering black locust trees bring bees in May and June, so avoid the park during this time if at risk for an allergic reaction. Management permits tents in all sites, but not on any grassy areas. Visit during late spring or early fall, when crowd volumes and temperatures and mild.

BASICS

Operated By: Washington State Parks & Recreation. **Open:** All year (fully operational Apr.–Sept.). **Site Assignment:** First come, first served; reservations(during on-season only, May 15-Sept. 15; Deposit-1 night plus non refundable reservation fee; refund: 48 hours cancellation). **Registration:** At park office or self-registration station. **Fee:** For 4 people, full: $20, standard (no hookups): $14, extra person: $2, extra vehicle (over 2): $6; V, MC, check, cash. **Parking:** At site.

FACILITIES

Number of RV-Only Sites: 18. **Number of Tent-Only Sites:** 180. **Hookups:** Electric (20, 30 amps), water, sewer. **Each Site:** Picnic table, fire ring. **Dump Station:** Yes. **Laundry:** No. **Pay Phone:** Yes. **Rest Rooms and Showers:** Yes. **Fuel:** No. **Propane:** No. **Internal Roads:** Paved. **RV Service:** No. **Market:** 5 mi. north in Coulee City. **Restaurant:** 5 mi. North in Coulee City. **General Store:** No. **Vending:** No. **Swimming Pool:** No. **Playground:** Yes. **Other:** Horseshoes, non-improved boat launch, golf course, row boat rental. **Activities:** Hiking, extensive fishing, swimming, golf, boating, metal detecting, bird-watching. **Nearby Attractions:** Grand Coulee Dam, tons of lakes for fishing, two golf courses, hiking trails, rock climbing, various local events, Coulee Dam Casino, Coville Tribes Museum, Dry Falls Visitor's Center, Lake Lenore Caves. **Additional Information:** Grand Coulee Dam Area Chamber of Commerce, (800) 268-5332.

RESTRICTIONS

Pets: On leash only (6 ft in length). **Fires:** In fire pits only. **Alcoholic Beverages:** At site only. **Vehicle Maximum Length:** None. **Other:** Be aware of "swimmer's itch" that may occur if swimming area is contaminated by snails; max stay 10 days during summer, 20 days during winter.

TO GET THERE

From the junction of Hwy. 17 and Hwy. 2 south of Coulee City: Drive 3.8 mi. SW on

Hwy. 17; 1.8 mi. south of Dry Falls Visitor Center, turn left onto Park Lake Rd. and go 1.1 mi., entrance on the left.

COUPEVILLE
Fort Ebey State Park

395 North Fort Ebey Rd., Coupeville 98239. T: (360) 678-4636; www.parks.wa.gov.

RV ★ Tent ★★★★

Beauty: ★★★★★	Site Privacy: ★★★
Spaciousness: ★★★★	Quiet: ★★★
Security: ★★★★★	Cleanliness: ★★★★
Insect Control: ★★	Facilities: ★★

Situated in relatively underdeveloped waterfront beauty, Fort Ebey is increasingly popular among tent campers and others looking to escape urban life. From a tent-camping perspective, Fort Ebey is decidedly the least developed. It is evident that every attempt has been made to retain the natural beauty of the area. Old-growth Douglas fir marks this region, and an undergrowth of salal, huckleberry, Scotch broom, and rhododendron isn't dense but provides pleasant greenbelts between campsites. There are plenty of activities within the 226-acre park. Beachcombing along the driftwood-laden shoreline. Hiking the wooded trails along the bluffline. Fishing for bass in freshwater Lake Pondilla. Watching a surprising variety of wildlife, including bald eagles, deer, geese, ducks, raccoons, rabbits, pheasant, and grouse. Seeking out the varieties of cactus (yes, cactus!) that grow in this unusual "banana belt" region of western Washington. Exploring the fort's old gun emplacements. If this doesn't satisfy you, there are several other state parks in the neighborhood, too.

BASICS

Operated By: Washington State Parks & Recreation Commission. **Open:** Late Feb.–Oct. 31. **Site Assignment:** First come, first served; reservations accepted mid–May–mid–Sept.; call (800) 452–5687; $6 reservation fee. **Registration:** At camp office. **Fee:** $12–$17. **Parking:** At site.

FACILITIES

Number of RV-Only Sites: Inquire at campground. **Number of Tent-Only Sites:** 0. **Number of Multipurpose Sites:** 50. **Hookups:** Electric (30 amps) at 4 sites. **Each Site:** Picnic table, fire grill, shade trees. **Dump Station:** No. **Laundry:** No. **Pay Phone:** Yes. **Rest Rooms and Showers:** Yes. **Fuel:** 2 mi. in Coupeville. **Propane:** 2 mi. **Internal Roads:** Paved. **RV Service:** No. **Market:** 2 mi. **Restaurant:** 2 mi. **General Store:** 2 mi. **Vending:** No. **Swimming Pool:** No. **Playground:** No. **Other:** Picnic area, boat launch. **Activities:** Fishing, boating, hiking, biking, badminton, bird-watching. **Nearby Attractions:** Lake Pondilla. **Additional Information:** www.parks.wa.gov.

RESTRICTIONS

Pets: On leash only. **Fires:** In fire pit. **Alcoholic Beverages:** Allowed. **Vehicle Maximum Length:** Call ahead for details.

TO GET THERE

From Seattle, drive north on I-5 and WA Rtes. 526 and 525 to Mukilteo and the Washington State Ferry terminal for Whidbey Island. Once on the island, follow SR 525 north, pick up US 20 at Keystone, and continue north to Libbey Rd. and signs to the park. Total driving distance on Whidbey Island is about 35 mi. An alternative route is to take US 20 west from I-5 at Burlington (just over 60 mi. north of Seattle), and drive down the northern half of Whidbey Island through scenic Deception Pass. This route allows you to avoid ferry lines.

DAVENPORT
Two Rivers RV Park

68 B. Hwy. 25S, Davenport 99129. T: (509) 722-4029

RV ★★★★ Tent ★★

Beauty: ★★★	Site Privacy: ★
Spaciousness: ★★★	Quiet: ★★★★
Security: ★★	Cleanliness: ★★★★
Insect Control: ★★	Facilities: ★★★★

Two Rivers RV Resort, a half hour north of Davenport on Hwy. 25, provides a convenient location for visiting the adjacent casino and Fort Spokane. The campground sits on high bluffs overlooking the giant, gray-blue Spokane River, with an organizational scheme of several loops plus two rows of campsites surrounded by lots of grass and some small flowering shrubs. The sites lack privacy or shade, but most have views of the surrounding semi-arid rolling highlands that fall towards the river; sites with views of the river exist on G and F loops. Half the sites in section E back into a hill, diminishing their scenic views.

The park has a few large pull-throughs, but it consists mostly of paved, spacious back-ins. The tent section of the campground has a cramped arrangement of picnic areas with some grassy patches for tents; sites 15–18 and 23–26 sit on the edge of bluffs overlooking the river. The park boasts two unusually large playground areas, but there's not much more in the way of on-site family recreation. Winters here are snowy and cold; visit during the late spring or summer for warm temperatures.

BASICS

Operated By: Spokane Tribe of Washington. **Open:** All year. **Site Assignment:** Reservations (deposit 1 night's stay; refund). **Registration:** At office, after hours pay in morning. **Fee:** For 6 people, full pull-through: $23, full Back in: $19, tent: $14, extra person: $2, 10 people site capacity; V, MC, check, cash. **Parking:** At site, some off site.

FACILITIES

Number of RV-Only Sites: 100. **Number of Tent-Only Sites:** 32. **Hookups:** Electric (20, 30, 50 amps), water, sewer. **Each Site:** Picnic table, grill. **Dump Station:** Yes. **Laundry:** Yes. **Pay Phone:** Yes. **Rest Rooms and Showers:** Yes. **Fuel:** Yes. **Propane:** Yes. **Internal Roads:** Paved & gravel. **RV Service:** No. **Market:** 25 mi. south in Davenport. **Restaurant:** 25 mi. south in Davenport. **General Store:** No. **Vending:** Yes. **Swimming Pool:** No. **Playground:** Yes. **Other:** Horseshoe pit, marina w/ houseboat rentals, casino. **Activities:** Fishing, 4th of Jul. fireworks show, hiking, swimming, gambling, boating. **Nearby Attractions:** Fort Spokane, Two River's Casino, hiking, fishing. **Additional Information:** Davenport Chamber of Commerce (509) 725-6711.

RESTRICTIONS

Pets: On leash only, pick up after pets. **Fires:** In fire pits only. **Alcoholic Beverages:** At site only. **Vehicle Maximum Length:** 40 ft. **Other:** No refund once checked in; 3-day minimum stay on holidays.

TO GET THERE

From the junction of Hwy. 2 and 25 on east side of Davenport: Drive 23.5 mi. north on Hwy. 25, then turn left on Confluence Dr. just after Fort Spokane and Spokane River Bridge, entrance to campground on left.

ELECTRIC CITY

Coulee Playland Resort

Box 457 Hwy. 155 No. 1, Electric City 99123.
T: (509) 633-2671; F: (509) 633-2133;
www.couleeplayland.com.

RV ★★★ Tent ★★

Beauty: ★★	Site Privacy: ★
Spaciousness: ★★★	Quiet: ★★
Security: ★	Cleanliness: ★★★
Insect Control: ★★★	Facilities: ★★★

Coulee Playland Resort, a couple of minutes south of Electric City, offers sites in a less crowded environment than Sunbanks resort down the road. Not as nicely furnished or landscaped as the latter, the grounds of the former consists of several rows of sites near or on the edge of Banks Lake. The general store is stocked with a wide array of fishing and boating accessories. Although the gravel RV sites lack both shade and privacy, most have the breathtaking views characteristic of the region. Water and electric sites 77–85 sit right on the water, with great views of contrasting bright-green sage and dull-colored shear coulee walls. Full-hookup sites 36–57 back into a hill, with more space than undesirable full hookups 1–18. Grassy tent sites B1–B7 sit on the deep blue lake's edge without shade or privacy. Particularly avoid water and electric back-ins 86–89, sitting as they do without a view of anything in what seems like a gravel pit. Spring, summer, and early fall make the best times to visit and avoid winter weather.

BASICS

Operated By: Coulee Playland Resort. **Open:** All year, fully operational Mar.–Oct. **Site Assignment:** First come, first served; reservations (one night stay deposit, 72 hour cancellation). **Registration:** At office, after hours at drop box in front of office. **Fee:** Full $20, standard: $17.50, B**Each Site:** $18, Beach Site w/ electric: $19, Yurt: $49; V , MC, AE, D, cash. **Parking:** At site.

FACILITIES

Number of RV-Only Sites: 59. **Number of Tent-Only Sites:** 8. **Hookups:** Electric (20, 30 amps), water, sewer. **Each Site:** Picnic table, grill. **Dump Station:** Yes. **Laundry:** Yes. **Pay Phone:** Yes. **Rest Rooms and Showers:** Yes. **Fuel:** Yes. **Propane:** No. **Internal Roads:** Gravel & paved.

RV Service: No. **Market:** 3 mi. north in Grand Coulee. **Restaurant:** 3 mi. north in Grand Coulee. **General Store:** Yes. **Vending:** No. **Swimming Pool:** No. **Playground:** Yes. **Other:** Boat launch & moorage, boat fuelling, store w/ fishing, boating supplies, & deli; 1 yurt, group picnic area, fishing licenses. **Activities:** Swimming, fishing, boating, picnicking. **Nearby Attractions:** Grand Coulee Dam, tons of lakes for fishing, 2 golf courses, Steamboat Rock State Park, hiking trails, rock climbing, various local events, Coulee Dam Casino, Coville Tribes Museum. **Additional Information:** Grand Coulee Dam Area Chamber of Commerce, (800) 268-5332.

Restrictions

Pets: On leash only. **Fires:** In fire pits only. **Alcoholic Beverages:** At site only. **Vehicle Maximum Length:** None. **Other:** Quiet Hours 10 p.m.–8 a.m.

To Get There

From the junction of Hwy. 174 and Hwy. 155 in Grand Coulee: Drive 1 mi. south on Hwy. 155, and take the second entrance on the right

ELECTRIC CITY

Steamboat Rock State Park Campground

P.O. Box 370, Electric City 99123-0352. T: (800) 233-0321 or reservations (800) 452-5687; www.parks.wa.gov; infocent@parks.wa.gov.

RV ★★★ Tent ★★★★

Beauty: ★★★★★	Site Privacy: ★
Spaciousness: ★★★	Quiet: ★★★★★
Security: ★★	Cleanliness: ★★★
Insect Control: ★★★	Facilities: ★★★

Steamboat Rock State Park Campground, 20 minutes south of Electric City, has the best local views of the surrounding coulee landscape of any campground in the area. The grounds lack shade or privacy, but this beneficially provides views of the shear, dark-toned, multicolored cliffs rising to the east and west. Site arrangement consists of cul-de-sacs of paved full-hookup sites, and standard sites on the avenues leading towards the cul-de sacs, all cut out of a grass field. The grounds sit on the shore of huge, blue Banks Lake, and the best sites with water views include full-hookup sites 81–90, 76–79, 55–57, 41–50, and standard sites 310–312. Tents must be erected within the designated dirt areas at each site, thus protecting the irrigated grass. The best time to visit is during the summer, since winters are cold and snowy.

Basics

Operated By: Washington State Parks & Recreation. **Open:** Year-round (some seasonal sites). **Site Assignment:** First come, first served; reservations (deposit: 1 night plus non refundable reservation fee; refund: 48 hours cancellation). **Registration:** At self pay station or front gate. **Fee:** For 4 people, Utility Site (Full Hookup) $20, standard $14, extra person $2 (max. 8 people per site), Extra Vehicle $6; V, MC, check, cash. **Parking:** At site.

Facilities

Number of RV-Only Sites: 100. **Number of Tent-Only Sites:** 26. **Hookups:** Electric (20, 30 amps), water, sewer. **Each Site:** Picnic table, fire ring. **Dump Station:** Yes. **Laundry:** No. **Pay Phone:** Yes. **Rest Rooms and Showers:** Yes. **Fuel:** No. **Propane:** No. **Internal Roads:** Paved in good condition. **RV Service:** No. **Market:** 11 mi. north in Electric City. **Restaurant:** 11 mi. north in Electric City. **General Store:** Yes, in day-use area. **Vending:** No. **Swimming Pool:** No. **Playground:** No. **Other:** In State Park complex: hiking trails, boat launch & dock. **Activities:** Hiking, fishing, swimming, canoeing, water skiing, mountain biking, hiking, rock climbing. **Nearby Attractions:** Grand Coulee Dam, tons of lakes for fishing, 2 golf courses, hiking trails, rock climbing, various local events, Coulee Dam Casino, Coville Tribes Museum. **Additional Information:** Grand Coulee Dam Area Chamber of Commerce, (800) 268-5332.

Restrictions

Pets: Leash Only (6 ft. long). **Fires:** In fire pits only. **Alcoholic Beverages:** At site only. **Vehicle Maximum Length:** 45 ft. **Other:** Quiet hours 11 p.m.–6:30 a.m.; max stay 10 days during summer, 20 days during winter; check in at 2:30 p.m., check out at 1 p.m.

To Get There

From the junction of Hwy. 155 and Hwy. 174, drive 7 mi. south on Hwy. 155, after state park boat launch, entrance is 3 mi. south on Hwy. 155. Take a right turn onto unnamed road indicated by a Washington Park Service sign. Follow this road northwest for 2 mi. until reaching park gate. Past the park gate, the campground is on the right.

ELECTRIC CITY

Sunbanks Resort

57662 Hwy. 155 N, Electric City 99123. T: (888) 822-7195; F: (509) 633-3472; www.sunbanksresort.com; info@sunbanksresort.com.

RV ★★★★ Tent ★★★

Beauty: ★★★★	Site Privacy: ★★
Spaciousness: ★★	Quiet: ★★★★
Security: ★★★	Cleanliness: ★★★★
Insect Control: ★★★	Facilities: ★★★★★

Sunbanks Resort, on the edge of deep, blue Banks Lake just south of Electric City, comes stocked with beautiful views of surrounding scenery and nicely furnished facilities. A mix of arid and irrigated areas creates an intriguing landscape inside the grounds. Sites consist of grass or gravel in a seemingly random organization running downhill to the lake's edge. The shady, gravel, back-in, full hookups sit in cramped, adjacent rows near the office. Most RV sites on the property have water and electric hookups; of these, sites 85–95, 60–63, and 68–74 make up the least-crowded areas. Sites A and B sit on a flat hill with a crow's-nest view of shear, jagged coulee walls and the lake, but they have no hookups and access limited by vehicle size. The best tent options, sites 1–39, sit on the shores of Banks Lake in a semi-shaded, grassy area. Inter-site privacy does not exist here, and the grounds become extremely cramped when full. Just before or after the summer season make the best times to visit and avoid crowds.

Basics

Operated By: Precision Mgmt. **Open:** All year; fully operational Apr. 1–Oct. **Site Assignment:** First come, first served; reservations (deposit: 1st night's stay, non-refundable). **Registration:** At gate or lodge; after hours pay in morning. **Fee:** For 6 people, Water-electric: $30, full: $34, Waterfront tent $34, Non-waterfront tent: $30, View site: $26. **Parking:** At site.

Facilities

Number of RV-Only Sites: 125. **Number of Tent-Only Sites:** 82. **Hookups:** Electric (20, 30, 50 amps), water, sewer. **Each Site:** Picnic table, grated fire pits. **Dump Station:** Yes. **Laundry:** Yes. **Pay Phone:** Yes. **Rest Rooms and Showers:** Yes. **Fuel:** No. **Propane:** No. **Internal Roads:** Well-maintained gravel. **RV Service:** No. **Market:** 5 mi. north in Electric City. **Restaurant:** 5 mi. North in Electric City. **General Store:** Yes. **Vending:** Yes. **Swimming Pool:** No. **Playground:** No. **Other:** Cafe, boat launch & moorage, outdoor stage, game room (2 pool tables), paddleboat rentals, horseshoes, play field. **Activities:** Swimming, fishing, boating, water skiing & other watersports (BYOB-Bring Your Own Boat). **Nearby Attractions:** Grand Coulee Dam, tons of lakes for fishing, 2 golf courses, Steamboat Rock State Park, hiking trails, rock climbing, various local events, Coulee Dam Casino, Coville Tribes Museum. **Additional Information:** Grand Coulee Dam Area Chamber of Commerce, (800) 268-5332.

Restrictions

Pets: Leash Only. **Fires:** In fire pits only. **Alcoholic Beverages:** At site only. **Vehicle Maximum Length:** None. **Other:** Watch for no pet areas; 2 night minimum stay on all reservations; site requests not guaranteed; tents must be moved every three days.

To Get There

From the junction of Hwy. 174 and Hwy. 155, go 3 mi. south on 155; entrance on right just before bridge.

ELLENSBURG

Ellensburg KOA

32 Thorp Hwy. South, Ellensburg 98926. T: (509)-925-9319; koa.com/where/wa/47129.htm.

RV ★★ Tent ★

Beauty: ★★★	Site Privacy: ★
Spaciousness: ★★	Quiet: ★
Security: ★★	Cleanliness: ★★★★
Insect Control: ★★	Facilities: ★★★

Ellensburg KOA, on the Yakima River, provides local access to unique recreation and sites on the river. Site arrangement consists of several parallel rows and sites on the perimeter of the grounds. The best gravel-grass perimetered full hookups, sites 4–20, sit on the banks of the green, swift river, shaded by weeping willows and pines. There also exist some quality tent spots on the river at sites T6–T13; unfortunately, these sites have a noise problem from the overpass that runs right next to site T13. Sites T1–T5 offer no shade, a definite minus in this area of intense sunlight.

Patchy grass provides thin ground cover around individual sites, but in the common areas the standard seems higher. The seasonal area has hot summers and mild winters; visit during milder spring or fall months if avoiding heat is desirable.

Basics

Operated By: Ellensburg KOA. **Open:** All year. **Site Assignment:** On arrival, reservations (deposit: 1 night's stay; refund: 24 hours cancellation). **Registration:** At office, after hours at drop by office. **Fee:** For 2 people, one camping vehicle, full $24.95, Water-electric $22.95, Tent $18, extra people/vehicle $3, Max per site 4 adults or 2 adults & 4 children (V, MC, cash). **Parking:** At site, limited off site.

Facilities

Number of RV-Only Sites: 90. **Number of Tent-Only Sites:** 30. **Hookups:** Electric (30, 50 amps), water, sewer. **Each Site:** Picnic table, fire pit. **Dump Station:** Yes. **Laundry:** Yes. **Pay Phone:** Yes. **Rest Rooms and Showers:** Yes. **Fuel:** No. **Propane:** No. **Internal Roads:** Gravel & paved. **RV Service:** No. **Market:** 4 mi. east in Ellensburg. **Restaurant:** 4 mi. east in Ellensburg. **General Store:** Yes. **Vending:** No. **Swimming Pool:** Yes. **Playground:** Yes. **Other:** Badminton, volleyball, horseshoes, arcade, boat ramp, kiddie pool, movie rentals. **Activities:** River fishing, swimming, boating. **Nearby Attractions:** Clymer Museum & Gallery, Gallery One, fly fishing, Ellensburg Bull Sculpture, Kittitas County Museum, Thorp Grist Mill, Chimpanzee & Human Communication Institute. **Additional Information:** Ellensburg Chamber of Commerce, (888) 925-2204.

Restrictions

Pets: On leash only. **Fires:** In fire pits only. **Alcoholic Beverages:** At site only. **Vehicle Maximum Length:** None. **Other:** No parking on grass areas.

To Get There

From I-90 Exit 106, turn south (if west-bound, turn left) and drive 0.2 mi. Turn left onto Thorp Hwy.; the entrance is on the left

ENUMCLAW

Corral Pass Campground

c/o White River Ranger District, Enumclaw 98022. T: (360) 825-6585; www.fs.fed.us/r6/mbs.

 n/a 

Beauty: ★★★★ Site Privacy: ★★★★★
Spaciousness: ★★★★★ Quiet: ★★★★★
Security: ★★ Cleanliness: ★★★
Insect Control: ★★★ Facilities: ★★

For your own personal, unsurpassed view of the north face of Mount Rainier and for a different perspective of Crystal Mountain Ski Area, take a hard left off WA Rte. 410 about 30 miles out of Enumclaw, onto FR 7174, to Corral Pass Campground. But bring plenty of water because there is no piped water here. Hopefully, you've come to Corral Pass for the backcountry hiking options, which are plentiful. Among a number of choices, there's Norse Peak Wilderness brushing the ridgetop just east of the campground, covering more than 50,000 acres of diverse terrain dissected by 52 miles of hiking trails. There is a surprising variety of wildlife and vegetation to enjoy as well—mountain goats, elk, and deer, to name a few. The wildflowers in the meadows around Noble Knob are known to rival those at Paradise on Mount Rainier's southern slope when in full bloom (late June to early August, depending on the elevation), and berry-picking is prime in late August and early September.

Basics

Operated By: Mount Baker-Snoqualmie National Forest. **Open:** Jul.–late Sept. **Site Assignment:** First come, first served. **Registration:** Not necessary. **Fee:** None. **Parking:** At site.

Facilities

Number of RV-Only Sites: 0. **Number of Tent-Only Sites:** 20. **Hookups:** None. **Each Site:** Picnic table, fire grill. **Dump Station:** No. **Laundry:** No. **Pay Phone:** No. **Rest Rooms and Showers:** Vault toilets. **Fuel:** No. **Propane:** No. **Internal Roads:** Call ahead for details. **RV Service:** No. **Market:** No. **Restaurant:** No. **General Store:** No. **Vending:** No. **Swimming Pool:** No. **Playground:** No. **Other:** Firewood. **Activities:** Hiking, fishing, horseback riding. **Nearby Attractions:** Norse Peak Wilderness, Noble Knob, Echo Lake/Greenwater River Trail, Naches Trail. **Additional Information:** www.fs.fed.us/r6/mbs.

Restrictions

Pets: On leash only. **Fires:** In fire pit. **Alcoholic Beverages:** Allowed. **Vehicle Maximum Length:** RVs & trailers not recommended. **Other:** No piped water.

TO GET THERE

From Enumclaw (roughly 40 mi. southeast of Seattle), take SR 410 southeast for about 30 mi. Turn left onto FS 7174 and follow to its end (6 mi.). The highway marker for FS 7174 can be obscured by overhanging foliage, so keep a sharp lookout for it on the right side of the road. If you find yourself at the turnoff to Crystal Mountain Ski Area and the entrance to Mount Rainier National Park, you've gone about 1 mi. too far.

FALL CITY

Snoqualmie River Campground and RV Park

P.O.Box 16, Fall City 98024. T: (425) 222-5545

RV ★★★ Tent ★★

Beauty: ★★★	Site Privacy: ★
Spaciousness: ★★★	Quiet: ★★★
Security: ★	Cleanliness: ★★★
Insect Control: ★★	Facilities: ★★

Snoqualmie River Campground and RV Park, about an hour east of Seattle off I-90 in Fall City, provides a rural, mountain setting between two rivers. A flat field with sites around the perimeter comprises the campground; the center of the park has lots of wide-open grassy space. RV sites have dirt surfaces, while tent sites consist of grass. No sites have privacy, but the best sites, pull-throughs 75–92, sit near one river (no views). Sites 110–117 make up the best tent sites; avoid sites 1–21, 38–40, and tent sites 101–109, as a fence provides the only separation between this side of the park and the golf course next door. Fishing from the river sounds good, with salmon among possible catches. Of course, seasons vary. The park does receive some noise from a nearby road; the best time to visit is during the summer. Salmon usually run in late spring to early summer. Call to find out about flood schedule (this park floods every year).

BASICS

Operated By: Snoqualmie River Campground. **Open:** Apr. 1–Oct. 31. **Site Assignment:** On arrival, reservation (deposit or credit card to hold). **Registration:** At office, after hours pay in morning. **Fee:** For 2 adults, Water electric $23, Tent $21, extra people $3.50, Children under 6 years of age-free, Day use fee $8 per car (max 5 people); V, MC, cash. **Parking:** At site & off site.

FACILITIES

Number of RV-Only Sites: 92. **Number of Tent-Only Sites:** 25. **Hookups:** Electric (30 amps), water, cable. **Each Site:** Picnic table, fire ring. **Dump Station:** Yes. **Laundry:** No. **Pay Phone:** Yes. **Rest Rooms and Showers:** Yes. **Fuel:** No. **Propane:** No. **Internal Roads:** Gravel. **RV Service:** No. **Market:** 5 mi. in Fall City. **Restaurant:** 5 mi. in Fall City. **General Store:** No. **Vending:** No. **Swimming Pool:** No. **Playground:** Yes. **Other:** Pavillion, river access nearby, large open field. **Activities:** Fishing (salmon & others, call about seasons). **Nearby Attractions:** Northwest Railway Museum, Snoqualmie Falls, fishing, rafting, river water sports, Seattle, Puget Sound, Snoqualmie Pass, Mt. Baker-Snoqualmie National Forest. **Additional Information:** Upper Snoqualmie Valley Chamber of Commerce, (425) 888-4440.

RESTRICTIONS

Pets: On leash only (no livestock please). **Fires:** In fire pits only. **Alcoholic Beverages:** At site only. **Vehicle Maximum Length:** None. **Other:** Make sure to call about flood season before arrival.

TO GET THERE

From I-90 Exit 22, drive north on Preston-Fall City Rd. for 4.5 mi., then turn right on SE 45th PL, and drive 1 mi. until road dead-ends into campground

FEDERAL WAY

Dash Point State Park

5700 Southwest Dash Point Rd., Federal Way 98023. T: (253) 593-2206; www.parks.wa.gov.

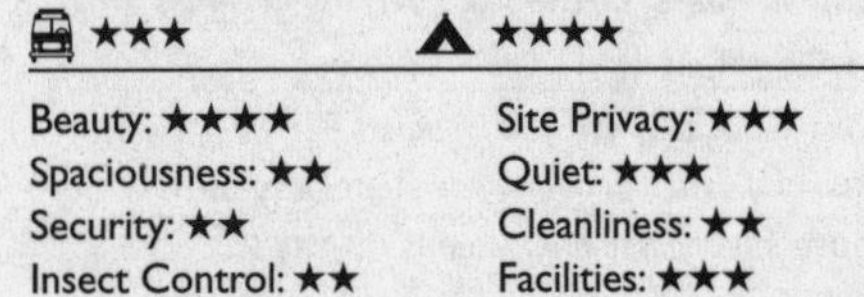

RV ★★★ Tent ★★★★

Beauty: ★★★★	Site Privacy: ★★★
Spaciousness: ★★	Quiet: ★★★
Security: ★★	Cleanliness: ★★
Insect Control: ★★	Facilities: ★★★

For a state park near the city, Dash Point State Park provides a nicely wooded camping environment just west of Tacoma. Set in a shady forest of fir and cedar and divided into two loops, the campground also has a trail leading down to a beach on Puget Sound. The lower loop better accomodates RVs; both loops provide amiable tent accomodations. In the lower loop, one finds some water and electric sites, paved parking in every site, and a dirt area for picnicking and tenting in each site; some sites have a layout more conducive to tents, with less density in a localized area. Utility sites sit in an area with a higher site density. Based on space and privacy, lower-loop utility sites 34–49 and non-utility sites 12–28 have the most of the aforementioned traits. The upper loop houses similar sites, but with dirt parking, no utilities, and much less room for all but small RVs. Sites 119–124 sit in a high-traffic area; sites in the upper loop vary in size and have much more foliage than lower-loop sites. Visit during the summer for the best weather, but the rainy season also has a beautiful, ethereal charm.

Basics

Operated By: Washington State Parks & Recreation. **Open:** All year, upper loop open only May–Sept. **Site Assignment:** On arrival, reservations. **Registration:** At gate or self pay station. **Fee:** Water electric $20, No hookups $14, extra car $6; V, MC, cash. **Parking:** At site.

Facilities

Number of RV-Only Sites: 27. **Number of Tent-Only Sites:** 114 non-utility. **Hookups:** Electric (20, 30 amps), water. **Each Site:** Picnic table, fire ring. **Dump Station:** Yes. **Laundry:** No. **Pay Phone:** Yes. **Rest Rooms and Showers:** Yes. **Fuel:** No. **Propane:** No. **Internal Roads:** Paved. **RV Service:** No. **Market:** In Federal Way, a few mi. **Restaurant:** In Federal Way, a few mi. **General Store:** No. **Vending:** Yes. **Swimming Pool:** No. **Playground:** No. **Other:** Amphitheater, hiking trails, biking trails, beach. **Activities:** Jr. Ranger programs during summer, hiking, biking. **Nearby Attractions:** Seattle, Tacoma, Olympia, Mt's. Rainier & St. Helens, skiing, Puget Sound. **Additional Information:** Seattle Visitor Info Center, (206) 461-5840; www.seeseattle.org.

Restrictions

Pets: On leash only (6 ft. max length). **Fires:** In fire pits only. **Alcoholic Beverages:** At site only. **Vehicle Maximum Length:** 40 ft. **Other:** Remember wildlife, plants, pretty much everything in park protected by law.

To Get There

From I-5: Exit at the 320th St. Exit (Exit 143). Take 320th St. west 4 mi. When 320th St. ends at a T-intersection, make a right onto 47th St. When 47th St. ends at another T-intersection, turn left onto Hwy. 509/Dash Point Rd. Drive 2 mi. to the park. (West side of street is the campground side, and east is the day-use area.)

FERNDALE
The Cedars RV Resort

6335 Portal Way, Ferndale 98248. T: (360) 384-2622; F: (360) 380-6365.

RV ★★★ Tent ★★

Beauty: ★ Site Privacy: ★★★★
Spaciousness: ★★ Quiet: ★★
Security: ★★★ Cleanliness: ★★★
Insect Control: ★★ Facilities: ★★★

The Cedars in Ferndale makes a great place to stop in northwest Washington for travelers seeking amenities. While the campground lacks any real connection with the surrounding natural environment, grass- and gravel-surfaced sites do have cedar hedges allowing some privacy for individual campers. Utility sections A and B and sites C1–C9 have the densest and tallest hedges, but only water and electric hookups. Full-hookup sites L9–L15 have the best view of the mountains to the east, but less privacy. A different story entirely, the tenting areas consist of open grass plots interspersed throughout the grounds in random locations. Summers here come in the Indian variety (July through Sept), but even then rain and cold abound. The area plays host to year-round tourism, as travel during winter seldom gets difficult.

Basics

Operated By: Holiday Trails Resorts. **Open:** All year. **Site Assignment:** On arrival, reservations. **Registration:** At general store. **Fee:** For 2 adults, 2 children, full $26, Water, electric $24, Dry camping $18, extra adult $3, Phone (nightly)–$2, Cable (nightly)–$2; V, MC, cash. **Parking:** At site.

Facilities

Number of RV-Only Sites: 117. **Number of Tent-Only Sites:** 0. **Hookups:** Electric (30, 50 amps), water, cable, phone. **Each Site:** Picnic table. **Dump Station:** Yes. **Laundry:** Yes. **Pay Phone:** Yes. **Rest Rooms and Showers:** Yes. **Fuel:** No. **Propane:** No. **Internal Roads:** Paved & gravel. **RV Service:** No. **Market:** 6 mi. south in Ferndale.

Restaurant: 6 mi. south in Ferndale. **General Store:** Yes. **Vending:** Yes. **Swimming Pool:** Yes. **Playground:** Yes. **Other:** Arcade, reception hall (max capacity 122 people), volleyball court. **Activities:** Horseshoes, badminton, volleyball, berry picking (in season), casino gambling (call about availability of shuttles to casinos). **Nearby Attractions:** Pioneer park, Hovander Homestead Park, Canada, The San Juan Islands, Victoria, whale-watching, fishing, Mt. Baker Ski Area & National Forest. **Additional Information:** Whatcom County Visitor's Bureau, (360) 671-3990, www.bellingham.org.

Restrictions

Pets: On leash only (no fighting breeds, no more than 2 dogs per site). **Fires:** In fire pits only. **Alcoholic Beverages:** At site, picnic areas only. **Vehicle Maximum Length:** 60 ft. **Other:** 7 day stay limit on dry camping, electric sites.

To Get There

From I-5 Exit 263, turn northeast on Portal Way, and drive 0.8 mi. The Cedars Resort will be on the left and clearly marked.

GIG HARBOR

Gig Harbor RV Resort

9515 Burnham Dr. Northwest, Gig Harbor 98332. T: (253) 858-8138 or (800) 526-8311; F: (253) 858-8399.

★★★ ★★

Beauty: ★★★	Site Privacy: ★★
Spaciousness: ★★★	Quiet: ★★★
Security: ★	Cleanliness: ★★★★
Insect Control: ★★	Facilities: ★★★

Gig Harbor RV Resort, located off Hwy. 16 and 45 minutes southwest of Seattle, provides lodging near a beautiful harbor area. Large terraced, gravel sites crown this park's accomodations. The park also has some adjacent sites at the top of the terraced hill. In the upper section, foliage provides a small amount of privacy; the actual terraces in the terraced section give a feeling of semi-privacy and open space. The upper section has some shade from trees; although ringed by forests of fir, the lower section has less shade and foliage among sites. Tenting within the park is limited, as the tenting area has small sites with no privacy and a little gravel, but lots of shade. Gig Harbor is a beautiful coastal area on Puget Sound. Visit during the summer for the best weather.

Basics

Operated By: PCF Mgmt. **Open:** All year. **Site Assignment:** On arrival, reservations. **Registration:** At office, after hours check welcome board out front. **Fee:** Full $37.81, Water electric $32.24, Tent $20, Cabins $30.85; V, MC, D, personal check, cash. **Parking:** At site, limited off site.

Facilities

Number of RV-Only Sites: 93. **Number of Tent-Only Sites:** 12. **Hookups:** Electric (20, 30, 50 amps), water, sewer. **Each Site:** Picnic table. **Dump Station:** Yes. **Laundry:** Yes. **Pay Phone:** Yes. **Rest Rooms and Showers:** Yes. **Fuel:** No. **Propane:** Yes. **Internal Roads:** Paved. **RV Service:** No. **Market:** 3 mi. west in Gig Harbor. **Restaurant:** 3 mi. west in Gig Harbor. **General Store:** Yes. **Vending:** Yes. **Swimming Pool:** Yes. **Playground:** Yes. **Other:** Basketball, volleyball, badminton, club room, horseshoes. **Activities:** Inquire at campground. **Nearby Attractions:** Scuba diving, sailing, kayaks, power boats, jet skis, wind surfing, water skiing, fishing, Seattle-Tacoma area, Puget Sound. **Additional Information:** Gig Harbor Chamber of Commerce, (253) 851-6865; Seattle Visitor Info Center, (206) 461-5840; www.seeseattle.org.

Restrictions

Pets: On leash only, no fencing or kenneling. **Fires:** No open fires, charcoal ok. **Alcoholic Beverages:** At site only. **Vehicle Maximum Length:** None.

To Get There

From I-5, take Exit 132 and follow Hwy. 16 west, cross the Tacoma Narrows Bridge. Turn right at Burnham Dr.-North Rosedale Exit. Drive 1.2 mi. on Burnham; entrance is on the left.

GOLDENDALE

Brooks Memorial State Park

2465 US Hwy. 97, Goldendale 98620. T: (509) 773-4611; www.parks.wa.gov.

 ★★★★

Beauty: ★★★★★	Site Privacy: ★★★
Spaciousness: ★★★	Quiet: ★★★★★
Security: ★★★★	Cleanliness: ★★★★★
Insect Control: ★★★	Facilities: ★★★

From its 3,000-foot location in the Simcoe Mountains, Brooks Memorial State Park is not only a good base for exploring the Klickitat Valley, but also for sights farther south to the Columbia River, west into the untamed Klickitat River region and Mount Adams, and north into the Yakima Indian Reservation and the viticultural lands of the Yakima Valley. Points of interest abound in all directions. Central to the area is Goldendale, a quiet community that is home to the Goldendale Observatory State Park Interpretive Center and has one of the largest telescopes available for public use in the country. Wildflowers bloom in the park from March until July, and there is quite a variety of park wildlife—turkeys, deer, raccoons, porcupines, beavers, bobcats, coyotes, red-tailed hawks, and owls. The Little Klickitat River follows US 97 from Brooks Memorial down into Goldendale, and it is not uncommon to observe beavers going about their business of damming the river.

Basics

Operated By: Washington State Parks & Recreation Commission. **Open:** All year. **Site Assignment:** First come, first served. **Registration:** Self-registration at self pay station across from the rest rooms. **Fee:** $11–$16. **Parking:** At site.

Facilities

Number of RV-Only Sites: 23. **Number of Tent-Only Sites:** 45. **Hookups:** Electric (20 amps), water. **Dump Station:** Yes. **Laundry:** No. **Pay Phone:** Yes. **Rest Rooms and Showers:** Yes. **Fuel:** 13 mi. In Goldendale. **Propane:** 13 mi. **Internal Roads:** Paved. **RV Service:** No. **Market:** 13 mi. In Goldendale. **Restaurant:** 13 mi. **General Store:** 13 mi. **Vending:** No. **Swimming Pool:** No. **Playground:** Yes. **Other:** Kitchen shelters w/ water & electricity, group accommodations. **Activities:** Hiking, fishing, nature talks in Environmental Learning Center upon request, horseshoe pit, softball field. **Nearby Attractions:** Goldendale Observatory, Maryhill Museum, historic Columbia Hwy. **Additional Information:** www.parks.wa.gov.

Restrictions

Pets: On leash only. **Fires:** In fire pit. **Alcoholic Beverages:** At site, picnic area. **Vehicle Maximum Length:** 40 ft. **Other:** No firewood gathering.

To Get There

From Yakima, follow US 97 south for 55 mi., crossing Satus Pass (elevation 3,107 ft.) to the park entrance.

GRAND COULEE

King's Court RV Park

P.O. Box 837, Grand Coulee 99133. T: (509) 633-3655 or (800) 759-2608; www.grandcouleedam.com/kingscourt; kingsco@televar.com.

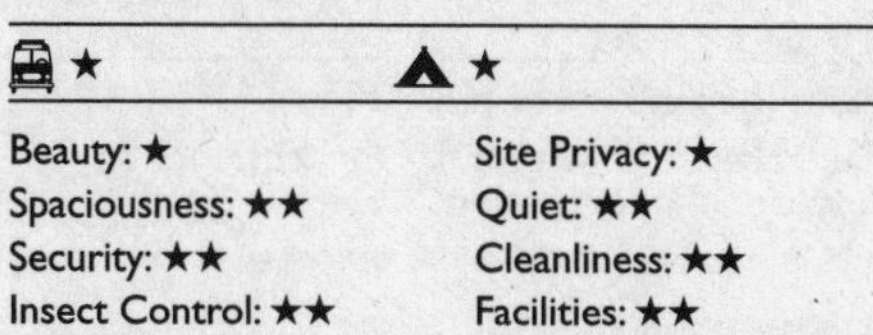

King's Court RV Park in Grand Coulee has a location very near Grand Coulee Dam and offers shuttles to the seasonal, nightly laser shows on the dam walls. This is the main advantage of staying at this small park. None of the small gravel sites avoid the noise of nearby roads, and facilities are dated and limited. The grounds have a nice view of the low bluffs across the highway, but sites lack privacy or much shade. The best sites, full hookups 1–12, sit furthest from the road. Avoid sites 15–28, as they are right next to the nearby highway. Visit during the summer season to avoid cold, snowy weather.

Basics

Operated By: The King's Court RV Park. **Open:** All year. **Site Assignment:** First come, first served; reservations (1 night stay deposit; 24 hour cancellation). **Registration:** At office across Hwy; After Hours see host or pay in morning. **Fee:** May 15–Sept. 15: $21, Sept. 16–May 14: $18; V, MC, AE, D, Cash. **Parking:** At site.

Facilities

Number of RV-Only Sites: 32. **Number of Tent-Only Sites:** n/a. **Hookups:** Electric (20, 30, 50 amps), water, sewer. **Each Site:** Picnic table. **Dump Station:** Yes. **Laundry:** Yes. **Pay Phone:** No. **Rest Rooms and Showers:** Yes. **Fuel:** No. **Propane:** Yes. **Internal Roads:** Gravel. **RV Service:** No. **Market:** 2 mi. south in Electric City. **Restaurant:** 2 mi. south in Electric City. **General Store:** No. **Vending:** Yes. **Swimming Pool:** No. **Playground:** No. **Other:** Shuttle to Grand Coulee Dam Laser Light Show. **Activities:** Laundry. **Nearby Attractions:** Grand Coulee Dam, tons of lakes for fishing, two golf courses, Steamboat Rock State Park, hiking trails, rock climbing, various local events, Coulee Dam Casino, Coville Tribes Museum. **Additional Information:** Grand

Coulee Dam Area Chamber of Commerce, (800) 268-5332.

Restrictions

Pets: On leash only. **Fires:** No open fires. **Alcoholic Beverages:** At site only. **Vehicle Maximum Length:** Forty ft. **Other:** Quiet Hours 10 p.m.–7 a.m.

To Get There

From the junction of Hwy. 155 and Hwy. 174: Take Hwy. 174 east for 0.7 mi.; entrance on right.

KETTLE FALLS

Hang Cove Campground

1368 South Kettle Park Rd., Kettle Falls 99141.T: (509) 738-6366; www.nps.gov/laro.

RV ★★★★ Tent ★★★★

Beauty: ★★★★★	Site Privacy: ★★★★
Spaciousness: ★★★★★	Quiet: ★★★★★
Security: ★★★	Cleanliness: ★★★★
Insect Control: ★★★	Facilities: ★★★

Set on the shore of Lake Roosevelt, against the sprawling backdrop of Colville National Forest—a 1,095,368-acre parcel in central northeastern Washington—Haag Cove is one of 32 campgrounds within the magnificent Coulee Dam National Recreation Area managed by the National Park Service. Deep canyons, sagebrush hills, and forested mountains are home to many kinds of animal and bird populations. One of the best spots for observing and shooting (with a camera) is just north of Haag Cove in Sherman Creek Habitat Management Area. The confluence of Sherman Creek and Lake Roosevelt produces a quality fly-fishing spot. The only other campground in the vicinity is Sherman Creek. However, it is boat-in only—one of the few campgrounds in eastern Washington accessible only via watercraft. Hiking options are plentiful and relatively uncrowded in Colville National Forest. A gentler terrain, drier climate, and longer season compared to the Cascade area make for ideal conditions for treks into the backcountry here.

Basics

Operated By: National Park Service. **Open:** All year. **Site Assignment:** First come, first served. **Registration:** Not necessary. **Fee:** $10; $5 winter. **Parking:** At site.

Facilities

Number of RV-Only Sites: Inquire at campground. **Number of Tent-Only Sites:** 0. **Number of Multipurpose Sites:** 16. **Hookups:** None. **Dump Station:** Yes. **Laundry:** No. **Pay Phone:** No. **Rest Rooms and Showers:** Vault toilets. **Fuel:** 3 mi. In Kettle Falls. **Propane:** 3 mi. **Internal Roads:** Paved. **RV Service:** No. **Market:** 3 mi. In Kettle Falls. **Restaurant:** 3 mi. **General Store:** 3 mi. **Vending:** No. **Swimming Pool:** No. **Playground:** No. **Other:** Boat launch (in Kettle Falls). **Activities:** Fishing, boating, hiking, biking, badminton, bird-watching. **Nearby Attractions:** Lake Roosevelt, Colville National Forest. **Additional Information:** www.nps.gov/laro.

Restrictions

Pets: On leash only. **Fires:** In fire pit. **Alcoholic Beverages:** At site only. **Vehicle Maximum Length:** 26 ft. **Other:** Fishing license & boat launch permit required.

To Get There

From Kettle Falls (81 mi. northwest of Spokane), drive west on SR 20 across this upper portion of the Columbia River, and stay on SR 20 as it turns south along the river to the turnoff for Inchelium-Kettle Falls Rd. at about 7 mi. Take Inchelium-Kettle Falls Rd. south for 5 mi. to the campground.

LA PUSH

Mora Campground

3283 Mora Rd., Forks 98331.T: (360) 374-5460; www.northolympic.com.

RV ★★★★ Tent ★★★★

Beauty: ★★★★★	Site Privacy: ★★★★
Spaciousness: ★★★★	Quiet: ★★★★★
Security: ★★★	Cleanliness: ★★★★
Insect Control: ★★★★★	Facilities: ★★★

Mora Campground, part of the network of well-attended Olympic National Park facilities, is among the elite when it comes to its location (only a mile or so from the Pacific Ocean). For a total of 57 unspoiled and challenging miles, the saltwater frontage of the Pacific Ocean is a panoply of protruding headlands, swirling tidepools, crashing surf, and stalwart "sea-stacks." Situated at sea level, Mora is open all year and is an ideal choice for off-season travel. Actually, winter months and early spring can be some of the best times weatherwise at the Washington coast. You'll have an opportunity to watch the migratory gray whales pass on their way to southern California and Mexico. A word of warning: Coastal hiking requires a tide table at all times of the year. The "Strip of Wilderness" brochure available at the Mora Ranger Station is full of information about the pleasures and precautions of coastal hiking. Check at either the Mora station or information stations along U.S. 101 for other options in this part of Olympic National Park and the surrounding National Forest. One last word: The Native American reservations that border the Park along the coast are private property.

Basics

Operated By: Olympic National Park, National Park Service, U.S Dept of Interior. **Open:** All year. **Site Assignment:** First come, first served. **Registration:** Self-registration. **Fee:** $10. **Parking:** At site.

Facilities

Number of RV-Only Sites: 6. **Number of Tent-Only Sites:** 94. **Hookups:** None. **Dump Station:** Yes. **Laundry:** No. **Pay Phone:** No. **Rest Rooms and Showers:** Yes. **Fuel:** 12 mi. In Forks. **Propane:** 12 mi. **Internal Roads:** Paved. **RV Service:** No. **Market:** 12 mi. in Fork. **Restaurant:** 12 mi. **General Store:** 1 mi. **Vending:** No. **Swimming Pool:** No (1 mi. to coast). **Playground:** No. **Other:** Amphitheater. **Activities:** Hiking, camp fire programs, tide pool walks. **Nearby Attractions:** Olympic Wilderness Area. **Additional Information:** www.northolympic.com.

Restrictions

Pets: On leash only. **Fires:** In fire pit. **Alcoholic Beverages:** Allowed. **Vehicle Maximum Length:** 21 ft. **Other:** No vehicles allowed off of park roads, permits required for extended hikes.

To Get There

From either north or south, take US 101 around the Olympic Peninsula to the town of Forks (between 125 and 200 mi. from Seattle, depending on which route you take). About 1 mi. north of Forks, turn west onto La Push Rd., and drive for about 10 mi. to Mora Rd. Turn right onto Mora Rd., and follow the signs to the campground.

LEAVENWORTH

Icicle River RV Resort

7305 Icicle Rd., Leavenworth 98826. T: (509) 548-5420; www.icicleriverrv.com; info@icicleriverrv.com.

RV: ★★★★★ Tent: n/a

Beauty: ★★★★★	Site Privacy: ★
Spaciousness: ★★★	Quiet: ★★★★★
Security: ★★★	Cleanliness: ★★★★
Insect Control: ★★	Facilities: ★

Icicle River RV Resort, a few minutes from the western edge of Leavenworth, has to have the most spectacular localized scenery of any RV park in Washington State. The grounds, partially shaded by birch and pines, sit very near Wenatchee National Forest boundaries and on a small alpine river, across which beautifully gray, rocky hills rise steeply towards the sky. No truly undesirable sites exist in this park; the best full-hookup options sit on the river (sites 15–28 and 59–62). Full-hookup sites 42–56 also have spectacular views. The park has a few water and electric sites, and some sites have gravel while others have concrete surfaces. Most sites have grass perimeters and some shade. The resort provides a very quiet, mellow place to relax away from the tourist hustle of Leavenworth, feeling worlds apart from the Bavarian tourist trap; the park seldom feels crowded, even when full. Mild mountain summers make up the best time to travel here; winters bring snow and cold weather.

Basics

Operated By: Icicle River RV. **Open:** Apr. 1–Nov 30. **Site Assignment:** On arrival, reservations (deposit: $25; refund: 48 hours cancellation). **Registration:** At office, after hours ring mgmt from facility outside office. **Fee:** For 2 people, full $27, full (50 amp)–$30, Water-electric $25, extra adults $4, extra child (6-16)–$3, extra vehicle $4 (V, MC, cash). **Parking:** At site, some off site.

Facilities

Number of RV-Only Sites: 106. **Number of Tent-Only Sites:** n/a. **Hookups:** Electric (20, 30, 50 amps), water, sewer, cable, central data port. **Each Site:** Picnic table. **Dump Station:** No. **Laundry:** Yes. **Pay Phone:** Yes. **Rest Rooms and Showers:** Yes. **Fuel:** No. **Propane:** Yes. **Internal Roads:** Paved, gravel. **RV Service:** No. **Market:** East 5 min. in Leavenworth. **Restaurant:** East 5 min. in Leavenworth. **General Store:** Yes. **Vending:** No. **Swimming Pool:** No. **Playground:** No. **Other:** Small creek-side beach, hot tub, two reserveable & fully enclosed pavilions, croquet, putting green. **Activities:** Putting, river fishing, hiking, biking, river swimming. **Nearby Attractions:** Wenatchee Nat'l Forest, Leavenworth Bavarian Village, Ohme Gardens, Icicle Junction Family Fun Center. Rocky Reach Dam. **Additional Information:** Leavenworth Chamber of Commerce, (509) 548-5807.

Restrictions

Pets: On leash only. **Fires:** In fire pits only. **Alcoholic Beverages:** At site only. **Vehicle Maximum Length:** None. **Other:** No tents.

To Get There

From the center of Leavenworth, go 1 mi. west on Hwy. 2, then turn left on Icicle Rd. Icicle River RV Resorts entrance is on the Left.

LEAVENWORTH

Lake Wenatchee State Park

21588A Hwy. 207, Leavenworth 98826. T: (509) 662-0420; www.parks.wa.gov.

RV ★★★ Tent ★★★★

Beauty: ★★★★★ Site Privacy: ★★★
Spaciousness: ★★★ Quiet: ★★★
Security: ★★★★ Cleanliness: ★★★★
Insect Control: ★★ Facilities: ★★★

Although it is quite large, Lake Wenatchee State Park is a pretty nice spot with spacious, secluded campsites and oodles of choices for enjoying the outdoor recreation of one of Washington State's most scenic and untainted areas. It is a sprawling 489-acre complex divided into north and south campgrounds. The sites are available on a first come, first served basis, and if you can manage it, go for the sites in the northern section. They're closer to the river and more spacious. On this eastern slope of the Cascades, summers are hot and dry. Thunderstorms materialize out of nowhere, and lightning strikes can quickly ignite the forests in late summer and early fall. Be aware of the fire danger at all times. Also be aware that this is bear country. Food should be stored in bear-proof containers (or at least the car) when not being consumed; a tent is not much of a deterrent to a hungry bear.

Basics

Operated By: Washington State Parks & Recreation Commission. **Open:** Apr.–Sept. w/ limited facilities Oct.–Mar. **Site Assignment:** First come, first served; reservations May 15–Sept. 15; call (800) 452-5687; $6 fee. **Registration:** Self-registration. **Fee:** $12. **Parking:** At site.

Facilities

Number of RV-Only Sites: Inquire at campground. **Number of Tent-Only Sites:** 0. **Number of Multipurpose Sites:** 197. **Hookups:** None. **Dump Station:** Yes. **Laundry:** No. **Pay Phone:** Yes. **Rest Rooms and Showers:** Yes. **Fuel:** 21 mi. In Leavenworh. **Propane:** 21 mi. **Internal Roads:** Paved. **RV Service:** No. **Market:** 21 mi. In Leavenworth. **Restaurant:** Yes. **General Store:** Yes. **Vending:** No. **Swimming Pool:** No. **Playground:** Yes. **Other:** Amphitheater, boat launch, boat rentals, group camp, firewood, kitchen shelters (without electricity). **Activities:** Boating, horseback riding, campfire programs, nature walks, golf junior ranger programs, rock climbing, volleyball field. **Nearby Attractions:** Alpine Lakes Wilderness. **Additional Information:** www.parks.wa.gov.

Restrictions

Pets: On leash only. **Fires:** In fire pit. **Alcoholic Beverages:** At site or picnic area. **Vehicle Maximum Length:** None. **Other:** No firewood gathering.

To Get There

From Leavenworth (23 mi. west of Wenatchee), take US 2 west for 16 mi. to SR 207. The state park and campground are 5 mi. up SR 207.

LEAVENWORTH

Pine Village KOA Kampground

11401 River Bend Rd., Leavenworth 98826. T: (509) 548-7709 or reservations (800) 562 5709; www.koa.com.

RV ★★★★ Tent ★★★

Beauty: ★★★★ Site Privacy: ★
Spaciousness: ★★★ Quiet: ★★★
Security: ★★ Cleanliness: ★★★
Insect Control: ★★ Facilities: ★★★★

KOA Pine Village, located minutes east of the tourist mecca of Leavenworth, has to be one of the busiest campgrounds in Washington State, mostly due to its scenic location. The nearby

Wenatchee National Forest houses some of the most beautiful alpine scenery around. Since it has an array of in-house recreation opportunities, the KOA stays buzzing with families, but the grounds do have some quieter areas amidst all the chaos. Sites have a seemingly arbitrary arrangement over a pine-shaded, hilly area near the Wenatchee River. Full-hookup RV sites 1–17 and 19–38 have a crowded feel, as do tent sites T4–T9 and T11–T24 located in and around a large field of grass. The least traffic-prone areas provide a less-crowded feel; gravel full-hookup sites H1–H8 and R1–R4 and and dirt tent sites R5–R21 make up the best of these. Be prepared for plenty of people regardless, as the common areas stay packed during the summer. Even so, summer provides the best season to visit this alpine area.

Basics

Operated By: Pine Village KOA. **Open:** Mar. 20–Nov. 1. **Site Assignment:** On arrival, reservations (deposit: 1 night's stay; refund: 5 days cancellation). **Registration:** At office, after hours at drop by office. **Fee:** For 2 people, full $36, Water-electric $34, Tent $29, extra adult $4.50, extra children 5-17 years old $4, extra vehicles $5, children younger than 5 stay free (V, MC, cash). **Parking:** At site, some off site.

Facilities

Number of RV-Only Sites: 135. **Number of Tent-Only Sites:** 45. **Hookups:** Electric (20, 30, 50 amps), water, sewer, cable. **Each Site:** Picnic table, grill. **Dump Station:** Yes. **Laundry:** Yes. **Pay Phone:** Yes. **Rest Rooms and Showers:** Yes. **Fuel:** No. **Propane:** No. **Internal Roads:** Paved. **RV Service:** No. **Market:** In Leavenworth 3 mi. west. **Restaurant:** In Leavenworth 3 mi. west. **General Store:** Yes. **Vending:** Yes. **Swimming Pool:** Yes. **Playground:** Yes. **Other:** Spa, game room, horseshoes, large covered pavillion, basketball, group areas, volleyball, horseshoes. **Activities:** Saturday night hay rides, train rides (small motorized cart pulling small cars), hiking, swimming, shuttle to Leavenworth, free coffee. **Nearby Attractions:** Ohme Gardens, Rocky Reach Dam, Icicle Junction Family Fun Center, Nutcracker Museum, North Central Washington Museum, Lake Wenatchee, Wenatchee National Forest. **Additional Information:** Leavenworth Chamber of Commerce, (509) 548-5807.

Restrictions

Pets: On leash only, not allowed in recreation areas. **Fires:** Fire pits, grills only. **Alcoholic Beverages:** At site only. **Vehicle Maximum Length:** None. **Other:** Don't tie clotheslines to trees or damage trees.

To Get There

From Hwy. 2 east of town heading west, turn right onto River Bend Dr., located by a Safeway. Follow signs for 0.5 mi.; entrance is on the right

LONG BEACH
Andersen's RV Park

1400 138th St., Long Beach 98631. T: (360) 642-2231 or (800) 645-6795; www.andersensrv.com; lorna@andersensrv.com.

RV ★★★ Tent ★★★

Beauty: ★★★★	Site Privacy: ★
Spaciousness: ★★	Quiet: ★★★
Security: ★★	Cleanliness: ★★★★
Insect Control: ★★	Facilities: ★★

Andersen's RV Park on the Long Beach Peninsula makes a good base for exploring the southwestern edge of the Olympic region. Natural attractions in the area draw more interest than organized recreation; the tourism infrastructure along all of the Washington Pacific Coast is, for lack of better words, second-rate and campy. Andersen's provides a small park consisting of two parallel rows of opposing back-ins, tent sites, and nearby beach access via a trail. The enormous Washington beaches form a straight line with the ocean's edge and run for miles; the surf looks like an impenetrable, high wall of fog. Everybody that has anything to say about it discourages swimming due to riptides and undertows. The gravel RV section of the campground has a slightly cramped feel and lacks shade or privacy. Tenters have it a little better; the grass sites are bigger and have more pronounced boundaries, but still no shade or privacy. Weather here aims to confuse on a daily basis, so be prepared for anything

Basics

Operated By: Andersen's RV Park. **Open:** All year. **Site Assignment:** On arrival, reservations (Encouraged; deposit: 1 night stay; refund: cancel by 12 noon on day of check-in). **Registration:** At office, after hours pay in morning. **Fee:** For 2 people, full $22, Tent $18, 6 people limit per tent site, extra people $2, Ages 6 & under free; V, MC, D, personal check, cash. **Parking:** At site.

Facilities

Number of RV-Only Sites: 58. **Number of Tent-Only Sites:** 18. **Hookups:** Electric (30 amps), water, sewer, cable. **Each Site:** Picnic table. **Dump Station:** No. **Laundry:** Yes. **Pay Phone:** Yes. **Rest Rooms and Showers:** Yes. **Fuel:** No. **Propane:** Yes. **Internal Roads:** Gravel. **RV Service:** No. **Market:** Nearby in Long Beach. **Restaurant:** Nearby in Long Beach. **General Store:** No. **Vending:** Yes. **Swimming Pool:** No. **Playground:** Yes. **Other:** Meeting room w/ pool table, fish cleaning station, beach access. **Activities:** Salt water fishing, swimming discouraged (rip tides & undertows). **Nearby Attractions:** Horseback Riding, sea kayaking, Cape Disappointment, fishing, clamming, beachcombing. **Additional Information:** Long Beach Peninsula Visitor' Info, (800) 451-2542 or (360) 642-2400.

Restrictions

Pets: On leash only. **Fires:** Not on ground in park, self contained raised fireplaces are o.k., get approval first from office. Bonfires allowed on beach, per regulation. Check w/ office. **Alcoholic Beverages:** At site only. **Vehicle Maximum Length:** None. **Other:** Do not play in driftwood, stay away from it, just leave it alone.

To Get There

Located just north of Long Beach on Hwy. 103 (northbound entrance is on the left between mile marker 4 and 5).

LONGMIRE

Cougar Rock Campground

Tahoma Woods, Star Rte., Ashford 98304-9751.
T: (360) 569-2211; www.nps.gov.

RV: ★★★ Tent: ★★★★

Beauty: ★★★★★ Site Privacy: ★★★
Spaciousness: ★ Quiet: ★★★
Security: ★★ Cleanliness: ★★★★★
Insect Control: ★★ Facilities: ★★★

Cougar Rock Campground, operated by the National Park Service and located on the west side of Mt. Rainier National Park, offers good semi-private sites and some views of Mt. Rainier. Organized into five loops, the heavily forested campground has small sites hemmed in with foliage. This creates semi-private sites, but it decreases site roominess. Since the property is better suited for smaller RVs and tents, large RVs have trouble being comfortable here. Natural beauty abounds in this campground, with gray, jagged, rocky terra firma carpeted by green moss. Sites E1–E10 and E21–30 have obscured views of Mt. Rainier, but not much privacy. D loop houses the most private sites. All sites have dirt and gravel surfaces and receive lots of shade from firs, cedars, and pines. Summer brings the best weather for visiting the area and the largest crowds; late spring and early fall have cooler weather and beautiful displays of seasonal foliage.

Basics

Operated By: National Park Service. **Open:** Mid May–Columbus Day. **Site Assignment:** On arrival, reservations. **Registration:** At office, at self pay station during off season. **Fee:** Reservation $15, Self pay $12; V, MC, D, cash. **Parking:** At site.

Facilities

Number of RV-Only Sites: 52. **Number of Tent-Only Sites:** 148 (tents & pop up campers). **Hookups:** None. **Each Site:** Picnic table, fire ring. **Dump Station:** Yes. **Laundry:** No. **Pay Phone:** Yes. **Rest Rooms and Showers:** No. **Fuel:** No. **Propane:** No. **Internal Roads:** paved. **RV Service:** No. **Market:** 15 mi. east. **Restaurant:** 15 mi. east. **General Store:** No. **Vending:** No. **Swimming Pool:** No. **Playground:** No. **Other:** Amphitheater, trails, ranger station. **Activities:** Interpretive programs (nightly during on-season). **Nearby Attractions:** Mount Rainier National Park. **Additional Information:** Mount Rainier Office, NPS (360) 569-2211.

Restrictions

Pets: On leash only (not on trails, can be walked on west side of main road). **Fires:** Pits only. **Alcoholic Beverages:** At site only. **Vehicle Maximum Length:** 35 ft. **Other:** Maximum of 6 people (or immediate family), 2 tents & 2 vehicles per site.

To Get There

At 2.3 mi. north of Longmire, enter park driving on SR 706 through southwest entrance gate (Nisqually entrance) and continue, following signs to campground. Campground is 9 mi. from entrance gate.

LOPEZ

Spencer Spit State Park

Rte. 2 Box 3600, Lopez 98261. T: (360) 468-2251; www.parks.wa.gov.

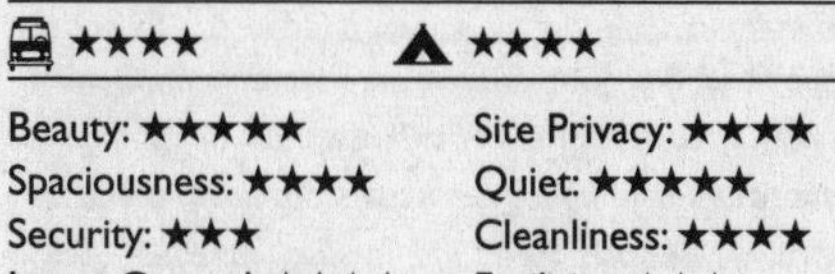

RV ★★★★ Tent ★★★★

Beauty: ★★★★★ Site Privacy: ★★★★
Spaciousness: ★★★★ Quiet: ★★★★★
Security: ★★★ Cleanliness: ★★★★
Insect Control: ★★★★ Facilities: ★★★

Spencer Spit is an excellent base camp for enjoying Lopez and its sister islands by car, foot, or bicycle. The only drawback to lovely little Spencer Spit is the Washington State ferry system. Plan on becoming a veritable scholar of the ferry schedule. One of the most appealing aspects of Spencer Spit State Park is that you can camp right on the beach—in designated areas, of course. You will have to pack your gear down from the parking lot above. Lopez Island is, in our opinion, the premier bicycling island of the San Juans and can easily be covered in a day of riding if you're accustomed to 40 miles or so. A terrific excursion on Lopez is to ride out to Shark Reef Park to watch the sea lions that sprawl en masse on the offshore rocks. You can also look far across the San Juan Channel to windswept Cattle Point on San Juan Island, where the only sand dunes in the entire island group exist.

Basics

Operated By: Washington State Parks & Recreation Commission. **Open:** Mar.–Oct. **Site Assignment:** Reservations required; call (800) 452-5687; $6. **Registration:** Self-registration. **Fee:** $6–$12. **Parking:** In campground & at some sites; parking for beach sites near trailhead.

Facilities

Number of Multipurpose Sites: 41. **Hookups:** Inquire at campground. **Dump Station:** Yes. **Laundry:** No. **Pay Phone:** No. **Rest Rooms and Showers:** Yes. **Fuel:** On island. **Propane:** On island. **Internal Roads:** Paved. **RV Service:** No. **Market:** On island. **Restaurant:** On island. **General Store:** On island. **Vending:** No. **Swimming Pool:** No. **Playground:** No. **Other:** 2 kitchen shelters without electricity. **Activities:** Boating, diving, fishing, clamming, crabbing, wildlife viewing, biking, water craft launch site, nightly moorage available for fee, San Juan Islands National Wildlife Refuge, Shark Reef Park, Cattle Point, Village of Lopez, Richardson & Mackay Harbor, Friday Harbor. **Nearby Attractions:** Inquire at campground. **Additional Information:** www.parks.wa.gov.

Restrictions

Pets: On leash only. **Fires:** In fire pit. **Alcoholic Beverages:** Allowed. **Vehicle Maximum Length:** 28 ft.

To Get There

From the ferry terminal at the north end of Lopez Island, take Ferry Rd. south, and follow the signs to the park. The total distance from the ferry terminal is barely 5 mi.

NORTH BEND

Denny Creek Campground

42404 Southeast North Bend Way, North Bend 98045. T: (888) 206-1421

RV ★★★★ Tent ★★★

Beauty: ★★★★★ Site Privacy: ★★
Spaciousness: ★★★ Quiet: ★★★★
Security: ★★ Cleanliness: ★★
Insect Control: ★★ Facilities: ★★

Denny Creek Campground, a National Forest Campground around an hour east of Seattle and in the vicinity of Snoqualmie Pass, provides a beautiful alpine forest landscape. The limited facilities include flush toilets only, and a few electric hookups; the park's facilities almost fit a description of rustic. Of the electric sites, paved pull-throughs 30–33 have the best location. Back-in sites 16–22 sit in an area with semi-privacy for each site and near a south fork of the Snoqualmie River. All back-in sites have paved parking, with a large adjacent area used for tenting. Shaded by firs and birch, the whole park provides a peaceful, quiet retreat. Summers bring the best time to visit the area, but nights can still be cool at this altitude.

Basics

Operated By: Recreational Resource Mgmt for National Forest Service. **Open:** Mid May–mid Oct. (weather permitting). **Site Assignment:** On arrival, reservations (877) 444-6777. **Registration:** At self pay station. **Fee:** No hookups $12, second vehicle $6, Electric $16, extra vehicle $8, Cash upon arrival. **Parking:** At site.

Facilities

Number of Multipurpose Sites: 33. **Hookups:** Electric (20 amps). **Each Site:** Picnic table, fire ring. **Dump Station:** No. **Laundry:** No. **Pay Phone:** No. **Rest Rooms and Showers:** Flush toilets only. **Fuel:** No. **Propane:** No. **Internal Roads:** Paved. **RV Service:** No. **Market:** Up the Interstate a few mi. **Restaurant:** Up the Interstate a few mi. **General Store:** No. **Vending:** No. **Swimming Pool:** No. **Playground:** No. **Activities:** Inquire at campground. **Nearby Attractions:** Hiking trails, Mt. Baker-Snoqualmie National Forest, skiing, fishing, golf, seattle. **Additional Information:** Washington State Tourism Office, (360) 725-5052.

Restrictions

Pets: On leash only (6 ft max length). **Fires:** In fire pits only. **Alcoholic Beverages:** At site only. **Vehicle Maximum Length:** 35 ft. (a few 40s). **Other:** Ask about collecting dead & down wood for campfires.

To Get There

Take Exit 47 off I-90. Go north, then turn right at the T intersection. Travel 0.25 mi. and turn left on Denny Creek Rd. 58. Continue for 2 mi. to the campground entrance on the left.

OCEAN PARK

Evergreen Court Campground

222nd Ave. & WA Rte. 103, Ocean Park 98640. T: (360) 665-6351

n/a ★★★

Beauty: ★★★ Site Privacy: ★★★
Spaciousness: ★★★ Quiet: ★★★★
Security: ★★★★★ Cleanliness: ★★★★★
Insect Control: ★★★★ Facilities: ★★

Long Beach Peninsula, so named by its claim to be the world's longest beach, struggles to find a workable balance between tourism promoters, real estate developers, oyster farmers, and cranberry harvesters. In the midst of this multiple-use stretch of surf and sand is Evergreen Court Campground, a five-acre haven for those willing to make the circuitous journey to this place of subtle beauty. Its proximity to Leadbetter Point State Park and the 11,000-acre Willapa National Wildlife Refuge makes Evergreen Court the perfect choice for those interested in all that these state- and federal-managed areas offer. For ocean access, Klipsan Beach Trail can be found about a half mile north of the campground, and a place to clean fish is provided for those who have a bit of luck at freshwater Loomis Lake, which is connected to the campground.

Basics

Operated By: John & Deanna Klattenhoff. **Open:** All year. **Site Assignment:** Reservations or first come first served. **Registration:** At camp office or by mail w/ deposit. **Fee:** $12 for 2 people; $1 each add'l. **Parking:** At site or in main lot.

Facilities

Number of RV-Only Sites: 0. **Number of Tent-Only Sites:** 8. **Hookups:** None. **Each Site:** Picnic table, fire pit w/ grill. **Dump Station:** No. **Laundry:** No. **Pay Phone:** Yes. **Rest Rooms and Showers:** Yes. **Fuel:** No. **Propane:** No. **Internal Roads:** Gravel. **RV Service:** No. **Market:** 2 mi. in Ocean Park. **Restaurant:** 2 mi. **General Store:** 2 mi. **Vending:** No. **Swimming Pool:** No. **Playground:** Yes. **Activities:** Year-round renters participate in "community" activities. **Nearby Attractions:** Willapa National Wildlife Refuge.

Restrictions

Pets: On leash only. **Fires:** In fire pit. **Alcoholic Beverages:** Allowed. **Vehicle Maximum Length:** Call ahead for details.

To Get There

From Seattle, take I-5 to Kelso/Longview (133 mi.). Go west on SR 4 for 62 mi. to Johnson's Landing. Turn south onto US 101 across the Naselle River and around the southern end of Willapa Bay to the turnoff for SR 103 and Long Beach Peninsula. Take SR 103 north. Evergreen Court Campground is 7 mi. north of Long Beach at the intersection of SR 103 and 222nd Ave. From Portland, take US 30 northwest along the Columbia River for 95 mi. to Astoria. Cross the bridge into Washington on US 101, turning left (west) onto SR 103 after 10 mi. From there, the directions are the same as from Seattle.

OLYMPIA

American Heritage Campground

9610 Kimmie St. Southwest, Olympia 98512. T: (360) 943-8778

Beauty: ★★★★ Site Privacy: ★★★★
Spaciousness: ★★★ Quiet: ★★
Security: ★ Cleanliness: ★★★
Insect Control: ★★ Facilities: ★★★★

American Heritage, the family-oriented sister campground of Olympia Campground, puts in a bid as a destination park. The older park has sites set within a well-manicured forest; the RV section has wide, paved sites, and the tenting section has a manicured yet unimproved feeling. Most sites create semi-private environments and receive lots of shade from tall conifers overhead. The best sites for both types of camping sit on the perimeters of their respective sections; sites on the medians of sections often lack any seclusion. As far as recreation goes, the "destination" section of the park kind of feels like a Florida reptile farm, but kids won't notice. The park has easy access to the interstate and a good amount of quiet; though it's only open during summer, travelers will still need a jacket for the cool western Washington nights.

Basics

Operated By: Olymia Campgrounds. **Open:** Memorial Day–Labor Day. **Site Assignment:** On arrival, reservations. **Registration:** At office, after hours see instructions outside office. **Fee:** For 2 adults, 2 children, full $27, Water-electric $26, Tent $19, extra person $4. **Parking:** At site.

Facilities

Number of RV-Only Sites: 74. **Number of Tent-Only Sites:** 25. **Hookups:** Electric (20, 30 amps), water, sewer. **Each Site:** Picnic table, fire ring. **Dump Station:** Yes. **Laundry:** Yes. **Pay Phone:** Yes. **Rest Rooms and Showers:** Yes. **Fuel:** No. **Propane:** Yes. **Internal Roads:** Paved. **RV Service:** No. **Market:** 5 mi. north in Olympia. **Restaurant:** 4 mi. North in Olympia. **General Store:** Yes. **Vending:** No. **Swimming Pool:** Yes. **Playground:** Yes. **Other:** Movie room, kiddie farm, playground, bike rentals, horseshoes, volleyball, badminton, rec hall, pavillion, bike track. **Activities:** Movies nightly, hay rides, various planned activities. **Nearby Attractions:** Olympia Farmers Market, Tumwater Falls Park, Monarch Sculpture Park, Yashiro Japanese Garden, Puget Sound, Seattle. **Additional Information:** Olympia Thurston County Visitor & Convention Bureau, (360) 704-7544 or (877) 704-7500.

Restrictions

Pets: On leash only, quiet. **Fires:** In fire pits only. **Alcoholic Beverages:** At site only. **Vehicle Maximum Length:** 40 ft. **Other:** Check in at 1p.m.

To Get There

Take Exit 99 off I-5, go 0.3 mi. east on 93rd Ave, then left on Kimmie St SW for 0.3 mi.; the road dead-ends into campground.

OLYMPIA
Olympia Campground

1441 83rd Ave. Southwest, Olympia 98512. T: (360) 352-2551

 ★★★ ▲ ★★★

Beauty: ★★★★ Site Privacy: ★★★
Spaciousness: ★★★ Quiet: ★★★
Security: ★★ Cleanliness: ★★★
Insect Control: ★★ Facilities: ★★★

Olympia Campground, located in the eponymous city, has flat, semiprivate sites with lots of shade. Watchtower-like Douglas firs all but block out the sky, and woody, deciduous shrubbery covers the ground in many spots and also provides some privacy among the gravel and dirt sites. Olympia Campground, like much of Olympia, has a heavily-forested but constantly upkept feel. The best sites sit in the back of the park, such as back-ins sites 50–80; the pull-through section sits near the front of the park in a more open area close to the office/convenience store/rec room/etc. This particular campground has a target audience of adults or older families; the owners have a sister park which is more family-oriented, but open summers only (see profile for American Heritage Campground). Facilities have an older, somewhat dated appearance. Weather in Olympia and all of the Puget Sound region has long, gray, wet, almost freezing winters, and short, mild summers, so a jacket (preferably of the rain-proof variety) is a good thing to keep handy.

Basics

Operated By: Olympia Campground. **Open:** All year. **Site Assignment:** On arrival, reservations. **Registration:** At convenience store. **Fee:** For 2 people, full $25, Water-electric $24, Tent $19, extra person $4; V, MC, cash. **Parking:** At site.

Facilities

Number of RV-Only Sites: 96. **Number of Tent-Only Sites:** 30. **Hookups:** Electric (20, 30 amps), water, sewer. **Each Site:** Picnic table, fire ring. **Dump Station:** Yes. **Laundry:** Yes. **Pay Phone:** Yes. **Rest Rooms and Showers:** Yes. **Fuel:** Yes. **Propane:** Yes. **Internal Roads:** Paved. **RV Service:** No. **Market:** 4 mi. away. **Restaurant:** 3 mi. away. **General Store:** Yes. **Vending:** No. **Swimming Pool:** Yes. **Playground:** Yes. **Other:** Badminton, horseshoes, rec room w/ arcade & pool table, video rentals, volleyball. **Activities:** Inquire at campground. **Nearby Attractions:** State Capital, Puget Sound Region, Volcanos, skiing, casinos, Seattle. **Additional Information:** Olympia Thurston County Visitor & Convention Bureau, (360) 704-7544 or (877) 704-7500.

Restrictions

Pets: On leash only, quiet. **Fires:** In fire pits only. **Alcoholic Beverages:** At site only. **Vehicle Maximum Length:** 40 ft. **Other:** Check in at 1p.m.

To Get There

Take I-5 Exit 101 (Airdustrial Way), drive 0.3 mi. east on Airdustrial, then turn right onto Center. Drive 1 mi. south on Center, then turn right onto 83rd and drive 0.2 mi. The entrance is on the left.

PACKWOOD

Ohanapecosh Campground (Mount Rainier National Park)

Tahoma Woods, Star Rte., Ashford 98304-9751. T: (360) 569-2211

★★★★ ★★★★

Beauty: ★★★★★ Site Privacy: ★★
Spaciousness: ★★★ Quiet: ★★★★
Security: ★★ Cleanliness: ★★★
Insect Control: ★★ Facilities: ★★★

Ohanapecosh Campground, on the east side of Mt. Rainier National Park, offers a more open feeling than Cougar Creek. Located in an old-growth forest near a rocky, cascading alpine river, the campground draws lots of campers year-round. Sites have less low-growing foliage than those at Cougar Creek, sacrificing privacy but creating a more spacious feeling below a canopy of tall evergreens. The campground has an organization of several shady loops; loop C has sites on the river, with several walk-in tent sites right on the banks. Other loops lack riverfront property but still provide a beautiful camping environment. The only loop to really avoid, B loop, has higher traffic and a location among campground facilities. Visit during the summer for the best temperatures, although a jacket still might be needed at night.

Basics

Operated By: National Park Service. **Open:** Late May–mid Oct. (weather permitting). **Site Assignment:** On arrival, reservations highly recommended & available Jul. 1–Labor Day, call 1-(800) 365-CAMP (deposit: 1 night stay; refund: 24 hours notice of cancellation less $13.25 cancellation fee). **Registration:** At self pay station. **Fee:** Site $15 reserved, $12 self-pay; V, MC, D, cash. **Parking:** At site.

Facilities

Number of Multipurpose Sites: 205. **Hookups:** n/a. **Each Site:** Picnic table, fire ring. **Dump Station:** Yes. **Laundry:** No. **Pay Phone:** Yes. **Rest Rooms and Showers:** No showers, but flush toilets. **Fuel:** No. **Propane:** No. **Internal Roads:** Paved, gravel. **RV Service:** No. **Market:** 11 mi. in Packwood. **Restaurant:** 11 mi. in Packwood. **General Store:** No. **Vending:** No. **Swimming Pool:** No. **Playground:** No. **Other:** Amphitheater, hiking trails, visitor's center. **Activities:** Interpretive programs, hiking. **Nearby Attractions:** Mount Rainier, hiking, fishing, backcountry camping. **Additional Information:** Ohanapecosh Visitor Center, (360) 569-2211, ext. 2352.

Restrictions

Pets: On leash only (6 ft. max length, pets not allowed on National Park trails). **Fires:** Fire pits only, keep them small & controlled. **Alcoholic Beverages:** At site only. **Vehicle Maximum Length:** 40 ft. **Other:** Maximum of 6 people (or immediate family), two tents & two vehicles per site.

To Get There

The campground is located off of Hwy. 123 in the southeast corner of the park, between mi. 4 and mi. 3. The road in the immediate area briefly changes to four lanes to accommodate park traffic; if headed southbound, campground entrance is on the right.

PASCO

Sandy Heights RV Park

P.O.Box 2487, Pasco 99301. T: (509) 542-1357 or (877) 894-1357; F: (509) 543-8335; sandyheightsrv@urx.com.

Beauty: ★★★ | Site Privacy: ★
Spaciousness: ★★★ | Quiet: ★★★
Security: ★★★★ | Cleanliness: ★★★★★
Insect Control: ★★ | Facilities: ★★★

Sandy Heights RV Park, off of I-182 in Pasco, provides a good base for exploring the tri-cities area. The grounds have a suburban park-like feel, lots of grass, the occasional red or green seedling, and newer, well-kept facilities. Recreational facilities include a basketball court with opposing goals and a large hot tub. The grass-perimetered, flat, paved, full-hookup sites come in both the pull-through and back-in variety. The park has no official "tent sites," but tents are allowed. The best back-in sites, 114–185, sit on the perimeter of the park with no neighbors to the rear; the pull-through sites lack any distinguishable differences. Security fences around the perimeter help to keep outsiders out, but also obscure views of the surrounding barren hills. Summers here stay hot, and winters stay cold; avoid visits during the hottest of summer months.

Basics

Operated By: Sandy Heights RV. **Open:** All year. **Site Assignment:** On arrival, reservation (deposit: 1 night stay; refund: 24 hours cancellation). **Registration:** At office, after hours pay in morning. **Fee:** For 2 people, RV $22.50, Tent $18, Phone $3, Exta adult $2.50, No charge for kids (V, MC, cash). **Parking:** At site, some off site.

Facilities

Number of RV-Only Sites: 185. **Number of Tent-Only Sites:** 0 (Can accommodate, though). **Hookups:** Electric (20, 30, 50 amps), water, sewer, cable, phone. **Each Site:** Picnic table. **Dump Station:** Yes. **Laundry:** Yes. **Pay Phone:** Yes. **Rest Rooms and Showers:** Yes. **Fuel:** No. **Propane:** Yes. **Internal Roads:** Paved. **RV Service:** No. **Market:** 5 mi. west on I-182. **Restaurant:** 5 mi. west on I-182. **General Store:** Yes. **Vending:** No. **Swimming Pool:** Yes. **Playground:** Yes. **Other:** Hot tub, basketball court, horseshoes, volleyball, BBQ area, reserveable meeting hall. **Activities:** Occasional potluck, ice cream socials on Sundays (seasonal). **Nearby Attractions:** Wineries, golf, rodeos, boating, water skiing, fishing, Oasis Waterworks (water park), Lewis & Clark Trail historical sites. **Additional Information:** Pasco Chamber of Commerce, (509) 547-9755.

Restrictions

Pets: On leash only. **Fires:** No open fires. **Alcoholic Beverages:** At site only. **Vehicle Maximum Length:** None. **Other:** Tent max stay 3 days.

To Get There

From I-182 Exit 7 (westbound, turn left) onto Broadmoor, drive 0.1 mi. south and turn at the first left onto St. Thomas Dr. Drive 1 mi. on St. Thomas, and the park is at the end of the road.

PORT ANGELES

Log Cabin Resort

3183 East Beach Rd., Port Angeles 98363. T: (360) 928-3325; F: (360) 928-2088; www.logcabinresort.net.

RV ★★★★ | Tent n/a

Beauty: ★★★★★ | Site Privacy: ★
Spaciousness: ★★ | Quiet: ★★★★
Security: ★ | Cleanliness: ★★★★
Insect Control: ★★ | Facilities: ★

Log Cabin Resort, west of Port Angeles and off Hwy. 101, has a small, no-frills RV area in a beautiful fishing lodge environment. The resort also has convenient access to much of Olympic National Park. Located on big, blue Lake Crescent, the shady, rust red-painted wood lodge has non powered boat and fishing gear rentals, a restaurant (open at volume), and a laundromat. When occupancy in the RV section is low, individual sites have an outstanding view; when full, such is only a short walk away. Across the cold-blue lake, the Olympic mountains rise into the sky. And the whole joint's pretty quiet too. The area has sunny, mild weather most of the time, summers being most pleasant.

Basics

Operated By: Log Cabin Resort for National Park Service. **Open:** Apr. 1–Oct. 31. **Site Assignment:** On arrival, reservations (deposit: one night stay; refund: full less $12 cancellation fee if 48 hours before scheduled arrival. **Registration:** At office, after hours see office door. **Fee:** Full $30.33, extra vehicle $5, Per pet $6.75, pay showers; V, MC, cash. **Parking:** At site.

Facilities

Number of RV-Only Sites: 38. **Number of Tent-Only Sites:** n/a. **Hookups:** Electric (30 amps), water, sewer. **Each Site:** Picnic table, fire ring. **Dump Station:** Yes. **Laundry:** Yes. **Pay Phone:** Yes. **Rest Rooms and Showers:** Yes. **Fuel:** No. **Propane:** No. **Internal Roads:** Gravel. **RV Service:** No. **Market:** East in Port Angeles. **Restaurant:** On site (May to Oct). **General Store:** Yes. **Vending:** No. **Swimming Pool:** No. **Playground:** No. **Other:** Non-powered boat rentals, fishing gear rentals, restaurant, lake access. **Activities:** Fishing, boating. **Nearby Attractions:** Olympic National Park, what else do you need?. **Additional Information:** ONP Info, (360) 452-0330; Port Angeles Chamber of Commerce, (360) 452-2363.

RESTRICTIONS

Pets: On leash only (6 ft. max length), not permitted on any trails within National Park. **Fires:** In fire pits only. **Alcoholic Beverages:** At site only. **Vehicle Maximum Length:** 40 ft. (limited capacity at that length). **Other:** No tents.

TO GET THERE

From Hwy. 101 west of Port Angeles, and if driving west, turn left just after mi. marker 232 onto East Beach Rd. Drive 3.2 mi., and the entrance is on the left.

PORT ANGELES
Shadow Mountain Campground

232951 Hwy. 101, Port Angeles 98363. T: (877) 928-3043; mountain@olypen.com.

RV ★★★ Tent ★★★

Beauty: ★★★★★	Site Privacy: ★
Spaciousness: ★★	Quiet: ★★★
Security: ★	Cleanliness: ★★★★
Insect Control: ★★	Facilities: ★★

Shadow Mountain RV Park, located west of Port Angeles on Hwy. 101, makes a good accommodation when visiting Olympic National Park. The campground lacks plush or lush amenities, but it has good views of the green Olympic Mountains to the south. Sizes vary among gravel, back-in, terraced sites; terrace site 4 (the highest on the hill) and sites 1–5 have the most roominess and best view. Also, a lake across the road provides swimming (it's Hwy. 101, cross carefully—logging trucks hurt); a deli and a 9-hole mini-golf course are also on site. Campites do not have much privacy, and the tenting area, although grassy, has some hills. Just before the on-season has the best traffic conditions for seeing the park and area; after the on-season (ends Labor Day), many services discontinue.

BASICS

Operated By: Shadow Mountain Campground. **Open:** All year. **Site Assignment:** Walkup, reservations (deposit: 1 night stay; refund: 24 hours cancellation. **Registration:** At store, after hours see kiosk out front. **Fee:** For 2 adults RV $18.50, Tent $13, extra adult $2, extra child $1, Pets $1 (V, MC, cash). **Parking:** At site.

FACILITIES

Number of RV-Only Sites: 40. **Number of Tent-Only Sites:** 10. **Hookups:** Electric (30 amps), water, sewer. **Each Site:** Picnic table, fire ring. **Dump Station:** Yes. **Laundry:** Yes. **Pay Phone:** Yes. **Rest Rooms and Showers:** Yes. **Fuel:** Yes. **Propane:** Yes. **Internal Roads:** Gravel. **RV Service:** No. **Market:** In Port Angeles. **Restaurant:** In Port Angeles. **General Store:** Yes. **Vending:** No. **Swimming Pool:** No. **Playground:** Yes. **Other:** Movie rentals, mini-golf, volleyball, badminton, basketball, horseshoes. **Activities:** swimming. **Nearby Attractions:** Port Angeles, Olympic National Park, Olympic National Forest, Dungeness Recreation Area, fishing, swimming, hiking. **Additional Information:** ONP Info, (360) 452-0330; Port Angeles Chamber of Commerce, (360) 452-2363.

RESTRICTIONS

Pets: On leash only. **Fires:** In fire pits only. **Alcoholic Beverages:** At site only. **Vehicle Maximum Length:** None.

TO GET THERE

Located on Hwy. 101 west of Port Angeles, the Texaco/campground office is at mi. 233.

PORT ANGELES
(Olympic National Park)
Altaire Campground

600 East Park Ave., Port Angeles 98362. T: (360) 452-4501; www.nps.gov.

RV ★★★ Tent ★★★★

Beauty: ★★★★★	Site Privacy: ★★
Spaciousness: ★★★	Quiet: ★★★★
Security: ★★	Cleanliness: ★★★★★
Insect Control: ★★	Facilities: ★

Altaire Campground in Olympic National Park has a beautiful setting in a less-trafficked area of the park. Surrounded by lush ferns, campsites sit among tall, vibrant, shady cedars. Sounds of the shallow, rushing Elwa River drift over the campground; the small propoerty makes up one of the river's banks. An entrance fee to the park must be paid to get to the campground, and no facilities come with the site fee, but the natural, local beauty of the surrounding landscape makes a man-made extras seem unneccessary. The site surfaces consist of dirt and fine-grit gravel. On-arrival-only registration makes it harder to obtain a specific site. Altaire also has some park-and-walk-in sites; it is a very short walk. Right after Labor Day, the National Park becomes a ghost town, and spectacular fall colors arrive shortly thereafter; just before or after the on-season provides an intimate setting to experience the Olympics.

BASICS

Operated By: National Park Service. **Open:** Closed during low volume. **Site Assignment:** On arrival. **Registration:** At self pay station. **Fee:** $10. **Parking:** At site.

FACILITIES

Number of Multipurpose Sites: 31. **Hookups:** None. **Each Site:** Picnic table, fire ring. **Dump Station:** No. **Laundry:** No. **Pay Phone:** No. **Rest Rooms and Showers:** Non-flush only. **Fuel:** No. **Propane:** No. **Internal Roads:** Paved. **RV Service:** No. **Market:** In Port Angeles (30–45 min. driving). **Restaurant:** In Port Angeles (30 to 45 min. driving). **General Store:** No. **Vending:** No. **Swimming Pool:** No. **Playground:** No. **Activities:** Resting. **Nearby Attractions:** Olympic National Park, Olympic National Forest, lakes w/ boating, Strait of Juan De Fuca. **Additional Information:** ONP Info, (360) 452-0330; Port Angeles Chamber of Commerce, (360) 452-2363.

RESTRICTIONS

Pets: On leash only (not allowed on National Park trails). **Fires:** Fire pits only, controlled & small. **Alcoholic Beverages:** At site only. **Vehicle Maximum Length:** 25 ft. **Other:** Store all food in a bear-proof location, wash all dishes promptly & don't drop food scraps.

TO GET THERE

From Hwy. 101 west of Port Angeles, turn Left on Olympic Hot Springs Rd., drive 2.1 mi. to entrance gate. From the park entrance, drive 2.4 mi. and the campground is on the right immediately across a bridge. Be alert, as it is not very well marked.

PORT ANGELES
(Olympic National Park)
Heart of the Hills Campground

600 East Park Ave., Port Angeles 98362-6798.
T: (360) 452-4501; www.nps.gov.

RV ★★★★ Tent ★★★★★

Beauty: ★★★★★	Site Privacy: ★★★
Spaciousness: ★★	Quiet: ★★★★
Security: ★★	Cleanliness: ★★★★
Insect Control: ★★	Facilities: ★

Heart o' the Hills Campground, the closest Olympic National Park campground in relation to Port Angeles (the largest city in the national park area), has the best variety in nearby recreation of any of the park campgrounds. Laid out over rolling hills, campsites sit under the canopy of an old-growth forest. Every site has a dirt area where a tent can be erected; parking areas have pavement. The surrounding forest has a vibrancy hard to find anywhere else, with lots of symbiotic plant and fungal relationships, wildlife, and atmosphere. Of the five single-loop sections, E loop has the least-open feel. All sites have at least a little privacy and lots of shade. Summers on the Olympic Peninsula bring lots of tourists, as the region has a look and feel like no other; if it's the on-season, be prepared for some crowds. Local weather is temperate ,and summers can be cool, so bring rain gear and cold-weather clothes.

BASICS

Operated By: National Park Service. **Open:** All year. **Site Assignment:** On arrival. **Registration:** At self pay station. **Fee:** $10. **Parking:** At site.

FACILITIES

Number of Multipurpose Sites: 103. **Hookups:** None. **Each Site:** Picnic table, fire ring. **Dump Station:** No. **Laundry:** No. **Pay Phone:** At park entrance. **Rest Rooms and Showers:** No showers. **Fuel:** No. **Propane:** No. **Internal Roads:** Paved. **RV Service:** No. **Market:** In Port Angeles. **Restaurant:** In Port Angeles. **General Store:** No. **Vending:** No. **Swimming Pool:** No. **Playground:** No. **Other:** Amphitheater. **Activities:** Hiking, interpretive programs. **Nearby Attractions:** Salt water fishing, boating, Olympic National Park, Hurricane Ridge. **Additional Information:** ONP Info, (360) 452-0330; Port Angeles Chamber of Commerce, (360) 452-2363.

Restrictions

Pets: On leash only (6 ft. max length, not allowed on any park trails). **Fires:** In fire pits only. **Alcoholic Beverages:** At site only. **Vehicle Maximum Length:** 21 ft., limited availability up to 32 ft. **Other:** Store all food in a bear-proof location, wash all dishes promptly & don't drop food scraps, In campgrounds where wood is not available, dead & down wood along public roads may be collected, Max occupancy 8 people per site, Max stay limit 14 days per year.

To Get There

From Hwy. 101 southbound in Port Angeles, turn left on Race St. (at traffic light). Drive 1 mi., and after NPS Visitor's Center road forks, follow the right side of the fork. Drive 5.5 mi., through the entrance gate, and the campground is on the left.

PORT ANGELES
(Olympic National Park)
Hoh Rain Forest Campground

600 East Park Ave., Port Angeles 98362-6798.
T: (360) 452-4501; www.nps.gov.

RV ★★★★★ Tent ★★★★★

Beauty: ★★★★★	Site Privacy: ★★★
Spaciousness: ★★	Quiet: ★★★★★
Security: ★★	Cleanliness: ★★★
Insect Control: ★★	Facilities: ★

Well off Hwy. 101, on the western edge of Olympic National Park sits the Hoh Rain Forest visitor's center, and close by, the Hoh Rain Forest Campground. Although a popular spot for tourists, the area has a quiet, private feel during the off-season and the surrounding natural environment breathes beauty year-round. The campground has three loops; B and C loops have a similar layout with dense foliage, paved parking, and gravel-and-grass mixed areas for tents on many sites. A loop has more grass than the others, but it also has more open sites. The benefits of such obscured views of the mountains are best reaped in sites A1–A15. Plant life throughout the area has a unique look and wide diversity; rivers and streams abound; and many hiking trails start at the visitor's center and are usually open even if the center is not. Summer provides the mildest time to visit (it still can be rainy), but be warned: the park has lots of visitors June 17 through Labor Day.

Basics

Operated By: National Park Service. **Open:** Year-round (some sections seasonal). **Site Assignment:** On arrival only. **Registration:** At self pay station. **Fee:** $10, Cash. **Parking:** At site, additional parking at visitor center.

Facilities

Number of Multipurpose Sites: 82. **Hookups:** None. **Each Site:** Picnic table, fire ring. **Dump Station:** Yes. **Laundry:** No. **Pay Phone:** No. **Rest Rooms and Showers:** Flush & Non-flush only (No shower). **Fuel:** No. **Propane:** No. **Internal Roads:** Paved. **RV Service:** No. **Market:** A long way. **Restaurant:** A long way. **General Store:** No. **Vending:** No. **Swimming Pool:** No. **Playground:** No. **Other:** Visitor center, interpretive programs. **Activities:** Interpretive programs, hiking. **Nearby Attractions:** Hoh Rain Forest, Hoh River, Olympic National Park, hiking, fishing. **Additional Information:** ONP Info, (360) 452-0330.

Restrictions

Pets: On leash only (6 ft. max length, not allowed on any park trails). **Fires:** In fire pits only. **Alcoholic Beverages:** At site only. **Vehicle Maximum Length:** 28 ft. **Other:** Store all food in a bear-proof location, wash all dishes promptly & don't drop food scraps, In campgrounds where wood is not available, dead & down wood along public roads may be collected, Max occupancy 8 people per site, Max stay limit 14 days per year.

To Get There

From Hwy. 101 southbound, turn left between mile markers 179 and 178; you're looking for an unnamed (and practically unmarked) access road. Drive 12.3 mi. to the park gate; proceed through gate and drive 5.4 mi.. Campground entrance is on the right.

PORT ANGELES
(Olympic National Park)
Sol Duc Resort

600 East Park Ave., Port Angeles 98362-6798.
T: (360) 452-4501; www.nps.gov.

RV ★★★ Tent ★★

Beauty: ★★★★★ Site Privacy: ★
Spaciousness: ★★ Quiet: ★★★★
Security: ★ Cleanliness: ★★★★
Insect Control: ★★ Facilities: ★★★★

Sol Duc Resort has a small RV area and, the main attraction, an acrid-smelling pool. The pool, fed by Sol Duc Hot Spring, smells that way due to high mineral content, as does much of the water in the immediate area. People come here to relax and "take the waters"; the resort also has an in-house massage therapy operation. The resort's accommodations consist of a lodge, some cabins, and a small, cramped RV area. Sites have no privacy and sit close together in a gravel parking area near the resort. Areas directly adjacent to the RV area have a much more natural and pristine setting. Most sites receive shade from the beautiful birch grove the RV section was cut from. Picnic tables and fire rings for each site sit under the birches. The surrounding area has lots of hiking, and even catch-and-release fishing in the nearby Sol Duc river (heavily regulated, get literature from official location). Summers bring the best weather to the area, but make sure to have rain gear handy anyway.

Basics

Operated By: Langsden Inc. under lease from NPS. **Open:** Mid Apr.–Oct. **Site Assignment:** On arrival, reservation (deposit: 1 night stay; refund: 48 hours notice of cancellation less $5 fee). **Registration:** At office (lodge), no after hours entry. **Fee:** $16, Pool use not included in fee;V, MC, cash. **Parking:** At site, some off site.

Facilities

Number of RV-Only Sites: 20. **Number of Tent-Only Sites:** n/a. **Hookups:** Electric (20, 30 amps), water. **Each Site:** Picnic table, fire ring. **Dump Station:** Yes. **Laundry:** No. **Pay Phone:** Yes. **Rest Rooms and Showers:** At pool. **Fuel:** No. **Propane:** No. **Internal Roads:** Gravel. **RV Service:** No. **Market:** In Port Angeles, 40 mi. east. **Restaurant:** In Port Angeles. **General Store:** Yes. **Vending:** No. **Swimming Pool:** Yes. **Playground:** No. **Other:** Hot springs pools, massage therapy, restaurant & deli. **Activities:** Taking the waters, relaxing, fishing, hiking. **Nearby Attractions:** Olympic National Park & Forest. **Additional Information:** ONP Info, (360) 452-0330; Port Angeles Chamber of Commerce, (360) 452-2363.

Restrictions

Pets: On leash only (6 ft. max length, not allowed on any park trails). **Fires:** In fire pits only. **Alcoholic Beverages:** At site only. **Vehicle Maximum Length:** 32 ft.

To Get There

On Hwy. 101 just east of the National Forest Boundary and just west of Crescent Lake, turn left on Duc Hot Springs Rd. Drive 0.3 mi. to park entrance gate. Pay fee (if applicable) and continue on 12 mi.,; campground entrance is on the right.

PORT TOWNSEND

Fort Flagler State Park

10542 Flagler Rd., Nordland 98358.T: (360) 385-1259; www.parks.wa.gov; infocent@parks.wa.gov.

RV ★★★★ Tent ★★★★★

Beauty: ★★★★★ Site Privacy: ★★★
Spaciousness: ★★★ Quiet: ★★★
Security: ★ Cleanliness: ★★★
Insect Control: ★★ Facilities: ★★

Fort Flagler, situated between Port Townsend Bay and Kilisut Harbor, has 19,100 feet of saltwater shoreline. The park has two campgrounds and both have good views. Better suited for RVs, the grassy lower campground also has better localized views than the upper. Gravel sites 97–116 have almost totally unobstructed 270° of water, horizon, and mountains (and smokestacks) rising from the Washington mainland. These sites don't have any shade; sites 52–76 have shade from short coastal pines but no view. All utility sites reside in the lower campground; the upper campground lacks utilities, is only open seasonally, and has a totally different vibe. Sitting on the edge of a lush, green, heavily forested cliff, the upper campground has limited views of the harbor below. With dirt site surfaces, narrow roads, semi-privacy, and shade, upper campground sites hold the most appeal for tent campers. Summers make the best time to visit here.

Basics

Operated By: Washington State Parks & Recreation. **Open:** Oct. 28–Mar. 1 open for day use only. **Site Assignment:** On arrival, reservations. **Registration:** At self pay station or entrance gate. **Fee:** For 4 adults, Utility $19, standard $13, Primitive $8, extra adult $2, extra vehicle $6; V, MC, cash. **Parking:** At site, off site.

FACILITIES

Number of RV-Only Sites: 14. **Number of Tent-Only Sites:** 101. **Hookups:** Electric (20, 30 amps), water. **Each Site:** Picnic table. **Dump Station:** Yes. **Laundry:** No. **Pay Phone:** No. **Rest Rooms and Showers:** Yes. **Fuel:** No. **Propane:** No. **Internal Roads:** Paved. **RV Service:** No. **Market:** In Port Townsend. **Restaurant:** In Port Townsend. **General Store:** No. **Vending:** No. **Swimming Pool:** No. **Playground:** No. **Other:** Fort Flagler Environmental Learning Center (call for info), boat ramp, moorage. **Activities:** Boating, fishing, swimming, crabbing, clamming. **Nearby Attractions:** The ocean, boating, fishing, water-sports plus salt, Fort Worden Military Park (Historical), Olympic National Park & Forest, ferries, golf, hiking, biking. **Additional Information:** Port Townsend Chamber of Commerce, (360) 385-2722.

RESTRICTIONS

Pets: On leash only (6 ft. max length). **Fires:** In fire pits only. **Alcoholic Beverages:** At site only. **Vehicle Maximum Length:** 40 ft. **Other:** Don't play in drift wood.

TO GET THERE

From the junction of Hwy. 20 and Hwy. 19 near Port Townsend, drive 5.4 mi. on Hwy. 19 south. Turn left onto SR 116 (Oak Bay Rd.). Go through Port Hadlock 2 mi. and take a sharp left, staying on SR 116. Follow to park entrance at end of highway. Park is about 10 mi. from Oak Bay Rd. turnoff.

PORT TOWNSEND

Fort Worden State Park

200 Battery Way, Port Townsend 98368. T: (360) 344-4400; F: (360) 385-7248; www.olympus.net/ftworden.

 ★★★★★ ▲ ★★★

Beauty: ★★★★★ Site Privacy: ★
Spaciousness: ★★★ Quiet: ★★★★
Security: ★★ Cleanliness: ★★
Insect Control: ★★ Facilities: ★★★★

Fort Worden State Park, a military history park in Port Townsend, has two campground sections. One has spectacular views—absolutely amazing views of the water and non-peninsular Washington beyond. Within the aptly titled "Beach Campground" sites, 1–17 have the most unobstructed views; sites 24–50 sit on a loop surrounded by dunes. The whole section hears the waves crashing on the flat beach, providing a peaceful aural backdrop. Waterfront areas have no shade or privacy to speak of; the upper area has some shade. Beach sites have flat, paved parking, while the upper campground sites have gravel parking, a few primitive sites, and no views. Weather here has a knack for changing, so bring cold-weather rain gear just in case.

BASICS

Operated By: Washington State Parks & Recreation. **Open:** All year. **Site Assignment:** On arrival, reservations. **Registration:** At park office or self pay station in campground. **Fee:** Apr. 1–Sept. 30 $20, Oct. 1-Mar. 30 $19, extra vehicle $6; V, MC, D, cash, check. **Parking:** At site.

FACILITIES

Number of RV-Only Sites: 85. **Number of Tent-Only Sites:** 5. **Number of Multipurpose Sites:** 35. **Hookups:** Electric (20, 30 amps), water, sewer. **Each Site:** Picnic table, fire ring. **Dump Station:** Yes. **Laundry:** No. **Pay Phone:** Yes. **Rest Rooms and Showers:** Yes. **Fuel:** No. **Propane:** No. **Internal Roads:** Paved. **RV Service:** No. **Market:** In Port Townsend, 5 mi. south. **Restaurant:** In Port Townsend, 5 mi. south. **General Store:** No. **Vending:** No. **Swimming Pool:** No. **Playground:** No. **Other:** Boat launch, beach, convention center, Military museums, hiking trails. **Activities:** Hiking, boating, fishing (check on regulations & seasons). **Nearby Attractions:** Whale-watching, fishing, boating, Olympic National Park, Olympic National Forest, shellfishing. **Additional Information:** Port Townsend Chamber of Commerce, (360) 385-2722.

RESTRICTIONS

Pets: On leash only (6 ft. max length). **Fires:** In fire pits only. **Alcoholic Beverages:** At site only. **Vehicle Maximum Length:** 40 ft. **Other:** Do not collect driftwood for fires, do not play in driftwood (very dangerous).

TO GET THERE

From I-20 east, follow hwy. into Port Towsend, turn left on Kearney St., drive 0.4 mi., then turn right on Blaine St. Drive 1 block and turn left on Walker, which changes names several times and even forks once (take the left side).

When the road dead-ends, turn right and drive 1 block; campground entrance is on the left.

RANDLE

Takhlakh Campground

Cowlitz Valley Ranger District, P.O. Box 670, Randle 98377. T: (360) 497-1120; www.fs.fed.us/gpnf.

RV: n/a | **Tent: ★★★★**

Beauty: ★★★★★	Site Privacy: ★★
Spaciousness: ★★★	Quiet: ★★★★★
Security: ★★★★	Cleanliness: ★★★★
Insect Control: ★★★	Facilities: ★★★

Just imagine: you're sitting at your site at Takhlakh Lake gazing out at a picture-perfect view of Mount Adams. Most of the 54 tent sites offer views of the lake and the mountain through stands of Douglas fir, Engelmann spruce, pine, and subalpine fir. There is a campground host in attendance at Takhlakh, so anything you can't find, feel free to inquire. There is no easy way to get to Takhlakh, which is part of its appeal. The confusing network of Forest Service roads can be downright irritating, too, if you don't have a good map of the area. If you've come in search of lazy fishing opportunities, Takhlakh is a treat. Only non-motorized boats are allowed on the glassy waters. With an Ansel Adams–like scene at your back, cast your line, and wait for the trout lurking in the frigid glacial depths to find you.

BASICS

Operated By: Northwest Land Management. **Open:** mid-Jun.–mid-Sept. **Site Assignment:** 70% of sites are reserveable; call (877) 444-6777; $8.25 fee. **Registration:** Not necessary. **Fee:** $11. **Parking:** At site.

FACILITIES

Number of Multipurpose Sites: 54. **Hookups:** Inquire at campground. **Dump Station:** Inquire at campground. **Laundry:** No. **Pay Phone:** No. **Rest Rooms and Showers:** No. **Fuel:** Inquire at campground. **Propane:** 3 mi. In Randle. **Internal Roads:** Paved. **RV Service:** No. **Market:** 3 mi. In Randle. **Restaurant:** 3 mi. **General Store:** Yes. **Vending:** No. **Swimming Pool:** No. **Playground:** No. **Other:** Campground host. **Activities:** Fishing, hiking, mountain biking. **Nearby Attractions:** Gifford Pinchot National Forest, Mount Adams Wilderness, Trout Lake, Lava Fields, New Takhtakh Meadow. **Additional Information:** www.fs.fed.us/gpnf.

RESTRICTIONS

Pets: On leash only. **Fires:** In fire pit. **Alcoholic Beverages:** Allowed. **Vehicle Maximum Length:** 21 ft. **Other:** Non-motorized boats only.

TO GET THERE

From Randle, take CR 3 off WA Rte. 12 at Randle. Go south for 2 mi. to FS 23. In another 29 mi., turn north onto FS 2329. The campground is a little over 1 mi. in. From Trout Lake, take FS 80 north to its intersection with FS 23. The campground is nearly the same distance from Trout Lake as from Randle, but the road twists and turns with vaguely marked intersections. The turnoff onto FS 2329 will be to the right coming from Trout Lake.

REPUBLIC

Swan Lake Campground

c/o Republic Ranger Station, P.O. Box 468, Republic 99166. T: (509) 775-3305; www.fs.fed.us/r6/colville.

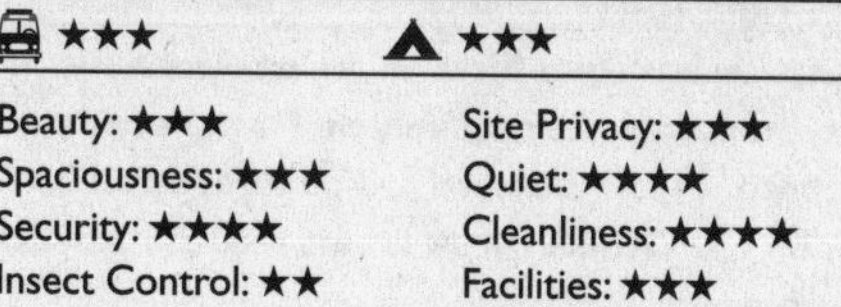

RV: ★★★ | **Tent: ★★★**

Beauty: ★★★	Site Privacy: ★★★
Spaciousness: ★★★	Quiet: ★★★★
Security: ★★★★	Cleanliness: ★★★★
Insect Control: ★★	Facilities: ★★★

The Swan Lake Campground has no headliner attractions. That's why people who have checked out the area come back year after year. It has a little bit of everything, but not enough of anything to attract crowds. Once a ranger station, Swan Lake retains much of the Civilian Conservation Corps' handiwork. The kitchen shelter built by the CCC in 1933 is the only structure of its kind on the Colville forest. The structure is the epicenter of all campground activit; it is a sanctuary in storms and the gathering place for everything from mountain biking groups to wedding parties. The nifty 2.2-mile trail circumnavigating the lake is particularly attractive to seniors and parents with kids. Although it's fun for mountain biking, most fat-tire enthusiasts head out to roughly 50 miles of single- and double-track trails that are blossoming on logging routes closed to motor vehicles. Popular routes go past beaver ponds, where the occasional moose can be found, and along Sheep Mountain, with views of the Kettle River Range.

Basics

Operated By: Colville National Forest. **Open:** Apr.–Oct., but water & garbage collection only from Memorial Day–Labor Day. **Site Assignment:** First come, first served. **Registration:** Not necessary. **Fee:** $8. **Parking:** At site & at boat launch & trailhead.

Facilities

Number of Multipurpose Sites: 25. **Hookups:** Inquire at campground. **Dump Station:** No. **Laundry:** No. **Pay Phone:** No. **Rest Rooms and Showers:** Vault toilets. **Fuel:** No. **Propane:** No. **Internal Roads:** Paved. **RV Service:** No. **Market:** No. **Restaurant:** No. **General Store:** No. **Vending:** No. **Swimming Pool:** No. **Playground:** No. **Other:** Group site, common cooking shelter, 12 water spigots, boat launch. **Activities:** Fishing, boating, biking, hiking. **Nearby Attractions:** Long Lake (dedicated to fly-fishing only), Stonerose Interpretive Center (in Republic). **Additional Information:** www.fs.fed.us/r6/colville.

Restrictions

Pets: On leash only. **Fires:** In fire pit. **Alcoholic Beverages:** At site only. **Vehicle Maximum Length:** 24 ft., but several pull-throughs available for big rigs. **Other:** Fishing license required, gas motors prohibited.

To Get There

From Republic on SR 20, drive south on SR 21 for 8.5 mi. and turn west on Scatter Creek Rd. (No. 53). Follow this paved road about 12 mi., turning right just before Long Lake to reach the Swan Lake Campground.

ROCHESTER
Outback RV Park

19100 Huntington St. Southwest, Rochester 98579. T: (360) 273-0585; www.outbackrvpark.com; outbackrvpark@hotmail.com.

 ★★★  ★

Beauty: ★	Site Privacy: ★
Spaciousness: ★★★	Quiet: ★★
Security: ★★★	Cleanliness: ★★★★
Insect Control: ★★	Facilities: ★★

Outback RV Park, located halfway between Seattle and Portland (its claim to fame), makes a good place to stay if getting off the road sounds attractive for a night. Recreational facilities are minimal, but the park has easy access to the interstate from a rural, low-traffic area. Arranged in several parallel rows across a flat field, sites have flat, gravel surfaces and easily navigable access. The grounds have a defoliated appearance, with little shade and only patches of grass. Sites 39–55 sit closer to a major road than some; otherwise sites are indistinguishable from one another. The campground stays open all year, winters in this part of Washington have relentlessly gray, rainy, cold weather.

Basics

Operated By: Outback RV Park. **Open:** All year. **Site Assignment:** On arrival, reservations. **Registration:** At office, after hours see info outside of office. **Fee:** For 4 people, 2 adults & 2 children, full $22, Tent $14, Phone $2, extra person $2; V, MC, personal checks, cash. **Parking:** At site, limited off site.

Facilities

Number of RV-Only Sites: 58. **Number of Tent-Only Sites:** 10. **Hookups:** Electric (20, 30, 50 amps), water, cable, phone. **Dump Station:** No. **Laundry:** Yes. **Pay Phone:** Yes. **Rest Rooms and Showers:** Yes. **Fuel:** No. **Propane:** Yes. **Internal Roads:** Paved, gravel. **RV Service:** No. **Market:** 2 mi. west in Rochester. **Restaurant:** 2 mi. west in Rochester. **General Store:** Yes. **Vending:** No. **Swimming Pool:** No. **Playground:** Yes. **Other:** Club room, exercise equipment (1 Stairmaster), basketball, horseshoes, video rentals. **Activities:** Inquire at campground. **Nearby Attractions:** Olympia, Seattle, Tacoma, Puget Sound, Mt. Rainier, Washington Pacific Coast. **Additional Information:** Washington State Tourism Board, (360) 725-5052.

Restrictions

Pets: On leash only. **Fires:** Portable fire enclosures, central fire pits only, ask mgmt. **Alcoholic Beverages:** At site only. **Vehicle Maximum Length:** None.

To Get There

From I-5 Exit 88, drive 2.6 mi. west on Hwy. 12 west; the entrance is on the left.

SEATTLE
Lake Pleasant RV Park

24025 Bothell Everett Hwy. Southeast, Bothell 98021. T: (800) 742-0386 or (425) 487-1785

RV ★★★ Tent n/a

Beauty: ★★★ Site Privacy: ★★★
Spaciousness: ★★ Quiet: ★★
Security: ★★★ Cleanliness: ★★★★
Insect Control: ★★ Facilities: ★★★

Lake Pleasant RV Park, off of I-405 in the northeast suburbs of Seattle, has to be the nicest RV park in the metro area. The garden-like grounds, surrounded by oak, pine, and blackberry bramble–covered hills, sit on the edge of small, manmade Lake Pleasant. The willows on the lake's edge, the occasional red Japanese maple, and the ducks only add to the charm of this very green park with paved, grass-encircled sites. The best back-ins (sites 1–14) and the best pull-throughs (sites 15–33) have privacy created by hedges of small pines and cedars, and they sit on the lake's edge. Most other sites also have some form of privacy hedging. The least-desirable sites (back-in sites 201–228) are cramped with no privacy. The quiet grounds' location in relation to downtown Seattle is less than 20 miles, but unless the day is Sunday at six in the morning, expect lots of traffic. Chilly temperatures and rain abound in all seasons except summer, making summers the best time to visit the Puget Sound area.

BASICS

Operated By: Lake Pleasant RV Park. **Open:** All Year. **Site Assignment:** First come, first served; reservations. **Registration:** At office, after hours at drop box in front of office. **Fee:** $28, Cash, check; V, MC. **Parking:** At site.

FACILITIES

Number of RV-Only Sites: 196. **Number of Tent-Only Sites:** n/a. **Hookups:** Electric (30 amps), water, sewer. **Each Site:** Picnic table. **Dump Station:** Yes. **Laundry:** Yes. **Pay Phone:** Yes. **Rest Rooms and Showers:** Yes. **Fuel:** No. **Propane:** Yes. **Internal Roads:** No. **RV Service:** No. **Market:** 2 mi. South in Bothell. **Restaurant:** 2 mi. south in Bothell. **General Store:** No. **Vending:** Yes. **Swimming Pool:** No. **Playground:** Yes. **Other:** Foot paths, volleyball net, horseshoe pit. **Activities:** Pancake breakfasts (monthly in summer), license-less fishing, blueberry picking, hiking. **Nearby Attractions:** Puget Sound, Seattle Center, Pike Place Market, fishing, night life, hiking, whale-watching charter. **Additional Information:** Greater Seattle Chamber of Commerce, (206) 389-7200.

RESTRICTIONS

Pets: On leash only, max length 8 ft.; no fighting breeds. **Fires:** No open fires. **Alcoholic Beverages:** At site only. **Vehicle Maximum Length:** None. **Other:** No swimming, boating in lake; no feeding of waterfowl.

TO GET THERE

From I-405 Exit 26, drive south on Hwy. 27 for 1.2 mi.; entrance on right.

SEATTLE
Trailer Inns RV Park

15531 Southeast 37th, Bellevue 98006. T: (425) 747-9181; trailerinnsrv.uswestdex.com/page3.html.

RV ★★★★ Tent ★

Beauty: ★★ Site Privacy: ★
Spaciousness: ★★★ Quiet: ★
Security: ★★ Cleanliness: ★★★★★
Insect Control: ★★ Facilities: ★★★★★

Trailer Inns, in the east Seattle suburb of Bellevue, offers the most amenities of any park near the city. A pool table, indoor pool, and sauna are just a few of the facilities that make this park stand out. Totally paved over, the flat camping area's layout of parallel rows doesn't have any grass, but it does have some trees and landscaping. The small campground makes good use of its allotted space; campsites have a good amount of room for an urban park. Recommended sites include back-ins 2–7 and 21–42. The pull-throughs here provide less room to the sides than back-ins do. Campsites 43–66, which are back-ins with no dividers in the rear, have more of a cramped feeling than other back-ins in the park. Like all urban parks, this one has some ambient urban noise, but it's not intolerable. Also, for pop-up tent trailers or pick-up piggy backs ,there are some smaller sites near the office. Visit Seattle during summer for the best weather.

BASICS

Operated By: Trailer Inns RV Park. **Open:** All year. **Site Assignment:** On arrival, reservations (deposit: $25; refund 24 hours notice for cancellation). **Registration:** At office, after hours see info at door. **Fee:** For 2 adults, 2 children & 2 pets, Supersite (largest)–$33, pull-through $31, Double $27, Single $22, Tent $18, extra people $5; V, MC, cash. **Parking:** At site.

Facilities

Number of RV-Only Sites: 109. **Number of Tent-Only Sites:** n/a. **Hookups:** Electric (30, 50 amps), water, sewer, cable. **Dump Station:** No. **Laundry:** Yes. **Pay Phone:** Yes. **Rest Rooms and Showers:** Yes. **Fuel:** No. **Propane:** Yes. **Internal Roads:** Paved. **RV Service:** No. **Market:** A few blocks west. **Restaurant:** A few blocks west. **General Store:** No. **Vending:** Yes. **Swimming Pool:** Yes. **Playground:** Yes. **Other:** Game room w/ pool table & arcade, indoor hot tub, indoor sauna, indoor BBQ, TV room w/ big screen & fireplace, outdoor gas grill. **Activities:** Inquire at campground. **Nearby Attractions:** Seattle & Puget Sound, Snoqualmie Falls, skiing. **Additional Information:** Seattle Visitor Info Center, (206) 461-5840; www.seeseattle.org.

Restrictions

Pets: On leash only, 2 pets max. **Fires:** No open fires, no charcoal. **Alcoholic Beverages:** At site only. **Vehicle Maximum Length:** None. **Other:** Properly maintained RVs only allowed on property.

To Get There

From I-90 Exit 11, take the third exit ramp to 150 Ave. SE. Drive south and turn left at first light onto Frontage Rd. Drive a few blocks on Frontage; when the road separates with a median, stay on far right. The campground entrance is the third driveway after the median starts.

SEATTLE (EVERETT)

Lakeside RV Park

12321 Hwy. 99 South, Everett 98204. T: (425) 347-2970 or (425) 742-7333 or reservations only (800) 468-7275; F: (425) 347-9052.

RV: ★★★ Tent: ★★

Beauty: ★★★	Site Privacy: ★★★
Spaciousness: ★★	Quiet: ★★
Security: ★★★	Cleanliness: ★★★★
Insect Control: ★★	Facilities: ★★

Lakeside RV Park, located in the suburban burg of Everett, has easy access to services (such as groceries and shopsl) and a quick route to Seattle, some 20 minutes south. The park has laundry, bathroom facilities, and a stocked lake for fishing (runoff feeds the lake, so eat your catch at your own risk). All back-in RV sites come with paved surfaces and are divided by cedar hedges that create a little privacy. The grounds have a cramped feeling but a good location. Back-in sites 127–139 back up to a hedge of deciduous shrubbery and provide the best space and privacy. Even-numbered sites 76–104 are the best paved pull-throughs (for space). Other than the above, the RV sites have a fairly homogenous layout, and sites 1–15 sit in a high traffic area. The tenting area has fine-grit gravel pads surrounded by grass, no privacy, and cannot accommodate large tents. Seattle has tourism year-round, but summer brings the best weather and avoids the stereotypical rains of winter.

Basics

Operated By: PFC Mgmt. **Open:** All year. **Site Assignment:** On arrival, reservations (deposit: 1 night stay; refund: 24 hours notice less $6 cancellation fee). **Registration:** At office, after hours pay in morning or drop in office door. **Fee:** Full $38.48, Tent $15.33 (V, MC, D, personal checks, cash). **Parking:** At site, additional parking available.

Facilities

Number of RV-Only Sites: 150. **Number of Tent-Only Sites:** 9. **Hookups:** Electric (20, 30, 50 amps), water, sewer, cable. **Dump Station:** No. **Laundry:** Yes. **Pay Phone:** Yes. **Rest Rooms and Showers:** Yes. **Fuel:** No. **Propane:** Yes. **Internal Roads:** Paved. **RV Service:** No. **Market:** South or north on Hwy. 99 (close by). **Restaurant:** South or North on Hwy. 99 (close by). **General Store:** No. **Vending:** Yes. **Swimming Pool:** No. **Playground:** Yes. **Other:** RV & boat storage, horseshoes, lake fishing, fishing dock, jogging path around lake, espresso stand (just in front of park, separate enterprise). **Activities:** Fishing (per fish charges & per site limits apply). **Nearby Attractions:** Seattle. **Additional Information:** Seattle Visitor Info Center, (206) 461-5840; www.seeseattle.org.

Restrictions

Pets: Short leash only. **Fires:** No open fires. **Alcoholic Beverages:** At site only. **Vehicle Maximum Length:** None. **Other:** Visitor parking for short term use (2 hours).

To Get There

From I-5 Exit 186 (128th St. SW) drive west on 128th for 1.3 mi. Turn left on Hwy. 99 at Home Depot.

SEATTLE
Twin Cedars RV Park

17826 Hwy. 99 North, Lynnwood 98037. T: (425) 742-5540 or (800) 878-9304; F: (425) 745-2200; twincedars@pcfre.com.

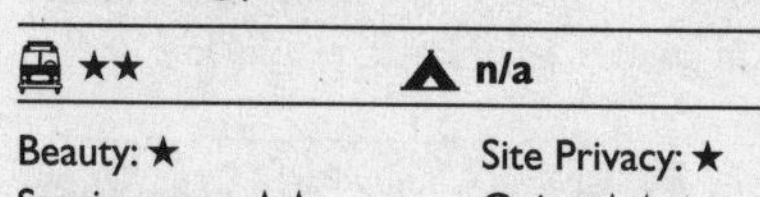

★★ n/a

Beauty: ★	Site Privacy: ★
Spaciousness: ★★	Quiet: ★★
Security: ★★	Cleanliness: ★
Insect Control: ★★	Facilities: ★

Twin Cedars RV Park in Lynnwood has a very convenient location on Hwy. 99 just north of Seattle; location is only draw here. Sites consist of gravel with a small amount of surrounding grass. The best campsites, sites 10–20, are the furthest from the loud industrial facility next door; conversely, the worst, sites 58–70, sit the closest to the industrial area. The park has no landscaping, a drainage ditch running through it, and patchy grass at best. In Seattle, the best weather happens during the summer, but the city has tourist attractions open year-round.

Basics

Operated By: PCF mgmt. **Open:** All year. **Site Assignment:** On arrival, reservations (deposit: 1 night stay; refund: 24 hours notice less $6 cancellation fee). **Registration:** At office, after hours check board at office, pay in morning. **Fee:** Full $35.08, 7th day free (V, MC, cash). **Parking:** At site, limited off site.

Facilities

Number of RV-Only Sites: 69. **Number of Tent-Only Sites:** n/a. **Hookups:** Electric (20, 30, 50 amps), water, sewer, cable. **Dump Station:** Yes. **Laundry:** Yes. **Pay Phone:** Yes. **Rest Rooms and Showers:** Yes. **Fuel:** No. **Propane:** Yes. **Internal Roads:** Paved. **RV Service:** No. **Market:** Across Hwy. 99. **Restaurant:** Across Hwy. 99. **General Store:** No. **Vending:** Yes. **Swimming Pool:** No. **Playground:** No. **Other:** Club house w/ TV, VCR, & small aerobic area; horseshoes, common picnic area. **Activities:** Inquire at campground. **Nearby Attractions:** Seattle. **Additional Information:** Seattle Visitor Info Center, (206) 461-5840; www.seeseattle.org.

Restrictions

Pets: On leash only. **Fires:** No open fires. **Alcoholic Beverages:** At site only. **Vehicle Maximum Length:** 40 ft.

To Get There

From I-5 Exit 183, drive west 1. 6 mi. on 164th Southwest. This turns into 44th Ave West. Drive 0.5 mi., turn right on 176th St. SW, and drive 0.3 mi., then turn left on SR 99, go 0.2 mi., and the entrance is on the right behind Avis Rent-A-Car.

SEATTLE/TACOMA
Seattle-Tacoma KOA

5801 South 212th St., Kent 98032. T: (253) 872-8652; F: (253) 395-1782; www.koa.com; seattlekoa@aol.com.

★★★ ★★

Beauty: ★★	Site Privacy: ★
Spaciousness: ★★★	Quiet: ★★
Security: ★	Cleanliness: ★★★
Insect Control: ★★	Facilities: ★★

KOA Seattle-Tacoma, located between the two cities in Kent, offers easy access to the metropolitan areas. The campground consists of a flat field of sites laid out in parallel rows with two different sections. One section has more shade, but it only has dirt- and gravel-surfaced sites. The other section has paved surfaces and a more maintained appearance, but no shade. No sites have privacy. The best sites in the first section (sites 26–36) have shade from tall, bushy Japanese maples. In the less-desirable section, sites 58–109 sit furthest from the traffic noise of a nearby road. The tenting area (sites 48–57) in the back of the park have grass and dirt surfaces and lots of shade. Sites 110–133 and 1–14 sit near a road and should be avoided due to noise. Weather-wise the best time to visit the area is during the summer.

Basics

Operated By: Seattle Tacoma KOA. **Open:** All year. **Site Assignment:** On arrival, reservations (deposit: 1 night stay; refund: 24 hours cancellation). **Registration:** At office, after hours register w/ security or pay in morning. **Fee:** For 2 people,

Deluxe Full (50 amp) $42.95, Regular Full $35.95, Water-electric $32.95, No hookup $24.95, extra people over the age of 5 $2.95 (V, MC, D, cash, personal checks). **Parking:** At site, limited off site.

Facilities

Number of RV-Only Sites: 160. **Number of Tent-Only Sites:** 20. **Hookups:** Electric (20, 30 amps), water, sewer, cable, phone. **Each Site:** Picnic table. **Dump Station:** Yes. **Laundry:** Yes. **Pay Phone:** Yes. **Rest Rooms and Showers:** Yes. **Fuel:** No. **Propane:** Yes. **Internal Roads:** Paved. **RV Service:** No. **Market:** South in Kent. **Restaurant:** South in Kent. **General Store:** Yes. **Vending:** No. **Swimming Pool:** Yes. **Playground:** Yes. **Other:** Arcade, day room (used for movies, breakfast), tour pickups & booking, vhs rentals, bike rentals (summer). **Activities:** Nightly movies, breakfast for sale in summer. **Nearby Attractions:** Seattle. **Additional Information:** Seattle Visitor Info Center, (206) 461-5840; www.seeseattle.org.

Restrictions

Pets: On leash only. **Fires:** No open fires, charcoal ok. **Alcoholic Beverages:** At site only. **Vehicle Maximum Length:** 60 ft.

To Get There

From I-5 Exit 152, take Orillia road and drive south to campground.

SEQUIM
Dungeness Recreation Area

223 East 4th St., Port Angeles 98362. T: (360) 417-2291; www.clallam.net/park/park_dungeness1.htm.

RV ★★★ Tent ★★★★

Beauty: ★★★★★	Site Privacy: ★★★★★
Spaciousness: ★★★★	Quiet: ★★★★
Security: ★★★★	Cleanliness: ★★★★
Insect Control: ★★★	Facilities: ★★

Dungeness Spit, the main attraction in the Dungeness Recreation Area/National Wildlife Refuge, is the longest natural sand spit in the United States. Arching nearly seven miles into the Strait of Juan de Fuca from the Olympic Peninsula, this unique landform averages only 100 yards wide for its entire length. The entire expanse of spits, tidelands, wetlands, landmarks, and adjoining surf forms Dungeness National Wildlife Refuge. The Dungeness Recreation Area campsites are well-designed around two loops, affording ultimate privacy with dense undergrowth between sites. About a third of the sites are spaced along a high bluff that overlooks the Strait of Juan de Fuca with million-dollar views. Despite the moderate year-round climate, the campground is open only from February 1 to October 1. Summer can be quite busy, so you may want to try the off-season. In addition to the ever-popular beachcombing, other activities in the park include horseback riding (separate equestrian trail and unloading area), game bird hunting in designated areas, and good old-fashioned picnicking.

Basics

Operated By: Clallam County Parks Dept. **Open:** Feb. 1–Oct. 1. **Site Assignment:** First come, first served. **Registration:** At park information booth from daylight-dusk. **Fee:** $10. **Parking:** At site.

Facilities

Number of RV-Only Sites: Inquire at campground. **Number of Tent-Only Sites:** 0. **Number of Multipurpose Sites:** 67. **Hookups:** None. **Each Site:** Picnic table, fire pit, shade trees. **Dump Station:** Yes. **Laundry:** No. **Pay Phone:** Yes. **Rest Rooms and Showers:** Yes. **Fuel:** 5 mi. in Sequim. **Propane:** 5 mi. **Internal Roads:** Paved. **RV Service:** No. **Market:** 5 mi. **Restaurant:** 5 mi. **General Store:** 5 mi. **Vending:** No. **Swimming Pool:** No. **Playground:** No. **Other:** Firewood. **Activities:** Equestrian trails, hiking, hunting, shell fishing, beachcombing. **Nearby Attractions:** Dungeness Wildlife Refuge, Agriculture Tour, Cungeness Lighthouse. **Additional Information:** www.clallam.net/park/park_dungeness1.htm.

Restrictions

Pets: On leash only. **Fires:** In fire pit. **Alcoholic Beverages:** Prohibited. **Vehicle Maximum Length:** None. **Other:** No dogs on beach.

To Get There

From Sequim (17 mi. east of Port Angeles), drive 5 mi. west on US 101 to Kitchen-Dick Ln. Turn north, and drive 3 mi., watching for signs to the recreation area campground entrance.

SEQUIM
Port Angeles-Sequim KOA

80 O'Brian Rd., Port Angeles 98362. T: (360) 457-5916; F: (360) 417-0759; www.koa.com; horizon@olypen.com.

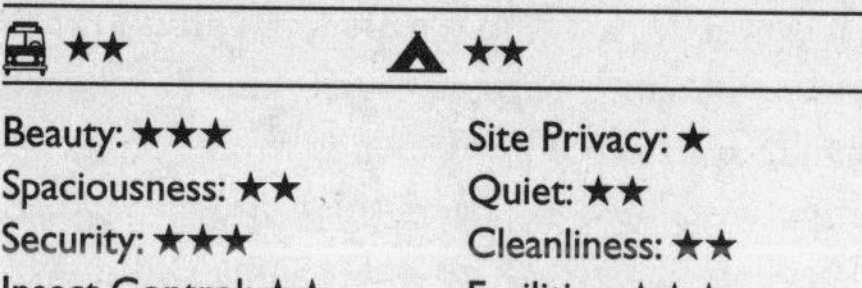

Beauty: ★★★
Site Privacy: ★
Spaciousness: ★★
Quiet: ★★
Security: ★★★
Cleanliness: ★★
Insect Control: ★★
Facilities: ★★★

KOA Port Angeles-Sequim, seven miles east of Port Angeles on Hwy. 101, has the most in-park recreational facilities near Dungeness Spit and Olympic National Park. The hotel-like recreation is not astounding, but it's an alternative to the natural or no-recreation parks that dot the rain shadow area of the northern Olympic Peninsula. The grass and gravel full hookup campsites (sites 1–18) have a view of the surrounding mountains, but they are situated without shade or privacy next to truck-heavy Hwy. 101. The quieter water and electric sites sit in grass and lightly shaded meadows with obscured or nonexistent views of the surrounding mountains. These campsites (sites 21–33) are the best, though cluttered; they sit near the next-best, which are no-hookup sites A–G. Campsites A–G have more space because they have no rear neighbors. Weather here stays mild and sunny, but most tourist attractions in the area are fully operational only in the summer.

Basics

Operated By: KOA Port Angeles-Sequim. **Open:** Apr. 1–Oct. 31. **Site Assignment:** First come, first served: Reservations (deposit: 1 night's stay; refund: 72 hours cancellation). **Registration:** At office, after hours see directions in office window. **Fee:** For 2 people, full: $29, Water-electric: $26, No hookup: $22, Tents: $22, extra person (greater than 5 years old): $4, extra vehicle (over 1 camping unit plus 1 vehicle): $5, V, MC, cash. **Parking:** At site.

Facilities

Number of RV-Only Sites: 84. **Number of Tent-Only Sites:** 11. **Hookups:** Electric (20, 30 amps), water, sewer, cable. **Each Site:** Picnic table, fire ring. **Dump Station:** Yes. **Laundry:** Yes. **Pay Phone:** Yes. **Rest Rooms and Showers:** Yes. **Fuel:** No. **Propane:** Yes. **Internal Roads:** Gravel. **RV Service:** No. **Market:** 7 mi. west in Sequim. **Restaurant:** 7 mi. west in Sequim. **General Store:** Yes. **Vending:** Yes. **Swimming Pool:** Yes. **Playground:** Yes. **Other:** Game room (w/ a pool table, video games, ping pong), hot tub, video rentals, badminton, volleyball, basketball, mini-golf, banana-seat bike rentals, horseshoes, tetherball. **Activities:** Kite flying, summer hay rides, planned activities. **Nearby Attractions:** Olympic National Park, scuba diving, boating, charter fishing, hiking, Dungeness Recreation Area, seasonal local events, Deer Park, Sol Duc valley. **Additional Information:** Port Angeles Chamber of Commerce (360) 452-2363.

Restrictions

Pets: On leash only. **Fires:** In fire pits only. **Alcoholic Beverages:** At site only. **Vehicle Maximum Length:** None. **Other:** Max 6 people per site.

To Get There

Located off Hwy. 101 7 mi. east of Port Angeles and 8 mi. west of Sequim very near the Washington State Patrol Sattelite office. If headed eastbound, turn right onto O'Brian Rd. and drive half a block; entrance is on right.

SEQUIM

Rainbow's End RV Park

261831 Hwy. 101, Sequim 98382. T: (360) 683-3863; rainborv@olypen.com.

RV ★★★ Tent ★★

Beauty: ★★★
Site Privacy: ★
Spaciousness: ★★
Quiet: ★★
Security: ★★★
Cleanliness: ★★★★
Insect Control: ★★
Facilities: ★★★★

Rainbow's End RV Park, a small, attractively landscaped RV park on Hwy. 101 near Sequim, lacks on-site recreation but provides a good location for access to the numerous Northern Olympic Peninsula attractions. Short coastal pines, weeping willows, and flowering hardwoods partially shade both the gravel sites and a small trout pond located in the middle of the park. The medium sized trout in the pond are for feeding only. Site layout creates a mildly cramped environment with the exception of the more spacious sites F–G. The quietest options, sites 11–21, sit furthest from the highway, and the shady tent area consists of a section of flat grass. All tent and RV sites lack privacy. The Northern Olympic Peninsula has mild weather all year, but its largest attraction—the national park,—is fully operational only in the summer.

Basics

Operated By: Rainbow's End RV Park. **Open:** All year. **Site Assignment:** First come, first served;

reservations (deposit 1 night's stay; refund: 72 hours cancellation). **Registration:** At office; after hours see host. **Fee:** For two people:, Full: $22.50, tent: $15, extra person>10 years old: $2, Under 10 years old, free. V, MC, cash, check. **Parking:** At site.

Facilities

Number of RV-Only Sites: 39. **Number of Tent-Only Sites:** 15. **Hookups:** Electric (20, 30, 50 amps), water, sewer, cable, phone, central data port. **Each Site:** Picnic table. **Dump Station:** Yes. **Laundry:** Yes. **Pay Phone:** Yes. **Rest Rooms and Showers:** Yes. **Fuel:** No. **Propane:** Yes. **Internal Roads:** Paved. **RV Service:** No. **Market:** 2 mi. east in Sequim. **Restaurant:** Two mi. east in Sequim. **General Store:** No. **Vending:** No. **Swimming Pool:** No. **Playground:** Yes. **Other:** Reserveable clubhouse, basketball goal, horseshoes, volleyball. **Activities:** Summer weekend BBQ's & potlucks, crafts based on tenants. **Nearby Attractions:** Olympic National Park, Dungeness Spit, Recreation area, & National Wildlife Refuge, Olympic Game Farm, Dungeness Lighthouse, local festivals. **Additional Information:** Sequim-Dungeness Chamber of Commerce, (800) 737-8462.

Restrictions

Pets: Well behaved & On leash only. **Fires:** In fire pits in tent area only. **Alcoholic Beverages:** At site only. **Vehicle Maximum Length:** Fifty ft. **Other:** Have to have a good time or you can't leave.

To Get There

The park is located 1.5 mi. west of the western-most Sequim Exit on Hwy. 101 on the coastal side. The park has a large sign and is surrounded by privacy fencing.

SILVER CREEK

Harmony Lakeside RV Park

563 Rte. 122, Silver Creek 98585. T: (360) 983-3804; F: (360) 983-8345; www.harmonylakesidervpark.com; info@harmonylakesidervpark.com.

▲ ★★

Beauty: ★★★★★	Site Privacy: ★★
Spaciousness: ★★★	Quiet: ★★★★
Security: ★	Cleanliness: ★★★★
Insect Control: ★★	Facilities: ★★★

Harmony Lakeside RV Park on Mayfield Lake is between I-5 and routes to Mt. Rainier and St. Helens. The beautifully manicured grounds run up to the lake's edge; the park also has several small, river-stone-lined ponds with fountains, brightly colored koi, and small bronze statues. The sites and roads are well-maintained gravel. There are no tent sites, but tent campers can set up in a water and electric site if they don't mind the gravel. Sites 1–27 stand on two loops in a grassy field with shade and painstakingly shaped hedges. This section is often reserved well in advance, making it hard to get into. Sites 1–8 have a beautiful view of the water. The second set of loops run through a manicured fairy tale–like forest of beautiful moss interspersed with grass, tall cedars, large dead tree trunks with beautiful secondary growth, and views of the lake some 20 feet below. Sites 66–69 in this section have lots of space and sit right on the edge of the cliffs. The bonsai-like artfulness of the groundskeepers makes this already small, quiet campground even more charming. Visit late in spring or early fall for the best weather and slowest-paced days.

Basics

Operated By: Harmony Lakeside RV. **Open:** All year. **Site Assignment:** On arrival, reservations. **Registration:** At office, after hours see drop. **Fee:** Full $27, Water electric $24, Pets $2 per pet per day, V, MC, cash. **Parking:** At site.

Facilities

Number of RV-Only Sites: 80. **Number of Tent-Only Sites:** 38. **Hookups:** Electric (20, 30, 50 amps), water, sewer, cable. **Each Site:** Picnic table, fire ring. **Dump Station:** Yes. **Laundry:** No. **Pay Phone:** Yes. **Rest Rooms and Showers:** Yes. **Fuel:** No. **Propane:** No. **Internal Roads:** Gravel. **RV Service:** No. **Market:** Near Mossyrock. **Restaurant:** Near Mossyrock. **General Store:** No. **Vending:** Yes. **Swimming Pool:** No. **Playground:** No. **Other:** Reception hall, both powered & non-powered boats, volleyball, badminton, horseshoes. **Activities:** Fishing, watersports. **Nearby Attractions:** Mt. Rainier, Mt. St. Helens, fish hatcheries, Seattle, Olympia. **Additional Information:** Washington State Tourism Board, (360) 725-5052.

Restrictions

Pets: Leash Only (fee required). **Fires:** In fire pits only. **Alcoholic Beverages:** At site only. **Vehicle Maximum Length:** None. **Other:** No firewood gathering.

To Get There

On I-5, drive to Exit 68 (Hwy. 12 Morton-Yakima). Once on US 12, go east 21 mi. At the Mossyrock blinker, turn left. Drive 2.5 mi. on SR 122 and the entrance is on the left.

SKAMANIA

Beacon Rock State Park

3483L WA Rte. 14, Skamania 98648. T: (360) 902-8844; www.parks.wa.gov.

RV ★★ Tent ★★★★

Beauty: ★★★★	Site Privacy: ★★★★
Spaciousness: ★★★★	Quiet: ★★★★★
Security: ★★★★	Cleanliness: ★★★★★
Insect Control: ★★	Facilities: ★★

The Northwest's longest and largest river, cutting a huge sea-level pass through the Cascade Mountains, teams with the world's second-largest monolith to produce the main attractions for campers at Beacon Rock State Park. Beacon Rock, once known as Castle Rock, towers 848 feet above the mighty Columbia River in the Columbia River Gorge National Scenic Area and is second only to the Rock of Gibraltar in size. Aside from the Beacon Rock trail (which is a must), a network of other paths throughout the park's interior offers destinations to Rodney Falls and Hardy Falls. Sitting beside the falls as they cascade down Hardy Creek, a forested mountain at your back, watching birds flit and chipmunks scamper, and enjoying the fragrant wisps of campfire smoke wafting past are all ingredients for as fine a Northwest outing as anyone could hope for. The campground is tucked against a forested hillside on the north side of WA Rte. 14. Tent sites are spaced comfortably around the circular paved drive that winds up from the river. The main camp area is an older camp in a forested setting suited more for tents than RVs. There are a limited number of sites that accommodate RVs over 20 feet.

Basics

Operated By: Washington State Parks & Recreation Commission. **Open:** Apr. 1–Oct. **Site Assignment:** Reservations for group camping only; otherwise first come first served. **Registration:** Self-registration. **Fee:** $11. **Parking:** At site.

Facilities

Number of RV-Only Sites: 6. **Number of Tent-Only Sites:** 29. **Hookups:** None. **Each Site:** Picnic table, fire grill, shade trees. **Dump Station:** Yes. **Laundry:** No. **Pay Phone:** Yes. **Rest Rooms and Showers:** Yes. **Fuel:** No. **Propane:** No. **Internal Roads:** Paved. **RV Service:** No. **Market:** No. **Restaurant:** No. **General Store:** No. **Vending:** No. **Swimming Pool:** No. **Playground:** Yes. **Other:** Kitchen, showers for fee, boat launch, clock. **Activities:** Hiking, boating, mountain biking, fishing, rock climbing. **Nearby Attractions:** Rodney Falls, Hardy Falls, Table Mountain, Hamilton Mountain. **Additional Information:** www.parks.wa.gov.

Restrictions

Pets: On leash only. **Fires:** In fire pit. **Alcoholic Beverages:** Allowed. **Vehicle Maximum Length:** 50 ft.

To Get There

Go east on SR 14 from its junction with I-205 at Ellsworth. The wide expanse of the Columbia is your constant companion as you drive approximately 30 mi. on the two-lane route (Lewis and Clark Hwy.) to the park's entrance. You'll pass the base of Beacon Rock as you are watching for the signs to the turnoff for the park. Be aware that the road signs around here are a bit confusing, and traffic gets congested when motorists slow to gawk at Beacon Rock.

SKYHOMISH

Beckler River Campground

c/o Skykomish Ranger District, Box 305, Skykomish 98288. T: (360) 677-2414; www.fs.fed.us/r6/mbs or www.reserveusa.com.

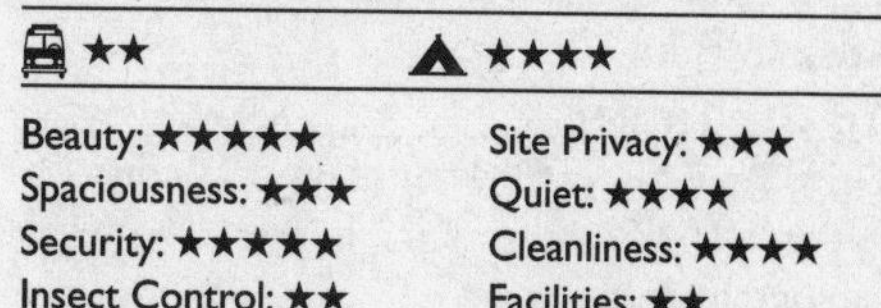

Only 60 miles from Seattle, Beckler sits on the banks of the Beckler River three miles from the town of Skykomish. A heavy canopy of western Washington foliage drapes the area around the campground as well as the numerous steep-sided river and creek valleys that drain their tributaries into the Beckler River. Trips into the Beckler backcountry should be prefaced by a visit to the

Skykomish Ranger Station. Heavy snow can often keep trails blocked longer than one would imagine. The Henry M. Jackson Wilderness (named for a former Washington State senator) lies to the north. It has 49 miles of hiking trails that were once the cross-Cascade routes used by early Native Americans and later by exploration teams. Follow the Forest Service road past Garland Hot Springs to reach the trailheads. To the south is the fabled Alpine Lakes Wilderness. Trailheads into Alpine Lakes are just west of Skykomish on Miller River Rd., which becomes FS 6412.

Basics

Operated By: Mount Baker-Snoqualmie National Forest. **Open:** Memorial Day–mid-Sept. **Site Assignment:** Reservations & fist come first served. **Registration:** At camp office. **Fee:** $12. **Parking:** At site.

Facilities

Number of RV-Only Sites: Inquire at campground. **Number of Tent-Only Sites:** 0. **Number of Multipurpose Sites:** 27. **Hookups:** None. **Each Site:** Picnic table, fire pit w/ grill, shade trees, piped water nearby. **Dump Station:** No. **Laundry:** No. **Pay Phone:** No. **Rest Rooms and Showers:** Vault toilets. **Fuel:** 1 mi. in Skykomish. **Propane:** 1 mi. **Internal Roads:** Paved. **RV Service:** No. **Market:** No. **Restaurant:** No. **General Store:** 1 mi. **Vending:** No. **Swimming Pool:** No. **Playground:** No. **Activities:** Fishing, hiking. **Nearby Attractions:** Mount Baker, Becker River. **Additional Information:** www.fs.fed.us/r6/mbs or www.reserveusa.com.

Restrictions

Pets: On leash only. **Fires:** In fire pit. **Alcoholic Beverages:** Allowed. **Vehicle Maximum Length:** 21 ft.

To Get There

Drive 1 mi. east of Skykomish on US 2, turn left onto FS 65, and go 2 mi. to the campground.

SPOKANE

Yogi Bear's Camp Resort

7520 South Thomas Mallen Rd., Cheney 99004. T: (509) 747-9415 or reservations (800) 494-PARK; www.jellystonewa.com; yogi@jellystonewa.com.

 ★★★★ 

Beauty: ★★	Site Privacy: ★
Spaciousness: ★★	Quiet: ★★★
Security: ★★★★★	Cleanliness: ★★★
Insect Control: ★★	Facilities: ★★★★★

Yogi Bear's Camp Resort, ten miles east of Spokane, offers a wide array of in house resort-like activities. The quality of the recreational facilities here far surpasses that of competitors, with tons of planned activities during the on-season and newly furbished facilities. These facilities include a well-kept mini-golf course with lots of flowing water under the shade of ponderosa pines. Within the shady grounds, sites vary in quality, and accommodations consist of both back-in and pull-through sites. Flat, gravel pull-through rows R, G, and B make up the best sites in the campground; avoid row Y. Back-in sites exist throughout the grounds, but unfortunately many are not totally flat. The tent sites at Yogi Bear's lack a Jellystone forest feel; all have gravel floors. Additionally, the camp resort offers several varieties of permanent fixture lodging, including bungalows and cabins. The busiest time to visit is June 16 through Labor Day; visit in the late spring or early fall to avoid the crowds.

Basics

Operated By: Private ownership of franchise rights to Jellystone Park Resorts. **Open:** All year. **Site Assignment:** First come, first served; reservations require a minimum 2 night stay (deposit 50% of total stay; refund on cancellation before 2 weeks, after 2 weeks no refund or rain check). **Registration:** At office; after hours must wait until morning-enter park. **Fee:** For 2 people Sun-Thurs, pull-through: $33, Back-in: $30, Tent site: $19, Friday or Saturday add $5-base, extra Adult: $8, extra Child: $3, extra Tent (1 per site) $11, $13 on weekends, extra Car (2 car max): $2, V, MC, cash. **Parking:** At site.

Facilities

Number of RV-Only Sites: 64. **Number of Tent-Only Sites:** 21. **Hookups:** Electric (20, 30, 50 amps), water, sewer, cable, phone. **Each Site:** Picnic table. **Dump Station:** Yes. **Laundry:** Yes. **Pay Phone:** Yes. **Rest Rooms and Showers:** Yes. **Fuel:** No. **Propane:** Yes. **Internal Roads:** Gravel. **RV Service:** No. **Market:** 5 mi. east on I-90. **Restaurant:** 5 mi. east on I-90. **General Store:** Yes. **Vending:** Yes. **Swimming Pool:** Yes. **Playground:** Yes. **Other:** Volleyball, pickleball, & basketball courts; 18 hole mini-golf, horseshoes, water balloon slingshot range, kiddie lagoon, hot tub, arcade w/ pool table, birthday party room, exercise room (small, equipped w/ weight, aerobic machines). **Activities:** Lots of planned activities every weekend, planned activities more frequently from Jun. 16–end of Aug. **Nearby Attractions:** Cheney Cowles Museum, Manito Park & Japanese Gardens, Riverfront Park, golf, Centennial Trail, regional special events. **Additional Information:** Spokane Chamber of Commerce (509) 624-1393.

RESTRICTIONS

Pets: On leash only. **Fires:** No open fires. **Alcoholic Beverages:** At site only. **Vehicle Maximum Length:** None. **Other:** All holiday weekends 3 night minimum stay.

TO GET THERE

From I-90 Exit 172 (eastbound turn right; westbound turn left), take next left at stop sign onto Westbow; road becomes Hallet St. Follow Hallet for 1.1 mi., and then turn right on Thomas Mallen Rd. Follow Thomas Mallen Road for 1.1 mi.; entrance is on right.

SWIFT

Lower Falls Recreation Area

42218 Northeast Yale Bridge Rd., Amboy 98601. T: (360) 247-3900; www.fs.fed.us/gpnf.

 ★★ ▲ ★★★★

Beauty: ★★★★★	Site Privacy: ★★★★
Spaciousness: ★★★★★	Quiet: ★★★★★
Security: ★★★	Cleanliness: ★★★★★
Insect Control: ★★★★	Facilities: ★★

Unfortunately, on cloudy days, there isn't much to look at on the way to the Lower Falls area except the expansive reservoirs and the clear-cut hills. However, if you are blessed with fewer clouds on your trip, views of Mount St. Helens appear at various points along the route. Once at the falls, the primary spectacle becomes a series of major waterfalls roaring off what are known geologically as "benches." Lower Falls Recreation Area has undergone some renovation recently and sports twice as many campsites as before. The original 20 sites are still the best because they are closer to the river and have more vegetation between them for ultimate privacy. Activities in the Lewis River valley include hiking, fishing, hunting, horsepacking, canoeing, and volcano watching. There are endless trails in the neighborhood. The Lewis River Trail is a popular, low-elevation meander for 13.6 miles. If you have time, check out the Mount St. Helens National Volcanic Monument Center in Swift.

BASICS

Operated By: Mount St. Helens National Volcanic Monument. **Open:** Memorial Day–Oct. **Site Assignment:** Reservations or first come first served. **Registration:** Self-registration. **Fee:** $12. **Parking:** At site.

FACILITIES

Number of RV-Only Sites: Inquire at campground. **Number of Tent-Only Sites:** 0. **Number of Multipurpose Sites:** 42. **Hookups:** None. **Each Site:** Fire pit, picnic table. **Dump Station:** No. **Laundry:** No. **Pay Phone:** No. **Rest Rooms and Showers:** Composting toilets. **Fuel:** No. **Propane:** No. **Internal Roads:** No. **RV Service:** No. **Market:** No. **Restaurant:** No. **General Store:** No. **Vending:** No. **Swimming Pool:** No. **Playground:** No. **Other:** Boardwalk to view falls. **Activities:** Hiking, fishing, wildlife viewing. **Nearby Attractions:** Indian Heaven Wilderness Area, Trout Lake, Mount St. Helens. **Additional Information:** www.fs.fed.us/gpnf.

RESTRICTIONS

Pets: On leash only. **Fires:** In fire pit. **Alcoholic Beverages:** Allowed. **Vehicle Maximum Length:** 20 ft. **Other:** Permits required for climbing Mount St. Helens.

TO GET THERE

Take the Woodland Exit off I-5, and follow SR 503 (Lewis River Rd.) to Cougar—about 45 mi. beyond Cougar, SR 503becomes FS 90. The campground is another 28 mi. past Cougar on FS 90.

VANCOUVER

Columbia Riverfront RV Resort

1881 Dike Rd., Woodland 98674. T: (360) 225-8051 or (800) 845-9842; www.columbiariverfrontrv resort.com; colriverfrontrv@aol.com.

★★★ ▲ n/a

Beauty: ★★★	Site Privacy: ★
Spaciousness: ★★★	Quiet: ★★★★
Security: ★★	Cleanliness: ★★★
Insect Control: ★★	Facilities: ★★★★

Columbia Riverfront RV Resort, a few minutes off I-5 and a half hour north of Vancouver, sits on the south shore of the Columbia in a rural area. Across the expansive Columbia stand rolling green hills and some industrial development. The partially landscaped gravel-covered grounds consist of back-in rows with views of the river. People come to this park to watch big ships navigate up and down the industrial corridor of the river, and the best campsites for this sit near the water (sites 1–10, 50–58, and 76). Other sites in the park have limited or no views of the water, and sites 17–25 and 32–40 have a road behind them. Still, the whole area is quiet and scenic with the local pastoral lands and RV park surrounded by blunt, tree-covered hills. Weather in the area stays mild and rainy during all seasons but the summer.

BASICS

Operated By: Columbia Riverfront RV Resort. **Open:** All year. **Site Assignment:** First come, first served; reservations. **Registration:** At office, after hours registration in front of office. **Fee:** Rates for 4 people, Riverfront Full: $26.27, Other Full: $24.08, extra vehicle **Fee:** $10, Pet: $1 per pet per day, extra person: $2, Cash, V, MC. **Parking:** At site.

FACILITIES

Number of RV-Only Sites: 76. **Number of Tent-Only Sites:** n/a. **Hookups:** Electric (20, 30, 50 amps), water, sewer, cable. **Each Site:** Picnic table. **Dump Station:** No. **Laundry:** Yes. **Pay Phone:** Yes. **Rest Rooms and Showers:** Yes. **Fuel:** No. **Propane:** Yes. **Internal Roads:** Wide, well-maintained gravel. **RV Service:** No. **Market:** 2 mi. east in Woodland. **Restaurant:** 2 mi. east in Woodland. **General Store:** No. **Vending:** No. **Swimming Pool:** Yes. **Playground:** Yes. **Other:** Riverfront beach, volleyball, horseshoe pits, clubhouse w/ kitchen (only reserveable). **Activities:** Fishing, swimming, ship watching, kite flying, hiking. **Nearby Attractions:** Golf, Mt. St. Helens, Hilda Klaegars' Lilac Gardens, The Old Grist Mill, the Columbia River, Ape Caves, Vancouver. **Additional Information:** Woodland Chamber of Commerce, (360) 225-9552.

RESTRICTIONS

Pets: On leash only. **Fires:** Beach only. **Alcoholic Beverages:** At site only. **Vehicle Maximum Length:** 40 ft. **Other:** No vehicle repairs or washing, no clotheslines, be aware of ship wakes & undertows.

TO GET THERE

From I-5 Exit 22: northbound turn left, southbound turn right onto Dike Access Rd., and follow west for 1.7 mi. When the road forks, take the left fork and follow for another 1.1 mi.; entrance is on the right.

VANCOUVER

Van Mall RV Park

10400 Northeast 53rd St., Vancouver 98662. T: (360) 891-1091 or (888) 941-0335; F: (360) 891-2033; www.vancouverrvparks.com; vanmallrvpark@juno.com.

RV ★★ Tent n/a

Beauty: ★	Site Privacy: ★
Spaciousness: ★	Quiet: ★★
Security: ★★★	Cleanliness: ★★★★
Insect Control: ★★	Facilities: ★★★★

Van Mall RV Park, in southeastern Vancouver off I-205, offers access to both Vancouver and Portland. The small, cramped, completely paved, urban park has an almost adjacent car dealership with a noisy loudspeaker. Even so, the car dealership closes in the evenings, and the convenient location's facilities stay in pristine condition. The quietest campsites in the park (sites 1–10) sit on the property's perimeter furthest from the dealership and nearby roads. The largest pull-through campsites (sites 37–47), form part of a row in the middle of the park. Avoid the extremely cramped sites 49–65 and 67–83. Common facilities are small but attractively decorated. The same owners operate a similar and larger facility, Vancouver RV Park (see profile), off I-5. Visit during the summer when the rains let up.

BASICS

Operated By: Vancouver RV Parks. **Open:** All year. **Site Assignment:** First come, first served; reservations (no deposit). **Registration:** At office, after hours pay in morning. **Fee:** For 2 people, pull-through: $25, Back-in: $22, extra person: $2, Cash, check. **Parking:** At site.

FACILITIES

Number of RV-Only Sites: 83. **Number of Tent-Only Sites:** n/a. **Hookups:** Electric (20, 30, 50 amps), water, sewer, cable. **Each Site:** Concrete & pebbles. **Dump Station:** No. **Laundry:** Yes. **Pay Phone:** Yes. **Rest Rooms and Showers:** Yes.

Fuel: No. **Propane:** No. **Internal Roads:** Paved. **RV Service:** Next door. **Market:** 1 mile east in Vancouver. **Restaurant:** 1 mi. east in Vancouver. **General Store:** No. **Vending:** Yes. **Swimming Pool:** No. **Playground:** No. **Other:** Nicely furbished reserveable rec room, horseshoes, small exercise room. **Activities:** Continental breakfast on Saturday, Sunday; Pot lucks once a month; Coffee every morning. **Nearby Attractions:** Fort Vancouver National Historic Site, Pearson Air Museum, Clark County Historic Museum, Portland, Mt. St Heles, Pomeroy Living History Farm. **Additional Information:** Southwest Washington Visitor's & Convention Bureau, (877) 600-0800.

RESTRICTIONS

Pets: On leash only. **Fires:** No fires. **Alcoholic Beverages:** At site only. **Vehicle Maximum Length:** 40 ft. **Other:** Vehicles must be (or appear) 10 years old or younger; Quiet hours 10 p.m.–7 a.m.; no firearms, fireworks, or auto repairs.

TO GET THERE

From I-205 Exit 30, Hwy. 500E, drive 0.5 mi. on NE Fourth Plain Blvd./500 E. Turn left onto NE Gher Rd. at traffic light (YMCA on far right corner of intersection), drive less than 1 block, and turn left at Kentucky Fried Chicken. Drive 2 blocks and turn left at State Farm office, continue for 0.2 mi., and the entrance is on the left.

VANCOUVER

Vancouver RV Park

7603 Northeast 13th Ave., Vancouver 98665. T: (360) 695-1158 or (877) 756-2972; F: (360) 735-8388; www.vancouverrvparks.com; vancouverrv@juno.com.

 ★★★  ★

Beauty: ★	Site Privacy: ★★
Spaciousness: ★★	Quiet: ★★
Security: ★★★★	Cleanliness: ★★★★
Insect Control: ★★	Facilities: ★★★★

Vancouver RV Park, located in Vancouver off of I-5, provides a quiet alternative for convenient access to Portland. RV parks in Vancouver lack the noise of northern Portland RV parks, but they do not have Portland public transit nearby. This paved park, operated by the owners of Van Mall RV Park (see profile), has better security and a little more room. A rarity in the city—the property has a few semi-private sites. Cedar hedges obscure views in back-in sites near the entrance to the park. The best of these, sites 3–19, sit further from local avenues. The largest pull-throughs, sites 62–72, also sit near the front but lack privacy. More expensive back-in deluxe sites (deluxe because they adjoin small grass islands) back into each other with a painted line on asphalt demarcating rear boundaries, creating a more cramped feeling even though these sites have more width than others. Vancouver RV Park's compact grounds waste very little space, and the new, attractive common facilities resemble their sister park's amenities with double the quantity available for double the sites.

BASICS

Operated By: Vancouver RV parks. **Open:** All year. **Site Assignment:** First come, first served; Reservations. **Registration:** At office; after hours pay in morning. **Fee:** For 2 people, one camping unit & one car, Value sites (2-46): $22, Back-ins (167-178): $28, Pull-throughs (61-72 & 153-166): $28, Deluxe Sites (107-151): $32, extra person (older than 3 years old): $2, Nightly phone (limited availability): $2/night, Cash/Check only. **Parking:** At site.

FACILITIES

Number of Multipurpose Sites: 178. **Hookups:** Electric (20, 30, 50 amps), water, sewer, cable, phone. **Each Site:** Concrete. **Dump Station:** Yes. **Laundry:** Yes. **Pay Phone:** Yes. **Rest Rooms and Showers:** Yes. **Fuel:** No. **Propane:** No. **Internal Roads:** Paved (wide). **RV Service:** No. **Market:** North on Hwy. 99. **Restaurant:** Near entrance. **General Store:** No. **Vending:** Yes. **Swimming Pool:** No. **Playground:** No. **Other:** Reserveable Club House w/ full kitchen, big screen TV; continental breakfast on weekends, coffee served every morning. **Activities:** Planned BBQs, potlucks. **Nearby Attractions:** Officer's Row, Rocket City Neon Advertising Museum, Two Rivers Heritage Museum, Water Resource Education Center. **Additional Information:** Southwest Washington Visitor's & Convention Bureau, (877) 600-0800.

RESTRICTIONS

Pets: On leash only. **Fires:** Charcoal grills only, no open fires. **Alcoholic Beverages:** At site only. **Vehicle Maximum Length:** None. **Other:** Quiet Hours 10 p.m.–7 a.m., No firearms, fireworks, auto repairs, pets in rest rooms.

To Get There

From I-5 Exit 4, drive east on NE 78th St.; at the second light (Kentucky Fried Chicken on corner) turn right onto NE 13th Ave.; drive 1 block, and entrance is on left.

WINTHROP

Winthrop-North Cascades National Park KOA

P.O.Box 305, Winthrop 98862. T: (509) 996-2258 or reservations (800) KOA-2158; www.methownet.com/koa; campkoa@methow.com.

RV ★★★ Tent ★★

Beauty: ★★★ Site Privacy: ★
Spaciousness: ★★ Quiet: ★★★
Security: ★★ Cleanliness: ★★★
Insect Control: ★★ Facilities: ★★★

Winthrop-North Cascades National Park KOA, located just east of the faux-Western town of Winthrop, provides convenient access to the eastern slopes of the North Cascades and nearby tourist attractions. The quiet campground consists of a grassy field surrounded by hardwoods on the banks of the narrow, glassy, rock-bottomed Methow River. None of the sites have privacy or shade. Furthest from the river sit the full-hookup options—wide pull-through sites 1–16. Most campsites on the property have water and electric or no hookups. On the river sit several no-hookup campsites (sites R8–R14) that can accept most RVs sideways, providing river views for more windows and creating some privacy. These grassy campsites, along with sites R1–R7, frequently get used as tent sites (they're the best tent options on the property). Avoid cramped water and electric sites 63–72 and the no-hookup sites 73–82. Visit during the summer; spring and fall nights can be chilly in this area, and much of the eastern side of the North Cascades stays snowed in during all but summer.

Basics

Operated By: Winthrop-North Cascades KOA under franchise from KOA. **Open:** Apr.–Nov. **Site Assignment:** First come, first served; reservations (deposit: $20 cash or credit; refund: 48 hours cancellation. **Registration:** At office; after hours at drop box in fron of office. **Fee:** For 2 people, full: $26, Water/electric: $23.50, No **Hookups:** $20, extra person ages 3-17: $2, Ages 18+: $4, Under three years old free, V, MC, AE, D, cash, check. **Parking:** At site.

Facilities

Number of RV-Only Sites: 68. **Number of Tent-Only Sites:** 35. **Hookups:** Electric (20, 30, 50 amps), water, sewer. **Each Site:** Picnic table, fire ring. **Dump Station:** Yes. **Laundry:** Yes. **Pay Phone:** Yes. **Rest Rooms and Showers:** Yes. **Fuel:** No. **Propane:** No. **Internal Roads:** Gravel. **RV Service:** No. **Market:** 0.5 mile west in Winthrop. **Restaurant:** 0.5 mi. west in Winthrop. **General Store:** Yes. **Vending:** No. **Swimming Pool:** Yes. **Playground:** Yes. **Other:** Horseshoes, volleyball, small game room, central data port, video rentals, bike rentals, shuttle service to Winthrop four times a day, local raft company drop point. **Activities:** swimming, fishing, rafting, hay rides, planned seasonal activities. **Nearby Attractions:** Shafer Museum, golf, hiking, mountain biking, North Cascades National Park, horseback riding, fish hatchery tours, Winthrop. **Additional Information:** Winthrop Chamber of Commerce, (888) 4METHOW.

Restrictions

Pets: On leash only (6 ft. max length); pick up after. **Fires:** In fire pits only. **Alcoholic Beverages:** At site only. **Vehicle Maximum Length:** None. **Other:** Quiet hours 10:30 p.m.–7 a.m., Do not tie anything–trees or shrubs.

To Get There

The campground ntrance is on Hwy. 20, 1 mi. east of downtown Winthrop (which is a remarkably small place), on the left side if traveling eastbound.

YAKIMA

Suntides RV Park

201 Pence Rd., Yakima 98908. T: (509) 966-7883

RV ★★ Tent n/a

Beauty: ★★ Site Privacy: ★
Spaciousness: ★★★ Quiet: ★
Security: ★★★ Cleanliness: ★★★
Insect Control: ★★ Facilities: ★★★★

Suntides RV Park, off Hwy. 12 in Yakima, provides convenient lodging for the avid golfer. The park stands adjacent to both a championship 18-hole putting course and an 18-hole full golf course. The green area looks like an oasis in the desert. Golf makes up the entireity of recreational activities at this location. The flat, paved, grass-perimetered sites lack shade, making for an intense noonday sun in the high desert. Accomodations consist of campsites in parallel rows; sites on row A sit closest to Hwy. 12 and a railroad, making them prone to noise. Sites 5D–14D are the best on the property. There are no tent-only campsites. Late spring and early fall are the best times to visit this park; summer heat here packs a punch.

BASICS

Operated By: Sun Tides, Inc. **Open:** All year. **Site Assignment:** On arrival, reservations (no deposit). **Registration:** At office, after hours pay in morning. **Fee:** For 2 people, full $19.37, extra person $1 (V, MC, check, cash). **Parking:** At site.

FACILITIES

Number of RV-Only Sites: 68. **Number of Tent-Only Sites:** n/a. **Hookups:** Electric (30, 50 amps), water, sewer. **Dump Station:** Yes. **Laundry:** Yes. **Pay Phone:** Yes. **Rest Rooms and Showers:** Yes. **Fuel:** No. **Propane:** No. **Internal Roads:** Paved. **RV Service:** No. **Market:** 2 mi. east. **Restaurant:** Next door. **General Store:** No. **Vending:** Yes. **Swimming Pool:** No. **Playground:** No. **Other:** 18 hole golf course, 18 hole putting course, restaurant, driving range. **Activities:** Golfing. **Nearby Attractions:** Elk feeding, golf, Central WA Agricultural Museum, Yakima Electric Railway Museum, Wineries. **Additional Information:** Yakima Chamber of Commerce, (509) 248-2021.

RESTRICTIONS

Pets: On leash only. **Fires:** No open fires. **Alcoholic Beverages:** At site only. **Vehicle Maximum Length:** None. **Other:** Check w/ office before washing vehicles.

TO GET THERE

From I-84 Exit 31 (Naches/12 West), drive 4.4 mi. on Hwy. 12 West and turn right onto Old Naches Hwy. Take an immediate right onto Pence Rd., drive 0.1 mi., and teh entrance is on the left.

YAKIMA
Trailer Inns RV Park

1610 North First St., Yakima 98901. T: (509) 451-9561 or reservations (800) 659-4784; trailerinnsrv.uswestdex.com/page3.html.

RV ★★★★ Tent ★★

Beauty: ★★	Site Privacy: ★
Spaciousness: ★★★	Quiet: ★★
Security: ★★★	Cleanliness: ★★★★★
Insect Control: ★★	Facilities: ★★★★★

Trailer Inns RV Park, right on the edge of downtown Yakima, offers convenient access to both the city and the interstate. The older, well-maintained facilities offer a wide array of furnishings. One of the more notable and above-average facilities, an indoor bar-b-que room, has two gas grills and a fireplace. Further, an indoor pool and two small hot tubs provide year-round swimming and relaxation. Regarding accomodations, the park's level, grassy tent sites lack shade or privacy and sit behind the office/clubhouse. The RV sites, predominately arranged into parallel rows, have some shade, and many also have adjacent grass areas. Avoid RV sites 55–71 because they lack shade and consist solely of blacktop. The best RV options are sites 103–115; they have shade, grass, and a reasonable amount of space. The high desert climate is arid and hot during the summers, and the sun's heat can be intense; visit during the spring, early summer, or early fall for optimal conditions.

BASICS

Operated By: Trailer Inns. **Open:** All year. **Site Assignment:** On arrival, reservations (deposit: 1 night stay, refund: 72 hours cancellation). **Registration:** At office, after hours pay at drop or in morning. **Fee:** Call for rates (V, MC, Cash). **Parking:** At site, limited off site.

FACILITIES

Number of RV-Only Sites: 60. **Number of Tent-Only Sites:** 22. **Hookups:** Electric (15, 30, 50 amps), water, sewer, cable. **Each Site:** Picnic table. **Dump Station:** Yes. **Laundry:** Yes. **Pay Phone:** Yes. **Rest Rooms and Showers:** Yes. **Fuel:** No. **Propane:** Yes. **Internal Roads:** Paved. **RV Service:** No. **Market:** Nearby in Yakima. **Restaurant:** Nearby in Yakima. **General Store:** Yes. **Vending:** Yes. **Swimming Pool:** Yes, indoor. **Playground:** Yes. **Other:** Arcade, TV room, indoor BBQ room, outdoor BBQ area, indoor hot tubs (2, small), outdoor porch, shuffleboard. **Activities:** Occasional potlucks (seasonal). **Nearby Attractions:** Golfing, hunting, fishing, rafting, horseback riding, wineries, Yakima Electric Railway Museum, Yakima Valley Museum. **Additional**

Information: Yakima Chamber of Commerce, (509) 248-2021.

Restrictions

Pets: On leash only, limit of 2 per space. **Fires:** No open fires, no charcoal. **Alcoholic Beverages:** At site only. **Vehicle Maximum Length:** None. **Other:** No eye-sore vehicles.

To Get There

From I-82 Exit 31, go 0.1 mi. south on First St. and the entrance is on the right.

YAKIMA

Yakama Nation Resort RV Park

280 Buster Rd., Toppenish 98948. T: (509) 865-2000 or (800) 874-3087; www.yakamanation.com; yakamarv@aol.com.

RV ★★★★ Tent ★★★

Beauty: ★★★ Site Privacy: ★
Spaciousness: ★★★ Quiet: ★★★
Security: ★★★ Cleanliness: ★★★★
Insect Control: ★★ Facilities: ★★★★★

The Yakama Nation RV Resort, located 20 miles south of Yakima off of I-84, provides easy access to Native American cultural events and obscured views of the surrounding arid hill country. The grounds consist of a flat field of grass, with paved avenues creating islands containing paved sites with grass; additional sites ring the park's perimeter. The grassy tent area has some shade from a few tall deciduous trees; the RV section has little protection from the high desert sun. The pull-through section consists of pavement with no surrounding grass. The best RV choices in the park (sites 30–54) sit furthest from nearby Hwy. 97 and on a perimeter with no rear neighbors. The park has nice and wide-ranging recreational facilities, including two very large unisex cedar saunas. The adjacent Yakama Nation Cultural Center adds to nearby recreational opportunities. Winters here stay cold and summers stay hot with cooler nights; the month of June has the largest number of Native American cultural events.

Basics

Operated By: Private Operator. **Open:** All year. **Site Assignment:** On arrival, reservations (no deposit). **Registration:** At office, after hours pay in morning. **Fee:** Full $23 (2 people), Additional People $2, teepee $30 (5 people), additional people (up to10 people) $5, cot rentals $2, tent area $16 (4 people), Additional people per tent $5, Three years & younger free (V, MC, cash, check). **Parking:** At site.

Facilities

Number of RV-Only Sites: 125. **Number of Tent-Only Sites:** 10. **Hookups:** Electric (20, 30, 50 amps), water, sewer, cable. **Each Site:** Picnic table. **Dump Station:** Yes. **Laundry:** Yes. **Pay Phone:** Yes. **Rest Rooms and Showers:** Yes. **Fuel:** No. **Propane:** Yes. **Internal Roads:** Paved. **RV Service:** No. **Market:** 1 mile north on 97. **Restaurant:** Next door. **General Store:** No. **Vending:** Yes. **Swimming Pool:** Yes. **Playground:** Yes. **Other:** Hot tub, large saunas (2), exercise room, arcade, volleyball, horseshoes, basketball, running trail, putting green, 2 reserveable meeting rooms, Cultural Center adjacent to park. **Activities:** Putting, running. **Nearby Attractions:** Yakama Nation Cultural Center, Old Depot Museum, American Hop Museum, Toppenish Murals (narrated wagon rides available Apr.-Oct), golf. **Additional Information:** Yakima Chamber of Commerce, (509) 248-2021.

Restrictions

Pets: On leash only. **Fires:** In fire pits only. **Alcoholic Beverages:** Absolutely not allowed. **Vehicle Maximum Length:** None. **Other:** Teepees don't come w/ bedding, required to supply your own.

To Get There

From I-82 Exit 50, drive 3.1 mi. southeast on Buena Way/East 22. Turn right at stoplight onto West 1st Ave and drive for 0.4 mi. Turn right at stoplight onto 97 North and follow 0.7 mi.; the entrance is on left through Yakima Nation Cultural Center.

Wyoming

Wyoming's clean, geometric borders belie the geographical variety found in its interior. With an amalgam of winding rivers, scenic gorges, vast plains, craggy mountain peaks, pristine lakes, and lonely buttes, Wyoming is a prime destination for campers and outdoor enthusiasts. Wyoming is probably most popular for containing the nation's first national park, **Yellowstone National Park,** whose **Old Faithful Geyser** is as popular as any theme park ride. However, if touring the state, it is important to give yourself plenty of time to visit the other points of interest available. In **Shoshone National Forest** on the eastern border of Yellowstone, you'll find the Absakora and Wind River Mountain Ranges as well as the Shoshone River's north and south forks. Camping here provides easy access to hiking, rafting, fishing, and exploration. Just south of Yellowstone on I-89 is the **Grand Teton National Park,** where the majestic Tetons stand 7,000 feet tall and shadow the famous ski area of **Jackson Hole.** Here, off I-191, are the headwaters of the Snake River, making this an ideal spot for campers interested in hiking, river rafting, and fishing. The **National Elk Preserve,** located in **Jackson,** might give you the opportunity to view a herd of elk or to hear their strange bugle call.

Farther south, the **Fossil Butte National Monument** is an interesting sight for curious observers and budding archeologists. **Flaming Gorge National Recreation Area** near the Green River is a veritable outdoors playground. Both the Flaming Gorge Lake, 90 miles long with 375 miles of shoreline, and the Green River provide limitless water recreation. Campers here enjoy watching the sun and shadows dance among the rock formations, transforming the area into a festival of lights and color. In the southeast corner of Wyoming is **Cheyenne,** the state's capital. The capitol building was modeled after its national equivalent in Washington, D.C.

Through central Wyoming, you can travel the **Oregon Trail** and view the land as Oregon-bound pioneers would have. There are a number of historical sites and opportunities for recreation. **Sinks Canyon State Park,** six miles south of Lander off Hwy. 131, is where the Popo Agie River flows from the Wind River Mountains into a limestone cavern in the Sink Canyon. The are offers numerous opportunities for camping, hiking, and fishing. **Casper,** Wyoming's second-largest city, is a nice stop too. In eastern Wyoming, you'll find **Thunder Basin National Grassland,** where a number of private campgrounds are located. And north from there, **Devil's Tower** and **Buffalo Bill Country** provide opportunity for picnics, scenic drives, fishing, and views of waterfalls. No matter the direction or destination, Wyoming is rich with opportunity to experience the beauty of a scenic outdoors.

Campground Profiles

BUFFALO
Buffalo KOA Kampground

P.O. Box 189, Buffalo 82834. T: (307) 684-5423 or (800) 562-5403; www.koa.com.

RV ★★★★ Tent ★★★★

Beauty: ★★★ Site Privacy: ★★★★
Spaciousness: ★★★★ Quiet: ★★★★
Security: ★★★★ Cleanliness: ★★★★
Insect Control: ★★★★ Facilities: ★★★★

Just east of town, set in an attractive and inviting atmosphere, is the Buffalo KOA Kampground. This KOA campground has truly earned its gold rating. In a state where grass is a luxury, this KOA is beautifully landscaped and impeccably kept. There are Russian olives and quaking aspen trees giving shade and adding warmth. Campsites are set in a series of rows, with a separate tenting area. All sites have a level parking pad, covered picnic table, and grill. There are both pull-through and back-in sites, most being pull-throughs. In addition, the campground has the only deluxe campsite in the KOA system with a private fence, yard, patio, and hot tub (special rates apply). The campground offers a daily pancake breakfast June–Aug., and propane service 8 a.m. to dusk. The weather is always windy, and summers are smoldering. The camp staff are friendly and happy to assist.

Basics

Operated By: Don and Sue Gill. **Open:** Apr.–Oct. **Site Assignment:** By reservation. **Registration:** In the camp store. **Fee:** Tent $17–$20, RVs $21–$28, per 2 people, extra people over age 6 $3. each. **Parking:** Yes, there is a $5 extra vehicle fee.

Facilities

Number of RV-Only Sites: 63. **Number of Tent-Only Sites:** 28. **Hookups:** Electric (20, 30, 50 amps), water, sewer. **Each Site:** Picnic tables, and a some fire pits. **Dump Station:** Yes. **Laundry:** Yes. **Pay Phone:** Yes. **Rest Rooms and Showers:** Yes. **Fuel:** No. **Propane:** Yes. **Internal Roads:** Gravel, in good condition. **RV Service:** Local service. **Market:** In town. **Restaurant:** In town. **General Store:** Yes. **Vending:** Yes. **Swimming Pool:** Yes w/ a hot tub. **Playground:** Yes. **Other:** 5 cabins, a fishing stream, covered picnic areas, camp kitchen, teepees, and a wonderful deluxe site w/ hot tub, Internet data port. **Activities:** Fishing, hiking, game room, playground, horseshoes, mini-golf. **Nearby Attractions:** The White Buffalo, Jim Gatchell Museum, the rodeo. **Additional Information:** Buffalo Chamber of Commerce, (307) 684-5544.

Restrictions

Pets: On leash. **Fires:** In fire rings only. **Alcoholic Beverages:** Yes. **Vehicle Maximum Length:** None.

To Get There

On Hwy. 16 between I-90 Exit 58 and I-25 Exit 299.

BUFFALO
Lake DeSmet, Lake Stop Resort

P.O.Box 578, Buffalo 82834. T: (307) 684-9051; lakeshop@vcn.com.

RV ★★★ Tent ★★★

Beauty: ★★★★ Site Privacy: ★★★★
Spaciousness: ★★★★ Quiet: ★★★★
Security: ★★★★ Cleanliness: ★★★
Insect Control: ★★★ Facilities: ★★★

Lake DeSmet, "the Lake Stop," is positioned at the base of the Big Horn Mountains on the splendid Lake DeSmet. This small lakeside campground is only a small part of the Lake Stop experience, which offers an 18-site circular campground with full hookups, pool, and clean facilities. The campsites are on a bed of red shale, and each have a table and light post. Although the campsites are not on the lake, there is lake access and boat launch. There is also a full-service bait/tack shop, cafe, motel, boat repair shop, professional fishing outfitters, and boat rentals. The Lake Stop has a small decorative pond up by the campground, and the motel beautifully landscaped with a nice grotto. The owners also have their own private residence across from the campground and are there to assist in any way. Lake DeSmet is six miles north of Buffalo, which is a nice community that offers a variety of activities, rodeos, and Native American history.

Basics

Operated By: Ted and Bambi Schumacher. **Open:** Year-round. **Site Assignment:** By reservation. **Registration:** In the lake shop. **Fee:** Tent $10, RV $19 per unit. **Parking:** At site.

Facilities

Number of RV-Only Sites: 18. **Number of Tent-Only Sites:** Open tent area. **Hookups:** Electric (20, 30, 50 amps), water, sewer. **Each Site:** Picnic tables, grills, and light posts. **Dump Station:** Yes. **Laundry:** Yes. **Pay Phone:** Yes. **Rest Rooms and Showers:** Yes. **Fuel:** Yes. **Propane:** Yes. **Internal Roads:** Red Shale. **RV Service:** Buffalo. **Market:** In town. **Restaurant:** On site. **General Store:** Yes. **Vending:** Yes. **Swimming Pool:** Yes. **Playground:** Yes. **Other:** Full service grocery store, tack shop, boat repair shop, boat ramp, motel, and a small pond w/ a grotto. **Activities:** Fishing (Rainbow, brown, and eagle lake trout), guided fishing tours, boating, jet skiing, basketball, volleyball, lake access. **Nearby Attractions:** 6 mi. from Buffalo, stream fishing, golf, scenic drives, rodeo. **Additional Information:** Buffalo Chamber of Commerce, (307) 684-5544.

Restrictions

Pets: On leash. **Fires:** Grills only. **Alcoholic Beverages:** Yes. **Vehicle Maximum Length:** 40 ft., limited room for extra long RV. **Other:** Fishing Packages.

To Get There

Off I-90 (Exit 51) then follow signs 7 mi. north.

CHEYENNE

A B Camping

1503 West College Dr., Cheyenne 82007. T: (307) 634-7035

RV ★★★ Tent ★★★

Beauty: ★★ Site Privacy: ★★★
Spaciousness: ★★★ Quiet: ★★★★
Security: ★★★★ Cleanliness: ★★★★
Insect Control: ★★★ Facilities: ★★★

The A.B. Campground is a quite, clean facility with a full array of camping amenities. The campground is configured in rows, with large gravel parking spurs at every site, lush green grass, and a perimeter of large pines that offer a nice buffer from the sun and wind. The campground has a large recreation area and playground with a covered pavilion and barbeque. The campground takes part in the annual Frontier Days Celebration (last ten days in July). The nearby city of Cheyenne is the capital of Wyoming, and it's also the largest city in the state, boasting a variety of activties and events. There are several state and federal parks in the area, as well as museums and galleries. Several tours of the area include downtown and the Wyoming state capitol building and grounds. Cheyenne has a very dry climate with relentless winds. The winters can be very harsh and the summers very warm.

Basics

Operated By: Larry and Kay Colboch. **Open:** Mar.–Oct. 31. **Site Assignment:** By reservation. **Registration:** In the camp store. **Fee:** Tent $13.50, RVs $14.50–$22.50, per 2 people, extra people over age of 5 $2 each. **Parking:** At site.

Facilities

Number of RV-Only Sites: 132. **Number of Tent-Only Sites:** Open tent area. **Hookups:** Electric (20, 30, 50 amps), water, sewer. **Each Site:** Picnic tables, and grills. **Dump Station:** Yes. **Laundry:** Yes. **Pay Phone:** Yes. **Rest Rooms and Showers:** Yes. **Fuel:** In town. **Propane:** Yes. **Internal Roads:** Gravel, in good condition. **RV Service:** Next door. **Market:** In town. **Restaurant:** In town. **General Store:** Yes. **Vending:** Yes. **Swimming Pool:** No. **Playground:** Yes. **Other:** 4 cabins, store, Internet dataport, pavilion w/ grills, movie rentals. **Activities:** Playground, horseshoes. **Nearby Attractions:** Golf, State Capitol, trolley tours. **Additional Information:** Cheyenne Chamber of Commerce, (307) 638-3388.

Restrictions

Pets: On leash. **Fires:** In fire rings only. **Alcoholic Beverages:** Yes. **Vehicle Maximum Length:** None. **Other:** Good Sam, AAA, AARP, special rates apply for Frontier Days and reservations need to be made up to a year in advance. (the last 10 days in July).

To Get There

From I-25 Exit 7, go east on SR 212 (W. College Dr.) about 1.7 mi. to the campground.

CHEYENNE

Cheyenne KOA

8800 Archer Frontage Rd., Cheyenne 82007. T: (307) 638-8840 or (800) 562-1507; F: (307) 432-9746; www.cheyennekoa.com; manager@cheyennekoa.com.

★★★★ 

Beauty: ★★★ Site Privacy: ★★★★
Spaciousness: ★★★★ Quiet: ★★★
Security: ★★★★ Cleanliness: ★★★★★
Insect Control: ★★★★ Facilities: ★★★★★

Conveniently located of I-80, the Cheyenne KOA presents a comfortable and well-maintained campground with full amenities to meet the entire family's needs. The Cheyenne KOA has reasonably sized gravel camping sites with some lawn and trees, configured into rows with both back-in and pull-through sites. The campground has several cabins, a snack bar, pool, and mini-golf. The nearby city of Cheyenne is the capital of Wyoming, and it's also the largest city in the state, boasting a variety of activties and events. There are several state and federal parks in the area, as well as museums and galleries. Several tours of the area include downtown and the Wyoming state capitol building and grounds. Cheyenne has a very dry climate with relentless winds. The winters can be very harsh and the summers very warm. The staff at the Cheyenne KOA are friendly and helpful, and the campground is secure.

BASICS

Operated By: Mike and Donna Lawrance and Don Lonergan. **Open:** Year-round. **Site Assignment:** By reservation. **Registration:** In the camp store. **Fee:** Tent $21, RVs $17–$28, per 2 people, extra people over age of 5 $3 each. **Parking:** At site.

FACILITIES

Number of RV-Only Sites: 42. **Number of Tent-Only Sites:** 11. **Hookups:** Electric (20, 30, 50 amps), water, sewer. **Each Site:** Picnic tables, and grills in the tent and cabin area. **Dump Station:** Yes. **Laundry:** Yes. **Pay Phone:** Yes. **Rest Rooms and Showers:** Yes. **Fuel:** 3 mi. east in town. **Propane:** Yes. **Internal Roads:** Gravel, in good condition. **RV Service:** Local service. **Market:** In town. **Restaurant:** In town. **General Store:** Yes. **Vending:** Yes. **Swimming Pool:** Yes. **Playground:** Yes. **Other:** 6 cabins, store, Internet dataport, pavilion w/ kitchen. **Activities:** Game room, playground, horseshoes, mini-golf, basketball. **Nearby Attractions:** Golf, State Capitol, trolley tours. **Additional Information:** Cheyenne Chamber of Commerce, (307) 638-3388.

RESTRICTIONS

Pets: On leash. **Fires:** In fire rings only. **Alcoholic Beverages:** Yes. **Vehicle Maximum Length:** None.

TO GET THERE

Right off I-80 Exit 367 on the north side.

CODY

Cody KOA

5561 Greybull Hwy., Cody 82414. T: (307) 587-2369 or (800) 562-8507; F: (307) 587-2369; www.koa.com; codykoa@aol.com.

★★★ 

Beauty: ★★★ Site Privacy: ★★★
Spaciousness: ★★★ Quiet: ★★★
Security: ★★★ Cleanliness: ★★★
Insect Control: ★★★ Facilities: ★★★

The Cody KOA is just east of Cody, conveniently located off Hwy 20. This full-service campground comes fully equipped to meet your needs. The campground offers close to 200 sites, 20 cabins, and a cottage. The comfortable sites come in both back-in and pull-through flavors, with quite a bit of grass and shade for the region. Each campsite has a gravel parking area. There is a large pool with a hot tub to escape Wyoming's blistering summer heat, as well as a game room and trail rides for your enjoyment. The community of Cody is warm and friendly, and there are a number of shops and restaurants to enjoy. Cody also conducts a nightly summer rodeo and serves as the east entrance to Yellowstone National Park.

BASICS

Operated By: Jean Mickelson- manager. **Open:** May–Oct. 1. **Site Assignment:** By reservation. **Registration:** In camp store. **Fee:** Tents $23–$29 RV $28–$36 per 2 people extra child $3, Adult $3. **Parking:** At site.

FACILITIES

Number of RV-Only Sites: 120. **Number of Tent-Only Sites:** 84. **Hookups:** Electric (20, 30 amps), water, sewer. **Each Site:** Picnic tables, and fire pits in tent sites. **Dump Station:** Yes. **Laundry:** Yes. **Pay Phone:** Yes. **Rest Rooms and Showers:** Yes. **Fuel:** No. **Propane:** Yes. **Internal Roads:** Gravel, in good condition. **RV Service:** In Cody. **Market:** In Cody. **Restaurant:** In Cody. **General Store:** Yes. **Vending;** Yes. **Swimming Pool:** Yes, w/ hot tub. **Playground:** Yes. **Other:** 20 cabins, 1 cottage, covered pavilion w/ 2 gas grills, game room w/ TV and cable, hot tub, dish sink, data port. **Activities:** Swimming, playground, games, trail rides, volleyball, horseshoes. **Nearby Attractions:** The east entrance to Yellowstone National Park, nightly summer rodeo, float trips, Buffalo Bills Historical Center. **Additional Information:** Cody Chamber of Commerce, (307) 587-2777.

Restrictions

Pets: On leash only. **Fires:** In fire pits only. **Alcoholic Beverages:** Yes. **Vehicle Maximum Length:** 45 ft.

To Get There

On US 20 just east of Cody.

CODY

Ponderosa Campground

1815 Yellowstone Ave., Cody 82414. T: (307) 587-9203; F: (307) 436-5779.

RV ★★★ Tent ★★★

Beauty: ★★★	Site Privacy: ★★
Spaciousness: ★★	Quiet: ★★★
Security: ★★★★	Cleanliness: ★★★
Insect Control: ★★★	Facilities: ★★★

Smack dab in the middle of Cody is the Ponderosa Campground. This large and busy place is in the center of all the activities Cody has to offer. There is shopping and fine dining just around the corner. In the summers, Cody host a nightly rodeo and other special events and festivals designed to entertain tourists. Cody is the main gate to Yellowstone National Park in the east, and the Ponderosa is the premiere full-service campground in the area. The Ponderosa's sites are relatively close together, and due to high traffic and hot dry weather, there is little grass. In addition, much for the same reason there are few trees, and little shade. The campground is well maintained, and the facilities are clean. It is recommended that reservations are made as far in advance as possible, since they do operate at full capacity most of the time. The campground is staffed around the clock, and they are very helpful and considerate.

Basics

Operated By: The Richardsons. **Open:** Apr.–Oct. 15. **Site Assignment:** By reservation. **Registration:** In the camp store. **Fee:** Tent $17, RV $27 per 2 people extra people over 8 $2. **Parking:** At site.

Facilities

Number of RV-Only Sites: 140. **Number of Tent-Only Sites:** Open tent area. **Hookups:** Electric (20, 30, 50 amps), water, sewer. **Each Site:** Picnic table. **Dump Station:** Yes. **Laundry:** Yes. **Pay Phone:** Yes. **Rest Rooms and Showers:** Yes. **Fuel:** No, down the street. **Propane:** No. **Internal Roads:** Gravel, in good condition. **RV Service:** In town. **Market:** In town. **Restaurant:** In town. **General Store:** Yes. **Vending:** Yes. **Swimming Pool:** No. **Playground:** Yes. **Other:** Arcade, trading post, store, 7 cabins, 6 teepees. **Activities:** Games, playground. **Nearby Attractions:** Yellowstone National Park, nightly summer rodeos, Horse Rides and Chuckwagon Dinner, Buffalo Bill Historical Center. **Additional Information:** Cody Chamber of Commerce, (307) 587-2297.

Restrictions

Pets: On leash. **Fires:** No fires in the city limit. **Alcoholic Beverages:** Yes. **Vehicle Maximum Length:** None. **Other:** Good Sam and AAA.

To Get There

Located on US 14 in Cody near 16th St. and Sheridan Ave.

DOUGLAS

Douglas Jackalope KOA Campground

P.O. Box 1190, Douglas 82007. T: (307) 358-2164 or (800) 562-2469; F: (307) 358-2164; www.koa.com.

RV ★★★ Tent ★★★

Beauty: ★★★	Site Privacy: ★★★
Spaciousness: ★★★	Quiet: ★★★
Security: ★★★	Cleanliness: ★★★
Insect Control: ★★★	Facilities: ★★★

If you are looking for a quiet place to stay or just passing through, the Douglas KOA is a delightful, well-maintained, and comfortable place to lodge. The Douglas KOA offers a more rustic, woodsy setting, with all the amenities you would expect from a full-service campground. The campsites are moderate in size and have gravel parking spurs; there are both pull-through and back-in sites. The community of Douglas is listed as number 72 in Norman Crampton's *The 100 Best Small Towns in America,* and it's home to Fort Fetterman and the Wyoming Pioneer Memorial Museum. This area of Wyoming is rich in Native American history, and the Oregon, Emigrant, Mormon, and Bozeman trails, which cross through the area, are full of untold stories. The Douglas KOA has a safe and secure atmosphere and a kind and caring staff.

Basics

Operated By: Bob and Delores Kessner. **Open:** Apr. 1–Nov. 1. **Site Assignment:** By reservation. **Registration:** In the camp store. **Fee:** Tent $17, RVs $22–$26, per 2 people, extra people $3 each. **Parking:** At site.

Facilities

Number of RV-Only Sites: 68. **Number of Tent-Only Sites:** 16. **Hookups:** Electric (20, 30, 50 amps), water, sewer, cable. **Each Site:** Picnic tables, and grills in the tent and cabin area. **Dump Station:** Yes. **Laundry:** Yes. **Pay Phone:** Yes. **Rest Rooms and Showers:** Yes. **Fuel:** No. **Propane:** Yes. **Internal Roads:** Gravel, in good condition. **RV Service:** Casper. **Market:** In town. **Restaurant:** In town. **General Store:** Yes. **Vending:** Yes. **Swimming Pool:** Yes. **Playground:** Yes. **Other:** 1 cabin, store, Internet dataport, pavilion. **Activities:** Game room, playground, horseshoes, mini-golf, basketball. **Nearby Attractions:** Pioneer Museum, natural bridge, national speedway, Ft Fetterman. **Additional Information:** Douglas Chamber of Commerce, (307) 358-2950.

Restrictions

Pets: On leash. **Fires:** No open wood fires. **Alcoholic Beverages:** Yes. **Vehicle Maximum Length:** None.

To Get There

From I-25 take Exit 140, go right on Hwy. 91, and drive for about 1.5 mi.

GLENROCK

Deer Creek Village RV Park

P.O. Box 1003, Glenrock 82637. T: (307) 436-8121; F: (307) 436-5779.

RV ★★★ Tent ★★

Beauty: ★★★	Site Privacy: ★★★
Spaciousness: ★★★	Quiet: ★★★
Security: ★★★	Cleanliness: ★★★
Insect Control: ★★★	Facilities: ★★

Deer Creek Village RV Park is nestled behind a large community park in Glenrock. Deer Creek has the advantage of activities offered by the Glenrock Community Park while maintaining a separate private area for its visitors. The Deer Creek RV Park has extra-large sites, with lush green grass and large, hearty shade trees. In addition, it offers full hookups and cable TV at an exceptionally reasonable price. The facilities are adequately maintained, and the owner resides on the property. The Glenrock Community Park has a large playground, baseball diamond, and tennis courts, all in walking distance from any campsite. There is plenty of room for children to ride bikes without the fear of major road traffic. There are a few full-time residents in the RV park as well as a few mobile homes. The weather has a tendency to be cool in the evening, and Wyoming is always windy.

Basics

Operated By: Cindy Yuker. **Open:** Mar. 15–Nov. 15. **Site Assignment:** By reservation. **Registration:** In the camp store. **Fee:** $12 no hookups, $16 w/ hookups, $1 extra for cable and $3-the heat. **Parking:** At site.

Facilities

Number of RV-Only Sites: 80. **Number of Tent-Only Sites:** 10. **Hookups:** Electric (20, 30, 50 amps), water, sewer, cable. **Each Site:** None. **Dump Station:** No. **Laundry:** Yes. **Pay Phone:** No. **Rest Rooms and Showers:** Yes. **Fuel:** No. **Propane:** Yes. **Internal Roads:** Gravel, in good condition. **RV Service:** In Casper. **Market:** In town. **Restaurant:** In town. **General Store:** Yes. **Vending:** Yes. **Swimming Pool:** No. **Playground:** Yes. **Other:** Gift shop. **Activities:** Next door to a nice city park w/ basketball, baseball, tennis, walking trails. **Nearby Attractions:** A Mane Attraction in Casper, Wagon Wheel Roller Skating in Mills. **Addi-**

tional Information: Glenrock Chamber of Commerce, (307) 436-5652.

Restrictions

Pets: On leash. **Fires:** In approved sites only. **Alcoholic Beverages:** Yes. **Vehicle Maximum Length:** None.

To Get There

From I-25, take US 20/26/87 into Glenrock. Campground is behind Glenrock Community Park.

GREYBULL

Greybull KOA Campground

P.O. Box 387, Greybull 82426. T: (307) 765-2555 or (800) 562-7508; F: (307) 765-2555; www.koa.com.

RV ★★★ Tent ★★★

Beauty: ★★★ Site Privacy: ★★★
Spaciousness: ★★★ Quiet: ★★★
Security: ★★★ Cleanliness: ★★★
Insect Control: ★★★ Facilities: ★★★

Situated just outside of the Big Horn National Forest and the Cloud Peak Wilderness, Greybull KOA, is an excellent base camp for the outdoor sports enthusiast. This area of Northeast Wyoming is renowned for its blue-ribbon trout fishing, its miles of hiking trails, and rocks that would challenge even the most experienced rock climbers. It offers excellent mountain biking for the serious biker, and there's also great snow in the winter for those who like to ski. Greybull KOA is a full-service RV park with full amenities, a pool, a snack bar, and cable TV. They offer a comfortable, affordable, well-maintained campground. The staff is friendly, helpful, and always willing to make your visit more pleasurable. The campground offers both pull-through and back-in sites, as well as gravel parking spurs. There is some grass; however, grass is not very common due to dry weather (so don't forget to pack the lotion).

Basics

Operated By: Bob and Marilyn Patterson. **Open:** Apr. 15–Oct. 30. **Site Assignment:** By reservation. **Registration:** In the camp store. **Fee:** Tent $20, RVs $25–$28, per 2 people, extra people over the age of 3 $3 each (no personal checks). **Parking:** At site.

Facilities

Number of RV-Only Sites: 33. **Number of Tent-Only Sites:** 24. **Hookups:** Electric (20, 30 amps), water, sewer, cable, phone, Internet. **Each Site:** Picnic tables, and grills. **Dump Station:** Yes. **Laundry:** Yes. **Pay Phone:** Yes. **Rest Rooms and Showers:** Yes. **Fuel:** No. **Propane:** Yes. **Internal Roads:** Gravel, in good condition. **RV Service:** In town. **Market:** In town. **Restaurant:** In town. **General Store:** Yes. **Vending:** No. **Swimming Pool:** Yes. **Playground:** Yes. **Other:** 3 cabins, store, café, Internet dataport. **Activities:** Game room, playground, horseshoes, volleyball, basketball. **Nearby Attractions:** Dinosaur Beds, Shell Falls, horseback riding. **Additional Information:** Greybull Chamber of Commerce (307) 765-2100.

Restrictions

Pets: On leash. **Fires:** In approved sites only. **Alcoholic Beverages:** Yes. **Vehicle Maximum Length:** None.

To Get There

Go four blocks north of Hwy. 14 off of 2nd St. or four blocks east of Hwy. 16/20 off 3rd Ave. in Greybull.

JACKSON HOLE

Snake River Park KOA (Jackson/Hoback Junction KOA)

9705 South Hwy. 89, Jackson Hole 83001. T: (307) 733-7078; F: (307) 733-0412; www.srkoa.com; srpinformation@aol.com.

RV ★★★★ Tent ★★★★

Beauty: ★★★★ Site Privacy: ★★★★
Spaciousness: ★★★★ Quiet: ★★★★
Security: ★★★★ Cleanliness: ★★★★
Insect Control: ★★★★ Facilities: ★★★★

Snake River Park KOA is positioned between the Snake River and Horse Creek only a few short miles south of Jackson Hole. The Snake River runs directly behind the facility and adds to the rustic atmosphere. The Snake River Park KOA is a full-service camping facility that offers grass sites and large shade trees along the water's edge. All sites have a gravel parking area, and both pull-through and back-in sites are available. This particular KOA is also a fully licensed float trip outfitter by the Bridger-Teton National Forest and specializes in packaged float trips both for individuals and for groups. They have Coast Guard–approved equipment and provide both food and transportation. The campground itself has a large convenience store, gift shop, game room, and snacks. This is a very lively KOA that caters to patrons utilizing their float service.

Basics

Operated By: Snake River Park, Inc. **Open:** Apr.–mid Oct. **Site Assignment:** By reservations, $30–$50 per site or cabin deposit required. Checks will be taken on deposits only until Apr. 1th. **Registration:** In camp store. **Fee:** Tents $30.95, RVs $39.95–$47.95 per 2 people, extra people over age 5 are $6 each w/ a max. of 6 people per site. **Parking:** Yes, but there is a $10 extra vehicle fee, campers are allowed 1 tow.

Facilities

Number of RV-Only Sites: 47. **Number of Tent-Only Sites:** 28. **Hookups:** Electric (30, 50 amps), water, sewer. **Each Site:** Picnic table, fire pits. **Dump Station:** Yes. **Laundry:** Yes. **Pay Phone:** Yes. **Rest Rooms and Showers:** Yes. **Fuel:** 1 mi. south in town. **Propane:** 1 mi. south in town. **Internal Roads:** Gravel, in good condition. **RV Service:** Mobile service from Jackson. **Market:** In Jackson. **Restaurant:** There is a café on site and another restaurant across the street, or in Jackson. **General Store:** Yes. **Vending:** General Store only. **Swimming Pool:** No. **Playground:** Yes. **Other:** River Access, whitewater rafting outfitters, 17 cabins, float packages. **Activities:** Rafting, fishing, tubing. **Nearby Attractions:** Jackson Hole, skiing, the Grand Tetons, Yellowstone National Park. **Additional Information:** Jackson Hole Chamber of Commerce, (307) 733-3316.

Restrictions

Pets: On Leash only. **Fires:** In approved sites only. **Alcoholic Beverages:** Yes. **Vehicle Maximum Length:** None. **Other:** 10 day max. stay, KOA discount.

To Get There

From Jackson, go south on US 26/89 for about 5 mi.; campground is on you right.

JACKSON HOLE
Virginian Lodge and RV Resort

P.O. Box 1052, Jackson 83001. T: (307) 733-7189 or (800) 321-6982 in the summer or (800) 262-4999 in the winter; F: (307) 733-4063; virginian@wyoming.com.

RV ★★★ Tent ★★

Beauty: ★★★
Spaciousness: ★★
Security: ★★★
Insect Control: ★★★
Site Privacy: ★★★
Quiet: ★★★
Cleanliness: ★★★
Facilities: ★★★

The Virginian Lodge and RV Resort is suitably located in downtown Jackson Hole. The property is convenientl to a vast number of novelty shops and excellent restaurants. The campground is open to RVs only and offers a full array of camping amenities. The campsites are gravel with some grass and shade. The facility offers both pull-through and back-in sites and has room to accommodate large RVs. There is a nice-sized swimming pool, hot tub, and full-service lodge. Jackson Hole is but a short drive from the Grand Teton National Park and serves as the south entrance to Yellowstone National Park. The area is a great base camp for those patrons wishing to experience the parks or take a float trip down the Snake River. The resort staff is very friendly and will be more than happy to assist with any needs. The weather can be a bit windy and dry, so it is always best to be prepared.

Basics

Operated By: Wayne and Lynn Simons. **Open:** May 1–Oct. 15. **Site Assignment:** By reservation. **Registration:** In camp registration office, located at the front gate. **Fee:** $37–$45 per unit (no personal checks). **Parking:** At site.

Facilities

Number of RV-Only Sites: 103. **Number of Tent-Only Sites:** 0. **Hookups:** Electric (20, 30, 50 amps), water, sewer, cable. **Each Site:** Picnic tables, and grills. **Dump Station:** Yes. **Laundry:** Yes. **Pay Phone:** Yes. **Rest Rooms and Showers:** Yes. **Fuel:** Less than a mi. in any direction. **Propane:** Same as above. **Internal Roads:** Gravel, in good condition. **RV Service:** 65 mi. west in Idaho Falls, ID. **Market:** In Jackson. **Restaurant:** On site or there is a large selection in town. **General Store:** No. **Vending:** Yes. **Swimming Pool:** Yes w/ Jacuzzi at the lodge. **Playground:** Yes. **Other:** Hotel, meeting rooms, central data port in office. **Activities:** There are no activities on site other than the pool and playground on site. **Nearby Attractions:** Yellowstone National Park, the Grand Tetons, Jackson Hole, Jackson National Fish Hatchery, National Museum of Wildlife Art, Snow King Mountain Ski Area, Jackson Hole Ski Area. **Additional Informa-**

tion: Jackson Hole Chamber of Commerce (307) 733-3316.

Restrictions

Pets: On leash only. **Fires:** No open fires, charcoal grills only. **Alcoholic Beverages:** Yes. **Vehicle Maximum Length:** 45 ft. **Other:** AAA, Good Sam.

To Get There

Once in Jackson Hole, US 26/89 will be W. Broadway. The campground is behind the lodge on Virginian Ln., heading northeast towards the Tetons.

LARAMIE

Laramie KOA

P.O. Box 1134, Laramie 82073. T: (307) 742-6553 or (800) 562-4153; www.koa.com; koalaramie.vcn.com.

RV ★★ Tent ★★

Beauty: ★★	Site Privacy: ★★
Spaciousness: ★★	Quiet: ★★★
Security: ★★★	Cleanliness: ★★★
Insect Control: ★★★	Facilities: ★★★

Directly off the highway, the Laramie KOA offers clean and affordable lodging. The Laramie KOA offers over 100 pull-through RV sites with cable and phone hookups. There is a playground, recreation hall, laundry, and locked rest rooms. The campground backs right up to I-80 and is behind a mobile home area. The campground is gravel for the most part—the exception being the cabin area, which has a small lawn and a flower garden. Sites are level and configured in long rows, resembling a large parking lot. The staff is very friendly, and they work hard to maintain a nice campground in a desert region. The Laramie area has many attractions and festivals, such as the fair in Aug., and the Wyoming Children's Museum & Nature Center. There is also the Laramie Wyoming Territorial Prison and Old West Park with a horse barn dinner theatre.

Basics

Operated By: Greg Milliken. **Open:** Apr.–Nov 1. **Site Assignment:** By reservation. **Registration:** In the camp store. **Fee:** Tent $15, RVs $23, per 2 people, extra people over age 8 $2 each. **Parking:** At site.

Facilities

Number of RV-Only Sites: 116. **Number of Tent-Only Sites:** Open tent area. **Hookups:** Electric (20, 30, 50 amps), water, sewer. **Each Site:** Picnic tables, and fire pits in the tent and cabin area. **Dump Station:** Yes. **Laundry:** Yes. **Pay Phone:** Yes. **Rest Rooms and Showers:** Yes. **Fuel:** No. **Propane:** Yes. **Internal Roads:** Gravel, in good condition. **RV Service:** Local service. **Market:** In town. **Restaurant:** In town. **General Store:** Yes. **Vending:** Yes. **Swimming Pool:** No. **Playground:** Yes. **Other:** 8 cabins, store, Internet data port, rec hall, garage, flower garden. **Activities:** Game room, playground, horseshoes. **Nearby Attractions:** Laramie Wyoming Territorial Prison and Old West Park, Medicine Bow-Routt National Forests and Thunder Basin National Grassland. **Additional Information:** Laramie Chamber of Commerce (307) 745-7339.

Restrictions

Pets: On leash. **Fires:** In fire rings only. **Alcoholic Beverages:** Yes. **Vehicle Maximum Length:** None.

To Get There

From I-80 take Exit 310, go east on Curtis St, then turn right on McCue St at the Pilot. The KOA can be seen from I-80.

LYMAN

Lyman KOA

HC 66 Box 55, Lyman 82937. T: (307) 786-2762 or (800) 562-2762; www.koa.com; larkmary@buea.net.

RV ★★★★ Tent ★★★

Beauty: ★★★	Site Privacy: ★★★
Spaciousness: ★★★	Quiet: ★★★★
Security: ★★★★	Cleanliness: ★★★
Insect Control: ★★★	Facilities: ★★★

Located between Evanston and Rock Springs is delightful medium-sized campground, set in a rural atmosphere. The Lyman KOA is charming and inviting. The campground has a beautiful green lawn, with just enough shade from a few large trees, and a large outdoor swimming pool. The owners are friendly and genuinely pleased to assist their customers. Each campsite has a gravel parking area, and both pull-through and back-in sites are available. There is a large covered pavilion great for family outings, along with a small basketball court and other games. The town of Lyman is small, and this is a great place to read a book and enjoy a nice spring breeze. The historic Ft. Bridger is only a short drive away, and the

Mountain Man Rendezvous is celebrated Labor Day weekend.

Basics

Operated By: Clark Anderson. **Open:** May 15–Oct. 1. **Site Assignment:** By reservation. **Registration:** In the camp store. **Fee:** Tent $17, RVs $21, per 2 people, extra people over age 4 $1.50 each. **Parking:** At site.

Facilities

Number of RV-Only Sites: 36. **Number of Tent-Only Sites:** 17. **Hookups:** Electric (20, 30, 50 amps), water, sewer. **Each Site:** Picnic tables, and a some fire pits. **Dump Station:** Yes. **Laundry:** Yes. **Pay Phone:** Yes. **Rest Rooms and Showers:** Yes. **Fuel:** No, 7 mi. in Mt. View. **Propane:** No, 7 mi. in Mt. View. **Internal Roads:** Gravel, in good condition. **RV Service:** Local service. **Market:** Mt. View. **Restaurant:** In town. **General Store:** Yes. **Vending:** Yes. **Swimming Pool:** Yes. **Playground:** Yes. **Other:** 2 cabins, pavilion w/ kitchen, horseshoes, Internet dataport. **Activities:** Game room, playground, horseshoes, basketball, volleyball. **Nearby Attractions:** Flaming Gorge, Rock City. **Additional Information:** Bridger Valley Chamber of Commerce, (307) 787-6738.

Restrictions

Pets: On leash. **Fires:** In fire rings only. **Alcoholic Beverages:** Yes. **Vehicle Maximum Length:** None.

To Get There

Campground is 1 mi. south of I-80 at Exit 44.

MOOSE
Grand Tetons

P.O. Drawer 170, Moose 83012. T: (307) 739-3300; F: (307) 739-3438; www.grand.teton.national-park.com; grte_info@nps.gov.

RV ★★★ Tent ★★★★

Beauty: ★★★★★	Site Privacy: ★★★
Spaciousness: ★★	Quiet: ★★★
Security: ★★★★	Cleanliness: ★★★
Insect Control: n/a	Facilities: ★★★

Regal and proud, the Grand Tetons stand tall over the Snake River and peer down from the heavens. This natural marvel represents most intact temperate ecosystem in North America. Renowned for its world-famous wildlife viewing and unparalleled beauty, the Grand Teton National Park portrays an image of strength and majesty unscathed by man. The park has a total of six large campgrounds with over 1,000 campsites among them. The sites range from primitive to modern, with Colter Bay Trailer Village offering full hookups. The Grand Teton Lodge Company is the in-park concessionaire and oversees the majority of guest services, including camping reservations in three of the six campgrounds. The campgrounds are configured in loops, with paved parking pads, potable water, and rest room facilities. Showers are available in the Colter Bay Service Area at the laundry. The Grand Tetons, like any national park, is home and refuge to many forms of wildlife—including bear, moose, and elk—and therefore it is very important for your safety to please follow all the regulations put forth by the National Park Service.

Basics

Operated By: National Park Service. **Open:** The park is open year round, most camping areas are open mid May–end of Sept. **Site Assignment:** Camping is first come, first served w/ the exception of Colter Bay Trailer Village (307) 739-3399 Visitor Information (There is a Colter Bay Campground and a Colter Bay Trailer Village, all in the Colter Bay Village Area). **Registration:** Each campground has a registration office. **Fee:** $10–$30. based on which campground is chosen and the amenities they provide. **Parking:** At site.

Facilities

Number of RV-Only Sites: 112. **Number of Tent-Only Sites:** 0. **Number of Multipurpose Sites:** 905. **Hookups:** Electric (20, 30, 50 amps), water, sewer in Colter Bay Trailer Village Park only. There are no hookups at the other 5 campgrounds inside the park. **Each Site:** Picnic tables, fire pits (except Colter Bay trailer Village). **Dump Station:** Yes, at Gros Ventre, Signal Mountain, and Colter Bay. **Laundry:** Yes, in the service area at Colter Bay. **Pay Phone:** Pay phones are located throughout the park, but Not necessarily at each campground, primarily in the service areas. **Rest Rooms and Showers:** There are rest rooms located in every campground, and showers in the service areas near Colter Bay for a fee. **Fuel:** Yes, there 3 service areas through out the park Colter Bay, Jenny Lake, and Moose Junction. **Propane:** Yes, in several service areas through out the park. **Internal Roads:** The majority are paved but in need of repair. **RV Service:** Minor repair service available at Colter Bay.

Market: There are several in the park, or in Jackson Hole, WY. **Restaurant:** There are several restaurants in the park, Jenny Lake Lodge, Signal Mountain Lodge, Jackson Lake Lodge and Flagg Ranch. **General Store:** There are 3 general stores at Colter Bay, Jenny Lake, Jackson Lake. **Vending:** Yes in the major service areas of the park. **Swimming Pool:** No. **Playground:** No. **Other:** The Grand Teton National Park is a its own community w/ lodging, food, transportation, laundry, stores, restaurants, and medical clinic. Each guest will be given a newsletter upon arrival w/ a complete listing of the parks amenities and services. **Activities:** Horseback riding, motor coach tours, photo safaris, hiking, backpacking, Ranger led programs, evening programs, photo hikes, lectures, boating tennis, golf, biking tours. **Nearby Attractions:** Yellowstone National Park, Jackson Hole, Jackson National Fish Hatchery, National Museum of Wildlife Art, Snow King Mountain Ski Area, Jackson Hole Ski Area. **Additional Information:** Grand Teton Lodge Company, (307) 543-2811; Jackson Hole Chamber of Commerce, (307) 733-3316; National Park Service US Dept. of the Interior, or there are over 50 Internet links to Yellowstone National Park through www.yahoo.com or www.google.com.

Restrictions

Pets: Although pets are allowed in The Grand Teton Nation; Park on a leash only, however we strongly discouraged bringing them. Pets are not allowed out of the camping ares areas or off the main roads. Pets are not allowed in the backcountry or in any public viewing area. **Fires:** In fire pits only (fires may be prohibited due to weather conditions, please ask before starting any open fire). **Alcoholic Beverages:** Yes. **Vehicle Maximum Length:** Depends on the campground of your choice but never longer than 45ft. **Other:** National Park passes honored for entrance fees, golden age and golden access cards are *not* honored at all the campgrounds, including Colter Bay Trailer Village.

To Get There

There are three main gates into the Grand Tetons.; the most popular is through Jackson on Hwy. 191.

MORAN

The Flagg Ranch Resort

P.O.Box 187, Moran 83013. T: (800) 443-2311 or (307) 543-2861; F: (307) 543-2356; www.flaggranch.com; info@flaggranch.com.

RV ★★★ Tent ★★★

Beauty: ★★★★★	Site Privacy: ★★★
Spaciousness: ★★★	Quiet: ★★★★
Security: ★★★	Cleanliness: ★★★
Insect Control: ★★★	Facilities: ★★★

The Flagg Ranch Resort Campground is in one of the most ideal locations in Wyoming. It is situated between the Grand Tetons National Park and the south entrance to Yellowstone National Park along Hwy 89. This campground is privately owned in conjunction with a full-service lodge and service station. The campground sits in a forest of large evergreens and offers a real sense of tranquility. A great base for visiting both national parks, this campground offers all the amenities expected of a full-service RV camp. Each campsite has a gravel parking pad, hookups, and fire ring, as well as a natural forest floor and towering pines. Due to the location of this camping facility and the fact that there is only one trailer campground with hookups in either park, reservations must be made far in advance. Also, there is no access to this campground except through one of the national parks; therefore, expect to pay a park entrance fee.

Basics

Operated By: Bob Walker. **Open:** Year-round. **Site Assignment:** By reservation. **Registration:** In camp store. **Fee:** Tents $20 RV $35 per 2 people, extra child $2, Adult $2. **Parking:** At site.

Facilities

Number of RV-Only Sites: 97. **Number of Tent-Only Sites:** 74. **Hookups:** Electric (20, 30 amps), water, sewer. **Each Site:** Picnic tables, and fire pits in tent sites. **Dump Station:** No. **Laundry:** Yes. **Pay Phone:** Yes. **Rest Rooms and Showers:** Yes. **Fuel:** Yes. **Propane:** Yes. **Internal Roads:** Gravel, in good condition. **RV Service:** At Colter Bay Village. **Market:** At Colter Bay Village. **Restaurant:** On site at the lodge. **General Store:** Yes. **Vending:** Yes. **Swimming Pool:** No. **Playground:** Yes. **Other:** Main lodge w/ dining area, fireplace, gift shop, store, service station, meeting rooms, cabins, hotel, Internet data ports. **Activities:** Fishing, hiking, float tours,biking, horseback riding, coach tours. **Nearby Attractions:** Yellowstone National Park, the Grand Tetons, Jackson Hole, Jackson National Fish Hatchery, National Museum of Wildlife Art, Snow King Mountain Ski Area, Jackson Hole Ski Area, fishing, float trips, covered wagon cookouts. **Additional Information:** Jackson Hole Chamber of Commerce, (307) 733-3316.

Restrictions

Pets: On leash only. **Fires:** In fire pits only. **Alcoholic Beverages:** Yes. **Vehicle Maximum Length:** 45 ft. **Other:** Expect to pay a national park entrance fee, unless you have a park pass.

To Get There

The campground is located directly between the south gate of Yellowstone National Park and north gate of the Grand Tetons National Park on Hwy. 89 (you will have to enter through one of the two parks, so expect to pay a park entrance fee).

MORAN

Grand Teton Park RV Resort

P.O.Box 83013, Moran 83013. T: (800) (563) 6469 or (307) 733-1980; F: (307) 543-0927; www.yellowstonerv.com; gtprv@blissnet.com.

RV ★★★ Tent ★★★

Beauty: ★★★★★ Site Privacy: ★★★
Spaciousness: ★★★ Quiet: ★★★★
Security: ★★★ Cleanliness: ★★★
Insect Control: ★★★ Facilities: ★★★

The Grand Teton Park RV Resort is just one mile east of the Grand Tetons National Park and 32 miles from the south gate of Yellowstone. Few other full-service RV campgrounds are more convenient to the national parks (though there is at least one—see profile for Flagg Ranch Resort). The Grand Teton Park RV Resort offers a spectacular panoramic view of the majestic Grand Tetons, in addition to comfortable and affordable lodging year-round. The campground offers over 200 campsites, large, open tenting areas, and five teepees. They have both pull-through and back-in sites, as well as level parking spaces. The campground has full amenities, including a deli, pizza, and fuel. The property also offers a variety of services such as snowmobile and van rentals. This campground is also in close proximity to the scenic Snake River and many rafting outfitters. The weather in summer is comfortable, and the winter is harsh—but regardless of season, this campground is always inviting, and the people are great.

Basics

Operated By: Private Operator. **Open:** Year-round. **Site Assignment:** By reservation. **Registration:** In camp store. **Fee:** Tents $29 RV $32–$40 per 2 people extra child $4, Adult $5. **Parking:** At site.

Facilities

Number of RV-Only Sites: 140. **Number of Tent-Only Sites:** 60. **Hookups:** Electric (20, 30, 50 amps), water, sewer. **Each Site:** Picnic tables, and fire pits in tent sites. **Dump Station:** Yes. **Laundry:** Yes. **Pay Phone:** Yes. **Rest Rooms and Showers:** Yes. **Fuel:** Yes. **Propane:** Yes. **Internal Roads:** Gravel, in good condition. **RV Service:** Mobile service. **Market:** 36 mi. southwest in Jackson. **Restaurant:** 2 mi. in any direction, but The Buffalo Valley Ranch Café is a wonderful find w/ good prices and excellent service. **General Store:** Yes. **Vending:** No. **Swimming Pool:** Yes w/ hot tub. **Playground:** Yes. **Other:** 18 cabins, game room, 5 tepees, Pizza and deli, central data port in office. **Activities:** There are no activities on site other than the pool and playground on site. **Nearby Attractions:** Yellowstone National Park, the Grand Tetons, Jackson Hole, Jackson National Fish Hatchery, National Museum of Wildlife Art, Snow King Mountain Ski Area, Jackson Hole Ski Area, fishing, float trips, covered wagon cookouts. **Additional Information:** Jackson Hole Chamber of Commerce, (307) 733-3316.

Restrictions

Pets: On leash only. **Fires:** In fire pits only. **Alcoholic Beverages:** Yes. **Vehicle Maximum Length:** 45 ft. **Other:** AAA, Good Sam, KOA discounts.

To Get There

The campground is 6 mi. east of the Moran junction on Hwy. 26 & 287.

RAWLINS
Rawlins KOA

205 East Hwy. 71, Rawlins 82301. T: (307) 328-2021 or (800) 562-7559; www.koa.com; gattfarr@vcn.com.

 ★★★  ★★

Beauty: ★★★ Site Privacy: ★★★
Spaciousness: ★★★ Quiet: ★★★
Security: ★★★★ Cleanliness: ★★★
Insect Control: ★★★ Facilities: ★★★★

The Rawlins KOA is located directly off I-80 and offers convenient lodging in a clean and well-maintained atmosphere. The Rawlins KOA is nicely landscaped in a desert area where it is hard for anything to grow. The campsites have recently been upgraded and lengthened to accommodate newer and longer RVs. Each site has a level, gravel parking area, as well as free cable TV. The tents sites have tent pads and wind shields. The weather is very dry, and there is a considerable amount of sand in this region. In addition, the campground has a nice swimming pool and a camp kitchen. There is fishing in the Seminoe Reservoir or the North Platte River nearby, and hunting for antelope and deer. The community of Rawlins is full of interesting places to see, such as the Frontier Prison or Fort Steele.

Basics

Operated By: Fran and Jean Farrell. **Open:** Apr.–Oct. 31. **Site Assignment:** By reservation. **Registration:** In the camp store. **Fee:** Tent $18, RVs $21–$23, per 2 people, extra people over age 5 $3 each. **Parking:** At site.

Facilities

Number of RV-Only Sites: 56. **Number of Tent-Only Sites:** 6. **Hookups:** Electric (20, 30, 50 amps), water, sewer. **Each Site:** Picnic tables, and fire pits in the tent and cabin area. **Dump Station:** Yes. **Laundry:** Yes. **Pay Phone:** Yes. **Rest Rooms and Showers:** Yes. **Fuel:** No. **Propane:** Yes. **Internal Roads:** Gravel, in good condition. **RV Service:** Larime. **Market:** In town. **Restaurant:** In town. **General Store:** Yes. **Vending:** Yes. **Swimming Pool:** Yes. **Playground:** Yes. **Other:** 5 cabin, store, Internet dataport. **Activities:** Game room, playground, horseshoes, basketball. **Nearby Attractions:** Carbon County Museum, Frontier Prison, Snowy Ridge Scenic Byway. **Additional Information:** Rawlins Chamber of Commerce, (307) 324-4111 or (800) 935-4821.

Restrictions

Pets: On leash. **Fires:** In fire rings only. **Alcoholic Beverages:** Yes. **Vehicle Maximum Length:** None.

To Get There

The campground is near Exit 214 off I-80 in central Rawlins.

RAWLINS
Western Hills Campground and Trailer Court

P.O. Box 760, Rawlins 82301. T: (307) 324-2592 or (888) 568-3040; members.tripod.com/~wyo_camping/index.htm#local; whc@trib.com.

★★★  ★★

Beauty: ★★ Site Privacy: ★★
Spaciousness: ★★★ Quiet: ★★★★
Security: ★★★ Cleanliness: ★★★
Insect Control: ★★★ Facilities: ★★★

Located directly off I-80 in Rawlins, Western Hills Campground is ideal for the night. The campground is clean and well maintained, with activities the entire family can enjoy. The campsites are mostly gravel with no trees, but this is very common for this particular part of Wyoming. The air is very hot in the summer, with little precipitation and large gusts of wind. The campground has a mini-golf course and wildlife viewing area. There is fishing in the Seminoe Reservoir or the North Platte River nearby, and hunting for antelope and deer. The community of Rawlins is full of interesting places to see, such as the Frontier Prison or Fort Steele. It is also home to several small museums. The Carbon County Fair and Rodeo are held the first week in Aug., an event well worth planning to attend.

Basics

Operated By: John and Doreen McDade. **Open:** Year-round w/ limited service Nov.–Mar. 1. **Site Assignment:** By reservation. **Registration:** In camp office. **Fee:** Tent $14, RV $18–$22 per 2 people, children under 5 stay free (cash, credit, check). **Parking:** At site.

Facilities

Number of RV-Only Sites: 139. **Number of Tent-Only Sites:** Open tent area. **Hookups:** Electric (30, 50 amps), water, sewer, cable, phone. **Each Site:** Picnic table. **Dump Station:** No. **Laundry:** Yes. **Pay Phone:** Yes. **Rest Rooms and Showers:** Yes. **Fuel:** No. **Propane:** No. **Internal Roads:** Gravel, in good condition. **RV Service:** 150 mi. east in Cheyenne. **Market:** 6 mi. east in town. **Restaurant:** There are over 30 restaurants in the Rawlins area. **General Store:** Yes w/ a photo shop. **Vending:** Yes. **Swimming Pool:** No. **Playground:** Yes. **Other:** Game room, dog walk, pavilion, wildlife viewing area. **Activities:** Games, horseshoes, mini-golf. **Nearby Attractions:** The Historic Fort Steele, The Carbon County Museum. **Additional Information:** Rawlins Chamber of Commerce, (800) 935-4821.

Restrictions

Pets: Yes on leash only. **Fires:** No open fires. **Alcoholic Beverages:** Yes. **Vehicle Maximum Length:** None. **Other:** Good Sam.

To Get There

From I-80 Exit 211, go west on W. Spruce St. (SR 789), then bear left onto S. Wagon Rd.

RIVERTON

Owl Creek

11124 US Hwy. 26/789, Riverton 82501. T: (307) 856-2869; campowlcreek@tcinc.net.

★★★★  ★★★★

Beauty: ★★★★ Site Privacy: ★★★★
Spaciousness: ★★★★ Quiet: ★★★★
Security: ★★★★ Cleanliness: ★★★★
Insect Control: ★★★★ Facilities: ★★★

Owl Creek Campground in Riverton is a lovely, established campground. Owl Creek was one of the original KOA campgrounds, and although it is no longer a member of the franchise, the original KOA structure and open breezeway still stand. The campground is one of the only campgrounds in Wyoming with thick, lush, green grass and mature, large, deciduous shade trees. The campground is beautifully maintained, but it has nostalgia for the past. This reminiscence is apparent in the owners' display of antiques and the older facilities. The owners' live in a large colonial home on the property, and the house the focal point of the park. Owl Creek caters to more mature visitors that appreciate the calm atmosphere and picturesque setting. Simply due to the age of this campground, sites needed to accommodate large RVs are very limited.

Basics

Operated By: Frank and Pat Petek. **Open:** May 15–Sept. 15. **Site Assignment:** By reservation. **Registration:** In the camp office. **Fee:** $18.50 per 2 people. **Parking:** At site.

Facilities

Number of RV-Only Sites: 21. **Number of Tent-Only Sites:** 20. **Number of Multipurpose Sites:** 11. **Hookups:** Electric (20, 30, 50 amps), water, sewer, a few phone. **Each Site:** Picnic tables, and grills. **Dump Station:** Yes. **Laundry:** Yes. **Pay Phone:** Yes. **Rest Rooms and Showers:** Yes. **Fuel:** No, but in town. **Propane:** No. **Internal Roads:** Paved. **RV Service:** Local service. **Market:** In town. **Restaurant:** In town. **General Store:** Yes. **Vending:** Yes. **Swimming Pool:** No. **Playground:** Yes. **Other:** Orchard, utility sink. **Activities:** Playground, tetherball. **Nearby Attractions:** Fishing, hunting, boating, biking, hiking, and scenic byways. **Additional Information:** Riverton Chamber of Commerce, (307) 856-4801.

Restrictions

Pets: On leash. **Fires:** In approved sites. **Alcoholic Beverages:** Yes. **Vehicle Maximum Length:** 40 ft., limited room for extra long RV.

To Get There

The campground is 5 mi. northeast of Riverton on Hwy. 26.

ROCK SPRINGS

Rock Springs KOA

P.O. Box 2910, Rock Springs 82902. T: (307) 362-3063 or (800) 562-8699; F: (307) 362-5799; www.koa.com.

★★★  ★

Beauty: ★★ Site Privacy: ★★
Spaciousness: ★★ Quiet: ★★
Security: ★★★★ Cleanliness: ★★★
Insect Control: ★★★ Facilities: ★★★

Welcome to the high desert, where the sun always shines, and there is seldom a drop of rain. The air is dry and wind is strong. Conveniently located off I-80 in Rock Springs, the Rock

Springs KOA is a full-service RV park with full amenities, a large swimming pool, store, and game room. This KOA is a large facility, well maintained and clean. The sites are gravel, and there is no grass anywhere in the park, including the tent sites or in front of the cabins. In addition, there are no trees, but we've been told there is great satellite television reception. The park does overlook some smaller mountains to the rear, but there is Conoco oil plant in the front. Sites are lined up in rows, with no real dividers. Rock City is a fairly large metropolis for Wyoming, offering movies, shopping, museums, and many special events and festivals.

BASICS

Operated By: Dale and Bonnie Whitley. **Open:** Apr. 1–Oct. 15. **Site Assignment:** By reservation. **Registration:** In the camp store. **Fee:** Tent $18, RVs $21–$28, per 2 people, extra people over age of 6 $3 each. **Parking:** At site.

FACILITIES

Number of RV-Only Sites: 86. **Number of Tent-Only Sites:** 10. **Number of Multipurpose Sites:** 11. **Hookups:** Electric (20, 30, 50 amps), water, sewer, cable. **Each Site:** Picnic tables, and grills in the tent and cabin area. **Dump Station:** Yes. **Laundry:** Yes. **Pay Phone:** Yes. **Rest Rooms and Showers:** Yes. **Fuel:** No, but in town. **Propane:** Yes. **Internal Roads:** Gravel, in good condition. **RV Service:** Local service. **Market:** In town. **Restaurant:** In town. **General Store:** Yes. **Vending:** Yes. **Swimming Pool:** Yes. **Playground:** Yes. **Other:** 6 cabins, store, Internet dataport, pavilion w/ kitchen, tent wind shelters, chuck wagon, hot tub. **Activities:** Game room, playground, horseshoes, basketball, nature trails. **Nearby Attractions:** Fort Bridger, shopping, stock car races, the rodeo, golf, museums, Flaming Gorge, and scenic byways. **Additional Information:** Rock Springs Chamber of Commerce (800) 46-DUNES.

RESTRICTIONS

Pets: On leash. **Fires:** No open fires. **Alcoholic Beverages:** Yes. **Vehicle Maximum Length:** None.

TO GET THERE

From I-80 Exit 99, follow signs for 1 mi. northeast.

THERMOPOLIS

Country Campin' RV Park

710 East Sunnyside Ln., Thermopolis 82443. T: (800) 609-2244; F: (307) 864-2416; w3.trib.com/~camp; camp@trib.com.

RV ★★★★★ Tent ★★★★

Beauty: ★★★★ Site Privacy: ★★★★
Spaciousness: ★★★★ Quiet: ★★★★★
Security: ★★★★★ Cleanliness: ★★★★★
Insect Control: ★★★★ Facilities: ★★★★

Located on the owners' private ranch, Country Campin' RV is a charming, small, private campground five miles north of Thermopolis. The campground offers full amenities with waterfront access. Campsites are mostly pull-throughs, large, level, and with gravel parking spurs. There is a small store and gift shop, laundry, and clean rest rooms and showers. The owners have a few farm animals for children to pet and two friendly dogs that watch over the campground. The campground is nicely landscaped, and the sprinklers are on frequently. There is a small boat dock for non-motorized boats, and there's great fishing along the Big Horn River. The campground has a large open common area, and it's decorated with large, colorful dinosaur statues. Thermopolis is home of the world's largest mineral hot springs, which are open 365 days a year, and Wyoming's Dinosaur Center.

BASICS

Operated By: Darvin and Spring Longwell. **Open:** May–Nov. 1. **Site Assignment:** By reservation. **Registration:** In the camp store. **Fee:** Tent $15, RV $20 per 2 people, extra people $1.50. **Parking:** At site.

FACILITIES

Number of RV-Only Sites: 42. **Number of Tent-Only Sites:** 12. **Hookups:** Electric (20, 30, 50 amps), water, sewer. **Each Site:** Picnic table. **Dump Station:** Yes. **Laundry:** Yes. **Pay Phone:** Yes. **Rest Rooms and Showers:** Yes. **Fuel:** No, but local. **Propane:** No. **Internal Roads:** Gravel, in good condition. **RV Service:** In town. **Market:** In town. **Restaurant:** In town. **General Store:** Yes. **Vending:** Yes. **Swimming Pool:** No, and please do Not swim in the river. **Playground:** Yes. **Other:** Boat launch, petting zoo, gift shop, teepees. **Activities:** playground, hiking, Blue Ribbon Trout

Fishing, boating. **Nearby Attractions:** World's largest mineral hot spring, Wyoming's Dinosaur Center. **Additional Information:** Thermopolis Chamber of Commerce, (307) 864-3192.

Restrictions

Pets: On leash. **Fires:** In approved areas and out by 10 p.m.. **Alcoholic Beverages:** Yes. **Vehicle Maximum Length:** None. **Other:** Good Sam and AAA.

To Get There

5.4 mi. north of Thermopolis off US 20 on E. Sunnyside Ln. This campground is on a private farm.

THERMOPOLIS

Eagle RV Park

204 Hwy. 20 South, Thermopolis 82443. T: (307) 864-2325 or (888) 865-5707; F: (307) 864-5262; www.eaglervpark.com; eaglervpark@wyoming.com.

★★★ 

Beauty: ★★★ Site Privacy: ★★★
Spaciousness: ★★★ Quiet: ★★★★
Security: ★★★★ Cleanliness: ★★★
Insect Control: ★★★ Facilities: ★★★

Eagle RV Park is located in the city of Thermopolis on Hwy. 20. Thermopolis is home of the worlds largest mineral pool and hot springs. Eagle RV Park is only a few miles from Hot Springs State Park, where visitors from all over the world come to see and enjoy the pools. The Eagle RV Park is convenient to the Big Horn River and offers float trip packages to its patrons. The campground is an older facility, but the owners are working diligently to update their facilities. Just in the past year, the internal roads have been asphalted, and a pool is being built for the new season. Rest rooms and showers are clean, and the grounds are well kept. Campites are being updated, but there was still a lot of work to be done when we visited. The owners are very gracious hosts, and they are always there to assist. The weather is dry here, and skin protection is always needed, especially in the mineral pools.

Basics

Operated By: The Schneider Family. **Open:** Year-round. **Site Assignment:** By reservation. **Registration:** In the camp office. **Fee:** Tent $13, RV $19 per 2 people, extra person $1.50. **Parking:** At site.

Facilities

Number of RV-Only Sites: 50. **Number of Tent-Only Sites:** 15. **Hookups:** Electric (20, 30, 50 amps), water, sewer, cable, phone. **Each Site:** Picnic tables, and grills. **Dump Station:** Yes. **Laundry:** Yes. **Pay Phone:** Yes. **Rest Rooms and Showers:** Yes. **Fuel:** No, but in town. **Propane:** Yes. **Internal Roads:** Paved asphalt. **RV Service:** Local service. **Market:** In town. **Restaurant:** In town. **General Store:** Yes. **Vending:** Yes. **Swimming Pool:** New pool!!! we hope. They were digging when we visited. **Playground:** Yes. **Other:** Tube rentals, float trips, 4 cabins. **Activities:** Playground, rafting. **Nearby Attractions:** Thermopolis hot springs, Wyoming Dinosaur Center, several small museums, blur ribbon trout fishing, golf, Hot Springs State Park. **Additional Information:** Thermopolis Chamber of Commerce, (307) 864-3192.

Restrictions

Pets: On leash. **Fires:** In approved sites. **Alcoholic Beverages:** Yes. **Vehicle Maximum Length:** 40 ft., limited room for extra long RV.

To Get There

The campground is ocated on Hwy. 20 on the south side of Thermopolis.

YELLOWSTONE

Fishing Bridge

P.O. Box 165, Yellowstone 82190. T: (307) 344-7311 or 303-338-6000; F: (307) 344-7456 or (303) 338-2045; www.travelyellowstone.com/fishing_bridge_campground; information@amfac.com or camp@travelyellowstone.com.

★★★ n/a

Beauty: ★★★ Site Privacy: ★
Spaciousness: ★ Quiet: ★★★
Security: ★★★★ Cleanliness: ★★★
Insect Control: ★★★ Facilities: ★★★

Fishing Bridge RV Park is one of 12 campgrounds inside Yellowstone National Park. However, Fishing Bridge is the only one to offer full hookups for hard-shelled RVs only. The campground itself is a simple, no-frills, concrete parking lot with 344 sites and barley enough room for slide-outs. There are no trees except on the outer perimeter, and trailers are parked back to back. On the upside of things, Fishing Bridge is in a very central location within Yellowstone and is in close proximity to fuel, groceries, showers, laundry, and an amphitheater with evening interpretive programs. It is also very close to the visitor's center and museum, as well as the Lake Hotel, which has a large dinning room and cafeteria. Amfac Parks and Resorts are the primary in-park concessionaire and provide the majority of guest services, which includes overseeing this campground.

Basics

Operated By: Amfac Parks & Resorts. **Open:** Mid May–mid Sept. **Site Assignment:** By reservations, reservations need to be made up to a year in advance. **Registration:** There is a registration desk. **Fee:** $30.24. **Parking:** Yes, but there is a vehicle fee for all vehicles.

Facilities

Number of RV-Only Sites: 334. **Number of Tent-Only Sites:** n/a. **Hookups:** Electric (20, 30, 50 amps), water, sewer. **Each Site:** A place to park. **Dump Station:** Yes. **Laundry:** Yes. **Pay Phone:** Yes. **Rest Rooms and Showers:** Yes, showers cost $3 and are open to the public. **Fuel:** Yes. **Propane:** Yes. **Internal Roads:** Paved. **RV Service:** Limited on site service. **Market:** In Yellowstone, about 2 blocks away at Hamiltons. **Restaurant:** There are several restaurants in Yellowstone a 3 close by. **General Store:** No. **Vending:** Yes. **Swimming Pool:** No. **Playground:** No. **Other:** Please see the profile on Yellowstone National Park. **Activities:** Please see the profile on Yellowstone National Park. **Nearby Attractions:** Jackson Hole, skiing, the Grand Tetons. **Additional Information:** Jackson Hole Chamber of Commerce, (307) 733-3316 or Yellowstone Visitor Information, (307) 344-7381, (TDD) (307) 344-2386.

Restrictions

Pets: On leash only, pets are not allowed off the main roads anywhere in Yellowstone. **Fires:** No open fires. **Alcoholic Beverages:** Yes. **Vehicle Maximum Length:** 40 ft. **Other:** Only hard-sided units only, Golden age and golden access discounts are *not* honored by Amfac.

To Get There

There are five entrances into Yellowstone; visit www.travelyellowstone.com for directions from the entrance of your choice, or call to request a map of the park.

YELLOWSTONE

Yellowstone National Park

P.O. Box 168, Yellowstone National Park 82190-0168. T: (307) 344-7381 or (TDD) (307) 344-2386; F: (307) 344-2005; www.nps.gov/yell/index.htm; yell_visitor_services@nps.gov or www.travelyellowstone.com.

RV ★★★ Tent ★★★★

Beauty: ★★★★★	Site Privacy: ★★★
Spaciousness: ★★	Quiet: ★★★
Security: ★★★★	Cleanliness: ★★★
Insect Control: n/a	Facilities: ★★★

Yellowstone National Park encompasses the entire northwestern corner of Wyoming, with over 2.2 million acres of federal land serving as the world's first and oldest national park. The park has five major entrances and a total of 12 campgrounds with over a 2,000 campsites among them. The campsites range from very primitive to full hookups. Most are RV-friendly, with level parking pads, grated fire pits, potable water, and rest rooms in a wooded location. Most all of the campgrounds are configured as large multiple loops. Amfac Parks and Resorts are the primary in-park concessionaire and provide the majority of guest services, overseeing the five major campgrounds. Campsites managed by Amfac maybe reserved up to a year in advance. Yellowstone Park is open year-round; however, there is very limited camping after Sept. Yellowstone National Park is wonderful natural attraction, but first and foremost it is a home and refuge to the wildlife that inhabit its land. Therefore, we are all guests of these majestic animals and must respect the regulations put forth by the National Park Service for our protection as well as that of the wildlife. If you're considering a trip to Yellowstone National Park, please plan far in advance and contact visitor services.

Basics

Operated By: National Park Service. **Open:** The park is open year round, most camping areas are open mid May–end of Sept. Mommoth is open all year. Fishing Lodge May 18–Sept. 23. **Site Assignment:** Bridge Bay, Canyon, Grant Village, Madison, and Fishing Bridge RV Park. Fishing Bridge RV Park are by reservation and concessioned by Amfac Parks and Resorts. For reservations call (800) 329-

9205 or (307) 344-7311. **Registration:** Each campground has a registration office. **Fee:** $10–$30. based on which campground is chosen and the amenities they provide. **Parking:** At site.

Facilities

Number of RV-Only Sites: 340 (Fishing Bridge Only). **Number of Tent-Only Sites:** 454. **Number of Multipurpose Sites:** 1406 both RV and tent w/no hookups. **Hookups:** Electric (20, 30, 50 amps), water, sewer at Fishing Bridge RV Park only. There are no hookups at the other 11 campgrounds inside the park. **Each Site:** Picnic tables, fire pits (except Fishing Bridge). **Dump Station:** Yes, at Bridge Bay, Canyon, Fishing Bridge, Grant Village, and Madison. **Laundry:** Yes, in the service area near Canyon, Fishing Bridge, and Grant Village. **Pay Phone:** Pay phones are located throughout the park, but Not necessarily at each campground. **Rest Rooms and Showers:** There are rest rooms located in every campground, and showers in the service areas near Canyon, Fishing Bridge, and Grants Village. **Fuel:** Yes, there a 8 service areas through out the park. **Propane:** Yes, in several service areas through out the park. **Internal Roads:** The majority are paved. **RV Service:** There are several repair stations in the park. **Market:** There are several in the park, or West Yellowstone, MT. **Restaurant:** There are 17 restaurants in the park, 5 by Old Faithful, 2 in Grants Village, 3 in Canyon Village, 3 in Lake Village, 2 in Tower Roosevelt. **General Store:** There are 13 general stores throughout the park. **Vending:** Yes in the major service areas of the park. **Swimming Pool:** No. **Playground:** No. **Other:** Yellowstone National Park is a its own community w/ lodging, food, transportation, laundry, stores, restaurants, and hospital. Each guest will be given a newsletter upon arrival w/ a complete listing of the parks amenities and services. **Activities:** Horseback riding, Stagecoach rides, Bridge Bay Guided Fishing Trips, motor coach tours, old West Cookouts, photo safaris, hiking, backpacking, Ranger led programs, evening programs, Yellowstone for kids, photo hikes, lectures,. **Nearby Attractions:** West Yellowstone, MT, visitors center, Imax, 15 museums, rodeos, the Grand Tetons, Jackson Hole, WY, Cody, WY, shopping. **Additional Information:** West Yellowstone Chamber of Commerce, (406) 646-7701, or there are over 45 Internet links to Yellowstone National Park through yahoo or google.com.

Restrictions

Pets: Although pets are allowed in Yellowstone National Park on a leash only, we strongly discouraged bringing them. Pets are not allowed out of the camping ares areas or off the main roads. Pets are not allowed in the backcountry or in any public viewing area. **Fires:** In fire pits only in approved areas, there are no open fires in Fishing Bridge (fires may be prohibited due to weather conditions, please ask before starting any open fire). **Alcoholic Beverages:** Yes. **Vehicle Maximum Length:** Depends on the campground of your choice, call and ask over the reservation line 800-329-9205 or 307-344-7311. **Other:** National Park passes are honored for entrance fees, golden age and golden access cards are NOT honored at all the campgrounds concessioned by Amfac, including Fishing Bridge.

To Get There

There are five entrances into Yellowstone; visit www.travelyellowstone.com for directions from the entrance of your choice, or call to request a map of the park.

British Columbia

The region of Southwest British Columbia, as covered in this book, extends from the southeast end of the Fraser Valley in Hope, through the start of the Coast Mountains just north of Vancouver and ending in Pemberton. Within this small section of the large province of British Columbia, travelers can find a diverse array of activities and sights from cosmopolitan to wilderness.

Squamish and **Whistler** provide the major eco-tourism and outdoor sport centers for southwest British Columbia. Squamish prides itself on being cheaper than Whistler, and yet it's only a short drive away. Squamish has the same outdoor opportunities as Whistler, with one exception—skiing. Whistler is the province's premier western ski resort town. Organized recreation north of Whistler exists, but on a smaller scale.

Finally, a note on customs. Some products commercially available in the United States will cause trouble at the border. Melatonin is one, alligator meat is another. Anything that seems like drugs or paraphernalia without prescription will cause trouble. *Do not* take weapons into Canada. If arrested by customs for anything, you will be summarily fined, detained until you pay the fine, and your vehicle will be impounded (to be extricated only by payment of another, usually larger fine). If the offense is deemed large enough, the RCMP will be called and criminal charges may also be brought.

Additional Information

If travelling between Whistler and Pemberton, make sure to have plenty of gas in the tank. Though the distance is short, filling stations come in short supply anywhere north of Whistler. In some of northern British Colubmia and the Yukon, it is a good idea to fill up at every gas station along the way.

When going from Vancouver to Alaska or the Yukon, travellers have an alternative to the British Columbia leg of the Alaska Highway. Take the Cassiar Highway (Highway 37) running south from Highway 1 near Upper Liard, Yukon to Highway 16 and continuing on to Prince George, However be advised, this road is extremely rugged (both in environment and construction), very long, and scarcely populated or traversed along the northernmost 550 miles. Services exist, but just barely.

Camping in northern British Columbia and the Yukon involves little more than stopping at a pull out (*do not* camp in a slow vehicle turn out). Empty septic tanks at designated dump stations only, pack *all* trash to a commercial waste disposal pickup (gas station, etc.), be aware of bears and other animals (consider any wild animal potentially dangerous upon approach or confrontation), help people out with car trouble in wilderness areas (other wise they may be stuck for hours), and carry plenty of water. But if time doesn't permit the lengthy trip through the north country, enjoy the stay in southwest British Columbia.

The following facilities accept payment in checks or cash only:

- Alice Lake Provincial Park, Squamish
- Brandywine Falls Provincial Park, Whistler/Squamish
- Gold Creek Campground (Golden Ears Provincial Park), Maple Ridge
- Nairn Falls Provincial Park, Pemberton
- Porteau Cove Provincial Park, Britannia Beach

Campground Profiles

ABBOTSFORD

Abbotsford Campground and RV

36114 Lower Sumas Mountain Rd., Abbotsford V3G 2J3. T: (604) 855-3330; F: (604) 855-7251.

RV ★★★★ Tent ★★★★

Beauty: ★★★★	Site Privacy: ★★★
Spaciousness: ★★★	Quiet: ★★★
Security: ★★★	Cleanliness: ★★★★
Insect Control: ★★	Facilities: ★★★

Abbotsford Campground, 10 minutes north of the Sumas border crossing and just off Hwy. 1, has attractive landscaping and private tent sites. The hilly grounds have an enormous pool, two smaller hot tubs, a little shade from cedar trees, beautifully maintained grass, and a subtle scheme of potted flowers and shrubs. RV sites come in several flavors: flat grass, gravel, or paved, each with full hookups, and all positioned over gently rolling hills. Most RV sites lack privacy; sites 53–59 lack the flatness most other sites provide. The best paved, grass sites with full hookups, 60–69, sit on the south edge of the park. Extremely thick, tall cedar hedges mark the bounderies for most grass tent sites, creating walls of privacy. On the south edge of the park, there is a hill providing a small viewpoint with a spectacular view of Snowy Mount Baker rising from the horizon (no individual sites have any particularly striking views). Tent sites A1–A10 have the best privacy with cedar hedges on two sides and a hill on the third. Summer provides the best weather for visiting the area, however some grass RV sites may be closed during rainy periods.

Basics

Operated By: Abbotsford Camp and RV Park. **Open:** All year. **Site Assignment:** Walk up, reservations (deposit: 1 night stay; refund: 72 hours cancellation). **Registration:** At office, after hours pay in morning. **Fee:** For 2 people, full $27, water-electric $25, tent $21, MC, V, cash, personal checks (Canadian). **Parking:** At site, limited off site.

Facilities

Number of RV-Only Sites: 71. **Number of Tent-Only Sites:** 17. **Hookups:** Electric (15, 30 amps), water, sewer, cable. **Each Site:** Picnic table. **Dump Station:** Inquire at campground. **Laundry:** Inquire at campground. **Pay Phone:** Inquire at campground. **Rest Rooms and Showers:** Inquire at campground. **Fuel:** Inquire at campground. **Propane:** Inquire at campground. **Internal Roads:** Call ahead for details. **RV Service:** No. **Market:** 4 mi. west. **Restaurant:** 1 mi. south. **General Store:** No. **Vending:** Yes. **Swimming Pool:** Yes. **Playground:** Yes. **Other:** 2 hot tubs, reservable cabin (meeting hall), view point. **Activities:** Swimming. **Nearby Attractions:** Vancouver (45 minutes east), BC Farm Machinery and Agricultural Museum, Aldergrove Telephone Museum, Cheam Lake Wetlands Regional Park, Minter Gardens, golf. **Additional Information:** Fraser Valley Guide, (604) 820-0206; www.fraservalleyguide.com (very good site).

Restrictions

Pets: Leash only. **Fires:** No open fires. **Alcoholic Beverages:** At site. **Vehicle Maximum Length:** None. **Other:** Gates closed 11 p.m. to 7 a.m.

To Get There

From Hwy. 1 Exit 95 (Whatcom Road), go north 3 mi. and take first right onto Lower Sumas Mountain, drive 0.1 mi. and entrance is on the right.

BRITANNIA BEACH

Porteau Cove Provincial Park

Box 220, Brackendale V0I 1H0.T: (604) 898-3678; F: (604) 898-4171; wlapwww.gov.bc.ca/bcparks/explore/parkpgs/porteau.htm; gsdinfo@victoria1.gov.bc.ca.

RV ★★★ Tent ★★★

Beauty: ★★★★★	Site Privacy: ★★
Spaciousness: ★★★	Quiet: ★
Security: ★★	Cleanliness: ★★★
Insect Control: ★★	Facilities: ★★

Porteau Cove Provincial Park, located between Squamish and Vancouver, offers a large number of waterfront sites with beautiful views of silty Howe Sound and cloud-ringed, steep, evergreen-forested mountains rising sharply from the sea to the sky. The down side to the campground sits just to the east—the BC Rail tracks runs right next to the campground. The best sites within the grounds definitely have to be those by the water; sites 10, 11, 13, 14, and 17 sit furthest from the tracks (but are still very close). Sites 24–30 sit closest to the railroad. The campground has 16 walk in tent sites, but they lack fire pits and picnic tables, sit too close together, have little privacy, are very near the train tracks, and the sites themselves are small. With the exception of the noise, the campgrounds provide a beautiful, mild summer experience of BC's unique scenery.

Basics

Operated By: Peak To Valley Recreations for BC Parks. **Open:** All year, fully operational (with flush bathrooms, showers) Mar. 1–Oct. 31. **Site Assignment:** Walk in, reservations (Reservation service and campsite fees must be paid in full by V or MC at time of booking, campers are charged a non-refundable reservation service fee of $6.42 per night to a max of $19.26; refund: cancellation 7 days prior to arrival less $6.42 cancellation fee). **Registration:** At gate or collected at sites by attendant or at self pay station. **Fee:** Prices for 4 adults, 4 children, Sites–$18.50, Extra vehicle–$9.25, Adults ages 16 and over if traveling by themselves, Cash. **Parking:** At site.

Facilities

Number of RV-Only Sites: 0. **Number of Tent-Only Sites:** 16. **Number of Multipurpose Sites:** 44. **Hookups:** None. **Each Site:** Picnic table, grated fire pits. **Dump Station:** Inquire at campground. **Laundry:** Inquire at campground. **Pay Phone:** Inquire at campground. **Rest Rooms and Showers:** Inquire at campground. **Fuel:** Inquire at campground. **Propane:** Inquire at campground. **Internal Roads:** Call ahead for details. **RV Service:** No. **Market:** 10 mi. north. **Restaurant:** 6 mi. north. **General Store:** No. **Vending:** No. **Swimming Pool:** No. **Playground:** No. **Other:** Boat ramp, amphitheater, beach. **Activities:** Hiking, boating, salt water swimming, fishing (off boats only), scuba diving. **Nearby Attractions:** Scuba diving, BC Museum of Mining, ecotourism, Vancouver, Squamish, Whistler. **Additional Information:** Squamish Chamber of Commerce, (604) 892-9244.

Restrictions

Pets: Leash only. **Fires:** Fire pits only. **Alcoholic Beverages:** At site. **Vehicle Maximum Length:** 40 ft. **Other:** Don't gather dead or downed wood.

To Get There

The park entrance, driving north bound on Hwy. 99, is on the left 38 km (23.6 mi.) north of Vancouver and 8.5 (5.2 mi.) km south of Britannia Beach. 20 km (12.4 mi.) south of Squamish.

BURNABY (VANCOUVER)

Burnaby Cariboo RV Park

8765 Cariboo Place, Burnaby V3N 4T2.T: (604) 420-1722 or reservations (800) 667-9901; F: (604) 420-4782; www.bcrvpark.com; camping@bcrvpark.com.

RV ★★★ Tent ★★

Beauty: ★★★	Site Privacy: ★★★
Spaciousness: ★★★	Quiet: ★
Security: ★★★	Cleanliness: ★★★★
Insect Control: ★★	Facilities: ★★★

Burnaby Cariboo RV Park, or BC RV, located within close proximity to downtown Vancouver, offers an array of well-furnished facilities in a convenient location. However, active railroad runs near the facility, so noise here can be a problem. Paved, grass-bordered RV sites offer a large amount of privacy with thick cedar hedges on at least two sides, making the park look like a maze.

The best RV sites ring the perimeter of the park with privacy on three sides and more area per site than those positioned on islands within the grounds; sites contained on islands vary greatly in size. Tenters have a small grassy area with open sites, and fine-grit gravel pads of varying sizes. Sites within the tenting area have little elbow room, but the section has a covered area with two large kitchen sinks for meal preparation. Vancouver has year-round tourist activities, but summer offers more amiable temperatures and less rain than the rest of the year.

Basics

Operated By: BCRV inc. **Open:** All year. **Site Assignment:** Walk up, reservations (deposit: 1 night stay; refund: 24 hours notice). **Registration:** At store, after hours see info on store front. **Fee:** For 2 people, Full–$34.75, Tent–$23, Cable–$2, Phone–$3, Ages 6 and younger–free, Ages 7-14–$2.50, Ages 15 and up–$3.50, RVs over 31 feet add $2.25/day, MC, V, D, Cash. **Parking:** At site and off site.

Facilities

Number of RV-Only Sites: 217. **Number of Tent-Only Sites:** 24. **Hookups:** Electric (30 amps), water, sewer, cable. **Each Site:** Picnic table. **Dump Station:** Inquire at campground. **Laundry:** Inquire at campground. **Pay Phone:** Inquire at campground. **Rest Rooms and Showers:** Inquire at campground. **Fuel:** Inquire at campground. **Propane:** Inquire at campground. **Internal Roads:** Call ahead for details. **RV Service:** No. **Market:** 4 mi. in Burnaby. **Restaurant:** 4 mi. in Burnaby. **General Store:** Yes. **Vending:** Yes. **Swimming Pool:** Yes, indoor. **Playground:** Yes. **Other:** Indoor pool, meeting room (large and nice), fitness room, Jacuzzi, sun bathing deck, tour bookings, rental car reservations, golf bookings, RV wash, horseshoes, outdoor cooking area. **Activities:** Aquafit classes once a week. **Nearby Attractions:** Golf, Simon Fraser University, Vancouver. **Additional Information:** Vancouver Tourist Info Center (604) 683-2000; www.tourism-vancouver.org.

Restrictions

Pets: Leash only, prefer small dogs. **Fires:** No open fires. **Alcoholic Beverages:** At site. **Vehicle Maximum Length:** 40 ft. **Other:** No boats in tow. No dogs in tenting area.

To Get There

From Hwy. 1, take Exit 37 and go north on Garlar and turn right at first light. Drive and turn left at first light onto Cariboo Rd. Drive 0.3 mi., turn right at light onto Cariboo Place and drive 0.1 mi., road dead ends into park.

CULTUS LAKE

Sunnyside Family Campground

3405 Columbia Valley Hwy., Cultus Lake V2R 5A3. T: (604) 858-5253; F: (604) 858-5263; www.cultuslake.bc.ca; cultuslake@dowco.com.

RV ★★★★ Tent ★★★

Beauty: ★★★★★	Site Privacy: ★
Spaciousness: ★★★	Quiet: ★★★
Security: ★★★★	Cleanliness: ★★★
Insect Control: ★★	Facilities: ★★★

Sunnyside Campground, a few minutes south of Hwy. 1 in the Fraser Valley, sits in the very popular vacation area of Cultus Lake. During summer, there exists no chance of entrance without a reservation; the campground teems with people and remains a cluttered sea of trailers and tents. The campground receives shade from a thick canopy of evergreens; individual sites consist of mostly dirt, with some gravel surfaces in the RV areas. In the overnighter area, RV sites sit arranged in parallel rows and tent sites line several avenues winding their way down to the lakefront. The best RV sites, numbered 1–18, back up to the northern perimeter of the park. Tent sites 121–127 sit very near the lake, isolated from the rest of the grounds; all tent sites have close neighbors and no privacy. The lengthy beach and some tent sites have beautiful vistas of the mountains that rise sharply beyond Cultus Lake's southern banks. In addition to the lake, the campground has an arcade, a large general store and a rec room frequently hosting family oriented planned activities. The best time for good weather and swimming is during the summer, and the best time to avoid crowds is a weekday during the off season.

Basics

Operated By: Cultus Lakes Parks Board. **Open:** Apr. 1–Oct. 1. **Site Assignment:** Walk up, reservations (highly recommended; deposit: 1 night or ten percent of reservation; refund: 7 days cancellation).

Registration: At gate, no after hours entrance without prior notification of office. **Fee:** For 2 people, Full–$30, Tenting regular–$22, Tenting, view–$25, Tenting waterfront–$28, Children under 16 free, Extra vehicle-1/2 of site charge, Extra RV or tent-Full site charge, Extra adults–$3, Pets–$2, MC, V, cash. **Parking:** At site.

FACILITIES

Number of RV-Only Sites: 104. **Number of Tent-Only Sites:** 132. **Hookups:** Electric (30 amps), water, sewer. **Each Site:** Picnic table, fire ring. **Dump Station:** Inquire at campground. **Laundry:** Inquire at campground. **Pay Phone:** Inquire at campground. **Rest Rooms and Showers:** Inquire at campground. **Fuel:** Inquire at campground. **Propane:** Inquire at campground. **Internal Roads:** Call ahead for details. **RV Service:** No. **Market:** 3 mi. north. **Restaurant:** 1.5 mi. North. **General Store:** Yes. **Vending:** Yes. **Swimming Pool:** No. **Playground:** Yes. **Other:** Boat launch, horseshoes, basketball, rec room, group BBQ, arcade, beach, moorage. **Activities:** Swimming, planned activities, daily kids programs. **Nearby Attractions:** Golf, water sports, hiking, Cultus Lake Provincial Park, Bridal Veil Falls, sport fishing, mountain biking, bird watching, mountain climbing, ATV's. **Additional Information:** Chilliwack Visitor Info Center (800) 567-9535; www.tourismchilliwack.com.

RESTRICTIONS

Pets: Leash only, not allowed on beach. **Fires:** Fire pits only. **Alcoholic Beverages:** At site. **Vehicle Maximum Length:** 45 ft. **Other:** No fishing from shore. No semi's pulling fifth wheels.

TO GET THERE

From Hwy. 1, take Exit 119B (Cultus Lake/Sardis), drive 3.8 mi. south on Vedder Rd. Turn left at light onto Cultus Lake Rd. Drive 2.8 mi. south on Cultus Lake, entrance on right with big wooden sign.

HARRISON HOT SPRINGS

Sasquatch Springs RV Resort

P.O.Box 400, Harrison Hot Springs V0M 1K0.
T: (604) 796-9228; F: (604) 796-2040.

★★★  ★★

Beauty: ★★★★ Site Privacy: ★
Spaciousness: ★★ Quiet: ★★★
Security: ★★ Cleanliness: ★★★★
Insect Control: ★★ Facilities: ★★★

Sasquatch Springs RV Resort, in scenic Harrison Hot Springs, provides nearby access to Harrison Lake and the hot springs pool a few blocks away. The green park sits in one of the many valleys of the beautiful Northern Cascades and the property backs up to a steep, forested hill; in front of the park flows the narrow, silty, meandering Meama River. Campers can rent canoes to explore the river. There also exist several other recreational opportunities. Sites receive a small amount of shade from cedars and Japanese maples; they contain a mixture of gravel and grass with manicured, grassy perimeters, but lack privacy. The best full-hookup sites, numbered 53–68, line the banks of the river. Grass tent sites T11–T16 also line the river, but these sites sit in a higher traffic area; grassy, electric sites 92–97 provide amicable tent accommodations, backing up to the steep mountain behind the park. Avoid full hookup sites 18–21 because of their close proximity to each other. Weather during the summers tends to be cool and often overcast, so don't forget rain gear.

BASICS

Operated By: Sasquatch Springs RV Park. **Open:** Mar. 15–Oct. 30. **Site Assignment:** Walk up, reservation (deposit: 100 percent of reservation; refund: 10 days cancellation for 90% of deposit) Two day minimum on reservations in July and August. **Registration:** At office, no entry after 10 p.m. **Fee:** For 2 people, Full mountain side–$24, Full riverbank–$26, No hookup and tent–$19, Extra persons age 6-12–$2.50, Extra persons age 13 and older–$3, Under 6 years old-free, Cable–$2.50, MC, V, cash. **Parking:** At site, limited off site.

FACILITIES

Number of RV-Only Sites: 78. **Number of Tent-Only Sites:** 22. **Hookups:** Electric (15, 20, 30 amps), water, sewer, cable. **Each Site:** Picnic table, fire ring. **Dump Station:** Inquire at campground. **Laundry:** Inquire at campground. **Pay Phone:** Inquire at campground. **Rest Rooms and Showers:** Inquire at campground. **Fuel:** Inquire at campground. **Propane:** Inquire at campground. **Internal Roads:** Call ahead for details. **RV Service:** No. **Market:** 1 block north. **Restaurant:** Across the street. **General Store:** Yes. **Vending:** Yes. **Swimming Pool:** No. **Playground:** No. **Other:** Small arcade, pool, ping pong, TV/rec room, canoe rentals, horseshoes, badmitton, lawn games. **Activities:** Occasional planned activities, boating (no power). **Nearby Attractions:** Harrison Lake, Agassiz-Harrison Museum, Agassiz Agriculture Research Center, Dino Town, Hells Gate Airtram, Hemlock Valley Ski Resort, Sandsculpture Competition (September). **Additional Information:** Harrison, Agassiz Chamber of Commerce (604) 796-3425; www.harrison.ca; Fraser Valley Guide (604) 820-0206; www.fraservalleyguide.com (very good site).

Restrictions

Pets: Leash only. **Fires:** Only use wood purchased from office; in fire pits only. **Alcoholic Beverages:** At site. **Vehicle Maximum Length:** None. **Other:** Check in 12 p.m. Gate closed 10 p.m. (11 p.m. weekends).

To Get There

From Hwy. 1 Exit 135, drive 10.7 mi. north on Hwy. 9. Hwy. 9 changes roads several times, the entrance is on the left just before downtown Harrison

HOPE

Hope Valley Campground

62280 Flood-Hope Rd., RR No. 2, Hope V0X 1L0. T: (604) 869-9857 or (866) 869-6660; F: (604) 869-7458.

RV ★★★ Tent ★★★

Beauty: ★★★★	Site Privacy: ★★★
Spaciousness: ★★★	Quiet: ★★★
Security: ★★	Cleanliness: ★★★
Insect Control: ★★	Facilities: ★★★

Hope Valley Campground, just off Hwy.1 in Hope, provides family-oriented accommodations on the edge of the wilderness. The melee of sites within the grounds have lots of thick shade and ground foliage, creating some privacy but sacrificing views; the older facilities have a well-maintained look. Consisting of pull-throughs near the front of the park, the small full hookup area has less of the rustic, woodland feel one finds throughout the rest of the park. Most RV sites have only water-electric hookups. The best water-electric sites consist of numbers 48–63 because of their privacy and intrasite spaciousness. Grass tent-only sites, T1–T22, along with water-electric sites 117–130, make up some of the most open sites on the property. All non T-prefixed sites consist of a mix of gravel and grass. Visit during the summer, but be aware that summers consist of cool and often rainy weather.

Basics

Operated By: Hope Valley Campground. **Open:** Mar. 1–Oct. 31. **Site Assignment:** Walk up, reservation (deposit: 1 night stay; refund: 24 hours cancellation, 48 on holidays). **Registration:** At office. **Fee:** For 2 people, Full–$25.50, Water-electric–$22.50, Extra children 4-17–$2, Extra adults–$3, Children under 3 free, MC, V, Cash. **Parking:** At site.

Facilities

Number of RV-Only Sites: 100. **Number of Tent-Only Sites:** 40. **Hookups:** Electric (15, 30 amps), water, sewer, cable. **Each Site:** Picnic table, fire ring. **Dump Station:** Inquire at campground. **Laundry:** Inquire at campground. **Pay Phone:** Inquire at campground. **Rest Rooms and Showers:** Inquire at campground. **Fuel:** Inquire at campground. **Propane:** Inquire at campground. **Internal Roads:** Call ahead for details. **RV Service:** No. **Market:** In Hope. **Restaurant:** In Hope. **General Store:** Yes. **Vending:** No. **Swimming Pool:** Yes. **Playground:** Yes. **Other:** Rec room with an arcade, 2 pool tables, volleyball, bike rentals. **Activities:** Swimming. **Nearby Attractions:** Chainsaw carvings, Cheam Lake Wetlands Regional Park, Coquihalla Canyon Provincial Park, Hell's Gate Air-Tram, golf, tons of ecotourism. **Additional Information:** Hope Visitor Info Center, (604) 869-2021; www.fraservalleyguide.com.

Restrictions

Pets: Leash only. **Fires:** Fire pits only. **Alcoholic Beverages:** Sites only. **Vehicle Maximum Length:** 45 ft. **Other:** Don't wash RVs.

To Get There

From Hwy. 1 west take Exit 165 and turn left off exit ramp. Road dead ends after 0.1 mi. Turn right onto Flood Hope Rd., drive 0.2 mi. and entrance is on the right. From Hwy. 1 East, take Exit 168 and turn right onto Flood Hope Rd., drive 1 mi. to entrance on left.

HOPE

Wild Rose Campground

62030 Flood Hope Rd., Hope V0X 1L2. T: (604) 869-9842; F: (604) 869-3171; wildrose@uniserve.com.

RV ★★★★ Tent ★★★

Beauty: ★★★★	Site Privacy: ★★
Spaciousness: ★★★	Quiet: ★★★
Security: ★★	Cleanliness: ★★★★
Insect Control: ★★	Facilities: ★★

Wild Rose Campground, off of Hwy.1 in Hope, offers a more adult-oriented setting in the beautiful, wild landscape of Hope. Lacking the in-house recreation most families seek, Wild Rose consists primarily of two rows of well manicured, grassy sites. Much of the grounds receives shade from numerous beautiful fir trees, and most sites have good views of the rugged mountains surrounding the Fraser Valley. The tent section, numbers 61–68, lacks an abundance of shade, but individual sites have some privacy created by cedars and the best, unobstructed mountain views. The largest RV sites, 22–26 and 41–45, have a mixture of shade and views. The pull-through section is extremely shady. The least attractive sites, 51-60, receive such a label due to their smaller size. Even during the summer the weather tends to be cool and rainy, so make sure and keep rain gear handy.

Basics

Operated By: Wild Rose Campground. **Open:** Apr. 1–Sept 30. **Site Assignment:** Walk up, reservations (deposit: 1 night stay; refund 48 hours cancellation). **Registration:** At office. **Fee:** For 2 people, Full–$24, No hookup–$20, Extra person–$2, MC, V, cash. **Parking:** At site.

Facilities

Number of RV-Only Sites: 60. **Number of Tent-Only Sites:** 8. **Hookups:** Electric (15, 30 amps), water, sewer, cable. **Each Site:** Picnic table. **Dump Station:** Inquire at campground. **Laundry:** Inquire at campground. **Pay Phone:** Inquire at campground. **Rest Rooms and Showers:** Inquire at campground. **Fuel:** Inquire at campground. **Propane:** Inquire at campground. **Internal Roads:** Call ahead for details. **RV Service:** No. **Market:** 3 mi. east in Hope. **Restaurant:** 0.1 mi. west. **General Store:** Yes. **Vending:** No. **Swimming Pool:** No. **Playground:** Yes. **Other:** Rec room, volleyball, horseshoes. **Activities:** Inquire at campground. **Nearby Attractions:** Dinotown, Hell's Gate AirTram, Hiking, Japanese Friendship Gardens, Trans-Canada Water Slide, (Rambo: First Blood was filmed in Hope). **Additional Information:** Hope Visitor Info Center, (604) 869-2021; www.fraservalleyguide.com.

Restrictions

Pets: Short leash only, quiet dogs only. **Fires:** Fire pits only. **Alcoholic Beverages:** At site. **Vehicle Maximum Length:** None. **Other:** No outdoor music.

To Get There

From Hwy. 1 west, take Exit 165 and turn left off exit ramp. Road dead ends after 0.1 mi.. Turn right onto Flood Hope road, drive 0.5 mi. and entrance is on the right From Hwy. 1 East, take Exit 168 and turn right onto Flood Hope Rd., drive 1.3 mi. and entrance on left.

MAPLE RIDGE

Gold Creek Campground (Golden Ears Provincial Park)

1610 Mt. Seymour Rd., North Vancouver V7G 2R9. T: (604) 924-2200; F: (604) 924-2244; wlapwww.gov.bc.ca/bcparks/explore/parkpgs/golden.htm; lmdinfo@victoria1.gov.bc.ca.

RV ★★★ Tent ★★★★

Beauty: ★★★★★	Site Privacy: ★★
Spaciousness: ★★★	Quiet: ★★★★
Security: ★★	Cleanliness: ★★★
Insect Control: ★★	Facilities: ★★

Golden Ears Provincial Park, located northeast of Vancouver, offers a very quiet, wilderness environment near the city. The park has three separate campgrounds, all close to one another; Gold Creek Campground has the only showers and flushers in the park. Sites have an arrangement on parallel, one-way avenues with numbers relative to the avenue's initials. All sites have the setting of a beautiful, heavily shaded cedar forest with a green floor resulting from moss and lichen growth on feeder logs, a very delicate environment to maintain effectively. The flat, gravel sites look like those of most provincial parks. This park is a highly popular and stays crowded during the summer, but two days after labor day the park turns into a ghost-town. The only sites to avoid sit on Trilium Drive, the main access loop to the rest of the grounds, and on Plantain Lane, another high traffic area. Sites do not adjoin, but they lack visual privacy due to the land formation in the campground. Summers here have cool temperatures, magnified by the shadiness of the area so make sure to pack accordingly.

Basics

Operated By: BC Parks. **Open:** All year, fully operational Apr. 6–Oct. 8. **Site Assignment:** Walk up, reservations available Apr. 6-Sept. 15 (Reservation service and campsite fees must be paid in full by V or MC at time of booking; campers are charged a non-refundable reservation service fee $6.42 per night to a max of $19.26; refund: cancellation 7 days prior to arrival less $6.42 cancellation fee). **Registration:** At gate or self pay stations. **Fee:** For four adults, Site–$18.50, extra vehicle–$9.25, rates for 4 adults and 4 children (under 16 years old, cash only upon arrival. **Parking:** At site.

Facilities

Number of RV-Only Sites: 0. **Number of Tent-Only Sites:** 0. **Number of Multipurpose Sites:** 138. **Hookups:** None. **Each Site:** Picnic table, fire ring. **Dump Station:** Inquire at campground. **Laundry:** Inquire at campground. **Pay Phone:** Inquire at campground. **Rest Rooms and Showers:** Inquire at campground. **Fuel:** Inquire at campground. **Propane:** Inquire at campground. **Internal Roads:** Call ahead for details. **RV Service:** No. **Market:** 20 mi. south in Maple Ridge. **Restaurant:** 20 mi. south in Maple Ridge. **General Store:** No. **Vending:** No. **Swimming Pool:** No. **Playground:** No. **Other:** Free firewood, hiking trails, interpretive trails, beach, Amphitheater. **Activities:** Interpretive programs in summer, hiking, swimming, biking. **Nearby Attractions:** Mountain Biking, canoeing, fishing, golfing, the Haney House (Homestead museum), hiking, horseback riding, skydiving, UBC Research Forest. **Additional Information:** Pitt Meadows Visitor Information Centre, (604) 460-8300.

Restrictions

Pets: Leash only. **Fires:** Fire pits only. **Alcoholic Beverages:** At site. **Vehicle Maximum Length:** 40 ft. **Other:** Don't gather dead or downed foliage.

To Get There

From Maple Ridge (located on Hwy. 7 north of Fraser River), drive east on Golden Ears Pkwy to entrance.

NORTH VANCOUVER

Capilano RV Park

295 North Tomahawk Ave., North Vancouver V7P 1C5. T: (604) 987-4722; F: (604) 987-2015; www.capilanorvpark.com; capilanorvpark.com.

RV: ★★★ Tent: ★★

Beauty: ★★	Site Privacy: ★
Spaciousness: ★★★	Quiet: ★★
Security: ★★★	Cleanliness: ★★★★
Insect Control: ★★	Facilities: ★★★★

Capilano RV Park, located in Metro Northwest Vancouver, offers convenient access to shopping and the city. The park has an indoor hot tub, a shopping mall within walking distance, and wide, easily navigable roads. Paved, grass perimetered back-in sites with full hookups sit back to back; cedar hedges provide some rear privacy, but no privacy on the sides or shade above. Sites 1-105 provide the best accommodations. A slight view of mountains to the north (largely eclipsed by tall condos) provides a backdrop for the urban campground, although individual sites have a view of little more than their neighbors. The tenting section lies on park's perimeter, with grass sites and gravel parking; sites 128-140 have partial shade. Because of its urban location, the park receives some noise from the surrounding city. Visit Vancouver during the summer, but even then weather can be crisp or rainy.

Basics

Operated By: Capilano RV Park. **Open:** All year. **Site Assignment:** Walk in, reservations (No deposit, will hold reservation after 6 p.m. on arrival date with credit card only; cancel as soon as possible). **Registration:** At office. **Fee:** For two people, Full–$38, Water-electric–$33, Extra vehicle–$10, Pet–$2/day, No hookup and tent–$28, Extra persons–$3.50, Five years old or younger–Free, V, MC, cash, Canadian travelers checks. **Parking:** At site, off site parking at additional charge.

Facilities

Number of RV-Only Sites: 208. **Number of Tent-Only Sites:** 29. **Hookups:** Electric (15, 30,

50 amps), water, sewer, cable. **Each Site:** Picnic table. **Dump Station:** Inquire at campground. **Laundry:** Inquire at campground. **Pay Phone:** Inquire at campground. **Rest Rooms and Showers:** Inquire at campground. **Fuel:** Inquire at campground. **Propane:** Inquire at campground. **Internal Roads:** Call ahead for details. **RV Service:** No. **Market:** Next door. **Restaurant:** Next door. **General Store:** No. **Vending:** Yes. **Swimming Pool:** Yes. **Playground:** Yes. **Other:** Small arcade, Jacuzzi, TV room. **Activities:** Swimming. **Nearby Attractions:** Lions Gate Bridge, False Creek, Point Grey, Stanley Park, Vancouver Harbor, Vancouver International Wine Festival, Capilano Salmon Hatchery, Chinatown, skiing. **Additional Information:** Vancouver Tourist Info Center, (604) 683-2000; www.tourism-vancouver.org.

Restrictions

Pets: Leash only. **Fires:** No open fires. **Alcoholic Beverages:** At site. **Vehicle Maximum Length:** 48 ft. **Other:** Quiet hours 9 p.m.–8 a.m.

To Get There

From Hwy. 99, take Exit 14 (just west of Lion's Gate Bridge) to Capilano Rd. Go south on Capilano 0.6 mi. and go through Marine intersection and take left fork. Drive 0.4 mi. to a stop and turn right on Welch Street. Drive 0.4 mi. to a stop and turn right following RV park signs. Drive 0.2 mi. and turn right following RV park signs, entrance is just across a right angle turn.

PEMBERTON

Nairn Falls Provincial Park

Box 220, Brackendale V0N 1H0. T: (604) 898-3678 or reservations (800) 689-9025; F: (604) 898-4171; www.env.gov.bc.ca/bcparks/explore/parkpgs/nairn.htm; gsdinfo@victoria1.gov.bc.ca.

RV ★★★★ | Tent ★★★★

Beauty: ★★★★★	Site Privacy: ★★★
Spaciousness: ★★★	Quiet: ★★★★
Security: ★★★	Cleanliness: ★★★
Insect Control: ★★	Facilities: ★★

Nairn Falls Provincial Park, just south of Pemberton, offers a quiet, wilderness setting just out of reach of the heavy tourist traffic found to the south in Whistler. Best described as primitive, the campground does not have flush toilets but does have potable water. Non-adjacent sites sit in an arrangement of parallel rows, creating a semi-private environment. Further, some sites have amazing views of nearby Green River and the mountains. These sites, 48–51, lack the privacy that can be found in the rest of the park and sit on a ridge, subject to a cold breeze at times. Sites with the most privacy sit on the exterior perimeters of the park and have no neighbors to the rear. All sites have gravel surfaces, a fair amount of room, and lots of shade from the overhead forest. The scenery here is incredible. The summers provide the best time to visit; even so, the mountain weather seldom gets very warm, so be prepared for cool temperatures.

Basics

Operated By: BC Parks. **Open:** May 1–Sept. 30. **Site Assignment:** Walk up, reservations (Reservation service and campsite fees must be paid in full by V or MC at time of booking, campers are charged a non-refundable reservation service fee $6.42 per night to a max of $19.26; refund: cancellation 7 days prior to arrival less $6.42 cancellation fee). **Registration:** Fees collected at sites by attendants, after hours pay in morning—host or drop box located by info station. **Fee:** For 4 adults, 4 children (under 16 years old), Site–$12, Extra vehicle–$6, cash only upon arrival. **Parking:** At site, limited off site.

Facilities

Number of RV-Only Sites: 0. **Number of Tent-Only Sites:** 0. **Number of Multipurpose Sites:** 88. **Hookups:** None. **Each Site:** Picnic table, fire ring. **Dump Station:** Inquire at campground. **Laundry:** Inquire at campground. **Pay Phone:** Inquire at campground. **Rest Rooms and Showers:** Inquire at campground. **Fuel:** Inquire at campground. **Propane:** Inquire at campground. **Internal Roads:** Call ahead for details. **RV Service:** No. **Market:** North in Pemberton; limited. **Restaurant:** North in Pemberton, limited. **General Store:** No. **Vending:** No. **Swimming Pool:** No. **Playground:** No. **Other:** Hiking trails. **Activities:** Fishing, hiking, wildlife viewing, birdwatching. **Nearby Attractions:** Horseback riding, river rafting, mountain biking, ecotourism. **Additional Information:** Pemberton and District Chamber of Commerce, (604) 894-6175.

Restrictions

Pets: Leash only. **Fires:** Fire pits only. **Alcoholic Beverages:** At site. **Vehicle Maximum Length:**

38 ft. **Other:** Be aware of areas designated no pets. Do not gather dead or down foliage, habitat sensitive. Use suitable grey water containers. Be aware of bear procedures.

To Get There

Driving north on Hwy. 99, entrance is on right just south of Pemberton and about 30 minutes north of Whistler

ROSEDALE (CHILLIWACK)

Chilliwack RV Park and Campground

50850 Hack Brown Rd., Rosedale V0X 1X0. T: (604) 794-7800; F: (604) 794-7800.

RV ★★★ Tent ★

Beauty: ★★★ Site Privacy: ★★
Spaciousness: ★★★ Quiet: ★★★
Security: ★★ Cleanliness: ★★★
Insect Control: ★★ Facilities: ★★

Chilliwack RV Park and Campground, just off the Trans-Canadian Highway in Chilliwack, provides a base for day trips to the surrounding areas. The park receives some noise from nearby Hwy. 1 and can be a little dusty, but also has beautiful panoramic views of the surrounding mountains. Limited recreational facilities make this property less family oriented than other parks in the area. Numbers 36–50, the best gravel full hookup sites, climb up a shady, gentle hill in the back of the park but have only obscured views of the surrounding scenery and no privacy. With less shade, sites 12–18 have some privacy provided by shrubbery and less obscured views of the distant scenery. The grass tent sites lack good shade or any privacy. The mild summers can be rainy here, so make sure to have rain gear handy.

Basics

Operated By: Chilliwack RV Park. **Open:** All year. **Site Assignment:** Walk up, reservation (deposit: 1 night stay; refund: 7 days notice of cancellation. **Registration:** At office, after hours pay in morning. **Fee:** For 2 people, Full–$22, Water-electric–$20, Tent–$18, Extra person–$2, Cable $2 extra, Pets–$1 per pet per day, Max 4 adults per site, MC, V, cash. **Parking:** At site.

Facilities

Number of RV-Only Sites: 58. **Number of Tent-Only Sites:** 15. **Hookups:** Electric (15, 30 amps), water, sewer, cable. **Each Site:** Picnic table, fire ring. **Dump Station:** Inquire at campground. **Laundry:** Inquire at campground. **Pay Phone:** Inquire at campground. **Rest Rooms and Showers:** Inquire at campground. **Fuel:** Inquire at campground. **Propane:** Inquire at campground. **Internal Roads:** Call ahead for details. **RV Service:** No. **Market:** 4 mi. north in Rosedale. **Restaurant:** 4 mi. North in Rosedale. **General Store:** Yes. **Vending:** No. **Swimming Pool:** No. **Playground:** Yes. **Other:** Horseshoe pits, meeting room, gazebo. **Activities:** Blackberry picking (in season). **Nearby Attractions:** Bridal Veil Falls Provincial Park, Minter Gardens, Trans Canada Water Slide, Harrison Watersports, Chilliwack River Rafting. **Additional Information:** Tourism Chilliwack Info Center (800) 567-9535; www.fraservalleyguide.com.

Restrictions

Pets: Leash only, max 2 per site. **Fires:** Fire pits only. **Alcoholic Beverages:** At site. **Vehicle Maximum Length:** None. **Other:** Inquire at campground.

To Get There

From Hwy. 1 Exit 129 (west bound turn left), cross Annis road, go down Hwy. 1 east entrance ramp and take right fork onto Hack-Brown Rd., drive 0.3 mi. and entrance is on right

SQUAMISH

Alice Lake Provincial Park

Box 220, Brackendale V0N 1H0. T: (604) 898-3678 or reservations (800) 689-9025; F: (604) 898-4171; www.env.gov.bc.ca/bcparks/explore/parkpgs/alicelk.htm; gsdinfo@victoria1.gov.bc.ca.

RV ★★★ Tent ★★★★

Beauty: ★★★★ Site Privacy: ★★
Spaciousness: ★★★ Quiet: ★★★★
Security: ★★★ Cleanliness: ★★★
Insect Control: ★★ Facilities: ★★

Alice Lake Provincial Park, just minutes north of Squamish, offers the widest array of facilities of any provincial park in the area. Translated, this means flush toilets and showers. The campground has an organization of loops off a main road and non-adjacent, shady, semi-private gravel sites in a beautifully forested area. Sites 56–96 make up a loop with less site density than the other main section, sites 1–55. Within the former, sites 79–86 have the most privacy of any in the grounds. There also exist some sites near

Alice Lake, numbered 61–68, but these get quite chilly with the wind they receive from the lake. In the latter section, sites 9–55 have a very high site density and not much privacy. The park has walk-in tent sites, and although these sit in an area slightly segregated from the main sections, they have no privacy within their area. Busy during the summer, the campground buzzes with families, especially on weekends. Otherwise, the campground stays free of ambient environmental noise. Summers are the best time to visit, but even then the weather has a crisp feel.

Basics

Operated By: Ben Hubbard for BC Parks. **Open:** Maintained with showers, flushers Mar. 1–Oct. 31; accessible all year. **Site Assignment:** Walk in, reservations highly recommended 90 days prior to arrival (Reservation service and campsite fees must be paid in full by V or MC at time of booking, campers are charged a non-refundable reservation service fee $6.42 per night to a max of $19.26; refund: cancellation 7 days prior to arrival less $6.42 cancellation fee). **Registration:** At gate, after hours pay in morning if entrance possible, sites available. **Fee:** For four adults, Site–$18.50, Extra vehicle–$9.25, rates for 4 adults and 4 children (under 16 years old), cash only upon arrival, reserved sites already paid in full upon arrival. **Parking:** At site.

Facilities

Number of RV-Only Sites: 0. **Number of Tent-Only Sites:** 11. **Number of Multipurpose Sites:** 96. **Hookups:** None. **Each Site:** Picnic table, fire ring. **Dump Station:** Inquire at campground. **Laundry:** Inquire at campground. **Pay Phone:** Inquire at campground. **Rest Rooms and Showers:** Inquire at campground. **Fuel:** Inquire at campground. **Propane:** Inquire at campground. **Internal Roads:** Call ahead for details. **RV Service:** No. **Market:** 10 min. south in Squamish. **Restaurant:** 10 min. south in Squamish. **General Store:** No. **Vending:** No. **Swimming Pool:** No. **Playground:** Yes. **Other:** Hiking trails, amphitheater, firewood (free), kayak rentals, changing rooms at beach. **Activities:** Hiking, interpretive programs (Thursday-Sunday in summers), fishing, swimming, mountain biking, kayaking, canoeing. **Nearby Attractions:** Hiking, mountain biking, fishing, rock climbing, adventure tours, ecotourism, Garibaldi Provincial Park. **Additional Information:** Squamish Chamber of Commerce, (604) 892-9244; www.squamishchamber.bc.ca/main.htm.

Restrictions

Pets: Leash only. **Fires:** Fire pits only. **Alcoholic Beverages:** At site. **Vehicle Maximum Length:** 40 ft. **Other:** Gates closed 11p.m. to 7 a.m., page security for entry. Be aware of areas designated no pets. Do not gather dead or down foliage, habitat sensitive. Use suitable grey water containers. Be aware of bear procedures.

To Get There

From Hwy. 99N, turn right on Alice Lake Rd. approx. 7 mi. north of Squamish. Drive 0.7 mi. and take left fork, drive 0.3 mi. further and entrance is on the right at gate house

SQUAMISH
Dryden Creek Resort and Campground

P.O.Box 1012, Garibaldi Highlands V0N 1T0.T: (604) 898-9726; F: (604) 898-9780; www.drydencreek.com; dryden@uniserve.com.

RV ★★★★ Tent ★★★

Beauty: ★★★★	Site Privacy: ★★
Spaciousness: ★★★	Quiet: ★★★
Security: ★★	Cleanliness: ★★★★
Insect Control: ★★	Facilities: ★★

Dryden Creek Resort and Campground, located just north of Squamish on Hwy. 99, offers close access to a plethora of outdoor recreation. The small campground has a quaint, enchanted forest feel, and offers a variety of sites. On top of backing up to a beautiful gray, rocky ridge forested with evergreens, the park also has a Salmon spawning creek running through it. RV sites in the west section of the park offer a more forested feel, but sit in a higher traffic area. The best gravel RV sites, E1–E8, sit in the east section of the park, half of which back up to the cliffs at the rear of the park. These sites have an open feel, no privacy, and grass perimeters. Within the tenting section there exist two types of sites, ones positioned in a grassy area with little shade or privacy, and ones that sit in a wooded area with more privacy but also gravel and dirt surfaces. The latter, sites N10–N14, have the most shade from tall cedars characteristic of the area. Surrounding areas provides year-round outdoor recreation, summers have mild and sometimes rainy weather, winters bring snow and world-class skiing.

Basics

Operated By: Dryden Creek Resorts. **Open:** All year. **Site Assignment:** Walk up, reservations (deposit: full cost of stay; refund: 48 hours less $6 cancellation fee). **Registration:** At office, after hours arrival call ahead before close. **Fee:** For 2 people, full $24, tent $18.50, weekly rates 10% off, extra people older than 18 or traveling without parents $2.20, extra people 18 and younger $1.12, V, MC, cash. **Parking:** At site.

Facilities

Number of RV-Only Sites: 29. **Number of Tent-Only Sites:** 20. **Hookups:** Electric (30 amps), water, sewer, cable. **Each Site:** Picnic table, fire ring. **Dump Station:** Inquire at campground. **Laundry:** Inquire at campground. **Pay Phone:** Inquire at campground. **Rest Rooms and Showers:** Inquire at campground. **Fuel:** Inquire at campground. **Propane:** Inquire at campground. **Internal Roads:** Call ahead for details. **RV Service:** No. **Market:** South in Squamish. **Restaurant:** South in Squamish. **General Store:** Yes. **Vending:** No. **Swimming Pool:** No. **Playground:** No. **Other:** Motel, group camping, one canoe for rental, German and Spanish speaking staff. **Activities:** Occasional church on Sundays, stream fishing. **Nearby Attractions:** Mountain Biking, wind surfing, rock climbing, salmon spawning trails, ecotourism. **Additional Information:** Squamish Chamber of Commerce, (604) 892-9244; www.squamishchamber.bc.ca.

Restrictions

Pets: Leash only. **Fires:** Fire pits only. **Alcoholic Beverages:** At site. **Vehicle Maximum Length:** 40 ft. **Other:** Check in 3 p.m. Stream regulated for fishing, check with office before fishing.

To Get There

On Hwy. 99, drive 1.7 mi. north of Burger King on north edge of Squamish/Brackendale. Turn right onto Depot Rd., take an almost immediate left and drive up entry drive into campground.

VANCOUVER (RICHMOND)

Richmond RV Park

6200 River Rd., Richmond V7C 5G1. T: (604) 270-7878 or voice mail (800) 755-4905; F: (604) 244-9713; www.richmondrvpark.com; richmondrv@aol.com.

RV ★★★ Tent ★★

Beauty: ★★	Site Privacy: ★
Spaciousness: ★★★	Quiet: ★★
Security: ★★★	Cleanliness: ★★★
Insect Control: ★★	Facilities: ★

Richmond RV Park, located in what can be considered downtown Vancouver, offers easy access to the city. The park has a good, relatively secure location. Constant, heavy traffic in surrounding areas and urban noise such as airliners overhead make the grounds unsuitable for travelers looking for exceptional quiet and slow moving relaxation; management assures the train tracks in the back of the park have been dead for some time. The pull-through sites 205–275 have a very cramped feeling. The grounds contain a multitude of back-ins with homogenous attributes; a flat field makes up the gravel and grass sites. The bare-bones park has a design lending itself to little more than a jumping off point for the city. Grass tent sites 276–292 (even numbered only) sit around the perimeter of the park; the best offer a reasonable amount of space. The bathrooms here have lots of stalls, no waiting in line for a shower. Vancouver has tourism year-round, but summer offers the most activities.

Basics

Operated By: Richmond RV Park. **Open:** Apr. 1–Oct. 31. **Site Assignment:** Walk in, reservations (deposit: 1 nights stay; refund: 24 hours notice). **Registration:** At office, after hours see instructions on office door. **Fee:** For 2 people, Back-in (RVs 22 feet and over)–$25, Back-in (RVs 21 feet and under)–$23, Pull-through–$27, No hookup and tent–$17, Additional persons 7 years and older–$3, Under 7 years old–free, V, MC, U.S and Canadian cash, travelers checks. **Parking:** At site, off site available.

Facilities

Number of RV-Only Sites: 200. **Number of Tent-Only Sites:** 75. **Hookups:** Electric (15, 30 amps), water. **Each Site:** Picnic table. **Dump Station:** Inquire at campground. **Laundry:** Inquire at campground. **Pay Phone:** Inquire at campground. **Rest Rooms and Showers:** Inquire at campground. **Fuel:** Inquire at campground. **Propane:** Inquire at campground. **Internal Roads:** Call ahead for details. **RV Service:** No. **Market:** 3 mi. east. **Restaurant:** 3 mi. east. **General Store:** Yes.

Vending: No. **Swimming Pool:** No. **Playground:** No. **Other:** Tour booking, gameroom, shuttle to Alaska Ferry Cruise dock and RV storage ($), mobile dump station, grill loans. **Activities:** Inquire at campground. **Nearby Attractions:** IMAX Theatre, Watermania, Steverson Fishing Village, Stanley Park, Lion's Gate Bridge, Queen Elizabeth Park, Gastown, Downtown Vancouver. **Additional Information:** Vancouver Tourist Info Center (604) 683-2000; www.tourism-vancouver.org.

Restrictions

Pets: Leash only. **Fires:** No open fires. **Alcoholic Beverages:** At site. **Vehicle Maximum Length:** None. **Other:** 30 day max stay limit.

To Get There

From Hwy. 99, take Exit 36 (Westminster Hwy., always high traffic) and drive 3.4 mi. west on Westminster Hwy. Turn right on No 2 Rd, drive less than 1 block and take off ramp to the right to River Road. Turn right onto River Road and drive 0.3 mi., entrance on the right

VANCOUVER (SURREY)

Dogwood Campground and RV Park

15151 112th Ave., Surrey V3R 6G8. T: (604) 583-5585; F: (604) 583-4725.

RV: ★★ Tent: ★★

Beauty: ★★	Site Privacy: ★
Spaciousness: ★★★	Quiet: ★★★
Security: ★★★	Cleanliness: ★
Insect Control: ★★	Facilities: ★★

Dogwood Campground in Surry, located about 20 minutes east of municipal Vancouver, offers a convenient location just outside the city. The park has areas for both overnight and seasonal accommodations, in addition to grassy tent sites that make up the perimeter of the park. The homogenous overnight section of the park consists of four rows of back-in sites, either grass or paved and surrounded by grass, open and adjacent on two sides. Overnighters can be put in a seasonal site if one is requested and available. Essential facilities have a clean, reasonably well kept interior appearance, but the grounds and building exteriors look quite run down and in need of cosmetic maintenance. Regarding tent sites, they lack privacy and many lack shade; the shadiest sites, 178–193, sit under oak and elm. Avoid tent sites 333–351 as they sit near the highway with some noise issues. Vancouver has a beautiful mild summer and rainy, cool to cold weather every other season.

Basics

Operated By: Dogwood Campground. **Open:** All year. **Site Assignment:** Walk in, reservations (deposit: 1 night stay; refund: 24 hour notice). **Registration:** At office, after hours see instructions posted outside office. **Fee:** Full–$30, For 2 people (regarding tents only), Tent–$19.50, Extra persons 12 years or older tenting–$3. **Parking:** At site.

Facilities

Number of RV-Only Sites: 209. **Number of Tent-Only Sites:** 150. **Hookups:** Electric (30 amps), water, sewer, cable. **Each Site:** Picnic table. **Dump Station:** Inquire at campground. **Laundry:** Inquire at campground. **Pay Phone:** Inquire at campground. **Rest Rooms and Showers:** Inquire at campground. **Fuel:** Inquire at campground. **Propane:** Inquire at campground. **Internal Roads:** Call ahead for details. **RV Service:** No. **Market:** 2 mi. east in Surrey. **Restaurant:** 2 mi. east in Surrey. **General Store:** Yes. **Vending:** Yes. **Swimming Pool:** Yes. **Playground:** Yes. **Other:** Jacuzzi, rec. hall, arcade, volleyball, badmitton, horseshoes, tour bookings, Gray Line tours pick-up. **Activities:** Swimming, lawn games. **Nearby Attractions:** Stanley Park and Aquarium, Vancouver Aquarium, Grouse Mountain Chairlift, Capilano Suspension Bridge, Downtown Vancouver. **Additional Information:** City of Surrey, (604) 591-4811; www.city.surrey.bc.ca; Vancouver Tourist Info Center (604) 683-2000; www.tourism-vancouver.org.

Restrictions

Pets: Leash only. **Fires:** No open fires. **Alcoholic Beverages:** At site. **Vehicle Maximum Length:** 45 ft.

To Get There

From the Hwy. 1 Exit, go north on 160th Street for 0.7 mi. and turn left on 108th Ave at the light with ScotiaBank. Follow 108th Ave for 1 mi., where it turns into 154th St. Drive 0.2 mi. on 154th St and turn left on 112th Ave which dead ends into the campground.

VANCOUVER (SURREY)

Hazelmere RV Park and Campground

18843 8th Ave., Surrey V4P 1M7. T: (604) 538-1167; F: (604) 538-1080; www.globalserve.net/~hazelmere; hazelmere@globalserve.net.

RV ★★★ Tent ★★

Beauty: ★★★	Site Privacy: ★
Spaciousness: ★★★	Quiet: ★★★
Security: ★★★	Cleanliness: ★★★★
Insect Control: ★★★	Facilities: ★★★★

Hazelmere RV Park, located in a rural area of Surrey and just south of Vancouver, offers large open spaces and a unique summer attraction. The campground has two large open grassy areas, accounting for much of the acreage; one field gets use as a group camping area and the other frequently hosts hot air balloon launches during the summer months. The park includes a large seasonal area (monthly rentals) and a smaller overnight section. Sites in the overnight section have gravel surfaces surrounded by grass, with a little shade and no privacy. The tent section consists of sites on the edge of the group camping area. The better RV sites, numbers 112–115 and 127–129, offer the best of the partial shade available. Sitting in the back of the park, the overnight section offers quiet, and backs up to a small river. Tent sites 152–155 sit on a slope and are not very flat. Summer is the best time to come to the Vancouver area.

BASICS

Operated By: Hazelmere RV Park. **Open:** All year. **Site Assignment:** Walk in, reservations (deposit: 1 night's stay; refund: cancel 4 days before arrival). **Registration:** At office, after hours at drop box or see caretaker. **Fee:** For 2 people: Full–$27.82, Electric-water RV–$24.61, Electric-water Tent–$23.54, Tent–$21.40, Extra people 7 years and up–$2, under 7 free, max 4 people per site, MC, V, cash. **Parking:** At site, limited off site.

FACILITIES

Number of RV-Only Sites: 160. **Number of Tent-Only Sites:** 8-plus. **Hookups:** Electric (15, 30 amps), water, sewer, cable. **Each Site:** Picnic table, fire ring. **Dump Station:** Inquire at campground. **Laundry:** Inquire at campground. **Pay Phone:** Inquire at campground. **Rest Rooms and Showers:** Inquire at campground. **Fuel:** Inquire at campground. **Propane:** Inquire at campground. **Internal Roads:** Call ahead for details. **RV Service:** No. **Market:** 10 min. north in Surrey. **Restaurant:** 10 min. North in Surrey. **General Store:** Yes. **Vending:** No. **Swimming Pool:** Yes. **Playground:** Yes. **Other:** Volleyball, basketball, soccer, horseshoes, rec room w/ pool table and 3 arcade games, picnic shelter, hot tub, exercise room, hot air balloon rides (summer), trails to fish hatchery. **Activities:** Ballooning, hiking. **Nearby Attractions:** Golf, Peace Arch Park, Bear Creek Park, Green Timbers Urban Forest, Redwood Park, Vancouver, Semiahmoo Fish Hatchery. **Additional Information:** City of Surrey, (604) 591-4811, www.city.surrey.bc.ca; Vancouver Tourist Info Center (604) 683-2000; www.tourism-vancouver.org.

RESTRICTIONS

Pets: Leash only (except for dog exercise area). **Fires:** Fire pits only. **Alcoholic Beverages:** At site, picnic areas. **Vehicle Maximum Length:** None. **Other:** Check in 12 p.m.

TO GET THERE

From Hwy. 15 just north of Blaine border crossing, turn right (east) on 8th Ave and drive 1.5 mi., entrance on the left. From Hwy. 99 just north of the border, take Exit 2 (8th Ave) and drive 2.5 mi. east, entrance on the left.

VANCOUVER (SURREY)

Peace Arch RV Park

14601 40th Ave., Surrey V4P 2J9. T: (604) 594-7009; F: (604) 597-4220; www.peacearchrvpark.com; info@peacearchrvpark.com.

RV ★★★★ Tent ★★

Beauty: ★★★	Site Privacy: ★★★★
Spaciousness: ★★★	Quiet: ★★★
Security: ★★★	Cleanliness: ★★★★
Insect Control: ★★	Facilities: ★★★★

Peace Arch RV Park, located about 10 minutes north of the Blaine, WA border crossing, houses beautiful, flowering shrubs and many private pull-throughs. Colored by densely packed flowers, the common areas stay in bloom throughout the summer. Facilities have a well-kept, clean appearance. The sites are arranged in many rows of gravel pull-throughs and back-ins parallel to each other. Back-in sites lack much shade or privacy, but all pull-through sites, rows B–D, have huge fir tree buffers on either side, creating a private, almost forest feeling and shade; they also have some grass within each site. The firs have an overgrown look, but do not encroach upon the spaciousness of the sites. Tent sites in the park sit in a small field without much shade or privacy; this field does, however, have many seedling hardwoods. Also, the tenting section has a small covered area with a sink for dishes. Summers bring flowers and the best time to visit the Vancouver area, but nights can be especially chilly even in August.

Basics

Operated By: Peace Arch RV Park. **Open:** All year. **Site Assignment:** Walk in, reservation (deposit: 1 night stay; refund: 24 hour cancellation policy). **Registration:** At office, after hours at drop box. **Fee:** For 2 people, Full–$24.50, Tents–$18.50, Extra people over 7 years old–$2, Under 7 years old-free, V, MC, US and Canadian cash and travelers checks. **Parking:** At site, off site.

Facilities

Number of RV-Only Sites: 202. **Number of Tent-Only Sites:** 50. **Hookups:** Electric (30 amps), water, sewer, phone (pull-throughs only), cable. **Each Site:** Picnic table. **Dump Station:** Inquire at campground. **Laundry:** Inquire at campground. **Pay Phone:** Inquire at campground. **Rest Rooms and Showers:** Inquire at campground. **Fuel:** Inquire at campground. **Propane:** Inquire at campground. **Internal Roads:** Call ahead for details. **RV Service:** No. **Market:** 5 min. north in Cloverdale. **Restaurant:** 5 min. North in Cloverdale. **General Store:** No. **Vending:** Yes. **Swimming Pool:** Yes. **Playground:** Yes. **Other:** Mini golf, horseshoes, basketball, rec room w/ pool table and 2 arcade games, RV storage. **Activities:** Winter social clubs, occasional BBQs in summer. **Nearby Attractions:** Stanley Park and Zoo, Vancouver Aquarium, Transportation Museum, Capilano Suspension Bridge, Gastown, White Rock Beach. **Additional Information:** City of Surrey, (604) 591-4811, www.city.surrey.bc.ca; Vancouver Tourist Info Center (604) 683-2000; www.tourism-vancouver.org.

Restrictions

Pets: Leash only. **Fires:** No Fires. **Alcoholic Beverages:** At site. **Vehicle Maximum Length:** None. **Other:** No parking on grass, do not tie any lines to trees.

To Get There

From Hwy. 99, take Exit 10, turn onto 99A northbound. After less than one block, turn right onto 40th Ave, drive 0.5 mi., entrance on the left

VANCOUVER (SURREY)

Tynehead RV Camp

16275 102nd Ave., Surrey V4N 2K7. T: (604) 589-1161; F: (604) 589-1161; www.tynehead.bc.ca.

RV: ★★★ Tent: ★★

Beauty: ★★★	Site Privacy: ★★
Spaciousness: ★★★	Quiet: ★★
Security: ★★★	Cleanliness: ★★★★
Insect Control: ★★	Facilities: ★★★

Tynehead RV Camp, located southeast of Vancouver in the suburb of Surrey, offers a quiet environment and easy access to Downtown Vancouver. Attractively landscaped and arranged in parallel rows, the park offers gravel pull-through and back-in full hookup sites with a small amount of privacy generated by cedar hedges. Still, there exists little shade for RV sites, and sites are not particularly flat. The best RV sites, back-ins 9–19, have the most shade and sit on a perimeter; the absence of rear neighbors creates more privacy. The back of the property has a little traffic noise. The tenting section consists of a grass field with sites interspersed throughout, none have particularly striking qualities. The best time to visit Vancouver has to be summer, when the weather is largely clear and mild.

Basics

Operated By: Tynehead RV Camp. **Open:** All year. **Site Assignment:** Walk in, reservations (deposit: 10% of stay or 1 night; refund: call about varying policy). **Registration:** At office, after hours ring buzzer outside. **Fee:** For 2 people, Full–$30, Partial–$27, Tent–$20, Extra person–$3, Large dogs–$2, Children 5 and under free, Group rate if more than 10 people in a tent site, MC, V, cash. **Parking:** At site, limited off site parking.

Facilities

Number of RV-Only Sites: 120. **Number of Tent-Only Sites:** 53. **Hookups:** Electric (30 amps), water, sewer, cable. **Each Site:** Picnic table. **Dump Station:** Inquire at campground. **Laundry:** Inquire at campground. **Pay Phone:** Inquire at campground. **Rest Rooms and Showers:** Inquire at campground. **Fuel:** Inquire at campground. **Propane:** Inquire at campground. **Internal Roads:** Call ahead for details. **RV Service:** No. **Market:** Nearby in Surrey. **Restaurant:** Nearby in Surrey. **General Store:** Yes. **Vending:** No. **Swimming Pool:** Yes. **Playground:** Yes. **Other:** Spa (indoor), mini-golf. **Activities:** Inquire at campground. **Nearby Attractions:** Greater Vancouver Zoological Centre, Science World, Queen Elizabeth and Bloedel Conservatory, Lynn Canyon Suspension Bridge, Chinatown, Vancouver. **Additional Information:** City of Surrey, (604) 591-4811; www.city.surrey.bc.ca; Vancouver Tourist Info Center (604) 683-2000; www.tourism-vancouver.org.

RESTRICTIONS

Pets: Leash only. **Fires:** In pits only. **Alcoholic Beverages:** At site. **Vehicle Maximum Length:** 40 ft. **Other:** Do not park vehicles on grass.

TO GET THERE

From Hwy. 1 Exit 501, turn south on 160th street and drive 0.15 mi.. Turn left on 103rd Ave. and drive 0.3 mi., then turn left on 102nd Ave and drive 0.2 mi., entrance on the left.

VANCOUVER (WHITE ROCK)

Seacrest Motel and RV Park

864 160th St. (Stayte Rd.), White Rock V4A 4W4. T: (604) 531-4720; F: (604) 531-4735; www.seacrestmotel.bc.ca; seacrest@uniserve.com.

RV ★★★ Tent n/a

Beauty: ★★	Site Privacy: ★
Spaciousness: ★★★	Quiet: ★★★
Security: ★★★	Cleanliness: ★★★★
Insect Control: ★★★	Facilities: ★★

Seacrest Motel and RV Park, just across the border in White Rock, has quiet, no frills lodging in a beach-side community about a half hour south of Vancouver. A walk to the beach takes only a few minutes. Sites exist in two rows in two sections on paved blacktop with no grass or privacy. The surrounding motel has attractive landscaping and a small laundry facility (one set of machines). The whole grounds have a very quaint, quiet feel to them, neither pretentious nor dated, perfect for people who want to see Vancouver but not stay within it's municipality. All sites have a pretty similar setting, with the exception of sites 101 and 107, which sit near a road. Visit during the summer for optimal meteorological conditions.

BASICS

Operated By: Seacrest Motel. **Open:** All year. **Site Assignment:** Walk in, reservations (deposit: 1 night stay; refund: 48 hours notice). **Registration:** At office, after hours pay in morning. **Fee:** Full–$24. **Parking:** At site.

FACILITIES

Number of RV-Only Sites: 32. **Number of Tent-Only Sites:** 0. **Hookups:** Electric (30 amps), water, sewer, cable. **Each Site:** Picnic table. **Dump Station:** Inquire at campground. **Laundry:** Inquire at campground. **Pay Phone:** Inquire at campground. **Rest Rooms and Showers:** Inquire at campground. **Fuel:** Inquire at campground. **Propane:** Inquire at campground. **Internal Roads:** Call ahead for details. **RV Service:** No. **Market:** a few mi. west in White Rock. **Restaurant:** A couple of blocks in either direction. **General Store:** No. **Vending:** No. **Swimming Pool:** No. **Playground:** No. **Other:** Inquire at campground. **Activities:** Inquire at campground. **Nearby Attractions:** White Rock Beach, pier and promenade, shopping and restaurants near waterfront, Peace Arch Park, Golf, fishing, crabbing, Vancouver. **Additional Information:** City of White Rock, (604) 541-2142, www.city.whiterock.bc.ca; Vancouver Tourist Info Center (604) 683-2000; www.tourism-vancouver.org.

RESTRICTIONS

Pets: Leash only, no loud dogs. **Fires:** No fires. **Alcoholic Beverages:** At site. **Vehicle Maximum Length:** 40 ft. **Other:** Check in at 1 p.m.

TO GET THERE

From Hwy. 99 Exit 2, drive 0.7 mi. west on 8th Ave. Turn right on Stayte Rd and drive less than 1 block; entrance is on the right

WHISTLER

Riverside RV Resort and Campground

8018 Mons Rd., Whistler V0N 1B0. T: (604) 905-5533 or (877) 905-5533; F: (604) 905-5539; www.whistlercamping.com; info@whistlercamping.com.

Beauty: ★★★★ Site Privacy: ★★★
Spaciousness: ★★ Quiet: ★★★
Security: ★★★ Cleanliness: ★★★★★
Insect Control: ★★ Facilities: ★★★★★

Riverside RV Resort and Campground, located in the expensive resort town of Whistler, provides convenient access to world class, year-round outdoor recreation, restaurants and clubs. This new campground has top-of-the-line, well equipped facilities and a variety of in-house recreation—notably a high-quality, all-grass, 18-hole putting course. Landscaping within the grounds is garden-like, well maintained, and classy. The RV section has obscured views of the surrounding mountains. In the RV section, consisting of several parallel rows of flat, paved back-in sites, the best sites, D1–D9 and E1–E8, sit toward the back of the grounds with some shade trees overhead and a little privacy. The tenting area, heavily shaded by pine and birch, consists of walk-in, semi-private dirt and gravel sites; the only sites to avoid, T1, T25, and T26, lack the privacy found in other sites. Any time makes a good time to visit Whistler; the town draws crowds for both summer and winter recreation.

Basics

Operated By: Riverside RV Resort. **Open:** All year. **Site Assignment:** Walk up, reservation (deposit: 1 night stay to hold; refund:cancel before 2 weeks for refund of *total* cost of stay, less than 2 weeks 50% of total stay, after 48 hours prior to arrival cancellation billed for total cost of stay). **Registration:** At office, after hours info in front of office. **Fee:** For 2 people, Full–$40, Overflow RV–$25, Extra RV adults–$5, Tent–$25, Extra tent adults–$7.50 (16 years and older, flexible for families). **Parking:** At site; tent sites walk-in with seperate parking lot.

Facilities

Number of RV-Only Sites: 60. **Number of Tent-Only Sites:** 31. **Hookups:** Electric (15, 30, 50 amps), water, sewer, cable ($2/day). **Each Site:** Picnic table, fire ring. **Dump Station:** Inquire at campground. **Laundry:** Inquire at campground. **Pay Phone:** Inquire at campground. **Rest Rooms and Showers:** Inquire at campground. **Fuel:** Inquire at campground. **Propane:** Inquire at campground. **Internal Roads:** Call ahead for details. **RV Service:** No. **Market:** Across street. **Restaurant:** On grounds. **General Store:** Yes. **Vending:** Yes. **Swimming Pool:** No. **Playground:** Yes. **Other:** PGA regulation 18-hole grass putting green, arcade with pool table, Internet terminal, cafe, rentals (roller blades, foot scooters, mountain bikes, movies, TVs, VCRs). **Activities:** Putting, volleyball, horseshoes, free shuttles to and from Whistler Village twice in morning and twice in afternoon. **Nearby Attractions:** Mountain biking, golf, hiking, fishing, tons of winter recreation (in winter), eco-tourism; restaurants, shopping, and nightlife at Whistler resort complex. **Additional Information:** Tourism Whistler, (800)-WHISTLER; www.tourism.whistler.com; Squamish Chamber of Commerce, (604) 892-9244; www.squamishchamber.bc.ca.

Restrictions

Pets: Leash only; not allowed in beach (stream), playground area. **Fires:** At site, in pits. **Alcoholic Beverages:** At site. **Vehicle Maximum Length:** None. **Other:** Be aware of bear regulations. No refunds for early departures.

To Get There

On Hwy. 99 heading north, drive 1.1 mi. north of Whistler Village (main entrance to the north edge of town) and turn right onto Spruce Grove Park/Blackcomb Way. Take an almost immediate left onto the access road and follow for 0.3 mi. to entrance

WHISTLER/SQUAMISH
Brandywine Falls Provincial Park

Box 220, Brackendale V0N 1H0. T: (604) 898-3678; F: (604) 898-4171; www.elp.gov.bc.ca/bcparks/explore/parkpgs/brandywi.htm; gsdinfo@victoria1.gov.bc.ca.

RV ★★ Tent ★★

Beauty: ★★★ Site Privacy: ★★
Spaciousness: ★★★ Quiet: ★★★
Security: ★ Cleanliness: ★★
Insect Control: ★★ Facilities: ★

Brandywine Falls Provincial Park, located about 15 minutes south of Whistler, offers an overflow area within a very busy tourist corridor. Blink and you'll miss this small campground of 15 sites. The campground consists of a loop with sites on the perimeter and a central island. Individual sites lack elbow room and privacy, but do have some shade from firs and cedars. Sites 1–6 sit near busy Hwy. 99, but sites 7–15 are more removed from the major provincial artery. There are no facilities of any kind save vault toilets. The provincial park itself seems more like a rest area than a park, but it does have a couple of trails to hike. Year-round outdoor recreation abounds in the surrounding areas.

Basics

Operated By: Markim Ventures for BC Parks. **Open:** May 15–Oct. 15, off season gate closed, can walk in; no services and no fees. **Site Assignment:** Walk up. **Registration:** Attendant will collect fees at site, or pay in morning-attendant (host) or at self-pay box by info station. **Fee:** For 4 adults, 4 children, Site–$12, Extra vehicle–$6, cash only upon arrival. **Parking:** At site.

Facilities

Number of RV-Only Sites: 0. **Number of Tent-Only Sites:** 0. **Number of Multipurpose Sites:** 15. **Hookups:** None. **Each Site:** Picnic table, fire ring. **Dump Station:** Inquire at campground. **Laundry:** Inquire at campground. **Pay Phone:** Inquire at campground. **Rest Rooms and Showers:** Inquire at campground. **Fuel:** Inquire at campground. **Propane:** Inquire at campground. **Internal Roads:** Call ahead for details. **RV Service:** No. **Market:** 15 min. north in Whistler. **Restaurant:** 15 min. North in Whistler. **General Store:** No. **Vending:** No. **Swimming Pool:** No. **Playground:** No. **Other:** Hiking trails to Brandywine Falls and surrounding areas. **Activities:** Hiking. **Nearby Attractions:** Whistler and Squamish areas with lots of ecotourism, outdoor sport activities. **Additional Information:** Tourism Whistler, (800)-WHISTLER; www.tourism.whistler.com; Squamish Chamber of Commerce, (604) 892-9244; www.squamishchamber.bc.ca.

Restrictions

Pets: Leash only. **Fires:** Fire pits only. **Alcoholic Beverages:** At site. **Vehicle Maximum Length:** 38 ft. **Other:** Pitch tents only in designated pads. Max stay 14 days.

To Get There

Located about 15 minutes south of Whistler. If travelling north on Hwy. 99, entrance is on the right.

Supplemental Directory of Campgrounds

ALASKA

Anchor Point

Kyllonen's RV Park, 74160 Anchor Point Beach Rd., 99556. T: (907) 235-7762 or (907) 235-7451. F: (907) 235-6435. www.kyllonenrvpark.com. susank@xyz.net. RV/tent: 23. $24. Hookups: electric (30 amps), water, sewer.

Anchorage

Centennial Campground, 8300 Glenn Hwy., 99519. T: (907) 343-4474. RV/tent: 129. $13–$15. Hookups: none.

Electronic Solutions Midtown RV Park, 545 East Northern Lights, Suite C, 99503. T: (907) 277-2407. RV/tent: 42. $22. Hookups: electric (20 amps), water, sewer.

Golden Nugget Camper Park, 4100 Debarr, 99508. T: (907) 333-2012 or (800) 449-2012. F: (907) 333-1016. www.alaskan.com/camperpark. Gnugget@alaska.net. RV/tent: 215. $17–$27. Hookups: electric (20, 30, 50 amps), water, sewer.

Hillside on Gambell Motel & RV Park, 2150 Gambell St., 99503. T: (907) 258-6006 or (800) 478-6005. F: (907) 279-8972. www.hillside-alaska.com. info@hillside-alaska.com. RV/tent: 67. $20–$24. Hookups: electric (20, 30, 50 amps), water, sewer.

Auke Bay

Auke Bay RV Park, 11930 Glacier Hwy., 99821. T: (907) 789-9467. RV/tent: 40. $22. Hookups: electric (20, 30 amps), water, sewer.

Cantwell

Cantwell RV Park, Mile 209.9 Parks Hwy., 99729. T: (907) 768-2210 (summer) or (800) 940-2210. F: (907) 262-5149. www.alaskaone.com/cantwellrv. jodinepp@corecom.net. RV/tent: 82. $10–$21. Hookups: water, electric (20, 30 amps).

Cooper Landing

Cooper Creek Campground, Sterling Hwy. Mile 51, 99572. T: (800) 280-CAMP. www.reserveusa.com. RV/tent: 29. $15. Hookups: none.

Russian River Campground, Mile 53 Sterling Hwy., 99572. T: (800) 280-CAMP. www.reserveusa.com. RV/tent: 110. $13–$20. Hookups: none.

Sunrise Inn RV Park, P.O. Box 832, 99572. T: (907) 595-1222. RV/tent: 27. $18–$22. Hookups: electric (20, 30, 50 amps), water, sewer.

Copper Center

Kenny Lake Mercantile/RV Park, Mile 7.5 Edgerton Hwy., 99573. T: (907) 822-3313. www.alaskaoutdoors.com/KennyLake. knnylake@alaska.net. RV/tent: 19. $15–$18. Hookups: electric (20 amps).

Delta Junction

Smith's Green Acres, 2428 Richardson Hwy. Mile 268, 99737. T: (907) 895-4369 or (800) 895-4369. F: (907) 895-4110. www.greenacresrvpark.com. garvpark@wildak.net. RV/tent: 97. $13–$22. Hookups: electric (30 amps), water, sewer.

Fairbanks

Chena Hotsprings Resort, P.O. Box 58740, 99711. T: (907) 452-7867 or (800) 478-4681. F: (907) 456-3122. www.chenahotsprings.com. chenahs@polarnet.com. RV/tent: 80. $20. Hookups: none.

Chena Marina RV Park, 1145 Shypoke Dr., 99709. T: (907) 479-4653. F: (907) 479-0575. www.chenarvpark.com. chenarv@mosquitonet.com. RV/tent: 67. $15–$32. Hookups: electric (30 amps), water, sewer, cable, phone.

ALASKA (continued)

Fairbanks (continued)

Tanana Valley Campground, 1800 College Rd., 99709. T: (907) 456-7956 (summer) or (907) 452-3750 (winter). F: (907) 456-7971. www.tananavalleyfair.org/campground. tvcg@tananavalleyfair.org. RV/tent: 50. $8–$15. Hookups: electric (30 amps).

Girdwood

GIRDWOOD, Crow Creek Mine, 99587. T: (907) 278-8060. F: (907) 278-8061. www.crowcreekgoldmine.com. cynthia2@ptialaska.net. RV/tent: 15. $5. Hookups: none.

Glennallen

Tazlina River RV Park, Mile 110.2 Richardson Hwy., 99588. T: (907) 822-3546. radigan@alaska.net. RV/tent: 12. $7–$15. Hookups: electric (20 amps), water.

Haines

Haines Hitch-Up RV Park, 851 Main St., 99827. T: (907) 766-2882. F: (907) 766-2515. www.hitchuprv.com. hitchuprv@aol.com. RV/tent: 92. $22-plus. Hookups: electric (30, 50 amps), water, sewer, cable, phone.

Port Chilkoot Camper Park, P.O. Box 1589, 99827. T: (907) 766-2755 or (800) 542-6363. F: (907) 766-2445. www.haines.ak.us/halsingland. halsinglan@aol.com. RV/tent: 25. $14–$19. Hookups: electric (20, 30, 50 amps), water, sewer.

Salmon Run Campground & Cabins, Mile 6.5 Lutak Rd., 99827. T: (907) 766-3240. salmonrun@whitebear.com. RV/tent: 30. $14. Hookups: none.

Healy

Carlo Creek Lodge and Campground, Mile 223.9 Parks Hwy., 99743. T: (907) 683-2576 (summer) or (907) 683-2573 (winter). F: (907) 683-2573. www.alaskaone.com/carlocreek. carlocreek@hotmail.com. RV/tent: 25. $17-plus. Hookups: electric (20 amps).

McKinley RV and Campground, Mile 248.3 Parks Hwy., 99743. T: (907) 683-2379 or (800) 478-2562. F: (907) 683-2281. RV/tent: 100. $18–$27. Hookups: electric (20, 30 amps), water, sewer.

Homer

Driftwood Inn RV Park, 135 West Bunnell Ave., 99603. T: (907) 235-8019 or (800) 478-8019. www.thedriftwoodinn.com. driftinn@xyz.net. RV/tent: 27. $26–$29. Hookups: electric (20, 30, 50 amps), water, sewer, cable.

Hope

Henry's One Stop, Mile 15.5 Hope Hwy., 99605. T: (907) 782-3222. RV/tent: 12. $17. Hookups: electric (20 amps), water, sewer.

Hyder

Camp Run-A-Muck, 1001 Premier Ave., 99923. T: (250) 636-9006 or (888) 393-1199. F: (250) 636-9003. www.sealaskainn.com. sealaskainn@yahoo.com. RV/tent: 65. $8–$17. Hookups: electric (30 amps), water, sewer.

Juneau

Spruce Meadow RV Park, 10200 Mendenhall Loop Rd., 99801. T: (907) 789-1990. F: (907) 790-7231. www.juneaurv.com. juneaurv@aol.com. RV/tent: 69. $24-plus. Hookups: electric (30 amps), water, sewer, cable.

Kasilof

Crooked Creek RV Park, 111 Sterling Hwy., 99610. T: (907) 262-1299. RV/tent: 45. $15–$20. Hookups: electric (20, 30, 50 amps), water, sewer.

Ketchikan

Clover Pass Resort, P.O. Box 7322, 99901. T: (907) 247-2234 or (800) 410-2234. F: (907) 247-0793. www.cloverpassresort.com. info@cloverpassresort.com. RV/tent: 32. $26. Hookups: electric (30 amps), water, sewer, cable.

Moose Pass

Moose Pass RV Park, Mile 29 Seward Hwy., 99631. T: (907) 288-5624. www.moosepassrvpark.com. moosepassrvpark@yahoo.com. RV/tent: 31. $12–$17. Hookups: electric (30 amps).

Ptarmigan Creek, Mile 23 Seward Hwy., 99631. T: (800) 280-CAMP. www.reserveusa.com. RV/tent: 16. $10. Hookups: none.

Trail River Campground, Mile 24 Seward Hwy., 99631. T: (800) 280-CAMP. www.reserveusa.com. RV/tent: 65. $10. Hookups: none.

Ninilchik

Alaskan Angler RV Resort, P.O. Box 39388, 99639. T: (907) 567-3393 or (800) 347-4114. F: (907) 347-4114. www.afishunt.com. info@afishunt.com. RV/tent: 70. $10–$27. Hookups: electric (20, 30, 50 amps), water, sewer, cable, phone.

North Pole

Riverview RV Park, 1316 Badger Rd., 99707. T: (907) 488-6281 or (888) 488-6392. F: (907) 488-0555. www.alaskaone.com/riverview. dfickes@mosquitonet.com. RV/tent: 180. $16–$24.95. Hookups: electric (20, 30, 50 amps), water, sewer, cable.

Road's End RV Park, 1463 Westcott Ln., 99705. T: (907) 488-0295. www.roadsendrvpark.com. kentgaverett@hotmail.com. RV/tent: 73. $10–$20. Hookups: electric (20, 30, 50 amps), water, sewer.

Santaland RV Park, 125 St. Nicholas Dr., 99705. T: (907) 488-9123 or (888) 488-9123. F: (907) 488-7947. www.santalandrv.com. info@santalandrv.com. RV/tent: 94. $15–$25. Hookups: electric (20, 30, 50 amps), water, sewer, cable.

ALASKA (continued)

Palmer

Grandview Lodge & RV Park, Mile 109.75 Glenn Hwy., 99645. T: (907) 746-4480. www.grandviewrv.com. RV/tent: 19. $18–$21. Hookups: electric (30, 50 amps), water, sewer.

The Homestead RV Park, P.O. Box 354, 99645. T: (907) 745-6005. RV/tent: 64. $21. Hookups: electric (30 amps), water.

Petersburg

Twin Creek RV Park, Mile 7 Mitkof Hwy., 99833. T: (907) 772-3244. RV/tent: 22. $16–$21. Hookups: electric (30 amps), water, sewer, cable.

Prince Wales Island

Log Cabin Resort, P.O. Box 54, 99925. T: (907) 755-2205 or (800) 544-2205. F: (907) 755-2218. www.logcabinresortandrv.com. lcresak@aptalaska.net. RV/tent: 14. $7-plus. Hookups: electric (30 amps), water, sewer.

Seward

Miller's Landing Campground, P.O. Box 81, 99664. T: (907) 224-5739. F: (907) 224-5739. www.millerslandingak.com. miland@ptialaska.net. RV/tent: 53. $20-plus. Hookups: electric (25 amps).

Sitka

Sitka Sportsman's Association RV Park, P.O. Box 3030, 99835. T: (907) 747-6033. www.ptialaska.net/~ssport. ssport@ptialaska.net. RV/tent: 16. $14–$18. Hookups: electric (30 amps), water.

Skagway

Garden City RV Park, P.O. Box 228, 99840. T: (907) 983-2378. F: (907) 983-3378. www.gardencityrv.com. gcrv@aptalaska.net. RV/tent: 96. $24. Hookups: electric (30 amps), water, sewer, cable.

Skagway Mountainview RV Park, 12th and Broadway, 99840. T: (907) 983-3333 or (888) 778-7700. F: (907) 983-2224. www.alaskarv.com. alaskarv@aol.com. RV/tent: 147. $14–$23. Hookups: electric (20, 30, 50 amps), water, sewer.

Soldotna

Diamond M Ranch, B&B, Cabins and RV Park, Mile 16.5 Kalifornsky Beach Rd., 99669. T: (907) 283-9424. F: (907) 283-9330. www.diamondmranch.com. martin@diamondmranch.com. RV/tent: 33. $20. Hookups: electric (30, 50 amps), water, sewer, phone.

Kasilof RV Park, P.O. Box 1333, 99669. T: (907) 262-0418 or (800) 264-0418. www.kasilofrvpark.com. kasilofrv@ak.net. RV/tent: 39. $18-plus. Hookups: electric (30 amps), water, sewer.

River Terrace RV Park, 44761 Sterling Hwy. (Kenai River Bridge), 99669. T: (907) 262-5593. F: (907) 262-8873. RV/tent: 70. $20–$35. Hookups: electric (20, 30, 50 amps), water, sewer.

Talkeetna

Talkeetna River Adventures Campground, P.O. Box 473, 99676. T: (907) 733-2604. RV/tent: 40. $12. Hookups: none.

Tok

Bull Shooter RV Park, 1313 Alaska Hwy., 99780. T: (907) 883-5625. F: (907) 883-5620. www.tokalaska.com. bullshooter@tokalaska.com. RV/tent: 25. $18–$20. Hookups: electric (30 amps), water, sewer.

Sourdough Campground, Mile 122.8 Tok Cutoff Rd., 99780. T: (907) 883-5543 or (800) 789-5543. www.tokalaska.com. sourdough@tokalaska.com. RV/tent: 75. $16–$24. Hookups: electric (20, 30 amps), water, sewer.

Tok RV Village, Mile 1313.4 Alaska Hwy., 99780. T: (907) 883-5877. F: (907) 883-5878. RV/tent: 150. $22–$25. Hookups: electric (30, 50 amps), water, sewer.

Tundra RV Park, Mile 1315 Alaska Hwy., 99780. T: (907) 883-7875 (summer) or (907) 883-5885 (winter). F: (907) 883-7876. www.tokalaska.com. tundrarv@aptalaska.net. RV/tent: 78. $14–$20. Hookups: electric (20, 30, 50 amps), water, sewer.

Two Rivers

Pleasant Valley RV Park, 7435 Chena Hot Springs Rd., 99716. T: (907) 488-8198. F: (907) 488-8198. RV/tent: 16. $20. Hookups: electric (30 amps), water.

Valdez

Bear Paw Camper Park, 101 North Harbor Dr., 99686. T: (907) 835-2530. F: (907) 835-5266. www.alaska.net/~bpawcamp. bpawcamp@alaska.net. RV/tent: 140. $17–$25. Hookups: electric (30 amps), water, sewer, cable.

Eagle's Rest RV Park, 630 East Pioneer Dr., 99686. T: (800) 553-7275 or (907) 835-2373. F: (907) 835-5267. www.eaglesrestrv.com. rvpark@alaska.net. RV/tent: 390. $17–$26. Hookups: electric (20, 30, 50 amps), water, sewer, cable, phone.

Wasilla

Bestview RV Park, 7701 Parks Hwy., 99687. T: (907) 745-7400 or (800) 478-6600. F: (907) 745-3512. RV/tent: 61. $18–$21. Hookups: electric (30 amps), water, sewer.

Iceworm RV Park & Country Store, Mile 50.2 Parks Hwy., 99687. T: (907) 892-8200. F: (907) 892-8200. RV/tent: 24. $18. Hookups: electric (30, 50 amps), water, sewer, phone.

ALASKA (continued)

Willow

Pioneer Lodge, Inc., Mile 71.4 Parks Hwy., 99688. T: (907) 495-1000. RV/tent: 47. $20. Hookups: electric (30 amps), water, sewer.

Susitna Landing, Mile 82.5 Parks Hwy., 99688. T: (907) 495-7700. F: (907) 495-5000. www.ronsriverboat.com. info@ronsriverboat.com. RV/tent: 30. $10–$16. Hookups: electric (30 amps).

Wrangell

Wrangell RV Park, P.O. Box 531, 99929. T: (907) 874-2444. F: (907) 874-3186. parksrec@aptak.net. RV/tent: 26. $6–$10. Hookups: electric (30 amps).

IDAHO

American Falls

Indian Springs RV Campground, 3249 Indian Springs Rd., 83211. T: (208) 226-2174. indian@gemstate.net. RV/tent: 125. $16–$18. Hookups: electric (15, 20, 30 amps), water, sewer.

Massacre Rocks State Park, 3592 North Park Ln., 83211. T: (208) 548-2672. mas@id.state.id.us. RV/tent: 48. $12–$16. Hookups: electric (30, 50 amps), water, sewer.

Willow Bay Recreation Area, 550 North Oregon Trail, 83211. T: (208) 226-2688. F: (208) 226-2548. RV/tent: 26. $11–$18. Hookups: electric (30 amps), water, sewer.

Arco

Landing Zone RV Park, 2424 No. 3000 West, 83213. T: (877) 563-0663. www.geocities.com/landing zone_2000. lzrvpark@ida.net. RV/tent: 37. $13–$16. Hookups: electric (30 amps), water, sewer, modem.

Mountain View RV Park, P.O. Box 284, 83213. T: (800) 845-1460 or (208) 527-3707. mtview@atcnet.net. RV/tent: 40. $15–$17. Hookups: electric (20, 30 amps), water, sewer, modem.

Ashton

Jessen's RV Park, Box 11, 83420. T: (800) 747-3356 or (208) 652-3356. RV/tent: 55. $15–$17. Hookups: electric (30 amps), water, sewer, modem.

Boise

Americana RV Park, 3600 Americana Ter., 83706. T: (208) 344-5733. www.americanarvpark.com. ak83706@cyberHwy.net. RV/tent: 107. $18. Hookups: electric (30, 50 amps), water, sewer, modem.

Fiesta RV Park, 11101 Fairview Ave., 83713. T: (888) 784-3246 or (208) 375-8207. F: (208) 322-2499. fiestarv@earthlink.net. RV/tent: 109. $23–$29. Hookups: electric (20, 30 amps), water, sewer, modem.

Hi Valley RV Park, 10555 Horshoe Bend Rd., 83703. T: (888) 457-5959 or (208) 939-8080. www.idahoheartland.net. RV/tent: 194. $23. Hookups: electric (30, 50 amps), water, sewer, cable, phone.

On The River RV Park, 6000 North Glenwood, 83714. T: (800) 375-7432. otrrvpark@internetoutlet.net. RV/tent: 223. $15–$22. Hookups: electric (30, 50 amps), water, sewer, cable, modem.

Bonners Ferry

Blue Lake Camp & RV Park, HCR 61 Box 277, 83847. T: (208) 267-2029. RV/tent: 55. $17–$20. Hookups: electric (20, 30 amps), water, sewer.

Deep Creek Resort, Rte. 4 Box 628, 83805. T: (800) 689-2729 or (208) 267-2729. RV/tent: 52. $9–$13. Hookups: electric, water, sewer.

Idyl Acres RV Park, HCR 61 Box 170, 83805. T: (208) 267-3629. RV/tent: 10. $15. Hookups: electric (20, 30 amps), water, sewer.

Caldwell

Caldwell Campground, 218 Town Cir., 83606. T: (888) 675-0279 or (208) 454-0279. RV/tent: 125. $17–$20. Hookups: electric (30, 50 amps), water, sewer, cable, modem.

Country Corners Campground, 17671 Oasis Rd., 83607. T: (208) 453-8791. www.rverschoice.com/id/countrycornersrv.park. RV/tent: 69. $18. Hookups: electric (30, 50 amps), water, sewer, cable, modem.

Challis

Challis Hot Springs Campground, HC Box 1779, 83226. T: (208) 879-4442. RV/tent: 36. $20. Hookups: electric (30 amps), water, modem.

Challis Valley RV Park, Box 928, 83226. T: (208) 879-2393. RV/tent: 48. $20. Hookups: electric (30, 50 amps), water, sewer, cable.

Clark Fork

River Delta Resort, 60190 Hwy. 200, 83811. T: (208) 266-1335. RV/tent: 57. $18. Hookups: electric (30, 50 amps), water, sewer.

IDAHO (continued)

River Lake RV Park, 145 North River Lake Rd., 83811. T: (208) 266-1115. RV/tent: 25. $16. Hookups: electric (30 amps), water, sewer.

Clayton

Torrey's Burnt Creek Inn, HC 67 Box 725, 83227. T: (208) 836-2313. RV/tent: 27. $15. Hookups: electric (30, 50 amps), water, sewer.

Cocolalla

Sandy Beach Resort, 4405 Loop Rd., 83813. T: (208) 263-4328. F: (208) 263-3253. RV/tent: 90. $16–$20. Hookups: electric, water, sewer.

Coeur d'Alene

Bambi RV Park, 3113 North Government Way, 83815. T: (877) 381-5534 or (208) 664-6527. RV/tent: 21. $16. Hookups: electric, water, sewer.

Blackwell Island RV Park, 800 South Marina Dr., 83814. T: (888) 571-2900 or (208) 665-1300. F: (208) 667-5853. www.idahorvpark.com. rvpark@ior.com. RV/tent: 122. $21–$30. Hookups: electric (20, 30, 50 amps), water, sewer, cable, modem.

River Walk RV Park, 1214 Mill Ave., 83814. T: (888) 567-8700 or (208) 765-6538. riverparkrvpark @yahoo.com. RV/tent: 42. $22–$26. Hookups: electric (30, 50 amps), water, sewer, cable, modem.

Robin Hood Campground & RV Park, 703 Lincoln Way, 83814. T: (208) 664-2306. RV/tent: 80. $19–$20. Hookups: electric (20, 30, 50 amps).

Shady Acres RV Park, 3630 North Government Way, 83814. T: (877) 212-0523 or (206) 664-3087. www.angelfire.com/id2/shadyacresrv. shadyacres rv@yahoo.com. RV/tent: 30. $17. Hookups: electric, water, sewer.

Squaw Bay Camping Resort, P.O. Box 174, 83816. T: (208) 664-6782. F: (208) 664-6728. RV/tent: 50. $15–$28. Hookups: electric, water, sewer, cable, modem.

Wolf Lodge Campground, 12425 East Interstate 90, 83814. T: (208) 664-2812. RV/tent: 100. $13–$23. Hookups: electric, water, sewer, cable, modem.

Declo

Travel Stop 216 RV Park, Exit 216 Interstate 84, 83323. T: (208) 654-2133. F: (208) 887-3525. www.travelstop216.com. manager@travel stop216.com. RV/tent: 165. $25. Hookups: electric (30, 50 amps), water, sewer, cable.

Donnelly

Chalet RV Resort, P.O. Box 100, 83615. T: (888) 457-5959 or (208) 325-8223. RV/tent: 76. $19. Hookups: electric (30 amps), water, sewer.

Mountain View RV Park, P.O. Box 488, 83615. T: (208) 325-8373. RV/tent: 40. $15-plus. Hookups: electric, water, sewer.

Southwestern Idaho Senior Citizens Recreation Association, P.O. Box 625, 83615. T: (208) 325-9518. RV/tent: 175. $3–$5. Hookups: electric, water, sewer.

Downey

Downata Hot Springs, 25900 Downata Rd., 83234. T: (208) 897-5736. F: (208) 897-5072. www.downatahotsprings.com. downata@poky.srv.net. RV/tent: 90. $16. Hookups: electric (20, 30 amps), water, modem.

Eden

Anderson Best Holiday Trav-L-Park, 1188 East 990 South, 83325. T: (888) 480-9400 or (208) 825-9800. F: (208) 825-9715. andercamo@cyber Hwy.net. RV/tent: 155. $19–$24. Hookups: electric (30, 50 amps), water, sewer, modem.

Fruitland

Neet Retreat RV Park, 2701 Alder Space, 83619. T: (800) 433-7806 or (208) 452-4324. RV/tent: 80. $20. Hookups: electric (30, 50 amps), water, sewer, cable, modem.

Glenns Ferry

Trails West RV Park, 510 North Bannock Ave., 83623. T: (208) 366-2002. RV/tent: 52. $10–$15. Hookups: electric, water, sewer, cable.

Grangeville

Mountain View RV Park, 127 Cunningham St. No. 4, 83530. T: (208) 983-2328. RV/tent: 75. $15. Hookups: electric (15, 30, 50 amps), water, sewer.

Hagerman

Hagerman RV Village, P.O. Box 297, 83332. T: (208) 837-4906 or (208) 837-4412. F: (208) 837-4551. RV/tent: 54. $17. Hookups: electric (30, 50 amps), water, sewer, modem.

Harvard

Pines RV Park & Campground, 4510 Hwy. 6, 83834. T: (208) 875-0831. RV/tent: 17. $12. Hookups: electric (15, 30 amps).

Hayden Lake

Coeur D'Alene North/Hayden Lake KOA, 4850 East Garwood Rd., 83825. T: (800) KOA-0250 or (208) 772-4557. RV/tent: 66. $16–$20. Hookups: electric (30 amps), water, sewer, modem.

Heise

Heise Hot Springs, 5116 Heise Rd. East, 83443. T: (208) 538-7312. www.srv.net/~heise/heise.html. heise@srv.net. RV/tent: 50. $15–$20. Hookups: electric, water, sewer.

IDAHO (continued)

Homedale

Snake River RV Resort, Rte. 1 Box 1062, 83628. T: (208) 337-3744. rvresort@cyberHwy.net. RV/tent: 52. $20. Hookups: electric (30, 50 amps), water, sewer, modem.

Hope

Beyond Hope Resort, 248 Beyond Hope, 83836. T: (877) 270-HOPE or (208) 264-5251. www.beyondhoperesort.com. bhresort@aol.com. RV/tent: 91. $24–$26. Hookups: electric (30, 50 amps), water, sewer, cable, modem.

Idaho Country Resort, 141 Idaho Country Rd., 83836. T: (800) (307) 3050 or (208) 264-5505. www.keokee.com/edahoresorts. RV/tent: 90. $15–$31. Hookups: electric (30 amps), water, sewer, cable.

Sam Owen Campground, Idaho Panhandle National Forest, 83836. T: 877-444-6777 or (208) 264-0209. www.reserveusa.com. claudia@americanll.com. RV/tent: 80. $12. Hookups: none.

Idaho Falls

Idaho Falls KOA, 1440 Lindsey Blvd., 83402. T: (800) 562-7644 or (208) 523-3362. RV/tent: 183. $24–$30. Hookups: electric (30 amps), water, sewer, modem.

Sunnyside Acres Park, 905 West Sunnyside Rd., 83401. T: (208) 523-8403. RV/tent: 25. $20. Hookups: electric (30, 50 amps), water, sewer.

Island Park

Aspen Lodge, HC 66 Box 269, 83429. T: (208) 558-7406. RV/tent: 8. $39. Hookups: electric, water, sewer.

Big Springs (Caribou National Forest), Big Springs Loop Rd., 83429. T: (208) 558-7301. RV/tent: 29. $7–$16. Hookups: none.

Red Rock RV & Camping Park, HC 66 Box 256, 83429. T: (800) 473-3762 or (208) 558-7442. www.8004redrock.com/.reservations@8004redrock.com. RV/tent: 52. $14–$16. Hookups: electric (20, 30 amps), water, sewer, modem.

Snowy River Campground, 3502 North Hwy. 20, 83429. T: (208) 558-7112 or (888) 797-3434. marleen@ida.net. RV/tent: 57. $15–$16. Hookups: electric (20, 30 amps), water, sewer, modem.

Valley View General Store & RV Park, HC 66 Box 26, 83429. T: (208) 558-7443. RV/tent: 53. $10–$20. Hookups: electric, water, sewer.

Jerome

Twin Falls/Jerone KOA, 5431 US 93, 83338. T: (800) 562-4169 or (208) 324-4169. RV/tent: 91. $24–$25. Hookups: electric (30, 50 amps), water, sewer, satelite, modem.

Kamiah

Lewis-Clark Resort, Rte. 1 Box 17X, 83536. T: (208) 935-2556. www.tenting-hostels.com/tvc. lcresort@camasnet.com. RV/tent: 190. $18. Hookups: electric (30 amps), water, sewer, modem.

Ketchum

Sun Valley RV Resort, P.O. Box 548, 83340. T: (208) 726-3429. RV/tent: 80. $19–$27. Hookups: electric, water, sewer, cable, modem.

The Meadows RV Park, P.O. Box 1440, 83353. T: (208) 726-5445. RV/tent: 45. $18. Hookups: electric (30 amps), water, sewer, cable.

Kooskia

Harpster Riverside RV Park, HC 66 Box 337, 83539. T: (800) 983-1918. RV/tent: 29. $18. Hookups: electric (30, 50 amps), water, sewer, satelite, modem.

River Junction RV Park, P.O. Box 413, 83539. T: (208) 926-7865. RV/tent: 29. $6–$14. Hookups: electric, water, sewer.

Lava Hot Springs

Cottonwood Family Campground, Box 307, 83246. T: (208) 776-5295. RV/tent: 116. $24–$27. Hookups: electric (20, 30 amps), water, sewer.

Lucille

Prospector's Gold RV & Campground, P.O. Box 313, 83542. T: (208) 628-3773. RV/tent: 24. $15. Hookups: electric (30, 50 amps), water, modem.

McCall

Lakeview Village RV Park, 8 Pearl St., 83638. T: (208) 634-5280. RV/tent: 84. $12–$16. Hookups: electric (30 amps), water, sewer.

McCall Campground, 190 Krahn Ln., 83638. T: (208) 634-5165. RV/tent: 36. $14–$16. Hookups: electric, water, sewer.

Melba

Given's Hot Springs, HC 79 Box 103, 83641. T: (800) 874-6046 or (208) 495-2000. F: (208) 286-0925. RV/tent: 18. $8–$13. Hookups: electric, water, sewer.

Meridian

The Playground RV Park, 1780 East Overland Rd., 83642. T: (800) 668-PLAY or (208) 887-1022. play groundrv@juno.com. RV/tent: 72. $20. Hookups: electric (30 amps), water, sewer, satellite, modem.

Montpelier

Emigration (Caribou National Forest), 322 North 4th, 83254. T: (877) 444-6777 or (208) 847-0375. RV/tent: 23. $8–$16. Hookups: none.

IDAHO (continued)

Montpelier Canyon (Caribou National Forest), 322 North 4th, 83254. T: (877) 444-6777 or (208) 847-0375. RV/tent: 14. $4. Hookups: none.

Scout Mountain (Caribou National Forest/Pocatello), 322 North 4th, 83254. T: (877) 444-6777 or (208) 236-7500. RV/tent: 32. $6–$18. Hookups: none.

Summit View (Caribou National Forest/Intermountain), 322 North 4th, 83254. T: (877) 444-6777 or (208) 847-0375. RV/tent: 19. $8. Hookups: none.

Willow Flat (Caribou National Forest/Preston), 322 North 4th, 83254. T: (877) 444-6777 or (208) 847-0375. RV/tent: 47. $4–$20. Hookups: none.

Moyle Springs

Herman Lake Campground, HCR 62 Box 246, 83845. T: (208) 267-1205. RV/tent: 10. $10–$25. Hookups: electric, water, sewer.

Twin Rivers Canyon Resort, HCR 62 Box 25, 83845. T: (208) 267-5932. RV/tent: 65. $13–$19. Hookups: electric, water, sewer.

Nampa

Garrity RV Park, 3515 Garrity Blvd., 83687. T: (877) 442-9090 or (208) 442-9000. F: (208) 442-1617. RV/tent: 98. $18–$20. Hookups: electric (30, 50 amps), water, sewer, cable, phone.

Mason Creek RV Park, 807 Franklin Blvd., 83687. T: (208) 465-7199. RV/tent: 88. $14–$19. Hookups: electric (30, 50 amps), water, sewer, cable, modem.

New Meadows

Meadows RV Park, P.O. Box 60, 83654. T: (208) 347-2325 or (800) 603-2325. RV/tent: 37. $17. Hookups: electric (30 amps), water, sewer, modem.

Zim's Hot Springs, P.O. Box 314, 83654. T: (208) 347-2686. RV/tent: 62. $10–$16. Hookups: electric (30 amps), water.

Nordman

Kaniksu Resort, HCO 1 Box 152, 83848. T: (208) 443-2121. F: (208) 443-3864. kaniksu@nidlink.com. RV/tent: 111. $18–$24. Hookups: electric (30, 50 amps), water, sewer.

North Fork

Wagonhammer Springs Campground, P.O. Box 173, 83466. T: (208) 865-2477. RV/tent: 28. $15–$17. Hookups: electric (20, 30 amps), water, sewer.

Obsidian

Sessions Lodge, HC 64 Box 9696, 83340. T: (208) 774-3366. RV/tent: 13. $12. Hookups: electric (30 amps), water, sewer.

Orofino

Freeman Creek Campground (Dworshak SP), P.O. Box 2028, 83544. T: (208) 476-5994. RV/tent: 108. $12–$16. Hookups: electric (20, 30 amps), water.

Osburn

Blue Anchor Trailer & RV Park, P.O. Box 645, 83849. T: (208) 752-3443. RV/tent: 38. $14–$20. Hookups: electric (30, 50 amps), water, sewer, cable.

Paris

Bear Lake State Park, P.O. Box 297, 83261. T: (208) 847-1045. F: (208) 847-1056. BEA@idpr.state.id/us. RV/tent: 100. 8–$16. Hookups: none.

Pinehurst

KOA Kellogg/Silver Valley Kampground, P.O. Box 949, 83850. T: (800) 562-0799. F: (208) 682-9464. kelloggkoa@aol.com. RV/tent: 57. $20–$29. Hookups: electric (20, 30, 50 amps), water, sewer, cable, modem.

Pocatello

Cowboy RV Park, 845 Barton Rd., 83204. T: (208) 232-4587. F: (208) 232-6731. RV/tent: 41. $22. Hookups: electric (30, 50 amps), water, sewer, cable, modem.

Post Falls

Suntree RV Park, 401 Idahine, 83854. T: (208) 773-9982. suntree@micron.net. RV/tent: 81. $23. Hookups: electric (30 amps), water, sewer, modem.

Priest Lake

Priest Lake RV Resort & Marina, HCR 5 Box 172, 83856. T: (208) 443-2405. F: (208) 443-2299. RV/tent: 16. $10–$13. Hookups: electric, water, sewer.

Priest River

Luby Bay (Idaho Panhandle National Forest), 5538 West Lakeshore Rd., 83856. T: (800) 280-2267 or (208) 443-1801. www.reserveusa.com. RV/tent: 50. $12. Hookups: none.

Rexburg

Rainbow Lake & Campground, 2245 South 2000 West, 83440. T: (208) 356-3681. RV/tent: 85. $15–$17. Hookups: electric (30 amps), water, sewer, modem.

Sheffield RV Park, 5362 South Hwy. 191, 83440. T: (208) 356-4182. sheffieldbb@msn.com. RV/tent: 27. $18. Hookups: electric (30, 50 amps), water, sewer, modem.

Ririe

7N Ranch, 5156 East Heise Rd., 83443. T: (208) 538-5097. RV/tent: 50. $12–$17. Hookups: electric (20, 30, 50 amps), water.

Mountain River Ranch RV Park, 98 North 5050 East, 83443. T: (208) 538-7337. RV/tent: 39. $17. Hookups: electric (30 amps), water.

Rogerson

Desert Hot Springs, General Delivery, 83302. T: (208) 857-2233. RV/tent: 12. $10–$15. Hookups: electric, water, sewer.

IDAHO (continued)

Sagle

Alpine Trailer Park, P.O. Box 585, 83860. T: (208) 265-0179. RV/tent: 15. $15. Hookups: electric, water, sewer.

Salmon

Century II Campground, 603 Hwy. 93 North, 83467. T: (208) 756-3063. RV/tent: 76. $17. Hookups: electric (30, 50 amps), water, sewer.

Heald's Haven, HC 61 Box 15, 83467. T: (208) 756-3929. RV/tent: 34. $12–$15. Hookups: electric (20, 30 amps), water.

Salmon Meadows

Salmon Meadows Campground, Rte. 1 Box 25AB, 83467. T: (888) 723-2640 or (208) 756-2640. F: (208) 756-3771. smeadows@ida.net. RV/tent: 71. $20. Hookups: electric (30, 50 amps), water, sewer, modem.

Sandpoint

Travel America Plaza, P.O. Box 199, 83860. T: (208) 263-6522. RV/tent: 79. $14–$15. Hookups: electric (20, 30, 50 amps), water, sewer, modem.

Spirit Lake

Silver Beach Resort, 8350 West Spirit Lake Rd., 83869. T: (208) 623-4842. www.silverbeach-resort.com. info@silver-beach-resort.com. RV/tent: 40. $17–$20. Hookups: electric, water, sewer.

St. Anthony

Riverside Campground (Targhee National Forest), P.O. Box 208, 83445. T: (208) 652-7442. RV/tent: 63. $8–$10. Hookups: none.

St. Charles

Bear Lake North RV Park & Campgrounds, P.O. Box 60, 83201. T: (208) 945-2941. brite_83272@yahoo.com. RV/tent: 66. $18. Hookups: electric (20, 30 amps), water.

Cedars & Shade Campground, P.O. Box 219, 83272. T: (208) 945-2608. RV/tent: 100. $8–$12. Hookups: none.

Twin Falls

Nat-Soo-Pah Hot Springs, 3738 East 2400 North, 83301. T: (208) 655-4337. RV/tent: 75. $12. Hookups: electric (30 amps), water.

Oregon Trail Campground & Family Fun Center, 2733 Kimberly Rd., 83301. T: (800) 733-0853 or (208) 733-0853. RV/tent: 50. $15. Hookups: electric, water, sewer.

Victor

Teton Valley Campground, 128 Hwy. 31 or P.O. Box 49, 83455. T: (877) 787-3036 or (208) 787-2647. F: (208) 787-3036. www.tenting-hostels.com/tve. tvcampground@pdt.net. RV/tent: 70. $20–$31. Hookups: electric (20, 30, 50 amps), water, sewer, modem.

Wallace

Down by the Depot RV Park, 108 Nine Mile Rd., 83873. T: (208) 753-7121. RV/tent: 43. $20–$22. Hookups: electric (30 amps), water, sewer, cable.

Weiser

Gateway RV Park, 229 East 7th St., 83672. T: (208) 549-2539. RV/tent: 24. $14–$18. Hookups: electric (20, 30 amps), water, sewer, cable.

Monroe Creek Campground & RV Park, 822 US Hwy. 95, 83672. T: (208) 549-2026. mccrvpark@rurainetwork.net. RV/tent: 66. $18. Hookups: electric (30 amps), water, modem.

Wendell

Intermountain RV Park, 1894 North Frontage Rd., 83355. T: (208) 536-2301. mike@idahorv.com. RV/tent: 55. $12. Hookups: electric (20, 30 amps), water, modem.

Wilder

Rivers Edge RV Park, 28522 Lower Pleasant Rd., 83676. T: (208) 482-6560. www.riversedgervpark.com. riverrv@riversedgervpark.com. RV/tent: 24. $13. Hookups: electric (30, 50 amps), water, sewer.

IOWA

Allerton

Bobwhite State Park, RR1 P.O. Box 124 A, 50008. T: (641) 873-4670. RV/tent: 32. $9–$14. Hookups: electric.

Amana

Amana Colonies RV Park, P.O. Box 400, 52203. T: (319) 622-7616. RV/tent: 144. $10–$18. Hookups: full.

Anita

Lake Anita State Park, RR1, 50020. T: (712) 762-3564. RV/tent: 144. $6–$14. Hookups: full.

Arnolds Park

City Park, P.O. Box 437, 51331. T: (712) 762-3564. RV/tent: 52. $9–$14. Hookups: electric.

IOWA (continued)

Auburn

Grants Park (Sac County Park), 3531 365th St., 51433. T: (712) 662-4530. RV/tent: 30. $9–$14. Hookups: electric, water.

Augusta

Lower Skunk River Access (Des Moines County Park), 512 North Main St., Burlington, 52601. T: (319) 753-8260. RV/tent: 47. $9–$14. Hookups: electric.

Avoca

Parkway Campground, 857 South Chestnut St., 51521. T: (712) 343-6652. RV/tent: 50. $15–$21. Hookups: full.

Bedford

Lake of Three Fires State Park, 2303 State Hwy. 49, 50833. T: (712) 523-2700. RV/tent: 140. $9–$14. Hookups: full.

Bellevue

Bellevue State Park, 21466 429th Ave., 52031. T: (563) 872-4019. RV/tent: 48. $9–$14. Hookups: electric, water.

Pleasant Creek, 11995 US Hwy. 52, 52031. T: (563) 872-5782. RV/tent: 60. $13–$17. Hookups: none.

Spruce Creek (Jackson County Park), Jackson County Courthouse, 52060. T: (563) 872-3621. RV/tent: 86. $9–$14. Hookups: electric (30 amps).

Blairstown

Hannen Park (Benton County Park), RR1 Box 37 B1, Vinton, 52349. T: (563) 454-6382. RV/tent: 55. $9–$14. Hookups: electric.

Bloomfield

Lakeside Village Campground, Rte. 3 Box 39, 52537. T: (647) 664-3364. RV/tent: 180. $10–$15. Hookups: full.

Boone

Ledges State Park, 1519 250th St., Madrid, 50126. T: (515) 432-1852. RV/tent: 94. $9–$14. Hookups: electric.

Brighton

Lake Darling State Park, 110 Lake Darling Rd., 52540. T: (319) 694-2323. RV/tent: 118. $9–$14. Hookups: electric.

Clermont

Skip-A-Way RV Park and Campground, Box 324, 52135. T: (800) 728-1167. RV/tent: 156. $13–$17. Hookups: electric (20, 30, 50 amps), water.

Colo

Twin Anchors RV Park, 68132 US Hwy. 30, 50023. T: (641) 372-2243. RV/tent: 210. $13–$20. Hookups: electric (30, 50 amps), water.

Council Bluffs

Bluffs Run RV Park, 2701 23rd Ave., 51501. T: (800) 238-2946. RV/tent: 123. $17–$20. Hookups: electric (20, 30, 50 amps), water.

Tomes Country Club Acres, 706 South Omaha Bridge Rd., 51501. T: (712) 366-0363. RV/tent: 25. $19. Hookups: electric (15, 20, 30 amps).

Crescent

Honey Creek Campground, 28120 145th St., 51526. T: (712) 545-9400. RV/tent: 66. $16–$18. Hookups: electric (20, 30, 50 amps), water.

Decorah

Chimney Rock Canoe Rental and Campground, 3312 Chimney Rock Rd., 52136. T: (319) 735-5786. RV/tent: 28. $10–$15. Hookups: electric (20 amps).

Des Moines

Timberline Best Holiday Trav-L-Park Campground, 3165 Ashworth Rd., 50263. T: (515) 987-1714. RV/tent: 100. $16–$22. Hookups: full.

Dubuque

Dubuque Yacht Basin and RV Park, 1630 East 16th, 52001. T: (319) 556-7708. RV/tent: 56. $21–$24. Hookups: full.

Forest City

Three Fingers Campground, 14300 355th St., 50436. T: (641) 581-5856. RV/tent: 75. $12. Hookups: electric, water.

Fort Madison

Hilltop Campground, 2182 US Hwy. 61, 52627. T: (319) 372-4227. RV/tent: 17. $10–$14. Hookups: electric (20, 30, 50 amps).

Garnavillo

J-Wood Campground, 31848 Clayton Rd., 52046. T: (319) 964-2236. RV/tent: 97. $15. Hookups: electric, water.

Paradise Valley, 19745 Keystone Rd. Unit 4, 52049. T: (319) 873-9632. RV/tent: 210. $11–$14. Hookups: electric (30 amps), water.

Harlan

Nielson RV Park, 1244 F32, 51537. T: (712) 627-4640. RV/tent: 17. $10–$15. Hookups: electric (20, 30 amps).

Kalona

Windmill Ridge Campground, P.O. Box 772, 52247. T: (319) 656-4488. RV/tent: 70. $8–$10. Hookups: electric (15, 30, 50 amps).

Kellogg

Lake Pla-Mor, 12725 Killdeer Ave., 50135. T: (641) 526-3169. RV/tent: 84. $7–$11. Hookups: electric (20, 30 amps), water.

IOWA (continued)

Keokuk

Hickory Haven Campground, 2413 353rd St., 52632. T: (800) 890-8469. RV/tent: 45. $13. Hookups: electric (20, 30, 50 amps), water.

Lansing

Red Barn Resort, 2609 Main St., 52151. T: (319) 538-4956. RV/tent: 117. $12–$20. Hookups: electric (20, 30, 50 amps), water.

Little Sioux

Woodland Campground, 1449 Benton Ln., 51545. T: (712) 649-2594. RV/tent: 27. $15. Hookups: electric (30 amps), water.

Marshalltown

Shady Oaks Camping, 2370 Shady Oaks Rd., 50138. T: (641) 752-2946. RV/tent: 22. $16. Hookups: electric (20, 30, 50 amps).

McCregor

Spook Cave and Campground, 13899 Spook Cave Rd., 52157. T: (319) 873-2114. RV/tent: 73. $10–$15. Hookups: electric (15, 20, 30, 50 amps), water.

Monticello

Walnut Acres, P.O. Box 624, 52310. T: (319) 465-4665. RV/tent: 255. $13–$20. Hookups: electric (20, 30 amps), water.

Mount Pleasant

J & J Camping, 105 North J & J Ln., 52641. T: (319) 986-6398. RV/tent: 100. $17. Hookups: electric, water.

Nashua

River Ranch Camping, 2575 Cheyenne Ave., 50658. T: (641) 435-2108. RV/tent: 111. $9–$14. Hookups: electric, water.

Newton

Rolling Acres RV Park and Campground, 1601 East 36th St. South, 50208. T: (641) 792-2428. RV/tent: 82. $17–$19. Hookups: electric (20, 30 , 50 amps), water.

North Liberty

Colony County Campground, 1275 Forevergreen Rd., Iowa City, 52240. T: (319) 626-2221. RV/tent: 45. $15–$22. Hookups: electric (20, 30 amps), water.

Jolly Roger Campground and Harper's Marina, 1858 Scales Bend Rd., 52317. T: (319) 626-2171. RV/tent: 190. $12–$20. Hookups: electric (15, 20, 30, 50 amps), water.

Onawa

Interchange RV Park, Box 324, 51040. T: (712) 423-1387. RV/tent: 28. $13–$16. Hookups: electric (20, 30, 50 amps), water.

Oxford

Sleepy Hollow RV Park and Campground, 3340 Black Hawk Ave., 52322. T: (319) 828-4400. RV/tent: 143. $14–$20. Hookups: electric (30, 50 amps), water.

MONTANA

Arlee

Jocko Hollow, Old Hwy. 93, 59821. T: (406) 726-3336. F: (406) 726-3334. RV/tent: 16. $15. Hookups: electric (20 amps).

Augusta

Lewis & Clark National Forest (Benchmark Campground), P.O. Box 869, 59403. T: (406) 466-5341. RV/tent: 25. $6. Hookups: none.

Basin

Merry Widow Health Mine Campground & Motel, Box 129, 59631. T: (406) 225-3220. RV/tent: 55. $6–$10. Hookups: electric (30 amps).

Big Sky

Gallatin/Red Cliff, US Hwy. 191, 59718. T: (406) 522-2520. RV/tent: 68. $9–$13. Hookups: electric, water.

Greek Creek/Deerlodge National Forest, US Rte. 191 North, 59718. T: (877) 444-6777. RV/tent: 14. $9. Hookups: none.

Big Timber

Spring Creek Campground and Trout Ranch, P.O. Box 1435, 59011. T: (406) 932-4387. RV/tent: 25. $15–$26. Hookups: full.

Bigfork

Outback Montana, 27202 East Lakeshore, 59911. T: (888) 900-6973 or (406) 837-6973. outback@cyberport.net. RV/tent: 50. $11–$16. Hookups: electric (20, 30, 50 amps), water, sewer.

Timbers RV Park & Campground, 8550 Hwy. 35 South, 59911. T: (800) 821-4546. RV/tent: 35. $18. Hookups: electric (20, 30, 50 amps), water, modem.

MONTANA (continued)

Billings

Big Sky Campground, 5516 Laurel Rd., 59101. T: (406) 259-4110. RV/tent: 54. $18–$23. Hookups: electric (30, 50 amps), water, sewer.

Bozeman

Bear Canyon Campground, 4000 Bozeman Trail Rd., 59715. T: (800) 438-1575 or (406) 587-1575. F: (406) 556-8133. www.bearcanyoncamp ground.com/. bearcc@gomontana.com. RV/tent: 130. $15–$22. Hookups: electric (30, 50 amps), water.

Sunrise Campground, 31842 Frontage Rd., 59715. T: (877) 437-2095. RV/tent: 70. $15–$19. Hookups: electric (20, 30, 50 amps), water, sewer, phone.

Broadus

Wayside Park, Box 568, 59317. T: (406) 436-2510. RV/tent: 21. $8–$12. Hookups: electric (20, 30, 50 amps), water.

White Buffalo Campground, P.O. Box 387, 59317. T: (406) 436-2595. RV/tent: 17. $12. Hookups: electric, water, sewer.

Browning

Chewing Black Bones Resort & Campground, P.O. Box 2809, 59417. T: (406) 732-9263. F: (406) 338-7206. RV/tent: 127. $12–$16. Hookups: electric, water, sewer, cable, phone.

Sleeping Wolf Campground, Box 607, 59417. T: (406) 338-7933. RV/tent: 21. $13–$18. Hookups: electric (20, 30, 50 amps), water.

Butte

2 Bar Lazy H RV Park, 122015 West Browns Gulch Rd., 59701. T: (406) 782-5464. RV/tent: 24. $18–$20. Hookups: electric (30, 50 amps), phone.

Choteau

Choteau KOA, 85 MT Hwy. 221, 59422. T: (800) 562-4156. F: (406) 466-5635. RV/tent: 55. $16–$22. Hookups: full.

Clancy

Alhambra RV Park, Hwy. 282 South No. 515, 59634. T: (406) 933-8020-. RV/tent: 38. $10–$16. Hookups: electric (20, 30 amps), water.

Clinton

Beaver Hill State Park, 3201 Spurgin Rd., 59804. T: (406) 542-5500. RV/tent: 28. $12. Hookups: none.

Elkhorn RV Ranch, 408 Rock Creek Rd., 59825. T: (406) 825-3220. www.montana.com/elkhorn. c/n3224@montana.com. RV/tent: 90. $20–$25. Hookups: electric (20, 30 amps), water, sewer, modem.

Columbia Falls

Glacer Mountain Shadows Resort, 7285 Hwy. 2 East, 59912. T: (406) 892-7686. RV/tent: 28. $16–$20. Hookups: electric (20, 30 amps), water, sewer, cable.

Glacier Peaks Campground, P.O. Box 492, 59912. T: (800) 268-4849. RV/tent: 76. $8–$19. Hookups: electric (30, 50 amps), water, cable, phone.

Dillon

Red Mountain Campgrounds, 1005 Selway Dr., 59725. T: (406) 683-2337. www.blm/for/state. RV/tent: 14. $5. Hookups: electric, water.

Sky-line RV Park Campground, 3525 North US Hwy. 91, 59725. T: (406) 683-4692. RV/tent: 34. $15. Hookups: electric (30 amps), water, sewer, cable.

Drummond

Good Time Camping & RV Park, 239 Frontage Rd. West, 59832. T: (406) 288-3608. RV/tent: 16. $15. Hookups: electric (20, 30, 50 amps), water, phone.

East Glacier Park

Firebrand Campground, P.O. Box 146, 59434. T: (406) 226-5573. RV/tent: 30. $10–$15. Hookups: electric (20, 30 amps).

Glacier/Two Medicine, P.O. Box 128, 59936. T: (406) 888-7800. RV/tent: 99. $14. Hookups: none.

Three Forks Campground, P.O. Box 124, 59434. T: (406) 226-4479. RV/tent: 42. $13–$16. Hookups: electric (20, 39 amps), water, sewer, modem.

Y Lazy R Camper Trailer Park, P.O. Box 146, 59434. T: (406) 226-5573. RV/tent: 41. $10–$15. Hookups: electric (20, 30 amps), water.

Gardiner

Rocky Mountain Campground, 14 Jardine Rd., 59030. T: (406) 848-7251. bertgini@earthlink.net. RV/tent: 87. $20–$26. Hookups: electric (30 amps), water, sewer, modem.

Georgetown

Georgetown Lake Lodge, 2015 Dentons Point Rd., 59711. T: (406) 563-6030. RV/tent: 63. $20–$25. Hookups: electric (30, 50 amps) water, sewer, modem.

Glasgow

Trails West Campground, Rte. 1-4404, 59230. T: (406) 228-2778. hrc@nemontel.net. RV/tent: 66. $13–$19. Hookups: electric (30, 50 amps), water, sewer, modem.

Glendive

Green Valley Campground, P.O. Box 1396, 59330. T: (406) 377-1944. RV/tent: 87. $13–$16. Hookups: electric (20, 30, 50 amps), water.

MONTANA (continued)

Great Falls

Dick's RV Park, 1403 11th St. South, 59404. T: (406) 452-0333. F: (406) 727-7340. RV/tent: 148. $22. Hookups: electric (30, 50 amps), water, sewer, modem.

Hamilton

Angler's Roost Campground, 815 US Hwy. 93 South, 59840. T: (406) 363-1268. RV/tent: 70. $19–$21. Hookups: full.

Bitterroot Family Campground, 1744 Hwy. 93 South, 59840. T: (800) 453-2430. RV/tent: 52. $10–$16. Hookups: electric (15, 20, 30 amps), water.

Lick Creek Campground, 2251 US Hwy. 93 South, 59840. T: (406) 821-3840. RV/tent: 54. $13–$15. Hookups: electric (20 amps), water, sewer.

Hardin

Grandview Campground, 1002 North Mitchell Ave., 59034. T: (406) 622-9890. www.grandviewcamp.com. grandviewcamp@mcn.net. RV/tent: 50. $13–$20. Hookups: electric (30, 50 amps), water, sewer, cable, modem.

Harlowton

Chief Joseph Park, Box 292, 59036. T: (406) 632-5523. RV/tent: 23. $3–$8. Hookups: electric (20, 30 amps).

Havre

Havre Family Campground, HC Box 200, 59501. T: (406) 265-9722. havrefamilycampground@hotmail.com. RV/tent: 108. $14–$18. Hookups: electric (30 amps), water, sewer.

Helena

Hauser Lake SRA/Black Sandy, 930 Custer Ave., 59620. T: (406) 444-4720. www.fwp.state.mt.us/. RV/tent: 33. $12. Hookups: electric, water.

Hungry Horse

Flathead/Lid Creek, Ranger District, Box 190340, 59919. T: (406) 387-5243. RV/tent: 22. $7. Hookups: electric, water.

Joliet

Cooney Reservoir State Park, P.O. Box 253, 59041. T: (406) 247-2940. www.fwp.state.mt.us/. RV/tent: 75. $7. Hookups: none.

Kalispell

Glacier Pines RV Park, 1850 Hwy. 35 East, 59901. T: (800) 533-4029 or (406) 752-2760. RV/tent: 160. $20–$22. Hookups: electric (20, 30 amps), modem.

Greenwood Village Campgrounds, 1100 East Oregon St., 59901. T: (406) 257-7719. RV/tent: 38. $11–$18. Hookups: electric (20, 30, 50 amps), phone.

Rocky Mountain HI Campground, 825 Helena Flats Rd., 59901. T: (800) 968-5637 or (406) 755-9573. F: (406) 755-8816. kalispell.bigsky.net/rmhc/. rmhc@bigsky.net. RV/tent: 102. $15–$20. Hookups: electric (20, 30 amps), water, TV, phone.

Spruce Park Campground, 1985 Hwy. 35, 59901. T: (888) 752-6321 or (406) 752-6321. F: (406) 756-0480. sprucepk@digisys.net. RV/tent: 160. $13–$18. Hookups: electric (15, 30, 50 amps), water, sewer, cable, phone.

Laurel

Clark's Riverfront Campground & Resort, 3001 Thiel Rd., 59044. T: (406) 628-2984. prk@imt.net. RV/tent: 33. $15. Hookups: electric.

Pelican's RV Campground, 3444 South Frontage Rd., 59044. T: (406) 628-4324. RV/tent: 54. $16. Hookups: electric (30, 50 amps), water, sewer.

Lewiston

Mountain Acres Campground, 103 Rocklyn Ave., 59457. T: (406) 538-7591. RV/tent: 36. $20. Hookups: electric (20, 30 amps), water, sewer.

Libby

Two Bit Outfit RV Park, 716 Hwy. 2 West, 59923. T: (406) 293-8323. www.twobitcamping.com. TwoBit@libby.org. RV/tent: 40. $12–$20. Hookups: electric.

Libby Mountain

Sportsman's RV Park, 11741 Hwy. 37, 59923. T: (406) 293-2267. RV/tent: 22. $16–$20. Hookups: full.

Livingston

Livingston Campground, 11 Rogers Ln., 59047. T: (406) 222-1122. livingstoncampground@hotmail.com. RV/tent: 42. $18–$26. Hookups: electric (20, 50 amps), water, sewer, cable.

Osen's Campground, 20 Merrill Ln., 59047. T: (406) 222-0591. RV/tent: 55. $18–$24. Hookups: electric (20, 30, 50 amps), water, sewer, cable+M60.

Rock Canyon Campground, 5070 US Hwy. 89 South, 59047. T: (406) 222-1096. RV/tent: 39. $17–$20. Hookups: electric (30 amps), water, sewer.

Lolo

Lolo Hot Springs RV Park & Campground, 38500 Hwy. 12 West, 59847. T: (406) 273-2294. www.lolohotsprings.net/. RV/tent: 116. $13–$19. Hookups: electric (20, 30 amps), water.

Square & Round Dance Center & RV Park, 9955 Hwy. 12 West, 59847. T: (406) 273-0141. missoula.bigsky.net/sqrdance. sqrdance@bigsky.net. RV/tent: 71. $12–$19. Hookups: electric (20, 30 amps), water, sewer, cable, modem.

MONTANA (continued)

Marion

Moose Crossing, 8405 Hwy. 2 West, 59925. T: (406) 854-2070. RV/tent: 22. $22. Hookups: electric, water, phone.

Miles City

Big Sky Camp & RV Park, RR 1 Hwy. 12, 59301. T: (406) 232-1511. RV/tent: 74. $11–$12. Hookups: electric (30 amps), water.

Missoula

Jim & Mary's RV Park, 9800 US Hwy. 93 North, 59802. T: (406) 549-4416. jimandmary@montana.com. RV/tent: 45. $19–$21. Hookups: electric (30, 50 amps), water, sewer, modem.

Outpost Campground, 11600 US Hwy. 93 North, 59802. T: (406) 549-2016. RV/tent: 65. $15–$16. Hookups: electric (20, 30 amps), water, sewer.

Yogi Bear's Jellystone Park, 10955 Hwy. 93 North, 59802. T: (406) 543- 9400 or (800) 318-9644. F: (406) 543-9400. www.campjellystonemt.com. RV/tent: 110. $21–$26. Hookups: electric (20, 30, 50 amps), water, sewer, phone.

Noxon

Cabinet Gorge RV Park & Campground, 30 Blue Jay Ln., 59853. T: (406) 847-2294. gardensock@blackfoot.netq. RV/tent: 26. $16. Hookups: electric (30, 50 amps), water, sewer, modem.

Philipsburg

Deerlodge/Piney Campground, Phillipsburg Ranger District H, 59851. T: (406) 859-3211. RV/tent: 47. $10. Hookups: none.

Polson

Flathead River Resort, P.O. Box 940, 59860. T: (406) 883-6400. RV/tent: 36. $24. Hookups: electric (20, 30, 50 amps), phone.

Paradise Pines Resort, 6913 East Shore Rte., 59860. T: (406) 887-2537. RV/tent: 87. $12–$18. Hookups: electric (20, 30 amps), water ,modem.

Red Lodge

Perry's RV Park & Campground, HC 49 Box 3586, 59068. T: (406) 446-2722. RV/tent: 40. $18. Hookups: electric (20 amps), water.

Rexford

Mariners Haven Campground, 101 Mariners Dr., 59930. T: (406) 296-3252. RV/tent: 65. $13–$20. Hookups: electric (20, 30 amps), water, sewer.

Ronan

Mission Meadows, 298 Mission Meadows Dr., 59364. T: (406) 676-5182. RV/tent: 42. $13–$18. Hookups: electric (20, 30 amps), water.

Pipestone Campground, 41 Bluebird Ln., 59759. T: (406) 287-5224. RV/tent: 75. $18–$22. Hookups: electric (20, 30, 50 amps), phone.

Shelby

Lake Shel-oole Campground, City of Shelby Box 743, 59474. T: (406) 434-5222. F: (406) 434-2143. RV/tent: 56. $12. Hookups: electric (30 amps), water.

Silver Star

Jefferson River Camp, 5162 State Hwy. 41, 59751. T: (406) 684-5225. RV/tent: 14. $15. Hookups: electric (20, 30 amps), water, phone.

St. Ignatius

St. Ignatius Campground & Hostel, 33076 Hwy. 93, 59865. T: (406) 745-3959. F: (406) 745-0024. campground@stignatius.net. RV/tent: 14. $16–$25. Hookups: electric (30 amps), water, sewer.

Sula

Lost Trail Hot Springs Resort, 8321 Hwy. 93 South, 59871. T: (800) 825-3574. RV/tent: 20. $20. Hookups: electric (20, 30 amps), phone.

Moosehead Campground, 6457 Hwy. 93 South, 59827. T: (406) 821-3327. RV/tent: 91. $20. Hookups: electric (20 amps), water, sewer.

Terry

Terry's RV Oasis, 510 Jane St., 59349. T: (406) 637-5520. RV/tent: 18. $12–$18. Hookups: electric (30, 50 amps), water, sewer, cable.

Thompson Falls

The Riverfront, P.O. Box 22, 59873. T: (406) 827-3460. RV/tent: 11. $19. Hookups: electric (20, 30, 50 amps), phone.

Three Forks

Fort Three Forks RV Park & Motel, 10776 Hwy. 287, 59752. T: (800) 477-5690 or (406) 285-3233. www.fortthreeforks.com. info@fortthreeforks.com. RV/tent: 12. $18. Hookups: electric (30, 50 amps) water, sewer.

Townsend

Roadrunner RV Park, 704 Nort Front Rd., 59644. T: (406) 266-9900. RV/tent: 25. $14. Hookups: electric (30, 50 amps), water, sewer.

Silos RV Park & Fishing Camp, 81 Silos Rd., 59644. T: (406) 266-3100. RV/tent: 41. $9–$14. Hookups: electric (30 amps), water, sewer.

Troy

Kootenai River Campground, 2898 Hwy. 2 North, 59935. T: (406) 295-4090. RV/tent: 48. $15–$18. Hookups: electric (20, 30 amps), water.

Valier

Lake Francis City Park Campground, P.O. Box 512, 59486. T: (406) 279-3361. RV/tent: 32. $8. Hookups: electric.

MONTANA (continued)

Virginia City

Virginia City Campground & RV Park, P.O. 188, 59755. T: (888) 833-5493. vccamp@3rivers.net. RV/tent: 17. $16–$32. Hookups: electric (30 amps), water, sewer.

West Glacier

San-Suz-Ed Trailer Park & Campground, P.O. Box 387, 59936. T: (800) 305-4616. www.san-suz-edrvpark.com. RV/tent: 68. $20–$22. Hookups: electric (30, 50 amps), water, phone.

Sundance RV Park & Campground, P.O. Box 130037, 59913. T: (406) 387-5016. RV/tent: 64. $16. Hookups: electric (20, 30 amps), water.

West Yellowstone

Gallatin/Beaver Creek, P.O. Box 520, 59758. T: (406) 646-7369. RV/tent: 65. $10. Hookups: none.

Hideaway RV Park, 310 Electric, 59758. T: (406) 646-9049. www.wyellowstone.com/hideaway. joe@hideawayrv.com. RV/tent: 17. $15–$25. Hookups: electric (20, 50 amps), water, sewer, cable.

Rustic Wagon RV, Campground & Cabins, 634 Hwy. 20 & Gibbon Ave., 59758. T: (406) 646-7387. www.wyellowstone.com/rusticwagon. rusticwagon@wyellowstone.com. RV/tent: 52. $20–$32. Hookups: electric (20, 30, 50 amps), water.

Wagon Wheel RV Campground & Cabins, 408 Gibbon Ave., 59758. T: (406) 646-7872. www.wyellowstone.com. wagonwheel@wyellowstone.com. RV/tent: 51. $28–$32. Hookups: electric (20, 30 amps), water, sewer, cable, modem.

Yellowstone Holiday RV Campground & Marina, P.O. Box 759, 59758. T: (877) 646-4242 or (406) 646-4242. F: (406) 646-4242. yhr@wyellowstone.com. RV/tent: 60. $15–$28. Hookups: electric (20, 30, 50 amps), water, sewer, modem.

White Sulpher Springs

Conestoga Campground, Box 508, 59645. T: (406) 547-3890 or (800) 548-2289. RV/tent: 77. $10–$17. Hookups: electric (20, 30, 50 amps), water.

Wolf Point

Rainbow Campground, P.O. Box C26456, 59201. T: (406) 525-3740. RV/tent: 9. $12–$18. Hookups: electric, water.

Rancho Campground, Hwy. 2, 59201. T: (406) 653-1382. RV/tent: 19. $16. Hookups: electric (30 amps), water, sewer.

NEBRASKA

Alliance

J&C RV Park, 2491 South US Hwy. 385, 69301. T: (308) 762-3860. RV/tent: 13. $20. Hookups: none.

Anselmo

Victoria Springs State Recreation Area, HC 69 P.O. Box 117, 68813. T: (308) 749-2235. RV/tent: 75. $8–$11. Hookups: electric.

Bellevue

Haworth Park, 210 West Misson Ave., 68005. T: (402) 293-3098. RV/tent: 129. $10. Hookups: electric, water.

Big Springs

McGreer Camper Park, Rte. 2 Box 96, 69122. T: (308) 889-3605. RV/tent: 40. $12–$16. Hookups: electric, water.

Bridgeport

Golden Acres Motel and RV Park, Rte. 1 Box 196, 69336. T: (308) 262-0410. RV/tent: 18. $14–$16. Hookups: electric, water.

Broken Bow

Wagon Wheel Motel and Campground, 1545 South "E" St., 68822. T: (308) 872-2433. RV/tent: 10. $11. Hookups: electric.

Brule

Riverside Park, 1000 South State St., 69127. T: (308) 287-2474. RV/tent: 38. $13–$17. Hookups: electric.

Burwell

Calamus Reservoir State Recreation Area, HC 79 P.O. Box 20-C, 68823. T: (308) 346-5666. RV/tent: 177. $4–$13. Hookups: electric.

Chadron

J&L RV Park, J&L No. 13, 69337. T: (308) 432-4349. RV/tent: 58. $12. Hookups: none.

Chappell

Creekside RV Park and Campground, P.O. Box 238, 69129. T: (308) 874-camp. RV/tent: 55. $18. Hookups: none.

NEBRASKA (continued)

Elm Creek

Sunny Meadows Campground, 234 East Front St., 68836. T: (308) 856-4792. RV/tent: 30. $12. Hookups: none.

Gibbon

Windmill State Recreation Area, 2625 Lowell Rd., 68840. T: (308) 468-5700. RV/tent: 89. $9–$13. Hookups: electric.

Grand Island

Grand Island KOA, 904 South B Rd., Doniphan, 68832. T: (402) 886-2249. RV/tent: 71. $17–$22. Hookups: none.

Gretna

West Omaha KOA, 14601 Hwy. 6, 68028. T: (402) 332-3010. RV/tent: 86. $18–$28. Hookups: electric, water.

Halsey

NA National Forest, P.O. Box 38, 69142. T: (308) 533-2257. RV/tent: 33. $8–$11. Hookups: none.

Harrison

Corral Campground, P.O. Box 115, 69346. T: (308) 668-2441. RV/tent: 12. $12. Hookups: none.

Hastings

Hastings Campground, 302 East 26th, 68901. T: (402) 462-5621. RV/tent: 63. $16–$21. Hookups: full.

Hemingford

Box Butte Reservoir State Recreation Area, P.O. Box 392, Crawford, 69339. T: (308) 665-2903. RV/tent: 50. $9–$17. Hookups: electric.

Kearrey

Claude and Vi's Campground, P.O. Box 834, 68848. T: (308) 234-1532. RV/tent: 110. $15–$20. Hookups: electric, water.

Kimball

KOA-Kimball, Rte. 1 Box 128 D, 69145. T: (308) 235-4404. RV/tent: 45. $17–$24. Hookups: electric, water.

Maxwell

Fort McPherson Campground, 12568 Valley View Rd., 69151. T: (308) 582-4320. RV/tent: 79. $14–$20. Hookups: electric.

Minden

Pioneer Village Motel and Campground, Harold Wrap Memorial Dr., 68959. T: (800) 445-4447. RV/tent: 165. $12–$23. Hookups: electric, water.

Nebraska City

Victorian Acres RV Park and Campground, 6591 Hwy. 2, 68410. T: (402) 873-6860. RV/tent: 70. $10–$15. Hookups: electric, water.

North Plate

A-1 Sunset RV Park, 3120 Rodeo Rd., 69101. T: (308) 532-9180. RV/tent: 24. $16. Hookups: none.

Holiday Park, 601 Hullingan Dr., 69101. T: (800) 424-4531. RV/tent: 98. $16–$22. Hookups: none.

The Rockin' DH Campground, 3800 Hadley Dr., 69101. T: (877) 994-2267. RV/tent: 57. $20. Hookups: electric, water.

Ogallala

Area's Finest Meyer Camper Court, 120 Rd. East 80, 69153. T: (308) 284-2415. RV/tent: 112. $12–$21. Hookups: none.

Corral Campground and RV Park, 221 Rd. East 85, 69153. T: (308) 284-4327. RV/tent: 68. $15–$17. Hookups: none.

Van's Lakeview Fishing Camp, No. 1 Lakeview, Brule, 69127. T: (308) 284-4965. RV/tent: 122. $17–$20. Hookups: electric, water.

Paxton

Ole's Lodge and RV Park, 851 Paxton-Elsie Rd., 69155. T: (308) 239-4510. RV/tent: 12. $10–$15. Hookups: full.

Schuyler

Schuyler Campground, 1103 B St., 68661. T: (402) 352-2057. RV/tent: 30. $5. Hookups: electric.

Shubert

Indian Cave State Park, RR 2 Box 30, 68437. T: (402) 883-2575. RV/tent: 274. $8–$13. Hookups: electric.

Sidney

Bear Family RV Park, 919 Greenwood, 69162. T: (308) 254-6000. RV/tent: 44. $17. Hookups: none.

Cabela's RV Park, 1 Anglers Ln., 69162. T: (308) 254-7177. RV/tent: 37. $25. Hookups: full.

South Sioux

Scenic Park, 1615 1st Ave., 68776. T: (402) 494-7531. RV/tent: 53. $10–$17. Hookups: full.

Sutherland

Oregon Trail Trading Post and Campground, Rte. 1 Box 606, 69165. T: (308) 386-4653. RV/tent: 30. $8. Hookups: electric.

Valentine

River of Life Camp, HC 37 Box 3, 96201. T: (402) 376-2958. RV/tent: 37. $15–$25. Hookups: electric, water.

Valentine Motel and RV Park, P.O. Box A, 69201. T: (800) 376-2450. RV/tent: 36. $20. Hookups: none.

NEBRASKA (continued)

Valentine (continued)

Wacky West Travel Park, 224 North Wood St., 69201. T: (402) 376-1771. RV/tent: 22. $17. Hookups: electric, water.

York

Double Nickel Campground and County Store, 907 Rd. South, 68460. T: (402) 728-5558. RV/tent: 110. $15–$23. Hookups: electric, water.

NORTH DAKOTA

Arvilla

Turtle River State Park, 3084 Park Ave., 58214. T: (701) 594-4445. F: (701) 594-2556. trsp@state.nd.us. RV/tent: 125. $5–$12. Hookups: electric (20, 30, 50 amps), water.

Beulah

Dakota Waters Resort, P.O. Box 576, 58523. T: (800) 473-5803. RV/tent: 45. $8–$12. Hookups: electric (30 amps).

Bismarck

Bismark KOA, 3720 Centennial Rd., 58501. T: (701) 575-4261. bismkoa@aol.com. RV/tent: 128. $18–$25. Hookups: electric (30, 50 amps), water, sewer, modem.

General Sibley RV Park, 5001 South Washington St., 58504. T: (701) 222-1844. RV/tent: 19. $15. Hookups: electric (20, 30 amps), water, sewer.

Hill Crest Acres Campground, 5700 East Main Ave., 58501. T: (701) 255-4334. RV/tent: 57. $14. Hookups: electric (30, 50 amps), water, sewer.

Bowman

Twin Butte Campground & Antiques, Box 983, 58623. T: (701) 523-5569. RV/tent: 26. $12. Hookups: electric (20, 30 amps).

Cavalier

Icelandic State Park, 13571 Hwy. 5, 58220. T: (800) 807-4723 or (701) 265-4561. isp@state.nd.us. RV/tent: 167. $7–$12. Hookups: electric (20, 30, 50 amps), water.

Church's Ferry

Wild Goose RV Park, HCR 1 Box 10, 58325. T: (701) 466-2324. RV/tent: 15. $10–$12. Hookups: electric (20, 30 amps).

Devils Lake

Graham's Island State Recreation Area, 152 South Duncan Dr., 58301. T: (800) 807-4723 or (701) 766-4015. www.state.nd.us/ndparks/Parks/DLSP.htm. dlsp@state.nd.us. RV/tent: 55. $3. Hookups: electric (30 amps), water.

Dickinson

Camp on the Heart, P.O. Box 1074, 58602. T: (701) 225-9600. camp@campontheheart.com. RV/tent: 18. $18–$26. Hookups: electric (20, 30, 50 amps), water, sewer, cable, modem.

Dunseith

International Peace Garden Campground, Rte. 1 Box 116, 58367. T: (701) 263-4390. RV/tent: 4. $9–$14. Hookups: electric (20 amps), water.

Eckelson

Praire Haven Family Campground, 10121 36th St. East, 58481. T: (701) 646-2267. prairhvn@ictc.com. RV/tent: 51. $20. Hookups: electric (20, 30, 50 amps), water, sewer, modem.

Grafton

Leistikow Park Campground, P.O. Box 122, 58237. T: (701) 352-1842. RV/tent: 38. $9–$12. Hookups: electric (30, 50 amps), water, sewer.

Grand Forks

Grand Forks Campground & RV Park, Rte. 1 Box 227, 58201. T: (701) 772-6108. RV/tent: 149. $19. Hookups: electric (20, 30, 50 amps), water, sewer, modem.

Hillsboro

Hillsboro Campground & RV Park, 203 6th St. Southwest, 58045. T: (888) 430-5205 or (701) 436-5205. www.gocampingamerica.com/hillsborocampground. hillsborocampground@gocampingamerica.com. RV/tent: 35. $15. Hookups: electric (20, 30 amps), water, sewer, modem.

Jamestown

Frontier Fort Campground, P.O. Box 143, 58401. T: (701) 252-7492. RV/tent: 71. $16. Hookups: electric (30, 50 amps), water, sewer.

Jamestown Dam/Lakeside Marina, 3225 East Lakeside Rd., 58401. T: (701) 252-9200. RV/tent: 48. $9–$14. Hookups: electric (20, 30 amps), water.

Jamestown KOA, 3605 80th Ave. North, 58401. T: (701) 752-6262. ahc@pocketmail.com. RV/tent: 68. $18–$27. Hookups: electric (30, 50 amps), water, sewer, modem.

NORTH DAKOTA (continued)

Lamoure

Lamoure County Memorial Park, P.O. Box 128, 58458. T: (701) 683-5856. RV/tent: 9. $8. Hookups: electric (15, 20 amps).

Linton

Sunrise Mobile Home Park & RV Camp, 146 Sunrise Ln., 58552. T: (701) 254-4439. RV/tent: 13. $8. Hookups: electric (30 amps).

Mandan

Colonial Campground, 4631 Memorial Hwy., 58554. T: (701) 663-9824 or (800) 377-9824. RV/tent: 42. $15. Hookups: electric (30, 50 amps).

Fort Abraham Lincoln State Park, 4480 Fort Lincoln Rd., 58554. T: (800) 807-4723 or (701) 663-9571. falsp@state.nd.us. RV/tent: 95. $11–$16. Hookups: electric (30 amps).

Medora

Medora Campground, P.O. Box 198, 58645. T: (800) 633-6721 or (701) 623-4444. RV/tent: 185. $22. Hookups: electric (20, 30, 50 amps), water, sewer, modem.

Red Trail Campground, Box 367 G, 58645. T: (800) 621-4317 or (701) 623-4317. F: (701) 623-4833. RV/tent: 98. $14–$26. Hookups: electric (20, 30, 50 amps), water, sewer, cable, modem.

Theodore Roosevelt/Cottonwood Campground, Watford City, 58854. T: (701) 842-2333 or (701) 623-4466. www.usparks.com/US_National_Parks/theodore/theodore_north_unit.shtml. RV/tent: 5. $10. Hookups: none.

Menoken

A Prairie Breeze RV Park, 2810 158th St. Northeast, 58558. T: (701) 224-8215. rafarm@btigate.com. RV/tent: 41. $12. Hookups: electric (30, 50 amps), water, sewer.

Minot

Casa Motel & Campground, 1900 Hwy. 2 & 52 West, 58701. T: (701) 852-2352. RV/tent: 15. $18. Hookups: electric (30 amps), water, sewer.

Minot KOA, 5261 Hwy. 52 South, 58701. T: (701) 839-7400. RV/tent: 74. $16–$20. Hookups: electric (30 amps), water, sewer, modem.

Pat's Motel & Campground, 2025 27th St. Southeast, 58701. T: (701) 838-5800. RV/tent: 45. $10–$16. Hookups: electric (30 amps), water, sewer.

Roughrider Campground, 500 54th St. West, 58703. T: (701) 852-8442. F: (701) 852-9482. www.minot.com/~roughrid. roughrid@minot.com. RV/tent: 94. $15–$21. Hookups: electric (30 amps), water, sewer, modem.

Ray

Red Mike's RV Park, Hwy. 1840, 58849. T: (701) 568-2600. www.redmike.com/. redmike@nccray.com. RV/tent: 13. $19. Hookups: electric (30, 50 amps), water, sewer.

Ross

Dakota West RV Park & General Store, P.O. Box 36, 58776. T: (701) 755-3407. RV/tent: 21. $10–$15. Hookups: electric (20, 30, 50 amps).

Steele

OK Motel & Campground, 301 3rd Ave. Northeast, 58482. T: (701) 475-2440. RV/tent: 17. $11. Hookups: electric (30, 50 amps).

Warwick

East Bay Campground, 3892 East Bay Rd., 58381. T: (701) 398-5184 or (701) 740-8368. www.eastbaycampground.com. woodfarm@stellarnet.com. RV/tent: 16. $14. Hookups: electric (20, 30 amps), water, sewer.

Williston

Buffalo Trails Campground, 6700 2nd Ave. West, 58801. T: (701) 572-3206. RV/tent: 149. $13–$19. Hookups: electric (20, 30, 50 amps), water, sewer, modem.

Prairie Acres RV Park, 13853 US Hwy. 2, 58801. T: (701) 572-4860. RV/tent: 37. $12. Hookups: electric (30, 50 amps), water, sewer.

OREGON

Agness

Agness RV Park, 04125 Agness Rd., 97406. T: (541) 247-2813. camping@agnessrv.com. RV/tent: 90. $17. Hookups: electric (30 amps), water.

Albany

Blue Ox RV Park, 4000 Blue Ox Dr. Southeast, 97321. T: (800) 336-2881. RV/tent: 149. $24. Hookups: full.

Ashland

Ashland Regency Inn and RV Park, 50 Lowe Rd., 97520. T: (800) 482-4701. RV/tent: 12. $17–$18. Hookups: electric (20, 30 amps), water.

Howard Prarie Lake Resort, P.O. Box 4709, Medford, 97501. T: (541) 482-1979. RV/tent: 268. $12–$19. Hookups: electric (20 amps), water, dump station.

OREGON (continued)

Ashland (continued)

Hyatt Lake Resort, 7979 Hyatt Prarie Rd., 97520. T: (541) 482-3331. RV/tent: 80. $20–$23. Hookups: electric (20, 30, 50 amps), water, dump station.

Astoria

Fort Stevens State Park, US 30, 97121. T: (503) 861-1671. park.info@state.or.us. RV/tent: 518. $18–$29. Hookups: full.

Baker City

Mountain View Holiday Trav-L-Park, 2845 Hughes Ln, 97814. T: (541) 523-4824. www.ohwy.com/or/m/mtviewrv.htm. RV/tent: 91. $21. Hookups: electric (20, 30, 50 amps).

Oregon Trails West RV Park, 42534 North Cedar Rd., 97814. T: (888) 523-3236. RV/tent: 61. $17. Hookups: full.

Wallowa-Whitman National Forest-Union Creek Campground, P.O. Box 907, 97814. T: (541) 894-2260. RV/tent: 58. $14–$19. Hookups: electric (20, 30 amps).

Bandon

Bandon-Port Orford-KOA, 46612 Hwy. 101, Langlois, 97450. T: (800) 562-3298. RV/tent: 72. $24–$26. Hookups: electric (20, 30 amps), water.

Bullards Beach State Park, Hwy. 101 North, 97411. T: (541) 347-2209. park.info@state.or.us. RV/tent: 185. $19. Hookups: full.

Beaver

Camper Cove, P.O. Box 42, 97108. T: (503) 398-5334. RV/tent: 18. $15–$18. Hookups: electric (20, 30, 50 amps), water.

Belknap Springs

Belknap Lodge and Hot Springs, Box No. 1, McKenzie Bridge, 97413. T: (541) 822-3512. RV/tent: 52. $12–$18. Hookups: electric (30), water.

Bend

Crane Prarie Campground (Deschutes National Forest), FR 4270, 97701. T: (541) 382-9443. RV/tent: 146. $13–$19. Hookups: none.

Crane Prarie Resort, Crane Prarie Lake Rd., 97701. T: (541) 383-3939. RV/tent: 39. $22. Hookups: full.

Crown Villa RV Park, 60801 Brosterhaus Rd., 97702. T: (541) 388-1131. RV/tent: 131. $17–$31. Hookups: full.

Curtis Lake Campground (Deschutes National Forest), FR 4635, 97701. T: (541) 382-9443. RV/tent: 55. $13–$19. Hookups: none.

Gull Point Campground (Deschutes National Forest), FR 4262, 97701. T: (541) 382-9443. RV/tent: 81. $13–$19. Hookups: none.

Lava Lake Campground (Deschutes National Forest), FR 514, 97701. T: (541) 382-9443. RV/tent: 45. $13–$19. Hookups: none.

Quinn River Campground (Deschutes National Forest), Hwy. 46, 97701. T: (541) 382-9443. RV/tent: 41. $13–$19. Hookups: none.

Rock Creek Campground (Deschutes National Forest), Hwy. 46, 97701. T: (541) 382-9443. RV/tent: 32. $13–$19. Hookups: none.

Scandia RV and Mobile Park, 61415 South Hwy. 97, 97702. T: (541) 382-6206. RV/tent: 75. $20. Hookups: full.

South Twin Lake Recreation Complex (Deschutes National Forest), FR 4260, 97701. T: (541) 382-9443. RV/tent: 45. $13–$19. Hookups: none.

Boardman

Driftwood RV Park, 800 West Kunze, 97818. T: (800) 684-5583. RV/tent: 123. $22–$28. Hookups: electric (20, 30, 50 amps).

Bonanza

Gerber Reservoir Campground, 2795 Anderson Ave., Klamath Falls, 97603. T: (541) 883-6916. RV/tent: 50. $13–$20. Hookups: none.

Brookings

Port of Brookings Harbor Beachfront RV Park, P.O. Box 848, 97415. T: (541) 469-5867. RV/tent: 147. $14–$27. Hookups: electric (30 amps), water.

At Rivers Edge RV Resort, 98203 South Bank Chetco, 97415. T: (888) 295-1441. RV/tent: 121. $20–$25. Hookups: electric (20, 30, 50 amps).

Portside RV Park, 16219 Lower Harbor Rd., 97415. T: (887) 787-2752. portsiderv@wave.net. RV/tent: 104. $16–$28. Hookups: full.

Whaleshead Beach Resort, 19921 Whaleshead Rd., 97415. T: (800) 943-4325. RV/tent: 110. $20–$25. Hookups: electric (30, 50 amps).

Canby

Riverside RV Park, 24310 Hwy. 99 East, 97013. T: (800) 425-2250. bj06990080@aol.com. RV/tent: 118. $22. Hookups: full.

Canyonville

Seven Feathers Casino Resort, 146 Chief Miwaleta Ln., 97417. T: (541) 839-1111. www.sevenfeathers.com. info@sevenfeathers.com. RV/tent: 32. $14–$16. Hookups: electric (20, 30 amps).

Stanton Park (Douglas County Park), P.O. Box 800, 97495. T: (541) 839-4483. RV/tent: 40. $11–$14. Hookups: none.

Cascade Summit

Shelter Cove Resort, West Odell Lake Rd., Hwy. 58, 97425. T: (800) 647-2729. RV/tent: 69. $12–$19. Hookups: electric (20, 30 amps).

Cave Junction

Country Hills, 7901 Caves Hwy., 97523. T: (541) 592-3406. RV/tent: 28. $17–$18. Hookups: electric (15, 20, 30 amps), water.

OREGON (continued)

Grayback US Forest and Campground, 11575 Caves Hwy., 97523. T: (541) 592-3311. RV/tent: 34. $15. Hookups: none.

Shady Acres RV Park, 27550 Redwood Hwy., 97523. T: (541) 592-3702. RV/tent: 30. $15. Hookups: electric (20, 30 amps).

Charleston

Sunset Bay State Park, 10965 Cape Arago Hwy., 97420. T: (541) 888-4902. RV/tent: 131. $15–$27. Hookups: electric, water.

Chiloquin

Agency Lake Resort, 37000 Modoc Point Rd., 97642. T: (541) 783-2489. RV/tent: 25. $16. Hookups: electric (20, 30 amps), water.

Melita's Highway 97 RV Park, 39500 Hwy. 97, 97624. T: (541) 783-2401. RV/tent: 27. $16. Hookups: electric (30 amps), water.

Walt's Cozy Camp, P.O. Box 243, 97624. T: (541) 783-2537. RV/tent: 34. $14. Hookups: electric (20 amps), water.

Water Wheel Campground, 200 Williamson River Dr., 97624. T: (541) 783-2738. RV/tent: 40. $15–$21. Hookups: electric (30, 50 amps), water.

Coos Bay

Alder Acres, 1800 28th Ct., 97420. T: (541) 269-0999. RV/tent: 33. $19. Hookups: electric (30, 50 amps).

Oregon Dunes KOA, 4135 Coast US Hwy.101, North Bend, 97459. T: (541) 756-4851. www.oregondunesKOA.com. RV/tent: 66. $26–$31. Hookups: electric (30, 50 amps), water.

Cottage Grove

Village Green RV Park, 725 Row River Rd., 97424. T: (541) 942-2491. RV/tent: 42. $24. Hookups: electric (20, 30, 50 amps).

Crater Lake

Mazama Campground, 1211 Ave. C., White City, 97503. T: (541) 594-2511. RV/tent: 196. $14. Hookups: none.

Crescent

Big Pines RV Park, 135151 Hwy. 97 North, 97733. T: (800) 351-2785. Bgpnsrvprk@aol.com. RV/tent: 21. $20. Hookups: full.

Williamette Pass Inn and RV, P.O. Box 35, 97425. T: (541) 443-2211. RV/tent: 19. $20. Hookups: electric (20, 30, 50 amps), water.

Dale

Meadowbrook Lodge Inc., P.O. Box 37, 97880. T: (541) 421-3104. RV/tent: 31. $18–$23. Hookups: electric (20 amps).

Depoe Bay

Fogarty Creek RV Park, 3340 North Hwy. 101, 97341. T: (888) 675-7034. RV/tent: 53. $17–$25. Hookups: electric (20, 30 amps).

Sea and Sand RV Park, US Hwy. 101, 97388. T: (541) 764-2313. RV/tent: 109. $21–$24. Hookups: full.

Detroit

Detroit Lake State Park, 711 North Santiam Hwy., 97342. T: (503) 854-3346. RV/tent: 238. $14–$22. Hookups: full.

Detroit RV Park, 100 Breinbenbush Rd., 97342. T: (503) 855-3002. RV/tent: 17. $17–$22. Hookups: full.

Dexter

Dexter Shores Mobile and RV Park, 39140 Dexter Rd., 97431. T: (541) 937-3711. RV/tent: 56. $24. Hookups: full.

Diamond Lake

Diamond Lake RV Park, 3500 Diamond Lake Loop, 97731. T: (541) 793-3318. F: (541) 793-3088. www.diamondlakervpark.com. RV/tent: 115. $22. Hookups: full.

Dodson

Ainsworth State Park, P.O. Box 100, 97019. T: (503) 695-2301. RV/tent: 50. $14–$19. Hookups: full.

Dufur

Dufur RV Park, P.O. Box 192, 97021. T: (541) 467-2449. RV/tent: 26. $14. Hookups: electric (20, 30 amps).

Elkton

Elkton RV Park, 450 River Dr., 97436. T: (541) 584-2832. RV/tent: 50. $20. Hookups: electric (20, 30, 50 amps).

Sawyers Rapids RV Resort, 24828 State Hwy. 38, 97436. T: (541) 584-2226. RV/tent: 32. $18. Hookups: full.

Enterprise

Outpost RV, 66258 Lewiston Hwy., 97828. T: (541) 426-4027. RV/tent: 60. $19. Hookups: full.

Estacada

Promontory Park, 40600 East Hwy. 224, 97023. T: (503) 630-7229. RV/tent: 48. $15. Hookups: none.

Silver Fox RV Park, 40505 Southeast Hwy. 224, 97023. T: (503) 630-7000. RV/tent: 70. $21. Hookups: electric (20, 30, 50 amps).

Eugene

Coburg Hills RV Park, 33022 Van Duyn Rd., 97408. T: (541) 686-3152. RV/tent: 141. $22. Hookups: full.

OREGON (continued)

Eugene (continued)

Deerwood RV Park, 35059 Seavey Loop Rd., 97405. T: (877) 988-1139. RV/tent: 50. $23–$26. Hookups: full.

KOA Sherwood Forest, 298 East Oregon Ave., Creswell, 97426. T: (541) 895-4110. RV/tent: 143. $17–$23. Hookups: electric, cable.

Shamrock Village, 4531 Franklin Blvd., 97403. T: (541) 747-7473. RV/tent: 115. $22. Hookups: electric (20, 30, 50 amps), water.

Fairview

Portland Fairview RV Park, 21401 Northeast Sandy Blvd., 97401. T: (503) 661-1047. www.portlandviewrv.com. info@portlandviewrv.com. RV/tent: 407. $25. Hookups: electric (20, 30, 50 amps), cable.

Rolling Hills Mobile Terrace and RV Park, 20145 Northeast Sandy Blvd., 97024. T: (503) 666-7282. RV/tent: 101. $22. Hookups: full.

Florence

Carl G. Washburne State Park, Hwy. 101 South, 97439. T: (541) 997-3641. RV/tent: 65. $14–$19. Hookups: full.

Darlings Resort and RV Park, 4879 Darlings Loop, 97439. T: (541) 997-2841. RV/tent: 41. $18. Hookups: electric (20, 30 amps).

Happy Place RV Park, 4044 Hwy. 101, 97439. T: (541) 997-1434. F: (541) 997-4044. happyplacerv@aol.com. RV/tent: 52. $25–$27. Hookups: full.

Lakeshore RV Park, 83763 US Hwy. 107, 97439. T: (541) 997-2741. RV/tent: 20. $18. Hookups: electric (30 amps).

Thousand Trails—South Jetty, 05010 South Jetty Rd., 97439. T: (541) 997-8333. RV/tent: 192. $20. Hookups: electric (20, 30 amps), water.

Woahink Lake RV Resort, 83570 Hwy. 101 South, 97439. T: (541) 997-6454. RV/tent: 76. $23. Hookups: electric (30, 50 amps).

Fort Klamath

Crater Lake Resort at Fort Creek Campground, 50711 State Hwy. 62, 97626. T: (541) 381-2349. RV/tent: 43. $16–$20. Hookups: electric (20, 30, 50 amps), water.

Fort Klamath Lodge and RV Park, P.O. Box 428, 97626. T: (541) 381-2234. RV/tent: 13. $15. Hookups: electric (20 amps).

Glendale

Meadow Wood RV and Campground, P.O. Box 885, 97442. T: (541) 832-3114. RV/tent: 64. $17–$19. Hookups: electric (20, 30, 50 amps), water.

Glide

Susan Creek (BLM), 777 Northwest Garden Valley Blvd., Roseburg, 97470. T: (541) 440-4930. RV/tent: 31. $11–$14. Hookups: none.

Gold Beach

Four Seasons RV Resort, 96526 North Bank Rogue, 97444. T: (800) 248-4503. www.fourseasonsrv.com. fourseasons@harbourside.com. RV/tent: 51. $22–$31. Hookups: full.

Honey Bear Campground, P.O. Box 97, 97464. T: (800) 822-4444. RV/tent: 120. $20–$22. Hookups: electric (20,30 amps), water.

Indian Creek, 94680 Jerry's Flat Rd., 97444. T: (541) 247-7704. RV/tent: 125. $22–$24. Hookups: electric (20, 30 amps), water.

Irelands Oceanview RV Park, 29272 Ellensburg Ave., 97444. T: (541) 247-0148. RV/tent: 33. $15–$22. Hookups: full.

Kimball Creek Bend RV Resort, North Bank Rogue River Rd., 97444. T: (541) 247-7580. RV/tent: 69. $23. Hookups: full.

Lucky Lodge RV Park, 32040 Watson Ln., 97444. T: (541) 247-7618. RV/tent: 36. $17–$22. Hookups: full.

Turtle Rock RV Resort, Hunter Creek Loop Rd., 97444. T: (800) 353-9754. www.turtlerockresorts.com. turtlerv@harbourside.com. RV/tent: 50. $18–$23. Hookups: full.

Gold Hill

KOA-Medford/Gold Hill, P.O. Box 320, 97525. T: (800) KOA-7608. RV/tent: 69. $19–$23. Hookups: electric (15, 20, 30 amps).

Lazy Acres RV Park and Motel, 1550 Second Ave., 97525. T: (541) 855-7000. RV/tent: 75. $16–$18. Hookups: electric (30, 50 amps), phone, modem, dump station.

Grants Pass

Moon Mountain RV Resort, 3290 Pearce Park Rd., 97526. T: (541) 479-1145. RV/tent: 50. $20. Hookups: electric (20, 30, 50 amps), water, dump station.

Rogue Valley Overnighters, 1806 Northwest Sixth, 97526. T: (541) 479-2208. RV/tent: 110. $20. Hookups: electric (20, 30, 50 amps), cable.

Twin Pines RV Park, 2630 Merlin Rd., 97526. T: (541) 956-0710. RV/tent: 22. $18. Hookups: electric (30, 50 amps).

Hermiston

Hat Rock Campground, Hat Rock Rd., 97838. T: (541) 567-0917. RV/tent: 65. $14–$15. Hookups: full.

Huntington

Farewell Bend State Park, Hwy. 30 East, 97907. T: (541) 869-2365. park.info@state.or.us. RV/tent: 136. $14–$23. Hookups: electric, water.

OREGON (continued)

Idleyld Park

Elk Have RV Resort, 22020 North Umpqua Hwy., 97477. T: (541) 496-3096. RV/tent: 42. $20. Hookups: electric (20, 30, 50 amps), water.

Klamath Falls

Klamath Falls KOA, 3435 Shasta Way, 97603. T: (800) KOA-9036. RV/tent: 84. $18–$23. Hookups: electric (20, 30, 50 amps), water, dump station, cable.

Lake of the Woods Resort, 950 Harriman Rte., 97601. T: (541) 949-8300. RV/tent: 39. $20. Hookups: electric (30, 50 amps).

Oregon 8 RV Park, 5225 Hwy. 97 North, 97601. T: (541) 883-3431. RV/tent: 30. $22. Hookups: electric (20, 30 amps), water.

La Grande

Hot Lake RV Resort, 65182 Hot Lake Ln., 97805. T: (800) 994-5253. RV/tent: 120. $23. Hookups: full.

La Pine

Cascade Meadows RV Resort, 53750 Hwy. 97, 97739. T: (541) 536-2244. F: (541) 536-2747. oregonrv@bendnet. RV/tent: 100. $17–$24. Hookups: full.

Lakeside

Eel Creek RV Park and Campground, 67760 Spin Reel Rd., 97449. T: (541) 759-4462. RV/tent: 41. $15. Hookups: full.

Osprey Point RV Resort, 1505 North Lake Rd., 97449. T: (541) 759-2801. RV/tent: 164. $18–$30. Hookups: full.

Lakeview

Goose Lake Park, US 395, 97630. T: (541) 937-3111. RV/tent: 47. $16–$22. Hookups: electric, water.

Hunter's RV Park, US 395, 97630. T: (541) 947-4968. RV/tent: 133. $15–$17. Hookups: full.

Lincoln City

Devils Lake State Park, 1450 Northeast 6th Dr., 97366. T: (541) 994-2002. RV/tent: 87. $22–$25. Hookups: full.

KOA-Lincoln City, 5298 Northeast Parklane, 97368. T: (541) 944-2961. www.koa.com. RV/tent: 76. $19. Hookups: full.

McMinnville

Mulkey RV Park, 1325 Southwest Hwy. 18, 97128. T: (887) 472-2475. RV/tent: 86. $15–$20. Hookups: full.

Olde Stone Village RV Park, 4155 Three Mile Ln., 97128. T: (503) 472-4315. RV/tent: 71. $20. Hookups: full.

Medford

Fish Lake Resort, P.O. Box 40, 97501. T: (541) 949-8500. RV/tent: 51. $15–$23. Hookups: electric (20, 30 amps).

Holiday RV Park, Box 1020, 97535. T: (800) 452-7970. RV/tent: 110. $25. Hookups: electric (20, 50 amps).

Lakewood RV Park, 2564 Merry Ln., White City, 97503. T: (541) 830-1957. RV/tent: 45. $22. Hookups: electric (20, 30, 50 amps).

Medford Oaks RV Park, 7049 State Hwy. 140, Eagle Point, 97524. T: (541) 826-5103. RV/tent: 70. $12–$23. Hookups: electric (20, 30, 50 amps), water, phone, modem.

Pear Tree Motel and RV Park, 3730 Fern Valley, 97504. T: (541) 535-4445. RV/tent: 31. $23. Hookups: electric (20, 30 50 amps).

Myrtle Creek

Rivers West RV Park, 333 Ruckles Dr., 97457. T: (888) 863-7602. RV/tent: 120. $20–$23. Hookups: electric (30, 50 amps), water.

Newport

Harbor Village RV Park, 923 Southeast Bay Blvd., 97365. T: (541) 265-5088. RV/tent: 140. $17. Hookups: full.

Pacific City

Cape Kiwanda RV Park, 33315 Cape Kiwanda Dr., 97135. T: (503) 965-6230. F: (503) 965-6235. pacificcity.net/capekiwandarvpark. capekiwanda@oregoncoast.com. RV/tent: 180. $21.50–$23. Hookups: full.

Pendleton

Mountain View RV Park, 1375 Southeast 3rd St., 97801. T: (541) 216-1041. F: (541) 966-8820. rvpark@oregontrail.com. RV/tent: 100. $20–$25. Hookups: full.

Prineville

Crook County RV Park, 1040 South Main, 97754. T: (800) 609-2599. RV/tent: 32. $19. Hookups: full.

Prospect

Rogue River National Forest (Farewell Bend Campground), 333 West Eighth St., 97501. T: (541) 560-3400. RV/tent: 61. $12–$17. Hookups: none.

Rogue River

Circle W RV Park, 8110 Rogue River Hwy., Grants Pass, 97527. T: (541) 582-1686. RV/tent: 25. $17–$22. Hookups: electric (20, 30, 50 amps), water, dump station.

Cypress Grove RV Park, 1679 Rogue River Hwy., Gold Hill, 97525. T: (800) 758-0719. RV/tent: 45. $20–$22. Hookups: electric (30, 50 amps), cable.

Roseburg

Mt. Nebo RV Park, 2071 Norheast Stephena, 97470. T: (541) 673-4108. RV/tent: 35. $17. Hookups: electric (30 amps).

Rising River RV Park, 5579 Grange Rd., 97470. T: (800) 854-4279. www.risingriverrv.com. risingrv@rosenet.net. RV/tent: 69. $20. Hookups: full.

OREGON (continued)

Roseburg (continued)

Twin Rivers Vacation Park, 433 River Forks Park Rd., 97470. T: (541) 673-3811. F: (541) 672-0261. twinrv@internetcds.com. RV/tent: 80. $15–$28. Hookups: full.

Western Star RV Park, 101 LADD, 97470. T: (541) 679-6159. RV/tent: 15. $16. Hookups: electric (20, 30, 50 amps).

Salem

Eola Bend RV Resort, 4700 Salem, Dallas Hwy. 22, 97304. T: (877) 364-9990. RV/tent: 180. $25. Hookups: full.

Salem Campground and RV, 3700 Hagers Grove Rd. Southeast, 97301. T: (800) 826-9605. F: (888) 827-9605. www.salemrv.com. salemrv@salemrv.com. RV/tent: 187. $14–$20. Hookups: full.

Shady Cove

Fly Casters RV Park, 21655 Crater Lake Hwy. 62, 97539. T: (800) 806-4705. RV/tent: 50. $18–$28. Hookups: electric (30, 50 amps), cable.

Rogue River RV Park and Resort, 21800 Crater Lake Hwy. 62, 97539. T: (541) 878-2404. RV/tent: 70. $18–$25. Hookups: electric (30, 50 amps).

Shady Trails RV Park and Campground, 1 Meadow Ln., 97539. T: (800) 606-2206. RV/tent: 50. $18–$22. Hookups: electric (20, 30 amps), water, dump station.

Sunny Valley

Grants Pass/Sunny Valley KOA, 140 Old Stage Rd., 97497. T: (800) 562-7557. RV/tent: 70. $17–$22. Hookups: electric (20, 40 amps), water, dump station.

Trail

Bear Mountain RV Park, 27301 Hwy. 62, 97541. T: (800) 586-2327. RV/tent: 43. $12–$16. Hookups: electric (20, 30, 50 amps), water.

Tualatin

Roamer's Rest RV Park, 17585 Southwest Pacific Hwy., 97062. T: (877) 4RV-PARK. RV/tent: 93. $23. Hookups: full.

Waldport

Waldport/Newport KOA, Hwy. 101—P.O. Box 397, 97394. T: (800) 562-3443. www.oregoncoastkoa.com. orcostkoa@casco.net. RV/tent: 84. $19–$30. Hookups: full.

Wilderville

Grants Pass/Redwood Hwy. KOA, 13370 Redwood Hwy., 97543. T: (541) 476-6508. RV/tent: 40. $17–$22. Hookups: electric (30, 50 amps), water, dump station.

Wilsonville

Pheasant Ridge RV Park, 8275 Southwest Elligen Rd., 97070. T: (800) 532-7829. RV/tent: 130. $26. Hookups: full.

Winston

On the River RV Park, P.O. Box 1614, 97470. T: (541) 679-6634. RV/tent: 36. $17–$21. Hookups: electric (20, 30 amps), water, dump station.

River Bend RV Park, 31 Southeast Thompson, 97496. T: (541) 679-4000. RV/tent: 63. $20. Hookups: electric (20, 30, 50 amps), dump station.

Umpqua Safari RV Park, P.O. Box 886, 97496. T: (541) 679-6328. RV/tent: 30. $17–$19. Hookups: electric (20, 30, 50 amps).

Wildlife Safari RV Area, P.O. Box 1600, 97496. T: (800) 350-4848. RV/tent: 24. $8–$10. Hookups: electric (20, 30 amps).

Wolf Creek

Creekside RV Resort, 999 Old Hwy. 99, 97497. T: (541) 866-2655. RV/tent: 42. $17.50. Hookups: electric (20, 30, 50 amps).

Woodburn

Woodburn I-5 RV Park, 115 North Arney Rd., 97071. T: (888) 988-0002. www.woodburnrv.com. RV/tent: 148. $21–$22. Hookups: full.

Yachats

Sea Perch Campground/RV Park, 95480 US 101 South, 97498. T: (541) 547-3505. RV/tent: 38. $28. Hookups: full.

Yamhill

Flying M Ranch, 23029 Northwest Flying M Rd., 97148. T: (503) 662-3222. RV/tent: 100. $12. Hookups: none.

SOUTH DAKOTA

Aberdeen

Wylie Park, 616 Southeast 10th Ave., 57401. T: (888) 326-9693. www.aberdeen.sd.us/parks/wylie.html. RV/tent: 92. $16. Hookups: electric (30, 50 amps), water, sewer.

Akaska

D & S Campground, Rte. Box 55H, 57420. T: (605) 229-1739. dscamp@hdc.net. RV/tent: 16. $15. Hookups: electric (30, 50 amps).

SOUTH DAKOTA (continued)

Belle Fourche

Riverside Campground & RV Park, 418 9th Ave., 57717. T: (605) 892-6446. www.ohwy.com/sd/r/rivecamp.htm. RV/tent: 75. $10–$15. Hookups: electric (15, 20, 30, 50 amps).

Beresford

Windmill Campground, 505 Southwest 13th St., 57004. T: (605) 763-2029. RV/tent: 53. $10–$18. Hookups: electric (20, 30, 50 amps), water.

Black Hawk

Fort WeLikIt Family Campground, P.O. Box 381, 57718. T: (888) 946-2267. www.blackhillssrv.com. gocamp@blackhillssrv.com. RV/tent: 100. $18–$27. Hookups: electric (20, 30, 50 amps), water, cable, sewer.

Chamberlain

Happy Campers Campground, 110 West Clemmer Ave., 57325. T: (888) 734-6655. RV/tent: 80. $10–$18. Hookups: electric (20, 30, 50 amps), water.

Custer

Beaver Lake Campground, 12005 West US Hwy. 16, 57730. T: (800) 346-4383. www.beaverlakecampground.net/. mailto:beaverlake@gwtc.net. RV/tent: 83. $16–$24. Hookups: electric (15,20,30 amps).

Big Pine Campground, Rte. 1 Box 52, 57730. T: (800) 235-3981. RV/tent: 90. $16–$20. Hookups: electric (20, 30 amps).

Custer-Crazy Horse Campground, Rte. 2 Box 3030, 57730. T: (866) 526-7377. RV/tent: 106. $17–$23. Hookups: electric (20, 30, 50 amps), water, sewer.

Deadwood

Fish'n Fry Campground, HC 73 Box 801, 57732. T: (605) 578-2150. www.deadwood.net/fishnfry/. fishnfry@deadwood.net. RV/tent: 65. $12–$14. Hookups: electric, water, sewer.

Hermosa

Heartland Campground and RV Park, 24743 Hwy. 79, 57744. T: (605) 255-5460. Rving@rapidnet.com. RV/tent: 150. $15–$25. Hookups: electric (20, 30, 50 amps), water, sewer, cable, phone.

Hot Springs

Angostura Reservoir, P.O. Box 131-A, 57747. T: (605) 745-6996. RV/tent: 159. $11–$13. Hookups: electric.

Larive Lake Resort and Campground, P.O. Box 33, 57747. T: (605) 745-3993. RV/tent: 40. $13–$21. Hookups: electric (20, 30 amps).

Interior

Badlands/White River KOA, HC 54 Box 1, 57750. T: (800) KOA-3897. RV/tent: 138. $18–$25. Hookups: electric (20, 30, 50 amps), water, phone.

Keystone

Spokane Creek Resort, P.O. Box 927, 57750. T: (800) 261-9331. www.spokanecreekresort.com. RV/tent: 15. $14–$24. Hookups: electric (15 amps).

Kimball

Parkway Campground, P.O. Box 136, 57355. T: (605) 778-6312. RV/tent: 26. $10–$15. Hookups: electric (20, 30, 50 amps).

Mitchell

R & R Campground, Box 867, 57301. T: (605) 996-8895. RV/tent: 53. $16–$22. Hookups: electric (20, 30, 50 amps), cable, water, sewer.

Mobridge

Kountry Kampging and Kabins, P.O. Box 907, 57601. T: (800) 648-2267. RV/tent: 33. $14–$16. Hookups: electric, water.

Murdo

Camp McKin-Z, P.O. Box 262, 57559. T: (605) 669-2573. RV/tent: 95. $15–$16. Hookups: electric (30, 50 amps), phone.

Oacoma

Familyland Campground, P.O. Box 97, 57365. T: (800) 675-6959. RV/tent: 100. $9–$13. Hookups: electric (30 amps), cable.

Oasis Campground, P.O. Box 97, 57365. T: (800) 675-6959. F: (605) 734-6927. RV/tent: 97. $12–$25. Hookups: electric (20,30, 50 amps), water, cable.

Pierre

Lighthouse Pointe, 19602 Lake Place, 57501. T: (888) 420-9340. www.lighthousepoint.com. lodge@lighthousepoint.com. RV/tent: 45. $12–$25. Hookups: electric (50 amps).

Rapid City

Lake Park Campground, 2850 Chapel Ln., 57702. T: (800) 644-2267. F: (605) 394-8871. campnelson @ rapidnet.com. RV/tent: 48. $19–$29. Hookups: electric (20, 30, 50 amps), water, sewer.

Salem

Camp America Campground, 25495 US Hwy. 57058, 57058. T: (605) 425-9085. cmpsalem@rapidnet.com. RV/tent: 62. $11–$18. Hookups: electric (30, 50 amps), water, phone, cable, modem.

Sisseton

Camp Dakotah, Rte. 1 Box 184, 57262. T: (877) 698-3507. RV/tent: 25. $10–$14. Hookups: electric (30, 50 amps), water, sewer.

Sturgis

Hog Heaven Resort, P.O. Box 477, 57785. T: (800) 551-1283. RV/tent: 100. $15–$35. Hookups: electric (30 & 50 amps), water, sewer.

SOUTH DAKOTA (continued)

Wall

Sleepy Hollow Campground, P.O. Box 101, 57790. T: (605) 279-2531. RV/tent: 93. $15–$20. Hookups: electric (20, 30 amps), water, cable, phone.

WASHINGTON

Amanda Park

Graves Creek Campground, 1835 Black Lake Blvd. SW, Olympia, 98512-5623. T: (360) 452-0330. RV/tent: 30. $10. Hookups: none.

American River

Bumping Lake Campground, 215 Melody Ln., 98801. T: (509) 653-2205. RV/tent: 45. $4–$8. Hookups: none.

Anacortes

Fidalgo Bay Resort, 7337 Miller Rd., 98221. T: (888) 777-5355. RV/tent: 67. $22–$25. Hookups: electric, water.

Artic

Artic RV Park and Campground, 893 US Hwy. 101, Cosmopolis, 98537. T: (360) 533-4470. RV/tent: 20. $14–$16. Hookups: full.

Ashford

Mouthaven Resort, 38210 State Hwy. 706 East, 98304. T: (800) 456-9380. RV/tent: 19. $20. Hookups: full.

Bay Center

KOA-Bay Center, P.O. Box 315, 98527. T: (800) 562-7810. RV/tent: 28. $21–$24. Hookups: electric, water.

Belfair

Snooze Junction RV Park, P.O. Box 880, 98528. T: (360) 275-2381. RV/tent: 36. $20. Hookups: full.

Birch Bay

Thousand Trails-Birch Bay, 8418 Harborview Rd., Blaine, 98230. T: (360) 371-7432. RV/tent: 180. $22. Hookups: full.

Burlington

KOA-Burlington, 6397 North Green Rd., 98233. T: (800) 562-9154. RV/tent: 40. $20. Hookups: electric, water.

Chehalis

Chehalis-KOA, 118 Hwy. 12, 98532. T: (800) KOA-9120. RV/tent: 19. $21–$24. Hookups: electric, water.

Cheney

Williams Lake Resort, 18607 Williams Lake Rd., 99004-9762. T: (509) 235-2391. RV/tent: 46. $15–$19. Hookups: electric, water.

Chinook

River's End Campground and RV Park, P.O. Box 280, 98614. T: (360) 777-8317. RV/tent: 72. $14–$18. Hookups: electric, water.

Clarkston

Granite Lake RV Resort, 306 Granite Lake Dr, 99403. T: (509) 751-1635. RV/tent: 75. $18–$26. Hookups: electric.

Conconully

Conconully Lake Resort, P.O. Box 131, 98819. T: (800) 850-0813. RV/tent: 11. $19. Hookups: electric.

Shady Pines Resort, P.O. Box 44, 98819. T: (800) 552-2287. RV/tent: 23. $19. Hookups: electric, water.

Concrete

Baker Lake Resort, 46110 East Main St., 98237. T: (360) 853-8341. RV/tent: 90. $15–$20. Hookups: electric, water.

Copalis Beach

Rod's Beach Resort, P.O. Box 507, 98535. T: (360) 289-2222. RV/tent: 90. $18. Hookups: electric.

Cougar

Lone Fit Resort, 16806 Lewis River Rd., 98616. T: (360) 238-5210. RV/tent: 31. $16. Hookups: electric.

Coulee

Laurent's Sun Village Resort, 33575 Park Lake Rd. Northeast, 99115. T: (888) 632-5664. RV/tent: 100. $18. Hookups: full.

Cusick

Blueslide Resort, 400041 Hwy. 20, 99119. T: (509) 445-1327. RV/tent: 56. $15–$16. Hookups: full.

Easton

RV Town, P.O. Box 1203, 98925. T: (509) 656-2360. RV/tent: 72. $18. Hookups: electric, water.

WASHINGTON (continued)

Eastsound

Moran State Park, SR Box 22, 98245. T: (360) 376-2326. RV/tent: 151. $13–$19. Hookups: none.

Ellensburg

KOA-Ellensburg, 32 Thorp Hwy. South, 98926. T: (800) 562-7616. RV/tent: 152. $23–$25. Hookups: full.

Elma

Elma RV Park, P.O. Box 1135, 98541. T: (360) 482-4053. RV/tent: 102. $18. Hookups: electric.

Essaquah EQ check this, there is an Issaquah

Blue Sky RV and Resorts, 9002 302nd Ave. Southeast, 98027. T: (425) 222-7910. RV/tent: 51. $28. Hookups: full.

Everett

Lakeside RV Park, 12321 Hwy. 99 South, 98204. T: (800) HOT-PARK. RV/tent: 164. $33. Hookups: electric.

Forks

Bogachiel State Park, Hwy. 101, 98331. T: (360) 374-6356. RV/tent: 42. $13–$19. Hookups: none.

Glacier

Yogi Bear Jellystone Park at Mt. Baker, 10443 Mt. Baker Hwy., 98244-0021. T: (360) 599-1908. RV/tent: 30. $21–$24. Hookups: full.

Goldendale

Maryhill State Park, 50 US Hwy. 97, 98620. T: (509) 773-5007. RV/tent: 70. $13–$19. Hookups: electric.

Graham

Benbow Campground, 32919 Benbow Dr. East, 98338. T: (360) 879-5426. RV/tent: 54. $18–$20. Hookups: full.

Granite Falls

Gold Basin Camground, 33515 Mt. Loop Hwy., 98252. T: (877) 444-6777. RV/tent: 94. $14–$24. Hookups: none.

Grayland

Ocean Gate Resort, P.O. Box 57, 98547. T: (800) 473-1956. RV/tent: 55. $19. Hookups: electric.

Ilwaco

Fort Canby State Park, P.O. Box 488, 98624. T: (360) 642-3078. RV/tent: 250. 23–$29. Hookups: full.

KOA-Ilwaco, P.O. Box 549, 98624. T: (360) 642-3292. RV/tent: 164. $3–$29. Hookups: full.

Inchelium

Rainbow Beach Resort, 18 North Twin Lakes Rd., 99138. T: (509) 722-5901. RV/tent: 19. $16. Hookups: full.

Ione

Colville National Forest, 755 South Main St., 99114. T: (509) 684-4557. RV/tent: 30. $14–$19. Hookups: none.

Kelso

Brookhollow RV Park, 2506 Allen St., 98626. T: (800) 867-0453. RV/tent: 132. $22. Hookups: electric.

Cedars RV Park, 115 Beauvais Rd., 98626. T: (360) 274-5136. RV/tent: 26. $15. Hookups: none.

Kent

KOA-Seattle/Tacoma, 5801 South 212th, 98032. T: (253) 872-8652. RV/tent: 160. $28–$40. Hookups: full.

La Conner

Blake's RV Park and Marina, 13739 Rawlins Rd., 98273. T: (360) 445-6533. RV/tent: 76. $15–$25. Hookups: full.

Thousand Trails La Conner, 16362 Shee Oosh Rd., 98257. T: (360) 446-3558. RV/tent: 298. $20. Hookups: electric (20, 30 amps), water.

La Push

Lonesome Creek RV Park, P.O. Box 250, 98350. T: (360) 374-4338. RV/tent: 55. $20–$29. Hookups: full.

Leavenworth

Blu-Shastin RV Park, 3300 Hwy. 97, 98826. T: (888) 548-4184. RV/tent: 82. $22. Hookups: full.

Thousand Trails, 20752-4 Chiwawa Loop Rd., 98826. T: (509) 7633217. RV/tent: 308. $20. Hookups: full.

Long Beach

Anderson's on the Ocean, 1400 138th St., 98631. T: (800) 645-6795. RV/tent: 75. $20. Hookups: full.

Driftwood RV Park, P.O. Box 296, 98631. T: (888) 567-1902. RV/tent: 55. $20. Hookups: full.

Loomis

Rainbow Resort, 761 Loomis Hwy., Tonasket, 98855. T: (509) 223-3700. RV/tent: 54. $16. Hookups: full.

Loon Lake

Deer Lake Resort, 3908 North Deer Lake Rd., 99148. T: (509) 233-2081. RV/tent: 65. $18. Hookups: full.

Shore Acres Resort, P.O. Box 900, 99148. T: (800) 900-2474. RV/tent: 30. $20. Hookups: electric.

Lynden

Lynden KOA, 8717 Line Rd., 98264. T: (800) 563-4779. RV/tent: 160. $28. Hookups: full.

Lynn Wood

Twin Cedars RV Park, 17826 Hwy. 99, 98037. T: (800) 878-9304. twincedar@pcfre.com. RV/tent: 69. $27–$30. Hookups: full.

WASHINGTON (continued)

Mazama

Okanogan National Forest, 1240 South 2nd Ave., 98840. T: (509) 996-4000. RV/tent: 46. $3–$8. Hookups: none.

Medical Lake

Rainbow Cove Resort, 12514 South Clear Lake Rd., 99022. T: (509) 299-3717. RV/tent: 17. $15–$18. Hookups: electric, water.

Montesano

Friends Landing, 300 Katon Rd., 98563. T: (360) 249-5117. RV/tent: 29. $20. Hookups: electric, water.

Lake Sylvia State Park, P.O. Box 701, 98563. T: (360) 249-3621. RV/tent: 35. $13–$19. Hookups: none.

Moses Lake

Mar Don Resort, 8198 State Hwy. 262 Southeast, Othello, 99344. T: (800) 416-2736. RV/tent: 273. $20. Hookups: full.

Mossyrock

Harmony Lakeside RV Park, 563 St. Rte. 122, Silver Creek, 98585. T: (360) 983-3804. RV/tent: 80. $19–$22. Hookups: electric, water.

Mount Vernon

Thousand Trails-Mount Vernon, 5409 North Darrk Ln., Bow, 98232. T: (360) 724-331. RV/tent: 240. $20. Hookups: electric, water.

Naches

Squaw Rock Resort, 45070 State Rte. 410, 98937. T: (509) 658-2926. RV/tent: 64. $20. Hookups: electric, water.

Neaah Bay

Snow Creek Campground, P.O. Box 248, 98357. T: (800) 883-1464. RV/tent: 81. $19–$23. Hookups: electric, water.

Newhalem

North Cascades NP-Ross Lake NRA, 810 St. Rte. 20, 98284. T: (360) 856-5700. RV/tent: 164. $10–$12. Hookups: none.

Newport

Thousand Trails-Little Diamond, 1002 McGowen Rd., 99156. T: (509) 447-4813. RV/tent: 312. $20. Hookups: electric, water.

North Bend

Denny Creek Campground, 33515 Mountain Loop Hwy., 98252. T: (877) 444-6777. RV/tent: 34. $12–$14. Hookups: none.

Tinkham Campground, 33515 Mountain Loop Hwy., Granite Falls, 98252. T: (877) 444-6777. RV/tent: 48. $12. Hookups: none.

Northport

Homeland RV Park and Camping, 4706 Northport Waneta Rd., 99157. T: (509) 732-4367. RV/tent: 28. $16. Hookups: none.

Oak Harbor

Military Park, 3515 Princeton St. Bldg. 2641, 98278-1900. T: (360) 257-2434. RV/tent: 26. $5–$10. Hookups: electric, water.

Ocean Park

Ocean Park Resort, P.O. Box 339, 98640. T: (800) 835-4634. info@opresort.com. RV/tent: 83. $18–$21. Hookups: full.

Ocean Shores

Yesterday's RV Park, 3377 Bethel Rd. Southeast 223, Port Orchard, 98366. T: (360) 289-9227. RV/tent: 48. $17–$20. Hookups: full.

Olympia

American Heritage Campground, 9610 Kimmie St. Southwest, 98512. T: (360) 943-8778. RV/tent: 99. $25–$26. Hookups: electric, water.

Olympia Campground, 1441 83rd Ave. Southwest, 98512. T: (360) 352-2551. RV/tent: 99. $20–$24. Hookups: electric, water.

Omak

Eastside Park, P.O. Box 1456, 98841. T: (509) 826-0804. RV/tent: 68. $7–$12. Hookups: full.

Orcas Island

West Beach Resort, 190 Waterfront Way, 98245. T: (360) 376-2240. RV/tent: 45. $30–$35. Hookups: electric, water.

Oroville

Orchard RV Park, 25A Thorndike Loop Rd., 98844. T: (509) 476-2669. RV/tent: 41. $13–$16. Hookups: full.

Sun Cove Resort and Guest Ranch, 93 East Wannacut Ln., 98844. T: (509) 476-2223. sun cove@nvinet.com. RV/tent: 38. $18. Hookups: full.

Pacific Beach

Pacific Beach State Park, 148 St. Rte. 115, Hoquiam, 98550. T: (360) 276-4297. RV/tent: 64. $13–$19. Hookups: electric.

Pasco

Arrowhead RV Park, 3120 Commercial Ave., 99301. T: (509) 545-8206. RV/tent: 64. $30. Hookups: none.

Sandy Heights RV Park, 8801 St. Thomas Dr., 99301. T: (877) 894-1357. sandyheightsrv@urx.com. RV/tent: 185. $20–$25. Hookups: full.

Pateros

Alta Lake State Park, 191A Alta Lake Rd., 98846. T: (509) 923-2473. RV/tent: 189. $3–$9. Hookups: none.

Port Angeles

Crescent Beach and RV Park, 2860 Crescent Beach Rd., 98363-8703. T: (360) 928-3344. RV/tent: 64. $30. Hookups: none.

WASHINGTON (continued)

Lyre River Park, 596 West Lyre River Rd., 98363. T: (360) 938-3436. RV/tent: 86. $17–$25. Hookups: full.

Peabody Creek RV Park, 127 South Lincoln, 98362. T: (800) 392-2361. patm@tenf. RV/tent: 44. $21. Hookups: full.

Port Orchard

Manchester State Park, P.O. Box 338, 98353. T: (360) 871-4065. RV/tent: 53. $13–$19. Hookups: none.

Poulsbo

Eagle Tree RV Park, 16280 St. Hwy. 305, 98370. T: (360) 598-5988. RV/tent: 93. $25. Hookups: electric.

Quinault

Lake Quinault's Rain Forest Resort Village, 516 South Shore Rd., Lake Quinault, 98575. T: (360) 288-2535. RV/tent: 30. $16. Hookups: electric, water.

Quincy

Crescent Bar Resort Campground, 8894 Crescent Bar Rd. Northwest, Suite 1, 98848. T: (800) 824-7090. RV/tent: 60. $30. Hookups: none.

Raymond

Timberland RV Park, 850 Crescent St., 98577. T: (800) 563-3325. RV/tent: 29. $15. Hookups: full.

Republic

Black Beach Resort, 80 Black Beach Rd., 99166. T: (509) 775-3989. bbresort@televar.com. RV/tent: 87. $16–$18. Hookups: full.

Pine Point Resort, 38 Pine Point Resort Rd., 99166. T: (877) 775-3643. RV/tent: 52. $17. Hookups: full.

Tiffany's Resort, 58 Tiffany Rd., 99166. T: (509) 775-3152. RV/tent: 17. $17. Hookups: full.

Riverside

Glenwood RV Park, P.O. Box 278, 98849. T: (509) 826-5228. RV/tent: 20. $15. Hookups: full.

Roosevelt

Crow Butte State Park, 1 Crow Butte State Park Rd., Paterson, 99345. T: (509) 875-2644. RV/tent: 50. $13–$19. Hookups: full.

Salkum

Barrier Dam Campground, 273 Fuller Rd., 98582. T: (360) 985-2495. RV/tent: 27. $20. Hookups: electric, water.

San Juan Island

Lakedale Resort, Friday Harbor, 98250. T: (800) 617-2267. RV/tent: 129. $23–$28. Hookups: none.

Seabeck

Scenic Beach State Park, P.O. Box 701, 98380. T: (360) 830-5079. RV/tent: 52. $13–$19. Hookups: none.

Seaview

Thousand Trails-Long Beach Preserve, 2215 Willows Rd., 98644. T: (360) 642-3091. RV/tent: 120. $20. Hookups: full.

Sekiu

Shipwreck Point Campground, 6850 Hwy. 112, 98381. T: (360) 963-2688. RV/tent: 48. $18. Hookups: none.

Selah

Stagecoach RV Park, P.O. Box 806, 98937. T: (509) 697-9650. RV/tent: 24. $15. Hookups: full.

Sequim

Dungeness Recreation Area, 554 Voice of America Rd., 98383. T: (360) 683-5847. RV/tent: 67. $13–$19. Hookups: none.

Shelton

Lake Nahatzel Resort, West 12900 Shelton Matlock Rd., 98584. T: (360) 426-8323. RV/tent: 17. $20–$22. Hookups: none.

Potlatch State Park, P.O. Box 1051, 98548-1051. T: (360) 877-5361. RV/tent: 35. $13–$19. Hookups: none.

Silver Lake

Seaquest State Park, 3030 Spirit Lake Hwy., 98611. T: (360) 274-8633. RV/tent: 92. $13–$19. Hookups: none.

Skamania

Beacon Rock Resort, 62 Moorage Rd., 98648. T: (509) 427-8473. RV/tent: 57. $15. Hookups: none.

South Prairie

Prairie Creek RV Park, P.O. Box 17, 98358. T: (888) 270-8465. RV/tent: 125. $18. Hookups: electric.

Spokane

KOA-Spokane, 3025 North Barker Rd., Otis Orchards, 99027. T: (509) 924-4722. RV/tent: 196. $23–$28. Hookups: electric, water.

Sprague

Four Sesasons Campround, 2384 North Bob Lee Rd., 99032. T: (509) 257-2332. RV/tent: 38. $17–$19. Hookups: none.

Stanwood

Cedar Grove Shores RV Park, 16529 West Lake Goodwin Rd., 98292. T: (360) 652-7083. RV/tent: 60. $19–$26. Hookups: electric, water.

Starbuck

Lyons Ferry Marina, P.O. Box 189, 99359. T: (509) 399-2001. RV/tent: 60. $14. Hookups: electric.

WASHINGTON (continued)

Sultan

Lake Bronson Club Family Nudist Park, P.O. Box 1135, 98294. T: (360) 793-0286. RV/tent: 26. $40–$50. Hookups: electric, water.

Sumas

Sumas RV Park and Campground, 9600 Easterbrook, 98295. T: (360) 988-8875. RV/tent: 60. $12–$18. Hookups: none.

Tenino

Offut Lake RV Resort, 4005 120th Ave. Southeast, 98589. T: (360) 264-2438. RV/tent: 66. $20. Hookups: none.

Tonasket

Spectacle Lake Resort, 10 McCammon Rd., 98855. T: (509) 223-3433. RV/tent: 40. $15. Hookups: none.

Toppenish

Yakama Nation RV Resort, 280 Buster Rd., 98948. T: (800) 874-3087. RV/tent: 125. $18–$25. Hookups: electric.

Trout Lake

Elk Meadows RV Park and Campground, 78 Trout Lake Creek Rd., 98650. T: (509) 395-2400. RV/tent: 63. $15–$17. Hookups: electric, water.

Twisp

Riverbend RV Park, 19961 Hwy. 20, 98856. T: (800) 686-4498. RV/tent: 104. $14–$19. Hookups: none.

Valley

Silver Beach Resort, 3323 Waitts Lake Rd., 99181. T: (509) 937-2811. RV/tent: 40. $19. Hookups: electric.

Winona Beach Resort, 33022 Winona Beach Rd., 99181. T: (509) 937-2231. RV/tent: 54. $19. Hookups: none.

Vantage

Vantage Riverstone Campground, P.O. Box 135, 98950. T: (509) 856-2800. RV/tent: 75. $21–$23. Hookups: electric.

Wanapum State Park, P.O. Box 1203, 98950. T: (509) 856-2700. RV/tent: 50. $13–$19. Hookups: none.

Walla Walla

RV Resort Four Seasons, 1440 Dallas Military Rd., 99362. T: (509) 529-6072. RV/tent: 89. $23. Hookups: electric.

Wenatchee

Daroga State Park, 1 South Daroga Park Rd., Orondo, 98843. T: (509) 664-6380. RV/tent: 28. $13–$19. Hookups: electric, water.

Lincoln Rock State Park, 1253 US Hwy. 2, 98802. T: (509) 884-8702. RV/tent: 93. $13–$19. Hookups: electric, water.

Westpoint

Jolly Rogers Fishing Camp, P.O. Box 342, 98595. T: (360) 268-0265. RV/tent: 22. $16–$18. Hookups: electric.

Westport

Coho RV Park, P.O. Box 1087, 98595. T: (800) 572-0177. RV/tent: 76. $18–$20. Hookups: electric.

Twin Harbors State Park, 420 St. Rte. 105, 98595. T: (360) 268-9717. RV/tent: 302. $13–$19. Hookups: electric, water.

White Salmon

Bridge RV Park and Campground, 65271 Hwy. 14, 98672. T: (509) 483-1111. RV/tent: 50. $21–$25. Hookups: electric.

Wilbur

Bell RV Park, 712 Southeast Railroad, 99185. T: (509) 647-5888. RV/tent: 30. $18. Hookups: electric.

Winthrop

Big Twin Lake Campground, Rt 2 Box 705, 98862. T: (509) 996-2650. RV/tent: 89. $18. Hookups: electric, water.

Jeffrey's Silberline Resort, 677 Bear Creek Rd., 98862. T: (509) 996-2448. RV/tent: 122. $18–$20. Hookups: none.

KOA-Methow River, P.O. Box 305, 98862. T: (800) 562-2158. RV/tent: 90. $20–$26. Hookups: electric, water.

Woodland

Columbia Riverfront RV Park, 1881 Dike Rd., 98674. T: (800) 845-9842. RV/tent: 76. $22–$24. Hookups: electric.

Paradise Point State Park, 33914 New Paradise Park Rd., Ridgefield, 98642. T: (360) 263-2350. RV/tent: 70. $13–$19. Hookups: electric, water.

Yakima

Circle H RV Ranch, 1107 South 18th St., 98901. T: (509) 457-3683. RV/tent: 76. $18. Hookups: electric.

Yakima-KOA, 1500 Keys, 98901. T: (800) 562-5773. RV/tent: 148. $22–$28. Hookups: electric, water.

WYOMING

Arlington

Arlington Outpost, Hwy. 13, 82083. T: (307) 378-2350. RV/tent: 76. $15–$17. Hookups: full.

Beulah

Camp Fish, Main St., 82712. T: (888) BEU-LAHW. RV/tent: 16. $15–$20. Hookups: electric (20, 30 amps), water.

Buffalo

Big Horn Mountains Campground, 8935 US 16 West, 82834. T: (307) 684-2307. RV/tent: 83. $15–$18. Hookups: full.

Buffalo KOA Campground, 87 Hwy. 16 East, 82443. T: (800) 562-5403. www.buffalokoa.com. RV/tent: 91. $20–$26. Hookups: full.

Deer Park, US 16, 82834. T: (800) 222-9960. information@deerparkrv.com. RV/tent: 97. $16–$25. Hookups: full.

Indian Campground, US 16, 82834. T: (307) 684-9601. steveng@trib.com. RV/tent: 122. $16–$25. Hookups: full.

Mountain View Motel, Cabins, and Campground, US 16, 82834. T: (307) 684-2881. RV/tent: 18. $15–$18. Hookups: full.

Caspar

Caspar KOA, 2800 East Yellowstone, 82609. T: (800) KOA-3259. www.koa.com. RV/tent: 110. $16–$20. Hookups: full.

Fort Caspar Campground, 4205 Fort Caspar Rd., 82604. T: (888) 243-7709. RV/tent: 165. $13–$19. Hookups: full.

Cheyenne

A B Camping, College Dr., 82207. T: (307) 634-7035. RV/tent: 194. $15–$21. Hookups: full.

Greenway Trailor Park, College Dr., 82207. T: (307) 634-6696. RV/tent: 42. $14. Hookups: full.

Jolley Rogers RV Campground, US 30, 82207. T: (307) 634-8457. RV/tent: 69. $15. Hookups: full.

KOA-Cheyenne, Campstool Rd., 82207. T: (307) 638-8840. manager@cheyennekoa.com. RV/tent: 53. $26–$28. Hookups: electric (20, 30, 50 amps), water.

Restway Travel Park, Whitney Rd., 82207. T: (800) 443-2751. RV/tent: 121. $15–$19. Hookups: full.

T-Joe's RV Park, P.O. Box 2267, 82003. T: (307) 635-8750. RV/tent: 54. $18–$20. Hookups: electric (20, 30, 50 amps), water.

WYC Campground, Box 5201, 82003. T: (307) 547-2244. RV/tent: 100. $15–$23. Hookups: electric (20, 30, 50 amps).

Chugwater

Diamond Guest Ranch, Box 236, 82210. T: (800) YEA-HAAA. RV/tent: 121. $18. Hookups: electric (20, 30, 50 amps), water.

Cody

7 K's RV Park, 232 West Yellowstone Ave., 82414. T: (307) 587-5890. RV/tent: 54. $20. Hookups: electric (20, 30 amps).

Absaroka Bay RV Park, P.O. Box 953, 82414. T: (800) 557-7440. www.cody-wy.com. campground@wyoming.com. RV/tent: 99. $19. Hookups: electric (30, 50).

Camp Cody Campground, 415 Yellowstone Ave., 82414. T: (888) 231-CAMP. RV/tent: 63. $15. Hookups: electric (20, 30, 50 amps), water.

Elk Valley Inn, RV Park, and Cabins, 3256 Yellowstone Hwy., 82414. T: (307) 587-4149. RV/tent: 70. $14–$23. Hookups: electric (20, 30, 50 amps), water.

Gateway Motel and Campground, P.O. Box 2348, 82414. T: (307) 587-2561. RV/tent: 87. $16–$20. Hookups: electric (20, 30 amps).

KOA-Cody, 5561 Greybull Hwy., 82414. T: (800) KOA-8507. RV/tent: 228. $22–$33. Hookups: electric (20, 30, 50 amps), water.

Parkway Village and RV Campground, 132 Yellowstone Ave., 82414. T: (307) 527-5927. RV/tent: 25. $10–$14. Hookups: electric (20, 30, 50 amps), water.

Ponderosa Campground, P.O. Box 1477, 82414. T: (307) 587-9203. RV/tent: 165. $17–$25. Hookups: electric (20, 30, 50 amps).

Dayton

Foothills Motel and Campground, Box 174, 82836. T: (307) 655-2347. www.fiberpip.net/~foothill/Home.htm. RV/tent: 45. $12–$17. Hookups: electric (20, 30, 50 amps), water.

Devils Tower

Fort Devils Tower Campground, 601 Hwy. 24, 82714. T: (307) 467-5655. RV/tent: 32. $15. Hookups: electric (20, 50 amps).

KOA—Devils Tower, P.O. Box 100, 82714. T: (800) 562-5785. RV/tent: 145. $20–$26. Hookups: electric (20, 30, 50 amps), water.

Douglas

Douglas Jackalope KOA Kampground, P.O. Box 1150, 82633. T: (800) 562-2469. RV/tent: 101. $21–$22. Hookups: electric (20, 30, 50 amps), water.

Dubois

Circle Up Camper Court, P.O. Box 1520, 82513. T: (307) 455-2238. RV/tent: 117. $17–$23. Hookups: electric (20, 30, 50 amps), water.

Pinnicale Buttes Lodge and Campground, 3577 US Hwy. 26, 82513. T: (800) 934-3569. RV/tent: 21. $12–$19. Hookups: electric (15. 20, 30, 50), water.

WYOMING (continued)

Evanston

Phillips RV Park, 225 Bear River Dr., 82930. T: (307) 789-3805. RV/tent: 58. $19. Hookups: electric (20, 30, 50).

Fort Bridger

Fort Bridger RV Camp, P.O. Box 244, 82933. T: (800) 578-6535. RV/tent: 23. $18. Hookups: electric (20, 30, 50 amps).

Fort Laramie

Chuckwagon RV Park, P.O. Box 142, 82212. T: (307) 837-2828. RV/tent: 12. $12. Hookups: electric (20, 30, 50 amps), water.

Pony Soldier RV Park, RR1 Box 33 US Hwy. 26, Lingle, 82223. T: (307) 837-3078. RV/tent: 65. $15–$16. Hookups: electric (20, 30, 50 amps), water.

Gillette

Green Tree's Crazy Woman Campground, 1001 West 2nd St., 82716. T: (307) 682-3665. RV/tent: 124. $16–$28. Hookups: electric (20, 30, 50 amps), water.

Glenrock

Deer Creek Village RV Park, P.O. Box 1003, 82637. T: (307) 436-8121. RV/tent: 95. $16. Hookups: electric (20, 30, 50 amps).

Green River

Buckbord Marina, HCR 65 Box 100, 82935. T: (307) 865-6927. RV/tent: 40. $22. Hookups: electric (30, 50 amps).

Tex's Travel Camp, Star Rte. 2 Box 101, 82935. T: (307) 875-2630. RV/tent: 89. $16–$25. Hookups: electric (20, 30, 50 amps), water.

Greybull

Green Oasis Campground, 540 12th Ave. North, 82426. T: (888) 765-2856. RV/tent: 32. $13–$21. Hookups: electric (20, 30, 50 amps), water.

KOA-Greybull, Box 387, 82426. T: (800) 562-7508. RV/tent: 57. $22–$23. Hookups: electric (30 amps), water.

Jackson

KOA-Snake River Park, 9705 South US Hwy. 89, 83001. T: (800) 562-1878. RV/tent: 96. $36–$39. Hookups: electric (20, 30, 50 amps), water.

Lone Eagle Resort, 13055 South US Hwy. 191, 83001. T: (800) 321-3800. RV/tent: 154. $41. Hookups: electric (20, 30 amps).

Lander

Hart Ranch Hideout RV Park and Campground, 7192 Hwy. 789/287, 82520. T: (800) 914-9226. RV/tent: 85. $23–$24. Hookups: electric (20, 30, 50 amps), water.

Maverick Mobile Home and RV Park, 1104 North 2nd St., 82520. T: (307) 332-3142. RV/tent: 45. $15. Hookups: electric (15, 20, 30 amps), water.

Rocky Acres Campground, P.O. Box 1565, 82520. T: (307) 332-6953. RV/tent: 30. $13. Hookups: electric (15,20, 30 amps).

Sleeping Bear RV Park and Campground, 715 East Main, 82520. T: (888) SLP-BEAR. RV/tent: 54. $26. Hookups: electric (20, 30 ,50 amps), water.

Laramie

KOA-Laramie, P.O. Box 1134, 82073. T: (800) KOA-4153. RV/tent: 146. $18–$22. Hookups: electric (20, 30, 50 amps).

Lusk

Prairie View Campground, Box 1168, 82225. T: (307) 334-3174. RV/tent: 29. $18. Hookups: electric (15, 20, 30 amps), water.

Lyman

KOA-Lyman, HC 66 Box 55, 82937. T: (307) 786-2188. RV/tent: 51. $16–$20. Hookups: electric (20, 30, 50 amps), water.

Madison Junction

Madison Junction Campground, P.O. Box 165, Yellowstone National Park, 82190. T: (307) 344-7311. RV/tent: 280. $15. Hookups: none.

Moran Junction

Colter Bay RV Park, P.O. Box 250, 83013. T: (800) 628-9988. RV/tent: 112. $32–$34. Hookups: electric (20, 30, 50 amps).

Grand Teton Park RV Resort, P.O. Box 92, 83013. T: (800) 563-6469. RV/tent: 204. $27–$38. Hookups: electric (20, 30, 50 amps), water.

Newcastle

Crystal Park Campground, 2 Fountain Plaza, 82701. T: (307) 746-3339. RV/tent: 100. $13–$16. Hookups: electric (20, 30 amps), water.

Rimrock RV, 2206 West Main, 82701. T: (307) 746-2007. RV/tent: 58. $15–$18. Hookups: electric (20, 30 amps), water.

Pine Bluffs

Pine Bluffs RV Park, P.O. Box 806, 82082. T: (800) 294-4968. RV/tent: 108. $20. Hookups: electric (20, 30, 50 amps).

Pinedale

Pinedale RV, P.O. Box 248, 82941. T: (307) 367-4555. RV/tent: 64. $18–$20. Hookups: electric (20, 30, 50 amps), water.

Ranchester

Lazy R Campground, P.O. Box 286, 82839. T: (888) 655-9284. RV/tent: 22. $15. Hookups: electric (30, 50 amps).

WYOMING (continued)

Rawlins

American Presidents Camp, 2346 West Spruce St., 82301. T: (307) 324-3218. RV/tent: 67. $8–$15. Hookups: electric (20, 30, 50 amps), water.

KOA-Rawlins, 205 East Hwy. 71, 82301. T: (800) 562-7559. RV/tent: 57. $15–$22. Hookups: electric (20, 30, 50 amps), water.

RV World Campground, P.O. Box 1282, 82301. T: (307) 328-1091. RV/tent: 60. $14–$20. Hookups: electric (20, 30, 50 amps), water.

Western Hills Campground, P.O. Box 760, 82301. T: (888) 568-3040. RV/tent: 179. $12–$17. Hookups: electric (20, 30, 50 amps).

Riverside

Lazy Acres Campground, P.O. Box 641, 82325. T: (307) 327-5968. RV/tent: 34. $13–$18. Hookups: electric (15, 20, 30, 50 amps).

Riverton

Owl Creek Kampground, 11124 US Hwy. 26, 82501. T: (307) 856-9769. RV/tent: 40. $17. Hookups: electric (20, 30 amps), water.

Rudy's Camper Court, 622 East Lincoln, 82501. T: (307) 856-9764. RV/tent: 24. $11–$18. Hookups: electric (20, 30 amps).

Wind River RV Park, 1618 East Park, 82501. T: (800) 528-3913. RV/tent: 60. $22–$25. Hookups: electric (20, 30, 50 amps).

Rock Springs

Rock Springs KOA, 86 Foothill Blvd., 82901. T: (800) 562-8699. RV/tent: 115. $18–$28. Hookups: full.

Thermopolis

Country Campin' RV and Tent Park, 710 East Sunnyside Ln., 82443. T: (800) 609-2244. RV/tent: 62. $18. Hookups: electric (20, 30, 50 amps), water.

Eagle RV Park, 204 Hwy. 20 South, 82443. T: (307) 864-5262. RV/tent: 45. $15–$18. Hookups: electric (20, 30 amps), water.

Fountain of Youth RV Park, 250 US Hwy. 20 North, 82443. T: (307) 864-3265. F: (307) 864-3388. w3.trib.com/~foyrvpark. foyrvpark@trib.com. RV/tent: 66. $19.50. Hookups: full.

The Wyoming Waltz RV Park, 720 Shoshoni Hwy. 20 South, 82443. T: (307) 864-2778. RV/tent: 13. $14. Hookups: full

BRITISH COLUMBIA

Balfour

Birch Grove Campground, RR 3 Site 33 Comp 18, Nelson, V1L 5P6. T: (250) 229-4275. RV/tent: 50. $19–$25. Hookups: full.

Barkerville

Becker's Lodge, P.O. Box 129, Wells, V0K 2R0. T: (800) 808-4761. becker@beckers.bc.ca. RV/tent: 17. $18–$20. Hookups: none.

Barriere

Dee Jay Camp and Trailer Park, 626 Yellowhead Hwy., V0E 1E0. T: (250) 672-5685. RV/tent: 75. $15–$18. Hookups: electric, water.

Bell II

Bell II Lodge, P.O. Box 1118, Vernon, V1T 6N4. T: (600) 700-3298. www.bell2lodge.com. info@bell2lodge.com. RV/tent: 10. $18. Hookups: full.

Blue River

Eleanor Lake Campsite, 1 Herb Bilton Way, V0E 1J0. T: (250) 673-8316. RV/tent: 60. $12–$19. Hookups: none.

Boston Bar

Blue Lake Resort, 63452 Blue Lake, V0K 1C0. T: (877) 867-9246. RV/tent: 75. $15–$20. Hookups: electric (15 amps), water.

Canyon Alpine RV Park & Campground, Hwy. 1, V0K 1C0. T: (800) 644-PARK. RV/tent: 31. $22. Hookups: full.

Boswell

Mountain Shores Resort and Marina, 13485 Hwy. 3A, V0B 1A0. T: (250) 223-8258. RV/tent: 87. $18–$24. Hookups: full.

Burnaby

Burnaby Cariboo RV Park, Cariboo Place, V5K 1A1. T: (604) 420-1722. camping@bcrvpark.com. RV/tent: 241. $22–$35. Hookups: full.

Burns Lake

Beaver Point Resort, P.O. Box 587, V0J 1E0. T: (250) 698-7665. RV/tent: 39. $13–$16. Hookups: electric, water.

Burns Lake KOA, P.O. Box 491, V0J 1E0. T: (800) 562-0905. RV/tent: 36. $16–$22. Hookups: full.

BRITISH COLUMBIA (continued)

Cache Creek

Brookside Campsite, P.O. Box 737, V0K 1H0. T: (250) 457-6633. RV/tent: 95. $12–$19. Hookups: none.

Campbell River

Shelter Bay Resort, 3860 South Island Hwy., V9H 1M2. T: (250) 923-5338. RV/tent: 50. $22. Hookups: full.

Canim Lake

Canim Lake Resort, P.O. Box 248, V0K 1J0. T: (250) 397-2355. RV/tent: 25. $15–$24. Hookups: full.

Reynolds Resort, North Canim Lake Rd., V0K 1M0. T: (250) 397-2244. RV/tent: 29. $13–$20. Hookups: full.

Castlegar

Pine Grove Resort, 1142 Pine Grove, Scotch Creek, V0E 3L0. T: (250) 955-2306. RV/tent: 15. $26. Hookups: full.

Chilanko Forks

Poplar Grove Resort, P.O. Box 70, V0L 1H0. T: (250) 481-1186. RV/tent: 18. $12–$15. Hookups: electric, water.

Chilliwack

Cottonwood Meadows RV Country Club, 44280 Luckakuck Way, V2R 4A7. T: (604) 824-7275. www.cottonwoodrvpark.com. camping@cottonwoodrvpark.com. RV/tent: 107. $19–$24. Hookups: full.

Christina Lake

Skands Court, 64 Johnson Rd., V0H 1V2. T: (250) 447-9295. RV/tent: 84. $19–$21. Hookups: electric, water.

Clearwater

Birch Island Campground, 88 Walker Rd., V0E 1NO. T: (250) 674-3991. RV/tent: 42. $15–$20. Hookups: full.

Clinton

Cache Creek, Cariboo Hwy., V0K 1H0. T: (250) 752-6707. RV/tent: 22. $14–$18. Hookups: full.

Courtenay

Hideaway Resort, 9413 Bracken Rd., Black Creek, V9I 1E3. T: (250) 337-5360. RV/tent: 67. $18–$20. Hookups: none.

Fairmont Hot Springs

Hoodoos Mountain Resort, P.O. Box 67, V0B 1L0. T: (250) 345-6631. www.realtystar.com/hoodoos. RV/tent: 75. $13–$20. Hookups: electric, water.

Spruce Grove Resort, P.O. Box 993, V0B 1L0. T: (250) 345-6561. www.sprucegroveresort.com. RV/tent: 160. $19–$27. Hookups: electric, water.

Fanny Bay

Pepper Land Outdoor Resort, 8256 South Island Hwy., V0R 1W0. T: (250) 336-1521. RV/tent: 24. $15–$19. Hookups: full.

Fort Fraser

Pipers Glen RV Resort, West Hwy. 16, V0J 1N0. T: (250) 690-7565. RV/tent: 32. $12–$15. Hookups: electric (15, 30 amps), water.

Fort Langley

Fort Camping, 9451 Glover Rd., V1M 352. T: (604) 888-3678. RV/tent: 300. $18–$21. Hookups: full.

Fort Nelson

Westend Campground, Mile 300.5 Alaska Hwy., V0C 1R0. T: (250) 774-2340. RV/tent: 139. $13–$20. Hookups: full.

Fort St. James

Pitka Bay Resort, Pitka Bay Rd., V0J 1P0. T: (250) 996-8585. RV/tent: 17. $12–$16. Hookups: full.

Stuart River Campground, Roberts Rd., V0J 1P0. T: (250) 996-8690. RV/tent: 34. $13–$15. Hookups: full.

Fort St. John

Sourdough Pete's RV Park, Box 6911, V1J 4J3. T: (800) 227-8388. RV/tent: 88. $12–$20. Hookups: full.

Fort Steele

Fort Steele Campground and RV Park, 335 Kelly Rd., V0B 1N0. T: (250) 426-5117. RV/tent: 63. $15–$21. Hookups: full.

Fraser Lake

Birch Bay Resort, Birch Bay Rd., V0J 1S0. T: (250) 699-8484. RV/tent: 31. $14–$17. Hookups: electric (15, 30 amps), water.

Francois Lake Resort, Francois Lake Rd., V0J 1S0. T: (250) 699-6551. RV/tent: 30. $14–$17. Hookups: full.

Nithi on the Lake, Francois Lake Rd., V0J 1S0. T: (250) 699-6675. RV/tent: 30. $13–$17. Hookups: full.

Golden

Whispering Spruce Campground and RV Park, 1430 Golden View Rd., V0A 1H1. T: (250) 344-6680. RV/tent: 135. $16–$21. Hookups: full.

Grand Forks

Riviera RV Park, 6331 Hwy. 3, V0H 1H0. T: (250) 442-2158. RV/tent: 36. $15–$20. Hookups: full.

Harrison Hot Springs

Bigfoot Campground, 670 Hot Springs, V0M 1K0. T: (604) 796-9767. RV/tent: 200. $16–$22. Hookups: full.

BRITISH COLUMBIA (continued)

Hixon

Canyon Creek Campgound, 39035 Hwy. 97 South, V0K 1S0. T: (250) 998-4384. www.canyoncreekcampground.com. rvpark@canyoncreekcampground.com. RV/tent: 55. $10–$18. Hookups: electric (30 amps), water.

Hope

Coquihalla Campsite, 800 Kawkawa Lake Rd., V0X 1L0. T: (604) 869-7119. RV/tent: 122. $16–$20. Hookups: electric (15, 30 amps), water,

Kawkawa Lake Resort, P.O. Box 788, V0X 1L0. T: (604) 869-9930. RV/tent: 120. $15–$25. Hookups: none.

Hornby Island

Bradsdadsland, 1980 Shingle Spit Rd., V0R 1Z0. T: (250) 335-0757. RV/tent: 50. $24–$27. Hookups: electric (15 amps), water.

Kaslo

Mirror Lake Campground, 5777 Arcola, V0G 1M0. T: (250) 353-7102. RV/tent: 114. $15–$17. Hookups: electric (15 amps), water.

Madeira Park

Sunshine Coast Resort, 12695 Hwy. 101, P.O. Box 213, V0N 2H0. T: (604) 883-9177. RV/tent: 30. $21–$28. Hookups: full.

Monte Lake

Heritage Campsite and RV Park, P.O. Box 42, V0E 2N0. T: (877) 881-5150. RV/tent: 36. $14–$17. Hookups: full.

Nakusp

Coachman Campsite, 1701 Hwy. 23, V0G 1R0. T: (250) 265-4212. RV/tent: 44. $24. Hookups: full.

Osoyoos

Wild Rapids Campground, RR 1 Lakeshore Dr., V0H 1R0. T: (250) 495-7696. RV/tent: 155. $19–$26. Hookups: electric, water.

Parksville

Park Sands Beach Resort, P.O. Box 179, 105 East Island Hwy., V9P 2G4. T: (250) 248-3171. www.parksands.com. RV/tent: 99. $20–$40. Hookups: full.

Port Alberni

Arrowvak Riverside Campground, 5955 Hector Rd., RR 3, V9Y 7L7. T: (250) 723-7948. RV/tent: 37. $15–$18. Hookups: none.

Prince George

Sintich Trailer Park, P.O. Box 1022, V2L 4V1. T: (250) 963-9862. www.sintichpark.bc.ca. info@sintichpark.bc.ca. RV/tent: 51. $15–$22. Hookups: full.

Quesnel

Cariboo Place Campsite, 6905 Hwy. 97 South, V2J 6M2. T: (250) 747-8555. RV/tent: 70. $14–$17. Hookups: electric, water.

Revelstoke

Williamson's Lake Campground, P.O. Box 1791, V0E 2S0. T: (250) 837-5512. RV/tent: 41. $15–$18. Hookups: none.

Salmon Arm

Salmon Arm KOA, 381 Hwy. 97 B, V1E 4M4. T: (250) 832-6489. RV/tent: 78. $26–$31. Hookups: electric, water.

Sicamous

Cedars Campground, P.O. Box 749, V0E 2V0. T: (250) 836-2265. cedars@sicamous.com. RV/tent: 105. $14. Hookups: electric, water.

Surrey

Dogwood Campground and Rv Park, 15151-112 Ave., V3R 6G8. T: (604) 583-5585. RV/tent: 300. $19.50–$30. Hookups: full.

Peace Arch RV Park, 14601 40th Ave., V4P 2J9. T: (604) 594-7009. RV/tent: 255. $19–$25. Hookups: full.

Victoria

Weir's Beach RV Resort, 5191 William Head Rd., V9C 4H5. T: (250) 478-3323. office@weirsbeachrvresort.bc.ca. RV/tent: 61. $25–$35. Hookups: full.

Westbay Marine Village RV Park, 453 Head St., V9A 5S1. T: (250) 385-1831. www.westbay.bc.ca. info@westbay.bc.ca. RV/tent: 61. $20–$35. Hookups: full.

Index

Alaska (continued)

Idaho

***Idaho** (continued)*

Iowa

***Iowa** (continued)*

Montana

Montana (continued)

Montana (continued)

Nebraska

North Dakota

North Dakota (continued)

Oregon

Oregon *(continued)*

Oregon (continued

South Dakota

South Dakota *(continued)*

Washington

***Washington** (continued)*

Washington (continued)

Wyoming

Wyoming (continued)

British Columbia